Framework Agreements Regarding the International Supply of Goods and the CISG

Global Trade Law Series

VOLUME 61

Series Editors

Prof. Ross P. Buckley, King & Wood Mallesons Professor of International Finance Law, Faculty of Law, University of New South Wales, Sydney, Australia
Prof. Andreas R. Ziegler, Faculty of Law, Criminal Sciences, and Public Administration, University of Lausanne, Switzerland

Introduction and Contents/Subjects

The *Global Trade Law Series* addresses key issues in international trade law. It covers a broad range of topics, including WTO dispute settlement, free trade agreements, investment law and arbitration, export control, and compliance with international trade obligations.

Objective & Readership

The volumes published in this series are aimed at offering high-quality analytical information and practical solutions, for practitioners, policy makers and academics.

Frequency of Publication

2-3 new volumes published each year.

The titles published in this series are listed at the end of this volume.

Framework Agreements Regarding the International Supply of Goods and the CISG

Julian Juhasz

Wolters Kluwer

Published by:
Kluwer Law International B.V.
PO Box 316
2400 AH Alphen aan den Rijn
The Netherlands
E-mail: lrs-sales@wolterskluwer.com
Website: www.wolterskluwer.com/en/solutions/kluwerlawinternational

Sold and distributed by:
Wolters Kluwer Legal & Regulatory U.S.
920 Links Avenue
Landisville, PA 17538
United States of America
E-mail: customer.service@wolterskluwer.com

ISBN 978-94-035-2079-7

e-Book: ISBN 978-94-035-2089-6
web-PDF: ISBN 978-94-035-2099-5

Table of Contents

Preface

The relationship between international framework agreements and the United Nations Convention on the International Sale of Goods (CISG) has long been debated, yet no clear approach or consensus has emerged in international case law or scholarship. Persistent uncertainty concerns both the question of applicability and the manner in which the CISG should be applied to such contracts.

This book addresses these questions comprehensively and proposes a systematic approach to the relationship between the CISG and international framework agreements. It examines when and under what conditions the CISG governs such agreements, and how its provisions should be applied to, for example, the non-sale obligations frequently included in them. The analysis further considers the interaction between the CISG and relevant domestic law provisions that may be of relevance in this context.

This book primarily proceeds on the basis of the established methodology under the CISG. Its arguments are further informed by comparative law perspectives derived from Switzerland, Germany, France, and the United States, as well as by private international law perspectives from Switzerland and the European Union.

The book's objective is to develop a clear and systematic approach to the interoperability of the CISG and framework agreements. This book is intended for scholars, practitioners, policymakers, and anyone interested in international trade law.

All sources are current as of September 2025. Any comments or feedback are welcome at julianjuhasz@yahoo.com.

Julian Juhasz
Basel, November 2025

Acknowledgements

This book is the result of my PhD thesis, which I completed during my time as a research and teaching assistant at the University of Basel in Switzerland. During the composition of the thesis, I was able to visit two outstanding institutions, namely the Max-Planck-Institute in Hamburg, Germany, and the UNIDROIT Library in Rome, Italy. I am very grateful to both institutions for this opportunity.

While there are numerous individuals to whom I would like to extend my thanks, I would first and foremost like to express my deepest gratitude to Professor Ulrich G. Schroeter for his exceptional academic mentorship, supervision of my thesis and guidance as a superior. He taught me in virtually every aspect of academic working, instilled a great deal of trust in me, enriched my thesis with countless, invaluable discussions and sparked my interest in research and teaching. I would also like to express my profound gratitude to Professor Christiana Fountoulakis for her invaluable insights and support as examiner of my thesis. In addition, I would like to extend my sincere thanks to Florian Mohs for setting aside time to deliberate on various aspects of my thesis and sharing profound insights with me, as well as acting as part of the doctoral committee.

In addition, I would like to extend my immense gratitude to Océane Kessler, Till Rau (born Maier-Lohmann), Patrick Platter, Cédric Pittet, Christapor Yacoubian and Raphael Dummermuth. They provided feedback on specific chapters, offering highly informative comments. Alissa Palumbo Högger provided the invaluable linguistic revisions of this thesis. Naturally, all errors remain my own.

Moreover, I would like to express my sincere thanks to Professor Ross Buckley and Professor Andreas Ziegler for their decision to include my book in their Global Trade Law Series. I also wish to express my thanks to Gwen de Vries and Simon Bellamy for their efforts in ensuring a smooth publication process with Kluwer, and to the editors of this book, in particular Radhika, Sharofina, Shamli, Sangeetha and Stella for their meticulous editing.

Finally, I would like to express my greatest thanks to my family, girlfriend and friends for their unwavering support during this period of my life.

List of Abbreviations

1955 Hague Convention	Convention on the law applicable to international sale of goods, done at the Hague, on 15 June 1955
1980 Rome Convention	1980 Rome Convention on the law applicable to contractual obligations (98/C 27/02)
6th Cir.	United States Court of Appeals for the Sixth Circuit
7th Cir.	United States Court of Appeals for the Seventh Circuit
8th Cir.	United States Court of Appeals for the Eighth Circuit
9th Cir.	United States Court of Appeals for the Ninth Circuit
AJP	Aktuelle Juristische Praxis (Switzerland)
Ala.	Alabama (USA)
All ER	All England Law Reports (United Kingdom)
Am. Soc. Rev.	American Sociological Review (USA)
AnwBl	Anwaltsblatt (Germany)
AP	Audiencia Provincial (Spanish Court of Appeal)
Ariz.	Arizona (USA)
Austral. Int'l L. J.	Australian International Law Journal (Australia)
AVV	Alleinvertriebsvertrag (sole distribution contract)
BB	Betriebs-Berater (Germany)
Belgrade L. Rev.	Belgrade Law Review (Serbia)

BGB	Bürgerliches Gesetzbuch in der Fassung der Bekanntmachung vom 2. January 2002 (German Civil Code in the version promulgated on 2 January 2002)
BGE	Entscheidungen des Schweizerischen Bundesgerichts (amtliche Sammlung) (official collection of decisions of the Swiss Federal Supreme Court)
BGer	Bundesgericht (Swiss Federal Supreme Court)
BGH	Bundesgerichtshof (German Supreme Court)
BK	Berner Kommentar (*see* Bibliography)
Brussels I Regulation	Council Regulation (EC) No. 44/2001 of 22 December 2000 on jurisdiction and the recognition and enforcement of judgments in civil and commercial matters
Brussels I Regulation (recast)	Regulation (EU) No. 1215/2012 of the European Parliament and of the Council of 12 December 2012 on jurisdiction and the recognition and enforcement of judgments in civil and commercial matters
BSK	Basler Kommentar (*see* Bibliography)
B. U. Int'l L. J.	Boston University International Law Journal (USA)
CA	Court of Appeal
Cali.	California (USA)
Cali. Rptr.	California Reporter (USA)
CC	Chamber of Commerce
Cc	Code Civil (France)
CHK	Handkommentar zum schweizerischen Privatrecht (*see* Bibliography)
CISG	Convention on the International Sale of Goods, adopted in Vienna on 11 April 1980
CISG-AC	CISG Advisory Council
Col.	Colorado (USA)
consid.	consideration
CR LDIP	Commentaire Romand, Loi sur le droit international privé (*see* Bibliography)
Ct.	Court
D.	Recueil Dalloz Sirey (France)
DCFR	Draft Common Frame of Reference

Diss.	Dissertation (doctoral thesis)
Dist. Ct.	District Court
DM	Deutsche Mark
Doc.	Document
Dr. prat. com. int.	Droit et pratique du commerce international/international trade law and practice (France)
ECJ	European Court of Justice
ED	Eastern District
EGBGB	Einführungsgesetz zum Bürgerlichen Gesetzbuch in der Fassung der Bekanntmachung vom 21. September 1994 (German Introductory Act to the Civil Code in the version promulgated on 21 September 1994)
Einl. vor	Einleitung vor (Introduction to)
EJLR	European Journal of Law Reform (the Netherlands)
ERCL	European Review of Contract Law (Germany)
ERPL	European Review of Private Law (Netherlands)
EU	European Union
EUR	Euro(s)
EuZW	Europäische Zeitschrift für Wirtschaftsrecht (Germany)
Fed. Cir.	United States Court of Appeals for the Federal Circuit
FIFA	Fédération Internationale De Football Association
FS	Festschrift
GWR	Gesellschafts- und Wirtschaftsrecht (Germany)
Harv. L. Rev.	Harvard Law Review (USA)
HCCH	Hague Conference on International Private Law
HGB	Handelsgesetzbuch vom 10. Mai 1897 (German Commercial Code of 10 May 1897)
HGer	Handelsgericht (Commercial Court)
Houst. J. Int'l L.	Houston Journal of International Law (USA)
ICC	International Chamber of Commerce
IHR	Internationales Handelsrecht, Zeischrift für das Recht des internationalen Warenkaufs und Warenvertriebs (Germany)

Indian J. Int'l Econ. L.	Indian Journal of International Economic Law (India)
Int'l	International
Int'l Trade & Bus. L. Rev.	International Trade and Business Law Review (Australia)
IPRax	Praxis des Internationalen Privat- und Verfahrensrechts (Germany)
IPRG/PILA	Bundesgesetz über das Internationale Privatrecht vom 18. Dezember 1987/Swiss Federal Act on Private International Law of 18 December 1987
IWRZ	Zeitschrift für Internationales Wirtschaftsrecht (Germany)
JCP G	Semaine Juridique (La), Édition générale
J. L. & Com.	Journal of Law and Commerce (USA)
J. L. & Soc.	Journal of Law and Society (Wales)
JPI	Juzgado de Primera Instancia (Spanish/Argentinian Court of First Instance)
KGer	Kantonsgericht (Swiss Court of Appeal; Swiss Court of First Instance)
KreisGer	Kreisgericht (Swiss Court of First Instance)
LG	Landgericht/Landesgericht (Austrian/German/Swiss District Court)
Loy. L.A. Int'l & Comp. L. Rev.	Loyola of Los Angeles International and Comparative Law Review (USA)
Mary.	Maryland
MD	Middle District
Mich.	Michigan (USA)
Misc.	Miscellaneous
MKAC	Tribunal of International Commercial Arbitration at the Russian Federation Chamber of Commerce and Industry
MPI	Max Planck Institute for Foreign Private and Private International Law (Hamburg, Germany)
MüKoBGB	Münchener Kommentar zum Bürgerlichen Gesetzbuch (*see* Bibliography)
MüKoHGB	Münchener Kommentar zum Handelsgesetzbuch (*see* Bibliography)
ND Ill.	Northern District of Illinois (USA)
NJ	New Jersey (USA)
NJOZ	Neue Juristische Online-Zeitschrift (Germany)

Nord. J. Comm. L.	Nordic Journal of Commercial Law (Denmark)
NY	New York (USA)
N.Y.U.L. Rev.	New York University Law Review (USA)
OFK	Orell Füssli Kommentar (*see* Bibliography)
OGer	Obergericht (Swiss Court of Appeal)
OGH	Oberster Gerichtshof (Austrian Supreme Court)
OLG	Oberlandesgericht (German/Austrian Court of Appeal)
Op.	Opinion
OR	Schweizerisches Obligationenrecht vom 30. März 1911 (Swiss Code of Obligations of 30 March 1911)
O.R.	Official Records
Pace Int'l L. Rev.	Pace International Law Review (USA)
PECL	Principles of European Contract Law
Penn.	Pennsylvania
RabelsZ	Rabels Zeitschrift für ausländisches und internationales Privatrecht (The Rabel Journal of Comparative and International Private Law) (Germany)
recht	recht, Zeitschrift für juristische Weiterbildung und Praxis (Switzerland)
Rev. Colomb. Der. Int.	Revista Colombiana Derecho Internacional (Colombia)
Riv. Dir. Int. Priv. Proc.	Rivista di Diritto Internazionale Private e Processuale (Italy)
Riv. Trim. Dir. Proced. Civ.	Rivista Trimestrale di Diritto e Procedura Civile (Italy)
RIW	Recht der Internationalen Wirtschaft (Germany)
R.L.R.	Ritsumeikan Law Review (Japan)
Rome I Regulation	Regulation (EC) No. 593/2008 of the European Parliament and of the Council of 17 June 2008 on the law applicable to contractual obligations (Rome I)
SCC	Arbitration Institute of the Stockholm Chamber of Commerce
S. Cal. L. Rev.	Southern California Law Review (USA)
SD	Southern District
Super. Ct.	Superior Court
Supr. Ct.	Supreme Court

Ten.	Tennessee (USA)
Transnat. L. & Pol'y	Journal of Transnational Law and Policy (USA)
Tulane J. Int'l & Comp. L.	Tulane Journal of International and Comparative Law (USA)
U. Pa. L. Rev.	University of Pennsylvania Law Review (USA)
UCC	Uniform Commercial Code
U.C.C. Rep. Serv.	Uniform Commercial Code Reporting Service
ULF	Convention relating to a Uniform Law on the International Sale of Goods, the Hague, 1 July 1964
ULIS	Convention relating to a Uniform Law on the Formation of Contracts for the International Sale of Goods, the Hague, 1 July 1964
UNCITRAL	United Nations Commission on International Trade Law
UNIDROIT	International Institute for the Unification of Private Law
Unif. L. Rev.	Uniform Law Review (UNIDROIT)
UNSW L. J.	University of New South Wales Law Journal (Australia)
UPICC	UNIDROIT Principles of International Commercial Contracts (2016 edition)
US	United States
USA	United States of America
VCLT	Vienna Convention on the Law of Treaties, adopted and open to signature on 23 May 1969
Vill. L. Rev.	Villanova Law Review (USA)
VJ	The Vindobona Journal of International Commercial Law and Arbitration (Austria)
Vorb./Vorbem.	Vorbemerkungen (preliminary remarks)
V.U.W. L. Rev.	Victoria University of Wellington Law Review (New Zealand)
WD	Western District
Wis. L. Rev.	Wisconsin Law Review (USA)
Yale J. Int'l L.	Yale Journal of International Law (USA)
Y.B.	Yearbook
ZEuP	Zeitschrift für Europäisches Privatrecht (Germany)
ZEuS	Zeitschrift für Europarechtliche Studien (Germany)

ZK	Zürcher Kommentar (*see* Bibliography)
ZSR	Zeitschrift für Schweizerisches Recht (Switzerland)
ZVertriebsR	Zeitschrift für Vertriebsrecht (Germany)

Chapter 1

Introduction

I. GENERAL

More than 40 years after the adoption of the Convention on the International Sale of Goods (CISG), the legal, technical and societal landscape has changed significantly.[1] These changes are, *inter alia*, illustrated by the fact that today's international commercial trade is characterised by networks of production and supply systems between highly specialised parties. This has led to the emergence of complex long-term contracts, especially so-called framework agreements.[2] Such contracts have been implemented in international supply relationships as they save time and costs.[3] Up to the present, there is neither a uniform international treaty dedicated to this type of agreement[4] nor a uniform definition or understanding.[5]

In the context of international trade, the question arises whether one of the most successful uniform instruments in the area of international commercial trade, the CISG, may be relied upon to deal with international framework agreements, thereby removing 'legal barriers in international trade' and promoting 'the development of international trade'.[6] In essence, the CISG only covers the international sale of goods. To be more precise, it merely does so in part, due to its limited substantive scope. International framework agreements in international supply relationships are indeed very much interrelated with sale of goods transactions.

1. The origins of the CISG even date back to the 1920s (*see* only *Schroeter*, RabelsZ 81 (2017), pp. 35 et seq.; *Schwenzer*, Challenges of the 2020s, p. 39; Staudinger/*Magnus*, Einleitung, paras 19 et seq.).
2. Cf. *Gass/Lange*, p. 1; *Hoffbauer*, pp. 1, 2.
3. UN Economic Commission for Europe, Trade Facilitation Implementation Guide, 'Framework agreements' (https://tfig.unece.org/domains/purchasing/purchasing/framework-agreements/, last checked September 2025).
4. With regard to distribution contracts: *Perales Viscasillas*, Extending the Scope, p. 118; *Perales Viscasillas*, Int'l Distribution Contracts and CISG, p. 46.
5. Cf. *UNCITRAL et al.*, Legal Guide, para. 431 (regarding distribution contracts).
6. Preamble of the CISG.

It is, therefore, not surprising that such contracts have been considered to be covered by the CISG, at least to some extent.[7] Although this issue has recurringly been dealt with in case law and legal writings, uncertainties remain whether the CISG is indeed applicable to international framework agreements – in particular international distribution contracts – and if so, under what conditions.[8] Moreover, it is uncertain whether the Convention is apt to deal with such complex long-term contracts, given that the majority of its provisions were drafted with one-off contracts in mind.[9]

In light of this and the practical importance of framework agreements, this study seeks to illuminate these questions. It will analyse the Convention's applicability to framework agreements and – assuming that the CISG will apply in some cases – the actual application of the CISG's substantive provisions to such contracts.

II. OUTLINE OF THIS STUDY

To this end, this study will start in Chapter 2 by outlining the notion of framework agreements as they are known in some domestic laws and proposing a definition on which this analysis will be based. Chapter 3 will examine whether framework agreements may be considered sales contracts under Art. 1 CISG. Taking into account the fact that framework agreements often contain non-sales elements, Chapter 4 will consider how the CISG deals with mixed framework contracts. Chapter 5 will analyse the additional challenges posed by framework agreements under the CISG in light of them being long-term contracts. Chapter 6 will then examine the potential implications of choice of law clauses contained in framework agreements on the Convention's applicability. Finally, Chapter 7 will outline this study's conclusions and results.

III. REMARKS ON METHODS

In assessing whether and, if so, how the CISG deals with framework agreements, this study will interpret the Convention's provisions in accordance with the interpretation principles pursuant to Art. 7(1) CISG and by relying on its methods of interpretation.[10]

1. Principles of Interpretation (Article 7(1) CISG)

Art. 7(1) CISG mentions the relevance of the CISG's international character, the need to promote uniformity in its application and the observance of good faith in international

7. *See* Chs 3 and 4 below.
8. *See* only *UNCITRAL et al.*, Legal Guide, para. 435: 'although this interpretation is not settled [...]'.
9. *Schroeter*, RabelsZ 81 (2017), p. 64.
10. On the distinction between principles and methods of interpretation: *Ferrari*, IHR 2013, p. 181; *Gruber*, p. 119; *B. Köhler*, p. 35; *B. Köhler*, Independent Development, p. 6; Schlechtriem/Schwenzer/Schroeter/*Ferrari*, 8th German ed., Art. 7 CISG, para. 8; Schlechtriem/Schwenzer/Schroeter/*Hachem*, 5th English ed., Art. 7 CISG, paras 7, 20; *Schroeter*, para. 139; *Schroeter*, RabelsZ 81 (2017), p. 48; Staudinger/*Magnus*, Art. 7 CISG, para. 30; cf. also Kröll *et al.*/*Perales Viscasillas*, Art. 7 CISG, paras 8, 10.

trade as principles of interpretation. Having regard to the CISG's international character is commonly understood to mean that the CISG must be interpreted autonomously.[11] The Convention must be interpreted on its own merits, without reference to domestic preconceptions such as legal concepts, principles, characterisations or definitions.[12] This principle of autonomous interpretation also requires the process of interpretation and the solutions developed to be acceptable in different legal systems.[13]

Moreover, regard is to be had to the need to promote uniformity in the Convention's application, according to Art. 7(1) CISG. This mandate is primarily addressed to courts and arbitral tribunals which are dealing with the interpretation and application of the CISG.[14] They are obliged[15] to take decisions or awards by other courts and arbitral tribunals into account as persuasive authority; the CISG does, however, not recognise the doctrine of *stare decisis*.[16] The need to promote uniformity also requires finding solutions under the CISG that are acceptable in different legal systems.[17] The third and final principle of interpretation under Art. 7(1) CISG requires the observance of good faith in international trade when interpreting the Convention.[18]

---

11. BeckOK/*Saenger*, Art. 7 CISG, para. 4; *Bridge*, Int'l Sale of Goods, para. 10.40; Brunner/Gottlieb/*Brunner/Wagner*, Art. 7 CISG, para. 3; *Ferrari*, IHR 2013, pp. 139, 140; Honsell/*Melis*, Art. 7 CISG, para. 5; *B. Köhler*, p. 36; Kröll *et al./Perales Viscasillas*, Art. 7 CISG, para. 18; *Schlechtriem*, Symposium Vischer, p. 9; Schlechtriem/Schwenzer/Schroeter/*Ferrari*, 8th German ed., Art. 7 CISG, para. 9; Schlechtriem/Schwenzer/Schroeter/*Hachem*, 5th English ed., Art. 7 CISG, para. 8; *Schroeter*, para. 126; *Schroeter*, RabelsZ 81 (2017), p. 48; Staudinger/*Magnus*, Art. 7 CISG, para. 12; *van Alstine*, (1998) 146 U. Pa. L. Rev., pp. 731, 732; *C. Witz*, para. 116.31; Witz/Salger/Lorenz/*W. Witz*, Art. 7 CISG, para. 8; *see also* BGer, 2 April 2015, CISG-online 2592, para. 78.
12. BGer, 28 May 2019, CISG-online 4463, para. 59; BeckOK/*Saenger*, Art. 7 CISG, para. 4; *Bridge*, Int'l Sale of Goods, para. 10.40; Brunner/Gottlieb/*Brunner/Wagner*, Art. 7 CISG, para. 3; *Ferrari*, IHR 2013, p. 140; Honsell/*Melis*, Art. 7 CISG, para. 5; *B. Köhler*, p. 36; *B. Köhler*, Independent Development, p. 6; Kröll *et al./Perales Viscasillas*, Art. 7 CISG, para. 18; *Schlechtriem*, Symposium Vischer, p. 9; Schlechtriem/Schwenzer/Schroeter/*Ferrari*, 8th German ed., Art. 7 CISG, para. 9; Schlechtriem/Schwenzer/Schroeter/*Hachem*, 5th English ed., Art. 7 CISG, para. 8; *Schroeter*, para. 126; *Schroeter*, RabelsZ 81 (2017), p. 48; Staudinger/*Magnus*, Art. 7 CISG, para. 12; *C. Witz*, para. 116.31; in general on the autonomous interpretation of uniform law: *Gruber*, pp. 80 et seq.
13. Gerechthof 's-Hertogenbosch, 16 October 2002, CISG-online 816, para. 14; *B. Köhler*, p. 36; Schlechtriem/Schwenzer/Schroeter/*Hachem*, 5th English ed., Art. 7 CISG, para. 8.
14. Honsell/*Melis*, Art. 7 CISG, para. 6; Schlechtriem/Schwenzer/Schroeter/*Hachem*, 5th English ed., Art. 7 CISG, para. 10; *Schroeter*, RabelsZ 81 (2017), p. 49; *van Alstine*, (1998) 146 U. Pa. L. Rev., p. 732; *see, e.g.*, AP Valencia, 7 June 2003, CISG-online 948; cf. also Brunner/Gottlieb/*Brunner/Wagner*, Art. 7 CISG, para. 4.
15. Schlechtriem/Schwenzer/Schroeter/*Hachem*, 5th English ed., Art. 7 CISG, para. 7 ('explicit command'); *Schroeter*, RabelsZ 81 (2017), p. 49.
16. *Bridge*, Int'l Sale of Goods, para. 10.40; Honsell/*Melis*, Art. 7 CISG, para. 6; *B. Köhler*, pp. 36, 37; *Schlechtriem*, Symposium Vischer, p. 9; Schlechtriem/Schwenzer/Schroeter/*Ferrari*, 8th German ed., Art. 7 CISG, para. 17; Schlechtriem/Schwenzer/Schroeter/*Hachem*, 5th English ed., Art. 7 CISG, paras 10, 13; *Schroeter*, para. 132; *Schroeter*, RabelsZ 81 (2017), p. 49; Staudinger/*Magnus*, Art. 7 CISG, para. 21; *C. Witz*, para. 116.41; cf. also Kröll *et al./Perales Viscasillas*, Art. 7 CISG, para. 45.
17. Gerechthof 's-Hertogenbosch, 16 October 2002, CISG-online 816, para. 14; BeckOK/*Saenger*, Art. 7 CISG, para. 5; *Gruber*, p. 104; *B. Köhler*, p. 36; Schlechtriem/Schwenzer/Schroeter/*Ferrari*, 8th German ed., Art. 7 CISG, para. 16; *Schwenzer*, Interpretation and gap-filling, p. 114; Staudinger/*Magnus*, Art. 7 CISG, para. 20; cf. also Schlechtriem/Schwenzer/Schroeter/*Hachem*, 5th English ed., Art. 7 CISG, para. 10; sceptical *Schroeter*, para. 146.
18. *See* Ch. 5 III. 1. a. ii. below on the controversial role of good faith under the CISG.

2. Methods of Interpretation

Although the CISG contains principles of interpretation, it is silent on how to achieve results that conform with these principles, i.e., the relevant methods of interpretation.[19]

a. Accepted Methods

Nevertheless, a consensus seems to have emerged about the relevant methods of interpretation.[20] The starting point for an interpretation of the CISG must be the wording of its text (literal interpretation).[21] In addition, the systematic position of a provision within the Convention and how the regulated issue is treated in other provisions must be taken into consideration (systematic interpretation).[22] A historical interpretation, which examines the genesis of a provision and the intentions of the drafters, is also recognised as a method of interpretation under the CISG (historical interpretation).[23] Finally, a teleological interpretation, which considers the purpose and aim of individual provisions and the Convention as a whole, is an accepted method of interpretation under the Convention (teleological interpretation).[24]

19. BeckOK/*Saenger*, Art. 7 CISG, para. 2; *Ferrari*, IHR 2013, p. 181; *Gruber*, p. 119; *B. Köhler*, p. 41; *B. Köhler*, Independent Development, p. 9; Kröll *et al./Perales Viscasillas*, Art. 7 CISG, para. 8; *Magnus*, Tracing Methodology, p. 40; MüKoBGB/*Gruber*, Art. 7 CISG, para. 6; Schlechtriem/Schwenzer/Schroeter/*Ferrari*, 8th German ed., Art. 7 CISG, para. 28; Schlechtriem/Schwenzer/Schroeter/*Hachem*, 5th English ed., Art. 7 CISG, para. 20; *Schroeter*, para. 139; *Schroeter*, RabelsZ 81 (2017), p. 48; Staudinger/*Magnus*, Art. 7 CISG, para. 30.
20. Brunner/Gottlieb/*Brunner/Wagner*, Art. 7 CISG, para. 6 ('widely accepted in doctrine'); *B. Köhler*, Independent Development, p. 9; *C. Witz*, para. 116.72.
21. OGH, 23 May 2005, CISG-online 1041, para. 19; BeckOK/*Saenger*, Art. 7 CISG, para. 2; *Bridge*, Int'l Sale of Goods, para. 10.41; Brunner/Gottlieb/*Brunner/Wagner*, Art. 7 CISG, para. 6; *B. Köhler*, p. 43; *B. Köhler*, Independent Development, p. 9; *Kröll et al./Perales Viscasillas*, Art. 7 CISG, para. 37; *Magnus*, Tracing Methodology, p. 53; MüKoBGB/*Gruber*, Art. 7 CISG, paras 14 et seq.; Schlechtriem/Schwenzer/Schroeter/*Ferrari*, 8th German ed., Art. 7 CISG, paras 30 et seq.; Schlechtriem/Schwenzer/Schroeter/*Hachem*, 5th English ed., Art. 7 CISG, para. 21; Staudinger/*Magnus*, Art. 7 CISG, para. 32; *van Alstine*, (1998) 146 U. Pa. L. Rev., p. 741; *C. Witz*, para. 116.81.
22. Brunner/Gottlieb/*Brunner/Wagner*, Art. 7 CISG, para. 6; *Ferrari*, IHR 2013, p. 186; *B. Köhler*, p. 44; *B. Köhler*, Independent Development, p. 10; *Magnus*, Tracing Methodology, p. 54; MüKoBGB/*Gruber*, Art. 7 CISG, para. 17; Schlechtriem/Schwenzer/Schroeter/*Ferrari*, 8th German ed., Art. 7 CISG, para. 37; Schlechtriem/Schwenzer/Schroeter/*Hachem*, 5th English ed., Art. 7 CISG, para. 21; *Schroeter*, para. 145; Staudinger/*Magnus*, Art. 7 CISG, para. 34; *C. Witz*, para. 116.81.
23. BeckOK/*Saenger*, Art. 7 CISG, para. 2; Brunner/Gottlieb/*Brunner/Wagner*, Art. 7 CISG, para. 6; Kröll *et al./Perales Viscasillas*, Art. 7 CISG, para. 39; *Magnus*, Tracing Methodology, p. 56; MüKoBGB/*Gruber*, Art. 7 CISG, paras 18 et seq.; Schlechtriem/Schwenzer/Schroeter/*Ferrari*, 8th German ed., Art. 7 CISG, para. 36; Schlechtriem/Schwenzer/Schroeter/*Hachem*, 5th English ed., Art. 7 CISG, para. 22; *Schroeter*, para. 141; Staudinger/*Magnus*, Art. 7 CISG, para. 35; *C. Witz*, para. 116.91.
24. *See* Brunner/Gottlieb/*Brunner/Wagner*, Art. 7 CISG, para. 6; Honsell/*Melis*, Art. 7 CISG, para. 11; *B. Köhler*, p. 47; *Magnus*, Tracing Methodology, pp. 56, 57; MüKoBGB/*Gruber*, Art. 7 CISG, para. 23; *Schroeter*, para. 144; Staudinger/*Magnus*, Art. 7 CISG, para. 36; *C. Witz*, para. 116.82.

b. *Comparative Law as an Auxiliary Method*

In contrast, it is disputed whether comparative law should be accepted as a method of interpretation under the CISG.[25] Some scholars have highlighted the potential value of comparative law as a method for interpreting the Convention, suggesting that it could assist in battling the so-called homeward trend.[26] Others disagree, stating that comparative law should not be considered a method of interpretation since it is incompatible with the CISG's principles of uniform and international interpretation.[27] It should be noted that this controversy may potentially be attributed to an inconsistent understanding of what comparative law as a method of interpretation exactly entails.[28]

In any case, the second view is justified in the sense that comparative law should certainly not be used as a means of transplanting domestic solutions or preconceptions into the CISG under the guise of interpretation.[29] Such an approach would be contrary to the principles of autonomous and uniform interpretation as per Art. 7(1) CISG.[30] Even then, there is still room for comparative law as an auxiliary method of interpretation, which complements the other methods, but should not be utilised to produce interpretative results on its own.[31]

There are three reasons militating for this view: first, a comparative law approach may assist in gaining a fundamental understanding of a specific CISG provision, which may itself have been the result of a compromise between various domestic laws.[32] Second, it may aid in identifying potential problems that have already been subject to discussion under domestic laws and might arise in a similar manner under the Convention.[33] The Convention's position on these problems must, naturally, still be found on the CISG's own merits without directly imposing domestic solutions or

25. *Gruber*, pp. 188 et seq.; MüKoBGB/*Gruber*, Art. 7 CISG, para. 24; *B. Köhler*, Independent Development, p. 11.
26. Brunner/Gottlieb/*Brunner/Wagner*, Art. 7 CISG, para. 6; *Gruber*, pp. 198, 199; Staudinger/*Magnus*, Art. 7 CISG, para. 37; highlighting the role of comparative law as a method of interpretation but based on a different reasoning: Schlechtriem/Schwenzer/Schroeter/*Hachem*, 5th English ed., Art. 7 CISG, para. 24; cf. also the comparative approach in Gerechtshof's-Hertogenbosch, 16 October 2002, CISG-online 816, paras 13 et seq.; more guardedly: Schlechtriem/Schwenzer/Schroeter/*Ferrari*, 8th German ed., Art. 7 CISG, para. 40.
27. *Janssen*, p. 323; *Schroeter*, para. 146.
28. In detail *Maier-Lohmann*, paras 29–32.
29. *B. Köhler*, pp. 47, 48; *B. Köhler*, Independent Development, p. 11; Schlechtriem/Schwenzer/Schroeter/*Ferrari*, 8th German ed., Art. 7 CISG, para. 40; Schlechtriem/Schwenzer/Schroeter/*Hachem*, 5th English ed., Art. 7 CISG, para. 24; *Schroeter*, para. 146.
30. *Janssen*, p. 242; *Schroeter*, para. 146; cf. also Honsell/*Melis*, Art. 7 CISG, para. 11; Schlechtriem/Schwenzer/Schroeter/*Ferrari*, 8th German ed., Art. 7 CISG, para. 40.
31. Cf. *Gruber*, pp. 223, 224, who holds a similar view but distinguishes between an objective and subjective comparative method – the latter is arguably part of the historical interpretation (cf. *Gruber*, pp. 188, 189); MüKoBGB/*Gruber*, Art. 7 CISG, paras 24, 25; *B. Köhler*, pp. 47, 48; *B. Köhler*, Independent Development, p. 11.
32. *Magnus*, Tracing Methodology, p. 57; MüKoBGB/*Gruber*, Art. 7 CISG, para. 24; Staudinger/*Magnus*, Art. 7 CISG, para. 37, who considers the CISG as 'coagulated comparative law'; cf. also *Gruber*, p. 199.
33. Cf. *Gruber*, pp. 199, 224; *B. Köhler*, Independent Development, pp. 11, 12.

concepts.[34] Third, comparative law may be utilised to ascertain whether a solution that has been developed based on other methods of interpretation is capable of being internationally accepted.[35] The principles of autonomous and uniform interpretation (Art. 7(1) CISG) require both the process of interpretation as well as the solutions developed to be acceptable in different legal systems.[36] Comparative law may therefore be helpful in finding interpretative results that are consistent with the CISG's international character and the need to promote uniformity in its application.[37]

On the basis of the aforementioned, this study will include occasional references to various domestic law provisions. These references may be partially helpful in identifying whether a particular understanding is likely to be accepted in other Contracting States. This may particularly be the case when it comes to questions of terminology. They are merely partially helpful because finding an international consensus would, strictly speaking, require analysis of the domestic laws of all relevant Contracting States[38] – which exceeds the scope of this study. In addition, references to domestic law rules will be used to identify and contextualise potential problems that might also arise in a similar manner under the CISG. For the same reasons, references to the UPICC will be made since they have been drafted on the basis of extensive comparative studies.[39] It is therefore possible that they may be helpful in identifying whether certain solutions are more likely to be internationally acceptable.[40]

Moreover, the relationship between the CISG and overlapping domestic law rules appears to be a particularly interesting topic that has not yet been the subject of much research. Hence, this study will address this relationship on several occasions.

3. Dynamic Versus Static Approach under the CISG

One of the crucial questions that arises in the interpretation of any international treaty is the determination of the specific moment in time that is decisive for the process of

34. *B. Köhler*, p. 48; *B. Köhler*, Independent Development, pp. 11, 12; *Magnus*, Tracing Methodology, p. 56; Schlechtriem/Schwenzer/Schroeter/*Hachem*, 5th English ed., Art. 7 CISG, para. 24.
35. *Gruber*, p. 199; *B. Köhler*, p. 48; *B. Köhler*, Independent Development, p. 11; Schlechtriem/Schwenzer/Schroeter/*Hachem*, 5th English ed., Art. 7 CISG, para. 24; *Schwenzer*, Interpretation and gap-filling, p. 114; cf. also Honsell/*Melis*, Art. 7 CISG, para. 11.
36. *See* Ch. 1 III. 1. above; Gerechthof 's-Hertogenbosch, 16 October 2002, CISG-online 816, para. 14; *B. Köhler*, p. 36; Schlechtriem/Schwenzer/Schroeter/*Hachem*, 5th English ed., Art. 7 CISG, para. 8 (with regard to the CISG's international character); with regard to the principle of uniform interpretation: BeckOK/*Saenger*, Art. 7 CISG, para. 5; *Gruber*, p. 104; Schlechtriem/Schwenzer/Schroeter/*Ferrari*, 8th German ed., Art. 7 CISG, para. 16; *Schwenzer*, Interpretation and gap-filling, p. 114; Staudinger/*Magnus*, Art. 7 CISG, para. 20; but *see Schroeter*, para. 146.
37. Cf. *Gruber*, p. 199; *B. Köhler*, Independent Development, p. 11; Schlechtriem/Schwenzer/Schroeter/*Hachem*, 5th English ed., Art. 7 CISG, para. 24; *Schwenzer*, Interpretation and gap-filling, p. 114.
38. Schlechtriem/Schwenzer/Schroeter/*Ferrari*, 8th German ed., Art. 7 CISG, para. 40; cf. also *Magnus*, Tracing Methodology, p. 57.
39. Some scholars have posited that the UPICC may indicate which solutions are capable of being internationally accepted, given that they have been drafted on the basis of extensive comparative studies: Brunner/Gottlieb/*Brunner/Wagner*, Art. 7 CISG, para. 11; Staudinger/*Magnus*, Art. 7 CISG, para. 14; cf. also *Magnus*, ZeuP 1999, p. 648.
40. Similarly, Schlechtriem/Schwenzer/Schroeter/*Hachem*, 5th English ed., Art. 7 CISG, para. 26.

treaty interpretation.[41] In this regard, two schools of thought can be distinguished:[42] according to the static approach, the original legislative purpose and the circumstances prevailing at the time of treaty conclusion are decisive for the interpretation.[43] According to the dynamic approach, the meaning of a treaty is to be established 'objectively' at the time of interpretation, i.e., in light of a changed societal and legal environment.[44] The dynamic approach considers the interpreter - i.e., the judge or arbitrator - to not be strictly bound by the original legislative intent.[45] As the dynamic approach may clash with the principle of uniform interpretation which is of outstanding importance in the context of international uniform law treaties,[46] it is subject to criticism.[47]

Despite the criticism, a dynamic approach to the interpretation of the CISG should be adopted for several reasons.[48] First of all, it is unlikely that a reform of the Convention or a successor to it will be implemented, given that all 97 Contracting States would need to agree to amendments or re-ratify a successor convention.[49] Developing the CISG by way of interpretation is thus virtually the only promising option.[50] Moreover, the CISG has been drafted in a way that makes it open to dynamic interpretation.[51] It contains broadly worded terms and general clauses which allow for a flexible and hence dynamic interpretation and application of its provisions.[52]

41. Dörr/Schmalenbach/*Dörr*, Art. 31 VCLT, para. 22; cf. also *Jiang*, p. 348.
42. Also relying on this dichotomy: Dörr/Schmalenbach/*Dörr*, Art. 31 VCLT, para. 22; *Jiang*, p. 348; *Neumann*, (2017) 21 VJ, p. 113; a comparable discussion has been conducted under the terms 'subjective' and 'objective' theory within the context of (domestic) German and Swiss methodology, *see* only *Gruber*, pp. 183, 184; *Kropholler*, p. 259; *Kramer*, pp. 148 et seq.
43. Dörr/Schmalenbach/*Dörr*, Art. 31 VCLT, para. 22; *Jiang*, p. 348; cf. also *Gruber*, pp. 184 et seq.; *Kramer*, pp. 139, 140; *Kropholler*, p. 259.
44. Dörr/Schmalenbach/*Dörr*, Art. 31 VCLT, para. 22; *Jiang*, p. 348; *van Alstine*, (1998) 146 U. Pa. L. Rev., p. 715; cf. also *Gruber*, pp. 186 et seq.; *Kramer*, p. 141; *Kropholler*, p. 259.
45. *Van Alstine*, (1998) 146 U. Pa. L. Rev., p. 715; cf. also *Gruber*, p. 186.
46. Cf. *Gruber*, pp. 186, 187; *B. Köhler*, Independent Development, p. 7; *O. Meyer*, Constructive Interpretation, p. 321.
47. *See* Dörr/Schmalenbach/*Dörr*, Art. 31 VCLT, para. 23, holding that the static approach represents the basic rule in international case law; *Gruber*, pp. 183 et seq.
48. Accord *O. Meyer*, Constructive Interpretation, pp. 319 et seq.; *Neumann*, (2017) 21 VJ, p. 113; *van Alstine*, (1998) 146 U. Pa. L. Rev., pp. 761 et seq.; cf. also *Honnold/Flechtner*, Salient Features of the 1980 Convention, para. 20.
49. *O. Meyer*, Constructive Interpretation, pp. 321, 322; *B. Köhler*, p. 63; *B. Köhler*, Independent Development, p. 4; Schlechtriem/Schwenzer/Schroeter/*Schroeter*, 8th German ed., Einleitung, paras 106, 107; *Schroeter*, RabelsZ 81 (2017), pp. 69, 70; cf. also *Neumann*, (2017) 21 VJ, p. 113.
50. Cf. *O. Meyer*, Constructive Interpretation, pp. 321, 322; *Neumann*, (2017) 21 VJ, p. 113; *Schroeter*, RabelsZ 81 (2017), pp. 69, 70.
51. *Honnold/Flechtner*, Salient Features of the 1980 Convention, paras 20 et seq.; Schlechtriem/Schwenzer/Schroeter/*Schroeter*, 8th German ed., Einleitung, paras 108 et seq.
52. *O. Meyer*, Constructive Interpretation, pp. 331, 332; *Neumann*, (2017) 21 VJ, p. 113; Schlechtriem/Schwenzer/Schroeter/*Schroeter*, 8th German ed., Einleitung, para. 110; cf. also *van Alstine*, (1998) 146 U. Pa. L. Rev., p. 777; a dynamic approach is typically considered to be appropriate for the interpretation of generic terms, *see* Dörr/Schmalenbach/*Dörr*, Art. 31 VCLT, para. 24; *Kramer*, pp. 152, 153.

Similarly, the CISG's general principles often merely provide for abstract normative guidelines, the content of which must be further specified, which again allows for a dynamic approach to the CISG's interpretation and application.[53] Additionally, the parties are free to decide how to deal with changing circumstances and needs as the CISG prioritises the contract concluded between the parties (Art. 6 CISG) and any practice they may have established between them (Art. 9 CISG).[54] All of this goes to show that a dynamic approach to the interpretation is suitable for the CISG.

Conversely, adherence to a static approach of interpreting the CISG would put the Convention at risk of becoming ossified.[55] In turn, judges or arbitrators may be tempted to have recourse to domestic laws more often instead of relying on the 'outdated' CISG.[56] In the long run, this would endanger the success of the CISG and undo the benefits achieved by the unification of international sales law.[57] Therefore, a dynamic approach to the interpretation of the CISG is generally preferable. This dynamic approach will underlie the remarks made in this study, even if it is not explicitly mentioned.

IV. DETERMINING THE CISG'S SUBSTANTIVE SCOPE OF APPLICATION AND GAP-FILLING

This study takes the position that the CISG may be applied to framework agreements in certain circumstances.[58] If the CISG does apply, it should be noted that the Convention typically does not address all aspects of such contracts. The CISG is, in fact, by nature fragmentary and non-exhaustive.[59] In addition, there might be concurrent rules of domestic laws that deal with specific aspects of framework agreements. Therefore, it is crucial to establish criteria to determine the CISG's substantive scope of application and to delineate the Convention's gap-filling mechanism in advance.

53. *See Karollus*, p. 17; *van Alstine*, (1998) 146 U. Pa. L. Rev., pp. 775 et seq.; cf. also *Muñoz*, (2019) 24 Unif. L. Rev., p. 285 (with regard to the question whether software may be characterised as 'goods').
54. *Honnold/Flechtner*, Salient Features of the 1980 Convention, para. 21; *O. Meyer*, Constructive Interpretation, pp. 331, 332; Schlechtriem/Schwenzer/Schroeter/*Schroeter*, 8th German ed., Einleitung, para. 109.
55. On the risk of ossification in a general manner: *B. Köhler*, Independent Development, p. 4; *O. Meyer*, Constructive Interpretation, pp. 320 et seq.; *Schroeter*, RabelsZ 81 (2017), pp. 69, 70; *van Alstine*, (1998) 146 U. Pa. L. Rev., p. 755.
56. Cf. *B. Köhler*, Independent Development, pp. 4, 5; *O. Meyer*, Constructive Interpretation, pp. 320, 321.
57. *B. Köhler*, Independent Development, p. 5.
58. *See* Chs 3 and 4 below.
59. *Schroeter*, para. 92; *Torsello*, pp. 206, 207.

1. Criteria to Determine the CISG's Substantive Scope

a. Limited Use of Article 4 CISG

Some courts and scholars have sought to determine the Convention's substantive sphere of application by reference to Art. 4 CISG.[60] This provision holds that the CISG governs 'only the formation of the contract of sale and the rights and obligations of the seller and buyer arising from such a contract'. It then goes on to state 'in particular, except as otherwise expressly provided in this Convention, it is not concerned with [...]' and lists the validity of the contract and the effects on property in the goods sold.

It has, however, been rightfully criticised that Art. 4 CISG by itself is of limited use for determining the Convention's substantive sphere of application.[61] The CISG not only governs the formation of sales contracts and rights and obligations that arise from them, but also, e.g., contracts to modify or terminate a sales contract[62] under Art. 29 CISG.[63] In addition, the second sentence of Art. 4 CISG is neither exclusive nor inclusive, as the CISG is also concerned with issues of validity in certain cases (e.g., formal validity in the sense of Art. 11 CISG), and there might be other issues that fall outside of its substantive scope of application beyond those explicitly mentioned.[64] This illustrates that Art. 4 CISG provides no precise guidelines to determine the Convention's substantive sphere of application.[65] Consequently, it is necessary to consider additional criteria in this context.

b. Two-Step Test

Schroeter has proposed a two-step test that offers more substantive criteria and takes the mandates enshrined in Art. 7(1) CISG into account.[66] According to this test, the first step is to ascertain whether the factual situation in question is covered by the CISG

60. *See Caterpillar, Inc. et al. v. Usinor Industeel et al.*, US Dist. Ct. ND Ill., 30 March 2005, CISG-online 1007, pp. 10 et seq.; OLG Hamm, 2 April 2009, CISG-online 1978, para. 59; *Hartnell*, (1993) 18 Yale J. Int'l L., pp. 14, 19; *Lookofsky*, Understanding the CISG, § 2.6; Witz/Salger/Lorenz/*W. Witz*, Art. 7 CISG, para. 26.
61. *Schroeter*, (2013) 58 Vill. L. Rev., pp. 553 et seq.; *Schroeter*, paras 151, 152; *Schroeter*, Unif. L. Rev. 2017, pp. 50 et seq.; cf. also *Janssen/Kiene*, p. 266; *B. Köhler*, Independent Development, pp. 13, 14.
62. *See* Ch. 3 II. 1. below.
63. Kröll *et al./Djordjevic*, Art. 4 CISG, para. 6; Schlechtriem/Schwenzer/Schroeter/*Ferrari*, 8th German ed., Art. 4 CISG, para. 8; Schlechtriem/Schwenzer/Schroeter/*Hachem*, 5th English ed., Art. 4 CISG, para. 2; *Schroeter*, (2013) 58 Vill. L. Rev., p. 557; *Schroeter*, para. 151; cf. also *B. Köhler*, Independent Development, pp. 12, 13.
64. *Schroeter*, (2013) 58 Vill. L. Rev., pp. 557, 558; *Schroeter*, para. 152; *Schroeter*, Unif. L. Rev. 2017, pp. 51, 52.
65. *Schroeter*, (2013) 58 Vill. L. Rev., p. 558; *Schroeter*, paras 151, 152; *Schroeter*, Unif. L. Rev. 2017, p. 52 (with regard to validity); cf. also *B. Köhler*, Independent Development, p. 13 (Art. 4 CISG is not an appropriate means of determining matters governed by the CISG 'in less evident cases').
66. In detail on the two-step approach: *Schroeter*, (2013) 58 Vill. L. Rev., pp. 556 et seq.; *Schroeter*, paras 160 et seq.; this approach is endorsed by: CISG-AC, Op. 23 *Beale*, Rule 3, Comments 3.5. et seq. (although in a different context); *B. Köhler*, pp. 51, 52; *B. Köhler*, Independent

(factual criterion).[67] This boils down to an interpretation of the Convention and its general principles in accordance with Art. 7(1) CISG.[68] In a second step, the factual criterion is to be supplemented by a 'normative' or legal criterion.[69] In accordance with the legal criterion, it is necessary to determine whether the CISG addresses a particular risk or attempts to reconcile conflicting interests within the covered factual scenario.[70] If both of these criteria are met, the CISG governs the matter and as a result will supersede any overlapping domestic law rules.[71]

The factual criterion has the advantage that it ignores dogmatic categories in characterising a factual situation and rather looks at its 'substance'.[72] In doing so, an international uniform solution in line with Art. 7(1) CISG is more likely to be found.[73] In addition, the legal criterion allows for a reasonable assessment whether a matter is governed by the CISG or not – without overly inflating the Convention's substantive sphere of application.[74] As the two-step test overall offers more accurate and nuanced criteria to determine whether a specific matter falls within the CISG's substantive scope of application, it will be relied upon in this study.

2. The Gap-Filling Mechanism Set Forth by Article 7(2) CISG

After it has been determined that a specific matter falls within the Convention's substantive scope of application, it may still be the case that the CISG does not provide an answer to all questions that might arise out of or in conjunction with this matter. In such cases, the mechanism enshrined in Art. 7(2) CISG may come into play. This provision holds that 'questions concerning matters governed by this Convention which are not expressly settled in it' are to be settled in conformity with the general principles underlying the CISG or in conformity with the law applicable by virtue of international private law rules. In the initial step, it is necessary to determine whether there is a question concerning a matter that is governed by the Convention but not expressly settled in it.[75] Subsequently, the identified question must be addressed in conformity with CISG's general principles or the applicable domestic law, as stipulated in Art. 7(2) CISG.

Development, p. 14; Schlechtriem/Schwenzer/Schroeter/*Hachem*, 5th English ed., Art. 4 CISG, para. 29; cf. also *C. Witz*, para. 114.12.

67. With more details on the factual criterion: *Schroeter*, Vill. L. Rev. 2013, pp. 564, 565; *Schroeter*, paras 161 et seq.
68. *Schroeter*, para. 161; *see also B. Köhler*, Independent Development, p. 14.
69. In detail: *Schroeter*, Vill. L. Rev. 2013, pp. 566 et seq.; *Schroeter*, paras 165 et seq.
70. *Schroeter*, Vill. L. Rev. 2013, pp. 566 et seq.; *Schroeter*, paras 165 et seq.; cf. also CISG-AC, Op. 23 *Beale*, Rule 3, Comments 3.14., 3.15. (purposes of the Convention and of the domestic rules must be 'broadly the same').
71. *Schroeter*, (2013) 58 Vill. L. Rev., p. 563; *Schroeter*, paras 148, 169.
72. *Schroeter*, (2013) 58 Vill. L. Rev., p. 564; cf. also *Honnold/Flechtner*, Art. 4 CISG, paras 87, 90.
73. CISG-AC, Op. 23 *Beale*, Rule 3, Comment 3.7.; *Schroeter*, (2013) 58 Vill. L. Rev., p. 564.
74. Cf. *B. Köhler*, Independent Development, p. 14; *Schroeter*, (2013) 58 Vill. L. Rev., p. 567.
75. *Janssen/Kiene*, p. 265; *B. Köhler*, Independent Development, p. 12; MüKoBGB/*Gruber*, Art. 7 CISG, para. 36; Schlechtriem/Schwenzer/Schroeter/*Ferrari*, 8th German ed., Art. 7 CISG, para. 43; *Schroeter*, para. 172.

a. *Questions Concerning Matters Governed by This Convention but Not Expressly Settled in It*

Art. 7(2) CISG distinguishes between 'matters' and 'questions', which could be interpreted to mean that a matter contains multiple questions, as merely some of the questions have been expressly settled.[76] Whether the Convention governs a matter essentially requires defining the CISG's substantive scope of application.[77] As stated above,[78] the two-step test should be employed in this context.

Once it has been established that the CISG governs a certain matter, Art. 7(2) CISG requires there to be a question within this matter which has not been expressly settled by the Convention.[79] A question is not expressly settled if it is not answered by an interpretation of the CISG's provisions in accordance with the CISG's principles and methods of interpretation.[80] Or put simply, there must be a 'gap' within the Convention.[81] Such gaps may result from the fact that the drafters of the Convention could not foresee later developments, e.g., technical changes, or that they simply have been overlooked.[82] If a gap has been identified in this way, the subsequent step is to fill it.

b. *Filling Gaps in the CISG*

Art. 7(2) CISG holds that gaps 'are to be settled in conformity with the general principles on which it is based [...]'. Although not specifically mentioned in this provision, the prevailing view advocates that gaps may also be filled by analogies to other provisions in the Convention.[83] Filling gaps by way of analogy should indeed be possible under the CISG based on the fundamental principle that comparable cases are

76. *Schroeter*, para. 172; *Schroeter*, Vill. L. Rev. 2013, p. 566.
77. *Gruber*, pp. 282 et seq.; *Janssen/Kiene*, p. 265; *B. Köhler*, Independent Development, p. 12; *Magnus*, RabelsZ 95 (1995), p. 475; MüKoBGB/*Gruber*, Art. 7 CISG, para. 36; Schlechtriem/Schwenzer/Schroeter/*Ferrari*, 8th German ed., Art. 7 CISG, para. 43; *Schroeter*, para. 172; Witz/Salger/Lorenz/*W. Witz*, Art. 7 CISG, paras 26 et seq.; cf. also *Himmen*, pp. 64, 79, 80; Staudinger/*Magnus*, Art. 7 CISG, para. 38.
78. *See* Ch. 1 IV. 1. b. above.
79. *Gruber*, p. 282; *Himmen*, p. 80; *Janssen/Kiene*, p. 265; *B. Köhler*, p. 52; *Magnus*, Tracing Methodology, p. 44; MüKoBGB/*Gruber*, Art. 7 CISG, para. 34; Schlechtriem/Schwenzer/Schroeter/*Ferrari*, 8th German ed., Art. 7 CISG, para. 43; *Schroeter*, para. 172; Staudinger/*Magnus*, Art. 7 CISG, para. 39; cf. also *C. Witz*, para. 116.142.
80. *Himmen*, p. 80; *B. Köhler*, p. 52; cf. also *Janssen/Kiene*, p. 266; *Schroeter*, para. 173; Witz/Salger/Lorenz/*W. Witz*, Art. 7 CISG, para. 29; *see* Ch. 1 III. 1., 2. above on the CISG's principles and methods of interpretation.
81. The CISG is not familiar with the term 'gap', *see Schroeter*, para. 172.
82. Schlechtriem/Schwenzer/Schroeter/*Hachem*, 5th English ed., Art. 7 CISG, para. 30; *Schroeter*, para. 173.
83. *Enderlein/Maskow*, Art. 7 CISG, note 9.1; *Ferrari*, IHR 2013, p. 189; *Gruber*, pp. 287 et seq.; *Herber/Czerwenka*, Art. 7 CISG, para. 11; *Himmen*, pp. 159 et seq.; *Neumann*, (2017) 21 VJ, p. 113; *Karner/Koziol*, para. 43; *B. Köhler*, pp. 53, 54; *B. Köhler*, Independent Development, p. 15; Kröll *et al./Perales Viscasillas*, Art. 7 CISG, para. 57; MüKoBGB/*Gruber*, Art. 7 CISG, para. 37; Schlechtriem/Schwenzer/Schroeter/*Ferrari*, 8th German ed., Art. 7 CISG, para. 47; Schlechtriem/Schwenzer/Schroeter/*Hachem*, 5th English ed., Art. 7 CISG, para. 31; *C. Witz*, para. 116.132; Witz/Salger/Lorenz/*W. Witz*, Art. 7 CISG, para. 30 (distinguishing between '*Einzelanalogie*' and '*Gesamtanalogie*').

to be treated alike.[84] Whether cases are comparable depends on the *ratio legis* of a specific provision which has to be determined on the grounds of the Convention and the principles it is based on.[85] A number of scholars hold that there is a hierarchy of gap-filling mechanisms, with filling gaps by analogy being of greater priority than having recourse to the general principles.[86] However, this view is not convincing as the boundaries between these two gap-filling mechanisms appear to be blurred.[87] Moreover, this distinction is hardly of any practical relevance.[88] This study will therefore rely on gap-filling by having recourse to the CISG's general principles and by analogy interchangeably.[89]

Beyond that, the CISG's general principles are to be found by subjecting the Convention's provisions to an inductive process.[90] In some cases, a literal and systematic interpretation of specific CISG provisions may reveal that they intend to establish more general principles for the entire Convention, such as the principle of party autonomy.[91] Apart from that, general principles may be based on one or multiple provisions in the CISG.[92] Some general principles may also follow from the Convention's overall context, such as the principle of *pacta sunt servanda* which is not explicitly mentioned in the CISG.[93] However, general principles may be merely based on the CISG itself ('on which it is based') and not on external rules, such as the

84. *Canaris*, Lücken, pp. 71 et seq.; *B. Köhler*, p. 54; *B. Köhler*, Independent Development, p. 15; *Kramer*, p. 230; *Kropholler*, pp. 293, 294.
85. *Gruber*, p. 292; *B. Köhler*, p. 54; *B. Köhler*, Independent Development, p. 15.
86. Bianca/Bonell/*Bonell*, Art. 7 CISG, note 2.3.2.1.; *Gruber*, p. 288; *Karner/Koziol*, para. 43; Kröll *et al./Perales Viscasillas*, Art. 7 CISG, para. 57; Schlechtriem/Schwenzer/Schroeter/*Ferrari*, 8th German ed., Art. 7 CISG, para. 47; cf. also *C. Witz*, para. 116.132.
87. *See Himmen*, pp. 159 et seq.; similarly, *Karollus*, p. 17 (the mechanism set forth in Art. 7(2) CISG can be considered an overall analogy ('*Rechts-/Gesamtanalogie*')); *B. Köhler*, p. 55; but *see* Bianca/Bonell/*Bonell*, Art. 7 CISG, notes 2.3.2.1., 2.3.2.2.
88. *Schlechtriem*, Symposium Vischer, p. 11; *Schroeter*, para. 173; *C. Witz*, para. 116.132.
89. Similarly *B. Köhler*, p. 55, holding that the most appropriate course of action is to rely on the method that is most compatible with the CISG's overall system and that most closely reflects the principles set forth in Art. 7(1) CISG with regard to a specific legal question.
90. *Bridge*, Int'l Sale of Goods, para. 10.46; *Karollus*, p. 16; *Schroeter*, para. 177; cf. also *Magnus*, RabelsZ 95 (1995), pp. 477, 478.
91. *Himmen*, pp. 106, 107; *Herber/Czerwenka*, Art. 7 CISG, para. 11; *Janssen/Kiene*, pp. 271 et seq.; *Magnus*, RabelsZ 95 (1995), p. 477; Staudinger/*Magnus*, Art. 7 CISG, para. 40; Witz/Salger/Lorenz/*W. Witz*, Art. 7 CISG, para. 30; cf. also *Bridge*, Int'l Sale of Goods, para. 10.46; *Schroeter*, para. 181; *van Alstine*, (1998) 146 U. Pa. L. Rev., p. 750.
92. *Himmen*, pp. 107, 108; *Janssen/Kiene*, pp. 273 et seq.; *Schroeter*, paras 177 et seq.; *B. Köhler*, p. 56; *B. Köhler*, Independent Development, pp. 15, 16; *Magnus*, RabelsZ 95 (1995), p. 478; Staudinger/*Magnus*, Art. 7 CISG, para. 40; providing a list of general principles under the CISG: BeckOK/*Saenger*, Art. 7 CISG, para. 7; *Janssen/Kiene*, pp. 271 et seq.; Kröll *et al./Perales Viscasillas*, Art. 7 CISG, paras 62 et seq.; *Magnus*, RabelsZ 95 (1995), pp. 480 et seq.; MüKoBGB/*Gruber*, Art. 7 CISG, para. 39; Schlechtriem/Schwenzer/Schroeter/*Ferrari*, 8th German ed., Art. 7 CISG, paras 48 et seq.; Schlechtriem/Schwenzer/Schroeter/*Hachem*, 5th English ed., Art. 7 CISG, paras 31 et seq.; Staudinger/*Magnus*, Art. 7 CISG, paras 41 et seq.; *C. Witz*, para. 116.143.
93. *Magnus*, RabelsZ 95 (1995), p. 478.

UPICC.[94] Once a general principle has been inductively derived, it must be assessed as to whether its abstract normative guidelines are apt for a concrete question.[95]

Where analogy to other provisions is not possible and there are no apt general principles to be applied to a specific question, Art. 7(2) CISG provides for recourse to 'the law applicable by virtue of the rules of private international law'.[96] Yet, having recourse to the applicable domestic law is merely an *ultima ratio*.[97] The CISG does not contain any rules on how to determine the applicable domestic law.[98] State courts thus have to turn to the relevant private international law rules in the forum state in order to determine the applicable domestic law.[99] In this context, the Rome I Regulation is of relevance within the European Union (*see* Arts 3 and 4 Rome I Regulation),[100] and the Swiss PILA in conjunction with the 1955 Hague Convention on the Law Applicable to International Sales Contracts within Switzerland (*see* Art. 118(1) PILA; Arts 3 and 4 of the 1955 Hague Convention).[101] Arbitral tribunals must turn to the applicable arbitral rules to determine the applicable domestic law.[102]

V. CONCLUSION

In determining whether and how the CISG deals with framework agreements, the Convention's provisions will be interpreted in accordance with its interpretation principles and by relying on its methods of interpretation. Art. 7(1) CISG refers to the relevance of the CISG's international character (autonomous interpretation), the need to promote uniformity in its application (uniform interpretation) and the observance of good faith in international trade as principles of interpretation.[103] Although the CISG is silent on how to achieve results that conform with these principles, there appears to be

94. BeckOK/*Saenger*, Art. 7 CISG, para. 7; *Himmen*, pp. 109 et seq.; MüKoBGB/*Gruber*, Art. 7 CISG, para. 39; Schlechtriem/Schwenzer/Schroeter/*Ferrari*, 8th German ed., Art. 7 CISG, paras 55, 62 et seq. (UPICC as persuasive authority and interpretative tool); Schlechtriem/Schwenzer/Schroeter/*Hachem*, 5th English ed., Art. 7 CISG, para. 36 (UPICC to find additional arguments); *Schroeter*, para. 179; *Schroeter*, RabelsZ 81 (2017), p. 65; but *see* Brunner/Gottlieb/*Brunner/Wagner*, Art. 7 CISG, para. 11; Kröll *et al./Perales Viscasillas*, Art. 7 CISG, para. 67; *Magnus*, RabelsZ 95 (1995), pp. 492, 493.
95. *Karollus*, p. 17; *B. Köhler*, Independent Development, p. 16.
96. BeckOK/*Saenger*, Art. 7 CISG, para. 8; MüKoBGB/*Gruber*, Art. 7 CISG, para. 40; Schlechtriem/Schwenzer/Schroeter/*Ferrari*, 8th German ed., Art. 7 CISG, para. 57; Schlechtriem/Schwenzer/Schroeter/*Hachem*, 5th English ed., Art. 7 CISG, para. 42; *Schroeter*, para. 186; Staudinger/*Magnus*, Art. 7 CISG, para. 58.
97. *Himmen*, p. 167; MüKoBGB/*Gruber*, Art. 7 CISG, para. 40; Schlechtriem/Schwenzer/Schroeter/*Ferrari*, 8th German ed., Art. 7 CISG, para. 58; Schlechtriem/Schwenzer/Schroeter/*Hachem*, 5th English ed., Art. 7 CISG, para. 42; Staudinger/*Magnus*, Art. 7 CISG, para. 58.
98. Schlechtriem/Schwenzer/Schroeter/*Hachem*, 5th English ed., Art. 7 CISG, para. 42.
99. Cf. *Schroeter*, para. 186; Staudinger/*Magnus*, Art. 7 CISG, para. 58; Schlechtriem/Schwenzer/Schroeter/*Hachem*, 5th English ed., Art. 7 CISG, para. 42.
100. With regard to Germany: BeckOK/*Saenger*, Art. 7 CISG, para. 8; MüKoBGB/*Gruber*, Art. 7 CISG, para. 40.
101. *See* Schlechtriem/Schwenzer/Schroeter/*Hachem*, 5th English ed., Art. 7 CISG, para. 42, who lists relevant private international law rules.
102. Schlechtriem/Schwenzer/Schroeter/*Hachem*, 5th English ed., Art. 7 CISG, para. 42.
103. *See* Ch. 1 III. 1. above.

consensus about the accepted methods of interpretation: The Convention's provisions are to be interpreted based on their wording (literal interpretation), their systematic position (systematic interpretation), their historical context (historical interpretation) and their purpose (teleological interpretation).[104]

More controversial is the role of comparative law in interpreting the CISG's provisions. Comparative law should be considered an auxiliary method of interpretation, which complements the other methods but should not be utilised to produce interpretative results on its own. Such an approach may assist in finding interpretative results that are capable of being internationally accepted and thus consistent with the CISG's international character and the need to promote uniformity in its application (Art. 7(1) CISG). This study will therefore include references to selected domestic law rules in order to ascertain whether a solution might be internationally acceptable. In addition, these references will help to identify and contextualise specific problems and to assess the CISG's relationship with domestic law rules which may concurrently apply. For the same reasons, references to the UNIDROIT Principles will be a part of this study.[105]

In the interpretation of any international treaty, a dispute concerns the question whether a treaty should be interpreted in a static or dynamic manner. A dynamic approach to the CISG's interpretation is generally preferable: the CISG is unlikely to ever be subject to amendments or have a successor, and hence the only promising option to develop it is by way of interpretation. Moreover, the CISG has been drafted in a way that makes it open to a dynamic approach. It contains broadly worded terms and general clauses which allow for a flexible and dynamic interpretation and application. Similarly, it includes abstract general principles which are equally open to a dynamic interpretation. A static approach, however, would endanger the Convention's long-term success and undo the benefits achieved by its unification.[106]

It will be argued in the course of this study that the CISG may be applied to framework agreements in certain circumstances. Even then, the Convention will not necessarily cover all aspects of such contracts, and there may be competing domestic law rules. It is thus crucial to determine the borders of the CISG's substantive scope of application. Art. 4 CISG is of limited use in that regard. Instead, a two-step test will be employed which requires both the application of a factual and legal criterion in order to determine the CISG's substantive sphere of application. This test has the advantage of offering more substantive and nuanced criteria in assessing whether the Convention governs a certain matter.[107]

Once it has been established that the CISG governs a certain matter, it is possible that the Convention does not provide an answer to a particular question. If so, Art. 7(2) CISG might come into play. According to this provision, there must be a question within a matter governed by the CISG which has not been expressly settled; or in other words, a gap. If a gap has been found, Art. 7(2) CISG primarily holds that it must be

104. *See* Ch. 1 III. 2. a. above.
105. *See* Ch. 1 III. 2. b. above.
106. *See* Ch. 1 III. 3. above.
107. *See* Ch. 1 IV. 1. above.

filled by relying on the CISG's general principles. Filling gaps under the CISG is possible by analogy as well as by having recourse to its general principles. Both methods will be referred to interchangeably, as the borders between them are blurred. The CISG's general principles normally follow inductively from one or multiple provisions in the Convention. In the absence of apt general principles that can be applied to a specific question, Art. 7(2) CISG holds that recourse should be had to the applicable domestic law, which must be determined in accordance with the relevant international private law rules in the forum state or the applicable arbitration rules.[108]

108. *See* Ch. 1 IV. 2. above.

CHAPTER 2

Notion of Framework Agreements

To begin, it is of paramount importance to establish an understanding of the notion of a 'framework agreement'. All analyses, evaluations and submissions made in the course of this study will be based on this understanding. The following section will therefore put forth a notion of framework agreements. It will first offer some general remarks and present a comparative overview of the understanding of framework agreements in selected domestic legal systems.

I. GENERAL REMARKS

1. No Mention in the CISG

The Convention itself does not define or even mention international framework agreements in any of its provisions. There is also no consistent terminology in academic writings that discuss the CISG's applicability to such contracts.[109] This further underlines the necessity of establishing a notion of framework agreements. Prior to this, a concise overview of the commercial background of framework agreements is warranted.

109. *See Honnold/Flechtner*, Art. 2 CISG, para. 71 footnote 41, acknowledging the inconsistent terminology; cf. further *Bridge*, Int'l Sale of Goods, para. 10.22 and Schlechtriem/Schwenzer/Schroeter/*Schroeter*, 5th English ed., Intro Arts 14–24 CISG, para. 24, who both seem to use a similar terminology ('framework contracts/agreements'); but *see Torsello*, pp. 240 et seq. (merely referring to '(preliminary) Distribution Agreements').

2. Commercial Background

Today's production and commercialisation of goods is characterised by economic cooperation between different market players.[110] For instance, the production of goods is typically divided into multiple subprocesses, each performed by a different company.[111] The same applies to the distribution and commercialisation of goods.[112] Such division of labour between several companies necessitates a significant number of delivery transactions.[113]

From a legal standpoint, one approach to these delivery transactions would be to conclude separate sales contracts for each transaction. However, the parties frequently seek to collaborate over an extended period of time for a number of reasons. Accordingly, this extended duration must also be reflected in their contract.[114] One of these reasons is that the buying party can ensure the acquisition of the goods with a consistent quality at a relatively stable price. The supplying party, however, can ensure having a trust- and creditworthy purchaser for its goods.[115] The conclusion of long-term agreements of any kind thus allows the involved parties to reliably plan ahead and improve the overall efficiency.[116] In light of the contract's duration, the parties might also be more incentivised to make large initial investments, the value of which will materialise over time.[117]

Similarly, the parties may have a reasonable interest in reacting to market fluctuations and therefore remain flexible in their supply relationship.[118] The ever-changing economic circumstances require modern merchants to remain relatively adaptable.[119] Hence, they may prefer not to enter into an agreement over fixed quantities of goods for an extended period of time.[120] Instead, one legal tool to combine the parties' interest in planning reliability with their interest in flexibility is the framework agreement.[121] Framework agreements facilitate the simplification and standardisation of the parties' contractual relationship by providing a uniform

110. *Gass/Lange*, p. 1; *Gebhardt*, pp. 13, 14; *Hoffbauer*, p. 1; from an economic perspective, each company has to make a 'make or buy'-decision, cf. *Gebhardt*, p. 14; *Saxinger*, pp. 29 et seq.
111. *Hoffbauer*, p. 1; *Wellenhofer-Klein*, p. 5.
112. Cf. *Hoffbauer*, p. 1; *Gass/Lange*, pp. 19, 20.
113. *Hoffbauer*, p. 1.
114. *Furrer/Lohri*, p. 22; *Gatsi*, pp. 2, 3; *Hoffbauer*, p. 1; *Weber*, ZSR 1987, p. 403; there are a number of reasons why parties enter into to long-term contracts: *Guo*, pp. 21, 22; cf. also the UN Economic Commission, Trade Facilitation Implementation Guide, 'Framework agreements' (https://tfig.unece.org/domains/purchasing/purchasing/framework-agreements/, last checked September 2025).
115. *Guo*, p. 21; cf. also *Budde/Geks*, ZVertriebsR 2012, p. 37.
116. *Budde/Geks*, ZVertriebsR 2012, p. 37; *Furrer/Lohri*, p. 23; *Gatsi*, p. 3; *Hoffbauer*, p. 1; cf. also Kull/Wildhaber/*Wildhaber*, paras 23 et seq.; *J. Schmidt*, (1983–1984) 6 Houst. J. Int'l L., p. 55; *Weber*, ZSR 1987, p. 403; UN Economic Commission for Europe, Trade Facilitation Implementation Guide, 'Framework agreements' (https://tfig.unece.org/domains/purchasing/purchasing/framework-agreements/, last checked September 2025).
117. Cf. Comment 5 on Art. 7.1.7 UPICC; *Guo*, p. 22.
118. *Gatsi*, p. 3; *Guo*, pp. 21, 22; *Hoffbauer*, pp. 1, 2; *Zuñiga Peralta*, (2021) 26 Unif. L. Rev., pp. 507, 508.
119. *Hoffbauer*, p. 94; *Lange*, NJOZ 2013, p. 577; *Zuñiga Peralta*, (2021) 26 Unif. L. Rev., p. 507.
120. *Hoffbauer*, pp. 1, 2; cf. also *Bremenkamp*, ZVertriebsR 2023, p. 207.
121. *Gatsi*, p. 3; *Hoffbauer*, p. 2; Sayag/*Pollaud-Dulian*, para. 20; *Weber*, ZSR 1986, p. 405.

frame;[122] thereby potentially reducing the administrative burden and associated costs.[123] Although the initial effort and expenses to establish such a contract may be greater than those required for other contracts, the downstream benefits will typically outweigh the initial efforts and expenses.[124]

II. COMPARATIVE OVERVIEW: UNDERSTANDING OF FRAMEWORK AGREEMENTS IN SELECTED DOMESTIC LEGAL SYSTEMS

The following overview will outline the notion of framework agreements in selected domestic legal systems. This overview is meant to provide perspective on domestic notions. Moreover, this information might be helpful in developing a notion of framework agreements for the purposes of this study that is capable of being internationally accepted (Art. 7(1) CISG).[125]

1. Germany

a. No Statutory Rules on Framework Agreements

There are no express statutory rules on framework agreements in German law.[126] Nonetheless, the term (*'Rahmenvertrag'*/*'Rahmenliefervertrag'*) has been used by scholars for a considerable amount of time.[127] This term describes an abstract category of contracts, primarily developed in academic writing.[128] It is important to note that scholars typically distinguish framework agreements from instalment contracts and precontracts under German law.[129]

A framework agreement may deal with a broad range of different factual circumstances, for example, with the accommodation of guests or with construction projects.[130] However, this study will focus on framework agreements that are related to the supply and distribution of goods.[131] Even within this category, a broad range of

122. *Mousseron/Seube*, D. 1973, p. 200; Sayag/*Pollaud-Dulian*, para. 17; *J. Schmidt*, (1983–1984) 6 Houst. J. Int'l L., p. 55.
123. *Hoffbauer*, p. 1; *Guo*, p. 22; UN Economic Commission for Europe, Trade Facilitation Implementation Guide, 'Framework agreements' (https://tfig.unece.org/domains/purchasing/purchasing/framework-agreements/, last checked September 2025).
124. UN Economic Commission for Europe, Trade Facilitation Implementation Guide, 'Framework agreements' (https://tfig.unece.org/domains/purchasing/purchasing/framework-agreements/, last checked September 2025).
125. *See* Ch. 1 III. 2. b. above (comparative law as an auxiliary method).
126. OLG München, 18 June 2018, CISG-online 3080; *Hoffbauer*, p. 7; *Muhl/Lüthge*, GWR 2016, p. 26.
127. *See, e.g., Ulmer*, pp. 300, 301 in 1969.
128. Cf. only *Hoffbauer*, p. 2; Jauernig/*Stadler*, § 311 BGB, para. 22; *Ulmer*, pp. 300, 301; *Wellenhofer-Klein*, p. 102.
129. *Hoffbauer*, pp. 20 et seq. with further references.
130. BGH, 30 April 1992, VII ZR 159/91; *Hoffbauer*, p. 2; *Weber*, ZSR 1987, p. 415.
131. With a similar distinction: *Hoffbauer*, p. 2; Martinek/Semler/Flohr/*Budde/Eckhoff*, § 40, paras 12, 13.

different contracts can be found in practice.[132] Nonetheless, common characteristics have been carved out.[133]

b. General Features

In general, framework agreements provide a 'roof' for multiple individual contracts subsequently concluded.[134] In the context of supply relationships, framework agreements are directed and tailored towards the conclusion of a series of individual sales contracts.[135] The framework agreement serves to link these individual sales contracts to a larger unit.[136] Nevertheless, it is necessary to differentiate between the framework agreement and the legally independent individual sales contracts.[137] There is a fundamental distinction between the framework agreement and the individual sales contracts.[138] Legal scholars refer to this approach as 'two-tier' ('*Zweistufigkeit*'), which is an essential feature of framework agreements under German law.[139]

Although a framework agreement is concerned with the parties' supply relationship, it does not contain delivery or payment obligations in the sense of § 433 of the German Civil Code (BGB).[140] These obligations will only be created once the individual sales contracts are concluded.[141] Framework agreements are characterised as contracts sui generis, not as a sub-type of sales contracts.[142] As a consequence, the general rules of the BGB and other general principles of the law of obligations are primarily applicable.[143]

132. OLG München, 18 June 2018, CISG-online 3080; *Budde/Geks*, ZVertriebsR 2012, p. 37; *Wellenhofer-Klein*, p. 105.
133. Cf. *Budde/Geks*, ZVertriebsR 2012, p. 37.
134. *Hoffbauer*, p. 5; cf. also *Gebhardt*, p. 42; *Muhl/Lüthge*, GWR 2016, p. 26; *Ulmer*, p. 300.
135. *Budde/Geks*, ZVertriebsR 2012, p. 37; *Hoffbauer*, pp. 1, 8; MüKoBGB/*Busche*, Vor § 145 BGB, para. 44 (framework agreements prepare and facilitate the conclusion of individual contracts); cf. also *Rother*, FS Larenz, p. 437.
136. *Fuchs-Wissemann*, p. 99; *Gass/Lange*, p. 14; Martinek/Semler/Flohr/*Budde/Eckhoff*, § 40, para. 11; *Ulmer*, pp. 300, 301; cf. *Rother*, FS Larenz, pp. 438, 439.
137. BGH, 4 April 1979, BGHZ 74, 136, 140 (in the context of distribution contracts).
138. Cf. OLG München, 18 June 2018, CISG-online 3080; BeckOGK/*Möslein*, § 145 BGB, para. 79; *Budde/Geks*, ZVertriebsR 2012, p. 37; *Gass/Lange*, pp. 14, 15; *Henrich*, p. 117; *Hoffbauer*, p. 6; Jauernig/*Stadler*, § 311 BGB, para. 22; Martinek/Semler/Flohr/*Budde/Eckhoff*, § 40, paras 8 et seq.; *Muhl/Lüthge*, GWR 2016, p. 26; *Ulmer*, p. 300.
139. *Budde/Geks*, ZVertriebsR 2012, p. 37; *Hoffbauer*, p. 13; *Iliou*, ZVertriebsR 2023, p. 81; Martinek/Semler/Flohr/*Budde/Eckhoff*, § 40, para. 8; *Muhl/Lüthge*, GWR 2016, p. 26.
140. *Budde/Geks*, ZVertriebsR 2012, p. 37; *Gass/Lange*, p. 14; *Hoffbauer*, pp. 13, 83 et seq. (holding that a framework agreement cannot contain payment and delivery obligations or else it must be characterised as a type of sales contract); *Iliou*, ZVertriebsR 2023, p. 81; Martinek/Semler/Flohr/*Budde/Eckhoff*, § 40, para. 8.
141. *Budde/Geks*, ZVertriebsR 2012, p. 37; *Hoffbauer*, p. 13; Martinek/Semler/Flohr/*Budde/Eckhoff*, § 40, paras 8, 9.
142. *Hoffbauer*, pp. 14, 15; BGH, 4 April 1979, BGHZ 74, 136, 140.
143. 'Atypical' contracts are, in principle, governed by the general rules of the BGB and laws of obligation: BeckOGK/*Herresthal*, § 311 BGB, para. 83; *Hoffbauer*, p. 15; MüKoBGB/*Emmerich*, § 311 BGB, para. 26 (in appropriate circumstances, atypical contracts may also be subject to the rules governing 'typical' contracts); *Rother*, FS Larenz, p. 437 (recourse to general principles necessary).

Moreover, framework agreements are intended to govern the parties' supply relationship for an extended period of time. They are usually concluded for a fixed period of time, sometimes even for an indefinite period of time.[144] Therefore, they are characterised as long-term contracts ('*Dauerschuldverhältnis*').[145] This characterisation implicates legal consequences, in particular for the termination of framework agreements.[146]

c. *Characteristic Obligations in Framework Agreements*

Framework agreements typically encompass a selection of predetermined terms for the individual sales contracts.[147] These terms are intended to be incorporated into each individual sales contract.[148] The idea is to ensure that all subsequent transactions are conducted under largely the same conditions.[149] Normally, the parties to the framework agreement are also the parties to the individual sales contracts.[150] Consequently, there is no need for renegotiation when the individual sales contracts are concluded.[151] Framework agreements usually contain an obligation to include these predetermined terms in the sales contracts subsequently concluded.[152]

In addition to terms relating to the sale of goods, framework agreements frequently contain general clauses pertaining to the cooperation between the parties.[153] For instance, the parties may include a non-disclosure obligation in their agreement which is binding regardless of the conclusion of individual contracts.[154]

The question whether framework agreements necessarily contain an obligation to conclude individual contracts is a matter of dispute.[155] One school of thought maintains that a framework agreement always obliges at least one or even both parties

144. *Gebhardt*, p. 42; *Henrich*, p. 117; cf. in the context of contract termination: *Muhl/Lüthge*, GWR 2016, p. 27.
145. OLG München, 18 June 2018, CISG-online 3080; *Budde/Geks*, ZVertriebsR 2012, p. 37; *Fuchs-Wissemann*, p. 101; *Hoffbauer*, p. 17; Martinek/Semler/Flohr/*Budde/Eckhoff*, § 40, para. 11; *Muhl/Lüthge*, GWR 2016, p. 26; *Saxinger*, p. 108; *Ulmer*, p. 301.
146. *Hoffbauer*, p. 15; *Muhl/Lüthge*, GWR 2016, p. 27; *Ulmer*, pp. 257 et seq.; *Wellenhofer-Klein*, p. 103 footnote 10.
147. OLG München, 18 June 2018, CISG-online 3080, p. 10; BGH, 4 April 1979, BGHZ 74, 136, 140; *Budde/Geks*, ZVertriebsR 2012, p. 37; *Gass/Lange*, p. 14; *Gebhardt*, p. 42; *Henrich*, p. 117; *Hoffbauer*, p. 5; Martinek/Semler/Flohr/*Budde/Eckhoff*, § 40, para. 11; *Muhl/Lüthge*, GWR 2016, p. 26; Staudinger/*Bork*, Vorbem. zu §§ 145–156 BGB, para. 54; *Ulmer*, p. 300; *Wellenhofer-Klein*, p. 103.
148. OLG München, 18 June 2018, CISG-online 3080, p. 10; *Budde/Geks*, ZVertriebsR 2012, p. 41; *Hoffbauer*, p. 5; *Saxinger*, p. 106.
149. OLG München, 18 June 2018, CISG-online 3080.
150. *Rother*, FS Larenz, p. 438.
151. OLG München, 18 June 2018, CISG-online 3080, p. 10; *Budde/Geks*, ZVertriebsR 2012, p. 41; *Hoffbauer*, p. 6.
152. *Hoffbauer*, p. 17.
153. *Hoffbauer*, pp. 12, 13.
154. *Hoffbauer*, pp. 13, 17.
155. Reproducing the discussion: *Hoffbauer*, pp. 89 et seq.; *Wellenhofer-Klein*, pp. 104, 105.

to conclude individual contracts.[156] According to this view, it is at the very core of framework agreements that the parties indicate their willingness to conclude individual contracts over a period of time.[157] The contrary and probably prevailing view holds that a framework agreement typically does not contain an obligation to conclude individual contracts, or at least that this obligation is not enforceable, since it lacks the required definiteness.[158] However, if a party refuses to conclude an individual contract, the opposing party might be entitled to damages based on a breach of the framework agreement ('*positive Vertragsverletzung*').[159] Furthermore, the absence of an obligation to conclude contracts distinguishes framework agreements from precontracts, according to this interpretation.[160] A third view proposes that there are framework agreements that include an obligation to conclude individual contracts, as well as framework agreements that do not include such an obligation; this should essentially be a matter of contract interpretation on a case-by-case basis.[161] The proponents of this view argue that the parties to a framework agreement intend to have as much flexibility as possible, and thus, it is up to them to determine whether they wish to include an obligation to conclude individual contracts.[162] For example, an obligation to conclude individual contracts may be assumed if the parties include a minimum purchase requirement in their framework agreement.[163] Furthermore, this view suggests that framework agreements can be distinguished from precontracts by using other criteria, primarily the contract's duration.[164]

d. Summary

Framework agreements are recognised under German law, despite the absence of an express statutory regulation. They intend to regulate an ongoing supply relationship between the parties. In addition, framework agreements are directed and tailored towards the conclusion of individual sales contracts. There is a fundamental distinction between the framework agreement and the individual sales contracts ('two-tier'). The framework agreement and the individual sales contracts form an economic unit but are

156. *Fuchs-Wissemann*, pp. 26 et seq.; *Saxinger*, p. 106; *Ulmer*, p. 300; cf. also *Henrich*, p. 117, who, however, asserts that the obligation to conclude individual contracts is unenforceable on the grounds that framework agreements lack the necessary definiteness required by German law.
157. *Fuchs-Wissemann*, p. 27, otherwise the agreement is a non-binding '*Normenvereinbarung*'; *Ulmer*, p. 301.
158. BGH, 30 April 1992, VII ZR 158/91 (architecture framework agreement); BeckOGK/*Möslein*, § 145 BGB, para. 79; BeckOK/*Eckert*, § 145 BGB, para. 27; *Gass/Lange*, p. 14; *Gebhardt*, pp. 42, 43; Erman/*Armbrüster*, Vor § 145 BGB, para. 55; *Neuner*, § 36, para. 16; Staudinger/*Bork*, Vorbem. zu § 145–156 BGB, para. 54.
159. Cf. only BGH, 30 April 1992, VII ZR 158/91; *Henrich*, p. 117.
160. *Gebhardt*, p. 42; Erman/*Armbrüster*, Vor § 145 BGB, para. 56; *Neuner*, § 36, para. 16.
161. *Budde/Geks*, ZVertriebsR 2012, p. 37; *Hoffbauer*, p. 94; Martinek/Semler/Flohr/*Budde/Eckhoff*, § 40, para. 9; *Muhl/Lüthge*, GWR 2016, p. 26; *Wellenhofer-Klein*, pp. 104, 105.
162. *Hoffbauer*, p. 94; *Wellenhofer-Klein*, p. 105.
163. *Budde/Geks*, ZVertriebsR 2012, p. 39 (with further examples pp. 38 et seq.); *Hoffbauer*, p. 101 (further examples pp. 96 et seq.).
164. *Fuchs-Wissemann*, pp. 22, 23; *Hoffbauer*, pp. 20 et seq.; *Wellenhofer-Klein*, pp. 103, 104; *Ulmer*, pp. 300, 301.

nevertheless independent contracts. Framework agreements are characterised as contracts sui generis and thus governed by general principles and the general part of the BGB. In addition, they are characterised as long-term contracts.

Framework agreements predetermine selected clauses pertaining to the sale of goods for the individual sales contracts. The parties are usually obliged to incorporate these terms into each individual sales contract. Furthermore, the framework agreement usually regulates specific aspects of the general cooperation between the parties, such as confidentiality. It is controversially discussed whether framework agreements oblige the parties to conclude individual sales contracts. The slightly predominant view maintains that framework agreements typically do not contain an obligation to conclude individual sales contracts, or at least that such an obligation is not enforceable.

2. Switzerland

a. No Statutory Rules on Framework Agreements

There is no statutory law on framework agreements in Switzerland.[165] However, the term is frequently mentioned in academic writing as well as case law.[166] Framework agreements are often discussed in the context of sole distribution contracts (‘*Alleinvertriebsvertrag*’),[167] which represent the most relevant form of framework agreements in practice.[168] In certain instances, they are also referenced in order to differentiate between precontracts and framework agreements, since the former are explicitly addressed in Art. 22 of the Swiss Code of Obligations (*CO* or *OR*).[169]

b. General Features

A framework agreement provides a legal bond and basis for a business relationship between the parties.[170] It establishes a unified legal environment for individual

165. *Weber*, ZSR 1987, p. 406.
166. *See, e.g.*, BGer, 26 July 2019, 4A_42/2019; *Bucher*, p. 109; *Furrer/Lohri*, pp. 20 et seq.; *von der Crone*, pp. 242 et seq.; *Weber*, ZSR 1987, pp. 403 et seq.
167. Cf. only BGer, 18 April 2024, CISG-online 6978, para. 12; BSK OR-I/*Amstutz/Morin*, Einl. vor Arts 184 ff. CO, paras 112 et seq.; CHK/*Jacobs*, Innominatverträge/AVV, para. 2; Kull/Wildhaber/*Wildhaber*, para. 202; *Oetiker/Weibel/Mata*, IHR 2022, p. 53; ZK OR/*Schönle*, Vorbem. Arts 184–551 CO, para. 32; critical of this terminology: *Fountoulakis*, p. 61; *Fountoulakis*, recht 2008, p. 224.
168. *See* for case law relating to distribution contracts (regarding different questions): BGer, 31 August 2018, 4A_241/2017; BGer, 18 June 2004, 4C.130/2004.
169. BSK OR-I/*Zellweger-Gutknecht*, Art. 22 CO, para. 29; KuKo OR/*Herzog*, Art. 22 CO, para. 7; BK OR/*Kramer*, Art. 22 CO, para. 76.
170. *Bucher*, p. 109; *Furrer/Lohri*, p. 24; *Weber*, ZSR 1987, p. 410.

contracts that will be concluded in the future.[171] Framework agreements have been referred to as a 'constitution' for the parties' collaboration.[172] In general, there is a fundamental distinction between the framework agreement and the individual sales contracts to be concluded at a later time.[173] The latter are concerned with the specifics of each individual sales transaction.[174]

Framework agreements are typically characterised as either contracts sui generis or mixed contracts.[175] Therefore, the general rules of the Swiss Code of Obligations as well as general principles from Swiss law of obligations are applicable to framework agreements.[176] In addition, the special rules of the Swiss Code of Obligations are applicable (by analogy) if a framework agreement is characterised as a mixed contract.[177] Furthermore, framework agreements are characterised as long-term contracts ('*Dauerschuldverhältnis*'),[178] which has legal implications, in particular with regard to the contract's termination and avoidance.[179] Given the close cooperation that is intended by the majority of parties to a framework agreement, some scholars highlight that the principle of good faith is of greater importance for the parties of such a contract in comparison to other agreements.[180]

171. *Weber*, ZSR 1987, p. 410.
172. *Furrer/Lohri*, p. 24.
173. BK OR/*Kramer*, Art. 22 CO, para. 76; BSK OR-I/*Zellweger-Gutknecht*, Vor Art. 1–40f CO, para. 40; BSK OR-I/*Zellweger-Gutknecht*, Art. 22 CO, para. 29; *Bucher*, p. 109; *Furrer/Lohri*, pp. 23, 24; KuKo OR/*Herzog*, Art. 22 CO, para. 7; Kull/Wildhaber/*Wildhaber*, para. 202; *von der Crone*, pp. 245, 246; *Weber*, ZSR 1987, p. 410; ZK OR/*Schönle*, Art. 184 CO, para. 104; ZK OR/*Schönle*, Vorbem. Arts 184–551 CO, para. 32.
174. *Bucher*, p. 109; *Furrer/Lohri*, p. 25; cf. also BSK OR-I/*Zellweger-Gutknecht*, Vor Art. 1–40f CO, para. 40; *Weber*, ZSR 1987, p. 410, who identifies a reificatory, specifying function of the individual contracts ('*ausfüllende, konkretisierende und spezifizierende Bedeutung*').
175. BGer, 31 August 2018, 4A_241/2017, note 3 (regarding sole distribution contracts); BSK OR-I/*Amstutz/Morin*, Einl. vor Arts 184 ff. CO, para. 115 (regarding sole distribution contracts); CHK/*Jacobs*, Innominatverträge/AVV, para. 18 (regarding sole distribution contracts); *Fountoulakis*, p. 62 (regarding sole distribution contracts); *Furrer/Lohri*, pp. 24, 25; Kull/Wildhaber/*Wildhaber*, para. 201; *Oetiker/Weibel/Mata*, IHR 2022, p. 53; *Weber*, ZSR 1987, p. 411; ZK/*Schönle*, Vorbem. Arts 184–551 CO, para. 32 (regarding sole distribution contracts).
176. *Furrer/Lohri*, p. 25; *Weber*, ZSR 1987, p. 411.
177. *Furrer/Lohri*, p. 25.
178. BGer, 18 April 2024, CISG-online 6978, para. 12; BSK OR-I/*Amstutz/Morin*, Einl. vor Arts 184 ff. CO, para. 115 (regarding sole distribution contracts); CHK/*Jacobs*, Innominatverträge/AVV, para. 19 (regarding sole distribution contracts); *Furrer/Lohri*, p. 24; *C. Meyer*, pp. 110, 111 (regarding sole distribution contracts); *Weber*, ZSR 1987, p. 410.
179. Cf. only ZK OR/*Schönle*, Vorbem. Arts 184–551 CO, para. 32 (regarding sole distribution contracts); BSK OR-I/*Amstutz/Morin*, Einl. vor Arts 184 ff. CO, para. 115 (regarding sole distribution contracts), who propose that the principles developed for instalment contracts should also be considered (*Sukzessivlieferungsvertrag*).
180. *Furrer/Lohri*, p. 24; *Weber*, ZSR 1987, p. 411.

c. *Characteristic Obligations in Framework Agreements*

The content of the individual sales contracts is partly derived from the framework agreement itself.[181] Accordingly, a framework agreement usually contains a selected number of terms which shall be incorporated into the individual sales contracts.[182]

A distinction between transactional clauses and relational clauses in framework agreements has occasionally been suggested: the former relate to individual sales contracts, while the latter relate to the general cooperation (or the relation) between the parties.[183] Although framework agreements predetermine certain clauses, the parties also purposely leave several terms open to be determined for each transaction by the individual sales contracts.[184] *Weber* posits that this does not contradict general principles of contract law but rather should be considered a characteristic feature of framework agreements.[185] The indefiniteness is a consequence of the flexibility typically desired by parties to a framework agreement.[186]

Legal scholars hold different opinions on the question whether framework agreements necessarily contain an obligation to conclude individual sales contracts. One school of thought puts forward that a framework agreement does not contain an obligation to conclude individual contracts, since this would distinguish them from precontracts.[187] The contrary view advocates that framework agreements at least oblige one of the parties to conclude individual sales contracts during the duration of the contract.[188] A third view holds that a framework agreement may include an obligation to conclude individual sales contracts but does not necessarily do so.[189]

181. BGer, 18 February 2016, BGE 142 III 239, consid. 5.2.3 (with regard to an arbitration clause); BK OR/*Kramer*, Art. 22 CO, para. 76; KuKo OR/*Herzog*, Art. 22 CO, para. 22; *Tritten*, para. 442; ZK OR/*Schönle*, Vorbem. Arts 184–551 CO, para. 32.
182. BK OR/*Kramer*, Art. 22 CO, para. 76; BSK OR-I/*Zellweger-Gutknecht*, Art. 22 CO, para. 29; *Furrer/Lohri*, p. 24; KuKo OR/*Herzog*, Art. 22 CO, para. 7; *Oetiker/Weibel/Mata*, IHR 2022, p. 53; ZK OR/*Schönle*, Vorbem. Arts 184–551 CO, para. 32; ZK OR/*Schönle*, Art. 184 CO, para. 104; with numerous examples: *Weber*, ZSR 1987, pp. 418 et seq.
183. Cf. Kull/Wildhaber/*Wildhaber*, para. 202; *C. Meyer*, p. 57; *Weber*, ZSR 1987, pp. 408, 409.
184. *Von der Crone*, p. 245; *Weber*, ZSR 1987, p. 413.
185. *Weber*, ZSR 1987, p. 413, in footnote 51 he posits that the requirement of sufficiently definite contracts should not be overstretched in the context of framework agreements.
186. *Von der Crone*, pp. 244, 245.
187. BSK OR-I/*Zellweger-Gutknecht*, Art. 22 CO, para. 29, who also cites BGer, 18 November 2015, 4A_390/2015 – the 'agreement' in this case does not constitute a framework agreement in the sense of this study, but rather a non-binding preliminary agreement; KuKo OR/*Herzog*, Art. 22 CO, para. 7; cf. also *Tritten*, para. 445 (no obligation to conclude future contracts, unless the parties specifically agree upon such an obligation).
188. *Weber*, ZSR 1987, p. 412 (although it is not enforceable); cf. also *Furrer/Lohri*, p. 31: permanent non-delivery under a framework agreement constitutes a breach of the suppliers' obligation to conclude individual sales contracts.
189. BK OR/*Kramer*, Art. 22 CO, para. 76; *Bucher*, p. 109; *von der Crone*, p. 249; probably also CHK/*Jacobs*, Innominatverträge/AVV, para. 19: sole distribution contracts may be characterised as precontracts if they contain an obligation to conclude individual sales contracts which is usually the case.

d. *Summary and Comparison*

The Swiss understanding of framework agreements appears to be relatively similar to the German understanding. A framework agreement is a contract that provides a legal bond and basis for the parties' supply relationship. Under Swiss law, it is characterised as a contract sui generis or mixed contract. Thus, the general provisions and principles of the Swiss Code of Obligations apply to framework agreements, as well as the special rules on specific types of contracts, if appropriate. Framework agreements are further characterised as long-term contracts, which primarily has implications for their termination and avoidance.

There is a fundamental distinction between a framework agreement and the individual sales contracts subsequently concluded. Typically, a framework agreement contains a number of clauses pertaining to the sale of goods which are supposed to be incorporated into each individual sales contract. Thus, the content of the individual sales contracts is partly derived from the framework agreement. In addition, framework agreements typically contain further clauses related to the general cooperation between the parties, such as confidentiality clauses. It is disputed whether they necessarily contain an obligation to conclude the individual sales contracts.

3. France

a. *Code Civil*

The revision of French contract law in 2016 introduced an explicit mention of framework agreements in the French Civil Code.[190] Art. 1111 of the French Civil Code (Cc) contains a definition of the so-called *contrat cadre* (framework agreement). This provision reads as follows:

> *Le contrat cadre est un accord par lequel les parties conviennent des caractéristiques générales de leurs relations contractuelles futures. Des contrats d'application en précisent les modalités d'exécution.*

This provision reveals that a framework agreement is an agreement by which the parties set out the general characteristics of their future contractual relations. In addition, it holds that individual contracts ('*contrats d'application*') then specify the modalities of performance.

b. *General Features*

The wording of Art. 1111 Cc indicates that there is a distinction between framework agreements ('*contrats cadre*') and individual contracts ('*contrats d'application*') in French law. This distinction is considered to be an essential feature of framework

190. 'Ordonnance du 16 février 2016'; cf. *Buffelan-Lanore/Larribau-Terneyre*, para. 974.

agreements.[191] The individual sales contracts are usually subordinate in relation to the framework agreement.[192]

Framework agreements are designed to establish and regulate a long-lasting, future relationship between the parties.[193] They are directed towards the conclusion of a series of individual contracts.[194] In terms of Art. 1111 Cc, the range of application of framework agreements is very broad.[195] This study will again only cover framework agreements within the context of the supply and distribution of goods.

Moreover, framework agreements are characterised as long-term contracts (Art. 1111-1 Cc: '*contrat à execution successive*'),[196] which has implications for the contract's termination.[197] In addition, they are occasionally described as 'preliminary' since they prepare the conclusion of individual contracts.[198] Due to their explicit regulation in Art. 1111 Cc, framework agreements constitute a category of contracts on their own.[199]

c. *Characteristic Obligations in Framework Agreements*

Framework agreements lay down a selected number of terms which shall be part of each individual sales contract subsequently concluded.[200] However, they also leave several terms open since it is not yet desired or possible to agree on these points.[201] The open terms will be specified by the individual sales contracts, for example, the exact date of delivery or the purchase price.[202] Typically, a framework agreement contains an obligation to implement the terms it already sets out in the individual sales contracts.[203]

Moreover, framework agreements usually contain clauses that are independent from the conclusion of individual sales contracts; they are rather concerned with the general cooperation between the parties.[204] So-called exclusivity obligations are a common example.[205]

---

191. *Gatsi*, paras 3, 4; *Malaurie/Aynès/Stoffel-Munck*, p. 244; Oertel/*Bruylant*, p. 59; Sayag/*Pollaud-Dulian*, para. 111.
192. *Gatsi*, paras 411 et seq.; Sayag/*Pollaud-Dulian*, para. 100.
193. *Bénabent*, para. 32; Sayag/*Pollaud-Dulian*, paras 17, 100.
194. *Gatsi*, para. 9; *J. Schmidt*, (1983–1984) 6 Houst. J. Int'l L., p. 54 (comparing French and US law).
195. Cf. *Gatsi*, paras 19 et seq.; *Malaurie/Aynès/Stoffel-Munck*, p. 244.
196. *Gatsi*, paras 223 et seq.; Oertel/*Bruylant*, p. 55; Sayag/*Pollaud-Dulian*, para. 100.
197. Cf. *Malaurie/Aynès/Stoffel-Munck*, pp. 216, 217; Sayag/*Pollaud-Dulian*, paras 222 et seq.
198. *Gatsi*, paras 285 et seq.; *Malaurie/Aynès/Stoffel-Munck*, pp. 243, 244; *Mousseron/Seube*, D. 1973, pp. 199, 200.
199. Cf. *Bénabent*, para. 32.
200. *Buffelan-Lanore/Larribau-Terneyre*, para. 1314; *Gatsi*, para. 383; *Malaurie/Aynès/Stoffel-Munck*, p. 244; *Mousseron/Seube*, D. 1973, p. 197; Oertel/*Bruylant*, p. 59; Sayag/*Pollaud-Dulian*, paras 100, 111.
201. Sayag/*Pollaud-Dulian*, para. 109.
202. *Buffelan-Lanore/Larribau-Terneyre*, para. 974; cf. *Gatsi*, para. 263.
203. Cf. *Buffelan-Lanore/Larribau-Terneyre*, para. 1314; *Gatsi*, para. 90; Sayag/*Pollaud-Dulian*, para. 109; *J. Schmidt*, (1983–1984) 6 Houst. J. Int'l L., pp. 56, 57.
204. *Malaurie/Aynès/Stoffel-Munck*, p. 244 ('*d'obligations de comportement*'); Sayag/*Pollaud-Dulian*, para. 108.
205. *Malaurie/Aynès/Stoffel-Munck*, p. 244; cf. also *Mousseron/Seube*, D. 1973, pp. 200 et seq.

The prevailing view further maintains that a framework agreement may, but does not have to, include an obligation to conclude individual contracts.[206] Another view holds that framework agreements, in particular distribution contracts, should invariably include an obligation to conclude individual contracts.[207] The parties to a framework agreement would (at least tacitly) imply such an obligation; otherwise, it would be questionable whether a binding contract is present at all, according to this view.[208]

d. *Problem of Indefinite Price*

For a considerable period of time, French case law held that framework agreements are invalid, on the grounds that they typically lacked a sufficiently definite purchase price.[209] This was deemed to contravene the former Art. 1129 Cc, which previously set out a general standard of definiteness for any contract.[210]

However, this position was subsequently overturned by a decision from the French Supreme Court. The '*assemblée plénière*' of the French Supreme Court ruled that the indeterminacy of the price in framework agreements should not affect their validity.[211] It also stated that one party may unilaterally fix the price, which is subject to judicial control *ex post*, in order to prevent abusive behaviour.[212]

This development in case law has essentially been restated in the revised Art. 1164 Cc.[213] Art. 1164 of the French Civil Code holds that a framework agreement may give one of the parties the power to unilaterally determine the price. The party exercising such a power must be able to justify the amount fixed. In addition, Art. 1164 Cc empowers judges to award damages or, in appropriate cases, terminate the contract in the event of abuse in the exercise of the unilateral power to fix the price. Apart from Art. 1111 of the Cc, Art. 1164 Cc is the only other provision that explicitly mentions framework agreements ('*dans les contrat cadre …*') within the French Civil Code.

e. *Summary and Comparison*

The French Civil Code includes an explicit definition of framework agreements in Art. 1111 Cc. According to this provision, framework agreements are contracts by which the parties set out the general characteristics of their future contractual relations. In addition, the provision holds that the individual contracts specify the modalities of

206. *Gatsi*, paras 14 et seq., distinguishing throughout their entire study between framework agreements with and without obligation to conclude individual contracts ('*sans obligations de contractor/avec obligation de contractor*'); *Malaurie/Aynès/Stoffel-Munck*, p. 244; *Mousseron/Seube*, D. 1973, p. 198.
207. Sayag/*Pollaud-Dulian*, para. 111.
208. Sayag/*Pollaud-Dulian*, paras 109 et seq.; criticising this view: Oertel/*Bruylant*, p. 60.
209. *Buffelan-Lanore/Larribau-Terneyre*, para. 1315; discussion and case law reproduced in: Oertel/*Bruylant*, pp. 55 et seq.; cf. also Sayag/*Pollaud-Dulian*, paras 137 et seq.
210. *See* '*Ancien* Art. 1129' (revised in 2016).
211. Cour de cassation, 1 December 1995, JCP G 1996, II., 22565.
212. Cour de cassation, 1 December 1995, JCP G 1996, II., 22565.
213. *Buffelan-Lanore/Larribau-Terneyre*, para. 1319.

performance. Consequently, there is a distinction between framework agreements and individual sales contracts. The former are long-term contracts directed at individual sales contracts.

Framework agreements usually contain an obligation to implement the conditions it sets out in the individual sales contracts. Moreover, they typically encompass more general clauses pertaining to the parties' collaboration. Framework agreements may also contain an obligation to conclude individual contracts, according to the prevailing view. Art. 1164 Cc clarifies that a framework agreement may give one of the parties a unilateral power to determine the price under the caveat of abuse (and providing a reason for the amount chosen). Overall, the comprehension of framework agreements appears to be similar to the notion of these contracts in German and Swiss law.

4. USA

a. No Notion of Framework Agreements

US scholars and case law seem to have no comparable concept or terminology of framework agreements as in civil law systems.[214] This becomes apparent when considering US case law on the CISG. In *Amco Ukservice & Promriladamco v. American Meter*, the Court cited German decisions that classified distribution contracts as 'framework agreements'; however, the Court placed the term used by the German courts in quotation marks and employed a different term, namely 'distributorship agreement'.[215] From the court's opinion, it can be inferred that the Court was aware of distribution contracts, yet appeared to be unfamiliar with the notion of framework agreements. It seems unlikely that the reason for this was the Court's ignorance. Rather, there is apparently no general concept of framework agreements under US law.[216]

The reasons behind the absence of a notion of framework agreement in the United States, as known in civil law systems, remain unclear. *Tallon* mentions three possible obstacles for a US-version of framework agreements as known in most European jurisdictions: the absence of the intention to be bound, the absence of consideration, and the uncertainty and incompleteness of framework agreements.[217] These possibilities can neither be clearly confirmed nor refuted.

214. *Amco Ukservice & Promriladamco v. American Meter Comp.*, US Dist. Ct. ED Penn., 29 March 2004, CISG-online 1664; Sayag/*Tallon*, paras 329 et seq.; cf. also *Newhouse/Tanaka*, R.L.R. 2012, pp. 18, 19, mentioning 'distributorship agreements, joint venture agreements, marketing contracts or franchising contracts' in the context of preliminary agreements; similarly, *Torsello*, pp. 240 et seq., who refers to '(Preliminary) Distribution Agreements'.
215. *Amco Ukservice & Promriladamco v. American Meter Comp.*, US Dist. Ct. ED Penn., 29 March 2004, CISG-online 1664: 'Two German appellate cases have similarly concluded that the CISG does not apply to distributorship agreements, which they termed "framework agreements", but does govern sales contracts that the parties enter pursuant to those agreements.'.
216. Sayag/*Tallon*, paras 329 et seq.; cf. also *Newhouse/Tanaka*, R.L.R. 2012, pp. 18, 19.
217. Sayag/*Tallon*, paras 338 et seq.

An additional explanation for the absence might be that US law simply deals differently with these sub-issues. This could explain why there might have been no necessity to develop an overarching notion of framework agreements. For instance, the issue of open terms in contracts has been extensively discussed under US law and found its way into the UCC (e.g., § 2-305 UCC). Moreover, distribution contracts – which are typically characterised as framework agreements in other legal systems – have also been addressed relatively extensively in the US. In the absence of other indications, the following part will focus on so-called open term contracts, which are similar to framework agreements (according to the European notion) in that they leave certain contractual terms open for a later agreement between the parties. In addition, this section will provide an overview of the manner in which US law deals with distribution contracts, which represent the most prevalent form of framework agreements in civil law jurisdictions.

b. *Open Term Contracts*

As a rule under US law, any contract must be sufficiently definite to be valid.[218] However, there are contracts in which the parties intentionally (for various reasons)[219] leave a number of terms open to be fixed by a later agreement between them.[220] Such so-called open term contracts[221] appear to be problematic in light of the requirement of sufficient definiteness. Although the parties are confident that they will reach an agreement on the open terms at a later point in time, there is often a lack of clarity regarding their expectations in the event of a failure to reach such an agreement.[222]

i. *Approach in the Past*

For this reason, open term contracts have historically been considered to be unenforceable under both the common law and the Uniform Sales Act.[223] This view was mainly based on two reasons: one of the reasons was that such contracts were too indefinite

218. *Farnsworth*, § 3.2, p. 201, arguing that this can be inferred from one of the objectives of contract law, namely the protection of the promisee's expectations; *see also Williston on Contracts*, § 4:21, pp. 634 et seq.
219. Outlining those (potential) reasons: *Farnsworth*, § 3.29, pp. 418 et seq.
220. *Farnsworth*, § 3.29, p. 431.
221. Cf. *Farnsworth*, § 3.29, pp. 431 et seq.; *Williston on Sales*, § 9:1, p. 464.
222. *Farnsworth*, § 3.29, p. 431; *Williston on Contracts*, § 4:29, pp. 851 et seq.
223. *Ohio Calculating, Inc. v. CPT Corp.*, 8th Cir., 10 May 1988, 846 F.2d 497: 'Such agreements generally are deemed unenforceable because they provide neither a basis for determining the existence of a breach nor for giving an appropriate remedy.' (regarding 'agreement to negotiate'); *In re Vylene Enterprises, Inc.*, 9th Cir., 29 June 1996, 90 F.3d 1472: 'although a promise may be sufficiently definite when it contains an option given to the promisor or promisee, yet if an essential element is reserved for the future agreement of both parties, the promise can give rise to no legal obligation until such future agreement. Since either party by the terms of the promise may refuse to agree to anything to which the other party will agree, it is impossible for the law to affix any obligation to such a promise'.; *Williston on Sales*, § 9:1, pp. 464, 465; cf. also *Crockett*, § 3:31, p. 319.

and incomplete to be enforceable.[224] The second reason was that the parties were still in the process of negotiating. A distinction between a preliminary bargain (i.e., the open term 'contract') and a final agreement was drawn.[225]

In this context, the notion of 'agreement to agree' was used to describe an unenforceable agreement between the parties, as opposed to a final and binding contract.[226] The general rule was that if an essential element of a promise was reserved for future agreement by both parties, the promise could not create a legal obligation until such future agreement had been reached.[227] Over time, the courts have become more liberal and have considered open term contracts to be enforceable.[228]

ii. *The UCC's Approach*

This increasingly liberal approach was incorporated into the Uniform Commercial Code,[229] which was first published in 1952.[230] § 2-204(3) UCC now expressly stipulates:

> Even though one or more terms are left open a contract for sale does not fail for indefiniteness if the parties have intended to make a contract and there is a reasonably certain basis for giving an appropriate remedy.

In addition, §§ 2-305 (regarding price), 2-306 (quantity), 2-308 (place of delivery) and 2-309 (contract duration and termination) UCC contain gap-filling provisions that function as dispositive contract law in the case of omitted terms.[231] Therefore, agreements with open terms may be binding and enforceable under the UCC.[232]

There are two requirements for an open term contract to be enforceable under the UCC: first, the parties must have an intent to form a contract.[233] The more open terms contained in the contract, the less likely it is to be enforceable.[234] Second, there must be a reasonably certain basis for granting an appropriate remedy, such as recovery of damages or specific performance.[235] A similar approach has been adopted in general

224. *Williston on Sales*, § 9:1, p. 465.
225. *Williston on Sales*, § 9:1, pp. 464, 465.
226. Cf. *Copeland v. Baskin Robbins U.S.A.*, CA Cali., 19 March 2002, 117 Cali. Rptr. 2d 875 (distinguishing an agreement to agree from an agreement to negotiate); *Sun Printing & Pub. Ass'n v. Remington Paper & Power Co.*, CA NY, 17 April 1923, 234 N.Y. 338; *Williston on Contracts*, § 4:29, pp. 855 et seq.
227. *City of Los Angeles v. Superior Court*, Supr. Ct. Cali., 13 January 1959, 51 Cal.2d 423; *Copeland v. Baskin Robbins U.S.A.*, CA Cal., 19 March 2002, 117 Cali. Rptr. 2d 875; *Williston on Contracts*, § 4:29, p. 851; cf. also *Crockett*, § 3:31, p. 319.
228. Cf. *Copeland v. Baskin Robbins U.S.A.*, CA Cali., 19 March 2002, 117 Cali. Rptr. 2d 875.
229. *Crockett*, § 3:31, p. 321; *Williston on Sales*, § 9:1, pp. 465 et seq.
230. For an historical overview of US sales law, *see*: *Palumbo*, pp. 15 et seq.; it is important to note that the UCC is not a federal commercial code, but rather a model law that has been adopted by each US state individually (*see Palumbo*, p. 5).
231. *Crockett*, § 3:31, p. 321; *White/Summers et al.*, §§ 3–4, p. 105.
232. *Crockett*, § 3:31, p. 321; cf. also *Farnsworth*, § 3.8a, p. 232.
233. *Williston on Sales*, § 9:1, pp. 466 et seq.
234. *See Intergraph Corp. v. Intel Corp.*, Fed. Cir., 5 November 1999, 195 F.3d 1346 (a letter containing virtually no obligations was considered to be too broad for gap-filling).
235. More detailed *Williston on Sales*, § 9:1, pp. 468 et seq.

contract law outside the UCC, as can be seen in § 33(2) Restatement Second of Contracts.[236]

It should be noted that the second 'stage of agreement', i.e., when the parties agree on the open terms, is not an actual agreement since the initial agreement is already binding on its own.[237] Accordingly, the two 'stages of agreement' are not considered to be separate contracts, contrary to the civil law concept of framework agreements.[238]

c. *Distribution Contracts in the US*

The majority of case law and scholars hold that the Uniform Commercial Code is applicable to distribution contracts.[239] Unlike in civil law systems, there is no distinction between distribution agreements and individual sales contracts. Notwithstanding, distribution agreements have been the subject of dispute for two main reasons.

First, courts have found that distribution agreements usually involve more than a 'typical' sales contract.[240] Therefore, they were categorised as hybrid contracts containing non-sales elements to which the 'predominance' test was applied (i.e., determining which part of the contract is predominant).[241] The majority of courts concluded that the sale of goods is usually the predominant purpose of distribution agreements.[242]

236. Cf. also *Williston on Contracts*, § 4:29, pp. 861, 862.
237. Cf. *Farnsworth*, § 3.8a, p. 232.
238. Sayag/*Tallon*, para. 332: no distinction between 'main contract' and 'collateral (*ou* accessory) contract'.
239. *Lorenz Supply Company v. American Standard, Inc.* (concurring opinion by Judge *Brickley*), Supr. Ct. Mich., 3 December 1984, UCC Rep. Serv. 1169; *Thermal Systems of Alabama v. Sigafoose*, Supr. Ct. Ala., 16 September 1988, 533 So. 2d 567; *Bausch Lomb v. Sonomed Technology*, US Dist. Ct. ED NY, 3 January 1992, 780 F. Supp. 943; *Custom Comm. Eng. v. EF Johnson*, Super. Ct. NJ, 30 December 1993, 636 A.2d 80; *SMR Technologies, Inc. v. Aircraft Parts International Combs, Inc.*, US Dist. Ct. WD Ten., 13 April 2001, 141 F. Supp.2d 923 (predominant purpose of distribution agreements is the sale of goods); *Precision Fitness Equipment, Inc. v. Nautilus, Inc.*, US Dist. Ct. Col., 2 February 2011, U.C.C. Rep. Serv. 2d 144 (primary purpose of distribution agreement was the sale of goods); *Watkins & Son Pet Supplies v. Iams Co.*, 6th Cir., 20 June 2001, 254 F.3d 607 (stating that the relationship in question was primarily about the sale of pet food, although service parts might be more significant in other cases); *Gruppo Essenziero Italiano, S.p.A. v. Aromi D'Italia, Inc.*, US Dist. Ct. Mary., 27 July 2011, CISG-online 2223 (comparing the UCC to the CISG); *Crockett*, § 1:4, pp. 41 et seq.; *Farnsworth*, § 1.9a, p. 53; *Newhouse/Tanaka*, R.L.R. 2012, p. 19; *Williston on Sales*, § 2:7, pp. 42, 43; more guardedly *White/Summers et al.*, § 1-1, p. 6 (UCC should be applied only by way of analogy to distributorship agreements).
240. *Sally Beauty Co. v. Nexxus Products Co., Inc.*, 7th Cir., 26 September 1986, 801 F.2d 1001 with further references; *SMR Technologies, Inc. v. Aircraft Parts International Combs, Inc.*, US Dist. Ct. WD Ten., 13 April 2001, 141 F. Supp.2d 923; *Precision Fitness Equipment, Inc. v. Nautilus, Inc.*, US Dist. Ct. Col., 2 February 2011, U.C.C. Rep. Serv. 2d 144.
241. *Sally Beauty Co. v. Nexxus Products Co., Inc.*, 7th Cir., 26 September 1986, 801 F.2d 1001; *SMR Technologies, Inc. v. Aircraft Parts International Combs, Inc.*, US Dist. Ct. WD Ten., 13 April 2001, 141 F. Supp.2d 923; *Precision Fitness Equipment, Inc. v. Nautilus, Inc.*, US Dist. Ct. Col., 2 February 2011, U.C.C. Rep. Serv. 2d 144; cf. also *White/Summers et al.*, § 1-1, p. 6.
242. Each case with further references: *Sally Beauty Co. v. Nexxus Products Co., Inc.*, 7th Cir., 26 September 1986, 801 F.2d 1001; *SMR Technologies, Inc. v. Aircraft Parts International Combs,*

The second dispute concerned the question whether distribution agreements are sufficiently definite with regard to the quantity of the goods.[243] The prevailing view holds that distribution and dealer agreements are sufficiently definite under § 2-306 UCC (even if they are relatively imprecise) because they usually measure the quantity by 'requirements of the buyer' or 'output of the seller'.[244] The official comment to § 2-306 UCC appears to confirm this view: 'It applies to such contracts of non-producing establishments such as dealers or distribution as well as to manufacturing contracts.'[245] Moreover, distribution agreements are valid even if they are indefinite with regard to their duration, as § 2-309 UCC will apply in such situations.[246]

Another related question is whether the Statute of Frauds (§ 2-201 UCC) should also apply to distribution agreements.[247] This rule sets out, *inter alia*, formal requirements for certain contracts containing a price of over USD 500 in order to be enforceable. They apply only to 'a contract for the sale of goods'. This term has sometimes been interpreted as narrower and more restrictive than the term 'transaction in goods' as stipulated in § 2-102 UCC, which refers to the UCC's general scope of application.[248] Nevertheless, the prevailing view in case law holds that distribution agreements should also be characterised as contracts for the sale of goods (§ 2-201 UCC).[249]

Inc., US Dist. Ct. WD Ten., 13 April 2001, 141 F. Supp.2d 923; *Watkins & Son Pet Supplies v. Iams Co.*, 6th Cir., 20 June 2001, 254 F.3d 607; *Precision Fitness Equipment, Inc. v. Nautilus, Inc.*, US Dist. Ct. Col., 2 February 2011, U.C.C. Rep. Serv. 2d 144.

243. *See* already Ch. 2 II. 4. b. above.
244. Cf. only *Lorenz Supply Company v. American Standard, Inc.* (concurring opinion by judge *Brickley*), Supr. Ct. Mich., 3 December 1984, U.C.C. Rep. Serv. 1169; but *see Cavalier Mobile Homes, Inc. v. Liberty Homes, Inc.*, CA Mary., 5 January 1983, 53 Md. App. 379: the Court ruled that the distribution contract in question was unenforceable due to its lack of sufficient definiteness regarding the quantity of the goods, in contravention of the Statute of Frauds.
245. *American Law Institute*, § 2-306, note 1.
246. With further references on case law: *White/Summers et al.*, §§3–6, pp. 113 et seq.
247. Cf. *Cavalier Mobile Homes, Inc. v. Liberty Homes, Inc.*, CA Mary., 5 January 1983, 53 Md. App. 379; *Lorenz Supply Company v. American Standard, Inc.* (concurring opinion by judge *Brickley*), Supr. Ct. Mich., 3 December 1984, U.C.C. Rep. Serv. 1169 (distribution agreement is 'transaction of goods' (§ 2-102 UCC) as well as 'contract for the sale of goods' (§ 2-201 UCC)); *Custom Comm. Eng. v. EF Johnson*, Super. Ct. NJ, 30 December 1993, 636 A.2d 80 (holding that distribution contracts generally fall under the broad notion of 'transaction in goods' (§ 2-102 UCC), but not every distribution contract should be considered a 'contract for the sale of goods' (§ 2-201 UCC)).
248. Cf. *Lorenz Supply Company v. American Standard, Inc.* (concurring opinion by judge *Brickley*), Supr. Ct. Mich., 3 December 1984, U.C.C. Rep. Serv. 1169: 'contract for the sale of goods is clearly more restrictive than the term transaction in goods'; *Custom Comm. Eng. v. EF Johnson*, Super. Ct. NJ, 30 December 1993, 636 A.2d 80: 'The statute of frauds provision is "designed for a pure sale of goods", whereas "transaction in goods" is a broad term (...)'.
249. *Cavalier Mobile Homes, Inc. v. Liberty Homes, Inc.*, CA Mary., 5 January 1983, 53 Md. App. 379 (distribution contract was deemed unenforceable due to the application of the Statute of Frauds); *De Filippo v. Ford Motor Co.*, 3rd Cir., 8 May 1975, 516 F.2d 1313; *Lorenz Supply Company v. American Standard, Inc.* (concurring opinion by judge *Brickley*), Supr. Ct. Mich., 3 December 1984, U.C.C. Rep. Serv. 1169; *Custom Comm. Eng. v. EF Johnson*, Super. Ct. NJ, 30 December 1993, 636 A.2d 80.

Although the UCC, as a special sales law in the US, is applied to domestic distribution agreements, it is noteworthy that most US courts have not applied the CISG to international distribution agreements.[250]

d. *Summary and Comparison*

Unlike Germany, Switzerland and France, US law is not familiar with a general concept of framework agreements. It deals in a different and more problem-oriented way with contracts that leave certain terms open for later determination, as well as distribution contracts.

In the past, open term contracts were considered to be invalid for their lack of definiteness. However, case law has developed an increasingly liberal approach to uphold such contracts. This development has been codified in the UCC, which expressly declares contracts with open terms to be binding and provides gap-filling provisions for such situations. It requires that the parties intend to enter into a contract and that there is a reasonably certain basis for remedies. It should be noted that the two stages of agreements, i.e., the original contract and the subsequent determination of open terms, are not considered to be separate contracts. Open term contracts are rather considered to be one single contract.

The prevailing view is that distribution contracts fall within the ambit of the UCC. They are mostly characterised as hybrid contracts with a predominant sales purpose. The quantity is usually determined by 'requirements' or 'output', which is sufficiently definite under § 2-306 UCC. The UCC also contains provisions for distribution agreements concluded for an indefinite period of time in § 2-309 UCC. Furthermore, distribution contracts are predominantly characterised as both 'transactions in goods' (§ 2-102 UCC) and 'contracts for the sale of goods' (§ 2-201 UCC).

III. UNDERSTANDING OF FRAMEWORK AGREEMENTS IN THIS STUDY

This study will be based on a rather broad notion of framework agreements, since there appears to be no universal definition, especially outside of European jurisdictions.[251] In addition, there are hardly any statutory regulations in domestic jurisdictions, let alone at an international level, that could serve as a model.[252] Framework agreements are

---

250. *See* Ch. 3 IV. 1. a. below.
251. *See* Ch. 2 II. 4. above on the US approach; *Perales Viscasillas*, Extending the Scope, p. 125 (in the context of distribution contracts); *Perales Viscasillas*, Int'l Distribution Contracts and CISG, p. 51 (in the context of distribution contracts).
252. The exception being Art. 1111 French Cc; cf. also UN Economic Commission for Europe, Trade Facilitation Implementation Guide, 'Framework agreements' with a description (*see* https://tfig.unece.org/domains/purchasing/purchasing/framework-agreements/, last checked September 2025).

therefore very heterogenous and their content varies considerably in practice depending on the circumstances and the parties' needs.[253] In order to take account of this heterogeneity, this study will rely on a broad understanding of framework agreements. Nevertheless, an important limitation must be made. In theory, a framework agreement may be concerned with all kinds of transactions.[254] However, this study will only deal with framework agreements relating to the international supply of goods.[255] Otherwise, the discussion of the CISG's applicability would be pointless *ab initio*.

Scholars have also not yet established a consistent terminology or notion when discussing the CISG's applicability to framework agreements.[256] It should be noted that one cannot rely on characterisations or definitions derived from domestic law (Art. 7(1) CISG) when discussing the CISG's applicability or actual application to such agreements.[257] In fact, the reference to the CISG's international character and the need to promote uniformity imply that an 'international definition' must be used, i.e., one that is capable of being accepted in various legal systems. In light of this, it is again submitted that a broad notion of framework agreements should be employed. This leads to the conclusion that the CISG's applicability to framework agreements cannot be affirmed or denied across the board, i.e., with regard to all types of framework agreements. Rather, it is suggested by this study that a determination should be made according to the content of each framework agreement.[258] Finally, the term framework agreement will be used as an umbrella term to cover all types of distribution contracts.[259]

1. General Features

In general, framework agreements provide a frame for an ongoing supply relationship between the parties.[260] They represent a uniform legal environment for a series of

253. Cf. *Perales Viscasillas*, Extending the Scope, p. 125 (in the context of distribution contracts); *Perales Viscasillas*, Int'l Distribution Contracts and CISG, p. 51 (in the context of distribution contracts); Schlechtriem/Schwenzer/Schroeter/*Fountoulakis*, 5th English ed., Art. 73 CISG, para. 8: 'Types and categories vary considerably, depending, among other things, on the trade branch concerned (cars, electronics, commodities, pharmaceuticals, clothes, etc'); *Weber*, ZSR 1987, pp. 410, 415; *C. Witz*, para. 112.61.
254. *Weber*, ZSR 1987, p. 415, providing numerous examples.
255. With regard to non-harmonised domestic law: *Hoffbauer*, p. 2; Martinek/Semler/Flohr/*Budde/Eckhoff*, § 40, para. 13; *Weber*, ZSR 1987, p. 415.
256. Cf. only *Bridge*, Int'l Sale of Goods, para. 10.22 and Schlechtriem/Schwenzer/Schroeter/*Schroeter*, 5th English ed., Intro Arts 14–24 CISG, para. 24, who appear to use a similar terminology; *Honnold/Flechtner*, Art. 2 CISG, para. 71 footnote 41 and *Torsello*, pp. 191 et seq., who rely on a different terminology.
257. *See Perales Viscasillas*, Extending the Scope, pp. 129, 130.
258. *See* Ch. 3 III. below in more detail.
259. *See* only *Budde/Geks*, ZVertriebsR 2012, p. 38; *Bridge*, Int'l Sale of Goods, para. 10.22; *Honnold/Flechtner*, Art. 2 CISG, para. 71 footnote 41, in reference to such an understanding as a 'framework agreement in a broader sense encompassing franchise and distributorship agreements', proceed to rely on a narrower term; *Schroeter*, para. 91; Schlechtriem/Schwenzer/Schroeter/*Hachem*, 5th English ed., Art. 1 CISG, para. 15.
260. Cf. Dist. Ct. Rzeszów, 28 February 2014, CISG-online 6752, paras 97, 98; OLG Graz, 28 September 2000, CISG-online 798, para. 38; *Bucher*, p. 109; *Furrer/Lohri*, p. 24; *Gebhardt*, p. 42; *Hoffbauer*, p. 5; *Muhl/Lüthge*, GWR 2016, p. 26; *Schwenzer/Muñoz*, para. 8.04; *Ulmer*, p. 300; *Weber*, ZSR 1987, p. 410.

transactions and are often directed and tailored towards the conclusion or delivery of individual sales transactions.[261] This will be considered an essential feature of framework agreements.

A framework agreement typically combines individual sales transactions into some form of economic unit.[262] In many jurisdictions and in an international context, there may be a distinction between the framework agreement and the individual sales contracts subsequently concluded.[263] This will be referred to as a 'two-tier structure'[264] and will also be part of this study's notion of framework agreements. Under this structure, it is only the individual sales contracts that will contain the actual delivery and payment obligations.[265] This type of framework agreement is equally relevant because the parties are generally free to structure their contract as they wish (freedom of contract).[266] Moreover, the parties may have a legitimate interest in delaying the conclusion of actual sales contracts, for example, in order to obtain an administrative authorisation or because of a (temporary) conflict with other legal positions.[267]

However, there are also cases in which specific modalities about the purchase and delivery of the goods are already embedded into the framework agreement itself (often merely in part).[268] If so, there may be no need to conclude separate individual sales contracts. Rather, the goods may be delivered by instalments or on demand but still as part of one single contract.[269] This type of contract will also be considered a

261. Cf. OLG Graz, 28 September 2000, CISG-online 798, para. 38; *Budde/Geks*, ZVertriebsR 2012, p. 37; *Hoffbauer*, p. 5; *Rother*, FS Larenz, p. 437; UN Economic Commission for Europe, Trade Facilitation Implementation Guide, 'Framework agreements' (https://tfig.unece.org/domains/purchasing/purchasing/framework-agreements/, last checked September 2025).
262. *Fuchs-Wissemann*, p. 99; *Gass/Lange*, p. 14; Martinek/Semler/Flohr/*Budde/Eckhoff*, § 40, para. 11; *Ulmer*, pp. 300, 301; cf. *Rother*, FS Larenz, pp. 438, 439.
263. Cf. Art. 1111 Cc; OLG München, 18 June 2018, CISG-online 3080; BeckOGK/*Möslein*, § 145 BGB, para. 79; BK OR/*Kramer*, Art. 22 CO, para. 76; BSK OR-I/*Zellweger-Gutknecht*, Vor Art. 1–40f CO, para. 40; BSK OR-I/*Zellweger-Gutknecht*, Art. 22 CO, para. 29; *Bucher*, p. 109; *Budde/Geks*, ZVertriebsR 2012, p. 37; *Furrer/Lohri*, pp. 23, 24; *Gass/Lange*, pp. 14, 15; *Henrich*, p. 117; *Hoffbauer*, p. 6; *Honnold/Flechtner*, Art. 2 CISG, para. 71; Jauernig/*Stadler*, § 311 BGB, para. 22; KuKo OR/*Herzog*, Art. 22 CO, para. 7; Martinek/Semler/Flohr/*Budde/Eckhoff*, § 40, paras 8 et seq.; *Muhl/Lüthge*, GWR 2016, p. 26; *Ulmer*, p. 300; *von der Crone*, pp. 245, 246; *Weber*, ZSR 1987, p. 410; ZK OR/*Schönle*, Art. 184 CO, para. 104; ZK OR/*Schönle*, Vorbem. Arts 184–551 CO, para. 32.
264. '*Zweistufigkeit*': *Budde/Geks*, ZVertriebsR 2012, p. 37; *Hoffbauer*, p. 13; Martinek/Semler/Flohr/*Budde/Eckhoff*, § 40, paras 8, 10; *Muhl/Lüthge*, GWR 2016, p. 26.
265. *Budde/Geks*, ZVertriebsR 2012, p. 37; *Hoffbauer*, p. 5; *Honnold/Flechtner*, Art. 2 CISG, para. 71; Martinek/Semler/Flohr/*Budde/Eckhoff*, § 40, para. 8; cf. also *Gass/Lange*, pp. 14, 15; *Torsello*, p. 192.
266. *See* Ch. 3 III. 1. a. below.
267. Cf. *Grunewald*, p. 27; *J. Schmidt*, (1983–1984) 6 Houst. J. Int'l L., p. 61 (in the context of preliminary agreements).
268. Cf. *Bridge*, Int'l Sale of Goods, para. 10.22; MüKoHGB/*B. Köhler*, Art. 1 CISG, para. 22 (regarding distribution contracts); MüKoHGB/*Sommerfeld*, Art. 73 CISG, para. 4, referring to 'qualified' framework contracts; Schlechtriem/Schwenzer/Schroeter/*Fountoulakis*, 5th English ed., Art. 73 CISG, para. 8; but *see Hoffbauer*, p. 34 (in accordance with German law, a framework agreement may not include sales obligations, as this would result in the agreement being characterised as a distinct type of contract).
269. Cf. *Bridge*, Int'l Sale of Goods, para. 10.22; MüKoHGB/*B. Köhler*, Art. 1 CISG, para. 22; MüKoHGB/*Sommerfeld*, Art. 73 CISG, para. 4; *Murray/Holloway/Timson-Hunt*, Schmitthoff's Law and Practice, para. 30-003 (on distribution contracts).

framework agreement for the purposes of this study, provided that it is an umbrella for a series of individual transactions.

In addition, framework agreements are usually characterised as long-term contracts, since they are to be performed over an extended period of time.[270] The framework agreement will not be terminated once the individual sales contracts are concluded.[271] Instead, framework contracts may be entered into for a fixed or indefinite period of time.[272]

Framework agreements are thus generally characterised by the fact that they form an umbrella for a series of individual sales transactions (individual sales contracts or mere deliveries) to be conducted over an extended period of time.

2. Characteristic Obligations in Framework Agreements

Framework agreements typically contain a number of, but not all, terms relating to the sale of goods, i.e., clauses relating to the individual sale of goods transactions to be concluded or delivered at a later point in time.[273] These specific clauses contained in the framework agreement are supposed to be incorporated into the individual sales contracts[274] if the latter are to be considered separate contracts. The idea is to ensure that all subsequent individual contracts are concluded on largely the same legal terms.[275] Consequently, framework agreements usually contain an obligation to incorporate the predetermined terms into the individual sales contracts concluded subsequently.[276] This presupposes, of course, that the parties to the framework agreement and the parties to the subsequent individual sales contracts are identical.[277]

The situation is different where the delivery obligation arises directly from the framework agreement. In such cases, there is no need to conclude individual sales

270. *See* Ch. 5 I., II. below; in agreement OLG München, 18 June 2018, CISG-online 3080; BSK OR-I/*Amstutz/Morin*, Einl. vor Arts 184 ff. CO, para. 115; *Budde/Geks*, ZVertriebsR 2012, p. 37; *Fuchs-Wissemann*, p. 101; *Furrer/Lohri*, p. 24; *C. Meyer*, pp. 110, 111; *Gatsi*, paras 223 et seq.; *Hoffbauer*, p. 17; Sayag/*Pollaud-Dulian*, para. 100; *Ulmer*, p. 301; *Weber*, ZSR 1987, p. 410.
271. *Saxinger*, p. 107; *Ulmer*, p. 301; *Wójtowicz*, ERCL 2018, p. 143 (on the Rome I Regulation).
272. DiMatteo *et al.*/*Saintier*, Ch. 27, paras 81 et seq.; *Muhl/Lüthge*, GWR 2016, p. 27; *Ulmer*, pp. 257 et seq.
273. Art. 1111 Cc ('*caractéristiques générales*'); OLG München, 18 June 2018, CISG-online 3080, p. 10; OLG Graz, 28 September 2000, CISG-online 798, para. 38; BK OR/*Kramer*, Art. 22 CO, para. 76; BSK OR-I/*Zellweger-Gutknecht*, Art. 22 CO, para. 29; *Budde/Geks*, ZVertriebsR 2012, p. 37; *Furrer/Lohri*, p. 24; *Gass/Lange*, p. 14; *Gebhardt*, p. 42; *Henrich*, p. 117; *Hoffbauer*, p. 5; Martinek/Semler/Flohr/*Budde/Eckhoff*, § 40, para. 11; *Muhl/Lüthge*, GWR 2016, p. 26; *Oetiker/Weibel/Mata*, IHR 2022, p. 53; Staudinger/*Bork*, Vorbem. zu §§ 145–156 BGB, para. 54; *Torsello*, pp. 192, 193; *Ulmer*, p. 300; *von Bar/Clive*, p. 2427 (DCFR); *Wellenhofer-Klein*, p. 103; ZK OR/*Schönle*, Vorbem. Arts 184–551 CO, para. 32; with numerous exemplary clauses: *Weber*, ZSR 1987, pp. 418 et seq.
274. OLG München, 18 June 2018, CISG-online 3080; *Saxinger*, p. 106; cf. also *J. Schmidt*, (1983–1984) 6 Houst. J. Int'l L., p. 55; *Torsello*, p. 226; *Weber*, ZSR 1987, p. 410.
275. OLG München, 18 June 2018, CISG-online 3080; UN Economic Commission for Europe, Trade Facilitation Implementation Guide, 'Framework agreements' (https://tfig.unece.org/domains/purchasing/purchasing/framework-agreements/, last checked September 2025).
276. Cf. *Buffelan-Lanore/Larribau-Terneyre*, para. 1314; *Gatsi*, para. 90; *Hoffbauer*, p. 17; Sayag/*Pollaud-Dulian*, para. 109; *J. Schmidt*, (1983–1984) 6 Houst. J. Int'l L., pp. 56, 57.
277. *Rother*, FS Larenz, p. 438.

contracts that are legally separate from the framework agreement.[278] Accordingly, the individual delivery – occasionally referred to as 'orders' or 'call-offs'[279] – will substantiate the obligations that already arise from the framework agreement itself.[280] There is no need for an obligation to implement the terms from the framework agreement into a separate contract.

Moreover, framework agreements often stipulate further terms, which are immediately binding upon the parties during the entirety of the contract's validity, even if an individual sales contract or 'call-off' is never concluded or made.[281] These clauses typically refer to the overall relationship and collaboration between the parties, e.g., confidentiality clauses, exclusivity, information, or distribution obligations and the like.[282] In order to distinguish between terms relating to the sale of goods and terms relating to the cooperation between the parties, they have been referred to as 'transactional' (relating to the sale of goods) and 'relational' (relating to the cooperation) clauses.[283]

This study assumes that a two-tier framework agreement, i.e., without delivery obligation, often contains an obligation to conclude individual sales contracts. However, such an obligation is not necessary for a contract to be characterised as a framework agreement. Thus, an obligation to conclude individual sales contracts may be included but is not required.[284] A framework agreement may merely set out terms for future deliveries without obliging any of the parties to conclude an individual sales contract. Whether a framework agreement contains an obligation to conclude an individual sales contract is a matter of contract interpretation.[285] In an international context, it should be noted that the enforceability of such an obligation may be assessed very differently depending on the applicable law of the forum.[286] In addition, a framework agreement may also 'directly' contain delivery and payment obligations.[287] In such a case, the two-tier structure is absent, and there is only one contract to be

278. Cf. MüKoHGB/*Sommerfeld*, Art. 73 CISG, para. 4.
279. *See* Gerechtshof Arnhem-Leeuwarden, 6 February 2024, CISG-online 6819, para. 4; CA Toulouse, 22 November 2023, CISG-online 6647, para. 24; OLG Hamm, 25 March 2019, CISG-online 5215, para. 2.
280. Schlechtriem/Schwenzer/Schroeter/*Fountoulakis*, 5th English ed., Art. 73 CISG, para. 8.
281. *Saxinger*, p. 106; Schlechtriem/Schwenzer/Schroeter/*Fountoulakis*, 5th English ed., Art. 73 CISG, para. 8; *Torsello*, pp. 225, 226; *Ulmer*, p. 301; *Weber*, ZSR 198, p. 410.
282. *Budde/Geks*, ZVertriebsR 2012, p. 37; *Hoffbauer*, pp. 12, 13; *Malaurie/Aynès/Stoffel-Munck*, p. 244; Sayag/*Pollaud-Dulian*, para. 108; *Weber*, ZSR 1987, pp. 408, 409; cf. also *Mousseron/Seube*, D. 1973, pp. 200 et seq.
283. Cf. *C. Meyer*, p. 57; *Weber*, ZSR 1987, pp. 408, 409.
284. Accord OLG München, 18 June 2018, CISG-online 3080; OLG Graz, 28 September 2000, CISG-online 798, para. 38; BK OR/*Kramer*, Art. 22 CO, para. 76; *Bucher*, p. 109; *Budde/Geks*, ZVertriebsR 2012, p. 37; *Hoffbauer*, p. 94; *Gatsi*, paras 14 et seq.; *Malaurie/Aynès/Stoffel-Munck*, p. 244; Martinek/Semler/Flohr/*Budde/Eckhoff*, § 40, para. 9; *Mousseron/Seube*, D. 1973, p. 198; *Muhl/Lüthge*, GWR 2016, p. 26; *von der Crone*, p. 249; *Wellenhofer-Klein*, pp. 104, 105.
285. Martinek/Semler/Flohr/*Budde/Eckhoff*, § 40, paras 38, 39; cf. further OLG München, 18 June 2018, CISG-online 3080; *Bude/Geks*, ZVertriebsR 2012, pp. 38 et seq.; *Muhl/Lüthge*, GWR 2016, pp. 26, 27; *see* Ch. 3 VI. below.
286. Cf. *Torsello*, p. 233; *J. Schmidt*, (1983–1984) 6 Houst. J. Int'l L., pp. 58 et seq.; *Wójtowicz*, ERCL 2018, p. 155, 156.
287. Cf. *Ulmer*, p. 243.

performed in deliveries. Consequently, there is no need to conclude an individual sales contract.[288] This illustrates that the characteristic obligations may vary depending on the type of framework agreement. Nonetheless, such contracts generally contain sales-related and non-sales-related terms and may or may not contain actual sales obligations or an obligation to conclude sales contracts.

3. Delimitations

Framework agreements must be distinguished from non-binding agreements that are entered into in the course of contract negotiations between the parties.[289] These agreements are similar to framework agreements in that they may anticipate the conclusion of further contracts. However, such agreements do not contractually bind the parties.[290] At best, they bind the parties on the basis of reputation or morals.[291] Handshake agreements, memoranda of understanding, and sometimes letters of intent may fall into this category.[292] Framework agreements, however, require the parties' intention to be contractually bound.[293]

Moreover, despite the (potentially) strong economic link between the parties to a framework agreement, they remain legally independent entities from each other.[294] No company between the parties is established simply by concluding a framework agreement.[295]

4. Distribution Contracts in Particular

This study considers distribution contracts as a subset of framework agreements. Distribution contracts are the most relevant form of framework agreements in practice.[296] A distribution contract typically involves a supplier, who undertakes to supply the goods on a continuing basis, and a distributor, who undertakes to distribute these

288. Cf. *Hoffbauer*, pp. 32, 33; MüKoHGB/*B. Köhler*, Art. 1 CISG, para. 22; MüKoHGB/*Sommerfeld*, Art. 73 CISG, para. 4; Soergel/*Kreße*, Art. 1 CISG, para. 22.
289. Cf. *Torsello*, pp. 217 et seq.; *Weber*, ZSR 1987, p. 413.
290. *Torsello*, p. 218; *Weber*, ZSR 1987, p. 413.
291. *Torsello*, p. 218; *Weber*, ZSR 1987, p. 413.
292. The relevant question is whether the parties had the intention to enter into a legally binding relationship. The terminology employed by scholars is inconsistent, cf. *Torsello*, pp. 217 et seq.; *Weber*, ZSR 1987, p. 413; cf. also *Gass/Lange*, pp. 23 et seq., who consider memoranda of understanding and letters of intent to be framework contracts.
293. *Weber*, ZSR 1987, p. 413.
294. Sayag/*Pollaud-Dulian*, para. 100; *Wójtowicz*, ERCL 2018, p. 143.
295. *C. Meyer*, Alleinvertrieb, pp. 466, 467; Sayag/*Pollaud-Dulian*, para. 100; *Wójtowicz*, ERCL 2018, p. 143; cf. also *Ulmer*, pp. 321 et seq.
296. Cf. *Budde/Geks*, ZVertriebsR 2012, p. 38; *Thieffry*, Dr. prat. com. int. 1993, p. 66, who recommends that the characterisation of distribution contracts as framework agreements should be taken into account when discussing the CISG's applicability.

goods to third parties in its own name and on its own behalf.[297] The distributor is legally independent, i.e., acts in its own name and on its own behalf, which distinguishes distribution contracts from all types of agency contracts.[298]

As is the case with any framework agreement,[299] distribution contracts usually contain only a number of predetermined terms regarding the delivery of goods, without containing all specific modalities.[300] In case of a two-tier distribution contract, the specific terms (e.g., quantity of the goods, time of delivery, etc.) are merely set out in the individual sales contracts that are subsequently concluded.[301] Whether a specific distribution contract contains an obligation to conclude these individual sales contracts is again a matter of contract interpretation. A distribution contract may also contain immediate delivery and payment obligations, and therefore, there may be no need to conclude separate sales contracts.[302]

Furthermore, by definition, a distribution contract encompasses a distribution obligation.[303] The distributor has to promote and resell the goods in order to maximise sales volume.[304] It is important to note that this study only covers the distribution of goods, not of services.[305] In addition, distribution contracts frequently contain some form of exclusivity obligation, which should not be regarded as an essential feature of distribution contracts.[306] Finally, distribution contracts are intended to be performed over an extended period of time. They should therefore be characterised as long-term contracts.[307]

IV. CONCLUSION

The CISG does not define or make any reference to framework agreements.[308] Such contracts are commercially attractive since they combine the parties' interest in reliable

297. Relying on a similar definition: DiMatteo *et al./Saintier*, Ch. 27, paras 62, 66; *Grieser*, p. 57; Münch/Passadelis/Lehne/*Rohn*, paras 4.18 et seq.; *Torsello*, p. 242; *Rothermel*, p. 244; *UNCITRAL et al.*, Legal Guide, pp. 95, 96; *van Houtte*, para. 5.02; *Wójtowicz*, ERCL 2018, pp. 140 et seq.
298. *Christou*, para. 4-01; *Ebenroth*, pp. 35, 36; Münch/Passadelis/Lehne/*Rohn*, para. 4.11; *Murray/Holloway/Timson-Hunt*, Schmitthoff's Law and Practice, para. 30-003; *Ulmer*, pp. 76, 77, 249; *Vischer/Huber/Oser*, para. 666; *von Bar/Clive*, pp. 2426, 2427; *Wójtowicz*, ERCL 2018, p. 142.
299. Distribution contracts as framework agreements, cf. only *UNCITRAL et al.*, Legal Guide, p. 96; *Wójtowicz*, ERCL 2018, p. 143; *von Bar/Clive*, p. 2427.
300. *See* Ch. 2 III. 2. above; cf. also *von Bar/Clive*, p. 2427.
301. *Von Bar/Clive*, pp. 2427, 2433.
302. E.g., ICC, 1 November 2016, CISG-online 5988; ICC, 18203/2013, CISG-online 2973, para. 31.
303. Cf. *Bridge*, Int'l Sale of Goods, para. 10.22; DiMatteo *et al./Saintier*, Ch. 27, para. 75; *Ebenroth*, p. 32; Schlechtriem/Schwenzer/Schroeter/*Fountoulakis*, 5th English ed., Art. 73 CISG, para. 8; *Ulmer*, p. 206; *UNCITRAL et al.*, Legal Guide, p. 95; *Vischer/Huber/Oser*, para. 667.
304. Cf. *Martinez-Luna*, Rev. Colomb. Der. Int. (2016), p. 258; Münch/Passadelis/Lehne/*Rohn*, para. 4.11; *Rothermel*, p. 244; *von Bar/Clive*, pp. 2444, 2445.
305. Unlike the DCFR, *see von Bar/Clive*, p. 2426; *Wójtowicz*, ERCL 2018, p. 141.
306. Accord *J. Hartmann*, pp. 9, 10; *von Bar/Clive*, p. 2425.
307. *See* Ch. 5 I. below on this study's notion of long-term contracts; in agreement BSK OR-I/*Amstutz/Morin*, Einl. vor Arts 184 ff. CO, para. 124 (regarding sole distribution contracts under Swiss law).
308. *See* Ch. 2 I. 1. above.

planning with their interest in flexibility. Framework agreements facilitate the standardisation and simplification of contractual supply relationships.[309]

There is a similar understanding of framework agreements in Germany, Switzerland and France. In these jurisdictions, a framework agreement sets out a general frame for an ongoing supply relationship between the parties. It contains selected terms relating to the sale of goods, which are intended to be incorporated into a series of sales contracts that are concluded at a later date. A distinction is made in these jurisdictions between a framework agreement and the subsequent individual sales contracts. A framework agreement usually contains an obligation to incorporate the predetermined terms into the individual sales contracts. In addition, it typically contains obligations relating to the overall cooperation between the parties, such as confidentiality or exclusivity obligations. In all three jurisdictions, it is controversial whether framework agreements must contain an obligation to conclude individual sales contracts. Moreover, framework agreements are typically characterised as long-term contracts as they are intended to govern an ongoing supply relationship. While framework agreements are explicitly mentioned in the French Civil Code, there are no comparable provisions in Switzerland or Germany. All three jurisdictions characterise distribution contracts as a subset of framework agreements (in practice, the most common and relevant form).[310]

There is no comparable concept of framework agreements under US law. There has been some discussion of contracts that leave several terms open for later determination, which may bear some similarities to framework agreements under the European concept. Historically, courts have been reluctant to validate such open terms contracts, although this has changed over time. This change was reflected in the UCC which explicitly declares open term contracts to be valid and provides gap-filling provisions. Under US law, distribution contracts are considered to be hybrid transactions to which sales law (i.e., the UCC) is applied for their predominant sales part. Their indefiniteness and incompleteness are no obstacle in light of the UCC's approach to open terms contracts.[311]

Since there is no universal concept, and in order to find an internationally acceptable solution, this study will be based on a broad notion of framework agreements: framework agreements are contracts which intend to provide an umbrella for a series of individual sales transactions to be conducted over an extended period of time. In some cases, there may be a distinction between the framework agreement and the individual sales contracts. If so, the framework agreement will usually contain sales terms, which are to be implemented into the individual sales subsequently concluded. They may also, but not necessarily have to, include an obligation to conclude these individual sales contracts. A framework agreement may also contain sales obligations in *sensu stricto*. If so, the individual deliveries will be based on the framework agreement itself and will specify the terms that were previously left open. In addition, a framework agreement often contains non-sales elements that relate to the parties'

309. *See* Ch. 2 I. 2. above.
310. *See* Ch. 2 II. 1., 2., 3. above.
311. *See* Ch. 2 II. 4. above.

overall relationship and cooperation. Furthermore, a framework agreement is typically to be performed over an extended period of time, which is why it will be considered a long-term contract. Distribution contracts – which are of particular practical relevance – will be contemplated as a subset of framework agreements.[312]

312. *See* Ch. 2 III. above.

CHAPTER 3

Framework Agreements as Sales Contracts under Art. 1 CISG?

Although the CISG does not mention framework agreements or distribution contracts, there is also no express exclusion of these contracts from its sphere of application, as can be found for other types of contracts in Art. 2 CISG. Therefore, it is necessary to analyse whether framework agreements fall within the Convention's ambit. First, the CISG's definition of sales contracts will be briefly outlined.

I. SALES CONTRACTS UNDER THE CONVENTION

1. No Express Definition

According to Art. 1(1) CISG, the 'Convention applies to contracts of sale of goods'. Apart from that, there is no express definition of sales contracts within the CISG.[313]

In endeavouring to explain the absence of an express definition, scholars have come to different conclusions. Some posit that the definitions of sales contracts as set forth in domestic laws at the time of drafting the Convention were strikingly similar, thereby rendering an express definition in the CISG superfluous.[314] Others contend that the definitions of sales contracts as delineated in domestic laws were largely different,

313. *Gabriel*, para. 2.1; Kröll *et al./Mistelis*, Art. 1 CISG, para. 25; MüKoBGB/*Huber*, Art. 1 CISG, para. 3; MüKoHGB/*B. Köhler*, Art. 1 CISG, para. 12; Schlechtriem/Schwenzer/Schroeter/*Ferrari*, 8th German ed., Art. 1 CISG, para. 12; Schlechtriem/Schwenzer/Schroeter/*Hachem*, 5th English ed., Art. 1 CISG, para. 9; Staudinger/*Magnus*, Art. 1 CISG, para. 13; *C. Witz*, para. 112.21.

314. *Memmo*, Riv. Trim. Dir. Proced. Civ. 1983, p. 189; *Padovini*, Riv. Dir. Int. Priv. Proc. 1987, p. 52; Schlechtriem/Schwenzer/Schroeter/*Ferrari*, 8th German ed., Art. 1 CISG, para. 12; cf. also *Klima*, RIW 1996, p. 1036; *Schwenzer/Muñoz*, para. 8.01 ('All legal systems examined in this work agree that a contract of sale usually implies that the seller is obliged to deliver the goods and transfer property (or cause to pass), and conversely the buyer has to pay the price').

rendering a uniform solution under the Convention unattainable.[315] A third approach attempts to explain the absence of an express definition by suggesting that the Convention is supposed to remain open to accommodate future developments.[316]

The exact reasoning remains unclear when viewed through the lens of the Convention's drafting history. A review of the drafting history merely reveals that a proposal to include an express definition of international sales contracts was unsuccessfully made.[317] The third approach has much to commend it, as it aligns with a dynamic approach to the interpretation of the CISG.[318] However, the explanation for the absence of an express definition can essentially be left open. Despite this absence, an autonomous definition of sales contracts under the CISG can be established.[319]

2. Prevailing Characterisation of Sales Contracts under the CISG

The prevailing view among scholars and courts is that such a definition can be found by reference to Arts 30 and 53 CISG. These provisions enshrine the main obligations of sellers (Art. 30 CISG) and buyers (Art. 53 CISG) under sales contracts governed by the CISG. Accordingly, a contract for the sale of goods is present if the seller is obliged to deliver the goods (as well as hand over any documents related to them) and transfer property in them, whereas the buyer is obliged to pay the purchase price and take delivery of the goods.[320] Recently, alternative definitions have been proposed which focus on material aspects of sales transactions in contrast to the more formalistic

315. Both with further references: Schlechtriem/Schwenzer/Schroeter/*Ferrari*, 8th German ed., Art. 1 CISG, para. 12; *Torsello*, p. 196.

316. *Maier-Lohmann*, para. 321, mentioning the sale of data; *Neumann*, (2017) 21 VJ, pp. 113, 114, with a focus on transactions involving modern software.

317. UNCITRAL Y.B. III (1972), Supplement, pp. 13, 14: the delegate of Guyana put forth the suggestion of including a definition in a sub-paragraph of Art. 1 CISG. The Austrian and Japanese delegates expressed their reservations and appeared to be opposed to the inclusion of such a definition. The chairman suggested that the proposal should be examined. Thereafter, the proposal was not mentioned again, indicating that it was dropped without further discussion.

318. *See* Ch. 1 III. 3. above on a dynamic approach under the CISG; similarly, *Maier-Lohmann*, para. 321.

319. Cf. only Gerechthof 's-Hertogenbosch, 18 January 2011, CISG-online 2179, para. 4.4.2; MüKoBGB/*Huber*, Art. 1 CISG, para. 3; Schlechtriem/Schwenzer/Schroeter/*Ferrari*, 8th German ed., Art. 1 CISG, para. 13; Staudinger/*Magnus*, Art. 1 CISG, para. 13.

320. BeckOK/*Saenger*, Art. 1 CISG, para. 4; *Gabriel*, para. 2.1; *Gillette/Walt*, p. 43; *Herber/Czerwenka*, Art. 1 CISG, para. 3; jurisPK-BGB/*Münch*, Art. 1 CISG, para. 27; Kröll *et al./Mistelis*, Art. 1 CISG, para. 25; Mankowski/*Mankowski*, Art. 1 CISG, para. 2; MüKoBGB/*Huber*, Art. 1 CISG, para. 3; *Muñoz*, (2019) 24 Unif. L. Rev., p. 287; *Perović*, (2011) 59 Belgrade L. Rev., p. 182; Schlechtriem/Schwenzer/Schroeter/*Ferrari*, 8th German ed., Art. 1 CISG, para. 13; *Schumacher*, IHR 2005, p. 149; Soergel/*Kreße*, Art. 1 CISG, para. 22; Staudinger/*Magnus*, Art. 1 CISG, para. 13; *Thiele*, IHR 2002, p. 10; *C. Witz*, para. 112.21; cf. *Huber/Mulis*, p. 43 (mentioning only the obligation to deliver); *see, e.g.*, in case law: Milan Chamber of Arbitration, 30 January 2019, CISG-online 5573, note 16; BGH, 28 May 2014, CISG-online 2513, para. 13; Supr. Ct. Lithuania, 9 March 2012, CISG-online 5111; Tribunale di Forli, 6 March 2012, CISG-online 2585, IHR 2013, p. 198; Gerechthof 's-Hertogenbosch, 18 January 2011, CISG-online 2179, para. 4.4.2; Tribunal Cantonal Valais, 27 October 2006, CISG-online 1563; High Commercial Ct. Croatia, 19 December 2006, CISG-online 3284; KGer Schaffhausen, 25 February 2002, CISG-online 723.

approach advocated by the prevailing view.[321] These alternative definitions have some advantages, especially in light of recent technical developments, for example, software and data trading.[322] Yet, it appears to be irrelevant which of these definitions is used as a starting point for the question whether the CISG is applicable to framework agreements. In order to facilitate clarity and comprehension, this study will utilise the prevailing definition of sales contracts under the CISG as a foundation for the subsequent analysis.

3. Contract's Label Is Irrelevant

Furthermore, the parties' labelling of a contract is of no consequence for the Convention's applicability.[323] Consequently, the parties are not required to explicitly label their contract as 'sales contract' or 'contract of sale of goods'. Rather, they are at liberty to refer to their contract by any label they choose. Regardless, the CISG may still be applicable, provided that the contract contains obligations in the sense of Arts 30 and 53 CISG.[324]

4. Broad Concept under the Convention

The Convention covers a broad range of contracts related to the sale of goods, irrespective of the modalities agreed upon on by the parties.[325] It expands upon the conventional view of sales contracts, which is prevalent in many domestic jurisdictions, by also covering contracts for the supply of goods to be manufactured and produced as well as mixed contracts according to Art. 3 CISG.[326] Furthermore, the CISG governs instalment contracts, as evidenced by Art. 73 CISG.[327]

Moreover, it should be noted that the Convention may also apply to contracts that do not contain sales obligations within the meaning of Arts 30 and 53 CISG. This could be an important expansion of the CISG, which might also influence its applicability to framework agreements. The following section will therefore focus on contracts without sales obligations in *sensu stricto*.

---

321. *See* the definitions proposed by *Maier-Lohmann*, paras 323 et seq. and *Neumann*, (2017) 21 VJ, pp. 109 et seq.
322. Cf. only *Hayward*, UNSW L. J. 2021, p. 907.
323. Gerechtshof Arnhem-Leeuwarden, 6 February 2024, CISG-online 6819, para. 9; *Hayward*, UNSW L. J. 2021, p. 907; *Nicolai*, p. 261; *Pavic/Djordjevic*, FS Rüßman, p. 911.
324. RB Midden-Nederland, 25 March 2015, CISG-online 2591, where the parties labelled a sales contract as 'License Agreement'; Tribunale di Forli, 6 March 2012, CISG-online 2585, IHR 2013, p. 198; Foreign Trade Ct. of Arbitration of the CC and Industry of Serbia, 15 July 2008, CISG-online 1795; Kröll *et al./Mistelis*, Art. 1 CISG, para. 25.
325. Cf. only *Achilles*, Art. 1 CISG, para. 2; Schlechtriem/Schwenzer/Schroeter/*Hachem*, 5th English ed., Art. 1 CISG, para. 10; Staudinger/*Magnus*, Art. 1 CISG, paras 15 et seq.
326. *Perales Viscasillas*, Extending the Scope, p. 128; *Schlechtriem*, (2005) 36 V.U.W. L. Rev., p. 787; Schlechtriem/Schwenzer/Schroeter/*Hachem*, 5th English ed., Art. 1 CISG, para. 10; *see* on mixed contracts under Art. 3(2) CISG Ch. 4 below.
327. Cf. only HGer Zürich, 22 November 2010, CISG-online 2160; Schlechtriem/Schwenzer/Schroeter/*Hachem*, 5th English ed., Art. 1 CISG, para. 10; Staudinger/*Magnus*, Art. 1 CISG, para. 15.

II. CONTRACTS WITHOUT SALES OBLIGATIONS UNDER THE CISG?

Upon initial examination, it might appear that contracts without sales obligations are not covered by the CISG. According to Art. 1 in conjunction with Arts 30 and 53 of the CISG, actual delivery and payment obligations are required for a contract to be characterised as a sales contract under the Convention.

However, such an interpretation is too narrow and inaccurate in its absolutism. There are two groups of contracts that do not necessarily contain delivery and payment obligations in *sensu stricto*, i.e., sales obligations within the meaning of Arts 30 and 53 CISG but are still considered to be within the CISG's sphere of application.

1. Agreements to Modify or Terminate Sales Contracts

A look at the Convention's text reveals that a contract may be modified or terminated by the mere agreement of the parties according to Art. 29 CISG. This provision refers to agreements that either modify, amend or terminate a sales contract governed by the CISG.

Art. 29 CISG refers to all types of agreements that intend to modify, amend or terminate an existing sales contract governed by the CISG,[328] including settlement agreements related to obligations arising from a CISG contract[329] and extension agreements ('*Stundungsvereinbarung*').[330] Such agreements may themselves be characterised as contracts which do not necessarily correspond with the Convention's conception of sales contracts in accordance with Art. 1 in conjunction with Arts 30 and 53 CISG.[331]

Nevertheless, the prevailing view is that any form of agreement to modify, amend or terminate a sales contract is governed by the CISG, in particular its provisions on contract formation pursuant to Arts 14–24 CISG.[332] The rationale provided is that these contracts directly affect the rights and obligations of the parties to a sales contract and

328. Cf. Schlechtriem/Schwenzer/Schroeter/*Schroeter*, 5th English ed., Art. 29 CISG, paras 20 et seq.; Staudinger/*Magnus*, Art. 29 CISG, para. 8.
329. HGer Zürich, 24 October 2003, CISG-online 857; LG Kassel, 15 February 1996, CISG-online 190; *Achilles*, Art. 1 CISG, para. 2; Brunner/Gottlieb/*Brunner/Brand*, Art. 29 CISG, para. 7; Honsell/*Gsell*, Art. 29 CISG, para. 5; MüKoBGB/*Gruber*, Art. 29 CISG, para. 5; Schlechtriem/Schwenzer/Schroeter/*Schroeter*, 5th English ed., Art. 29 CISG, para. 32; Staudinger/*Magnus*, Art. 29 CISG, para. 8; Staudinger/*Magnus*, Art. 4 CISG, para. 62; but *see* OLG Köln, 21 November 2012, CISG-online 2401, paras 58, 59; LG Aachen, 14 May 1993, CISG-online 86.
330. LG Hamburg, 26 September 1990, CISG-online 21, paras 35, 36; MüKoHGB/*Benicke*, Art. 29 CISG, para. 2; Staudinger/*Magnus*, Art. 29 CISG, para. 8.
331. Honsell/*Dornis*, Vorbem. Arts 14–24 CISG, para. 2; cf. also jurisPK-BGB/*Hlawon*, Art. 14 CISG, para. 8, referring to contracts containing sales elements in a broader sense ('*Verträge mit kaufrechtlichem Inhalt im weiteren Sinne*'); BeckOGK/*Buchwitz*, Art. 14 CISG, para. 15.
332. OLG Köln, 22 February 1994, CISG-online 127; AG Sursee, 12 September 2008, CISG-online 1728, note 4.1; LG Hamburg, 26 September 1990, CISG-online 21; *Achilles*, Art. 29 CISG, para. 2; BeckOGK/*Buchwitz*, Art. 14 CISG, para. 15; BeckOK/*Saenger*, Art. 29 CISG, para. 2; Brunner/Gottlieb/*Brunner/Pfisterer/Köster*, Intro Arts 14–24 CISG, para. 20; Honsell/*Dornis*, Vorbem. Arts 14–24 CISG, para. 2; jurisPK-BGB/*Hlawon*, Art. 14 CISG, para. 8; Schlechtriem/Schwenzer/Schroeter/*Schroeter*, 5th English ed., Art. 29 CISG, para. 10; Staudinger/*Magnus*, Art. 29 CISG, para. 8; Witz/Salger/Lorenz/*Salger*, Art. 29 CISG, para. 9.

therefore they should also be governed by the Convention.[333] This could be considered evidence for the CISG's applicability to contracts that are closely linked or related to actual sales contracts within the meaning of Art. 1 CISG, despite these related contracts not meeting all of the criteria of a sales contract.[334]

Agreements to modify or terminate sales contracts admittedly differ from framework agreements. However, Art. 29 CISG underlines that not only contracts that contain sales rights and obligations in the sense of Arts 30 and 53 CISG may be governed by the Convention.[335] Consequently, framework agreements that do not contain sales obligations in *sensu stricto* should not a priori be excluded from the Convention's sphere of application. Instead, it should be considered whether such agreements are closely related to the sale of goods.[336] In addition to agreements to modify or terminate sales contracts, one further group of contracts without actual sales obligations is commonly considered to fall within the Convention's sphere of applicability.

2. Preliminary Agreements

In practice, sales contracts are often not concluded by simply exchanging an offer and acceptance. Instead, a lengthy process of negotiating precedes their conclusion.[337] In such cases, the parties may want to find security outside the 'final' sales contract and allocate the risks of the process leading up to it.[338] For that reason, the parties may have recourse to so-called preliminary agreements, especially when it comes to complex transactions.[339] Preliminary agreements allow the parties to pin down the most relevant terms for their future contract and to roughly allocate investment tasks.[340]

It should be noted that there is no established international terminology when it comes to preliminary agreements.[341] Rather, the notion covers a broad and heterogeneous spectrum of agreements.[342] The common feature of all agreements within the spectrum is that they anticipate and prepare the conclusion of one or multiple contracts.[343] This study will exclusively refer to preliminary agreements that anticipate the conclusion of sales contracts.

333. *Ferrari*, p. 78; jurisPK-BGB/*Hlawon*, Art. 14 CISG, para. 8.
334. Cf. also *Ferrari*, p. 78.
335. Cf. Honsell/*Dornis*, Vorbem. Arts 14–24 CISG, para. 2.
336. *See* Ch. 3 III. 1. b. ii. below.
337. Cf. *Farnsworth*, (1987) 87 Col. L. Rev., pp. 218, 219; *J. Schmidt*, (1983–1984) 6 Houst. J. Int'l L., p. 37.
338. *Farnsworth*, (1987) 87 Col. L. Rev., p. 220; *J. Schmidt*, (1983–1984) 6 Houst. J. Int'l L., p. 62.
339. *Bonell*, RIW 1990, p. 696; Ferrari *et. al./Mankowski*, Vorbem. Arts 14–24 CISG, para. 15.
340. Brunner/Gottlieb/*Brunner/Pfisterer/Köster*, Art. 14 CISG, para. 7; Schlechtriem/Schwenzer/Schroeter/*Schroeter*, 5th English ed., Art. 14 CISG, para. 109; *Torsello*, p. 215; from a Law and Economics point of view: *Schwartz/Scott*, (2007) 661 Harv. L. Rev., pp. 1 et seq.
341. *Torsello*, p. 192; for a different terminology *see*: *Farnsworth*, (1987) 87 Col. L. Rev., pp. 219 et seq.; *J. Schmidt*, (1983–1984) 6 Houst. J. Int'l L., pp. 37 et seq.
342. *Bonell*, RIW 1990, p. 696; *J. Schmidt*, (1983–1984) 6 Houst. J. Int'l L., p. 37; *Torsello*, p. 192; cf. Hof van Beroep Gent, 15 May 2002, CISG-online 745, note 6.2, holding that there is no precise legal meaning of the term 'letter of intent'.
343. *J. Schmidt*, (1983–1984) 6 Houst. J. Int'l L., p. 37; *Torsello*, p. 192.

The CISG primarily deals with actual sales contracts that provide for the delivery of goods, transfer of property and payment of the purchase price.[344] Accordingly, preliminary agreements are not expressly mentioned within the Convention.[345] If the general notion of sales contracts as set out in the context of the CISG is applied, one might conclude that preliminary agreements differ from a CISG contract. They do not contain obligations to deliver the goods, transfer property in them and pay the purchase price.[346] In fact, they are only preparing and anticipating the conclusion of sales contracts that contain such typical sales obligations. This may indicate that the Convention is not applicable to preliminary agreements, as there is no express provision and they do not follow the conventional sales structure as per Art. 1 in conjunction with Arts 30 and 53 CISG.

However, preliminary agreements may be considered closely related or linked to CISG contracts.[347] Preliminary agreements prepare and anticipate one or multiple sales contracts.[348] It is therefore pertinent to inquire as to whether preliminary agreements should be covered by the Convention based on their close link and relation to CISG contracts. Similar to agreements in the sense of Art. 29 CISG, preliminary agreements may directly affect or establish rights and obligations under a sales contract. Consequently, they may be regarded as a further group of contracts without actual sales obligations that still falls within the Convention's sphere of applicability. The Convention's applicability to preliminary agreements may be of particular relevance with regard to framework agreements, given that these types of agreements share some similarities.[349]

In order to ascertain the CISG's applicability to preliminary agreements, it is necessary to distinguish between different types of preliminary agreements based on their content.[350] The terminology chosen by the parties (or even courts) is not decisive but rather the content of the respective agreement.[351] This study will use the term 'preliminary agreement' in reference to any 'agreement' that is anticipating or preparing the conclusion of a sales contract – whether or not it is legally binding.[352]

344. Ferrari *et. al./Mankowski*, Vorbem. Arts 14–24 CISG, para. 16; cf. also *Torsello*, p. 208, 209 (CISG contracts as 'discrete' contracts).
345. Ferrari *et. al./Mankowski*, Vorbem. Arts 14–24 CISG, para. 16.
346. *Torsello*, p. 233.
347. Cf. *Torsello*, p. 192.
348. *Bonell*, RIW 1990, p. 696.
349. *See* Ch. 3 III. 1. b. ii. 2) b) below.
350. Hof van Beroep Gent, 15 May 2002, CISG-online 745, note 6.2; also distinguishing between different types of preliminary agreements but employing different terminologies: *Farnsworth*, (1987) 87 Col. L. Rev., pp. 249 et seq.; *J. Schmidt*, (1983–1984) 6 Houst. J. Int'l L., pp. 51 et seq.; *Torsello*, pp. 214 et seq.
351. Cf. *J. Schmidt*, (1983–1984) 6 Houst. J. Int'l L., p. 37; *Torsello*, p. 216.
352. *See Farnsworth*, (1987) 87 Col. L. Rev., p. 250.

a. Non-binding Preliminary Agreements

The first type of preliminary agreements discussed here is labelled in various ways. These include letter of intent, memorandum of understanding, gentlemen's agreement or agreement in principle.[353]

i. Characteristics

These agreements are distinguished by the fact that they do not yet bind the parties to a sales contract.[354] In fact, the parties to such an agreement often merely wish to express their willingness to negotiate a sales contract.[355] They may wish to memorialise certain points that have been discussed but remain unsettled or to pin down those points that have already been successfully discussed (i.e., intermediate results).[356] The parties to such an agreement typically intend to remain free to decide whether or not to conclude a final contract and do not include an obligation to conclude a contract.[357] Consequently, such agreements are usually non-contractual and not legally binding.[358]

In some borderline cases, it may not be entirely clear whether the parties intended to be legally bound or not.[359] This is essentially a matter of characterisation by interpreting the wording of the respective agreement and all surrounding circumstances.[360] The question whether a sales contract governed by the CISG exists in such cases should be assessed on the basis of the Convention itself, in particular by having recourse to Art. 8(2) and Art. 8(3) CISG.[361]

353. *See Bonell*, RIW 1990, p. 696; *Torsello*, pp. 217, 218.
354. *Torsello*, p. 218; cf. also *Farnsworth*, (1987) 87 Col. L. Rev., p. 251.
355. *Bonell*, RIW 1990, p. 696; Ferrari *et al./Mankowski*, Vorbem. Arts 14–24 CISG, para. 16.
356. BeckOK/*Saenger*, Art. 14 CISG, para. 6; Brunner/Gottlieb/*Brunner/Pfisterer/Köster*, Art. 14 CISG, para. 7; Schlechtriem/Schwenzer/Schroeter/*Schroeter*, 5th English ed., Art. 14 CISG, para. 109; Staudinger/*Magnus*, Art. 14 CISG, para. 15; *Torsello*, p. 218; cf. also *Farnsworth*, (1987) 87 Col. L. Rev., p. 251; comparing domestic laws with regard to this type of agreement: *Henrich*, § 9, p. 101.
357. Cf. Staudinger/*Magnus*, Art. 14 CISG, para. 15.
358. *Benedick*, para. 142; *Torsello*, p. 218.
359. *Bonell*, RIW 1990, p. 696; Brunner/Gottlieb/*Brunner/Pfisterer/Köster*, Art. 14 CISG, para. 7; Schlechtriem/Schwenzer/Schroeter/*Schroeter*, 5th English ed., Art. 14 CISG, para. 109; *Torsello*, p. 109; Staudinger/*Magnus*, Art. 14 CISG, para. 15.
360. Cf. *Hanwha Corp. v. Cedar Petrochemicals, Inc.*, US Dist. Ct. SD NY, 18 January 2011, CISG-online 2178 (no intention to be bound since the parties agreed on 'two-step process' and only the second step established a final contract); BeckOK/*Saenger*, Art. 14 CISG, para. 6; *Bonell*, RIW 1990, p. 696; Brunner/Gottlieb/*Brunner/Pfisterer/Köster*, Art. 14 CISG, para. 7; Ferrari *et al./Mankowski*, Vorbem. Arts 14–24 CISG, para. 17; *Piltz*, NJW 2000, p. 2060 (providing examples); Staudinger/*Magnus*, Art. 14 CISG, para. 15.
361. Schlechtriem/Schwenzer/Schroeter/*Schroeter*, 5th English ed., Art. 14 CISG, para. 109; *Torsello*, p. 220.

ii. *Applicability of the CISG*

The CISG should generally not be applied to non-binding preliminary agreements.[362] First of all, Art. 1 CISG refers to 'contracts'. Non-binding preliminary agreements do not bind the parties legally and therefore do not constitute a contract within the meaning of Art. 1 CISG. To be more specific, the parties to such preliminary agreements lack the intention to be bound by their agreement which is explicitly mentioned in Art. 14(1), sentence 1 CISG.[363] For the same reason, this type of preliminary agreement cannot be interpreted as an offer from one party to the other.[364] Therefore, they fall outside the Convention's sphere of application.

Nonetheless, non-binding preliminary agreements may still be relevant for a CISG contract subsequently concluded, namely in terms of its interpretation.[365] Art. 8(3) CISG holds that 'due consideration is to be given to all relevant circumstances of the case including the negotiations [...]'. A non-binding preliminary agreement might provide clues about the course of the negotiation and might thus be taken into consideration as a 'relevant circumstance' pursuant to Art. 8(3) CISG.[366] Consequently, a final contract governed by the CISG might be interpreted in light of the preliminary agreement.[367] If the parties wish to prevent their preliminary agreement from being taken into account, they are free to include a corresponding clause in their final contract. Art. 6 CISG allows derogation or variance from the provision in Art. 8(3) CISG.[368]

b. *Preliminary Agreements Relating to the Negotiations*

The second type of preliminary agreements relate to the negotiations preceding the conclusion of a sales contract.[369] As with the previous type of preliminary agreements, there is no established terminology. Rather, it is necessary to consider the content of the respective preliminary agreement.

i. *Characteristics*

This type of preliminary agreement may oblige the parties to engage in further negotiations.[370] Such preliminary agreements prevent either party from withdrawing

362. *Bonell*, RIW 1990, p. 696; *Torsello*, p. 218; cf. also Kröll *et al./Ferrari*, Art. 14 CISG, para. 14.
363. Cf. Brunner/Gottlieb/*Brunner/Pfisterer/Köster*, Art. 14 CISG, para. 7; Kröll *et al./Ferrari*, Art. 14 CISG, para. 14; MüKoBGB/*Gruber*, Art. 14 CISG, para. 9.
364. *Torsello*, p. 219.
365. *Torsello*, p. 222.
366. *Torsello*, p. 222; cf. also Schlechtriem/Schwenzer/Schroeter/*Schroeter*, 5th English ed., Intro Arts 14–24 CISG, para. 121.
367. *Torsello*, p. 222.
368. *Torsello*, p. 222; cf. also *Bonell*, RIW 1990, p. 698; MüKoHGB/*Ferrari*, Art. 8 CISG, para. 14; Schlechtriem/Schwenzer/Schroeter/*Schmidt-Kessel*, 8th German ed., Art. 8 CISG, para. 35; Staudinger/*Magnus*, Art. 8 CISG, para. 23.
369. With a similar distinction: *J. Schmidt*, (1983–1984) 6 Houst. J. Int'l L., pp. 39 et seq.
370. *J. Schmidt*, (1983–1984) 6 Houst. J. Int'l L., pp. 39 et seq.; *Torsello*, pp. 223 et seq.

from the negotiations.[371] This is of particular interest to the parties if one or both parties have made investments in light of the relationship between them.[372] The parties to such an agreement are typically still uncertain about the eventual conclusion of a final contract.[373] A possible reason not to enter into a contract obliging the parties to conclude a final contract might, for example, be that the contract's profitability cannot yet be properly evaluated.[374] Therefore, the parties intend to continue the negotiations and not be bound to conclude a final agreement; they are merely obliged to negotiate, not to actually reach an agreement.[375]

Moreover, preliminary agreements relating to the negotiations may establish specific obligations that regulate the conduct of the negotiations.[376] For example, the parties frequently agree on confidentiality clauses in a preliminary agreement.[377] Such clauses are relevant if the negotiations involve the disclosure of confidential information, e.g., know-how, etc.[378] The disclosing party wants to ensure that their confidential information is not shared with third parties, whereas the opposing party wants to have more information about their future contract before making any (financial) commitment.[379] For that reason, the parties frequently agree on confidentiality obligations that do not end with the conclusion of a final contract but rather last during its performance and sometimes even beyond.[380] They do so by implementing the confidentiality obligation into the final contract, e.g., by including an explicit reference clause in the final contract.[381]

In contrast to the type of preliminary agreements previously discussed,[382] preliminary agreements obliging the parties to negotiate are usually legally binding, i.e., they constitute a contract.[383] This at least appears to be recognised in most civil law jurisdictions.[384] However, common law jurisdictions are more sceptical with regard to the legally binding nature (or at least enforceability) of such preliminary agreements.[385] The specific obligations that may be established by a preliminary agreement relating to

371. *Torsello*, p. 223.
372. *Torsello*, p. 223.
373. *Torsello*, p. 223.
374. *Torsello*, p. 223.
375. Cf. *Farnsworth*, (1987) 87 Col. L. Rev., p. 251.
376. *J. Schmidt*, (1983–1984) 6 Houst. J. Int'l L., p. 49; *Torsello*, p. 225.
377. *J. Schmidt*, (1983–1984) 6 Houst. J. Int'l L., p. 49; *Torsello*, p. 226; cf. also *Farnsworth*, (1987) 87 Col. L. Rev., pp. 278, 279.
378. *J. Schmidt*, (1983–1984) 6 Houst. J. Int'l L., p. 49; *Torsello*, p. 226.
379. Cf. *Farnsworth*, (1987) 87 Col. L. Rev., pp. 277 et seq.; *J. Schmidt*, (1983–1984) 6 Houst. J. Int'l L., p. 49.
380. *Torsello*, p. 226.
381. *Torsello*, p. 226.
382. *See* Ch. 3 II. 2. a. above.
383. *Torsello*, p. 223.
384. *J. Schmidt*, (1983–1984) 6 Houst. J. Int'l L., pp. 40, 41; *Torsello*, p. 223.
385. The decision in *Courtney and Fairbairn Ltd. v. Tolaini Brothers (Hotels) Ltd.*, [1975] 1 All ER 716, offers an illustration: in this case, *Lord Denning* held that a contract to negotiate 'is too uncertain to have any binding force'; *Chitty on contracts*, para. 4-169; *J. Schmidt*, (1983–1984) 6 Houst. J. Int'l L., p. 41; *Torsello*, p. 223.

the negotiations are typically binding for the parties during the course of the negotiations.[386]

ii. Applicability of the CISG

Preliminary agreements that merely relate to the negotiations should not be governed by the CISG.[387] They do not follow the conventional structure of CISG contracts in the sense of Art. 1 in conjunction with Arts 30 and 53 CISG.[388]

As evidenced by the Convention's applicability to agreements to modify or terminate sales contracts,[389] the CISG extends beyond conventional sales contracts and also covers closely related or linked contracts under certain circumstances.[390] It is put forth by this study that this generally requires the closely linked contract to either establish or directly affect the parties' rights and obligations under the CISG contract.[391]

A preliminary agreement relating to the negotiations does not establish rights and obligations under a CISG contract. In fact, the parties of such a preliminary agreement may still be uncertain whether they will ultimately agree on an international sales contract.[392] The parties do not commit themselves to conclude a sales contract but rather oblige themselves to negotiate or they may agree on obligations that are limited to the course of negotiations. At most, they may agree that if a sales contract is concluded, it will include certain terms, such as a confidentiality obligation. However, these obligations are merely incorporated into the final agreement if the parties conclude a sales contract, which they are not bound to do.[393] Thus, the parties do not even indirectly establish rights and obligations under a CISG contract because it is uncertain whether they will ever enter into such an agreement.

Moreover, preliminary agreements that relate to the negotiations do not directly affect the parties' rights and obligations under a CISG contract. In many instances, such agreements merely refer to the negotiations between the parties.[394] Yet, it could be argued that a preliminary agreement that sets out obligations to be incorporated into the final agreement directly affects a CISG contract. This connection should not be considered to directly affect the parties' rights and obligations under a CISG contract. For purposes of comparison, an agreement in the sense of Art. 29 CISG directly affects the parties' rights and obligations under a sales contract by modifying or terminating them.[395] This illustrates that the concept of 'affecting the parties' rights and obligations' necessitates the existence of a CISG contract, which is directly influenced by the related

---

386. *Torsello*, p. 225.
387. Accord *Torsello*, pp. 223 et seq.
388. Cf. *Torsello*, p. 223.
389. Cf. Honsell/*Dornis*, Vorbem. Arts 14–24 CISG, para. 2.
390. *See* Ch. 3 II. 1. above.
391. Cf. *Ferrari*, p. 78 ('*affectent directement les droits et obligations des parties à un contrat international de vente*'); jurisPK-BGB/*Hlawon*, Art. 14 CISG, para. 8 ('alle *Vereinbarungen, welche kaufvertragliche Rechte und Pflichten berühren oder begründen*').
392. *See Torsello*, pp. 223, 224, 229.
393. Cf. *Torsello*, p. 229.
394. Cf. RB Utrecht, 19 November 2003, CISG-online 4613, note 5.3; *Torsello*, p. 224.
395. *See* Ch. 3 II. 1. above; cf. *Ferrari*, p. 78.

contract. Neither is the case if the parties have predetermined specific terms to be incorporated into the final contract, as there is not yet a sales contract and a further step, namely incorporation of these terms, is necessary. Hence, there is no room to apply the CISG to this type of preliminary agreement, despite the possibility that it may be considered a preparatory act for a CISG contract.[396]

Nevertheless, preliminary agreements relating to the negotiations might be a relevant circumstance within the meaning of Art. 8(3) CISG, which is relevant for the interpretation of an international sales contract subsequently concluded.[397] This is of particular relevance in cases where the parties establish obligations to be incorporated into the final contract.[398] Moreover, the parties might include clauses in their preliminary agreement with regard to the conclusion of the future contract. Thereby, they might derogate from the rules on contract formation set out in the CISG (Arts 14–24 CISG), which they are free to do in accordance with Art. 6 CISG.[399]

A case decided by the District Court Utrecht is illustrative. The Court held that the CISG was not applicable to a letter of intent concluded between a Belgian seller and a Dutch buyer.[400] In this case, the parties signed a letter of intent to bridge the period until they would conclude a contract for the licensing, installation and maintenance of a payment software. The Court held that the subject matter of this letter of intent was the regulation of the parties' relationship before the final contract was concluded as well as the supply of services.[401] According to the Court, both subjects could not be characterised as sale of movable goods and thus it held that the CISG did not apply.[402] Furthermore, the Court stated that the characterisation of the final agreement and the CISG's application to it were irrelevant for the Convention's applicability to the letter of intent.[403]

c. *Preliminary Agreements Obliging the Parties to Conclude a Sales Contract*

The remaining group of preliminary agreements to be discussed here are preliminary agreements that obligate the parties to conclude a sales contract.[404] There are various reasons parties enter into such a preliminary agreement instead of immediately concluding a final sales contract. If both parties are convinced that the core points of the contract have been agreed on, they may wish to find security by concluding a preliminary agreement binding them to conclude a final contract.[405] This allows each

396. *Torsello*, p. 223.
397. *See* Ch. 3 II. 2. a. ii. above; cf. also *Newhouse/Tanaka*, R.L.R. 2012, p. 18.
398. *See Newhouse/Tanaka*, R.L.R. 2012, p. 18.
399. *See Torsello*, p. 224; cf. also Hof van Beroep Gent, 15 May 2002, CISG-online 746, note 6.1.
400. RB Utrecht, 19 November 2003, CISG-online 4613.
401. RB Utrecht, 19 November 2003, CISG-online 4613, note 5.3.
402. RB Utrecht, 19 November 2003, CISG-online 4613, note 5.3.
403. RB Utrecht, 19 November 2003, CISG-online 4613, note 5.3.
404. Cf. *J. Schmidt*, (1983–1984) 6 Houst. J. Int'l L., pp. 58 et seq. (comparing different domestic laws with regard to such agreements); *Torsello*, p. 231.
405. *Torsello*, p. 231.

party to hold the opposing party to the deal.[406] Furthermore, such preliminary agreements might provide security for the investments that have already been made by both parties.[407] The parties might even be incentivised to make further investments if they conclude a binding preliminary agreement.[408] Moreover, such preliminary agreements may be interesting for both parties if they have further reason to postpone the conclusion of a final sales contract: one potential example is where the parties are unable to immediately conclude the final contract due to the necessity of first acquiring an administrative authorisation.[409]

i. Characteristics

The parties to such preliminary agreements express their intention to conclude the sales contract at a later date.[410] The parties do not intend the preliminary agreement to be a final sales contract.[411] Their intention to be bound is limited to the obligation to conclude a sales contract in the future and does not (yet) extend to the exchange of goods against money.[412] Thus, the parties still need to find another consensus for there to be a sales contract in *sensu stricto*. The preliminary agreement itself is nonetheless legally binding.[413] The parties agree on the future conclusion of a final sales contract under more or less predetermined conditions.[414] Consequently, the preliminary agreement is performed by concluding a sales contract, specifically by exchanging offer and acceptance.[415] Therefore, such preliminary agreements are also referred to as 'agreements to agree' or 'contracts to contract'.[416] Typically, both contracting parties are obliged to conclude a final contract; however, the obligation can also be limited to one of the parties.[417] Furthermore, the parties' obligation to conclude a contract can be conditional upon the parties' agreement on the outstanding points or upon taking specific action, such as requesting an administrative authorisation.[418]

The preliminary agreements discussed here may vary in the level of detail provided regarding the specifics of the final contract. It is possible that the parties to a

406. *Torsello*, p. 231.
407. *Ben-Shahar*, (2004) 389 Wis. L. Rev., pp. 389, 406, 407; cf. also *Farnsworth*, (1987) 87 Col. L. Rev., p. 250.
408. *Ben-Shahar*, (2004) 389 Wis. L. Rev., pp. 389, 406, 407.
409. Cf. *J. Schmidt*, (1983–1984) 6 Houst. J. Int'l L., p. 61.
410. *Bonell*, RIW 1990, p. 696; *J. Schmidt*, (1983–1984) 6 Houst. J. Int'l L., pp. 58 et seq. (comparing different domestic laws with regard to such agreements); *Torsello*, p. 231.
411. *Torsello*, p. 232.
412. Cf. *Benedick*, para. 141; *Torsello*, pp. 231, 232; *see also Farnsworth*, (1987) 87 Col. L. Rev., p. 253.
413. *Bonell*, RIW 1990, p. 696.
414. *Bonell*, RIW 1990, p. 696; *Schroeter*, para. 90.
415. *Henrich*, pp. 184 et seq.; cf. also *Ferrari*, EuLF 2000/01, p. 9 (in the context of framework agreements).
416. *See Knapp*, (1969) 44 N.Y.U.L. Rev., p. 676; Flechtner/*Schlechtriem*, (1999) 18 J. L. & Com., p. 222; Schlechtriem/Schwenzer/Schroeter/*Schroeter*, 5th English ed., Intro Arts 14–24 CISG, para. 23.
417. *See Henrich*, p. 1; *Ritzinger*, NJW 1990, p. 1201; *J. Schmidt*, (1983–1984) 6 Houst. J. Int'l L., p. 58.
418. *Henrich*, p. 184; *Torsello*, p. 233.

preliminary agreement have not yet agreed on all aspects of the final contract.[419] In such cases, the parties intend to have further negotiations and frequently agree on an additional obligation to carry out the subsequent negotiations in good faith.[420] At the same time, they believe that the basics of the contract have been sufficiently agreed upon and hence agree on an obligation to conclude the final contract.[421] In practice, the parties may choose to leave terms of their agreement open when the responsibility is divided between merchants and lawyers – the merchants deal with the essential basics of their transaction while leaving the discussion and conclusion of a more detailed, final contract to their lawyers.[422]

Moreover, preliminary agreements that oblige the parties to conclude a contract may also contain virtually all substantive aspects of the final contract and merely postpone its conclusion.[423] Such preliminary agreements are sometimes referred to as precontracts or '*Vorvertrag*' in German-speaking jurisdictions.[424] The parties to such a preliminary agreement are at a more advanced stage of the negotiations as they have agreed on (almost) all aspects of their future transaction but still decide not to yet enter into a final contract.[425] In such cases, it is not always clear whether the agreement should still be considered a preliminary agreement or as a final contract.[426] The parties' intention is decisive for this question which must be determined by way of interpretation.[427] The mere reproduction of a contract that has previously been agreed upon in all of its essential aspects should not be characterised as a preliminary agreement obliging the parties to conclude a sales contract.[428] In fact, a final contract may already be concluded if a 'meeting of the minds' on all essential aspects of the final contract occurs.[429] The formalisation of the contract is primarily for evidentiary purposes in such a situation.[430] Even if the parties agree upon all aspects of the final transaction, they may still want to agree on a preliminary agreement which is to be followed by a final contract; ultimately, the parties' intention is decisive.[431]

419. In detail *Farnsworth*, (1987) 87 Col. L. Rev., pp. 253 ('agreements with open terms'); *see also Torsello*, p. 231 ('incomplete preliminary agreements').
420. *Farnsworth*, (1987) 87 Col. L. Rev., pp. 253, 254; cf. also Flechtner/*Schlechtriem*, (1999) 18 J. L. & Com, p. 222.
421. *Torsello*, p. 231.
422. Cf. *Farnsworth*, (1987) 87 Col. L. Rev., p. 253.
423. *Torsello*, p. 231.
424. Cf. only *Bonell*, RIW 1990, p. 696; *Torsello*, pp. 237 et seq.; *see also* the explicit rule in Art. 22 Swiss Code of Obligations; *Henrich*, passim, particularly with regard to the concept of a precontract ('*Vorvertrag*') under German law.
425. *Torsello*, p. 237.
426. Cf. *Farnsworth*, (1987) 87 Col. L. Rev., p. 253.
427. *Farnsworth*, (1987) 87 Col. L. Rev., p. 253; *Torsello*, pp. 231, 232; cf. also Flechtner/*Schlechtriem*, (1999) 18 J. L. & Com., pp. 222, 223.
428. *Torsello*, pp. 237, 238; cf. also *Bonell*, RIW 1990, p. 698.
429. *Bonell*, RIW 1990, p. 698; Flechtner/*Schlechtriem*, (1999) 18 J. L. & Com., p. 222; *Torsello*, p. 238; but *see* Witz/Salger/Lorenz/*W. Witz*, Art. 14 CISG, para. 26 (no intention to be bound if the parties agree on 'formal agreements to follow').
430. With more detail: *Bonell*, RIW 1990, pp. 697, 698.
431. *Henrich*, pp. 77, 78.

ii. Applicability of the CISG

1) Reasons to Not Apply the Convention?

Upon initial examination, the Convention does not contain any provisions that refer to preliminary agreements.[432] The CISG's silence on this matter could suggest its non-applicability.

Furthermore, it could be contended that preliminary agreements obliging the parties to conclude a sales contract cannot be characterised as sales contract in the sense of Art. 1 CISG and are therefore beyond the Convention's sphere of application.[433] This approach posits that the parties to such a preliminary agreement do not undertake – at least not yet – sales obligations, i.e., obligations to deliver the goods, transfer property and pay the purchase price as per Arts 30 and 53 CISG.[434] Instead, the parties merely agree to conclude a contract in the future, which will include such sales obligations.[435] The obligation to conclude a sales contract is arguably significantly different from the obligations undertaken by the parties to a final sales contract.[436] Because of these differences, one scholar has proposed that the parties to a preliminary agreement binding them to conclude a sales contract cannot yet be considered buyer or seller.[437] Moreover, the Convention's provisions only deal with final sales contracts.[438] Consequently, it has been argued that the CISG, in particular its provisions on remedies, is not appropriate to deal with the preliminary agreements discussed here.[439]

2) Prevailing View

In contrast, the majority view advocates that preliminary agreements obliging the parties to conclude a sales contract – sometimes referred to as precontracts – should also be governed by the Convention.[440] In this context, it has been submitted that

432. Cf. *Bonell*, RIW 1990, pp. 696, 697; Ferrari *et al./Mankowski*, Vorbem. Arts 14–24 CISG, para. 16; Schlechtriem/Schwenzer/*Schlechtriem*, Intro Arts 14–24 CISG, para. 7; W. Witz/Salger/Lorenz/*W. Witz*, Vor Arts 14–24 CISG, para. 9.
433. *Newhouse/Tanaka*, R.L.R. 2012, p. 18, who generally hold that 'preliminary contracts between the parties fall outside the scope of the CISG'; cf. also *Torsello*, p. 233.
434. *Bonell*, RIW 1990, p. 696; *Höß*, p. 64; *Torsello*, p. 233.
435. *Bonell*, RIW 1990, p. 696; *Höß*, p. 64; *Torsello*, p. 233.
436. Cf. *Höß*, p. 64; *Torsello*, p. 233 ('Indeed, the obligation to conclude a contract is radically different from the obligation to transfer property or to pay a purchase price').
437. *Höß*, p. 64.
438. Ferrari *et al./Mankowski*, Vorbem. Arts 14–24 CISG, para. 16; cf. also *Höß*, pp. 64, 65, who mentions that the CISG's remedies are not an appropriate means of resolving disputes related to such preliminary agreements; *Thieffry*, Dr. prat. com. int. 1993, p. 65, maintaining that the Convention simply does not take a position on the parties' obligation to conclude a sales contract.
439. *Höß*, pp. 64, 65.
440. BeckOGK/*Buchwitz*, Art. 14 CISG, para. 16; *Benedick*, para. 141; *Bonell*, RIW 1990, p. 697; Brunner/Gottlieb/*Brunner/Pfisterer/Köster*, Intro Arts 14–24 CISG, para. 19; Ferrari *et al./Mankowski*, Vorbem. Arts 14–24 CISG, para. 16; *Grunewald*, p. 38; Honsell/*Dornis*, Vorbem. Arts 14–24 CISG, para. 2; *Janssen/Wahnschaffe*, EuZW 2021, p. 878; jurisPK-BGB/*Hlawon*, Art. 14 CISG, para. 8; MüKoBGB/*Huber*, Art. 1 CISG, para. 5; MüKoBGB/*Gruber*,

merely considering the different nature and structure of the obligations set out in a preliminary agreement in comparison to those in a sales contract would be too formalistic.[441] Rather, the focus should be on the 'economic substance' of the transaction.[442] While the direct object of a preliminary agreement is the conclusion of a future contract, the indirect, but economically more substantial, object is the exchange of goods against money.[443] At their core, such preliminary agreements already contain obligations to deliver the goods and pay the purchase price.[444]

Similarly, scholars have emphasised the close link between preliminary agreements binding the parties to conclude a contract and the final sales contract.[445] Based on this close link, the preliminary agreement should also be governed by the Convention if the main sales contract is governed by the CISG.[446]

Furthermore, *Torsello* highlights that a preliminary agreement binding the parties to conclude a sales contract in the future is essentially comparable to a final sales contract providing for postponed performance; in both cases, the likelihood of an exchange of goods against money in the future is reasonably high.[447] He therefore submits that the CISG should be applied to preliminary agreements that oblige the parties to conclude a sales contract.[448]

This raises the question of prerequisites that must be met for a preliminary agreement to be governed by the Convention. Upfront, it is important to note that preliminary agreements must be related to a final sales contract governed by the CISG.[449] Furthermore, a number of scholars hold that the CISG is applicable to preliminary agreements to the extent that they contain an obligation to conclude one or multiple sales contracts.[450]

Vor Art. 14 CISG, para. 5; MüKoHGB/*B. Köhler*, Art. 1 CISG, para. 13; *Piltz*, AnwBl 1991, p. 58; Schlechtriem/Schwenzer/Schroeter/*Ferrari*, 8th German ed., Art. 1 CISG, para. 21; Soergel/*Kreße*, Vor Arts 14–24 CISG, para. 4; Staudinger/*Magnus*, Art. 1 CISG, para. 41; *Torsello*, pp. 233 et seq.; *C. Witz*, para. 112.71; Witz/Salger/Lorenz/*W. Witz*, Vor Arts 14–24 CISG, para. 9.

441. *Torsello*, p. 233.
442. *Torsello*, p. 233; cf. with regard to hire purchase agreements: *Fogt*, IPRax 2003, pp. 368, 369; *Honnold/Flechtner*, Art. 3 CISG, para. 82.
443. *Torsello*, pp. 233, 234; cf. also *Grunewald*, p. 38.
444. *Grunewald*, p. 38.
445. *Grunewald*, p. 38, who argues that it would not be sensible to apply different laws to the preliminary agreement and the main contract; *Janssen/Wahnschaffe*, EuZW 2021, p. 878; Schlechtriem/Schwenzer/Schroeter/*Ferrari*, 8th German ed., Art. 1 CISG, para. 21; cf. also BeckOGK/*Buchwitz*, Art. 14 CISG, para. 16, who maintains that preliminary agreements are merely a 'minus' to the conclusion of a sales contract; MüKoBGB/*Huber*, Art. 1 CISG, para. 5.
446. *Achilles*, Art. 1 CISG, para. 2; Staudinger/*Magnus*, Art. 1 CISG, para. 41; cf. also Schlechtriem/Schwenzer/Schroeter/*Ferrari*, 8th German ed., Art. 1 CISG, para. 21.
447. *Torsello*, p. 234.
448. *Torsello*, pp. 233, 234.
449. Cf. only *Achilles*, Art. 1 CISG, para. 2; Staudinger/*Magnus*, Art. 1 CISG, para. 41.
450. Brunner/Gottlieb/*Brunner/Pfisterer/Köster*, Intro Arts 14–24 CISG, para. 19; Ferrari *et al./Mankowski*, Vorbem. Arts 14–24 CISG, para. 16; *Grunewald*, p. 38; MüKoBGB/*Gruber*, Vor Art. 14 CISG, para. 5; *C. Witz*, para. 112.71; Witz/Salger/Lorenz/*W. Witz*, Vor Arts 14–24 CISG, para. 9; cf. also *Bonell*, RIW 1990, pp. 696, 697; cf. further (without expressly mentioning the obligation to conclude a sales contract): *Piltz*, para. 2-30; Schlechtriem/Schwenzer/Schroeter/*Schroeter*, 5th English ed., Intro Arts 14–24 CISG, para. 23; Schlechtriem/Schwenzer/Schroeter/*Schroeter*, 8th German ed., Vorbem. Arts 14–24 CISG, para. 112.

3) Preferable View

The view that preliminary agreements containing an obligation to conclude a sales contract should be governed by the CISG is preferable.[451] Indeed, there is no explicit provision within the Convention addressing this type of agreement.

The Convention, nonetheless, generally regulates which type of contracts fall within its sphere of application. It does not expressly settle whether it applies to closely related or linked contracts apart from agreements to modify, terminate or amend a contract in the sense of Art. 29 CISG.[452] It is submitted that a general principle can be derived from Art. 29 CISG. According to this general principle, the Convention applies to closely related or linked contracts. This requires that the closely linked contract either establishes or directly affects the parties' rights and obligations under a CISG contract.[453] A preliminary agreement that obliges the parties to enter into a sales contract may be considered to establish the parties' rights and obligations under a CISG contract. In comparison, an agreement amending a contract, e.g., an addendum, may equally establish rights and obligations under a CISG contract.

Admittedly, the preliminary agreement itself does not, strictly speaking, establish rights and obligations of sale in *sensu stricto*; only the final sales contract does so.[454] However, such preliminary agreements have similar effects as the parties bind themselves to agree on a contract containing sales obligations.[455] Even though an additional step is needed, both parties indicate that they are willing to carry out the bargain and that they are certain to reach a final agreement.[456] It could therefore be argued that preliminary agreements obliging the parties to conclude a sales contract in substance already contain sales obligations.[457] They can be considered sales contracts with specific modalities, similar to option contracts and comparable contracts.[458] One might even compare the situation to a final sales contract providing for postponed performance.[459] For these reasons, this study argues that the preliminary agreements under discussion in substance establish rights and obligations under a CISG contract.

451. Accord Brunner/Gottlieb/*Brunner/Pfisterer/Köster*, Intro Arts 14–24 CISG, para. 19; Ferrari *et al./Mankowski*, Vorbem. Arts 14–24 CISG, para. 16; MüKoBGB/*Gruber*, Vor Art. 14 CISG, para. 5; *C. Witz*, para. 112.71; Witz/Salger/Lorenz/*W. Witz*, Vor Arts 14–24 CISG, para. 9; cf. also *Bonell*, RIW 1990, pp. 696, 697; cf. also (without expressly mentioning the obligation to conclude a sales contract): *Piltz*, para. 2-30; Schlechtriem/Schwenzer/Schroeter/*Schroeter*, 5th English ed., Intro Arts 14–24 CISG, para. 23; Schlechtriem/Schwenzer/Schroeter/*Schroeter*, 8th German ed., Vorbem. Arts 14–24 CISG, para. 112.
452. *See* Ch. 1 IV. 2. above on the CISG's gap-filling mechanism.
453. *See* already Ch. 3 II. 2. b. ii. above.
454. *See* Ch. 3 II. 2. c. i. above.
455. Cf. *Benedick*, para. 141.
456. Cf. *Torsello*, p. 231.
457. *Grunewald*, p. 38; Schlechtriem/Schwenzer/Schroeter/*Schroeter*, 8th German ed., Vorbem. Arts 14–24 CISG, para. 112 ('*wenn sie der Sache nach bereits Verpflichtungen zwischen Vertragspartnern in verschiedenen Staaten zur Lieferung beweglicher Güter begründen* [...]'); cf. also Staudinger/*Magnus*, Art. 1 CISG, para. 41.
458. Cf. Schlechtriem/Schwenzer/Schroeter/*Schroeter*, 5th English ed., Intro Arts 14–24 CISG, para. 23; Schlechtriem/Schwenzer/Schroeter/*Schroeter*, 8th German ed., Vorbem. Arts 14–24 CISG, para. 112; Staudinger/*Magnus*, Art. 1 CISG, para. 41.
459. *Torsello*, p. 234.

Indeed, the main purpose of such agreements is to establish rights and obligations under a sales contract. Apart from this main purpose, the indirect purpose, namely the exchange of goods against money, should be taken into account.[460] Therefore, preliminary agreements obliging the parties to conclude a sales contract should be considered closely linked contracts falling within the CISG's scope.

It should be noted that the CISG is not only applicable to preliminary agreements if the parties ultimately conclude a sales contract governed by the Convention.[461] In fact, the close link and relation to a (potential) international sales contract is sufficient for the CISG to apply, even if the parties fail to find a final agreement.[462]

In conclusion, the CISG may be applicable to preliminary agreements that bind the parties to conclude a sales contract, since they are closely related contracts that, at least in substance, establish rights and obligations under a sales contract.

iii. Consequences of the CISG's Applicability

The differing structure of preliminary agreements in comparison to traditional sales contracts[463] raises the question whether the CISG's remedies are suitable for governing preliminary agreements. It would not make sense to apply the Convention if the results of its application were unsatisfactory.[464]

Indeed, the CISG is primarily tailored to final sales contracts; it does not explicitly refer to preliminary agreements.[465] In light of this, some scholars have proposed an analogous application of the Convention to preliminary agreements.[466] However, it is more persuasive to conclude that a number of CISG provisions, in particular those pertaining to remedies,[467] are sufficiently flexible to be applied directly to preliminary agreements. The Convention also contains provisions which are not specifically tailored to sales contracts but rather may be juxtaposed with general international contract law.[468] If the CISG's provisions cannot be applied in a specific case, it is first necessary to determine whether the matter falls within the Convention's substantive scope. Once that has been determined, the mechanism provided for in Art. 7(2) CISG might apply.[469]

460. *Grunewald*, p. 38; *Torsello*, p. 234.
461. Cf. *Torsello*, p. 235.
462. Cf. *Torsello*, pp. 234, 235.
463. *See* Ch. 3 II. 2. c. i. above.
464. *Torsello*, p. 234.
465. *Bonell*, RIW 1990, pp. 696, 697; Ferrari *et al./Mankowski*, Vorbem. Arts 14–24 CISG, para. 16; Schlechtriem/Schwenzer/Schroeter/*Schroeter*, 5th English ed., Intro Arts 14–24 CISG, para. 23; Witz/Salger/Lorenz/*W. Witz*, Vor Arts 14–24 CISG, para. 9.
466. *Benedick*, para. 141; *Bonell*, RIW 1990, pp. 696, 697.
467. Cf. *Magnus*, Remedies, p. 259, holding that 'most CISG remedies can be viewed as constituting general remedies, which apply to any breach of a CISG contract by either party'.
468. Cf. *Perales Viscasillas*, Extending the Scope, pp. 115, 116; Schlechtriem/Schwenzer/Schroeter/*Schroeter*, 5th English ed., Intro Arts 14–24 CISG, para. 6; *Schroeter*, UN-Kaufrecht und Europ. Gemeinschaftsrecht, § 18, para. 30.
469. *See* Ch. 1 IV. 1., 2. above.

The following part will outline the consequences of the CISG's applicability to preliminary agreements without attempting to provide a comprehensive overview of this topic. Instead, it will focus on a selection of key questions.

1) Contract Formation (Articles 14–24 CISG)

Arts 14–24 CISG (Part II of the Convention) govern the formation of any contract that is governed by the Convention.[470] Consequently, the formation of a preliminary agreement governed by the CISG is also subject to Arts 14–24 CISG.[471] The provisions on contract formation in Arts 14–24 CISG are suitable to regulate all kinds of contractual agreements, not just international sales contracts.[472] They resemble general international contract law (with some exceptions).[473] The application of Part II of the Convention to preliminary agreements therefore appears to be unproblematic for the most part.

It is conceivable that an issue might be identified with the 'definiteness' of a preliminary agreement, in particular if it leaves several terms open to be agreed on in the final sales contract, which might be deemed insufficient in light of the definiteness that is required by Art. 14(1) CISG. While preliminary agreements must indeed also meet the minimum content requirements set forth by Art. 14(1) CISG,[474] these requirements should be interpreted in a liberal manner.[475] The requirements are met in the event that certain elements are only subsequently determined within the final sales contract.[476] In addition, the parties may derogate from any standard set forth by Art. 14(1) CISG in accordance with Art. 6 CISG.[477] Consequently, the application of Arts 14–24 CISG to preliminary agreements does not present any issues.

470. Schlechtriem/Schwenzer/Schroeter/*Schroeter*, 5th English ed., Intro Arts 14–24 CISG, para. 19.
471. Brunner/Gottlieb/*Brunner/Pfisterer/Köster*, Intro Arts 14–24 CISG, para. 19; Ferrari *et al./Mankowski*, Vorbem. Arts 14–24 CISG, para. 16; MüKoBGB/*Gruber*, Vor Art. 14 CISG, para. 5; Schlechtriem/Schwenzer/Schroeter/*Schroeter*, 5th English ed., Intro Arts 14–24 CISG, para. 23; Witz/Salger/Lorenz/*W. Witz*, Vor Arts 14–24 CISG, para. 9.
472. Schlechtriem/Schwenzer/Schroeter/*Schroeter*, 5th English ed., Intro Arts 14–24 CISG, para. 6.
473. *Perales Viscasillas*, Extending the Scope, p. 115; Schlechtriem/Schwenzer/Schroeter/*Schroeter*, 5th English ed., Intro Arts 14–24 CISG, para. 6.
474. *See* MüKoBGB/*Gruber*, Vor Art. 14 CISG, para. 5; *Torsello*, p. 234; Witz/Salger/Lorenz/*W. Witz*, Vor Arts 14–24 CISG, para. 9.
475. *See* Ch. 3 IV. below.
476. Cf. Schlechtriem/Schwenzer/*Schlechtriem*, 2nd English ed., Intro Arts 14–24 CISG, para. 7; Schlechtriem/Schwenzer/Schroeter/*Schroeter*, 5th English ed., Intro Arts 14–24 CISG, para. 23; Schlechtriem/Schwenzer/Schroeter/*Schroeter*, 8th German ed., Vorbem. Arts 14–24 CISG, para. 112.
477. Mankowski/*Spagnolo*, Art. 14 CISG, para. 8; MüKoBGB/*Gruber*, Art. 14 CISG, para. 16; Schlechtriem/Schwenzer/Schroeter/*Schroeter*, 5th English ed., Art. 14 CISG, para. 25; Soergel/*Kreße*, Art. 14 CISG, para. 4; Staudinger/*Magnus*, Art. 14 CISG, para. 3; Witz/Salger/Lorenz/*W. Witz*, Art. 14 CISG, para. 13.

2) Breach of the Obligation to Conclude a Sales Contract

A more pressing issue may be the breach of the obligation to conclude a final sales contract. This obligation is not a characteristic part of 'conventional' sales contracts under the Convention, as can be deduced from Arts 30 and 53 CISG.[478] Therefore, it may be debatable whether the CISG's provisions are apt to deal with a breach of this type of obligation. A breach might occur if one of the parties expressly refuses to conclude the final sales contract.[479] Alternatively, one of the parties may fail to comply with the conditions that have been predetermined in the preliminary agreement when making an offer, e.g., by including a lower price for the goods in the offer.[480]

It is not possible to distinguish between the remedies of the seller and the remedies of the buyer in this context since the obligation may apply to both parties (provided it is not unilateral), irrespective of their role under the future sales contract. This is unproblematic as most CISG remedies apply equally to both parties of the contract under the same conditions.[481]

Furthermore, it is submitted that Arts 38 and 39 CISG should not be applied to a breach of the obligation to conclude a sales contract. The provisions in Arts 38 and 39 CISG refer to goods that have been delivered to the buyer. Consequently, the obligation to examine the goods and give notice about any non-conformity necessitates the delivery of goods.[482] The obligation to conclude a sales contract does not involve the delivery of goods and hence an application of Arts 38 and 39 CISG appears to be inapt.[483] Accordingly, the aggrieved party is not required to give notice to the breaching party if the obligation to conclude a sales contract has been breached.[484]

Otherwise, the CISG's provisions, in particular its remedies, can by and large be applied to a breach of the obligation to conclude a sales contract, as will be illustrated below.

a) Specific Performance

Should the aggrieved party be willing to hold on to the bargain, they may be interested in pursuing a claim for specific performance, i.e., the conclusion of an international sales contract in accordance with the preliminary agreement.[485] The Convention confers upon each party the right to demand specific performance in Arts 46(1) and 62

478. With regard to the different structure of a preliminary agreement: *Bonell*, RIW 1990, pp. 696, 697; *Ferrari*, EuLF 2000/01, p. 9 (in the context of framework agreements); cf. also *Schroeter*, para. 90.
479. Cf. *Torsello*, p. 235.
480. Cf. *Henrich*, pp. 182 et seq.
481. *Magnus*, Remedies, p. 259.
482. Cf. *Schroeter*, para. 477; more extensively Staudinger/*Magnus*, Art. 3 CISG, para. 9 (e.g., application by analogy to documents that represent the goods).
483. *See* Ch. 4 III. 2. a. ii. 2) below (in the context of breaches of service obligations).
484. Cf. also Staudinger/*Magnus*, Art. 38 CISG, para. 9 and Art. 39 CISG, para. 12, who posits that Arts 38 and 39 CISG do not extend to 'other' breaches of contract, such as breaches of service obligations; but *see* with regard to service obligations Schlechtriem/Schwenzer/Schroeter/*Hachem*, 5th English ed., Art. 7 CISG, para. 37.
485. *See Torsello*, p. 235.

CISG. Both of these provisions refer in a general manner to the other party's obligations.[486] The broad wording of these provisions implies that the parties to a preliminary agreement also have the right to demand specific performance of the other party's obligation to conclude a contract. The aggrieved party may raise such a claim for the conclusion of a sales contract if the other party refuses to conclude it. This is also applicable in case one of the parties fails to comply with the terms set out in the preliminary agreement.

In accordance with the obligations agreed upon, the parties to a preliminary agreement are not permitted to immediately claim for delivery of the goods or payment of the purchase price without first concluding a sales contract under the CISG.[487] It is important to acknowledge that some domestic procedural laws permit the combination of a claim for contract conclusion with a claim for delivery of the goods in the same proceedings; this is primarily a matter of procedural efficiency.[488] While the CISG grants a claim for specific performance under both a preliminary agreement and a final sales contract, it is up to the domestic procedural law to determine whether these claims may be combined. Such questions lie outside the Convention's substantive scope of application.

Furthermore, the Convention does not provide for a uniform solution as to the enforceability of a claim for specific performance.[489] Rather, Art. 28 CISG refers to the *lex fori*.[490] Parties to a preliminary agreement governed by the CISG may have a claim for specific performance but its enforceability may be limited by the applicable law of the forum.[491]

b) Avoidance

The aggrieved party may wish to avoid the preliminary agreement entirely if the obligation to conclude a contract has been breached. Arts 49(1)(a) and 64(1)(a) CISG are broadly worded and merely refer to the failure to perform 'any of his obligations'. This may also include the failure to perform the obligation to conclude a sales contract. The decisive factor for avoidance under the Convention is whether a contract has been fundamentally breached.[492]

If the breach of the obligation to conclude a sales contract constitutes a fundamental breach of the preliminary agreement, the aggrieved party may consequently declare the contract avoided.[493] In case one party is unwilling to conclude a sales contract in its entirety or under specified conditions, this may frequently be deemed a fundamental breach in the sense of Art. 25 CISG. The obligation to conclude a sales

486. Art. 46(1) CISG: 'The buyer may require performance by the seller of his obligations [...]'; Art. 62 CISG: 'The seller may require the buyer to pay the price, take delivery or perform his other obligations [...]'.
487. Cf. *Henrich*, pp. 188 et seq. (a similar situation exists under German domestic law, whereas the circumstances appears to be distinct under Italian domestic law).
488. Cf. on German law *Henrich*, p. 187.
489. Cf. *Janssen/Ahuja*, IHR 2020, p. 6; *Torsello*, p. 236.
490. *Torsello*, p. 236.
491. *Torsello*, p. 236.
492. Cf. *Magnus*, Remedies, pp. 269 et seq.
493. *See* Arts 49(1)(a) and 64(1)(a) in conjunction with Art. 25 CISG.

contract will typically be the most important obligation for both parties to a preliminary agreement; the contractual expectation of the non-breaching party is one of the decisive criteria under Art. 25 CISG.[494] Consequently, the aggrieved party is generally entitled to avoid the contract if the obligation to conclude a sales contract has been breached. However, the individual circumstances of each case will be crucial in determining whether a preliminary agreement has been fundamentally breached.

c) Damages

If a preliminary agreement has been breached, the aggrieved party may also wish to pursue a claim for damages. The CISG stipulates a claim for damages in Arts 45(1)(b) and 61(1)(b) CISG. These provisions require one of the parties' failure to 'perform any of his obligations'. It is therefore irrelevant which obligation under a CISG contract has been breached.[495] Accordingly, the claim for damages, like the claim for specific performance and the remedy of avoidance, can be directly applied in cases where there has been a breach of the obligation to conclude a sales contract under a preliminary agreement governed by the Convention.

With regard to the scope and calculation of damages, Art. 74 CISG is primarily relevant.[496] If the breaching party is in breach of their obligation to conclude a sales contract, the aggrieved party may wish to claim damages arising from the (subsequent) non-performance of the final sales contract.[497] The aggrieved party should be entitled to claim damages for this type of loss, provided that the additional requirements of Art. 74 CISG are met, in particular the foreseeability rule.[498] Thus, the CISG's provisions on damages are appropriate and sufficiently flexible to deal with a claim for damages in the cases discussed here.[499]

The same can also be said of most of the other provisions of the CISG; the Convention is generally well suited to govern preliminary agreements. Its provisions on contract formation and most of its remedies are sufficiently flexible to be applied to any CISG contract and its breach. It should be noted that disputes arising out of international preliminary agreements appear to be relatively rare, as evidenced by the lack of CISG-related case law.

3. Conclusion

It follows that the CISG does not only apply to contracts containing sales obligations in the narrower sense. Art. 29 CISG explicitly mentions contracts to modify, amend or

494. Cf. only Schlechtriem/Schwenzer/Schroeter/*Schroeter*, 5th English ed., Art. 25 CISG, para. 28.
495. *Magnus*, Remedies, p. 260.
496. *See Magnus*, Remedies, p. 263; Schlechtriem/Schwenzer/Schroeter/*Schwenzer*, 5th English ed., Art. 74 CISG, para. 1; *Schroeter*, paras 814 et seq.
497. With regard to this issue under German domestic law: *Henrich*, pp. 214 et seq.
498. Similar under German domestic law: *Henrich*, pp. 214 et seq.; on the limitation of damages to foreseeable losses under Art. 74 CISG: *Magnus*, Remedies, p. 264; Schlechtriem/Schwenzer/Schroeter/*Schwenzer*, 5th English ed., Art. 74 CISG, paras 47 et seq.; *Schroeter*, paras 818 et seq.
499. Cf. *Bonell*, RIW 1990, p. 701.

terminate a CISG contract. These agreements may themselves not resemble a conventional sales contract but are nonetheless governed by the Convention. It is submitted that a general principle can be derived from this provision according to which the CISG covers closely related or linked contracts. This requires that these contracts either establish or directly affect the parties' rights and obligations under one or multiple CISG contracts.

On this basis, the CISG could also cover preliminary agreements. However, it is necessary to distinguish between different types of preliminary agreements on the basis of their content, as there is no international consensus on this term. Non-binding preliminary 'agreements' should not be covered by the Convention, since the CISG requires a contract for its applicability. Such agreements may still be relevant for the interpretation of the individual sales contract subsequently concluded (Art. 8(3) CISG). Likewise, the CISG should not be applied to preliminary agreements relating to the negotiations between the parties. Although such agreements may set out terms to be included in the final sales contract, they should not be regarded as directly affecting the parties' rights and obligations under a CISG contract, since an additional step is required (e.g., compared to agreements modifying a CISG contract). Moreover, they do not establish rights and obligations under a sales contract.

The situation is different in the case of preliminary agreements that oblige the parties to conclude a CISG contract. Indeed, such agreements do not correspond to the autonomous definition of sales contracts derived from Art. 1 in conjunction with Arts 30 and 53 CISG. However, in substance, they establish rights and obligations under a CISG contract. It is the main purpose of such contracts to establish rights and obligations under a sales contract by binding the parties to conclude a final sales contract in the future. They should hence be governed by the CISG as they trigger the general principle according to which the Convention applies to closely related or linked contracts. The CISG's applicability to such contracts is also supported by the prevailing view.

Of course, it would be unsound to apply the CISG to such agreements if its application did not lead to satisfactory results. However, most of the Convention's provisions, such as the provisions on contract formation and the remedies of specific performance, avoidance and damages, can be applied directly to this type of preliminary agreement because they are drafted in a sufficiently flexible manner. Accordingly, the majority of the CISG's provisions are suitable for dealing with this type of agreement.

III. FRAMEWORK AGREEMENTS UNDER THE CONVENTION

The next part will analyse whether framework agreements fall within the CISG's sphere of application which has been outlined above. It is important to note that framework agreements are rather heterogeneous and vary in content.[500] Consequently, it is not

500. Cf. BGH, 5 November 1986, NJW-RR 1987, p. 306 (regarding a framework leasing agreement); *Perales Viscasillas*, Extending the Scope, p. 125; *Perales Viscasillas*, Int'l Distribution Contracts

possible to provide a general answer to the question of whether the CISG covers framework agreements.[501]

This study will distinguish between two groups of framework agreements in order to analyse the CISG's applicability. The first group will be referred to as framework agreements that are binding with regard to individual transactions. The second group will be referred to as framework agreements that are not binding with regard to individual transactions.

1. Framework Agreements That Are Binding with Regard to Individual Transactions

Framework agreements permit commercial parties to merge their interest in reliable planning with their interest in remaining flexible.[502] On the one hand, the parties to a framework agreement intend to remain relatively flexible in light of changing economic markets.[503] On the other hand, the parties to a framework agreement may wish to have planning reliability by concluding a binding long-term contract.[504] These two objectives may occasionally conflict with each other.[505] While both parties generally assume that they will always be interested in carrying out the transactions, this may not be the case under certain circumstances.[506] To illustrate, in the event of a substantial decline in the overall market demand for the goods in question, a buyer may no longer be interested in purchasing goods from a seller, given the possibility of being unable to resell the goods.[507] This may give rise to a dispute with the seller who may have assumed that the parties would proceed with the transaction regardless of the surrounding circumstances.

In order to preclude the possibility of such disputes, the parties may include provisions in their framework agreement which regulate the question of whether they are bound to conduct the individual transactions.[508] In case the parties have a particular interest in planning reliability, they should agree to (contractually) bind themselves to carry out transactions in the future, at least to some extent.[509] By doing

and CISG, p. 51; Schlechtriem/Schwenzer/Schroeter/*Fountoulakis*, 5th English ed., Art. 73 CISG, para. 8: 'Types and categories [of framework agreements] vary considerably, depending, among other things, on the trade branch concerned (cars, electronics, commodities, pharmaceuticals, clothes, etc)'; *Weber*, ZSR 1987, pp. 410, 415; *Wellenhofer-Klein*, pp. 102–105; *C. Witz*, para. 112.61.

501. Huber/Mulis/*Huber*, p. 48: 'Distribution contracts need to be analysed on a case-by-case basis [...]'; *Perales Viscasillas*, Extending the Scope, p. 120; *Perović*, (2011) 59 Belgrade L. Rev., p. 190: 'problems of applicability of the CISG to the international distribution contract are to be solved on the basis of the facts of each particular transaction [...]'; *C. Witz*, para. 112.61.
502. *Gatsi*, p. 3; *Hoffbauer*, pp. 2, 94; Sayag/*Pollaud-Dulian*, para. 20; *Weber*, ZSR 1986, p. 433; *see* Ch. 2 I. 2. above.
503. *Hoffbauer*, p. 94; *Weber*, ZSR 1987, p. 405.
504. *Hoffbauer*, p. 94; *Weber*, ZSR 1987, p. 405.
505. *Weber*, ZSR 1987, p. 405.
506. *Budde/Geks*, ZVertriebsR 2012, p. 38.
507. *Budde/Geks*, ZVertriebsR 2012, p. 38.
508. *Budde/Geks*, ZVertriebsR 2012, p. 38.
509. Cf. *Hoffbauer*, pp. 94, 95.

so, they agree about the 'if' of their future transactions. Conversely, the parties, at least partially, relinquish their freedom to decide whether they will carry out individual transactions at a later point in time.

This will be considered to be the decisive feature of the first group of framework agreements discussed here: the parties bind themselves in their framework agreement to carry out future transactions, at least to some extent. In addition, these framework agreements share the general characteristics of any framework agreement. They are long-term contracts which aim to provide a regulatory framework for an ongoing supply relationship between the parties. The parties intend to have recurring sales transactions under largely the same conditions.[510] The framework agreements often contain clauses pertaining to the future sale of goods as well as clauses pertaining to the overall cooperation and relationship between the parties.[511]

a. *Two Typical Structures*

i. *Characteristics*

There are primarily two 'structures' for framework agreements that are binding with regard to the individual transactions:[512] first, the parties may include an obligation to conclude separate individual sales contracts in their framework agreement.[513] Second, the parties may incorporate immediate delivery and payment obligations into the framework agreement itself.[514] In both cases, the parties bind themselves to execute individual transactions, frequently with a quantifiable volume and purchase price.

Under the first structure, the framework agreement includes an obligation to conclude individual sales contracts. It is thus evident that there is a distinction between the framework agreement and the individual sales contracts. Only the latter contain delivery and payment obligations, i.e., sales obligations.[515] In such cases, the contract follows a so-called two-tier structure. This entails the superordinate framework

510. OLG München, 18 June 2018, CISG-online 3080.
511. *See* Ch. 2 III 2. above.
512. These two structures are also distinguished with regard to long-term supply agreements ('*Zulieferverträge*') under German law: *Bremenkamp*, p. 46; *Hoffbauer*, p. 42 (distinguishing long-term supply agreements from framework agreements); Hopt/*Leyens*, Einl. vor § 373 HGB, para. 30; *Lange*, NJOZ 2013, pp. 578 et seq.; Staudinger/*Beckmann*, vor § 433 BGB, para. 215e.
513. OLG München, 18 June 2018, CISG-online 3080; BK OR/*Kramer*, Art. 22 CO, para. 76; *Bucher*, p. 109; *Budde/Geks*, ZVertriebsR 2012, p. 37; *Hoffbauer*, p. 94; *Gatsi*, paras 14 et seq.; *Malaurie/Aynès/Stoffel-Munck*, p. 244; Martinek/Semler/Flohr/*Budde/Eckhoff*, § 40, para. 9; *Mousseron/Seube*, D. 1973, p. 198; *Muhl/Lüthge*, GWR 2016, p. 26; *von der Crone*, p. 249; *Wellenhofer-Klein*, pp. 104, 105.
514. Cf. BGH, 25 April 1960, BB 1960, p. 574; MüKoHGB/*Sommerfeld*, Art. 73 CISG, para. 4, referring to 'qualified' framework contracts; Schlechtriem/Schwenzer/Schroeter/*Fountoulakis*, 5th English ed., Art. 73 CISG, para. 8; *Ulmer*, p. 243; employing a more narrow terminology: *Hoffbauer*, pp. 84 et seq.
515. *Budde/Geks*, ZVertriebsR 2012, p. 37; *Hoffbauer*, p. 5; Martinek/Semler/Flohr/*Budde/Eckhoff*, § 40, paras 8, 9; Staudinger/*Beckmann*, Vorbem. § 433 BGB, para. 215e; *von Scheven*, p. 19.

agreement being followed by individual sales contracts, which are concluded on the basis of the framework agreement.[516]

Under the second structure, the framework agreement already contains sales obligations in *sensu stricto*. If this is the case, it is not necessary to conclude separate individual sales contracts.[517] Instead, the individual deliveries are made on the basis of one uniform contract and do not constitute independent contracts.[518]

The parties are generally free to agree on either structure for their contract. The relevant question is whether they intend to include actual sales obligations in their agreement or to conclude separate sales contracts.[519] This is essentially a matter of contract interpretation[520] to be determined on a case-by-case basis.[521]

ii. Distinction

A number of factors may be relevant in distinguishing between the two structures. It is first necessary to consider the wording of the framework agreement.[522] However, it is common for this issue not to be explicitly regulated in the framework agreement. Furthermore, it should be noted that the label given to the contract by the parties is not by itself a decisive factor. Even if the parties refer to the individual transactions as separate contracts, there may still be one uniform contract.[523]

Another indication may be the definiteness of the framework agreement. In the event of uncertainty regarding essential terms of the delivery of the goods or the number of future transactions to be carried out, it may be preferable for the parties to opt for a two-tier structure.[524] Consequently, in case an agreement contains few details and is relatively indefinite with regard to the goods, their quantity and the purchase price, the parties may intend to discuss these open points once more and conclude a more detailed agreement at a later stage.[525] In contrast, there is more likely to be one single contract, which provides for sales obligations in the narrower sense, in instances

516. *See* Ch. 2 III. 1. above.
517. *Hoffbauer*, pp. 32, 33; MüKoHGB/*Sommerfeld*, Art. 73 CISG, para. 4.
518. Cf. *Hoffbauer*, pp. 32, 33; MüKoHGB/*B. Köhler*, Art. 1 CISG, para. 22.
519. Cf. BGH, 5 November 1986, NJW-RR 1987, p. 306.
520. BGH, 5 November 1986, NJW-RR 1987, p. 306; *Hoffbauer*, pp. 70 et seq.
521. Cf. *Wellenhofer-Klein*, pp. 105 et seq. (in a different context).
522. RB Zeeland-West-Brabant, 15 February 2023, CISG-online 6231, para. 49: in this case, the Court determined that the language of the 'Framework Supply Agreement' indicated that the parties intended to enter into separate purchase agreements based on the framework agreement; BGH, 5 November 1986, NJW-RR 1987, p. 306.
523. Cf. Arbitral Tribunal of the Exchange for Agricultural Products in Vienna, 10 December 1997, CISG-online 351; CC Zürich, 31 May 1996, CISG-online 1291.
524. *See Hoffbauer*, p. 84; *Grunewald*, p. 27; *Torsello*, p. 243; cf. also *Lange*, NJOZ 2013, p. 577; *Piltz*, Rahmen-Verkaufsvertrag, para. 1; *Piltz*, Rahmen-Einkaufsvertrag, para. 1.
525. *Fuchs-Wissemann*, pp. 66, 67; *Lange*, NJOZ 2013, pp. 578, 579; *Schumacher*, IHR 2005, p. 148; *Torsello*, p. 243; cf. further Kröll *et al.*/*Saidov*, Art. 73 CISG, para. 6; *von Scheven*, p. 21. *Weber*, ZSR 1987, p. 414; *Wellenhofer-Klein*, pp. 111.

where the agreement encompasses details regarding the goods, their quantity and the purchase price.[526]

Moreover, the parties may wish to postpone the conclusion of actual sales contracts for similar reasons to those motivating the conclusion of preliminary agreements that bind the parties to conclude a sales contract.[527] To illustrate, the parties may not be able to immediately conclude individual sales contracts, as they first need to obtain an administrative authorisation or because of a (temporary) conflict with other legal positions.[528] In order to find some security, the parties may still wish to bind each other to the bargain by agreeing on an obligation to conclude individual sales, rather than immediately agreeing on sales obligations.

Despite the differences between these two structures, it is not essential to distinguish between them in order to determine whether the CISG is applicable. Framework agreements that are binding with regard to the individual transactions should be treated equally with regard to the CISG's applicability, regardless of their structure.[529] However, it should be noted that the distinction between these two structures may nevertheless be relevant in certain respects, as will be demonstrated throughout the course of this study.

b. Applicability of the CISG

The CISG's applicability to framework agreements that are binding with regard to individual transactions will be examined hereinafter. In general, the aforementioned principles apply.[530] In a first step, it is necessary to ascertain whether such agreements contain delivery, transfer of property and payment obligations as set forth in Arts 30 and 53 CISG in order to determine if there is a sales contract within the meaning of Art. 1 CISG.[531]

526. OLG München, 18 June 2018, CISG-online 3080; Hopt/*Leyens*, Einl. vor § 373 HGB, para. 30; Kröll *et al./Saidov*, Art. 73 CISG, para. 6; Schlechtriem/Schwenzer/Schroeter/*Fountoulakis*, 5th English ed., Art. 73 CISG, para. 8; Staudinger/*Magnus*, Art. 73 CISG, para. 7; *Wellenhofer-Klein*, p. 111.
527. *See* Ch. 3 II. 2. c. above; cf. also *Grunewald*, p. 27.
528. Cf. *Grunewald*, p. 27; *J. Schmidt*, (1983–1984) 6 Houst. J. Int'l L., p. 61 (in the context of preliminary agreements).
529. *See* Ch. 3 III. 1. b. below.
530. *See* Ch. 3 I., II. above; cf. also Tribunale di Forli, 6 March 2012, CISG-online 2585, IHR 2013, p. 198; High Commercial Ct. Croatia, 19 December 2006, CISG-online 3284; KGer Schaffhausen, 25 February 2002, CISG-online 723.
531. Cf. only Gerechtshof Arnhem-Leeuwarden, 6 February 2024, CISG-online 6819, para. 9 (affirmed with regard to a 'framework consignment agreement'); RB Midden-Nederland, 25 March 2015, CISG-online 2591, para. 21; Dist. Ct. Szczecin, 13 February 2015, CISG-online 6807, para. 74 (negated with regard to a framework agreement); Tribunale di Forli, 6 March 2012, CISG-online 2585, IHR 2013, pp. 198, 199; High Commercial Ct. Croatia, 19 December 2006, CISG-online 3284; KGer Schaffhausen, 25 February 2002, CISG-online 723.

i. Framework Agreements Containing Sales Obligations

Framework agreements that are binding with regard to the individual transactions may contain immediate sales obligations.[532] In such cases, there is no need to subsequently conclude individual sales contracts.[533] Rather, the individual deliveries, which are sometimes referred to as 'orders' or 'call-offs',[534] are made on the basis of one single contract and do not constitute independent contracts.[535] They may be purely sales-related or contain further obligations and rights of the parties.[536] In practice, such a framework agreement is, e.g., referred to as 'Master Sales Agreement'.[537]

As such framework agreements contain obligations to deliver goods, transfer property and pay the purchase price, they should be characterised as sales contracts within the meaning of Art. 1 in conjunction with Arts 30 and 53 CISG.[538] Consequently, the Convention is applicable to such agreements, provided that all of the additional requirements for its applicability are met and the parties have not excluded its application.[539]

There are no provisions in Part I or elsewhere in the Convention that expressly exclude framework agreements from its sphere of application.[540] Furthermore, the characterisation of such agreements under domestic law is irrelevant; the CISG's concept of sales contracts must be found autonomously without having recourse to domestic law.[541] On that note, the prevailing view among legal scholars convincingly advocates that framework agreements may be governed by the CISG if they contain specific and immediate sales obligations.[542]

532. *See* Ch. 3 III. 1. a. above.
533. Cf. *Hoffbauer*, pp. 32, 33; MüKoHGB/*B. Köhler*, Art. 1 CISG, para. 22; MüKoHGB/*Sommerfeld*, Art. 73 CISG, para. 4; Soergel/*Kreße*, Art. 1 CISG, para. 22.
534. *See* Gerechtshof Arnhem-Leeuwarden, 6 February 2024, CISG-online 6819, para. 4; CA Toulouse, 22 November 2023, CISG-online 6647, para. 24; OLG Hamm, 25 March 2019, CISG-online 5215, para. 2.
535. Cf. *Hoffbauer*, pp. 32, 33; MüKoHGB/*B. Köhler*, Art. 1 CISG, para. 22; MüKoHGB/*Sommerfeld*, Art. 73 CISG, para. 4.
536. Cf. Ch. 2 III. 2. above; BeckOGK/*Buchwitz*, Art. 14 CISG, para. 19, who refers to purely sales-related framework agreements.
537. Supr. Ct. Poland, 27 January 2006, CISG-online 1399.
538. *Juhasz*, IHR 2025, p. 43.
539. *Juhasz*, IHR 2025, pp. 43, 44; Schlechtriem/Schwenzer/*Schlechtriem*, 2nd English ed., Intro Arts 14–24 CISG, para. 7; cf. also Gerechtshof Arnhem-Leeuwarden, 6 February 2024, CISG-online 6819, para. 14.
540. Cf. Supr. Ct. Poland, 27 January 2006, CISG-online 1399.
541. Gerechtshof Arnhem-Leeuwarden, 6 February 2024, CISG-online 6819, para. 9; Tribunale di Forli, 6 March 2012, CISG-online 2585, IHR 2013, p. 198; Tribunale di Padova, 11 January 2005, CISG-online 967; *Perales Viscasillas*, Extending the Scope, pp. 129, 130.
542. *Grunewald*, p. 57; *Höß*, p. 65; *Klima*, RIW 1996, p. 1036; *Magnus*, ZEuP 1997, pp. 829, 830, adding that Art. 3(2) CISG must be taken into consideration; similarly, MüKoBGB/*Huber*, Art. 1 CISG, para. 11; MüKoHGB/*B. Köhler*, Art. 1 CISG, paras 22, 23; *Newhouse/Tanaka*, R.L.R. 2012, p. 18; Ostendorf/*Ostendorf/Sauthoff*, § 18, para. 208; *Perales Viscasillas*, Extending the Scope, pp. 123, 124; *Piltz*, para. 2-30; *Piltz*, Int. Wirtschaftsrecht, § 18, para. 9; Reithmann/Martiny/*Fabig*, para. 37.67; *Schlechtriem/Butler*, para. 24a; *Schroeter*, para. 92; Schlechtriem/Schwenzer/Schroeter/*Schroeter*, 5th English ed., Intro Arts 14–24 CISG, para. 24; Schlechtriem/Schwenzer/Schroeter/*Schroeter*, 8th German ed., Vorbem. Arts 14–24 CISG, para. 20; *Schwenzer*, Challenges of the 2020s, p. 44; *Schwenzer/Fountoulakis/Dimsey*, p. 702;

The prevailing view in literature has also been shared by a considerable number of courts in cases where the CISG's applicability to framework agreements was in question.[543] For instance, in a case before a Swiss Court of Appeal, the CISG was, *inter alia*, applied because the framework agreement contained an obligation to deliver a specific product in exchange for payment of a purchase price.[544] Similarly, an Italian District Court applied the CISG to a distribution contract, given that one of the parties undertook the obligation to supply the goods and the other party undertook the obligations to buy and resell the goods.[545] The Court further held that the CISG may not be applied to distribution contracts in their conventional scheme, but did find that it could be applied to the particular distribution contract under consideration, as it took the form of a supply agreement.[546] This decision highlights that the CISG's applicability to framework agreements must be determined on a case-by-case basis.[547]

In contrast, the position taken by some courts and scholars appears to be overly broad, as they have simply held that distribution contracts, a subtype of framework agreements, are outside the CISG's sphere of application.[548] Rather, it is necessary to

---

Schwenzer/Mohs, IHR 2006, p. 240; Soergel/*Lutzi*, Art. 73 CISG, para. 2; Staudinger/*Magnus*, Art. 1 CISG, para. 37; *Thiele*, IHR 2002, p. 11; *UNCITRAL et al.*, Legal Guide, p. 96, para. 435, noting that 'this interpretation is not settled'; *Vischer/Huber/Oser*, para. 669; *C. Witz*, para. 112.61.

543. RB Den Haag, 20 August 2025, CISG-online 7590, paras 24 et seq.; Gerechtshof Arnhem-Leeuwarden, 6 February 2024, CISG-online 6819, paras 7 et seq. (the Court characterised the framework agreement in question as a purchase agreement); OLG Hamm, 25 March 2019, CISG-online 5215, para. 38 (the Court characterised the framework contracts in dispute as '*Bezugsverträge*', i.e., requirement contracts); ICC, 1 November 2016, CISG-online 5988 (regarding a distribution agreement that contained a 'supply obligation'); ICC, 18203/2013, CISG-online 2973, para. 31 ('Distribution Agreement' was characterised as international sale of goods); CA Reims, 4 September 2012, CISG-online 3141; Tribunale di Forli, 6 March 2012, CISG-online 2585, IHR 2013, pp. 198, 199; OLG Frankfurt, 20 November 2012, CISG-online 2481 (the Court ruled that the parties had agreed upon a framework sales agreement ('*Kauf-Rahmenvertrag*'), which is governed by the CISG); CA Geneva, 20 May 2011, CISG-online 2429, note. 4; Supr. Ct. Poland, 27 January 2006, CISG-online 1399; Cour de Cassation, 30 June 2004, CISG-online 870; Supr. Ct. Italy, 14 December 1999, CISG-online 1314 (the specifics of the framework agreement in question remain unclear from the decision); ICC, 9448/1999, CISG-online 707; LG München I, 9 December 1996, CISG-online 405, paras 14, 15 (regarding a dealer agreement that contained delivery obligations); applying the CISG without further reasoning: *Medical Marketing Int'l, Inc. v. Internazionale Medico Scientifica, S.r.l.*, US Dist. Ct. ED Louisiana, 17 May 1999, CISG-online 387 ('Business License Agreement') and Metropolitan Ct. Budapest, 17 June 1997, CISG-online 288 ('distribution contract'), both criticised by Schlechtriem/Schwenzer/*Schlechtriem*, 2nd English ed., Intro Arts 14–24 CISG, para. 7 in footnote 38; cf. also BGer, 18 April 2024, CISG-online 6978 (the applicability of the CISG was left open due to the fact that both parties and the lower court assumed the applicability of the Swiss Code of Obligations, *see* para. 14); OLG Jena, 8 December 2015, CISG-online 2663 (structure of long-term contract not entirely clear); *Fryer Holdings Pty Ltd. v. Liaoing MEC Group Co Ltd. et al.*, Supr. Ct. New South Wales, 30 January 2012, CISG-online 2325 (unclear whether the transactions in question were individual sales contracts or orders); Ct. of Arbitration of the Hamburg CC, 21 March 1996, CISG-online 187, paras 38 et seq.
544. CA Geneva, 20 May 2011, CISG-online 2429, note 4.
545. Tribunale di Forli, 6 March 2012, CISG-online 2585, IHR 2013, p. 199.
546. Tribunale di Forli, 6 March 2012, CISG-online 2585, IHR 2013, p. 199.
547. *Juhasz*, IHR 2025, p. 44; cf. also Huber/Mulis/*Huber*, p. 48; *Perović*, (2011) 59 Belgrade L. Rev., p. 190.
548. *See* KCAB, 2017, CISG-online 5463; High Ct. Singapore, 16 September 2015, CISG-online 2939; CA Warsaw, 15 May 2015, CISG-online 2783; High Commercial Ct. Serbia, 22 April 2008,

consider the content of framework agreements, including distribution contracts, in a given case in order to determine whether the CISG may be applied. However, with regard to distribution contracts, Art. 3(2) CISG must typically be taken into consideration.[549]

In certain cases, it may not be apparent whether a framework agreement includes sales obligations. This must be determined through contract interpretation, which will again depend on the specific circumstances of each case.[550] If the CISG's applicability is in question, the relevant standard for this interpretation should be found within the Convention itself, in particular Art. 8 CISG.[551]

ii. *Framework Agreements Containing an Obligation to Conclude Individual Sales Contracts*

The parties may also bind themselves to execute individual transactions by including an obligation to conclude individual sales contracts.[552] In such instances, it is necessary to distinguish between the framework agreement and the individual sales contracts subsequently concluded.[553] These contracts are considered to be separate and legally independent from each other.[554] Only the individual sales contracts contain delivery,

CISG-online 1990; Metropolitan Ct. Budapest, 19 May 1996, CISG-online 289; *Achilles*, Art. 1 CISG, para. 3; Ferrari, EuLF 2002, p. 9; *Gabriel*, para. 2.8; *Lookofsky*, para. 58; Witz/Salger/Lorenz/*Lorenz*, Art. 1 CISG, para. 7.

549. *See* Ch. 4 below.
550. *See* Gerechtshof Arnhem-Leeuwarden, 6 February 2024, CISG-online 6819, paras 7 et seq., where the Court determined the parties' rights and obligations under a framework agreement by relying on Art. 8 CISG.
551. Gerechtshof Arnhem-Leeuwarden, 6 February 2024, CISG-online 6819, para. 9; cf. also Cour de Cassation, 30 June 2004, CISG-online 870; *Perales Viscasillas*, Extending the Scope, p. 132.
552. *See* OLG München, 18 June 2018, CISG-online 3080; OLG Graz, 28 September 2000, CISG-online 798, para. 38; BK OR/*Kramer*, Art. 22 CO, para. 76; *Bucher*, p. 109; *Budde/Geks*, ZVertriebsR 2012, p. 37; *Hoffbauer*, p. 94; *Gatsi*, paras 14 et seq.; *Klima*, RIW 1996, p. 1036; *Malaurie/Aynès/Stoffel-Munck*, p. 244; Martinek/Semler/Flohr/*Budde/Eckhoff*, § 40, para. 9; *Mousseron/Seube*, D. 1973, p. 198; *Muhl/Lüthge*, GWR 2016, p. 26; *von der Crone*, p. 249; *Wellenhofer-Klein*, pp. 104, 105.
553. Cf. on this two-tier structure: Art. 1111 French Cc; OLG München, 18 June 2018, CISG-online 3080; Supr. Ct. Italy, 20 September 2004, CISG-online 1015; OLG Düsseldorf, 11 July 1996, CISG-online 201; BeckOGK/*Möslein*, § 145, para. 79; BK OR/*Kramer*, Art. 22 CO, para. 76; BSK OR-I/*Zellweger-Gutknecht*, Vor Art. 1-40f CO, para. 40; BSK OR-I/*Zellweger-Gutknecht*, Art. 22 CO, para. 29; *Bucher*, p. 109; *Budde/Geks*, ZVertriebsR 2012, p. 37; *Furrer/Lohri*, pp. 23, 24; *Gass/Lange*, pp. 14, 15; *Henrich*, p. 117; *Hoffbauer*, p. 6; Jauernig/*Stadler*, § 311 BGB, para. 22; KuKo OR/*Herzog*, Art. 22 CO, para. 7; Martinek/Semler/Flohr/*Budde/Eckhoff*, § 40, para. 9; *Muhl/Lüthge*, GWR 2016, p. 26; *Schlechtriem/Butler*, para. 24a; *Ulmer*, p. 300; *von der Crone*, pp. 245, 246; *Weber*, ZSR 1987, p. 410; ZK OR/*Schönle*, Art. 184 CO, para. 104; ZK OR/*Schönle*, Vorbem. Arts 184–551 CO, para. 32.
554. Cf. *Fuchs-Wissemann*, p. 99; *Gass/Lange*, p. 14; Martinek/Semler/Flohr/*Budde/Eckhoff*, § 40, para. 10; *Rother*, FS Larenz, pp. 438, 439; Sayag/*Pollaud-Dulian*, para. 100; *Ulmer*, pp. 300, 301.

transfer of property and payment obligations.[555] The framework agreement, in comparison, may contain an obligation for one or both parties to conclude such individual sales contracts.

1) Non-applicability of the CISG?

The CISG's applicability to framework agreements containing an obligation to conclude individual sales contracts appears to be uncertain when the 'general test' under Art. 1 in conjunction with Arts 30 and 53 CISG is applied: they do not include obligations to deliver the goods, transfer property in them and pay the purchase price as per Arts 30 and 53 CISG.[556] These obligations will only be established through the conclusion of the individual sales contracts.[557] In fact, the obligations assumed by the parties in such a framework agreement diverge from those typically found in a conventional sales contract.[558] One such obligation is that the parties frequently agree to conclude multiple sales contracts in the future.[559] Additionally, the parties often agree on non-sales obligations that relate to their overall cooperation (relational clauses).[560]

a) Scholarly Writings

Some scholars have reached the conclusion that the CISG is not applicable to such framework agreements based on their structure.[561] *Saenger*, for example, maintains that the Convention is not applicable to distribution contracts, a subtype of framework agreements, on the grounds that they do not include any (specific) delivery obligations.[562] In addition, *Ferrari, inter alia,* holds that distribution contracts are not performed by delivering goods and transferring property in them.[563] Instead, these

555. Cf. *Budde/Geks*, ZVertriebsR 2012, p. 37; *Hoffbauer*, p. 5; *Klima*, RIW 1996, p. 1036; *Magnus*, FS Bonell, p. 1779; Martinek/Semler/Flohr/*Budde/Eckhoff*, § 40, para. 8; MüKoHGB/*Sommerfeld*, Art. 73 CISG, para. 4; *von Scheven*, p. 19; cf. also *Gass/Lange*, pp. 14, 15; *Torsello*, p. 192.
556. Cf. BeckOK/*Saenger*, Art. 1 CISG, para. 6; *Ferrari*, EuLF 2000/01, p. 9; *Grieser*, pp. 124, 125, 134; *Magnus*, FS Bonell, p. 1779; Mankowski/*Dornis*, Art. 73 CISG, para. 3; MüKoBGB/*Huber*, Art. 1 CISG, para. 11; *Piltz*, Int. Wirtschaftsrecht, § 18, para. 7; Reithmann/Martiny/*Fabig*, § 37, para. 37.65; *Torsello*, p. 233 (on preliminary agreements); but *see Bridge*, Int'l Sale of Goods, para. 10.22 *in fine*.
557. Cf. *Budde/Geks*, ZVertriebsR 2012, p. 37; *Hoffbauer*, p. 5; *Grieser*, p. 134; *Klima*, RIW 1996, p. 1036; *Magnus*, FS Bonell, p. 1779; Martinek/Semler/Flohr/*Budde/Eckhoff*, § 40, paras 8; MüKoHGB/*Sommerfeld*, Art. 73 CISG, para. 4; *von Scheven*, p. 19.
558. But *see Thieffry*, Dr. prat. com. int. 1993, pp. 64, 65, who posits that the standard clauses typically included in distribution contracts are essentially comparable to the provisions set forth in the CISG. Consequently, he concludes that the Convention includes provisions that are directly applicable to distribution contracts.
559. *Ferrari*, EuLF 2000/01, p. 9: a distribution contract is performed through the conclusion of individual contracts; MüKoHGB/*Sommerfeld*, Art. 73 CISG, para. 4; *Piltz*, Int. Wirtschaftsrecht, § 18, para. 7; *Piltz*, NJW 2019, p. 2517; cf. also *Torsello*, p. 233.
560. *See* Ch. 2 III. 2. above.
561. *Newhouse/Tanaka*, R.L.R. 2012, p. 18 (distribution agreements as preliminary agreements that fall outside the CISG's sphere of applicability); but *see Torsello*, pp. 243, 244.
562. BeckOK/*Saenger*, Art. 1 CISG, para. 6.
563. *Ferrari*, EuLF 2000/01, p. 9.

agreements are performed by concluding individual sales contracts.[564] Consequently, he posits that they should not fall within the CISG's sphere of application.[565] Similarly, *Magnus* asserts that framework contracts 'do not establish immediately binding sales obligations'.[566] He maintains that this precludes the Convention's applicability to the framework agreement, whereas the individual sales contracts may still be covered by the CISG.[567] *Klima* further asserts that framework agreements fall outside the Convention's sphere of application pursuant to Art. 1 CISG, since they may contain an obligation to conclude individual sales contracts, but not actual sales obligations.[568] *Huber* argues that the CISG is generally not applicable to the framework agreement in instances where the framework and the individual sales are regarded as separate contracts; he suggests that the CISG should be applied solely to the individual sales contracts, rather than the underlying framework agreement.[569] Along those lines, it could be argued that the Convention is not applicable to a contract if an additional consensus of the parties is required for there to be sales obligations in *sensu stricto*.[570]

b) Case Law

A comparable view can also be found in case law: for instance, the District Court of The Hague reached the conclusion that the CISG was not applicable to a distribution contract.[571] It held that the most important elements of a sale were only laid down in a sales contract that was subsequently concluded on the basis of the framework agreement.[572] Consequently, the Court reasoned that the framework agreement itself could not be characterised as a sales contract.[573] A similar conclusion was reached by the Swedish Supreme Court. In its decision, the Court held that the CISG requires a contract for the transfer of movable property against payment for it to be applicable.[574] The contract in dispute, which was labelled as a 'Purchase Agreement' by the parties, was characterised as a framework agreement that did not oblige the supplier to sell a certain quantity of goods and also did not oblige the other party to purchase these

564. *Ferrari*, EuLF 2000/01, p. 9.
565. *Ferrari*, EuLF 2000/01, p. 9; accord *Honnold/Flechtner*, Art. 2 CISG, para. 71 (if framework agreements do not involve the delivery of goods, they are not governed by the CISG); Reithmann/Martiny/*Fabig*, para. 37.65.
566. *Magnus*, FS Bonell, p. 1779.
567. *Magnus*, FS Bonell, p. 1799; cf. also Reithmann/Martiny/*Fabig*, paras 37.65, 37.66.
568. *Klima*, RIW 1996, p. 1036, while stating that the CISG should be applicable to a framework agreement if it (exceptionally) falls under the conventional definition of a sales contract under the CISG, i.e., if the agreement contains sales obligations in *sensu stricto*; similarly, Honsell/*Siehr*, Art. 2 CISG, para. 8 (CISG is not suitable to govern framework agreements that merely contain an obligation to conclude individual sales contracts); Mankowski/*Dornis*, Art. 73 CISG, para. 3.
569. MüKoBGB/*Huber*, Art. 1 CISG, para. 11.
570. Cf. *Schumacher*, IHR 2005, p. 149.
571. RB Gravenhage, 2 July 1997, CISG-online 1331.
572. RB Gravenhage, 2 July 1997, CISG-online 1331.
573. RB Gravenhage, 2 July 1997, CISG-online 1331; left open in: RB Rotterdam, 17 October 2018, CISG-online 2018.
574. Supr. Ct. Sweden, 29 May 2020, CISG-online 5500, Comment 3 by Justice Councillor Johny Herre.

goods, according to the Court.[575] In other words, the Court determined that the contract in dispute did not contain sales obligations within the meaning of Art. 1 in conjunction with Arts 30 and 53 CISG. The Supreme Court thus concluded that the framework agreement was not a sales contract within the meaning of Art. 1 CISG, which resulted in the Convention's non-applicability.[576]

Without providing a detailed rationale, a part of case law simply followed the formula that the CISG does not apply to the framework agreement itself, but it does apply to the individual sales contracts concluded under the umbrella of this framework agreement.[577]

2) Preferable View: The CISG Is Applicable

There are admittedly certain merits to the argument that such framework agreements do not resemble a contract of sale of goods within the meaning of Art. 1 in conjunction with Arts 30 and 53 CISG, based on their rights and obligations. They are rather preparing and obliging the parties to conclude such sales contracts. Nevertheless, there are compelling reasons in favour of applying the CISG to this type of framework agreements.[578] In addition, the assertion found in case law that the Convention is applicable to the individual sales contracts but not to the framework agreement itself is too general and oversimplified.

a) Separation Between Framework Agreement and Individual Sales Contracts Does Not Hinder the CISG's Applicability

The argument that the CISG should be applied solely to the individual sales contracts whenever the framework and the individual sales are considered to be separate contracts is not, in itself, a compelling one.[579] To put it another way, the fact that there is a distinction between the framework agreement and the individual sales contracts does not, in and of itself, preclude the CISG from applying to the framework agreement.[580] In comparison, preliminary agreements follow a similar structure, which does not prevent the Convention from being applicable to them.[581] Instead, it must be assessed whether the CISG covers such framework agreements *ratione materiae*.

575. Supr. Ct. Sweden, 29 May 2020, CISG-online 5500, Comment 3 by Justice Councillor Johny Herre.
576. Supr. Ct. Sweden, 29 May 2020, CISG-online 5500, Comment 3 by Justice Councillor Johny Herre (the CISG was, however, applied to the individual sales contracts).
577. Dist. Ct. Szczecin, 13 February 2015, CISG-online 6807, paras 73, 74; Dist. Ct. Rzeszów, 28 February 2014, CISG-online 6752, para. 95; Foreign Trade Ct. of Arbitration of the CC and Industry of Serbia, 28 January 2009, CISG-online 1856; CA Versailles, 19 February 2004, CISG-online 3345; HGer Zürich, 8 April 1999, CISG-online 489; KGer Schaffhausen, 23 April 2002, CISG-online 731.
578. *Juhasz*, IHR 2025, pp. 45, 46.
579. Probably *contra* MüKoBGB/*Huber*, Art. 1 CISG, para. 11.
580. *Torsello*, pp. 233, 234 (in the context of preliminary agreements); cf. also RB Zeeland-West-Brabant, 23 February 2023, CISG-online 6231; OLG Graz, 28 September 2000, CISG-online 798, para. 40 (CISG applied to framework agreement and the individual sales contracts).
581. *See* Ch. 3 II. 2. c. ii. above.

b) Comparison with Preliminary Agreements

Although the framework agreements discussed here do not contain actual sales obligations, the CISG may still be applicable. This study proposes a general principle according to which the CISG may be applied to related or closely linked contracts, provided that they establish or directly affect the parties' rights and obligations under a CISG contract.[582] Examples of such contracts include agreements to modify, amend or terminate a sales contract and preliminary agreements that oblige the parties to conclude a CISG contract.[583] Framework agreements that contain an obligation to conclude individual sales contracts are, in essence, very similar to preliminary agreements that bind the parties to conclude a sales contract.[584]

In light of this, the CISG should also be applied to this type of framework agreements, in accordance with a similar rationale that supports the Convention's applicability to preliminary agreements that oblige the parties to conclude a sales contract.[585] By including an obligation to conclude international sales contracts, the framework agreements under discussion, in substance, establish rights and obligations under multiple CISG contracts.[586] While these contracts technically only create the obligation to conclude individual sales contracts and not sales obligations in *sensu stricto*, they manifest the parties' intentions to establish sales obligations under a number of sales contracts.[587] It is, in fact, one of the main purposes of these contracts to create sales obligations under a variety of individual transactions.

In addition, the indirect or economic object of these framework agreements is the actual sale of goods, i.e., exchange of goods against money on multiple occasions.[588] In

582. *Juhasz*, IHR 2025, p. 45.
583. *See* Ch. 3 II. 1., 2. c. above.
584. Cf. Dist. Ct. Rzeszów, 28 February 2014, CISG-online 6752, paras 97, 98; *Canaris*, § 17, para. 11; *Fuchs-Wissemann*, p. 96; *Grunewald*, pp. 38, 57; *Newhouse/Tanaka*, R.L.R. 2012, p. 18; *Schluep*, p. 26; *Torsello*, p. 242; *C. Witz*, para. 112.71; *Zubović/Filipović*, p. 162; the differences between framework agreements and preliminary agreements are irrelevant in this context (framework agreements are established for the conclusion of a relatively large number of future sales contracts over an extended period of time, whereas preliminary agreements usually end once the final contract has been concluded; *see* for further details on these differences: *Budde/Geks*, ZVertriebsR 2012, p. 38; *Henrich*, pp. 213, 214; *Hoffbauer*, p. 22; *Weber*, ZSR 1987, p. 414).
585. *Juhasz*, IHR 2025, pp. 45, 46; similarly, *Grunewald*, p. 57; sceptical with regard to distribution contracts: *Canaris*, § 17, para. 11; *contra Newhouse/Tanaka*, R.L.R. 2012, p. 18: as distribution agreements 'are normally looked upon as preliminary agreement to the sales of goods transactions', they fall outside the CISG's scope of application.
586. Cf. *Canaris*, § 17, paras 10 et seq., referring to a sales element ('*kaufrechtliche Komponente*'); *Grunewald*, pp. 38, 57, holding that framework agreements are precontracts and precontracts essentially already contain sales obligations ('*im Kern bereits die Verpflichtung zur Lieferung und Zahlung enthält*'); jurisPK-BGB/*Hlawon*, Art. 14 CISG, para. 8; *see also* Ch. 3 II. 2. c. ii. 3) above.
587. *See Bridge*, Int'l Sale of Goods, para. 10.22 ('It seems pedantic to effect a sharp separation between individual sales and the framework contract, the former being "contracts of sale of goods" and the latter contracts *for* the sale of goods'); but *see Newhouse/Tanaka*, R.L.R. 2012, p. 18.
588. Cf. RB Zeeland-West-Brabant, 15 February 2023, CISG-online 6231; Supr. Ct. Italy, 14 December 1999, CISG-online 1314, note 2; *Canaris*, § 17, para. 10; *Perales Viscasillas*, Extending the Scope, p. 126; *Perales Viscasillas*, Int'l Distribution Contracts and CISG, p. 52; cf. also *Thieffry*, Dr. prat. com. int. 1993, p. 68.

general, there exists a close link between such framework agreements and the subsequent sales contracts.[589] It is therefore proposed here that framework agreements which oblige the parties to conclude future sales contracts should be governed by the CISG.

c) Commentators and Case Law

A number of commentators share the view that the CISG is applicable to framework agreements containing an obligation to conclude individual sales contracts.[590] Furthermore, in a case before the Court of Appeal Graz, the parties had agreed on a framework distribution contract that, *inter alia*, contained a minimum purchase requirement for three years.[591] Consequently, the framework agreement arguably included an obligation to conclude individual sales contracts to that extent.[592] In its decision, the Court of Appeal simply held that the CISG is applicable to framework agreements regulating the sale of goods according to 'doctrine and case law'.[593]

The Court of Appeal Munich reached a comparable conclusion: it was disputed between the parties whether the German seller was obliged to supply the goods to the buyer under a framework distribution agreement in a case before the Court.[594] The Court held that such a 'supply obligation' is a fundamental prerequisite for the conclusion of individual sales contracts. It further stated that the question of whether the seller is obliged to deliver the goods on the basis of the framework agreement is closely linked to the individual sales contracts.[595] Consequently, it concluded that the CISG should be applied to the framework distribution agreement in question.[596]

This decision was criticised in a note by *Klima*: he put forth that the 'abstract' delivery and acceptance obligations that arise from a framework agreement, which are

589. *See* RB Zeeland-West-Brabant, 15 February 2023, CISG-online 6231; OLG München, 22 September 1995, CISG-online 208.
590. Brunner/Gottlieb/*Brunner/Pfisterer/Köster*, Intro Arts 14–24 CISG, para. 19; *Grunewald*, p. 57; *Hoffbauer*, p. 48; Kröll *et al./Mistelis*, Art. 1 CISG, para. 28; MüKoBGB/*Gruber*, Vor Art. 14, para. 5; Ostendorf//*Ostendorf/Sauthoff*, § 18, para. 208; *Schlechtriem*, 4th ed., para. 24b; *Schlechtriem/Butler*, para. 24b; *Schumacher*, IHR 2005, p. 149; *C. Witz*, para. 112.71; Witz/Salger/Lorenz/*W. Witz*, Vor Arts 14–24, para. 9; *Zubović/Filipović*, p. 162; without explicitly mentioning the obligation to conclude individual sales contracts: *Bridge*, Int'l Sale of Goods, para. 10.22 ('contracts *for* the sale of goods'); *Thiele*, IHR 2002, p. 11; Ferrari *et al.*/Mankowski, Vorbem. Arts 14–24 CISG, paras 18, 19; Schlechtriem/Schwenzer/Schroeter/*Schroeter*, 5th English ed., Intro Arts 14–24 CISG, para. 24; *Schroeter*, para. 92.
591. OLG Graz, 28 September 2000, CISG-online 798, para. 2; cf. also Court of Appeal Krakow, 22 June 2015, CISG-online 5471, where the parties had agreed on an annual minimum purchase requirement, stipulating that the value of orders for rain gutters must be at least EUR 2.5 million per annum.
592. *See* Ch. 3 VI. 2. below.
593. OLG Graz, 28 September 2000, CISG-online 798, para. 38, referencing OGH, 15 December 1998, CISG-online 1535 – the Austrian Supreme Court held in para. 15 that requirement contracts, framework agreements and option contracts fall within the CISG's sphere of application; similarly, CA Krakow, 22 June 2015, CISG-online 5471, where the Court upheld the previous instance's decision to base its ruling on the CISG.
594. OLG München, 22 September 1995, CISG-online 208.
595. OLG München, 22 September 1995, CISG-online 208.
596. OLG München, 22 September 1995, CISG-online 208.

performed by concluding individual sales contracts, are not governed by the CISG.[597] Only the 'concrete' obligations that follow from the individual sales contracts fall within the CISG's sphere of application.[598] However, the preferable view is that framework agreements, which include an obligation to conclude individual sales contracts (i.e., 'abstract' sales obligations), should fall within the CISG's sphere of application. This is based on a general principle according to which closely linked or related contracts are covered by the Convention. The reasoning and result of the Court of Appeal Munich is therefore more convincing.[599] The criticism of this decision fails to acknowledge that the Convention goes beyond conventional sales contracts and also covers closely linked or related contracts if they establish or directly affect the parties' rights and obligations under a CISG contract. This is the case when it comes to framework agreements that oblige the parties to conclude individual sales contracts.

The District Court Zeeland-West-Brabant rendered a similar decision to the ones mentioned above. In this case, the parties, *inter alia*, entered into a 'Framework Supply Agreement' (FSA), which obliged them to conclude individual sales contracts.[600] At the outset, the District Court held that the CISG was applicable to the individual contracts because they were contracts for the sale of movable goods concluded between two parties from Contracting States in accordance with Art. 1(1)(a) CISG.[601] The Court also ruled that the framework agreement itself should be governed by the CISG, as the provisions of the FSA were closely related to the obligations arising out of the individual sales contracts.[602] This decision is in line with the view taken by this study: the Court not only applied the CISG to a framework agreement containing an obligation to conclude individual sales contracts, but also acknowledged the close link between the framework agreement and the individual sales contracts.

d) Equal Treatment of Comparable Situations

Beyond the arguments mentioned above, it is submitted that framework agreements obliging the parties to conclude individual sales contracts and framework agreements that contain actual sales obligations should be treated equally when it comes to the CISG's applicability. Despite the differences in the structure of these contracts, they both bind the parties to conduct individual transactions. The practical differences between these two types of contracts, e.g., in terms of legal proceedings, are relatively minor,[603] although this may vary from one jurisdiction to another. These factually comparable situations should thus be treated in the same way with regard to the Convention's applicability.

This approach considers the perspective of the commercial parties involved in such transactions. The Preamble of the Convention reveals that it was primarily drafted

597. *Klima*, RIW 1996, p. 1036.
598. *Klima*, RIW 1996, p. 1036.
599. Also in agreement *Thiele*, IHR 2002, p. 11.
600. RB Zeeland-West-Brabant, 15 February 2023, CISG-online 6231, paras 47 et seq.
601. RB Zeeland-West-Brabant, 15 February 2023, CISG-online 6231, para. 49.
602. RB Zeeland-West-Brabant, 15 February 2023, CISG-online 6231, para. 49.
603. *Hoffbauer*, p. 94 (with regard to German law).

for the benefit of merchants involved in international trade.[604] From their perspective, it is important to know which factual circumstances will result in what kind of legal consequences. The legal consequences will naturally depend on the applicable law.[605] By determining the applicable law based on the factual circumstances of the case, the parties are more likely to be able to foresee which law will be applied to their case.[606] This also means that factually comparable cases should result in the applicability of the same law. A framework agreement that binds the parties to conduct individual transactions should therefore be governed by the CISG, regardless of the theoretical classification of the contract, i.e., whether it is structured as one single contract or a contract that is followed by multiple individual contracts. Moreover, this approach offers the benefit of rendering difficult and ambiguous delineation issues unnecessary.[607]

e) Flexibility of the Convention's Provisions

It should further be noted that the different structure of the framework agreements under discussion, compared to conventional sales contracts, is not an obstacle to the CISG's applicability.[608] Rather, the CISG's flexible provisions can be applied to most questions if interpreted adequately and not too strictly.[609] An example can be found in a decision rendered by the Court of Appeal Krakow: in this case, the buyer in a framework agreement was obliged to order gutter systems from the seller with a value of not less than EUR 2.5 million per annum, which they failed to do.[610] Consequently, the Court granted damages to the seller for lost profits due to the lack of an adequate order, based on Art. 74 in conjunction with Art. 61(1)(b) CISG.[611]

Even if the Convention does not provide an answer to a specific question, the mechanism enshrined in Art. 7(2) CISG will typically lead to satisfactory results, provided that the CISG regulates the matter in the first place.[612] With regard to the non-sales elements in such framework agreements, Art. 3(2) CISG is relevant: as long as the non-sales obligations do not constitute the preponderant obligations, the CISG may still be applicable.[613]

604. Cf. *Schroeter*, (2013) 58 Vill. L. Rev., p. 564.
605. *Schroeter*, (2013) 58 Vill. L. Rev., p. 564.
606. *Schroeter*, (2013) 58 Vill. L. Rev., p. 564.
607. Cf. *Bridge*, Int'l Sale of Goods, para. 10.22; *Hoffbauer*, p. 94.
608. *Contra* Honsell/*Siehr*, Art. 2 CISG, para. 8: the CISG is unsuitable for distribution agreements that merely oblige the parties to conclude individual sales contracts.
609. In this regard, it is pertinent to refer to the previous remarks on preliminary agreements, as there are no discrepancies with regard to the breach of the obligation to conclude sales contracts: *see* Ch. 3 II. 2. c. iii. above; but *see* Honsell/*Siehr*, Art. 2 CISG, para. 8.
610. CA Krakow, 22 June 2015, CISG-online 5471.
611. CA Krakow, 22 June 2015, CISG-online 5471.
612. *See* Ch. 1 IV. above.
613. *Magnus*, ZEuP 1997, p. 829; Schlechtriem/Schwenzer/Schroeter/*Schroeter*, 5th English ed., Intro Arts 14–24 CISG, para. 24; Schlechtriem/Schwenzer/*Schlechtriem*, 2nd English ed., Intro Arts 14–24 CISG, para. 7; *see* Ch. 4 below for more detail.

f) Summary

Framework agreements that contain an obligation to conclude individual sales contracts should generally fall within the CISG's sphere of application. The fact that there is a separation between the framework agreement and the individual sales contracts does not, in and of itself, preclude the CISG from applying to the framework agreement. Essentially, this type of framework agreement is comparable to a preliminary agreement that obliges one or both parties to conclude a sales contract. Both types of contracts, in substance, establish rights and obligations under one or multiple CISG contracts. They should therefore be governed by the CISG in line with a general principle that the Convention may apply to related or closely linked contracts, on the condition that such agreements establish or directly affect the parties' rights and obligations under a CISG contract. From a practical perspective, there are only minor differences when the parties agree on a framework agreement containing an obligation to conclude individual sales contracts compared to a framework agreement containing actual sales obligations. The CISG should thus be applicable in both cases, as both contracts oblige the parties to carry out individual transactions. Considering that the type of framework agreements discussed here are structured differently from conventional sales contracts, the CISG's provisions must be applied carefully, e.g., in terms of the obligation to conclude individual sales contracts. However, in the majority of cases, the CISG's provisions are sufficiently flexible to deal with such issues.

2. Framework Agreements That Are Not Binding with Regard to Individual Transactions

In contrast to the aforementioned framework agreements, the parties may wish to remain free from any commitment towards the individual transactions. They may prioritise flexibility over planning reliability.[614] In such instances, the parties may conclude a framework agreement that is not binding with regard to the individual transactions, meaning they are not obliged to carry out individual transactions.[615]

a. Characteristics

The parties to such a framework agreement retain the freedom to decide whether they wish to proceed with any individual sales. If one of the parties refuses to conclude an individual sales contract, no legal consequences follow from the framework agreement.[616] Nevertheless, the legitimate expectation of the party regarding the conclusion of individual sales contracts may be safeguarded under some domestic laws.[617] The

614. *Hoffbauer*, p. 94.
615. *See Fikentscher/Heinemann*, para. 136; *Hoffbauer*, pp. 107 et seq.; Martinek/Semler/Flohr/*Budde/Eckhoff*, § 40, para. 9; *K. Schmidt*, § 20, para. 12; cf. also RB Zeeland-West-Brabant, 14 February 2023, CISG-online 6231, para. 51; *Piltz*, Rahmen-Einkaufsvertrag, paras 2, 6, 10; *Piltz*, Rahmen-Verkaufsvertrag, paras 2, 6, 10.
616. *Hoffbauer*, p. 107.
617. With regard to German law: *Hoffbauer*, p. 108; cf. *K. Schmidt*, § 20, paras 38 et seq.

aggrieved party may, for instance, be entitled to claim damages based on domestic legal remedies such as *culpa in contrahendo*.[618]

Framework agreements that are not binding with regard to individual transactions contain neither sales obligations in the strict sense nor obligations to conclude individual sales contracts. Obligations to deliver the goods and pay the purchase price are only established once the parties agree to conclude individual sales contracts.[619] It is therefore necessary to distinguish between the framework agreement and the individual sales contracts that might be subsequently concluded.[620]

In their framework agreement, the parties typically (pre-)agree on specific details pertaining to the future sale contracts, without including sales obligations or obliging themselves to conclude individual sales contracts.[621] Put differently, such framework agreements may set out the terms or the content of future sales contracts, without regulating whether the parties will carry out such individual sales transactions.[622] To illustrate, the parties may agree on quality standards or warranties for future sales contracts.[623] The objective is to incorporate these terms in the individual sales contracts if the parties eventually find an agreement.[624] Thus, these clauses remain 'dead letters' until the parties integrate them into the respective individual sales contracts.[625]

Apart from predetermining certain clauses and conditions for future sales contracts, the parties may include additional clauses in their framework agreement. They frequently agree on relational clauses that refer to their overall relationship and cooperation.[626] Examples of such clauses include confidentiality clauses, information obligations, clauses referring to the distribution of the goods and many more.[627]

618. *Hoffbauer*, p. 108; cf. also *Honnold/Flechtner*, Art. 2 CISG, para. 71.
619. *Budde/Geks*, ZVertriebsR 2012, p. 37; *Hoffbauer*, p. 5; Martinek/Semler/Flohr/*Budde/Eckhoff*, § 40, para. 8; cf. also *Gass/Lange*, pp. 14, 15; *Piltz*, Rahmen-Einkaufsvertrag, paras 2, 6; *Piltz*, Rahmen-Verkaufsvertrag, paras 2, 6; *Torsello*, pp. 243, 244.
620. Cf. OLG München, 18 June 2018, CISG-online 3080; Supr. Ct. Italy, 20 September 2004, CISG-online 1015; OLG Düsseldorf, 23 July 1997, CISG-online 276; OLG Düsseldorf, 11 July 1996, CISG-online 201; BGH, 4 April 1979, BGHZ 74, 136, 140 (the distribution contract must be distinguished from the individual sales contracts); *Budde/Geks*, ZVertriebsR 2012, p. 37; *Fikentscher/Heinemann*, para. 136; Martinek/Semler/Flohr/*Budde/Eckhoff*, § 40, para. 9; *Schwenzer*, Challenges of the 2020s, p. 44.
621. *Fikentscher/Heinemann*, para. 136; Martinek/Semler/Flohr/*Budde/Eckhoff*, § 40, para. 9; *K. Schmidt*, § 20, para. 12; Staudinger/Bork/*Herrler*, Vorbem. zu §§ 145 ff. BGB, para. 54; cf. also CA Paris, 5 March 2019, CISG-online 5765, paras 82 et seq.; OLG München, 18 June 2018, CISG-online 3080; *Piltz*, NJW 2019, p. 2517; *Schroeter*, para. 91; *Torsello*, p. 246.
622. Martinek/Semler/Flohr/*Budde/Eckhoff*, § 40, para. 9; *K. Schmidt*, § 20, para. 12; cf. also RB Zeeland-West-Brabant, 14 February 2023, CISG-online 6231, para. 51; *Gillette/Walt*, p. 62; *Piltz*, Rahmen-Einkaufsvertrag, paras 2, 6, 10; *Piltz*, Rahmen-Verkaufsvertrag, paras 2, 6, 10.
623. *Gass/Lange*, p. 14; *Piltz*, Rahmen-Einkaufsvertrag, para. 6; *Piltz*, Rahmen-Verkaufsvertrag, para. 6.
624. *Fikentscher/Heinemann*, para. 136; *Torsello*, p. 246.
625. Cf. Ostendorf/*Ostendorf/Sauthoff*, § 18, para. 210; *Piltz*, para. 2-41; *Piltz*, Int. Wirtschaftsrecht, § 18, para. 9.
626. RB Zeeland-West-Brabant, 14 February 2023, CISG-online 6231, para. 51 (the contract in dispute, *inter alia*, contained clauses regarding the 'Cooperation strategy' and the 'Working culture').
627. *Budde/Geks*, ZVertriebsR 2012, p. 37; *Hoffbauer*, pp. 12, 13; Martinek/Semler/Flohr/*Budde/Eckhoff*, § 40, para. 11; Sayag/*Pollaud-Dulian*, para. 108; *Torsello*, pp. 225, 226; *Weber*,

Moreover, the parties may agree on obligations to negotiate the conclusion of individual sales contracts, without obliging them to effectively find an agreement.[628]

b. Applicability of the CISG

These framework agreements do not fall within the 'conventional' definition of a sales contract under the CISG: they do not contain obligations to deliver goods, transfer property in them and pay the purchase price as per Arts 30 and 53 in conjunction with Art. 1 CISG. This could imply the CISG's non-applicability to these agreements.

i. Sufficiently Close Connection?

Before excluding this type of framework agreement from the CISG's sphere of application, it is necessary to consider whether these contracts are nevertheless covered by the Convention based on the general principle that closely linked or related contracts may be governed by the CISG. This requires a sufficiently close connection, which means that the framework agreement must directly affect or establish the parties' rights and obligations under CISG contracts.[629] By way of comparison, the framework agreements outlined above, in substance, establish the parties' rights and obligations under CISG contracts, since they include an obligation to conclude individual sales contracts.[630] Consequently, the CISG is applicable to them in accordance with this general principle.

The same assertion cannot be made about framework agreements that are not binding with regard to the individual transactions.[631] Such framework agreements do not include sales obligations in *sensu stricto,* and they lack an obligation to conclude individual sales contracts. They therefore do not establish any rights and obligations under CISG contracts. Rather, further negotiations between the parties are typically required; they still need to find an (uncertain) additional agreement on each individual sales contract.[632] Both parties still retain the option of declining to conclude any individual sales contracts without facing legal consequences that follow from the framework agreement.[633] The parties essentially indicate their intention not to yet establish sales obligations under a number of sales contracts by agreeing on such a framework agreement.[634] In light of this, the framework agreements discussed here should not be considered closely linked or related contracts in accordance with the aforementioned general principle.

ZSR 1987, p. 409; cf. also *Mousseron/Seube*, D. 1973, pp. 200 et seq.; Schlechtriem/Schwenzer/Schroeter/*Fountoulakis*, 5th English ed., Art. 73 CISG, para. 8.

628. *Hoffbauer*, pp. 108, 109.
629. *See* already Ch. 3 II. 2. b. ii. above.
630. *See* Ch. 3 II. 2. c. ii. 3) above.
631. Cf. RB Zeeland-West-Brabant, 14 February 2023, CISG-online 6231, paras 47 et seq.
632. Cf. *Fikentscher/Heinemann*, para. 136; MüKoHGB/*B. Köhler*, Art. 1 CISG, para. 13 (with regard to preliminary agreements).
633. *Hoffbauer*, p. 107.
634. *Juhasz*, IHR 2025, p. 47; cf. also RB Zeeland-West-Brabant, 14 February 2023, CISG-online 6231, para. 51; *Grunewald*, p. 57.

Notwithstanding, framework agreements that are not binding with regard to the individual transactions may still be deemed to affect the individual sales contracts subsequently concluded: in their framework agreement, the parties may predetermine specific details about the future sale of goods, which are to be implemented into the individual sales contracts.[635] These clauses that have been pre-agreed upon become legally effective once the parties decide to enter into individual sales contracts.[636] It could thus be argued that the framework agreement affects the rights and obligations under the individual sales contracts by predetermining a number of sales terms, which are to be implemented into each individual contract.[637]

Nevertheless, merely predetermining clauses should not be construed as directly affecting the parties' rights and obligations under a CISG contract.[638] Affecting the parties' rights and obligations generally requires an existing CISG contract that is directly influenced by the linked contract. Neither is the case if the parties predetermine certain (mostly sales-related) terms to be included in the individual contracts: there are typically no individual sales contracts, yet when the parties conclude the framework agreement, i.e., no CISG contracts exist. If the parties decide not to enter into any individual sales contracts, these terms remain without any relevance.[639] In other words, the predetermined terms may retain no legal significance for the individual sales contracts at all.[640] Moreover, the predetermined terms do not directly influence the individual sales contracts as they merely become relevant by virtue of an additional agreement by the parties to incorporate them.[641] Put differently, these clauses only 'come to life' if the parties undertake further steps and conclude an individual sales contract with specific content.[642]

For all of these reasons, the CISG should not apply to this group of framework agreements.[643] This applies to all forms of framework agreements that are not binding with regard to the individual transactions, e.g., framework agreements that merely

635. *See* OLG München, 18 June 2018, CISG-online 3080; *Budde/Geks*, ZVertriebsR 2012, p. 37; *Fikentscher/Heinemann*, para. 136; *Hoffbauer*, p. 5; *K. Schmidt*, § 20, para. 12; *Schroeter*, para. 91; *Piltz*, NJW 2019, p. 2517; *Piltz*, Rahmen-Einkaufsvertrag, para. 2; *Piltz*, Rahmen-Verkaufsvertrag, para. 2; *Torsello*, p. 246.
636. *Piltz*, Int. Wirtschaftsrecht, § 18, para. 7; cf. also *Piltz*, NJW 2019, p. 2517; *Piltz*, Rahmen-Einkaufsvertrag, para. 6; *Piltz*, Rahmen-Verkaufsvertrag, para. 6.
637. Similarly, *Piltz*, Int. Wirtschaftsrecht, § 18, para. 7; *Piltz*, Rahmen-Einkaufsvertrag, paras 2, 59; *Piltz*, Rahmen-Verkaufsvertrag, paras 2, 63; *Torsello*, p. 246.
638. *Juhasz*, IHR 2025, p. 47.
639. *See Piltz*, para. 2-41; *Piltz*, Int. Wirtschaftsrecht, § 18, para. 9; *Torsello*, p. 246; cf. also *Klima*, RIW 1996, p. 1036.
640. But *see Piltz*, Int. Wirtschaftsrecht, § 18, para. 9, who invokes the legal significance of the predetermined terms for the individual sales contracts governed by the CISG, thus substantiating the argument that the framework agreement should also be governed by the Convention; similarly, *Piltz*, Rahmen-Einkaufsvertrag, paras 2, 59; *Piltz*, Rahmen-Verkaufsvertrag, paras 2, 63.
641. Ostendorf/*Ostendorf/Sauthoff*, § 18, para. 210; cf. also *Schumacher*, IHR 2005, p. 149.
642. Ostendorf/*Ostendorf/Sauthoff*, § 18, para. 210; *Piltz*, para. 2-41; *Piltz*, Int. Wirtschaftsrecht, § 18, para. 9, employing a distinction between framework sales agreements and framework distribution agreements in his argumentation.
643. Accord RB Zeeland-West-Brabant, 14 February 2023, CISG-online 6231, para. 51; *Grunewald*, p. 57; *Hoffbauer*, p. 49; Ostendorf/*Ostendorf/Sauthoff*, § 18, para. 210; *Schumacher*, IHR 2005, p. 149; *Schroeter*, para. 93; cf. also *Honnold/Flechtner*, Art. 2 CISG, para. 71 (framework

contain sales-related terms as well as distribution or franchise agreements, provided that they do not bind the parties to proceed with the individual sales. As a consequence, these framework agreements will be governed by domestic law applicable by virtue of international private law rules.[644] In contrast to the aforementioned framework agreements, the contracts under discussion lack an obligation to conclude individual sales contracts or sales obligations in *sensu stricto*.[645]

This position is supported by a case decided by the District Court Zeeland-West-Brabant: while the Court applied the CISG to a 'Framework Supply Agreement' that obliged the parties to enter into individual sales contracts, it came to a different conclusion with regard to a 'Project Specific Contract'.[646] Both contracts in this case could arguably be characterised as framework agreements under the broad definition applied in this study. However, in contrast to the 'Framework Supply Agreement', the 'Project Specific Contract' merely sets out the parties' objectives for their future cooperation.[647] The Court established that it did not contain any commitments with regard to the sale of the goods.[648] In establishing the applicable law to the 'Project Specific Contract', the Court determined that it was not possible to employ the same reasoning as in the case of the 'Framework Supply Agreement'. With regard to the latter, it had previously reasoned the CISG's applicability based on the framework agreement's close connection to the individual sales contracts.[649] Ultimately, the Court applied domestic Dutch law to the 'Project Specific Contract'.[650] The Court's nuanced decision is convincing. The CISG should be applied to framework agreements only when they are binding with regard to the individual transactions. In contrast, framework agreements that do not contain any commitments towards the individual transactions should remain outside the Convention's sphere of application and be governed by the otherwise applicable domestic law. Such agreements demonstrate an absence of sufficient close linkage for the CISG to be applicable.

ii. 'Indirect Relevance' of the CISG

Although framework agreements that are not binding with regard to the individual transactions generally do not fall within the Convention's ambit, the CISG may still be

agreement 'without more' does not fall under Art. 1 CISG); *C. Witz*, paras 112.61, 112.71; but *see Piltz*, Rahmen-Einkaufsvertrag, para. 59; *Piltz*, Rahmen-Verkaufsvertrag, para. 63.

644. RB Zeeland-West-Brabant, 14 February 2023, CISG-online 6231, paras 51 et seq. (Rome I Regulation led to the applicability of Dutch law); *Hoffbauer*, p. 49; Schlechtriem/Schwenzer/Schroeter/*Schroeter*, 5th English ed., Intro Arts 14–24 CISG, para. 25; Schlechtriem/Schwenzer/Schroeter/*Schroeter*, 8th German ed., Vorbem. Arts 14–24 CISG, para. 20.
645. *See* already Ch. 3 II. 2. a. ii., b. ii. above regarding preliminary agreements without an obligation to conclude a sales contract.
646. RB Zeeland-West-Brabant, 14 February 2023, CISG-online 6231, paras 47 et seq.
647. RB Zeeland-West-Brabant, 14 February 2023, CISG-online 6231, para. 51.
648. RB Zeeland-West-Brabant, 14 February 2023, CISG-online 6231, para. 51.
649. RB Zeeland-West-Brabant, 14 February 2023, CISG-online 6231, paras 47 et seq.
650. RB Zeeland-West-Brabant, 14 February 2023, CISG-online 6231, paras 51 et seq.

'indirectly' relevant for these contracts.[651] This is due to the fact that the individual sales contracts concluded under the umbrella of such a framework agreement may nevertheless be governed by the Convention, given that they meet the prerequisites for its applicability.[652]

The content of these individual sales contracts governed by the CISG may be derived from the framework agreement containing predetermined sales clauses, which, as such, still remains outside the Convention's ambit.[653] Similar to standard terms,[654] the parties may agree on a reference to the framework agreement's terms when concluding an individual sales contract.[655] Moreover, an interpretation of the individual sales contract under Art. 8(3) CISG may reveal that the parties intended to implement the framework agreement's terms into the individual sales contracts.[656] The framework agreement may then be a relevant circumstance, in particular a 'practice', to be considered in accordance with Art. 8(3) CISG.[657] In this context, the framework agreement and its drafting history may be relevant in determining the meaning of specific terms under the individual sales contract. The predetermined terms contained in the framework agreement may also be incorporated into the individual sales contracts based on a 'practice' in the sense of Art. 9(1) CISG.[658] The terms incorporated in this way may, e.g., relate to the remedies available under the individual sales contracts.[659]

The parties may also agree on the basis of a framework agreement, which could again be considered a 'practice' under Art. 8(3) CISG or Art. 9(1) CISG, to derogate from the CISG's provisions on contract formation with regard to the individual sales

651. *Juhasz*, IHR 2025, p. 48.
652. Dist. Ct. Szczecin, 13 February 2015, CISG-online 6807, para. 74; OLG Hamburg, 15 July 2010, CISG-online 2448; Foreign Trade Ct. of Arbitration of the CC and Industry of Serbia, 28 January 2009, CISG-online 1856; CA Versailles, 19 February 2004, CISG-online 3345 confirmed by the Cour de Cassation, 20 February 2007, CISG-online 1492; OGer Luzern, 8 January 1997, CISG-online 228; OLG Koblenz, 17 September 1993, CISG-online 91, para. 42; not entirely clear OGH, 26 November 2018, CISG-online 3912; cf. also RB Zeeland-West-Brabant, 17 April 2024, CISG-online 6940, para. 6; *Fryer Holdings Pty Ltd. v. Liaoing MEC Group Co Ltd. et al.*, Supr. Ct. New South Wales, 30 January 2012, CISG-online 2325 (unclear whether the transactions in question were individual sales contracts or orders); *Grunewald*, p. 57; *Hoffbauer*, p. 49; Schlechtriem/Schwenzer/Schroeter/*Schroeter*, 5th English ed., Intro Arts 14–24 CISG, para. 25; Schlechtriem/Schwenzer/Schroeter/*Schroeter*, 8th German ed., Vorbem. Arts 14–24 CISG, para. 20; *Schroeter*, para. 94; Staudinger/*Magnus*, Art. 1 CISG, para. 37; *Walt*, p. 85; *C. Witz*, para. 112.61; but *see C. Meyer*, Alleinvertrieb, p. 470; *C. Meyer*, Jusletter 2 May 2016, para. 23.
653. *Honnold/Flechtner*, Art. 2 CISG, para. 71; Schlechtriem/Schwenzer/Schroeter/*Hachem*, 5th English ed., Art. 1 CISG, para. 15; *Schroeter*, paras 93, 94; cf. also Honsell/*Dornis*, Art. 14 CISG, para. 12; Ostendorf/*Ostendorf/Sauthoff*, § 18, para. 210.
654. Cf. only Schlechtriem/Schwenzer/Schroeter/*Schroeter*, 5th English ed., Art. 14 CISG, paras 125 et seq.
655. OLG München, 18 June 2018, CISG-online 3080, mentioning an explicit or implicit reference to the framework agreement ('*ausdrückliche oder konkludente Bezugnahme auf den Rahmenvertrag*').
656. Schlechtriem/Schwenzer/Schroeter/*Schmidt-Kessel*, 5th English ed., Art. 8 CISG, para. 50; *Schroeter*, para. 94; cf. RB Zeeland-West-Brabant, 17 April 2024, CISG-online 6940.
657. Schlechtriem/Schwenzer/Schroeter/*Schmidt-Kessel*, 5th English ed., Art. 8 CISG, para. 50 (framework agreements as practice in the sense of Art. 8(3) CISG).
658. *Juhasz*, IHR 2025, p. 48; *Schroeter*, para. 94.
659. *Hoffbauer*, pp. 114, 115; Ostendorf/*Ostendorf/Sauthoff*, § 18, para. 210.

contracts.[660] For example, the parties may derogate from the rule enshrined in Art. 18(1) CISG and stipulate that silence amounts to acceptance of an offer under certain circumstances.[661] An individual sales contract may then already be concluded if the receiving party does not respond to an offer, e.g., an 'order', within a certain period of time.[662]

In all of these cases, the Convention merely applies to the individual sales contracts, whereas the framework agreement as such remains outside the CISG's sphere of application. However, the sales-related terms set out in the framework agreement become an integral part of the individual sales contracts that are in turn governed by the CISG.[663] Furthermore, it may be necessary to consider the framework agreement in order to gain a deeper understanding of an individual sales contract for the purposes of contract interpretation. Consequently, the CISG may be applicable to questions arising from the individual sales contracts, yet still relate to the framework agreement.[664] Therefore, it can be posited that the CISG is indirectly relevant to the framework agreement. The parties are, for instance, well advised to draft the terms contained in the framework agreement in respect of the fact that they will be incorporated into CISG contracts.

3. Conclusion

To conclude, framework agreements that are binding with regard to the individual transactions should be governed by the CISG, regardless of their exact structure. In this context, this study proposes distinguishing between framework agreements containing sales obligations in *sensu stricto* and framework agreements that contain an obligation to conclude individual sales obligations.

If framework agreements include sales obligations in the strict sense, the CISG will apply to such contracts based on Art. 1 in conjunction with Arts 30 and 53 CISG. There is no explicit provision within the Convention that would preclude this interpretation. Moreover, the characterisation of such agreements under domestic law is irrelevant, as the Convention determines its sphere of applicability autonomously.

The Convention should also be applicable to framework agreements that contain an obligation to conclude individual sales contracts. The fact that there is a separation between the framework agreement and the individual sales contracts does not preclude

660. Cf. *Honnold/Flechtner*, Intro Arts 14–24 CISG, para. 178; *Piltz*, para. 2-41; *Piltz*, Rahmen-Einkaufsvertrag, paras 9, 13; *Piltz*, Rahmen-Verkaufsvertrag, para. 9; Schlechtriem/Schwenzer/Schroeter/*Schroeter*, 5th English ed., Art. 14 CISG, para. 72.
661. Kröll *et al./Ferrari*, Art. 18 CISG, para. 11; MüKoHGB/*Ferrari*, Art. 18 CISG, para. 10; Schlechtriem/Schwenzer/Schroeter/*Schroeter*, 5th English ed., Art. 18 CISG, paras 48, 84; cf. also Secretariat's Commentary, Art. 16, No. 4, Example 16B.
662. *See* Secretariat's Commentary, Art. 16, No. 4, Example 16B (no response within 14 days after receipt).
663. Cf. RB Zeeland-West-Brabant, 17 April 2024, CISG-online 6940; Ostendorf/*Ostendorf/Sauthoff*, § 18, para. 210; *Piltz*, para. 2-41; Schlechtriem/Schwenzer/Schroeter/*Hachem*, 5th English ed., Art. 1 CISG, para. 15.
664. *Juhasz*, IHR 2025, p. 48.

the Convention from applying to the former contract. This type of framework agreements is essentially comparable to preliminary agreements that oblige one or both parties to conclude a sales contract. Both types of contracts, in substance, establish rights and obligations under one or multiple CISG contracts. They should therefore be governed by the CISG in accordance with the general principle that the CISG may apply to related or closely linked contracts, provided that such contracts establish or directly affect the parties' rights and obligations under a CISG contract. Furthermore, the practical differences between such a framework agreement compared to a framework agreement containing actual sales obligations are relatively insignificant, which is why they should be treated equally in terms of the Convention's applicability. The CISG's provisions are sufficiently flexible to deal with both types of framework agreements, including breaches of the obligation to conclude individual sales contracts and the like.

In contrast, it is necessary to distinguish the aforementioned contracts from framework agreements that are not binding with regard to the individual transactions. Such framework agreements that are not binding with regard to the individual transactions should not be governed by the CISG. Although they may predetermine certain terms to be incorporated into the individual sales contracts (comparable to standard terms), they do not directly affect the parties' rights and obligations under these CISG contracts, as the parties must find an additional agreement to incorporate these terms. Furthermore, they do not establish rights and obligations because both parties retain the freedom to decide whether or not to conclude any individual sales contracts without any legal consequences.

The CISG may nonetheless be indirectly relevant for such framework agreements, which, as such, remain outside its sphere of application: if the parties decide to enter into individual sales contracts under the umbrella of the framework agreement, the individual sales contracts may be subject to the Convention. The framework agreement may then be relevant for the interpretation of the individual sales contracts (Art. 8(3) CISG). It may further be considered a practice within the meaning of Art. 9(1) CISG or constitute a derogation from certain provisions of the Convention (e.g., Art. 18(1) CISG). The parties are therefore well advised to draft the terms of the framework agreement in respect of the fact that they may be incorporated into sales contracts governed by the CISG.

IV. SUFFICIENT DEFINITENESS IN FRAMEWORK AGREEMENTS

Now that it has been outlined under which circumstances a framework agreement should be characterised as a contract of sale of goods or a closely related contract to which the CISG applies, an additional concern is worth addressing.

Framework agreements typically leave one or several terms regarding the sale of goods open or indefinite for a later determination, i.e., when actual orders or call-offs of the goods are made. This has led to the proposition that framework agreements are not sufficiently definite to fall within the CISG's sphere of application.

The following part will illustrate this concern in more detail. Thereafter, it will outline the CISG's standard of definiteness in a general manner. Finally, this standard will be applied to framework agreements, revealing that open terms in framework agreements should not be considered an obstacle to the CISG's applicability.

1. Are Framework Agreements Too Indefinite to Be Governed by the CISG?

A significant amount of case law and scholars hold that framework agreements are not sufficiently definite to be governed by the CISG.[665] In particular, several US courts have identified the indefiniteness of framework agreements as a reason to reject the CISG's applicability.

a. US Case Law

In this context, *Helen Kaminski v. Marketing Australian Products (MAP)* decided by the US District Court for the Southern District of New York is an important precedent.[666] In this case, an Australian supplier concluded a distribution agreement with a US distributor for fashion accessories.[667] The distribution contract included sales-related terms as well as a minimum purchase requirement.[668] The parties amended the agreement to address the sale of specific goods already located in the US.[669] A few months later, the distributor issued purchase orders for additional products (not explicitly mentioned in the amendment).[670] Subsequently, the distributor failed to pay the purchase price for these orders, whereupon the supplier initiated legal proceedings.[671] Meanwhile, the distributor filed for insolvency, and the competent bankruptcy court ordered a stay on the prior proceedings as well as an extension of the distributor's time limit to cure any defects.[672]

This prompted the supplier to appeal against the aforementioned decision. The supplier maintained that the CISG was applicable to the contract at hand, thereby

665. *See* Ch. 3 IV. 1. a. and b. below.
666. *Helen Kaminski Pty. Ltd. v. Marketing Australian Products, Inc.*, US Dist. Ct. SD NY, 21 July 1997, CISG-online 297 with notes by: *Genys*, (1997/98) 17 J. L. & Com., pp. 415 et seq.; *Harjani*, (2004) 23:1 Houst. J. Int'l L., pp. 81 et seq.; *Kilian*, (2011) 11 Transnat. L. & Pol'y, pp. 235 et seq.; *Thiele*, IHR 2002, pp. 10, 11.
667. *Helen Kaminski Pty. Ltd. v. Marketing Australian Products, Inc.*, US Dist. Ct. SD NY, 21 July 1997, CISG-online 297.
668. *Helen Kaminski Pty. Ltd. v. Marketing Australian Products, Inc.*, US Dist. Ct. SD NY, 21 July 1997, CISG-online 297, p. 1: 'a total of U.S. Dollar 2 million worth of products from February 1, 1996 to January 31, 1997'.
669. *Helen Kaminski Pty. Ltd. v. Marketing Australian Products, Inc.*, US Dist. Ct. SD NY, 21 July 1997, CISG-online 297, p. 1.
670. *Helen Kaminski Pty. Ltd. v. Marketing Australian Products, Inc.*, US Dist. Ct. SD NY, 21 July 1997, CISG-online 297, p. 1.
671. *Helen Kaminski Pty. Ltd. v. Marketing Australian Products, Inc.*, US Dist. Ct. SD NY, 21 July 1997, CISG-online 297, p. 1.
672. *Helen Kaminski Pty. Ltd. v. Marketing Australian Products, Inc.*, US Dist. Ct. SD NY, 21 July 1997, CISG-online 297, p. 2.

superseding US insolvency law.[673] It elaborated that the contract was sufficiently definite with regard to the terms for the parties' commercial relationship, thus falling within the ambit of the Convention.[674] In contrast, the distributor argued that the contract was merely a framework agreement, which was not covered by the CISG, given that it did not identify the ordered goods by type, date or price.[675] According to the distributor, the CISG requires an enforceable contract with definite terms regarding quantity and price.[676]

The Court held that both parties concurred that the CISG's applicability depends on the question of whether the distribution agreement can be characterised as a sales contract, which requires that it contains definite terms for specified goods.[677] Accordingly, the Court analysed whether the distribution agreement in dispute contained sufficiently definite terms. With regard to the products additionally ordered, it held that the dispute concerned goods 'not specifically identified in the Distributor Agreement'.[678] Based on this lack of definiteness, the Court found the CISG to not be applicable.[679] It further stated that 'the identification in the Distributor Agreement of certain goods – about which there is no claim of breach – is insufficient to bring the Distributor Agreement within coverage of the CISG […]'.[680]

In *Viva Vino Import v. Franese Vini*, the US District Court for the Eastern District of Pennsylvania simply agreed with the rationale adopted in *Helen Kaminski v. MAP* and concluded that the CISG was not applicable to the distribution contract in question, as it did 'not cover the sale of specific goods and contain definite terms regarding price and quantity'.[681]

Similarly, in *Gruppo Essenziero Italiano v. Aromi D'Italia*, the US District Court for the District of Maryland did not apply the CISG to a distribution contract, since such agreements fail to establish specific terms for the quantity and price of the goods.[682] It

673. *Helen Kaminski Pty. Ltd. v. Marketing Australian Products, Inc.*, US Dist. Ct. SD NY, 21 July 1997, CISG-online 297, p. 2.
674. *Helen Kaminski Pty. Ltd. v. Marketing Australian Products, Inc.*, US Dist. Ct. SD NY, 21 July 1997, CISG-online 297, p. 3.
675. *Helen Kaminski Pty. Ltd. v. Marketing Australian Products, Inc.*, US Dist. Ct. SD NY, 21 July 1997, CISG-online 297, p. 3.
676. *Helen Kaminski Pty. Ltd. v. Marketing Australian Products, Inc.*, US Dist. Ct. SD NY, 21 July 1997, CISG-online 297, p. 3; cf. also SCC, January 2020, CISG-online 6368.
677. *Helen Kaminski Pty. Ltd. v. Marketing Australian Products, Inc.*, US Dist. Ct. SD NY, 21 July 1997, CISG-online 297, p. 3.
678. *Helen Kaminski Pty. Ltd. v. Marketing Australian Products, Inc.*, US Dist. Ct. SD NY, 21 July 1997, CISG-online 297, p. 3.
679. *Helen Kaminski Pty. Ltd. v. Marketing Australian Products, Inc.*, US Dist. Ct. SD NY, 21 July 1997, CISG-online 297, p. 3; criticism by *Thiele*, IHR 2002, p. 11.
680. *Helen Kaminski Pty. Ltd. v. Marketing Australian Products, Inc.*, US Dist. Ct. SD NY, 21 July 1997, CISG-online 297, p. 3.
681. *Viva Vino Import Corp. v. Franese Vini S.r.l.*, US Dist. Ct. ED Penn., 29 August 2000, CISG-online 675, p. 2: 'This court agrees with the rationale adopted by the court in Kaminski and concludes that the CISG does not apply to distributorship contracts that do not cover the sale of specific goods and contain definite terms regarding quantity and price'; cf. also more recently regarding a 'Membership Agreement': *Reecon North America, LLC v. Du-Hope Int'l Group et al.*, US Dist. Ct. WD Penn., 20 June 2019, CISG-online 4425.
682. *Gruppo Essenziero Italiano, S.p.A. v. Aromi D'Italia, Inc.*, US Dist. Ct. Mary., 27 July 2011, CISG-online 2223, p. 4.

supported this position by referencing Art. 14(1) CISG: an offer under the Convention requires sufficiently definite terms for determining the price and the quantity of the goods.[683]

Finally, the US District Court for the District of Arizona in *Adonia Holdings v. Adonia Organics* did not apply the CISG to an exclusive distribution agreement because it did not specify the goods or the types of goods that are to be sold.[684]

b. *Scholarly Writings*

Similar to the cases outlined above, some scholars reject the CISG's applicability to framework agreements based on their lack of sufficient definiteness. *Gillette* and *Walt* hold that, in accordance with Art. 23 CISG, a contract is concluded when an acceptance of an offer becomes effective.[685] Art. 14(1) CISG further stipulates that a proposal constitutes an offer if it, *inter alia,* fixes the quantity and the price of the goods.[686] These scholars argue that a framework agreement does not fix the quantity and the price of the goods as required by these provisions.[687] Therefore, they conclude that unlike the individual sales contracts, framework agreements are not to be characterised as sales contracts and that the CISG should not be applicable to them.[688]

In a similar way, *Genys* refers to Art. 14 CISG as a requirement for any sales contract under the CISG.[689] According to her, a contract for the sale of goods, in accordance with Art. 1 CISG in conjunction with Arts 30 and 53 CISG, must be sufficiently definite as set out by Art. 14(1) CISG.[690] In reference to *Helen Kaminski v. MAP*, she posits that the 'indefiniteness' of the distribution agreement in that case indicated the CISG's non-applicability.[691] She therefore essentially agrees with the Court's decision and adds that the requirement of sufficient definiteness can, *inter alia*, be derived from Art. 14 CISG.[692]

In reference to a decision by the OLG Munich, *Kreße* notes that according to that Court's more expansive interpretation, the CISG is applicable to framework agreements in cases where they establish 'abstract' sales obligations that are to be specified at a

683. *Gruppo Essenziero Italiano, S.p.A. v. Aromi D'Italia, Inc.*, US Dist. Ct. Mary., 27 July 2011, CISG-online 2223, p. 4.
684. *Adonia Holding GmbH v. Adonia Organics LLC,* US Dist. Ct. Ariz., 16 December 2014, CISG-online 2951, pp. 4, 5 (it is worth noting that the distribution agreement in this case contained a minimum purchase requirement).
685. *Gillette/Walt*, p. 62.
686. *Gillette/Walt*, p. 62.
687. *Gillette/Walt*, p. 62.
688. *Gillette/Walt*, p. 62; in agreement *Walt*, pp. 84, 85.
689. *Genys*, (1997/98) 17 J. L. & Com., p. 421: 'CISG Article 14, concerning the prerequisites for finding an offer, is also illuminating as to the requirements of the eventual contract for sale'; cf. also *Grieser*, p. 134.
690. *Genys*, (1997/98) 17 J. L. & Com., pp. 421, 422.
691. *Genys*, (1997/98) 17 J. L. & Com., pp. 421, 422.
692. *Genys*, (1997/98) 17 J. L. & Com., pp. 422 et seq. (however, the author critiques the Court's decision, contending that it was reached without any references to case law, scholars or CISG provisions).

later date.[693] He admits that Art. 14 CISG permits a subsequent determination of the goods' quantity and the purchase price.[694] However, he criticises the fact that the parties to a framework agreement are typically required to conclude individual sales contracts that are independent from the framework agreement.[695] In his view, the CISG can only be applied to a framework agreement if the contract is sufficiently definite, such that there is no necessity to conclude separate individual sales contracts.[696] This interpretation implies that a subsequent determination of open terms in separate contracts does not meet the Convention's standards.

In the same vein, *B. Köhler* posits that a distribution contract shall be governed by the Convention only if it is sufficiently definite regarding the price and the quantity of the goods, thus rendering the need to conclude individual sales contracts superfluous.[697] In contrast, if the framework agreement is followed by individual sales contracts, the Convention shall be applicable only to these individual sales contracts.[698]

c. *Implications of This View*

In conclusion, three main implications follow from this view held in case law and among scholars. First, the CISG generally requires sufficiently definite contracts for it to be applicable.[699] Second, framework agreements are typically not sufficiently definite with regard to the quantity of the goods and the purchase price, which is why the Convention is deemed inapplicable to them. Third, the Convention's standard of sufficient definiteness is not met if the quantity of the goods and the purchase price are to be subsequently determined in separate sales contracts. The CISG may be applicable to a framework agreement only if the framework agreement itself is sufficiently definite, thus rendering the need to conclude separate sales contracts superfluous.

2. Standard of Definiteness in CISG Contracts

Art. 14(1) CISG requires a proposal for contract conclusion to be sufficiently definite. Art. 14(1), sentence 2 CISG elaborates on this requirement: a proposal is sufficiently definite if it indicates the goods and expressly or implicitly fixes or makes provisions for determining the quantity and price. Upon closer examination of this provision's wording, it seems to set out a stricter standard for the goods ('indicates') in comparison

693. Soergel/*Kreße*, Art. 1 CISG, para. 22, in reference to the decision in OLG München, 22 September 1995, CISG-online 208; cf. also *Grieser*, p. 133.
694. Soergel/*Kreße*, Art. 1 CISG, para. 22.
695. Soergel/*Kreße*, Art. 1 CISG, para. 22; *see also Grieser*, pp. 133, 134.
696. Soergel/*Kreße*, Art. 1 CISG, para. 22; accord *Grieser*, p. 134.
697. MüKoHGB/*B. Köhler*, Art. 1 CISG, para. 22; cf. also MüKoHGB/*Sommerfeld*, Art. 73 CISG, para. 4.
698. MüKoHGB/*B. Köhler*, Art. 1 CISG, para. 22.
699. Cf. also *Perales Viscasillas*, Extending the Scope, pp. 122, 123 (referencing US case law).

to the quantity and the price ('expressly or implicitly fixes or makes provisions ...').[700] However, the prevailing view among commentators convincingly holds that the difference in the provision's wording should not be considered a relevant factor and that the goods can also be indicated implicitly or by making provisions for their determination.[701] There is no compelling reason, substantive or historical, to apply a stricter standard to the indication of goods.[702] Instead, an equal standard should apply to all the minimum elements listed in Art. 14(1), sentence 2 CISG.

As the offer shapes the content of the entire transaction,[703] Art. 14(1) CISG indirectly outlines the minimum content of any CISG contract.[704]

a. Explicit or Implicit Determination

Art. 14(1), sentence 2 CISG holds that the quantity and price can be fixed explicitly or implicitly. Consequently, an offer can explicitly fix the quantity and price,[705] or it can implicitly fix these minimum requirements.[706] In the *Chinchilla furs* case, the Austrian Supreme Court held that the pivotal question for an implicit determination is whether the *essentialia contractus* can be discerned from the circumstances by a reasonable third person in the sense of Art. 8 CISG.[707]

b. Determinability

Furthermore, Art. 14(1), sentence 2 CISG states that it is sufficient for an offer to provide a means for determining the price and quantity (so-called determinability).[708] The fact that implicit determination as well as determinability of the minimum elements meet the standard of sufficient definiteness under Art. 14(1), sentence 2 CISG

700. Schlechtriem/Schwenzer/Schroeter/*Schroeter*, 5th English ed., Art. 14 CISG, para. 42; Staudinger/*Magnus*, Art. 14 CISG, para. 20.
701. Brunner/Gottlieb/*Brunner/Pfisterer/Köster*, Art. 14 CISG, para. 14 footnote 572; Kröll *et al./Ferrari*, Art. 14 CISG, para. 21; MüKoHGB/*Ferrari*, Art. 14 CISG, para. 21; Schlechtriem/Schwenzer/Schroeter/*Schroeter*, 5th English ed., Art. 14 CISG, para. 42; Schlechtriem/Schwenzer/Schroeter/*Schroeter*, 8th German ed., Art. 14 CISG, para. 41; Staudinger/*Magnus*, Art. 14 CISG, para. 20; Witz/Salger/Lorenz/*W. Witz*, Art. 14 CISG, para. 30.
702. Schlechtriem/Schwenzer/Schroeter/*Schroeter*, 5th English ed., Art. 14 CISG, para. 42; Staudinger/*Magnus*, Art. 14 CISG, para. 20.
703. Cf. Schlechtriem/Schwenzer/Schroeter/*Schroeter*, 5th English ed., Art. 14 CISG, para. 16; Schlechtriem/Schwenzer/Schroeter/*Schroeter*, 8th German ed., Art. 14 CISG, para. 15.
704. *Genys*, (1997/98) 17 J. L. & Com., p. 421; cf. also *Grieser*, p. 134; Staudinger/*Magnus*, Art. 14 CISG, para. 3.
705. *See* Honsell/*Dornis*, Art. 14 CISG, para. 15; Schlechtriem/Schwenzer/Schroeter/*Schroeter*, 5th English ed., Art. 14 CISG, para. 71; Schlechtriem/Schwenzer/Schroeter/*Schroeter*, 8th German ed., Art. 14 CISG, para. 64.
706. OGH, 10 November 1994, CISG-online 117, para. 14; Metropolitan Ct. Budapest, 24 March 1992, CISG-online 61: the Court established the *essentialia negotii* of the sales contract based on the circumstances; *Fogt*, p. 191; Schlechtriem/Schwenzer/Schroeter/*Schroeter*, 5th English ed., Art. 14 CISG, para. 71.
707. OGH, 10 November 1994, CISG-online 117, paras 14 et seq.; cf. also *Fogt*, p. 191; *Schroeter*, paras 301, 302.
708. Schlechtriem/Schwenzer/Schroeter/*Schroeter*, 5th English ed., Art. 14 CISG, para. 76; *C. Witz*, para. 231.41.

serves to illustrate the underlying purpose that this provision should generally be construed in a liberal way.[709] An overly strict interpretation of Art. 14(1) CISG must be avoided.[710]

i. *Reference to Existing or Future Objective Factors*

The minimum elements required by Art. 14(1), sentence 2 CISG are determinable if the offer includes a reference to existing objective factors.[711] Moreover, the prevailing view among commentators posits that a reference to future objective factors is equally sufficient under Art. 14(1), sentence 2 CISG.[712] A reference to future objective factors may, for instance, include a reference to market prices at the time of delivery or a reference to the harvest from a certain area in the following year.[713] In such cases, a reference is made to an objective factor that is not yet present at the time the offer is made.[714] In other words, the minimum content remains uncertain when the offer is made (and accepted) until the factor in question comes into existence.[715]

This still meets the liberal standard of sufficient definiteness under Art. 14(1) CISG, if this provision is being interpreted literally. The second sentence of this provision merely requires that the offer 'makes provisions for determining' without specifying any limitations in terms of time, such as determinability or determination at the time of contract conclusion.[716]

709. *Fogt*, p. 191 ('wide latitude'); Witz/Salger/Lorenz/*W. Witz*, Art. 14 CISG, para. 29 (the purpose of the terminology chosen is to ensure a liberal interpretation of this provision); cf. also *Schulze*, Ch. 8, para. 29.
710. *Schroeter*, para. 304, who issues a cautionary note regarding a narrow-minded ('*engherzig*') interpretation of Art. 14(1), sentence 2 CISG; Schlechtriem/Schwenzer/Schroeter/*Schroeter*, 5th English ed., Art. 14 CISG, para. 54 (in the context of an implicitly fixed price).
711. *Enderlein/Maskow*, Art. 14 CISG, note 12; Schlechtriem/Schwenzer/Schroeter/*Schroeter*, 5th English ed., Art. 14 CISG, para. 77; e.g., a reference to price lists or a catalogue (cf. OLG Rostock, 10 October 2001, CISG-online 671; *Herber/Czerwenka*, Art. 14 CISG, para. 5; Mankowski/*Spagnolo*, Art. 14 CISG, para. 3; Schlechtriem/Schwenzer/Schroeter/*Schroeter*, 5th English ed., Art. 14 CISG, para. 77).
712. Honsell/*Dornis*, Art. 14 CISG, para. 18; Mankowski/*Spagnolo*, Art. 14 CISG, para. 3; MüKoBGB/*Gruber*, Art. 14 CISG, para. 19; Schlechtriem/Schwenzer/Schroeter/*Schroeter*, 5th English ed., Art. 14 CISG, para. 78; but *see Fogt*, p. 191; Kröll *et al.*/*Ferrari*, Art. 14 CISG, para. 24.
713. OLG Brandenburg, 3 July 2014, CISG-online 2543: the 'goods' were the harvest from cuttings in the following year; Bianca/Bonell/*Eörsi*, Art. 14 CISG, note 2.2.4.3; *Enderlein/Maskow*, Art. 14 CISG, note 12; Mankowski/*Spagnolo*, Art. 14 CISG, para. 3; Schlechtriem/Schwenzer/Schroeter/*Schroeter*, 5th English ed., Art. 14 CISG, paras 78, 79; cf. also Secretariat's Commentary, Art. 12, Nos 11 et seq.
714. MüKoBGB/*Gruber*, Art. 14 CISG, para. 19; Secretariat's Commentary, Art. 12, No. 11; Schlechtriem/Schwenzer/Schroeter/*Schroeter*, 5th English ed., Art. 14 CISG, para. 78.
715. Schlechtriem/Schwenzer/Schroeter/*Schroeter*, 5th English ed., Art. 14 CISG, para. 78; cf. also *Honnold/Flechtner*, Art. 14 CISG, para. 185.
716. Cf. Schlechtriem/Schwenzer/Schroeter/*Schroeter*, 5th English ed., Art. 14 CISG, para. 78, who, however, also mentions that the authentic French text might lead to a different conclusion; *contra*: *Fogt*, p. 191.

ii. *Power of Determination*

Furthermore, the prevailing view holds that the minimum content is also determinable if a party is authorised to fix the minimum content; or, put another way, the offer includes a 'power of determination'.[717] The minimum content will then again be uncertain until the respective power is exercised. As such cases are similar to cases of reference to future objective factors, this nonetheless meets the liberal standard under Art. 14(1) CISG,[718] based on a literal interpretation of this provision and taking into account that it should not be construed overly strictly.

1) Determination by a Third Party or a Contracting Party

The offer could, for instance, authorise a third party to fix the minimum content, such as the price.[719] Equally, the offer could authorise one of the contracting parties to unilaterally stipulate the minimum content, which would also be sufficiently definite.[720]

In practice, such a unilateral power of determination often refers to the quantity of the goods, in particular when it comes to long-term contracts:[721] under so-called requirement contracts, the buyer determines the quantity of the goods according to their needs.[722] Under so-called output contracts, the seller determines the quantities

717. Schlechtriem/Schwenzer/Schroeter/*Schroeter*, 5th English ed., Art. 14 CISG, para. 80; *see also Fogt*, p. 191; Mankowski/*Spagnolo*, Art. 14 CISG, para. 3; MüKoBGB/*Gruber*, Art. 14 CISG, para. 20; cf. also Cour de Cassation, 30 June 2004, CISG-online 870; with different reasoning: Honsell/*Dornis*, Art. 14 CISG, para. 19; Witz/Salger/Lorenz/*W. Witz*, Art. 14 CISG, paras 31, 45: a power of determination does not fulfil the requirements of Art. 14(1), sentence 2 CISG, but the parties may derogate from this provision in accordance with Art. 6 CISG.

718. *See* Schlechtriem/Schwenzer/Schroeter/*Schroeter*, 5th English ed., Art. 14 CISG, para. 80.

719. Bianca/Bonell/*Eörsi*, Art. 14 CISG, note 2.2.4.3; BeckOK/*Saenger*, Art. 14 CISG, para. 4; Brunner/*Pfisterer/Köster*, Art. 14 CISG, para. 9; *Enderlein/Maskow*, Art. 14 CISG, note 12; *Fogt*, p. 191; *Herber/Czerwenka*, Art. 14 CISG, para. 5; Mankowski/*Spagnolo*, Art. 14 CISG, para. 3; MüKoBGB/*Gruber*, Art. 14 CISG, para. 20; *Piltz*, para. 3-23; Schlechtriem/Schwenzer/Schroeter/*Schroeter*, 5th English ed., Art. 14 CISG, para. 81; regarding the quantity: Staudinger/*Magnus*, Art. 14 CISG, para. 22; but *see* Witz/Salger/Lorenz/*W. Witz*, Art. 14 CISG, para. 49 (derogation under Art. 6 CISG necessary).

720. Cf. *Solae, LLC v. Hershey Canada, Inc.*, US Dist. Ct. Dela., 9 May 2008, CISG-online 1769; Cour de Cassation, 30 June 2004, CISG-online 870; HGer Zürich, 10 July 1996, CISG-online 227 (the seller was allowed to diverge up to 10% from the ordered goods according to the contract); Brunner/Gottlieb/*Brunner/Pfisterer/Köster*, Art. 14 CISG, para. 11; *Enderlein/Maskow*, Art. 14 CISG, note 12; *Herber/Czerwenka*, Art. 14 CISG, para. 5; Mankowksi/*Spagnolo*, Art. 14 CISG, para. 3; MüKoBGB/*Gruber*, Art. 14 CISG, para. 20; Ostendorf/*Ostendorf/Sauthoff*, § 18, para. 209; *Piltz*, para. 3-23; Schlechtriem/Schwenzer/Schroeter/*Schroeter*, 5th English ed., Art. 14 CISG, para. 84; Staudinger/*Magnus*, Art. 14 CISG, para. 22 (regarding quantity); *contra*: Witz/Salger/Lorenz/*W. Witz*, Art. 14 CISG, para. 45.

721. Cf. *Solae, LLC v. Hershey Canada, Inc.*, US Dist. Ct. Dela., 9 May 2008, CISG-online 1769; HGer Zürich, 10 July 1996, CISG-online 227; *Honnold/Flechtner*, Art. 14 CISG, para. 185; Schlechtriem/Schwenzer/Schroeter/*Schroeter*, 5th English ed., Art. 14 CISG, para. 84.

722. *See* Ch. 3 VI. 1. below on requirement clauses; on requirement contracts under the UCC: *White/Summers et al.*, §§ 3–9, pp. 129 et seq.

according to their output, frequently within certain limits contractually stipulated.[723] Both types of contracts give one party the power to unilaterally determine the quantity of goods.[724] As this suffices under Art. 14(1)'s determinability requirement, output and requirement contracts are sufficiently definite under the CISG.[725] Depending on the individual circumstances, a framework agreement may also be characterised as a requirement or output contract,[726] or at least include a requirement clause.[727] It can therefore be concluded that Art. 14(1) CISG is not an obstacle to the CISG's applicability to such framework agreements.[728]

Beyond that, it is doubtful whether the Convention attempts to regulate or contains general principles (Art. 7(2) CISG) on the issue of how a unilateral power should be exercised or on other limitations to such a power of determination; consequently, it is more convincing that the relevant domestic law should apply in that regard.[729]

2) Joint Determination by Both Parties

Lastly, an offer may contain a power of determination authorising both parties to jointly agree on the goods, their quantity or the purchase price at a later point in time.[730] In a case before the MKAC, a proposal for contract conclusion suggested that the price of the goods was to be agreed upon 10 days prior to the beginning of the new year.[731] The Tribunal maintained that this could not be interpreted as making provision for determining the price of the goods.[732] It held that this clause was too indefinite,

723. Schlechtriem/Schwenzer/Schroeter/*Schroeter*, 5th English ed., Art. 14 CISG, paras 50, 84; *see also* the explicit provision in § 2-306 UCC 'Output, requirements and exclusive dealings'.
724. Schlechtriem/Schwenzer/Schroeter/*Schroeter*, 5th English ed., Art. 14 CISG, para. 50.
725. Cf. Cour de Cassation, 30 June 2004, CISG-online 870; *Bridge*, Int'l Sale of Goods, para. 10.22; *Fogt*, p. 193; *Honnold/Flechtner*, Art. 14 CISG, para. 185; Schlechtriem/Schwenzer/Schroeter/*Schroeter*, 5th English ed., Intro Arts 14–24 CISG, para. 20; Schlechtriem/Schwenzer/Schroeter/*Schroeter*, 5th English ed., Art. 14 CISG, para. 50; *von Scheven*, pp. 105 et seq.; *C. Witz*, para. 231.42.
726. *See Bridge*, Int'l Sale of Goods, para. 10.22; Schlechtriem/Schwenzer/Schroeter/*Schroeter*, 5th English ed., Art. 14 CISG, para. 50 footnote 130.
727. *See* Ch. 3 VI. 1. below.
728. *Bridge*, Int'l Sale of Goods, para. 10.22: no reason to exclude such contracts from the CISG's sphere of application.
729. Ostendorf/*Ostendorf/Sauthoff*, § 18, para. 209; Schlechtriem/Schwenzer/Schroeter/*Schroeter*, 5th English ed., Art. 14 CISG, para. 85; Soergel/*Kreße*, Art. 14 CISG, para. 4; Witz/Salger/Lorenz/*W. Witz*, Art. 14 CISG, para. 48; differently, Brunner/Gottlieb/*Brunner/Pfisterer/Köster*, Art. 14 CISG, para. 11 (discretion must be exercised within the limits of good faith); *Honnold/Flechter*, Art. 14 CISG, para. 185 (the principles enshrined in Arts 8 and 7(1) CISG are 'tools to cope with these problems'); but *see C. Witz*, paras 231.65 et seq. (in particular with regard to Art. 1164(2) of the French Code Civil).
730. Brunner/Gottlieb/*Brunner/Pfisterer/Köster*, Art. 14 CISG, para. 11; Mankowski/*Spagnolo*, Art. 14 CISG, para. 3, Schlechtriem/Schwenzer/Schroeter/*Schroeter*, 5th English ed., Art. 14 CISG, para. 82; but *see Gillette/Walt*, p. 105; *Tallon*, § 7.03, s. 7.13.
731. MKAC, 3 March 1995, CISG-online 204.
732. MKAC, 3 March 1995, CISG-online 204; also sceptical with regard to clauses calling for joint determination of the price: *Gillette/Walt*, p. 105; *Tallon*, § 7.03, section 7.13.

since it merely expressed that the price shall be subject to a future agreement between the parties.[733]

In contrast, the prevailing view considers comparable clauses as 'making provision for determining' the price or other essential elements in accordance with Art. 14(1), sentence 2 CISG.[734] Once more, the requirements under Art. 14(1) CISG must be construed liberally and its broad wording should be taken into account. The approach of the prevailing view is thus more convincing than the aforementioned decision; clauses that call for a joint determination of the minimum requirements are sufficiently definite under Art. 14(1) CISG.

c. *Possibility of Modification and Derogation (Article 6 CISG)*

Regardless of the remarks above, the parties are free to derogate from any standard of sufficient definiteness set forth by Art. 14(1) CISG in accordance with Art. 6 CISG. Art. 14(1) CISG is not mandatory and subject to derogations or variations pursuant to Art. 6 CISG.[735] Consequently, the parties are free to derogate from or vary the minimum content required by this provision.[736] Such derogation or variations require nothing more than an agreement by the parties.[737] The parties can even implicitly agree on a derogation from or on a variation of the minimum content as per Art. 14(1), sentence 2 CISG.[738] This must, however, be proven by the party relying on such a deviation.[739]

This implies that some of the disputes concerning the standard of definiteness under Art. 14(1) CISG are of little practical relevance. For instance, if one were to adopt the view that a reference to future objective factors or a power of determination is not

733. MKAC, 3 March 1995, CISG-online 204; similarly, Witz/Salger/Lorenz/*W. Witz*, Art. 14 CISG, para. 31.
734. CIETAC, 25 December 1998, CISG-online 1135: price 'to be mutually agreed' – sufficiently definite proposal in accordance with Art. 14 CISG; Mankowski/*Spagnolo*, Art. 14 CISG, para. 3, Schlechtriem/Schwenzer/Schroeter/*Schroeter*, 5th English ed., Art. 14 CISG, para. 82; Schlechtriem/Schwenzer/Schroeter/*Schroeter*, 8th German ed., Art. 14 CISG, para. 72.
735. With the exception of the intention to be bound, which cannot be derogated from in a logical sense, *see* Schlechtriem/Schwenzer/Schroeter/*Schroeter*, 5th English ed., Art. 14 CISG, para. 26.
736. *Bridge*, Int'l Sale of Goods, para. 11.15; Brunner/Gottlieb/*Brunner/Pfisterer/Köster*, Art. 14 CISG, para. 12; *Honnold/Flechtner*, Art. 14 CISG, paras 188, 189; Mankowski/*Spagnolo*, Art. 14 CISG, para. 8; MüKoBGB/*Gruber*, Art. 14 CISG, para. 16; Ostendorf/*Ostendorf/Sauthoff*, § 18, para. 209; Schlechtriem/Schwenzer/Schroeter/*Schroeter*, 5th English ed., Art. 14 CISG, para. 25; Soergel/*Kreße*, Art. 14 CISG, para. 4; Staudinger/*Magnus*, Art. 14 CISG, para. 3; Witz/Salger/Lorenz/*W. Witz*, Art. 14 CISG, para. 13; pointing out issues of logic: *Honnold/Flechtner*, Intro Arts 14–24 CISG, para. 178.
737. *Bridge*, Int'l Sale of Goods, para. 11.15; Schlechtriem/Schwenzer/Schroeter/*Schroeter*, 5th English ed., Art. 14 CISG, para. 25; Witz/Salger/Lorenz/*W. Witz*, Art. 14 CISG, para. 13.
738. Mankowski/*Spagnolo*, Art. 14 CISG, para. 8; Witz/Salger/Lorenz/*W. Witz*, Art. 14 CISG, para. 13; cf. MüKoBGB/*Gruber*, Art. 14 CISG, para. 17; Schlechtriem/Schwenzer/Schroeter/*Schroeter*, 5th English ed., Art. 14 CISG, para. 25.
739. BeckOK/*Saenger*, Art. 6 CISG, para. 9; Brunner/Gottlieb/*Manner/Schmitt*, Art. 6 CISG, para. 11; Schlechtriem/Schwenzer/Schroeter/*Schroeter*, 5th English ed., Art. 14 CISG, para. 25; Schlechtriem/Schwenzer/Schroeter/*Ferrari*, 8th German ed., Art. 6 CISG, para. 38; cf. also OLG Linz, 23 January 2006, CISG-online 1377 (with regard to an exclusion of the CISG); CA Paris, 6 November 2001, CISG-online 677 (with regard to an exclusion of the CISG).

sufficiently definite under Art. 14(1), sentence 2 CISG, an offer could nevertheless be present, as the parties are free to agree on a derogation or variation of the provision in accordance with Art. 6 CISG. It is submitted that the standard of definiteness under the CISG should not be interpreted in an overly strict manner. It is not only sufficient to provide means for the determination of price and quantity, but the parties are also free to deviate from any standard set forth by Art. 14(1) CISG in accordance with Art. 6 CISG.

3. Preferable View: Article 14 CISG Does Not Hinder the CISG's Applicability to Framework Agreements

In light of this standard of sufficient definiteness, the following section will reconsider the decision in *Helen Kaminski v. MAP* and the related US cases.

a. *Rethinking* Helen Kaminski v. MAP & *Related US Cases*

The Court in *Helen Kaminski v. MAP* denied the CISG's applicability to a distribution agreement, as the contract did not contain sufficiently definite terms with regard to the goods.[740] It should, however, be noted that the parties in this case agreed upon a minimum purchase requirement for the purchase of fashion accessories for a total of USD 2 million per year.[741] Nonetheless, the seller advanced the argument that the distribution contract did not contain sufficiently definite terms with regard to the goods.[742] This view was apparently adopted by the Court.[743]

i. *Thorough Interpretation of Articles 14(1) and 6 CISG Was Neglected*

The court's reasoning is not convincing. To begin with, it is submitted that the parties typically bind themselves to carry out the individual transactions if they agree upon a minimum purchase requirement;[744] this was the case here. Consequently, the distribution contract in question would generally fall within the CISG's sphere of application.[745] Furthermore, a minimum purchase requirement normally permits drawing

740. *Helen Kaminski Pty. Ltd. v. Marketing Australian Products, Inc.*, US Dist. Ct. SD NY, 21 July 1997, CISG-online 297.
741. *Helen Kaminski Pty. Ltd. v. Marketing Australian Products, Inc.*, US Dist. Ct. SD NY, 21 July 1997, CISG-online 297.
742. *Helen Kaminski Pty. Ltd. v. Marketing Australian Products, Inc.*, US Dist. Ct. SD NY, 21 July 1997, CISG-online 297, p. 3.
743. *Helen Kaminski Pty. Ltd. v. Marketing Australian Products, Inc.*, US Dist. Ct. SD NY, 21 July 1997, CISG-online 297, p. 3 (although the minimum purchase requirement was not explicitly mentioned).
744. *See* Ch. 3 VI. 2. below.
745. *See* Ch. 3 III. 1 b. above.

conclusions regarding the quantity of the goods, as it specifies the quantity of the goods to a certain extent.[746]

Moreover, it can be posited that the parties granted the distributor (buyer) the power to unilaterally determine the terms regarding the goods at any time they issued an order for the supply of goods. Likewise, it is conceivable that the parties may have agreed to jointly determine specifics regarding the goods for each order issued by the distributor. Both scenarios would meet the standard set forth by Art. 14(1), sentence 2 CISG.[747] The Court should have had regard to the broad wording of Art. 14(1) CISG ('provisions for determining ...') and its flexible application as endorsed by the prevailing view.[748]

Alternatively, the parties may have implicitly derogated from the standard under Art. 14(1), sentence 2 CISG in accordance with Art. 6 CISG, thus deviating from the necessity to address specifics regarding the goods in the distribution agreement altogether.[749] Such a derogation could have been inferred from the circumstances and the fact that the framework agreement was being performed by both parties through the individual sales contracts.[750] Overall, the Court applied an overly strict standard of definiteness and is not convincing in its reasoning for not applying the CISG to the distribution contract.[751]

The decisions in *Viva Vino Import v. Franese Vini*,[752] *Gruppo Essenziero Italiano v. Aromi D'Italia*[753] and *Adonia Holding v. Adonia Organics*[754] are equally unconvincing:[755] these courts each relied on the position originally adopted by the Court in *Helen*

746. *Perales Viscasillas*, Extending the Scope, p. 123; *Perales Viscasillas*, Int'l Distribution Contracts and CISG, p. 50; cf. also OLG Graz, 28 September 2000, CISG-online 798.
747. Cf. Ostendorf/*Ostendorf/Sauthoff*, § 18, para. 209; *Perales Viscasillas*, Extending the Scope, p. 123; *Perales Viscasillas*, Int'l Distribution Contracts and CISG, p. 50; *see also* Schlechtriem/Schwenzer/Schroeter/*Schroeter*, 5th English ed., Intro Arts 14–24 CISG, para. 25; Schlechtriem/Schwenzer/Schroeter/*Schroeter*, 8th German ed., Vorbem. Arts 14–24 CISG, para. 20; *Schroeter*, para. 92.
748. HGer Aargau, 26 September 1997, CISG-online 329: the contract was concluded, although not all of the relevant terms had been addressed by the parties, such as the purchase price; cf. also Ostendorf/*Ostendorf/Sauthoff*, § 18, para. 209; *Perales Viscasillas*, Extending the Scope, pp. 123 et seq.; *Perales Viscasillas*, Int'l Distribution Contracts and CISG, pp. 56, 57; *see* Ch. 3 IV. 2. above for further references.
749. Ostendorf/*Ostendorf/Sauthoff*, § 18, para. 209; *Perales Viscasillas*, Extending the Scope, p. 131; *Perales Viscasillas*, Int'l Distribution Contracts and CISG, p. 57.
750. *Perales Viscasillas*, Extending the Scope, p. 130; *Perales Viscasillas*, Int'l Distribution Contracts and CISG, p. 57; cf. also Brunner/Gottlieb/*Brunner/Pfisterer/Köster*, Art. 14 CISG, para. 12; MüKoBGB/*Gruber*, Art. 14 CISG, para. 17: performance of the contract by both parties as a deviation from Art. 14(1) CISG.
751. Accord *Thiele*, IHR 2002, p. 11; *contra*: *Genys*, (1997/98) 17 J. L. & Com., pp. 420 et seq.
752. *Viva Vino Import Corp. v. Franese Vini S.r.l.*, US Dist. Ct. ED Penn., 29 August 2000, CISG-online 675.
753. *Gruppo Essenziero Italiano, S.p.A. v. Aromi D'Italia, Inc.*, US Dist. Ct. Mary., 27 July 2011, CISG-online 2223 (the US District Court for the District of Maryland did indeed make reference to the wording of Art. 14(1) CISG but unfortunately failed to provide an in-depth analysis of this provision).
754. *Adonia Holding GmbH v. Adonia Organics LLC*, US Dist. Ct. Ariz., 16 December 2014, CISG-online 2951.
755. In agreement *Bridge*, Int'l Sale of Goods, para. 10.22 in footnote 192: 'A reason that might be cited to conclude that an agreement is too uncertain to be enforced is a poor reason for concluding that a contract falls outside the CISG.'

Kaminski v. MAP and held that the CISG requires specific terms regarding goods, quantity and price for its applicability.[756] However, a thorough interpretation of Art. 14(1), sentence 2 CISG could have revealed that the parties may have agreed to unilaterally or jointly determine the quantity and price of the goods at a later point in time, or at least to derogate from or vary any standard set forth by this provision in accordance with Art. 6 CISG.[757] The CISG therefore does not necessitate specific terms regarding goods, quantity and price for its applicability.[758]

ii. *Article 14(1) CISG Is Not an 'Invalidating Provision'*

For the same reasons noted above, the decision in *Amco Ukservice & Promriladamco v. American Meter* is similarly unsatisfactory.[759] Furthermore, the Court in this case raised an additional consideration worth noting: it held that it would be challenging to conclude a framework agreement without triggering the CISG's 'invalidating provisions'.[760] With this phrase, it was referring to Art. 14(1)'s minimum content requirement.

Such a reading of Art. 14(1) CISG is inappropriate. This provision should not be characterised as an 'invalidating provision'.[761] Art. 14(1), sentence 2 CISG does not stipulate that the agreement is void or unenforceable if it is not sufficiently definite.[762] Moreover, it does not employ mandatory language but merely states that a proposal is sufficiently definite under certain circumstances.[763] Art. 14(1), sentence 2 CISG rather establishes a default 'guideline' that can be derogated from or modified in accordance with Art. 6 CISG.[764] The Convention also acknowledges offers that do not meet the

756. *Gruppo Essenziero Italiano, S.p.A. v. Aromi D'Italia, Inc.*, US Dist. Ct. Mary., 27 July 2011, CISG-online 2223, p. 4; *Adonia Holding GmbH v. Adonia Organics LLC*, US Dist. Ct. Ariz., 16 December 2014, CISG-online 2951, p. 4.
757. Accord *Thiele*, IHR 2002, p. 11; *see also* Ostendorf/*Ostendorf/Sauthoff*, § 18, para. 209; *Perales Viscasillas*, Extending the Scope, pp. 123 et seq., 130, 131; *Perales Viscasillas*, Int'l Distribution Contracts and CISG, pp. 56, 57.
758. Cf. *Genpharm Inc. v. Pliva-Lachema A.S., Pliva d.d.*, US Dist. Ct. ED NY, 19 March 2005, CISG-online 1006, para. 20; *Bridge*, Int'l Sale of Goods, para. 10.22 n 209, 11.14; *Perales Viscasillas*, Extending the Scope, pp. 130, 131; *Perales Viscasillas*, Int'l Distribution Contracts and CISG, pp. 56, 57; *Schumacher*, IHR 2005, p. 149.
759. *Amco Ukservice & Promriladamco v. American Meter Comp.*, US Dist. Ct. ED Penn., 29 March 2004, CISG-online 1664; but *see Gillette/Walt*, pp. 62, 63, agreeing with this decision.
760. *Amco Ukservice & Promriladamco v. American Meter Comp.*, US Dist. Ct. ED Penn., 29 March 2004, CISG-online 1664, p. 5.
761. Accord *Honnold/Flechtner*, Art. 14 CISG, para. 189.
762. With regard to the price: *Bridge*, Int'l Sale of Goods, para. 11.14: 'Yet it is noticeable that the approach of the CISG is unlike that of the common law: it does not say that the agreement is void or unenforceable. Rather, it focuses upon the offer and, even here, does not say that the offer is void or ineffectual.'; *Honnold/Flechtner*, Art. 14 CISG, para. 189; cf. also Soergel/*Kreße*, Art. 14 CISG, para. 4 (Art. 14 CISG cannot be re-interpreted as mandatory law).
763. *Honnold/Flechtner*, Art. 14 CISG, para. 189: Art. 14(1) CISG does not use the word 'must' which would have clarified that it is a 'rule of validity'.
764. Cf. *Bridge*, Int'l Sale of Goods, para. 11.14; Brunner/Gottlieb/*Brunner/Pfisterer/Köster*, Art. 14 CISG, para. 12; Mankowski/*Spagnolo*, Art. 14 CISG, para. 8; MüKoBGB/*Gruber*, Art. 14 CISG, para. 16; Schlechtriem/Schwenzer/Schroeter/*Schroeter*, 5th English ed., Art. 14 CISG, para. 25;

requirements of Art. 14(1), sentence 2 CISG,[765] suggesting that this provision is not directly related to the CISG's sphere of application.[766]

For all of these reasons, the approach in US case law is not convincing. A thorough interpretation of Art. 14(1) CISG could have led to other outcomes or at least a more satisfying examination of the rationale that has been reproduced ever since the decision in *Helen Kaminski v. MAP*. The view held by this study has also been supported by one US Court in *Genpharm v. Pliva-Lachemak*.[767] The US District Court for the Eastern District of New York stated that 'the applicability of the CISG is not restricted to contracts after formation or contracts containing definite prices or quantities.'[768] Indeed, the Convention does not merely apply to sales contracts after their formation. Part II of the Convention governs the formation of the contract. If the Convention *ab initio* required a fully concluded contract, this part would be superfluous.[769] Moreover, the Court correctly noted that the Convention's applicability is not restricted to contracts containing definite prices or quantities.[770] However, this decision unfortunately appears to have been overlooked in subsequent decisions by US Courts.[771]

b. Open Terms in Framework Agreements Are Not an Obstacle for the CISG's Applicability

Based on the previous remarks, this study holds that the lack of sufficient definiteness with regard to the goods, their quantity and the purchase price as per Art. 14(1) CISG is not an obstacle to the Convention's applicability to framework agreements.[772] The

Soergel/*Kreße*, Art. 14 CISG, para. 4; Staudinger/*Magnus*, Art. 14 CISG, para. 3; Witz/Salger/Lorenz/*W. Witz*, Art. 14 CISG, para. 13.

765. *Bridge*, Int'l Sale of Goods, paras 11.14, 11.15.
766. *See Perales Viscasillas*, Extending the Scope, pp. 126, 130, 131; *Perales Viscasillas*, Int'l Distribution Contracts and CISG, pp. 53, 56, 57.
767. *Genpharm Inc. v. Pliva-Lachema A.S., Pliva d.d.*, US Dist. Ct. ED NY, 19 March 2005, CISG-online 1006 (although the reasoning of the Court is doubtful, as it, *inter alia*, relied on the UCC).
768. *Genpharm Inc. v. Pliva-Lachema A.S., Pliva d.d.*, US Dist. Ct. ED NY, 19 March 2005, CISG-online 1006, para. 20.
769. *Schumacher*, IHR 2005, p. 149; cf. also Schlechtriem/Schwenzer/Schroeter/*Schroeter*, 5th English ed., Intro Arts 14–24 CISG, para. 78.
770. *Genpharm Inc. v. Pliva-Lachema A.S., Pliva d.d.*, US Dist. Ct. ED NY, 19 March 2005, CISG-online 1006, para. 20; cf. also *Bridge*, Int'l Sale of Goods, para. 10.22 n 209, 11.14; *Perales Viscasillas*, Extending the Scope, pp. 124, 125; *Perales Viscasillas*, Int'l Distribution Contracts and CISG, pp. 56, 57; *Schumacher*, IHR 2005, p. 149.
771. *See Reecon North America, LLC v. Du-Hope Int'l Group et al.*, US Dist. Ct. WD Penn., 20 June 2019, CISG-online 4425; *Adonia Holding GmbH v. Adonia Organics LLC*, US Dist. Ct. Ariz., 16 December 2014, CISG-online 2951; *Gruppo Essenziero Italiano, S.p.A. v. Aromi D'Italia, Inc.*, US Dist. Ct. Mary., 27 July 2011, CISG-online 2223; *Claus Ettensberger Corp. v. TechArt Automobildesign GmbH*, US Dist. Ct. CD Cali., 4 May 2011, CISG-online 4648; left open in *W.W. Sports Importadora Exportadora e Comercial Ltda v. BPI Sports, LLC et al.*, US Dist. Ct. SD Florida, 10 August 2016, CISG-online 3999, para. 10.
772. Accord Supr. Ct. Poland, 27 January 2006, CISG-online 1399; OLG München, 22 September 1995, CISG-online 208; *Perales Viscasillas*, Extending the Scope, pp. 130, 131; *Perales Viscasillas*, Int'l Distribution Contracts and CISG, pp. 56, 57 Schlechtriem/Schwenzer/*Schlechtriem*,

standard of sufficient definiteness is typically met even in instances where a framework agreement leaves several terms open to be agreed upon in the individual sales contracts or individual orders.[773] This position must be substantiated in two ways.

i. Subsequent Determination in Individual Contracts Suffices under the CISG

Some scholars highlight that the CISG can only be applied to a framework agreement if the contract is sufficiently definite regarding the price and quantity of the goods, so that there is no need to conclude individual sales contracts.[774] This view implies that a framework agreement is not sufficiently definite if the minimum content is determined solely in the individual sales contracts concluded on the basis of the framework agreement.[775] A framework agreement that includes an obligation to conclude individual sales contracts but leaves some essential terms open (e.g., the price) would not be sufficiently definite and would not fall within the CISG's sphere of application if one were to follow this approach.

The more preferable view is that the standard of definiteness under Art. 14(1) CISG, sentence 2 CISG is also met in cases where the essential terms are merely stipulated in the individual sales contracts concluded on the basis of the framework agreement.[776] The provisions agreed upon by the parties for subsequent determination of the minimum content are in accordance with the standard set forth by Art. 14(1), sentence 2 CISG.[777] Art. 14(1) CISG does not present any obstacles to such an approach.[778] In any case, the parties are free to partially exclude Art. 14(1) CISG in line with Art. 6 CISG. This may arguably be the case if they agree to conclude individual sales contracts in the future and to subsequently determine the minimum content of these contracts.

The opposing view is not consistent with the treatment of preliminary agreements under the Convention: such agreements are governed by the CISG, even if the

---

2nd English ed., Intro Arts 14-24 CISG, para. 7; Schlechtriem/Schwenzer/Schroeter/*Schroeter*, 5th English ed., Intro Arts 14-24 CISG, para. 25; Schlechtriem/Schwenzer/Schroeter/*Schroeter*, 8th German ed., Vorbem. Arts 14-24 CISG, para. 20; *Schroeter*, para. 92; *see also* Ostendorf/*Ostendorf/Sauthoff*, § 18, para. 209; *C. Witz*, para. 112.61.

773. Schlechtriem/Schwenzer/*Schlechtriem*, 2nd English ed., Intro Arts 14-24 CISG, para. 7; Schlechtriem/Schwenzer/Schroeter/*Schroeter*, 5th English ed., Intro Arts 14-24 CISG, para. 25; Schlechtriem/Schwenzer/Schroeter/*Schroeter*, 8th German ed., Vorbem. Arts 14-24 CISG, para. 20; *Schroeter*, para. 92; cf. also Supr. Ct. Poland, 27 January 2006, CISG-online 1399; OLG München, 22 September 1995, CISG-online 208; *C. Witz*, para. 112.61.
774. MüKoHGB/*B. Köhler*, Art. 1 CISG, para. 21; MüKoHGB/*Sommerfeld*, Art. 73 CISG, para. 4; Soergel/*Kreße*, Art. 1 CISG, para. 22; *see also Grieser*, p. 134.
775. Cf. Soergel/*Kreße*, Art. 1 CISG, para. 22.
776. Schlechtriem/Schwenzer/*Schlechtriem*, 2nd English ed., Intro Arts 14-24 CISG, para. 7; Schlechtriem/Schwenzer/Schroeter/*Schroeter*, 8th German ed., Vorbem. Arts 14-24 CISG, para. 20; cf. also Schlechtriem/Schwenzer/Schroeter/*Schroeter*, 5th English ed., Intro Arts 14-24 CISG, para. 25; *Schroeter*, para. 92.
777. Cf. Schlechtriem/Schwenzer/Schroeter/*Schroeter*, 5th English ed., Intro Arts 14-24 CISG, paras 23, 24; *see also* OLG München, 22 September 1995, CISG-online 208 ('*Eine spätere Konkretisierung genügt* […]').
778. Cf. Supr. Ct. Poland, 27 January 2006, CISG-online 1399, p. 8.

minimum content (Art. 14(1) CISG) is stipulated merely in the main sales contract.[779] For the purposes of Art. 14(1) CISG, it is sufficient for the necessary minimum content to be determined in the main sales contract,[780] which is a separate contract from the preliminary agreement.

ii. Contract Formation Is Typically Not Disputed

It is typically clear in the cases under discussion that a framework agreement has been concluded and is being performed through the individual sales; contract formation will only rarely be the matter of dispute.[781] As Art. 14(1) CISG is not an 'invalidating provision' that is directly related to the Convention's sphere of application, sufficient definiteness is usually not a problem, provided that it is otherwise evident that a CISG contract has been concluded.[782] The aforementioned discussion therefore misses the crucial point: the relevant question is whether there is a framework agreement that falls within the CISG's sphere of application.[783] This, *inter alia*, depends on the fact whether the parties bound themselves to carry out the individual transactions; this is the case if the parties include sales obligations in *sensu stricto* or an obligation to conclude individual sales contracts in their agreement.[784]

Whether the parties bound themselves to carry out the individual transactions is essentially a matter of contract interpretation and will turn on the individual content of a framework agreement. In cases where a framework agreement is rather definite with regard to the essential sales elements, this may be considered an indication that the parties bound themselves to carry out the individual transactions, and vice versa, the absence of definiteness may indicate the opposite. A lack of sufficient definiteness is, however, irrelevant if it is evident from other circumstances that the parties have bound themselves to conduct the individual transactions.[785] The definiteness of a framework agreement is thus one of multiple circumstances that is relevant for the

779. Schlechtriem/Schwenzer/*Schlechtriem*, 2nd English ed., Intro Arts 14–24 CISG, para. 7; Schlechtriem/Schwenzer/Schroeter/*Schroeter*, 5th English ed., Intro Arts 14–24 CISG, para. 23.
780. Schlechtriem/Schwenzer/Schroeter/*Schroeter*, 5th English ed., Intro Arts 14–24 CISG, para. 23 (citing Cour de Cassation, 30 June 2004, CISG-online 870 and *Genpharm Inc. v. Pliva-Lachema A.S., Pliva d.d.*, US Dist. Ct. ED NY, 19 March 2005, CISG-online 1006); cf. also Schlechtriem/Schwenzer/*Schlechtriem*, 2nd English ed., Intro Arts 14–24 CISG, para. 7.
781. *Perales Viscasillas*, Extending the Scope, p. 130; *Perales Viscasillas*, Int'l Distribution Contracts and CISG, p. 57; cf. also HGer Aargau, 26 September 1997, CISG-online 329, where the Court held that a contract was undoubtedly concluded and that the respondent merely tried to get out of the contract by invoking its insufficient definiteness.
782. *See* Ch. 3 IV. 3. a. ii. above.
783. *Perales Viscasillas*, Extending the Scope, p. 130; *Perales Viscasillas*, Int'l Distribution Contracts and CISG, p. 57: 'The issue is a different one [not one of contract conclusion] and it is related to the scope of application of the Vienna Convention.'
784. *See* Ch. 3 III. 1. above; in addition, it must be determined whether the sales or the non-sales part constitutes the preponderant part of the framework agreement, *see* Ch. 4 below on this issue.
785. Cf. *Perales Viscasillas*, Extending the Scope, p. 131; *Perales Viscasillas*, Int'l Distribution Contracts and CISG, p. 57.

assessment whether a particular framework agreement binds the parties to carry out the individual transactions.[786]

4. Conclusion

Multiple scholars and in particular US courts maintain that framework agreements should not be governed by the CISG, reasoning that they are not sufficiently definite with regard to the goods, their quantity and/or the purchase price. This view primarily relies on Art. 14(1) CISG, which indirectly outlines the minimum content requirements for any CISG contract. However, Art. 14(1) CISG allows parties to make 'provisions for determining the quantity and the price'. This sentence is generally interpreted in a liberal manner. A contract is sufficiently definite if it makes references to objective factors or includes a unilateral or bilateral power of determination. Furthermore, the parties are free to derogate from any standard set out by Art. 14(1) CISG in accordance with Art. 6 CISG.

In light of this liberal standard, the view held by US courts and certain scholars appears to be overly strict. The preferable view is that open or indefinite terms in a framework agreement should not present an obstacle to the CISG's applicability. For the purposes of Art. 14(1) CISG, it is sufficient for the necessary minimum content to be determined solely in the individual orders or even in the individual sales contracts. In any event, the parties are free to derogate from the standard of definiteness set out by Art. 14(1) CISG in accordance with Art. 6 CISG.

Essentially, this discussion misses the crucial point; the relevant question is whether framework agreements fall within the CISG's sphere of application. The CISG is not restricted to contracts that contain sufficiently definite terms but is rather flexible in that regard. The 'sufficient definiteness' requirement is, in fact, not directly related to the CISG's sphere of application. Art. 14(1) CISG is not an 'invalidating provision'.

V. RELATIONSHIP BETWEEN THE LAW APPLICABLE TO THE FRAMEWORK AGREEMENT AND THE LAW APPLICABLE TO THE INDIVIDUAL CONTRACTS

This study has previously analysed the applicability of the CISG to different types of framework agreements. It has also been established that the Convention may, in any event, be applicable to the individual sales contracts concluded on the basis of a framework agreement.[787] In cases where the CISG is merely applicable to the individual

786. Moreover, it can indicate the structure of the framework agreement, i.e., whether the parties agreed on sales obligations *stricto sensu* or merely an obligation to conclude individual sales contracts, *see* Ch. 3 III. 1. a. ii. above.

787. CA Reims, 30 April 2013, CISG-online 2479; OLG Hamburg, 15 July 2010, CISG-online 2448; Foreign Trade Ct. of Arbitration of the CC and Industry of Serbia, 28 January 2009, CISG-online 1856; CA Versailles, 19 February 2004, CISG-online 3345, confirmed by Cour de Cassation, 20 February 2007, CISG-online 1492; CA Vaud, 8 December 2000, CISG-online 1841; OGer Luzern, 8 January 1997, CISG-online 228; OLG Koblenz, 17 September 1993, CISG-online 91, para. 42; *Hoffbauer*, p. 49; Schlechtriem/Schwenzer/Schroeter/*Schroeter*, 5th English ed., Intro Arts

sales contracts, while domestic law is applicable to the framework agreement, different laws would govern economically related contracts.[788] One might inquire as to whether there should be any relation between the laws applicable to these contracts, given their interconnection. The interplay between the law governing the framework agreement and the law applicable to the individual sales contracts will be examined in the next section.

1. Necessity to Apply the CISG to All Related Contracts?

In the context of discussing the CISG's applicability to framework agreements, some scholars have put forth the argument that the CISG should be applicable to a framework agreement in cases where it is applicable to the individual sales contracts.[789] This view posits that applying the CISG solely to the individual sales contracts, but not to the framework agreement itself, results in inconsistencies.[790] Consequently, this approach essentially attempts to extend the application of the CISG not only to the individual sales contracts but also to the framework agreement.

More specifically, *Schwenzer* holds that there may be issues if the CISG were applied merely to the individual sales contracts, but not to the framework agreement itself.[791] She illustrates her concerns with the case of hardship as a practical example: the prerequisites for the seller to be exempted from their obligations based on hardship may differ significantly under the framework agreement governed by domestic law compared to the prerequisites under the individual sales contracts governed by the CISG.[792] She posits that these issues are related and should be addressed through similar solutions, namely by applying the same law.[793] Thus, *Schwenzer* concludes that

14–24 CISG, para. 25; Schlechtriem/Schwenzer/Schroeter/*Schroeter*, 8th German ed., Vorbem. Arts 14–24 CISG, para. 20; *Schroeter*, para. 94; Staudinger/*Magnus*, Art. 1 CISG, para. 37; *Walt*, p. 85.

788. *Perović*, (2011) 59 Belgrade L. Rev., p. 188; *Torsello*, p. 246; *Walt*, p. 85; cf. on Swiss private international law: *Furrer/Lohri*, pp. 40 et seq.
789. *Schwenzer*, Challenges of the 2020s, p. 44; *Piltz*, NJW 2019, p. 2517; *Piltz*, Int. Wirtschaftsrecht, § 18, para. 7; cf. also *Thieffry*, Dr. prat. com. int. 1993, pp. 67 et seq.
790. *Schwenzer*, Challenges of the 2020s, p. 44; *Piltz*, NJW 2019, p. 2517; cf. also *Schwenzer/Munoz*, para. 8.05; *Thieffry*, Dr. prat. com. int. 1993, p. 67; *Walt*, p. 85, mentioning that this discrepancy in law is inconsequential when the applicable domestic law and the CISG are identical – however, in certain domestic jurisdictions there may be more rigorous formal requirements.
791. *Schwenzer*, Challenges of the 2020s, p. 44; *Bridge*, Choice of Law and the CISG, p. 96.
792. *Schwenzer*, Challenges of the 2020s, p. 44; this example is also mentioned by *Bridge*, Choice of Law and the CISG, p. 96 ('for example, the seller of the goods might be able to plead an exception under Art. 79 CISG with regard to the particular sale when the law governing the framework agreement itself, an output contract for example, would not regard the seller's general duty to deliver as having been excused, discharged or suspended.').
793. *Schwenzer*, Challenges of the 2020s, p. 44; cf. also *Bridge*, Choice of Law and the CISG, p. 96, who, however, arrives at a different conclusion (*quasi-depeçage*).

the Convention should also apply to the framework agreement in any instance where it is applicable to the individual sales contracts.[794]

Piltz presents a slightly different perspective, suggesting that the law applicable to the framework agreement and the law applicable to the individual sales contracts should be determined in a consistent manner. He maintains that this requires the framework agreement predetermining clauses for the individual sales contracts, which remain without any legal relevance as long as they are not 'activated' by concluding individual sales contracts.[795] He draws the conclusion that the CISG should also govern the framework agreement if it is applicable to the individual sales contracts.[796]

Both scholars derive conclusions from the CISG's applicability to the individual sales contracts with regard to the applicability of the Convention to the framework agreement itself. This view implies that there is an interplay between the law governing the individual sales contracts and the law applicable to the framework agreement.

2. Discussion under the Rome I Regulation and Swiss International Private Law Rules

The interplay of the law applicable to the framework agreement and the law governing the individual sales contracts has also been discussed under international private law rules, such as the Rome I Regulation and Swiss international private law rules. Comparable to the discussion under the CISG, it has been debated whether the framework agreement and the individual contracts should be governed by the same law. The current legal situation under the Rome I Regulation and Swiss international private law rules will be briefly outlined in the following.

Under Art. 4(1)(f) Rome I Regulation as well as Art. 117 PILA, distribution agreements, which are a subtype of framework agreements, are subject to the law at the habitual residence of the distributor (i.e., the buyer) in the absence of a law chosen by the parties.[797] In contrast, the law applicable to the individual sales contracts must be determined separately, according to the prevailing view.[798] The individual sales contracts are either governed by the CISG or the law of the seller's country of habitual

794. *Schwenzer*, Challenges of the 2020s, p. 44, who holds that she is convinced 'that the CISG is suitable to govern service contracts', suggesting that certain (distribution) framework agreements might be characterised as service contracts.
795. *Piltz*, NJW 2019, p. 2517; *Piltz*, Int. Wirtschaftsrecht, § 18, para. 7.
796. *Piltz*, NJW 2019, p. 2517; cf. also *Piltz*, Int. Wirtschaftsrecht, § 18, para. 7.
797. OLG Düsseldorf, 11 July 1996, CISG-online 201; Kronke *et al./Killias/Marzorati*, Teil G, para. 343; MüKoBGB/*Martiny*, Art. 4 Rome I Regulation, para. 157; Staudinger/*Magnus*, Art. 4 Rome I Regulation, para. 77; Reithmann/Martiny/*Häuslschmid*, paras 2050 et seq.; *Wójtowicz*, ERCL 2018, p. 147; BSK IPRG/*Amstustz/Wang/Silvan Gohari*, Art. 117 PILA, para. 64; CR LDIP/*Bonomi*, Art. 117 PILA, para. 40; *Vischer/Huber/Oser*, para. 667; ZK IPRG/*Kren Kostkiewicz*, Art. 117 PILA, para. 193.
798. OLG Jena, 27 August 2008, CISG-online 1820; *Amco Ukservice & Promriladamco v. American Meter Comp.*, US Dist. Ct. ED Penn., 29 March 2004, CISG-online 1664; KGer Schaffhausen, 23 April 2002, CISG-online 731; OLG Hamm, 5 November 1997, CISG-online 381; OLG Düsseldorf, 11 July 1996, CISG-online 201; BGH, 28 March 1979, NJW 1979, 1782 (on the ULIS); CHK/*Jacobs*, Innominatverträge/AVV, para. 44; *Hoffbauer*, p. 47; Kronke *et al./Killias/Marzorati*, Teil G, para. 347; Reithmann/Martiny/*Fabig*, para. 37.146;

residence in accordance with Art. 4(1)(a) Rome I Regulation and Art. 3(1) 1955 Hague Convention in conjunction with Art. 118(1) PILA.[799] The underlying rationale is that the characteristic performance under the framework agreement and the characteristic performance under the individual sales contracts are considered to be different.[800]

Nevertheless, a number of scholars advance the argument that the law applicable to the framework agreement should also be applicable to the individual sales contracts subsequently concluded.[801] This school of thought posits that these contracts are linked and should thus be governed by the same law.[802] Under the Rome I Regulation, this could arguably be based on Art. 4(3) Rome I Regulation (so-called escape clause), thereby deviating from the rules in Art. 4(1)(a) and 4(1)(f) Rome I Regulation.[803] Moreover, it has sometimes been highlighted that the framework agreement is, *inter alia*, performed by concluding individual sales contracts.[804] It would therefore be coherent to apply the same law to the framework agreement as well as the individual sales contracts, given that the obligations under these contracts are intertwined.[805] Finally, it has been mentioned that a breach of an individual sales contract may also be relevant for the framework agreement, which is another reason why one single law should be applied to such 'overlapping' issues.[806]

In response to that, the proponents of the opposing and probably prevailing view emphasise that the framework agreement and the individual sales contracts are legally independent contracts, and hence the applicable law must be determined independently.[807] Even though the framework agreement and the individual sales contracts are linked and may be related in terms of their content, they may still diverge with regard

Staudinger/*Magnus*, Art. 4 Rome I Regulation, paras 72, 76, 78; *Vischer/Huber/Oser*, para. 669; cf. also *Magnus*, FS Bonell, p. 1779.

799. OLG Düsseldorf, 11 July 1996, CISG-online 201; CHK/*Jacobs*, Innominatverträge/AVV, para. 44; Kronke *et al.*/*Killias/Marzorati*, Teil G, para. 347; Reithmann/Martiny/*Häuslschmid*, para. 2046; Staudinger/*Magnus*, Art. 4 Rome I Regulation, para. 78; cf. also BSK IPRG/*Amstutz/Wang/Gohari*, Art. 118 PILA, paras 10, 11.
800. Cf. *Hoffbauer*, p. 47.
801. *Furrer/Lohri*, pp. 45, 46; *Jayme*, p. 319; MüKoBGB/*Martiny*, Art. 4 Rome I Regulation, paras 158, 325; *Rehbinder*, IPRax 1982, p. 7; *Wójtowicz*, ERCL 2018, pp. 146 et seq.; *Vischer/Huber/Oser*, para. 669.
802. *Furrer/Lohri*, p. 45; MüKoBGB/*Martiny*, Art. 4 Rome I Regulation, paras 158, 325; *Rehbinder*, IPRax 1982, p. 7; Staudinger/*Magnus*, Art. 4 Rome I Regulation, para. 136; *Wójtowicz*, ERCL 2018, p. 146 (with regard to cases where a distribution contract includes a choice of law clause).
803. Staudinger/*Magnus*, Art. 4 Rome I Regulation, para. 136; *Wójtowicz*, ERCL 2018, pp. 147, 148.
804. *Vischer/Huber/Oser*, para. 669; *Wójtowicz*, ERCL 2018, p. 146 (with regard to cases where a distribution contract contains a choice of law clause).
805. *Vischer/Huber/Oser*, para. 669; *Wójtowicz*, ERCL 2018, p. 146; cf. also *Rehbinder*, IPRax 1982, p. 7.
806. *Wójtowicz*, ERCL 2018, p. 156.
807. OLG Jena, 27 August 2008, CISG-online 1820, para. 16; *Amco Ukservice & Promriladamco v. American Meter Comp.*, 29 March 2004, CISG-online 1664; OLG Hamm, 5 November 1997, CISG-online 381; OLG Düsseldorf, 11 July 1996, CISG-online 201; BGH, 4 April 1979, BGHZ 74, 136, 140 (distribution contract must be distinguished from individual sales contracts); *Hoffbauer*, pp. 47, 48; Kronke *et al.*/*Killias/Marzorati*, Teil G, para. 347; Reithmann/Martiny/*Häuslschmid*, para. 2046; cf. also Foreign Trade Ct. of Arbitration of the CC and Industry of Serbia, 28 January 2009, CISG-online 1856.

to the characteristic performance.[808] Furthermore, it is possible to address performance, any breaches or other disputes related to the contracts separately from each other.[809]

3. Preferable View

The subsequent section will discuss whether the law applicable to the framework agreement and to the individual sales contracts should generally be determined separately or unitarily. This study has distinguished between various types of framework agreements, given that a broad notion of framework agreements has been adopted. The following discussion will refer to these various types of framework agreements.

a. *The Applicable Law Should Generally Be Determined Separately*

If a framework agreement contains sales obligations *stricto sensu*, the individual transactions are part of the framework agreement and do not constitute independent contracts.[810] Consequently, there will only be one singular contract, subject to one law. The identification of the applicable law is less problematic in such cases. If the prerequisites for the CISG's application are met, the Convention will govern the framework agreement as well as the individual orders, which are part of the contract.[811] If the CISG is not applicable, for instance, based on Art. 3(2) CISG, and the parties have not included a choice of law clause in their contract, the applicable domestic law will typically depend on the characteristic performance of the contract in accordance with the relevant rules of private international law.[812]

If a framework agreement includes an obligation to conclude individual sales contracts, a distinction between the framework agreement and the individual sales contracts is implied.[813] It has been submitted that such framework agreements generally fall within the CISG's sphere of application. This is based on a general principle that the CISG may apply to related or closely linked contracts, provided that they establish or directly affect the parties' rights and obligations under a CISG contract. Framework agreements that contain an obligation to conclude multiple sales contracts governed by the Convention, in substance, establish rights and obligations under CISG contracts. To put it another way, the CISG's application can be justified by reference to the precontractual element of such framework agreements.[814] There is thus merit to the argument that the framework agreement is, *inter alia*, performed by concluding individual sales contracts, which is why the obligations under these

808. OLG Düsseldorf, 11 July 1996, CISG-online 201; OLG Hamm, 5 November 1997, CISG-online 381; *Hoffbauer*, pp. 47, 48; Kronke *et al./Killias/Marzorati*, Teil G, para. 347.
809. Cf. *Hoffbauer*, p. 47; Kronke *et al./Killias/Marzorati*, Teil G, para. 347.
810. *See* Ch. 2 III. 1. above.
811. In addition to Art. 1 CISG, it is also necessary to consider Art. 3 CISG, *see* Ch. 4 below.
812. *See* Art. 4 Rome I Regulation and Art. 117 Swiss PIL.
813. *See* Ch. 2 III. 1 above.
814. *See* Ch. 3 III. 1. b. ii. 2) b) above.

contracts are closely intertwined.[815] Yet, the conclusion reached by the proponents of this argument is not persuasive. It is not appropriate to apply a single law to both the framework agreement and the individual sales contracts by default, even if the former agreement includes a precontractual element.

The framework agreement may include additional obligations that outweigh its (precontractual) sales part.[816] In such cases, the CISG is not applicable to the framework agreement according to Art. 3(2) CISG, as the non-sales part is preponderant.[817] Nevertheless, the Convention may be applicable to the individual sales contracts if they meet the requirements for its application.[818] Outside of the CISG, the characteristic performance under a framework agreement may diverge from that under the individual sales contracts in instances where the framework agreement includes substantial non-sales obligations. This would result in the applicability of a different law to the framework agreement in comparison to the individual sales contracts.[819] Accordingly, even if a framework agreement is closely linked or related to the individual sales contracts, it is not appropriate to determine the law unitarily for all linked contracts. In fact, the contracts may still significantly differ from each other.[820] It is therefore preferable to conclude that the law applicable to framework agreements that contain an obligation to conclude individual sales contracts and to the individual sales contracts must be determined separately. By doing so, the specific circumstances of each case can be taken into consideration.[821] In some cases this may, nevertheless, result in the applicability of the same law to all related contracts.

If framework agreements are not binding with regard to the individual transaction, there is likewise a distinction between the framework agreement and the individual sales contracts.[822] The law applicable to these contracts should also be determined separately.[823] In contrast to the aforementioned framework agreements, these framework agreements lack a precontractual element and therefore do not fall within the scope of the general principle according to which closely linked or related contracts may be governed by the CISG. Therefore, this study has advanced the argument that these contracts are generally outside the Convention's sphere of application.[824] Although the framework agreement as such falls outside the CISG's

815. With this argument: *C. Meyer*, Alleinvertrieb, pp. 463 et seq.; *Vischer/Huber/Oser*, para. 669; cf. also *Rehbinder*, IPRax 1982, p. 7; *Wójtowicz*, ERCL 2018, p. 146.
816. OLG Düsseldorf, 11 July 1996, CISG-online 201; OLG Hamm, 5 November 1997, CISG-online 381; *Hoffbauer*, pp. 47, 48; Kronke *et al./Killias/Marzorati*, Teil G, para. 347.
817. *See* Ch. 4 below for more detail.
818. *See* only CA Reims, 30 April 2013, CISG-online 2479; HGer Aargau, 10 March 2010, CISG-online 2176; OGer Luzern, 8 January 1997, CISG-online 228; *Magnus*, FS Bonell, p. 1779: 'They [the individual sales contracts] are not necessarily subject to the same law as the framework contract [...]'; Reithmann/Martiny/*Fabig*, para. 37.68.
819. Cf. OLG Düsseldorf, 11 July 1996, CISG-online 201; *Hoffbauer*, pp. 47, 48; Kronke *et al./Killias/Marzorati*, Teil G, para. 347.
820. Cf. *Hoffbauer*, p. 48.
821. *See* already *Hoffbauer*, p. 48.
822. Cf. only OLG Düsseldorf, 23 July 1997, CISG-online 276; *Budde/Geks*, ZVertriebsR 2012, p. 37; Martinek/Semler/Flohr/*Budde/Eckhoff*, § 40, para. 9.
823. Accord OLG Jena, 27 August 2008, CISG-online 1820, para. 16; OLG Hamm, 5 November 1997, CISG-online 381; OLG Düsseldorf, 11 July 1996, CISG-online 201; *Hoffbauer*, pp. 47, 48.
824. *See* Ch. 3 III. 2. b. i. above.

sphere of application, the individual sales contracts may still be governed by the Convention, provided that all prerequisites for its application are met.[825] In this context, the Court of Appeal Versailles explicitly held that it is irrelevant for the CISG's application whether the individual sales contracts were concluded on the basis of a distribution contract, which itself fell outside the Convention's sphere of application.[826] Outside of the CISG, there equally appears to be no reason to apply the same law to these contracts under the relevant private international law rules. Furthermore, the autonomy of the contracts is not affected by the fact that the framework agreement may partially predetermine the content of the individual sales contracts.[827]

b. No Necessity to Apply the Same Law to the Framework Agreement and the Individual Sales Contracts

Contrary to some of the views outlined above,[828] it is not necessary to apply one unitary law to the framework agreement and the individual sales contracts for the sake of coherence. To illustrate, consider the case of hardship. At the outset, it should be noted that there is some controversy surrounding the question of whether the Convention covers hardship and, if so, to what extent.[829] For the purposes of this example, this study will assume that the Convention covers hardship.[830]

One of the criticisms was that the prerequisites for an exemption based on hardship may differ in cases where the framework agreement is governed by domestic law, while the individual sales contracts are governed by the CISG.[831] This is, however, not necessarily an issue. The nature of the obligations set forth in the framework agreement may diverge significantly from the nature of the obligations set forth in the

825. Almost undisputed: CA Reims, 30 April 2013, CISG-online 2479; HGer Aargau, 10 March 2010, CISG-online 2176, para. 22; Foreign Trade Ct. of Arbitration of the CC and Industry of Serbia, 28 January 2009, CISG-online 1856; CA Versailles, 19 February 2004, CISG-online 3345, confirmed by Cour de Cassation, 20 February 2007, CISG-online 1492; KGer Schaffhausen, 23 April 2002, CISG-online 731; CA Vaud, 8 December 2000, CISG-online 1841; HGer Zürich, 8 April 1999, CISG-online 489; OGer Luzern, 8 January 1997, CISG-online 228; ICC, 23 January 1997, CISG-online 236; OLG Koblenz, 17 September 1993, CISG-online 91; *Achilles*, Art. 1 CISG, para. 3; Ferrari *et al./Saenger*, Art. 1 CISG, para. 5; Kröll *et al./Mistelis*, Art. 1 CISG, para. 33; *Magnus*, FS Bonell, p. 1779; MüKoBGB/*Huber*, Art. 1 CISG, para. 11; Schlechtriem/Schwenzer/Schroeter/*Ferrari*, 8th German ed., Art. 1 CISG, para. 31; Schlechtriem/Schwenzer/Schroeter/*Hachem*, 5th English ed., Art. 1 CISG, para. 15; *C. Witz*, para. 112.61; but *see C. Meyer*, Alleinvertrieb, p. 470; *C. Meyer*, Jusletter 2 May 2016, para. 23.

826. CA Versailles, 19 February 2004, CISG-online 3345: '*Considérant qu'il est indifférent que les commandes litigieuses aient été passées dans le cadre d'un contrat de distribution, lui-même non soumis à la Convention de Vienne, les articles 1 à 6 de celle-ci ne prévoyant aucune exclusion de son champ d'application pour ce motif*'; this decision was upheld by the Cour de Cassation, 20 February 2007, CISG-online 1492.

827. OLG Hamm, 5 November 1997, CISG-online 381; *Klima*, RIW 1996, p. 1036; cf. also Kronke *et al./Killias/Marzorati*, Teil G, para. 347.

828. *See Schwenzer*, Challenges of the 2020s, p. 44: 'similar problems should call for similar solutions'; cf. also *Rehbinder*, IPRax 1982, p. 7; *Wójtowicz*, ERCL 2018, pp. 155, 156 and Ch. 3 V. 1., 2. above.

829. *See* Ch. 5 III. 3. b. below.

830. *See* Ch. 5 III. 3. b. ii. below.

831. *Schwenzer*, Challenges of the 2020s, p. 44.

sales contracts. For instance, the obligations under the framework agreement may primarily relate to the parties' overall cooperation. Put differently, the interests under the framework agreement may differ from those under the individual sales contracts.[832] Accordingly, the seller may be exempted from their obligation to deliver the goods in accordance with Art. 79 CISG on the grounds of hardship. At the same time however, they might not be exempted from their obligations arising from the framework agreement, which are subject to the applicable domestic law. Even if the affected obligations are similar, it should typically not be problematic if different laws are being applied. Given the potential differences between the contracts, it is more sensible to determine the applicable law separately for each contract, taking into account the specific circumstances of each case. Consequently, it is not convincing to extend the application of the CISG from the individual sales contracts to the framework agreement in every scenario.

Moreover, most other disputes arising from the framework agreement and/or the individual sales contracts can be dealt with separately.[833] To illustrate, in cases where a seller demands payment of outstanding purchase prices, the legal basis will be the individual sales contracts.[834] In contrast, if one of the parties claims damages based on a wrongful termination of a distribution agreement, the legal basis for their claim will be the framework agreement.[835] In cases where the goods delivered are non-conforming, have been delivered late or not delivered at all, the breach can usually be

832. *Hoffbauer*, pp. 47, 48; cf. also OLG Düsseldorf, 11 July 1996, CISG-online 201; Kronke *et al./Killias/Marzorati*, Teil G, para. 347.
833. Cf. CA Paris, 5 March 2019, CISG-online 5765; CA Vaud, 8 December 2000, CISG-online 1841; Ct. of Arbitration of the Hamburg CC, 21 March 1996, CISG-online 187, where the Court distinguished between the claims for damages based on the individual sales contracts and the claims for damages based on the framework agreement (the exact characterisation of this contract remains unclear); *Hoffbauer*, pp. 114 et seq.; *Perović*, (2011) 59 Belgrade L. Rev., pp. 190, 191; more guardedly *C. Meyer*, Alleinvertrieb, p. 467.
834. Cf. Milan Chamber of Arbitration, 15 January 2020, CISG-online 5554: payment claims were based on the 'individual purchase orders' (apart from this, the extent of the CISG's application is not entirely clear); Supr. Ct. Norway, 6 February 2019, CISG-online 4318: dispute concerned a right of stoppage under an individual sales contract (CISG was applied); OLG Köln, 29 January 2010, CISG-online 2172: the claim for payment of the outstanding purchase price arising from individual sales contracts was assessed under the CISG, while other questions relating to the distribution contract were considered under German law; Foreign Trade Ct. of Arbitration of the CC and Industry of Serbia, 28 January 2009, CISG-online 1856: the Court ruled that the seller's claim for payment of the purchase price was based on individual transactions, rather than the framework agreement as a whole; Supr. Ct. China, 21 September 2005, CISG-online 1611: the Court held that only those disputes that arise from the 'placing of orders or thereafter' relate to the sales relationship and thus fall within the CISG's sphere of application; Supr. Ct. Italy, 20 September 2004, CISG-online 1015: the claim for performance was based on the individual sales contracts; *Perović*, (2011) 59 Belgrade L. Rev., pp. 190, 191.
835. *Gruppo Essenziero Italiano, S.p.A. v. Aromi D'Italia, Inc.*, US Dist. Ct. Mary., 27 July 2011, CISG-online 2223: the buyer sought damages for the wrongful termination of an exclusive distribution agreement. The Court ruled that this issue was related to the distribution agreement and not the individual sales contracts. Consequently, it left open the question of whether the CISG was applicable to the individual sales contracts; cf. also CA Warsaw, 15 May 2015, CISG-online 2783: breach of an exclusivity obligation set forth in a distribution contract (the CISG was deemed inapplicable in either case); *C. Meyer*, Alleinvertrieb, p. 466, mentioning a breach of the buyer's right of sole distribution; cf. also CA Paris, 5 March 2019, CISG-online 5765.

assigned to one or multiple individual sales contracts.[836] Consequently, the aggrieved party may pursue a claim based on the relevant individual sales contract(s) without affecting the contractual relationship established under the framework agreement.[837] These related contracts can therefore essentially be dealt with separately, even if the disputes appear to be 'overlapping' at first glance.

c. *Summary*

In summary, this study proposes that various types of framework agreements be distinguished: framework agreements that contain sales obligations should be regarded as a single contract, subject to one law. If there is a distinction between the framework agreement and the individual sales contracts, the preferable view is that the applicable law should be determined separately. In cases where a framework agreement includes an obligation to conclude individual sales contracts, there is indeed a close link between these contracts. However, such framework agreements may also contain further non-sales obligations. It is therefore submitted that the applicable law must be determined separately; this may, nevertheless, result in the applicability of the same law in some cases. By doing so, the specific circumstances of each case can be taken into consideration. Framework agreements that are not binding with regard to the individual transactions lack a comparable close link to the individual contracts. In light of this, it can be concluded that the applicable law must be determined independently for each contract. This is not changed by the fact that the framework agreement may predetermine certain clauses to be incorporated into the individual sales contracts.

Furthermore, it is not a persuasive argument to apply the same law to the framework agreement and the individual sales contracts on the basis that the standards set out in different applicable laws may differ in certain cases, such as in the case of hardship. In fact, the interests under these contracts may diverge, suggesting that it is more compelling to determine the applicable law separately for each contract. This applies to any other breach of contract. In most cases, such disputes can either be assigned to the framework agreement or to one or multiple individual sales contracts.

4. Conclusion

Some scholars advocate that the CISG should apply to all related contracts, i.e., the framework agreement and the individual sales contracts. This view is based on the idea that these contracts should be treated equally in the event of a dispute and that their obligations are intertwined. A similar discussion has been led under the Rome I Regulation and Swiss PIL. With comparable arguments, some scholars endorse the application of one single law to the framework agreement as well as the individual sales

836. Cf. *Hoffbauer*, p. 115; more guardedly *C. Meyer*, Alleinvertrieb, p. 463; *see* Ch. 5 III. 5. c. i. below.
837. *Hoffbauer*, p. 116; *C. Meyer*, Alleinvertrieb, pp. 328 et seq., 463, 467.

contracts concluded under its umbrella. However, the prevailing view holds that the law applicable to the framework agreement and to the individual sales contracts must generally be found separately, as the characteristic performance and the parties' interests may differ under these contracts.

This view is also more convincing with regard to the CISG's applicability to framework agreements. In this context, this study proposes distinguishing between the different types of framework agreements mentioned above. Framework agreements that contain sales obligations should be characterised as one single contract that is governed by one law.

In instances where there is a distinction between the framework agreement and the individual sales contracts, the applicable law should generally be determined separately. The obligations set out in these contracts may indeed be somewhat intertwined, especially if the framework agreement includes an obligation to conclude individual sales contracts. Nevertheless, even in such cases, the framework agreement may contain additional obligations that are not sales-related. Thus, determining the law separately is a more convincing approach, as it allows for the specific circumstances of each case to be taken into account. This may still lead to the CISG's applicability to both the framework agreement as well as the individual sales contract.

VI. TYPICAL CLAUSES IN FRAMEWORK AGREEMENTS AND THEIR EFFECTS ON THE CISG'S APPLICABILITY

It has been submitted that the CISG is generally applicable to framework agreements that bind the parties to carry out the individual transactions, either by including actual sales obligations or by including an obligation to conclude individual sales contracts (two-tier structure). In contrast, the CISG should not apply to framework agreements that leave it open whether the parties will actually carry out the individual transactions. It is therefore crucial to determine whether the parties bound themselves to carry out the individual transactions in their framework agreement. Essentially, this is a matter of contract interpretation in light of the specific circumstances of each case.[838]

Whenever the characterisation of a contract and thus the CISG's applicability is in question, the relevant interpretation standards should be drawn from the Convention itself.[839] The reason for this is that the CISG autonomously determines its own scope of application.[840] Accordingly, Art. 8 CISG, in particular its paragraph 2, must be taken into account for the interpretation and characterisation of an international framework

838. High Ct. Singapore, 13 March 2019, CISG-online 4108, paras 23 et seq. (original arbitral award: ICC, 10 December 2015, CISG-online 4106); *Hoffbauer*, p. 96.
839. Gerechtshof Arnhem-Leeuwarden, 6 February 2024, CISG-online 6819, para. 9; Schlechtriem/Schwenzer/Schroeter/*Schmidt-Kessel*, 5th English ed., Art. 8 CISG, para. 4; cf. also HGer Aargau, 5 February 2008, CISG-online 1740, para. 44 (mentioning Art. 8(3) CISG); *Perales Viscasillas*, Extending the Scope, p. 132.
840. Reliant upon this argument in a different context: Schlechtriem/Schwenzer/Schroeter/*Hachem*, Art. 3 CISG, para. 12.

agreement in order to ascertain whether the CISG applies.[841] Naturally, the individual circumstances of each case will be decisive for this characterisation. There are, however, clauses that are frequently included in framework agreements.[842] The following part will outline these typical clauses and their effects. In this context, the following section will merely refer to the typical meaning of such clauses under Art. 8 CISG which may, of course, differ under certain circumstances.

1. Requirement Clauses

The parties may include a so-called requirement clause in their framework agreement. Under requirement clauses, the buyer agrees to purchase the entirety or a part of their requirements solely from the seller and/or the seller agrees to deliver the quantities of goods requested by the buyer.[843]

Such clauses may give rise to a relationship of dependency between the parties, depending on the extent of the respective obligation. A buyer who agrees to buy solely from one seller may be economically dependent on the fact that the latter will actually deliver the ordered goods, particularly if the buyer agrees to buy their entire requirement from the seller.[844] The same may apply to the seller, depending on the (economic) extent of their obligation. If they agree to deliver the quantities of goods requested by the buyer, their production may be oriented towards the buyer's needs, especially in cases where the buyer purchases a significant proportion of the seller's overall output. In such cases, there may be severe economic consequences for the seller if the buyer unexpectedly does not call for the delivery of goods.[845]

There may accordingly be significant consequences for both parties if they agree to include a requirement clause in their framework agreement, depending on the extent of such a clause. In light of these consequences, a reasonable third person in the same type of business (Art. 8(2) CISG) would understand that the parties intended to be bound to carry out the individual transactions by incorporating such a clause into their agreement.[846] This applies in particular in cases where the requirement clauses give rise to a relationship of dependency, namely when the buyer agrees to purchase all of their requirements from the seller or when the seller agrees to sell their entire output to the buyer. Even in instances where a requirement clause merely refers to a part of the buyer's requirements, e.g., a percentage of their annual needs, and where the consequences for the parties appear to be less significant, the parties typically indicate their willingness to supply and/or to purchase to this extent.[847] A reasonable third

841. *See* Gerechtshof Arnhem-Leeuwarden, 6 February 2024, CISG-online 6819, para. 9; Cour de Cassation, 30 June 2004, CISG-online 870.
842. *Budde/Geks*, ZVertriebsR 2012, pp. 38, 39; *Hoffbauer*, pp. 96 et seq.
843. *Hoffbauer*, p. 98; cf. on requirement contracts: *Bridge*, Int'l Sale of Goods, para. 10.22; *Fawcett/Harris/Bridge*, para. 16.95; Schlechtriem/Schwenzer/Schroeter/*Schroeter*, 5th English ed., Intro Arts 14–24 CISG, para. 20.
844. *Hoffbauer*, p. 98; cf. CA Warsaw, 15 May 2015, CISG-online 2783.
845. *Hoffbauer*, p. 98.
846. Cf. *Budde/Geks*, ZVertriebsR, p. 39; *Hoffbauer*, p. 98.
847. *Budde/Geks*, ZVertriebsR, p. 39.

person would thus understand such a clause in the same way, namely that the parties committed themselves to carry out the individual transactions to the extent agreed upon in the requirement clause.

Therefore, the parties typically bind themselves to conduct individual transactions to a certain extent by including a requirement clause in their framework agreement. Such a clause gives rise to either sales obligations in the strict sense or an obligation to conclude individual sales contracts. A framework agreement that includes a requirement clause may therefore generally fall within the CISG's sphere of application.[848] In addition, all other requirements for the Convention's application must be met, and the specific circumstances of each case must be taken into careful consideration.

It should be noted that the seller typically is only bound to carry out the individual transaction if the buyer is in need of the goods. In the event of a dispute, the buyer may be required to prove that they are in need of the goods as well as the required quantity.[849] Furthermore, a requirement clause may be agreed upon under a resolutive condition. If a third party makes a more attractive offer to the buyer, the buyer may be permitted to purchase the goods from the third party, provided that the seller does not subsequently make an offer under equal conditions. The purpose of such an additional term is to weaken the buyer's dependency on the seller.[850]

2. Minimum Purchase Requirements

Framework agreements very frequently include clauses that stipulate a minimum purchase requirement.[851] Under such clauses, the parties agree that the buyer must purchase a minimum quantity of goods over a particular period of time.[852] To illustrate, the parties to a framework agreement for the supply of beverages may agree that the buyer must purchase a minimum of 300 litres of beverages per year during the contract's duration.[853] The inclusion of a minimum purchase requirement clause in the agreement indicates the parties' interest in establishing a limited degree of planning reliability.[854] The buyer's objective is to maintain a fixed supply, while the seller's objective is to maintain a fixed order at the minimum quantity to be purchased.[855]

848. To that effect: Court of Arbitration of the Hamburg CC, 21 March 1996, CISG-online 187, paras 38 et seq.
849. *Hoffbauer*, p. 98.
850. *Hoffbauer*, p. 99.
851. Cf. *Hoffbauer*, p. 101; Münch/Passadelis/Lehne/*Rohn*, paras 4.58 et seq.; *Schluep*, p. 20; *Ulmer*, p. 290.
852. Cf. CA Krakow, 22 June 2015, CISG-online 5471 (annual order of rain gutter must have a value of at least EUR 2.5 million); CA Geneva, 20 May 2011, CISG-online 2429; Cour de Cassation, 30 June 2004, CISG-online 870; OLG Graz, 28 September 2000, CISG-online 798; BGH, 4 December 1996, NJW 1997, p. 934; *Hoffbauer*, p. 101; *Ulmer*, p. 112.
853. BGH, 4 December 1996, NJW 1997, p. 934; *see also* Cour de Cassation, 30 June 2004, CISG-online 870; OLG Graz, 28 September 2000, CISG-online 798; BGH, 12 July 1995, NJW-RR 1995, p. 1328 (a minimum of 500 units of the contracted goods must be purchased annually over a two-year period).
854. *Hoffbauer*, p. 101.
855. OLG Graz, 28 September 2000, CISG-online 798; *Hoffbauer*, p. 101.

Minimum purchase requirement clauses may vary with regard to the quantity to be delivered and the price to be paid.[856] In a distribution agreement, the minimum purchase requirement may be considered the 'counterpart' to the buyer's sole right of distribution; for instance, the buyer may be granted the right to exclusively sell the goods in a particular geographical area, and in return, they must purchase a certain minimum from the seller.[857]

A reasonable person in the same type of business (Art. 8(2) CISG) would understand that the parties intended to be bound with regard to the individual transactions by incorporating a minimum purchase requirement into their contract.[858] Agreeing on a minimum purchase requirement would be meaningless in the absence of binding (sales) obligations being established.[859] Thus, by agreeing on such a clause, the parties indicate their willingness to commit themselves to carrying out the individual transactions, albeit within defined limits. They are free to decide whether they would like to conduct further individual transactions beyond the agreed minimum quantity, as they are only bound to the extent of the minimum purchase quantity.[860] Accordingly, a framework agreement that includes such a clause may generally fall within the CISG's sphere of application.[861]

The same conclusion was essentially drawn by the Court of Appeal Geneva: in its decision, the Court, *inter alia,* held that the CISG was applicable to the framework agreement in dispute as it contained a *'l'obligation d'achat minimum'*, i.e., a minimum purchase requirement. Under this minimum purchase requirement, the buyer was obliged to buy at least 150,000 units of the goods per year.[862] Similarly, the Court of Appeal Krakow applied the CISG to a framework agreement containing a minimum purchase requirement, which obliged the buyer to place orders for the goods (rain gutters) in the amount of a minimum of EUR 2.5 million per year.[863] These decisions are convincing and fall in line with the interpretation of such clauses proposed by this study.

856. Cf. *Hoffbauer*, p. 101; *Ulmer*, pp. 112, 113.
857. BGH, 12 July 1995, NJW-RR 1995, p. 1329.
858. Cf. CA Krakow, 22 June 2015, CISG-online 5471; Cour de Cassation, 30 June 2004, CISG-online 870; OLG Graz, 28 September 2000, CISG-online 798; BGH, 12 July 1995, NJW-RR 1995, p. 1329; *Hoffbauer*, p. 101; cf. also BGH, 4 December 1996, NJW 1997, p. 934; *Perales Viscasillas*, Extending the Scope, p. 123; but *see Ulmer*, pp. 112, 113, 290, 310.
859. Cf. *Hoffbauer*, p. 101.
860. *Hoffbauer*, p. 101.
861. Schlechtriem/Schwenzer/Schroeter/*Schroeter*, 5th English ed., Intro Arts 14–24 CISG, para. 25: 'if [...] the formation of the framework agreement itself is also governed by Part II of the CISG (as e.g. in case of a minimum amount of deliveries having been fixed in the framework contract) [...]'.
862. CA Geneva, 20 May 2011, CISG-online 2429; in agreement Cour de Cassation, 30 June 2004, CISG-online 870: over the course of eight years, a minimum of 20,000 units were required to be supplied in accordance with the buyer's requirements.
863. CA Krakow, 22 June 2015, CISG-online 5471.

3. Forecast Clauses

Moreover, the parties may agree on forecast clauses in framework agreements.[864] Under such clauses, the buyer shares the forecasted purchase quantity, based on their internal planning, with the seller.[865] The forecast is typically limited to a certain period of time, e.g., to the next six months.

If the parties agree on a forecast clause, they are usually not willing to make any definitive commitments at that point. Rather, the purpose of such a clause is to give the seller of the goods some predictability so that they can plan accordingly.[866] Put differently, the parties indicate that they are still uncertain about the future transactions by including a forecast clause in their framework agreement.[867] A reasonable third person in the sense of Art. 8(2) CISG would therefore understand that forecast clauses are typically not binding with regard to the individual transactions, unless the wording of the clause explicitly suggests otherwise.[868] Accordingly, a framework agreement should not fall within the CISG's sphere of application solely based on this type of clause.[869]

A similar result was reached by an Arbitral tribunal in *BVU v. BVX*:[870] in this case, the parties concluded a framework agreement for the sale of food (a minimum of 1 million tons per year), which contained a choice of law clause in favour of the CISG. It was, *inter alia*, disputed whether the framework agreement obliged the buyer to place purchase orders, i.e., whether the parties bound themselves with regard to the individual transactions. The framework agreement contained a clause, which obliged the buyer to forecast their demand and 'use its best commercially reasonable effort to order and purchase' goods within this forecasted range.[871] In interpreting the contract under Art. 8 CISG, the tribunal concluded that the framework agreement did not bind the buyer to place purchase orders in accordance with the parties' intentions as expressed in the contract.[872]

The situation may be different if a forecast clause refers to a temporal interval that is proximate: in cases where a buyer communicates their forecasted demand for the next month, the seller might buy the required materials and manufacture the demanded goods; it might thus be essential for the seller that the transactions under the

864. *See* CA Paris, 5 March 2019, CISG-online 5765, paras 57 et seq.; ICC, 10 December 2015, CISG-online 4106 (confirmed in High Ct. Singapore, 13 March 2019, CISG-online 4108).
865. *Budde/Geks*, ZVertriebsR, p. 39; *Hoffbauer*, pp. 99, 100.
866. *Hoffbauer*, p. 100.
867. *Budde/Geks*, ZVertriebsR, p. 39; *Hoffbauer*, p. 100; cf. also High Ct. Singapore, 13 March 2019, CISG-online 4108, paras 26, 27.
868. *Budde/Geks*, ZVertriebsR, p. 39; *Hoffbauer*, pp. 99, 100; cf. also CA Paris, 5 March 2019, CISG-online 5765, paras 59 et seq.; *Piltz*, Rahmen-Einkaufsvertrag, para. 10.
869. It is possible that the interpretation of the framework agreement in its entirety may still result in the CISG being applicable.
870. ICC, 10 December 2015, CISG-online 4106 – the arbitral award has been reproduced by the High Ct. Singapore, 13 March 2019, CISG-online 4108, paras 20 et seq.
871. High Ct. Singapore, 13 March 2019, CISG-online 4108, para. 4 (where clause (d) of the contract can be found).
872. High Ct. Singapore, 13 March 2019, CISG-online 4108, paras 26, 27.

framework agreement will be carried out.[873] A reasonable person in the same type of business (Art. 8(2) CISG) would understand that the seller has a significant interest in the clause being binding with regard to the individual transactions. Consequently, such a clause may be binding at least on the buyer if it refers to the following month or an even more immediate period.[874] Nevertheless, most forecast clauses are not binding with regard to individual transactions. In any event, the parties are well advised to clarify the legal consequences of a forecast clause in their contract in order to remove any ambiguities.[875]

4. Exclusivity Clauses

Distribution contracts, as a subset of framework agreements, frequently include so-called exclusivity clauses. Such exclusivity clauses can take various forms: the seller may be obliged to only sell the goods to distributors that meet certain requirements, a group of distributors or to one distributor in a certain geographical area.[876] An exclusivity clause may also give the buyer (distributor) the sole right to distribute, i.e., re-sell, the goods in a specific market – often in a geographical sense.

In many cases, the parties do not intend to bind themselves to carry out the individual transactions merely by including such clauses. A reasonable person under comparable circumstances in the sense of Art. 8(2) CISG would thus not conclude that such clauses are meant to bind the parties to carry out the individual transactions, unless other circumstances indicate so.[877] However, this interpretation is contingent on the specific nature of the exclusivity obligation in question.

An exclusivity clause may also oblige the buyer to exclusively buy the goods from the seller.[878] This type of clause can essentially be juxtaposed with requirement clauses that have been referred to above.[879] A distributor who agrees to exclusively purchase from the seller is economically dependent on the latter's ability and willingness to deliver the ordered goods.[880] A reasonable third person in the same type of business (Art. 8(2) CISG) would hence understand that the parties intended to be bound to carry out the individual transactions by incorporating such a clause.[881] Consequently, a framework agreement that contains this form of exclusivity clause may generally fall in

873. Cf. *Budde/Geks*, ZVertriebsR, p. 39.
874. Cf. *Budde/Geks*, ZVertriebsR, p. 39, proposing that the supplier may have a claim for compensation if a forecast refers to the following two to six months.
875. *Budde/Geks*, ZVertriebsR, p. 39.
876. *See Perales Viscasillas*, Extending the Scope, p. 126; *Schluep*, pp. 20 et seq.
877. This was the case in ICC, 1 November 2016, CISG-online 5988: the 'supply obligation' under the Distribution Agreement, *inter alia*, followed from the nature of the agreement, the warranty clauses contained in the agreement and the terms relating to the shipping of the goods.
878. CA Warsaw, 15 May 2015, CISG-online 2783: the buyer of a distribution contract agreed to buy dietary products only from the seller; *Perales Viscasillas*, Extending the Scope, p. 126; *Perales Viscasillas*, Int'l Distribution Contracts and CISG, p. 52.
879. *See* Ch. 3 VI. 1. above.
880. *Hoffbauer*, p. 98.
881. Cf. *Budde/Geks*, ZVertriebsR, p. 39; *Hoffbauer*, p. 98.

the CISG's sphere of application, provided that all other prerequisites for its applicability are met.

VII. CONCLUSION

Sales contracts under the CISG are generally defined as contracts that contain obligations to deliver the goods, transfer property in them and pay the purchase price in accordance with Art. 1 in conjunction with Arts 30 and 53 CISG.[882] That being said, the Convention also covers agreements to modify or terminate sales contracts as evidenced by Art. 29 CISG. Strictly speaking, such agreements are not in line with the general definition of sales contracts. From this example, a general principle can be derived that the Convention applies to closely linked or related contracts. For this to be the case, the closely linked contracts must establish or directly affect the parties' rights and obligations under one or multiple CISG contracts.[883]

Having regard to this general principle, the CISG also applies to preliminary agreements that contain an obligation to conclude a 'final' sales contract, but not sales obligations in *sensu stricto*. Such contracts, in substance, establish rights and obligations under a CISG contract. The Convention should, in contrast, not apply to non-binding preliminary 'agreements' and preliminary agreements that merely relate to the negotiations between the parties.[884]

From the aforementioned considerations, it is possible to derive conclusions regarding the CISG's applicability to framework agreements. In this context, this study proposes distinguishing between framework agreements that bind the parties to carry out the individual transactions and framework agreements that do not bind the parties in that regard. The first group of contracts either contains immediate sales obligations or an obligation to conclude individual sales contracts. A framework agreement that contains sales obligations in the narrower sense may unproblematically be governed by the CISG in accordance with Art. 1 in conjunction with Arts 30 and 53 CISG. Furthermore, the CISG should also be applicable to framework agreements that merely contain an obligation to conclude individual sales contracts. Although they do not contain sales obligations, they are closely linked to CISG contracts based on their obligation to conclude such contracts. They, in substance, establish rights and obligations under multiple CISG contracts and thus fall within the scope of the aforementioned general principle. In this regard, they are comparable to preliminary agreements and should be treated in a similar manner.[885]

In contrast, the CISG should not be applicable to framework agreements that are not binding with regard to the individual transactions. Such agreements lack a comparable close link to the individual sales contracts, as they do not establish or directly affect the parties' rights and obligations under the CISG contracts. This is because the parties are free to decide whether they eventually conclude individual

882. *See* Ch. 3 I. above.
883. *See* Ch. 3 II. 1., 2. above.
884. *See* Ch. 3 II. 2. above.
885. *See* Ch. 3 III 1. above.

sales contracts. Furthermore, it is insufficient that such framework agreements may predetermine certain terms to be incorporated into the individual sales contracts, since the parties must still agree to include these terms in the contracts subsequently concluded. The CISG may nevertheless be indirectly relevant for such framework agreements, which as such remain outside its sphere of application. If the parties decide to enter into individual sales contracts under the umbrella of the framework agreement, the individual sales contracts may be governed by the Convention. The framework agreement may then be relevant for the interpretation of the individual sales contracts (Art. 8(3) CISG). Furthermore, the framework agreement may be considered a practice within the meaning of Art. 9(1) CISG or constitute a derogation from certain provisions of the Convention (e.g., Art. 18(1) CISG).[886]

Some scholars and in particular US courts have held that framework agreements do not fall within the Convention's sphere of application for their insufficient definiteness (Art. 14(1) CISG). A thorough interpretation of Art. 14(1), sentence 1 CISG reveals that it does not set a strict, but rather a liberal standard of sufficient definiteness. This view is therefore not persuasive and overly restrictive in its interpretation of the Convention's sphere of application. It should not be an obstacle to the CISG's applicability that framework agreements leave some terms open or indefinite. For the purposes of Art. 14(1) CISG, it is sufficient for the minimum content to be stipulated in the individual orders or even in the individual sales contracts. In any case, the parties are free to derogate from the standard of definiteness set out in Art. 14(1) CISG in accordance with Art. 6 CISG. The CISG is not restricted to contracts that contain sufficiently definite terms but is rather flexible in that regard. Consequently, the requirement of sufficient definiteness is generally not directly related to the CISG's sphere of application; Art. 14(1) CISG is not an 'invalidating provision'.[887]

Beyond that, several scholars have posited that the same law should by default be applied to the framework agreement and the individual sales contracts, given their close relationship. This argument has been advanced with regard to the CISG as well as private international law rules in the European Union and Switzerland. However, the preferable view is that the law applicable to the framework agreement and to the individual sales contracts should generally be determined independently. Even though there may be significant relationships in some cases, which could suggest applying one law to all related contracts, it is preferable to determine the applicable law separately for each contract. This approach enables the specific circumstances of each case to be taken into account. Even if a framework agreement is closely related to the individual sales contracts, it may contain additional non-sales elements that could alter its focus.[888]

The approach proposed by this study leads to the conclusion that the CISG's applicability will depend on whether a framework agreement is binding with regard to the individual transactions. Whenever the characterisation of a contract, and thus the CISG's applicability, is in question, the relevant interpretation standards should be

886. *See* Ch. 3 III 2. above.
887. *See* Ch. 3 IV. above.
888. *See* Ch. 3 V. above.

drawn from the Convention itself, since the Convention autonomously regulates its own sphere of application. From the perspective of a reasonable third person (Art. 8(2) CISG), it can be assumed that requirement clauses and minimum purchase requirements will typically indicate a commitment by the parties to carry out the individual transactions. It is not typical for forecast clauses to indicate this. With regard to exclusivity clauses, the commitment by the parties may depend on the specific nature of the exclusivity obligation contained in the framework agreement. Ultimately, the specific circumstances of each case will be decisive for this question of characterisation, which must be resolved in accordance with the provisions of the CISG itself, in particular Art. 8 CISG.[889]

889. *See* Ch. 3 VI. above.

CHAPTER 4
Framework Agreements as Mixed Contracts under the CISG

A framework agreement generally falls within the CISG's sphere of application if it contains sales obligations or an obligation to conclude individual sales contracts.[890] However, there may be an obstacle to the Convention's applicability as well as its actual application. Framework agreements often contain 'non-sales' rights and obligations.[891] In particular, distribution contracts, a subtype of framework agreements, may include various non-sales obligations.[892] The following chapter will analyse whether these obligations constitute an obstacle to the CISG's applicability. Moreover, it will address the consequences of the CISG's application to mixed framework agreements.

I. GENERAL REMARKS

The Convention extends beyond the mere sale of goods and also addresses contracts that combine sales and non-sales related rights and obligations.[893] Art. 3 CISG explicitly refers to contracts that combine different kinds of obligations beyond the mere sale of goods. This provision must be taken into consideration when determining the CISG's sphere of application.[894]

890. *See* Ch. 3 III. above.
891. Schlechtriem/Schwenzer/Schroeter/*Schroeter*, 5th English ed., Intro Arts 14–24 CISG, para. 24; cf. also OLG Graz, 28 September 2000, CISG-online 798 (regarding a framework agreement that, *inter alia*, included a sole right of distribution in favour of the distributor/buyer); cf. also *Fountoulakis*, pp. 54 et seq.
892. Cf. only RB Utrecht, 29 December 2010, CISG-online 5325; Supr. Ct. Italy, 14 December 1999, CISG-online 1314; OGer Luzern, 8 January 1997, CISG-online 228; *Perales Viscasillas*, Extending the Scope, p. 129; *Perales Viscasillas*, Int'l Distribution Contracts and CISG, p. 55; *Piltz*, Rahmen-Einkaufsvertrag, para. 2.
893. *Fogt*, IPRax 2003, p. 367; *Karner/Koziol*, para. 16; *Perales Viscasillas*, Extending the Scope, p. 128; *Schlechtriem*, (2005) 36 V.U.W. L. Rev., p. 787; Staudinger/*Magnus*, Art. 3 CISG, para. 1; *Thieffry*, Dr. prat. com. int. 1993, p. 62.
894. Cf. *Thieffry*, Dr. prat. com. int. 1993, p. 62.

1. Article 3 CISG

Art. 3(1) CISG stipulates that contracts for the supply of goods to be manufactured or produced are also considered to be sales. Even more crucial with regard to framework agreements is paragraph 2 of Art. 3 CISG. This provision deals with mixed contracts where the seller undertakes sales obligations as well as labour or other service obligations in the same agreement.[895] It holds that the CISG does not apply to contracts in which the preponderant part of the obligations of the party who furnishes the goods consists in the supply of labour or other services. *E contrario*, the CISG is applicable to mixed contracts, provided that the non-sales part does not constitute the preponderant part of the agreement.[896] Consequently, the CISG may be generally applicable to framework agreements that combine different kinds of obligations.[897]

2. Scope of Article 3(2) CISG

The provision in Art. 3(2) CISG expressly refers to the 'supply of labour or other services'. Any mixed contract that includes both sales obligations and labour or other service obligations is, in general, within the scope of this provision. Yet, the Convention is silent on cases where the seller undertakes sales obligations and further non-sales obligations other than service or labour obligations.[898] It has been convincingly submitted that a general principle can be derived from Art. 3(2) CISG within the meaning of Art. 7(2) CISG.[899] As long as a mixed contract combines any non-sales obligations that fall outside the Convention's scope with sales obligations that fall within the CISG's scope, the legal concept behind Art. 3(2) CISG should be applicable.[900]

---

895. Schlechtriem/Schwenzer/Schroeter/*Hachem*, 5th English ed., Art. 3 CISG, para. 11; Soergel/*Kreße*, Art. 3 CISG, para. 4; *Thieffry*, Dr. prat. com. int. 1993, p. 62; *C. Witz*, para. 112.61.
896. Milan Chamber of Arbitration, 30 January 2019, CISG-online 5573, note 19; *Enderlein/Maskow*, Art. 3 CISG, note 7; MüKoHGB/*B. Köhler*, Art. 3 CISG, paras 12, 13; *Pavic/Djordjevic*, FS Rüßmann, p. 909; Schlechtriem/Schwenzer/Schroeter/*Ferrari*, 8th German ed., Art. 3 CISG, para. 13; *Schwenzer/Ranetunge/Tafur*, (2019) 10 Indian J. Int'l Econ. L., p. 172; *Schwenzer/Ranetunge/Tafur*, (2019/20) 39 J. L. & Com., p. 305; Staudinger/*Magnus*, Art. 3 CISG, paras 3, 21.
897. RB Utrecht, 29 December 2010, CISG-online 5325; OLG Graz, 28 September 2000, CISG-online 798, para. 40; Supr. Ct. Italy, 14 December 1999, CISG-online 1314, note 2; *Bridge*, Int'l Sale of Goods, para. 10.22; MüKoBGB/*Huber*, Art. 1 CISG, para. 11; *Perales Viscasillas*, Extending the Scope, p. 128; Schlechtriem/Schwenzer/Schroeter/*Schroeter*, 5th English ed., Intro Arts 14–24 CISG, para. 24; *C. Witz*, para. 112.61; cf. also ICC, 8817/1997, CISG-online 750.
898. Huber/Mullis/*Huber*, p. 42; cf. also MüKoBGB/*Huber*, Art. 3 CISG, para. 3.
899. Huber/Mullis/*Huber*, p. 42; MüKoBGB/*Huber*, Art. 3 CISG, para. 3; cf. also *Piltz*, para. 2-34; *Schroeter*, para. 107; Staudinger/*Magnus*, Art. 3 CISG, para. 30; *C. Witz*, para. 112.132.
900. Huber/Mullis/*Huber*, p. 42; *Piltz*, para. 2-34; *Schroeter*, para. 107; reaching the same outcome through a different line of reasoning (application by analogy): *Herber/Czerwenka*, Art. 3 CISG, para. 6; MüKoHGB/*B. Köhler*, Art. 3 CISG, para. 17; Schlechtriem/Schwenzer/Schroeter/*Ferrari*, 8th German ed., Art. 3 CISG, para. 19; Schlechtriem/Schwenzer/Schroeter/*Hachem*, 5th English ed., Art. 3 CISG, para. 22; cf. also *C. Witz*, para. 112.132.

The following section will analyse the specific non-sales obligations that are frequently included in mixed framework agreements and determine whether Art. 3(2) CISG is applicable to them. In this context, a distinction between service or labour obligations in the narrower sense and exclusivity obligations or non-competition clauses will be made.

a. Non-sales Obligations in Framework Agreements

i. Service or Labour Obligations

Framework agreements frequently contain service or labour obligations in the narrower sense.[901] In particular, distribution contracts often include service or labour obligations. They may, e.g., include obligations to market, advertise and promote the goods, to provide technical assistance, to provide customer service and advice, to stock spare parts, etc.[902]

Depending on the specifics of the distribution contract, it may be the seller who undertakes such service obligations in addition to their sales obligations.[903] If so, Art. 3(2) CISG is applicable to such a contract.[904] In contrast, it is also possible that the buyer of a distribution contract may undertake service obligations in addition to their sales obligations.[905] In such a scenario, it could be argued that the provision enshrined in Art. 3(2) CISG is not applicable in this instance, as it – if read literally – refers to cases in which the seller undertakes additional service or labour obligations ('party who furnishes the goods [...]').[906]

It is submitted that the general principle derived from Art. 3(2) CISG[907] should also apply if it is the buyer undertaking non-sales obligations in addition to sales obligations. Although the provision solely refers to one specific situation, the underlying idea should be applied to any other scenario in which a mixed contract combines non-sales obligations that fall outside the CISG's scope with sales obligations that fall

901. *Grunewald*, p. 57; Schlechtriem/Schwenzer/Schroeter/*Schroeter*, 5th English ed., Intro Arts 14–24 CISG, para. 24.
902. Cf. Gerechtshof Arhem-Leeuwarden, 6 February 2024, CISG-online 6819; OLG Graz, 28 September 2000, CISG-online 798; OLG Köln, 15 February 2000, CISG-online 3036; *Grieser*, p. 126; *Perales Viscasillas*, Extending the Scope, p. 128; *Perović*, (2011) 59 Belgrade L. Rev., p. 189; Schlechtriem/Schwenzer/Schroeter/*Schroeter*, 5th English ed., Intro Arts 14–24 CISG, para. 24; *Schluep*, pp. 20 et seq.; *UNCITRAL et al.*, Legal Guide, para. 432.
903. *Magnus*, ZEuP 1997, pp. 829, 830; *Perales Viscasillas*, Extending the Scope, p. 128; *Perović*, (2011) 59 Belgrade L. Rev., p. 189; cf. also Gerechtshof Arhem-Leeuwarden, 6 February 2024, CISG-online 6819, para. 12 (obligation of the seller to make warehouse available for the storage of the goods).
904. Cf. only *Grunewald*, p. 57; *Grieser*, pp. 126, 127 (however, not convincing in his result); *Magnus*, ZEuP 1997, pp. 829, 830.
905. Cf. *Grieser*, p. 126; *Thieffry*, Dr. prat. com. int. 1993, p. 62; *Perales Viscasillas*, Extending the Scope, p. 128; *Perović*, (2011) 59 Belgrade L. Rev., p. 189; *UNCITRAL et al.*, Legal Guide, para. 432.
906. *See Thieffry*, Dr. prat. com. int. 1993, p. 62; cf. also *Gillette/Walt*, p. 64.
907. *See* Ch. 4 I. 2. above.

within the CISG's scope.[908] In each instance, it is necessary to determine which part of the contract is preponderant.[909] If the non-sales part is preponderant, the CISG is not applicable to the respective agreement.[910]

It can be inferred from the aforementioned that framework agreements are generally within the scope of Art. 3(2) CISG if they include service and sales obligations.[911] Consequently, the CISG may be applicable to such framework agreements, provided that its non-sales part is not preponderant.[912]

ii. Exclusivity or Non-competition Clauses

Furthermore, framework agreements frequently include exclusivity obligations or non-competition clauses.[913] Some scholars have proposed that these obligations do not qualify as 'labour or other services' within the meaning of Art. 3(2) CISG, and thus they should not be considered when determining the preponderant part.[914] This view is based on the following reasons: Art. 3(2) CISG merely focuses on labour or services and not on additional obligations that are closely related to the sales obligations, such as exclusivity and non-competition obligations.[915] This type of obligations is inseparable from the sales part of the contract, and thus it cannot be considered an indication to not apply sales law (the CISG).[916] According to this view, the CISG should be applicable to mixed contracts that, *inter alia*, include exclusivity and non-competition clauses, without the necessity of resorting to the determination set forth in Art. 3(2) CISG.[917]

Moreover, it has been highlighted that, if read literally, Art. 3(2) CISG merely refers to 'the supply of labour or other services'.[918] Both of these variants (labour or

908. Cf. *Czerwenka*, p. 146; Huber/Mullis/*Huber*, p. 42; MüKoBGB/*Huber*, Art. 1 CISG, para. 11.
909. Huber/Mullis/*Huber*, p. 42; cf. also OLG Dresden, 11 June 2007, CISG-online 1720, paras 46 et seq.: in essence, the Court compared Art. 3(2) CISG with the centre of gravity theory as it is understood within the context of international private law doctrine.
910. Huber/Mullis/*Huber*, p. 42.
911. *Grunewald*, p. 57; MüKoBGB/*Huber*, Art. 1 CISG, para. 11; cf. also *Grieser*, pp. 126, 127; *C. Witz*, para. 112.61.
912. *See* RB Utrecht, 29 December 2010, CISG-online 5325; OLG Graz, 28 September 2000, CISG-online 798, para. 40; Supr. Ct. Italy, 14 December 1999, CISG-online 1314, note 2; *Bridge*, Int'l Sale of Goods, para. 10.22; *Magnus*, ZEuP 1997, p. 830; MüKoBGB/*Huber*, Art. 1 CISG, para. 11; Schlechtriem/Schwenzer/Schroeter/*Schroeter*, 5th English ed., Intro Arts 14–24 CISG, para. 24; *Schwenzer*, Challenges of the 2020s, p. 45; cf. OLG Dresden, 11 June 2007, CISG-online 1720, paras 46 et seq.; OLG Köln, 15 February 2000, CISG-online 3036, para. 26 (CISG, *inter alia*, deemed inapplicable due to the preponderance of the non-sales obligations).
913. *Perales Viscasillas*, Extending the Scope, p. 128; *Thieffry*, Dr. prat. com. int. 1993, p. 63; *UNCITRAL et al.*, Legal Guide, para. 432.
914. *Grunewald*, p. 59; *Magnus*, FS Bonell, p. 1778; Staudinger/*Magnus*, Art. 3 CISG, para. 23; cf. also *Gillette/Walt*, p. 64.
915. *Grunewald*, p. 59.
916. Cf. *Grunewald*, p. 59.
917. *Grunewald*, p. 59; in case law: CA Reims, 4 September 2012, CISG-online 3141: the Court applied the CISG to a sales contract that contained an exclusivity clause in accordance with Art. 1(1)(a) CISG and held that the exclusivity clause was only 'secondary' to the transaction; cf. also ICC, 9448/1999, CISG-online 707; Court of Arbitration of the Hamburg CC, 21 March 1996, CISG-online 187.
918. Cf. *Herber*, p. 40; Staudinger/*Magnus*, Art. 3 CISG, para. 23.

other services) involve an obligation to do something, whereas exclusivity obligations and non-competition clauses oblige the parties to refrain from certain activities, i.e., to not do something.[919] In light of this, the proponents of this view maintain that exclusivity and non-competition obligations cannot be qualified as 'labour or other services' within the meaning of Art. 3(2) CISG.[920]

This view is not persuasive, particularly in its conclusion. Although exclusivity or non-competition clauses may indeed be interrelated with the sales obligations under a mixed contract,[921] there is no reason to refrain from determining the preponderant part in accordance with Art. 3(2) CISG; or, more precisely, the general principle underlying this provision.[922] After all, exclusivity and non-competition clauses establish non-sales obligations between the parties. Such non-sales obligations are, at least to some extent, invariably interrelated with the sales obligations, provided that they are combined in one single contract.[923] It also appears to be unclear where to draw the line between non-sales obligations that are interrelated and those that are not. Therefore, any non-sales obligations should simply be regarded as a non-sales element that may require determining the preponderant part.

Furthermore, a literal interpretation of Art. 3(2) CISG could indeed lead to the conclusion that this provision does not address cases where a mixed contract involves obligations to refrain from certain activities, such as exclusivity or non-competition obligations. Consequently, it is accurate to state that Art. 3(2) CISG cannot be applied directly to such cases.[924] Nevertheless, despite the wording of this provision, it is still possible to rely on the general principle underlying Art. 3(2) CISG, according to which the Convention is not applicable if the non-sales elements in a mixed contract are preponderant.[925] This general principle is applicable to every case that involves a mixed contract combining any type of non-sales obligations that fall outside the Convention's scope with sales obligations that fall within the CISG's scope.[926] For these reasons, this study does not share the view outlined above. As with any other non-sales elements, exclusivity and non-competition obligations should trigger the general

919. Staudinger/*Magnus*, Art. 3 CISG, para. 23; *see also* RB Utrecht, 29 December 2010, CISG-online 5325, para. 26 (classifying an exclusivity obligation as an obligation to not do something).
920. Staudinger/*Magnus*, Art. 3 CISG, para. 23; cf. also *Gillette/Walt*, p. 64; *Magnus*, FS Bonell, p. 1778.
921. Cf. *Perales Viscasillas*, Extending the Scope, p. 126; *Perales Viscasillas*, Int'l Distribution Contracts and CISG, p. 52.
922. *See* Ch. 4 I. 2. above.
923. Art. 3(2) CISG presupposes that sales and non-sales obligations have been combined in one single contract, *see* Ch. 4 III. 1. c. ii. below.
924. Cf. *Magnus*, FS Bonell, p. 1778; Staudinger/*Magnus*, Art. 3 CISG, para. 23.
925. Huber/Mullis/*Huber*, p. 42; MüKoBGB/*Huber*, Art. 3 CISG, para. 3; cf. also Schlechtriem/Schwenzer/Schroeter/*Ferrari*, 8th German ed., Art. 3 CISG, para. 19 (relying on an analogy).
926. Huber/Mullis/*Huber*, p. 42; *Piltz*, para. 2-34; *Schroeter*, para. 107; reaching the same outcome through a different line of reasoning (Art. 3(2) CISG by analogy): MüKoHGB/*B. Köhler*, Art. 3 CISG, para. 17; Schlechtriem/Schwenzer/Schroeter/*Ferrari*, 8th German ed., Art. 3 CISG, para. 19; Schlechtriem/Schwenzer/Schroeter/*Hachem*, 5th English ed., Art. 3 CISG, para. 22.

principle underlying Art. 3(2) CISG and should thus be considered non-sales elements to be taken into account for determining the preponderant part.[927]

b. *Preliminary Agreements Excluded?*

In a similar vein, *B. Köhler* posits that Art. 3(2) CISG should be applied by analogy to other mixed contracts where the non-sales part does not consist of the supply of labour or other services.[928] However, he makes two exceptions for barter contracts and preliminary agreements – Art. 3(2) CISG should not be applied to these contracts.[929] Adhering to this view would potentially lead to the conclusion that Art. 3(2) CISG is also not applicable to framework agreements that contain an obligation to conclude individual sales contracts, as these contracts may (partially) be characterised as preliminary agreements or at least contain a preliminary element.[930]

Yet, this view is not convincing and not supported by this study. Preliminary agreements as well as framework agreements may fall within the Convention's sphere of application if they contain an obligation to conclude one or multiple CISG contracts.[931] In light of this, such agreements should be treated as any other contract within the CISG's ambit. If they combine non-sales obligations that fall outside the Convention's scope with the obligation to conclude one or multiple sales contracts, Art. 3(2) CISG or at least the general principle underlying this provision should be applicable.[932]

II. DETERMINING THE PREPONDERANT PART

In light of the fact that Art. 3(2) CISG or the general principle derived from this provision may be applicable to framework agreements, the CISG's applicability to such contracts may depend on determining the preponderant part. However, the Convention does not provide any further clarification on how to determine the preponderant

927. Cf. also *Perales Viscasillas*, Extending the Scope, p. 128 and *Perales Viscasillas*, Int'l Distribution Contracts and CISG, pp. 54, 55, who refers to exclusivity obligations as an example of non-sales obligations that are commonly included in distribution contracts; *Schroeter*, para. 107, who maintains that the breach of a non-competition obligation may result in consequences and remedies under the CISG, provided that they are part of a mixed contract with a preponderant sales part.
928. MüKoHGB/*B. Köhler*, Art. 3 CISG, para. 17.
929. MüKoHGB/*B. Köhler*, Art. 3 CISG, para. 17.
930. BK OR/*Kramer*, Art. 22 CO, para. 76; *Canaris*, § 17, para. 11; CHK/*Jacobs*, Innominatverträge/AVV, para. 19; *Fikentscher/Heinemann*, para. 136; *Grunewald*, p. 57; *Hoffbauer*, pp. 23, 104 et seq.; *K. Schmidt*, § 20, para. 8; *Torsello*, pp. 240 et seq., referring to '(preliminary) distribution agreements'; *Zubović/Filipović*, p. 162; cf. also *Henrich*, p. 117 (provided that the framework agreement is sufficiently definite).
931. *See* Ch. 3 II. 2. c. ii., III. 1 b. above.
932. Cf. OLG Graz, 28 September 2000, CISG-online 798, para. 40 (however, not explicitly mentioning Art. 3(2) CISG); *Grunewald*, p. 57; Schlechtriem/Schwenzer/Schroeter/*Schroeter*, 5th English ed., Intro Arts 14–24 CISG, para. 24; *Zubović/Filipović*, p. 162: if a distribution/franchise agreement is deemed to constitute a precontract, it must be subjected to the preponderant test in order to ascertain whether the CISG is applicable.

part of a mixed contract in accordance with Art. 3(2) CISG.[933] Accordingly, the term 'preponderant' is open to autonomous interpretation. There are mainly two approaches to this interpretation that have been established in case law and by scholarly writings.

1. Economic Value Test

The first approach will be referred to as the 'economic value test', as it relies on criteria that are related to the economic value of the parties' obligations. The following section will outline this test, the required threshold and potential difficulties that may arise in the context of framework agreements.

a. Comparison of Value Ratios

Under the economic value test, the value of the non-sales obligations must be compared to the value of the goods in light of the entire agreement; put differently, the respective value ratios must be compared.[934] The value of the goods and the value of the non-sales elements must be assessed on the basis of hypothetical prices that could have been obtained had the parties concluded separate contracts for the sales and non-sales obligations, respectively.[935] The relevant point in time for determining the value ratio is the time of contract conclusion.[936] The rationale for this is that this point in time is the date at which the parties must be aware of which law is applicable to their agreement.[937] Consequently, changes in value prior to or subsequent to contract conclusion are deemed irrelevant under the economic value test.[938]

933. Kröll *et al./Mistelis/Raymond*, Art. 3 CISG, para. 17.
934. Milan Chamber of Arbitration, 30 January 2019, CISG-online 5573, note 20; KGer Zug, 14 December 2009, CISG-online 2026; OGer Aargau, 3 March 2009, CISG-online 2013; Tribunale Forli, 16 February 2009, CISG-online 1780; cf. also RB Noord-Holland, 6 October 2021, CISG-online 5692; BGer, 16 July 2012, CISG-online 2371; OLG Stuttgart, 18 April 2011, CISG-online 2226; OLG München, 3 December 1999, CISG-online 585; *Bridge*, Int'l Sale of Goods, para. 10.20; Brunner/Gottlieb/*Brunner/Feit*, Art. 3 CISG, para. 8; CISG-AC, Op. 4 *Perales Viscasillas*, Comments 3.3, 3.4; *Gabriel*, para. 2.57; *Gillette/Walt*, p. 61; Huber/Mullis/*Huber*, p. 46; Kröll *et al./Mistelis/Raymond*, Art. 3 CISG, para. 18; *Piltz*, AnwBl 1991, p. 59; Schlechtriem/Schwenzer/Schroeter/*Hachem*, 5th English ed., Art. 3 CISG, para. 18; Schlechtriem/Schwenzer/Schroeter/*Ferrari*, 8th German ed., Art. 3 CISG, para. 13; *Schroeter*, para. 101; Soergel/*Kreße*, Art. 3 CISG, para. 4; Staudinger/*Magnus*, Art. 3 CISG, para. 21; *C. Witz*, para. 112.41.
935. Milan Chamber of Arbitration, 30 January 2019, CISG-online 5573, note 20; KGer Zug, 14 December 2009, CISG-online 2026, para. 72; Schlechtriem/Schwenzer/Schroeter/*Hachem*, 5th English ed., Art. 3 CISG, para. 18.
936. OGer Aargau, 3 March 2009, CISG-online 2013; *Achilles*, Art. 3 CISG, para. 12; BeckOK/*Saenger*, Art. 3 CISG, para. 6; CISG-AC, Op. 4 *Perales Viscasillas*, Comment 3.3; Mankowski/*Mankowski*, Art. 3 CISG, para. 11; Schlechtriem/Schwenzer/Schroeter/*Hachem*, 5th English ed., Art. 3 CISG, para. 19; Schlechtriem/Schwenzer/Schroeter/*Ferrari*, 8th German ed., Art. 3 CISG, para. 13; Staudinger/*Magnus*, Art. 3 CISG, para. 25; *C. Witz*, para. 112.41.
937. Mankowski/*Mankowski*, Art. 3 CISG, para. 11; Schlechtriem/Schwenzer/Schroeter/*Hachem*, 5th English ed., Art. 3 CISG, para. 19; Staudinger/*Magnus*, Art. 3 CISG, para. 25.
938. *Achilles*, Art. 3 CISG, para. 12; BeckOK/*Saenger*, Art. 3 CISG, para. 6; Ferrari *et al./Saenger*, Art. 3 CISG, para. 6; Staudinger/*Magnus*, Art. 3 CISG, para. 22.

In some instances, the parties may explicitly stipulate the value of the goods and the value of the non-sales elements in their agreement, or break down the price structure in light of the different obligations.[939] It may also follow from other circumstances, such as subsequent invoices or payments, that the value of one part of the contract is preponderant compared to the other part.[940] The relevant values may further be derived from one party's cost accounting, provided that this is recognisable to the other party.[941]

Yet, in other cases, an explicit stipulation or other circumstances may be absent. For instance, the parties may agree on a lump sum in their contract, without providing further details.[942] In such a scenario, it can be challenging, if not impossible, to determine the respective value ratios.[943] One potential solution could be to utilise the market value of comparable goods or services.[944] However, a market value for services or even some types of goods will often be impossible to determine, which makes this solution appear impractical in many cases.[945] Consequently, the economic value test encounters difficulties in cases where it is not possible to determine the respective value ratios from the contract and its surrounding circumstances.[946]

b. *Required Threshold*

The majority of case law and scholarly writings hold that the non-sales obligations must exceed 50 % of the value ratio in order to be preponderant under Art. 3 (2) CISG.[947]

939. RB Kortrijk, 12 December 2007, CISG-online 3709: the value of goods in the amount of EUR 52,000 was significantly greater than the value of the services in the amount of EUR 15,700; CA Grenoble, 26 April 1995, CISG-online 154: the value of the goods in the amount of 381,200 French Francs was significantly greater than the value of the services in the amount of 118,800 French Francs; CISG-AC, Op. 4 *Perales Viscasillas*, Comment 3.4; Huber/Mullis/*Huber*, p. 47; *Perales Viscasillas*, Extending the Scope, p. 132; Schlechtriem/Schwenzer/Schroeter/*Hachem*, 5th English ed., Art. 3 CISG, para. 19.
940. Cf. RB Noord-Holland, 6 October 2021, CISG-online 5692, with a note by *Bens*, IHR 2022, p. 64; Milan Chamber of Arbitration, 30 January 2019, CISG-online 5573: the circumstances indicated that the value of the services was preponderant; LG München I, 16 November 2000, CISG-online 667: the Court ruled that the services parts were not subject to separate charges, which indicated the preponderance of the sales part; OLG München, 3 December 1999, CISG-online 585: the value of the services provided constituted a mere fraction of the total costs for the plant in the amount of DM 1,245,000; CISG-AC, Op. 4 *Perales Viscasillas*, Comment 3.4.
941. Cf. Soergel/*Kreße*, Art. 3 CISG, para. 4; similarly, MüKoHGB/*B. Köhler*, Art. 3 CISG, para. 13.
942. Schlechtriem/Schwenzer/Schroeter/*Hachem*, 5th English ed., Art. 3 CISG, para. 19.
943. LG Mainz, 26 November 1998, CISG-online 563; Brunner/Gottlieb/*Brunner/Feit*, Art. 3 CISG, para. 8; Schlechtriem/Schwenzer/Schroeter/*Hachem*, 5th English ed., Art. 3 CISG, para. 18.
944. *Achilles*, Art. 3 CISG, para. 8; MüKoBGB/*Huber*, Art. 3 CISG, para. 13.
945. But *see Achilles*, Art. 3 CISG, para. 8, proposing to rely on performance related prices and charge rates.
946. Cf. LG Mainz, 26 November 1998, CISG-online 563; CISG-AC, Op. 4 *Perales Viscasillas*, Comment 3.3; *see* Ch. 4 II. 1. c. i. below.
947. KGer Zug, 14 December 2009, CISG-online 2026; Tribunale Forli, 16 February 2009, CISG-online 1780; Brunner/Gottlieb/*Brunner/Feit*, Art. 3 CISG, para. 8; CISG-AC, Op. 4 *Perales Viscasillas*, Comment 3.4; *Enderlein/Maskow*, Art. 3 CISG, note 5; Ferrari *et al./Saenger*, Art. 3 CISG, para. 6; Huber/Mullis/*Huber*, pp. 46, 47; Kröll *et al./Mistelis/Raymond*, Art. 3 CISG, para. 18; MüKoBGB/*Huber*, Art. 3 CISG, para. 15; MüKoHGB/*B. Köhler*, Art. 3 CISG, para. 13;

If the value ratios of the non-sales obligations and the goods are roughly equivalent, the Convention should still be applicable.[948]

Another view maintains that the non-sales elements must significantly exceed 50% in order to constitute the preponderant part of the contract.[949] This view mainly contends that such an approach would facilitate an assessment of the CISG's applicability and eliminate uncertainties in borderline cases.[950] The opponents of this view argue that such an approach would in fact create further uncertainty, since it remains unclear which exact percentage would satisfy the threshold and trigger the application of the Convention.[951]

This study supports the second view. It falls in line with a *pro Conventionis* approach - in cases of doubt, the Convention should be applied.[952] It must be acknowledged that the concerns of those who oppose this view have some merit, given that the precise threshold in percentages remains unclear under this expansive view. However, this counter-argument is based on the premise that one should rely on fixed percentages in order to determine the CISG's applicability in accordance with the preponderance test. The preferable view is that a hard and fast rule that includes fixed percentages is not an appropriate means of determining the preponderant part according to Art. 3(2) CISG.[953] The economic value test should rather be conducted on a case-by-case basis, taking into account the specific circumstances of each case.[954]

c. *Difficulties with Framework Agreements*

The majority of cases that have explicitly or implicitly relied on Art. 3(2) CISG in the context of a framework agreement have not relied on the economic value test.[955] This

---

Nicolai, p. 284; Schlechtriem/Schwenzer/Schroeter/*Ferrari*, 8th German ed., Art. 3 CISG, para. 15; Staudinger/*Magnus*, Art. 3 CISG, para. 22; *C. Witz*, para. 112.41.

948. OLG München, 3 December 1995, CISG-online 585, para. 17; *Achilles*, Art. 3 CISG, para. 7; CISG-AC, Op. 4 *Perales Viscasillas*, Comment 3.4; Huber/Mullis/*Huber*, p. 46; Staudinger/*Magnus*, Art. 3 CISG, para. 22.
949. KGer Zug, 25 February 1999, CISG-online 490, para. 5; KreisGer Bern-Laupen, 29 January 1999, CISG-online 701, para. 35; Schlechtriem/Schwenzer/Schroeter/*Hachem*, 5th English ed., Art. 3 CISG, para. 20; *Schroeter*, (2001) 5 VJ, p. 77 ('clearly in excess of 50 percent'); cf. also CISG-AC, Op. 4 *Perales Viscasillas*, Comment 3.4 (a non-sales part that is slightly above 50% does not preclude the CISG's applicability).
950. BGH, 7 December 2017, CISG-online 2961, para. 44; OGH, 8 November 2005, CISG-online 1156, para. 24 ('*deutlich überwiegt*'); KGer Zug, 25 February 1999, CISG-online 490, para. 5 ('*deutlich überwiegt*'); KreisGer Bern-Laupen, 29 January 1999, CISG-online 701, para. 35; Schlechtriem/Schwenzer/Schroeter/*Hachem*, 5th English ed., Art. 3 CISG, para. 20; Soergel/*Kreße*, Art. 3 CISG, para. 4.
951. MüKoBGB/*Huber*, Art. 3 CISG, para. 15; *Nicolai*, p. 284; Staudinger/*Magnus*, Art. 3 CISG, para. 22.
952. Cf. CISG-AC, Op. 4 *Perales Viscasillas*, Comment 4.4; *Fogt*, IPRax 2003, p. 369; *Perales Viscasillas*, Extending the Scope, p. 130.
953. Schlechtriem/Schwenzer/Schroeter/*Hachem*, 5th English ed., Art. 3 CISG, para. 19; cf. also MüKoBGB/*Huber*, Art. 3 CISG, para. 15.
954. Huber/Mullis/*Huber*, p. 47.
955. Cf. RB Utrecht, 29 December 2010, CISG-online 2010, para. 17 (no explicit mention of Art. 3(2) CISG); HGer Aargau, 10 March 2010, CISG-online 2176; ICC, 12173/2004, CISG-online 2066 (no explicit mention of Art. 3(2) CISG); OLG Graz, 28 September 2000, CISG-online 798, para. 40

indicates that the economic value test is of limited use when determining the preponderant part in framework agreements. There are two main reasons that support this assumption.

i. Determination of Value Ratios Not Possible

First, framework agreements often do not explicitly stipulate the value of different obligations. With regard to the goods, it may be possible to rely on a market price, comparable prices or charge rates.[956] However, this will rarely be possible with regard to the service obligations that may also be part of a framework agreement. For instance, the determination of the value of an obligation to advertise and market goods is hardly achievable and will greatly depend on the specific circumstances of each case. Consequently, it is typically not possible to rely on market prices, comparable prices or charge rates to determine the value of the framework agreement's service part if there are no explicit or implicit stipulations.[957]

ii. Open Terms in Framework Agreements

Second, it may not (yet) be feasible to determine the value of the goods under a framework agreement at the time of contract conclusion, which is the relevant point in time for the economic value test.[958] This is due to the fact that the parties to a framework agreement often leave terms regarding the goods, their quantity or their price open for later determination. These open terms will then be stipulated once the goods are ordered or the individual sales contracts are concluded,[959] i.e., after the framework agreement has already been concluded. In light of this, it may not yet be possible to determine the precise value of the goods at the time of the framework agreement's conclusion. To illustrate this point, if the parties agree on a requirement clause, the precise quantity of the goods and accordingly their overall value may not yet be fixed at the time of contract conclusion.

The aforementioned considerations demonstrate that the economic value test is of limited use when determining the preponderant part in framework agreements. Therefore, additional criteria may be relevant in determining the preponderant part in framework agreements.

(no explicit mention of Art. 3(2) CISG); Supr. Ct. Italy, 14 December 1999, CISG-online 1314 (no explicit mention of Art. 3(2) CISG); ICC, 8817/1997, CISG-online 750; OGer Luzern, 8 January 1997, CISG-online 228, para. 11.

956. Cf. *Achilles*, Art. 3 CISG, para. 8; MüKoBGB/*Huber*, Art. 3 CISG, para. 13.
957. *Karner/Koziol*, para. 66, 81, who highlight the challenges of establishing a market price for services in a different context.
958. OGer Aargau, 3 March 2009, CISG-online 2013; *Achilles*, Art. 3 CISG, para. 12; BeckOK/*Saenger*, Art. 3 CISG, para. 6; CISG-AC, Op. 4 *Perales Viscasillas*, Comment 3.3; Mankowski/*Mankowski*, Art. 3 CISG, para. 11; Schlechtriem/Schwenzer/Schroeter/*Hachem*, 5th English ed., Art. 3 CISG, para. 19; Schlechtriem/Schwenzer/Schroeter/*Ferrari*, 8th German ed., Art. 3 CISG, para. 13; Staudinger/*Magnus*, Art. 3 CISG, para. 25.
959. Such open terms do, however, not hinder the CISG's applicability, *see* Ch. 3 IV. above.

2. Additional Criteria: Overall Assessment

The prevailing view among scholars and case law appears to be that the economic value test should be supplemented or even revised by additional criteria, such as the parties' intentions as expressed in the contract or surrounding circumstances.[960] This is particularly relevant in cases where the value ratio is difficult or impossible to establish.[961]

This view is supported by the drafting history of the Convention:[962] a proposal by a UK delegate to replace the word 'preponderant' with 'major value in practice' was withdrawn.[963] In particular, *Farnsworth*, a US delegate, expressed his concerns that 'contracts for the supply of services would be treated as sale of goods simply because the materials used in the process were very expensive'.[964] To illustrate, *Farnsworth* referred to a contract to paint a ceiling with gold leaf; in such a contract, the parties are more interested in the labour elements, even though the price for the gold leaf may be higher and thus preponderant in the sense of Art. 3(2) CISG.[965]

a. Relevant Factors

Among the aforementioned additional criteria are primarily the intentions of the parties and the parties' interests as set out in the contract and the surrounding circumstances.[966] Naturally, this is a matter of interpretation in each specific case. Consequently, a case-by-case analysis of the entire contract as well as all surrounding circumstances is necessary in order to determine the preponderant part, i.e., an overall

960. Cf. BGH, 7 December 2017, CISG-online 2961, para. 44; OGH, 22 November 2011, CISG-online 2239, para. 19; OLG Stuttgart, 18 April 2011, CISG-online 2226, para. 44; KGer Zug, 14 December 2009, CISG-online 2026, para. 72; OLG Innsbruck, 18 December 2007, CISG-online 1735, para. 60; OLG Dresden, 11 June 2007, CISG-online 1720, para. 47; Hof van Beroep Gent, 24 November 2004, CISG-online 966; OLG München, 3 December 1999, CISG-online 585, para. 17; LG Mainz, 26 November 1998, CISG-online 563, para. 19; Brunner/Gottlieb/*Brunner/Feit*, Art. 3 CISG, para. 8; CISG-AC, Op. 4 *Perales Viscasillas*, Comment 3.4; Kröll *et al./Mistelis/Raymond*, Art. 3 CISG, para. 19; MüKoBGB/*Huber*, Art. 3 CISG, para. 14; MüKoHGB/*B. Köhler*, Art. 3 CISG, para. 13; *Piltz*, AnwBl 1991, p. 59; Schlechtriem/Schwenzer/Schroeter/*Hachem*, 5th English ed., Art. 3 CISG, para. 18; Schlechtriem/Schwenzer/Schroeter/*Ferrari*, 8th German ed., Art. 3 CISG, para. 14; *Schroeter*, (2005) 5 VJ, p. 78; *Schroeter*, para. 101; Staudinger/*Magnus*, Art. 3 CISG, para. 21; *C. Witz*, para. 112.41.
961. LG Mainz, 26 November 1998, CISG-online 563; cf. also Brunner/Gottlieb/*Brunner/Feit*, Art. 3 CISG, para. 8; CISG-AC, Op. 4 *Perales Viscasillas*, Comment 3.3.
962. Accord MüKoBGB/*Huber*, Art. 3 CISG, para. 14; MüKoHGB/*B. Köhler*, Art. 3 CISG, para. 13; Schlechtriem/Schwenzer/Schroeter/*Ferrari*, 8th German ed., Art. 3 CISG, para. 14; Staudinger/*Magnus*, Art. 3 CISG, para. 21; but *see Grunewald*, p. 59 in footnote 131.
963. O.R., pp. 241 et seq.
964. O.R., p. 242, para. 37 (*Farnsworth*).
965. O.R., p. 242, para. 37 (*Farnsworth*).
966. BGH, 7 December 2017, CISG-online 2961, para. 44; OGH, 22 November 2011, CISG-online 2239, para. 19; KGer Zug, 14 December 2009, CISG-online 2026, para. 72; OLG Innsbruck, 18 December 2007, CISG-online 1735, para. 60; OLG Dresden, 11 June 2007, CISG-online 1720, para. 47; OGH, 8 November 2005, CISG-online 1156, para. 24; Hof van Beroep Gent, 24 November 2004, CISG-online 966; OLG München, 3 December 1999, CISG-online 585, para. 17; ICC, 7153/1992, CISG-online 35; Brunner/Gottlieb/*Brunner/Feit*, Art. 3 CISG, para. 8; *Czerwenka*, p. 144; Kröll *et al./Mistelis/Raymond*, Art. 3 CISG, para. 19; MüKoBGB/*Huber*, Art. 3

assessment.[967] The text of a contract itself may be a starting point for this overall assessment.[968] In this context, it is essential to consider the weight given by the parties to the different contractual obligations.[969] This may be deducted from the degree of detail that the parties have allocated to each obligation in the contract.[970] Moreover, other circumstances surrounding the contract conclusion should be taken into account.[971]

Finally, the primary purpose of the contract should be found in order to determine the preponderant part in accordance with Art. 3(2) CISG.[972] In this context, it has been posited that the service obligations are preponderant if they constitute the 'characteristic obligation' under the contract.[973] This is problematic insofar as one cannot rely on characterisations and distinctions originating from domestic or regional law, such as the relevant private international law rules, in order to identify the 'characteristic obligation'. For instance, distribution contracts are presumably characterised as service contracts under the Brussels I Regulation (recast) and Rome I Regulation.[974] Such characterisations and distinctions that originate from regional law must be disregarded under the CISG.[975] Instead, the Convention's scope of application must be interpreted autonomously, without having recourse to characterisations of regional or domestic law.[976]

CISG, para. 14; MüKoHGB/*B. Köhler*, Art. 3 CISG, para. 13; *Piltz*, AnwBl 1991, p. 59; Schlechtriem/Schwenzer/Schroeter/*Ferrari*, 8th German ed., Art. 3 CISG, para. 14; cf. also ICC, 12173/2004, CISG-online 2066.

967. OLG Innsbruck, 18 December 2007, CISG-online 1735, para. 60; OGH, 8 November 2005, CISG-online 1156, para. 24; MüKoBGB/*Huber*, Art. 3 CISG, para. 14, proposing an 'overall assessment' of the relevant circumstances; MüKoHGB/*B. Köhler*, Art. 3 CISG, para. 13; Schlechtriem/Schwenzer/Schroeter/*Hachem*, 5th English ed., Art. 3 CISG, para. 19.
968. LG Mainz, 26 November 1998, CISG-online 563, para. 20; ICC, 7153/1992, CISG-online 35.
969. ICC, 7153/1992, CISG-online 35; CISG-AC, Op. 4 *Perales Viscasillas*, Comment 3.4; Schlechtriem/Schwenzer/Schroeter/*Hachem*, 5th English ed., Art. 3 CISG, para. 18; cf. also *C. Witz*, para. 112.61 (*'le centre du gravité du contrat'*).
970. LG Mainz, 26 November 1998, CISG-online 563, para. 20; Huber/Mullis/*Huber*, p. 47; cf. also Soergel/*Kreße*, Art. 3 CISG, para. 4.
971. Milan Chamber of Arbitration, 30 January 2019, CISG-online 5573, note 20; LG Mainz, 26 November 1998, CISG-online 563, para. 19.
972. Milan Chamber of Arbitration, 30 January 2019, CISG-online 5573, note 20; Supr. Ct. Italy, 9 June 1995, CISG-online 314; cf. further Hof van Beroep Gent, 24 November 2004, CISG-online 966; MüKoBGB/*Huber*, Art. 3 CISG, para. 14; *Piltz*, AnwBl 1991, p. 59; Soergel/*Kreße*, Art. 3 CISG, para. 4; *Torsello*, p. 244.
973. OLG München, 3 December 1999, CISG-online 585, para. 17: the preponderant part is contingent upon the characteristic obligation of the contract; KreisGer Bern-Laupen, 29 January 1999, CISG-online 701, para. 35; *Czerwenka*, pp. 144, 145; Schlechtriem/*Herber*, 1st English ed., Art. 3 CISG, para. 5; Witz/Salger/Lorenz/*Lorenz*, Art. 3 CISG, para. 4.
974. ECJ, 31 January 2013, C-9/12 (with regard to the Brussels I Regulation prior to its recasting); Rome I Regulation, preliminary remark No. (17); *Magnus*, IHR 2018, p. 50.
975. *Perales Viscasillas*, Extending the Scope, p. 130; *Perales Viscasillas*, Int'l Distribution Contracts and CISG, p. 56.
976. Cf. Tribunale di Forli, 6 March 2012, CISG-online 2585, IHR 2013, p. 198; Tribunale di Padova, 11 January 2005, CISG-online 967; *Perales Viscasillas*, Extending the Scope, pp. 129, 130.

b. *Modification under Article 6 CISG?*

The aforementioned considerations demonstrate that the intentions of the parties and their interests as expressed in the contract and the surrounding circumstances should prevail when determining the preponderant part under Art. 3(2) CISG.[977] In this context, *Hachem* holds that the parties' intentions would also prevail if one were to assume a modification of Art. 3 CISG in line with Art. 6 CISG – the same result could be achieved this way.[978] This assertion should be approached with a degree of scepticism. Indeed, the parties' intentions are a relevant factor under the preponderance test enshrined in Art. 3(2) CISG.

However, this follows from an autonomous interpretation of the term 'preponderant',[979] which must be distinguished from a modification in accordance with Art. 6 CISG. The latter provision permits the parties to exclude the Convention's applicability or to modify its rules, provided that the CISG applies in the first place.[980] If the CISG is not applicable, e.g., based on a preponderant non-sales part of the contract, the parties should not be able to invoke Art. 6 CISG to derogate from Art. 3(2) CISG, thereby effectively extending the Convention's sphere of application.[981] This is due to the fact that the Convention does not deal with extensions of its own sphere of application.[982] Opting into the Convention in cases where it is not applicable must be evaluated in accordance with the relevant international private law rules; the parties should not be able to circumvent these rules by relying on a modification or derogation under Art. 6 CISG in order to extend the Convention's sphere of application.[983] In any case, Art. 6 CISG presupposes the CISG's applicability before it can be invoked by the parties.[984] For these reasons, the CISG's provisions on its sphere of application have been referred to as 'fundamental rules [...] that stand outside the zone accorded by Article 6 to party autonomy'.[985] It should therefore not be possible to extend the CISG's sphere of application 'through the backdoor' by allowing a modification of Art. 3 CISG in accordance with Art. 6 CISG.

977. BGH, 7 December 2017, CISG-online 2961, para. 44; OGH, 22 November 2011, CISG-online 2239, para. 19; KGer Zug, 14 December 2009, CISG-online 2026, para. 72; OLG Innsbruck, 18 December 2007, CISG-online 1735, para. 60; OLG Dresden, 11 June 2007, CISG-online 1720, para. 47; OGH, 8 November 2005, CISG-online 1156, para. 24; Hof van Beroep Gent, 24 November 2004, CISG-online 966; OLG München, 3 December 1999, CISG-online 585, para. 17; ICC, 7153/1992, CISG-online 35; Brunner/Gottlieb/*Brunner/Feit*, Art. 3 CISG, para. 8; *Czerwenka*, p. 144; Kröll *et al./Mistelis/Raymond*, Art. 3 CISG, para. 19; MüKoBGB/*Huber*, Art. 3 CISG, para. 14; MükoHGB/*B. Köhler*, Art. 3 CISG, para. 13; *Piltz*, AnwBl 1991, p. 59; Schlechtriem/Schwenzer/Schroeter/*Ferrari*, 8th German ed., Art. 3 CISG, para. 14; cf. also ICC, 12173/2004, CISG-online 2066.
978. Schlechtriem/Schwenzer/Schroeter/*Hachem*, 5th English ed., Art. 3 CISG, para. 19.
979. *See* Ch. 4 II. 1, 2. a. above.
980. *Maier-Lohmann*, para. 526.
981. Cf. *Bridge*, Int'l Sale of Goods, para. 10.54; *Maier-Lohmann*, para. 526.
982. *Bridge*, Int'l Sale of Goods, para. 10.54; *Piltz*, AnwBl 1990, p. 61; *Maier-Lohmann*, para. 526.
983. *Maier-Lohmann*, paras 314, 315, 526; cf. also *Bridge*, Int'l Sale of Goods, para. 10.54; *Lindbach*, pp. 76, 77; Mankowski/*Mankowski*, Art. 3 CISG, para. 3.
984. *Bridge*, Int'l Sale of Goods, para. 10.54.
985. *Bridge*, Int'l Sale of Goods, para. 10.54; cf. also *Lindbach*, pp. 76, 77.

c. *Overall Assessment with Regard to Framework Agreements*

As outlined above, the preponderant part in framework agreements usually cannot be determined solely by relying on the economic value test.[986] Consequently, it is necessary to consider additional criteria in order to determine the preponderant part in framework agreements, namely, an overall assessment. Among those criteria are the parties' intentions and their interests, the agreement's wording, the weight given by the parties to the obligations, and the circumstances surrounding the contract conclusion.[987]

It is additionally vital to acknowledge that framework agreements are long-term contracts, with the contract's preponderant part being subject to change over time. The intended duration of the agreement, later extensions and prolongation agreements should thus be sufficiently regarded when determining the preponderant part.[988] If parties were to modify, amend or supplement the framework agreement in question by adding further non-sales-related terms, it may be necessary to determine the preponderant part once more in accordance with Art. 3(2) CISG.[989]

Consequently, the preponderant part of a framework agreement and, thus, the CISG's applicability will depend on the specific circumstances of each case.[990] In contrast, a number of courts have simply held that distribution contracts are excluded from the CISG based on their typical content in accordance with Art. 3(2) CISG, without conducting an in-depth analysis of the distribution contracts in dispute.[991] These decisions are excessively broad and not persuasive. The better approach is to resort to an overall assessment in light of the surrounding circumstances, which is to be applied on a case-by-case basis.[992]

---

986. *See* Ch. 4 II. 1. c. above; but *see Magnus*, ZEuP 1997, p. 830 (sales part must be preponderant in terms of value).
987. *See* Ch. 4 II. 2. a. above.
988. Mankowski/*Mankowski*, Art. 3 CISG, para. 11.
989. *See* Schlechtriem/Schwenzer/Schroeter/*Schroeter*, 5th English ed., Art. 29 CISG, para. 34; Schlechtriem/Schwenzer/Schroeter/*Schroeter*, 8th German ed., Art. 29 CISG, para. 23.
990. Cf. Tribunale di Forli, 6 March 2012, CISG-online 2585, IHR 2013, p. 199 (the CISG was applicable to the distribution contract based on the specific obligations agreed upon); *Bridge*, Int'l Sale of Goods, para. 10.22; Huber/Mullis/*Huber*, p. 48; *Perales Viscasillas*, Extending the Scope, p. 128 ('need to study the contractual obligations agreed to by the parties'); *Perović*, (2011) 59 Belgrade L. Rev., pp. 190, 191; *Zubović/Filipović*, p. 162; but *see* Brunner/Gottlieb/*Brunner/Feit*, Art. 3 CISG, para. 14 (non-sales elements are generally preponderant in framework agreements).
991. CA Reims, 30 April 2013, CISG-online 2479, para. 19; HGer Aargau, 10 March 2013, CISG-online 2176, para. 22; OGer Luzern, 8 January 1997, CISG-online 228, para. 11; cf. also Brunner/Gottlieb/*Brunner/Feit*, Art. 3 CISG, para. 14 (non-sales elements generally preponderant in framework agreements).
992. *Bridge*, Int'l Sale of Goods, para. 10.22; Huber/Mullis/*Huber*, p. 48; *Perales Viscasillas*, Extending the Scope, p. 128; *Perović*, (2011) 59 Belgrade L. Rev., p. 190; *Zubović/Filipović*, p. 162; primarily in relation to turn-key contracts, but also with regard to Art. 3(2) CISG: *Mahnken*, IHR 2020, p. 242; *see also C. Witz*, para. 112.61, proposing that many distribution contracts should be governed by the CISG, with the exception of franchise contracts ('*Il en résulte que de nombreux contrats de distribution ont vocation à être régis par la Convention, notamment les contrats de distribution sélective ou les contrats d'approvisionnement exclusifs, alors que les contrats de franchise par exemple, axés sur la transmission d'un savoir-faire, devraient échapper à la Convention*').

This approach has the advantage that the particularities of each specific contract can be taken into consideration.[993] It must be acknowledged that the application of a case-by-case approach will inevitably result in legal uncertainty for the parties. This is justified, however, by the fact that framework agreements are inherently heterogenous and vary considerably. The obligations included in such agreements may differ from case to case, especially as there is no uniform understanding on an international level.[994] Consequently, the CISG should neither be indiscriminately applied to nor universally excluded from all types of framework agreements, including distribution contracts.

i. The Primary Purpose in Particular

Similarly, the primary purpose of a framework agreement should also be determined in light of the specific circumstances of each case.[995] In this context, some decisions and commentators have held that the primary purpose of distribution contracts is to implement a sales concept (e.g., marketing strategy), organise distribution and other framework conditions, rather than to sell goods.[996]

The determination of the primary purpose of distribution contracts on a general level is not a convincing proposition. Although some distribution contracts may indeed have such a primary purpose, not all types of distribution agreements are alike.[997] Furthermore, one might respond to this view that distribution contracts are ultimately always for the sale of goods, and that all other obligations are interrelated with that; this could suggest that their primary purpose is in fact the sale of goods.[998]

Neither of the two generalisations is persuasive. The primary purpose of a specific distribution contract or any other framework agreement must be determined in light of the particular circumstances of each case.[999] This assessment presupposes that the framework agreement falls within the CISG's sphere of application (Art. 1 CISG) in

993. *See Zubović/Filipović*, p. 162.
994. Cf. *Bridge*, Int'l Sale of Goods, para. 10.22; *C. Witz*, para. 112.61.
995. Cf. Milan Chamber of Arbitration, 30 January 2019, CISG-online 5573.
996. CA Reims, 30 April 2013, CISG-online 2479, para. 13; OGer Luzern, 8 January 1997, CISG-online 228, para. 11; OLG Düsseldorf, 11 July 1996, CISG-online 201; *see also* Kröll *et al./Mistelis*, Art. 1 CISG, para. 33; *Piltz*, AnwBl 1991, p. 59; Schlechtriem/Schwenzer/Schroeter/*Ferrari*, 8th German ed., Art. 1 CISG, para. 31; *C. Witz*, para. 112.61.
997. *See* Tribunale di Forli, 6 March 2012, CISG-online 2585, IHR 2013, p. 199; *Zubović/Filipović*, p. 162.
998. *Perales Viscasillas*, Extending the Scope, p. 126; cf. also Supr. Ct. Italy, 14 December 1999, CISG-online 1314; *Thieffry*, Dr. prat. com. int. 1993, p. 64, who highlights that the clauses typically included in a distribution contract bear resemblance to the provisions set forth in the CISG.
999. *Bridge*, Int'l Sale of Goods, para. 10.22; Huber/Mullis/*Huber*, p. 48; *Perović*, (2011) 59 Belgrade L. Rev., pp. 190, 191; *Zubović/Filipović*, p. 162; cf. also Supr. Ct. Italy, 14 December 1999, CISG-online 1314.

the first place.[1000] In this context, it is essential to refrain from relying on characterisations and distinctions known under domestic or regional law.[1001]

ii. *Issues with the Two-Tier Structure?*

Some framework agreements are structured in a manner that may be described as two-tier. This structure entails the framework agreement being followed by individual sales contracts that are concluded on the basis of the former.[1002] Should a framework agreement be structured in this manner, it may be questionable whether Art. 3(2) CISG can be applied. The reason is that Art. 3(2) CISG requires sales and service obligations to be combined in one single contract.[1003]

If a framework agreement follows a two-tier structure, there is not one unified contract, but rather a separation between sales contracts and the framework agreement. In light of this distinction, some case law and scholars have proposed a simple formula with regard to the CISG's applicability to framework agreements: the CISG does not apply to the framework agreement itself, but it does apply to the individual sales contracts concluded in execution of this framework agreement.[1004]

Bridge, *Fawcett* and *Harris* refer to this approach as 'a type of *dépecage*', given that different laws would apply to contracts that are closely related.[1005] They suggest avoiding this outcome by treating the framework agreement and the individual sales contract as one whole contract, weighing the sales obligations against the distribution obligations in accordance with the preponderance test (Art. 3(2) CISG).[1006]

Such an holistic approach is not necessary. As held above, only framework agreements that at least contain an obligation to conclude individual sales contracts

1000. *See* Ch. 3 III. above.
1001. *Perales Viscasillas*, Extending the Scope, p. 130; *Perales Viscasillas*, Int'l Distribution Contracts and CISG, p. 56.
1002. *See* Ch. 2 III. 1. above.
1003. *Gabriel*, para. 2.58; *Honnold/Flechtner*, Art. 3 CISG, para. 79; jurisPK-BGB/*Münch*, Art. 3 CISG, para. 8; Mankowski/*Mankowski*, Art. 3 CISG, para. 13; MüKoBGB/*Huber*, Art. 3 CISG, para. 11; MüKoHGB/*B. Köhler*, Art. 3 CISG, para. 16; *Piltz*, para. 2-35; Schlechtriem/Schwenzer/Schroeter/*Ferrari*, 8th German ed., Art. 3 CISG, para. 12; Schlechtriem/Schwenzer/Schroeter/*Hachem*, 5th English ed., Art. 3 CISG, para. 12; Staudinger/*Magnus*, Art. 3 CISG, para. 9; Witz/Salger/Lorenz/*Lorenz*, Art. 3 CISG, para. 5.
1004. Dist. Ct. Szczecin, 13 February 2015, CISG-online 6807, paras 73, 74; Dist. Ct. Rzeszów, 28 February 2014, CISG-online 6752, para. 95; Foreign Trade Court of Arbitration of the CC and Industry of Serbia, 28 January 2009, CISG-online 1856; HGer Aargau, 10 March 2010, CISG-online 2176, para. 22; CA Versailles, 19 February 2004, CISG-online 3345; OLG Düsseldorf, 11 July 1996, CISG-online 201; HGer Zürich, 8 April 1999, CISG-online 489; KGer Schaffhausen, 23 April 2002, CISG-online 731; OGer Luzern, 8 January 1997, CISG-online 228; cf. Schlechtriem/Schwenzer/Schroeter/*Ferrari*, Art. 1 CISG, para. 31; Kröll *et al.*/*Mistelis*, Art. 1 CISG, para. 33; BeckOK/*Saenger*, Art. 1 CISG, para. 6 (with different reasoning); MüKoBGB/*Huber*, Art. 1 CISG, para. 11; *C. Witz*, para. 112.61.
1005. *Bridge*, Choice of Law and the CISG, p. 96 ('quasi-*dépecage*'); *Fawcett/Harris/Bridge*, para. 16.95.
1006. *Bridge*, Choice of Law and the CISG, p. 96; *Fawcett/Harris/Bridge*, para. 16.95; but *see* Mankowski/*Mankowski*, Art. 3 CISG, para. 13 (separate contracts should not be considered an overarching transaction).

should fall within the CISG's scope of application.[1007] Such framework agreements contain a sales element, namely the obligation to conclude individual sales contracts (precontractual sales element).[1008] Consequently, it is the framework agreement itself that combines sales obligations with non-sales obligations when it includes non-sales elements in addition to the obligation to conclude individual sales contracts. If this is the case, the obligation to conclude sales contracts must be weighed against the non-sales obligations in order to determine the preponderant part.[1009]

Even if a framework agreement that falls under the Convention's ambit follows a two-tier structure, the preponderant part of this framework agreement can and should be determined on its own, without having regard to the individual sales contracts. If its non-sales part is not preponderant, the CISG may be applied not only to the individual sales contracts but also to the framework itself.[1010]

d. *Examples from Case Law Applying the CISG*

In order to illustrate the CISG's application to framework agreements that combine a sales part with a non-sales part, the following will outline a number of cases.

One illustrative example can be found in a case decided by the Court of Appeal Graz, where the Court applied the CISG to a framework agreement that obliged the parties to conclude individual sales contracts.[1011] The framework agreement in this case, *inter alia,* included an obligation of the seller to abstain from direct sales in Austria as well as an obligation of the buyer (distributor) to maintain storage for the goods.[1012] Although these obligations may not directly fall under Art. 3(2) CISG,[1013] they may nevertheless be considered non-sales elements under the general principle derived from Art. 3(2) CISG. Ultimately, the Court concluded that the framework agreement had a preponderant sales part, without giving a detailed reasoning.[1014]

Moreover, the District Court Utrecht rendered a decision pertaining to a distribution agreement that incorporated sales obligations in *sensu stricto,* along with exclusivity and advertising obligations of the seller.[1015] In this case, the Court simply held that the contract primarily involved sale obligations, i.e., the sale and purchase of movable goods.[1016]

Finally, the Italian Supreme Court addressed an agreement that combined sales obligations with non-sales distribution obligations.[1017] It held that the transaction in

1007. *See* Ch. 3 III. above.
1008. *See* Ch. 3 III. 1. b. ii. above.
1009. Cf. OLG Graz, 28 September 2000, CISG-online 798, para. 40; *Zubović/Filipović,* p. 162.
1010. Cf. only OLG Graz, 28 September 2000, CISG-online 798, para. 40; *Grunewald,* p. 57; Schlechtriem/Schwenzer/Schroeter/*Schroeter,* 5th English ed., Intro Arts 14–24 CISG, para. 24; *Zubović/Filipović,* p. 162.
1011. OLG Graz, 28 September 2000, CISG-online 798, paras 2, 38.
1012. OLG Graz, 28 September 2000, CISG-online 798, para. 2.
1013. *See* Ch. 4 I. 2. a. above.
1014. OLG Graz, 28 September 2000, CISG-online 798, para. 40.
1015. RB Utrecht, 29 December 2010, CISG-online 5325, para. 16.
1016. RB Utrecht, 29 December 2010, CISG-online 5325, para. 17.
1017. Supr. Ct. Italy, 14 December 1999, CISG-online 1314, note 2.

question was atypical and, in fact, constituted a sales contract with an ancillary distribution part.[1018] The Court further explained that the primary purpose of the contract was the sale of goods, which were subsequently to be distributed in the United Kingdom, as evidenced by a letter.[1019] Consequently, the Court found the CISG to be applicable, which was relevant in order to determine the Italian Court's jurisdiction over the dispute.[1020]

It is worth noting that none of the aforementioned courts explicitly referenced Art. 3(2) CISG. However, they did address its substance, as they essentially determined the preponderant part of each mixed framework agreement. The outcomes of these decisions are, therefore, convincing; although one could criticise that they should have included an explicit reference to Art. 3(2) CISG or the general principle underlying this provision.

3. Conclusion

Framework agreements that combine sales obligations that fall within the CISG's scope with service or labour obligations that fall outside the CISG's scope are subject to the assessment set forth in Art. 3(2) CISG. The same applies to mixed framework agreements that combine other non-sales obligations, such as exclusivity or non-competition obligations, with sales obligations. Although Art. 3(2) CISG is not directly applicable in such cases, the principle derived from this provision may nonetheless be applicable. Art. 3(2) CISG or at least the general principle derived from this provision should equally apply to preliminary agreements as well as framework agreements that combine the obligation to conclude individual sales contracts with non-sales obligations.

In order to determine the preponderant part, the economic value ratios of the different contractual obligations must be compared. With regard to the threshold, the preferable view is that the non-sales part of the contract must significantly exceed the threshold of 50% in order to be considered the preponderant part. Yet, framework agreements often lack an explicit stipulation of the relevant value ratios. In addition, framework agreements frequently contain open or indefinite terms regarding the goods, their quantity and the price, which are to be determined only after the contract has already been concluded. Consequently, it may be challenging or even impossible to establish the relevant value ratios at the time of contract conclusion. For these reasons, the economic value test is of limited use for determining the preponderant part in framework agreements.

Apart from the economic value test, additional criteria should be taken into account when determining the preponderant part, namely, an overall assessment. Among these criteria for an overall assessment are, *inter alia*, the parties' intentions and interests, the text of the contract, the weight given to the different obligations, the

1018. Supr. Ct. Italy, 14 December 1999, CISG-online 1314, note 2.
1019. Supr. Ct. Italy, 14 December 1999, CISG-online 1314, note 2.
1020. Supr. Ct. Italy, 14 December 1999, CISG-online 1314, note 3.

intended duration of the contract, the circumstances surrounding the contract conclusion, and the primary purpose of the contract. It should, however, be noted that one cannot rely on characterisations and distinctions that originate from domestic or regional law in order to find the 'characteristic obligations' of a framework agreement.

With regard to framework agreements, it is typically not possible to determine the preponderant part solely by relying on the economic value test. Therefore, it is necessary to rely on additional criteria, namely an overall assessment. Consequently, the CISG's applicability will depend on the particular circumstances of each case. This approach appears to be justified with regard to framework agreements, given the considerable heterogeneity of such contracts. It does not pose any problems that some framework agreements follow a two-tier structure. The preponderant part of such framework agreements must still be determined on its own, without having regard to the individual sales contracts. A number of decisions have demonstrated that the Convention may be applicable to mixed framework agreements based on their preponderant sales part.

III. CONSEQUENCES OF THE CISG'S APPLICABILITY TO MIXED FRAMEWORK AGREEMENTS

Upon determining the preponderant part of a framework agreement, one may conclude that the CISG is applicable, as the non-sales part is not preponderant in the sense of Art. 3(2) CISG. This prompts the question of the extent to which the CISG governs such mixed framework agreements, and whether it applies to the entire agreement. If the Convention does apply to the entire agreement, it may be unclear how it deals with the non-sales obligations included in a mixed framework agreement. The following part will address these issues.

1. Extent of the CISG's Applicability

The extent of the CISG's applicability to a particular mixed framework agreement is subject to dispute among scholars. Two basic positions can be distinguished. The first position holds that the CISG should be applied only to the sales obligations in a mixed framework agreement.[1021] According to the second position, the CISG should be applied to the entire agreement including the non-sales obligations.[1022]

1021. CA Grenoble, 26 April 1995, CISG-online 153; *Bridge*, Int'l Sale of Goods, para. 10.22; Reithmann/Martiny/*Fabig*, para. 37.67 *in fine*; *Thieffry*, Dr. prat. com. int. 1993, pp. 64 et seq.; *Torsello*, p. 246; identifying these two basic positions under various domestic laws: *Schwenzer/Ranetunge/Tafur*, (2019) 10 Indian J. Int'l Econ. L., pp. 178, 179; *Schwenzer/Ranetunge/Tafur*, (2019/20) 39 J. L. & Com., p. 312.

1022. Cf. RB Utrecht, 29 December 2010, CISG-online 5325; OLG Graz, 28 September 2000, CISG-online 798, paras 38 et seq.; MüKoBGB/*Huber*, Art. 1 CISG, para. 11; *Perales Viscasillas*, Extending the Scope, pp. 128, 129; *Perales Viscasillas*, Int'l Distribution Contracts and CISG, p. 55; *Piltz*, AnwBl 1990, p. 59; *Schroeter*, para. 92; *Schwenzer*, Challenges of the 2020s, pp. 44, 45; cf. also *Schwenzer/Ranetunge/Tafur*, (2019) 10 Indian J. Int'l Econ. L., pp. 178, 179; *Schwenzer/Ranetunge/Tafur*, (2019/20) 39 J. L. & Com., p. 312.

a. *Approach 1: The CISG Applies Only to the Sales Part of a Framework Agreement*

The first approach entails the application of the CISG exclusively to the sales part of a mixed framework agreement. In contrast, the non-sales part is subject to the relevant domestic law, which results in a form of *dépeçage*.[1023] This position is supported by *Thieffry*, *Torsello* and a French Court of Appeal.

i. Thieffry's *Suggestion*

Thieffry points out that distribution contracts typically include sales terms that are strikingly similar to the provisions set forth in the CISG.[1024] Consequently, he concludes that the Convention contains provisions that may be directly applied to distribution contracts.[1025] At the same time, he admits that the CISG was not drafted to address other questions pertaining to such contracts, such as the performance or termination of exclusive distribution contracts.[1026] Therefore, *Thieffry* proposes that the CISG should generally be applicable to the sales part of an international distribution contract, whereas domestic law should govern the non-sales part.[1027] He posits that this would align with the parties' intentions:[1028] they are typically interested in the existence of uniform standards for the sales part of their transaction in order to avoid clashes between different domestic laws.[1029] Furthermore, *Thieffry* rejects the view that the CISG should be applied solely to the individual sales contracts but not to the framework agreement, arguing that this approach is impractical and fails to align with the parties' true intentions.[1030]

ii. Torsello's *Position*

Similarly, *Torsello* maintains that a *dépeçage* should be applied to international distribution agreements, provided that this is supported by the parties' intentions and that the contract includes both sales terms and non-sales terms.[1031] He argues that it would typically not align with the parties' intentions to deny the CISG's applicability to the sales part of the distribution agreement – at least when the parties have made it

1023. Cf. on the term in this context *Bridge*, Int'l Sale of Goods, para. 10.22; *Thieffry*, Dr. prat. com. int. 1993, p. 65.
1024. *Thieffry*, Dr. prat. com. int. 1993, p. 64.
1025. *Thieffry*, Dr. prat. com. int. 1993, p. 65.
1026. *Thieffry*, Dr. prat. com. int. 1993, p. 63.
1027. *Thieffry*, Dr. prat. com. int. 1993, p. 65; similarly, *Bridge*, Int'l Sale of Goods, para. 10.22, holding that such a *dépeçage* 'has much to commend it'; *Gillette/Walt*, pp. 62, 63: 'In that case the main contract will be both a framework and a sales contract. However, the CIGS only governs the latter contract'; Reithmann/Martiny/*Fabig*, para. 37.67 *in fine* ('*Vielmehr sind die vertriebsrechtlichen Fragestellungen nie dem CISG zu unterstellen* […]').
1028. *Thieffry*, Dr. prat. com. int. 1993, p. 65.
1029. *Thieffry*, Dr. prat. com. int. 1993, p. 67.
1030. *Thieffry*, Dr. prat. com. int. 1993, pp. 66, 67; cf. also *Bridge*, Int'l Sale of Goods, para. 10.22.
1031. *Torsello*, p. 246.

clear 'that they believe the conclusion of individual sales contracts to be a certain future occurrence'.[1032] Furthermore, such a *dépeçage* would be consistent with the need to have recourse to domestic law with regard to the non-sales obligations in distribution agreements, according to *Torsello*.[1033]

iii. Société E. Ambrosio v. Entreprise Alain Veyron

The Court of Appeal Grenoble has held that the CISG was applicable to the sales part of a 'commercial collaboration agreement', whereas the non-sales part was to be governed by domestic French law.[1034] The agreement provided, among other things, for the sale of goods and the representation and promotion of the goods in return for a commission,[1035] making it somewhat comparable to international distribution agreements. The Court essentially relied on a *dépeçage* and split the obligations under the contract with respect to the applicable law.[1036]

In summary, all of these authorities concurred that the CISG should be applied solely to the sales obligations set forth in framework agreements, whereas the non-sales obligations should be governed by domestic law.

b. Approach 2: The CISG Applies to the Entire Framework Agreement

The second approach entails the application of the CISG to the framework agreement as a whole.[1037] Consequently, the sales obligations as well as the non-sales obligations would be subject to the Convention.

Huber holds that a mixed framework agreement should fall in its entirety under the CISG, provided that the non-sales part is not preponderant in the sense of Art. 3(2) CISG, as this would align with a general principle derived from this provision.[1038] He further elaborates that the CISG's gap-filling mechanism should be applied if the Convention does not contain rules for the non-sales obligations included in mixed framework agreements: 'internal' gaps are to be settled in conformity with the CISG's general principles, whereas 'external' gaps should be settled by the domestic law that is applicable by virtue of international private law rules in accordance with Art. 7(2) CISG.[1039]

Perales Viscasillas relies on a 'unitary contractual approach' under Art. 3 CISG: the Convention should be applied to the entire contract if the non-sales obligations in

1032. *Torsello*, p. 246.
1033. *Torsello*, p. 247.
1034. CA Grenoble, 26 April 1995, CISG-online 153.
1035. CA Grenoble, 26 April 1995, CISG-online 153.
1036. CA Grenoble, 26 April 1995, CISG-online 153.
1037. To that effect: RB Utrecht, 29 December 2010, CISG-online 5325; OLG Graz, 28 September 2000, CISG-online 798, paras 38 et seq.
1038. MüKoBGB/*Huber*, Art. 1 CISG, paras 10, 11; cf. also *Piltz*, AnwBl 1990, p. 59.
1039. MüKoBGB/*Huber*, Art. 1 CISG, para. 11; cf. also *Piltz*, AnwBl 1990, p. 59; *Schroeter*, para. 92.

a mixed framework agreement are not preponderant as per Art. 3(2) CISG.[1040] She argues, *inter alia*, that the CISG contains rules that are generally applicable and suitable to govern any international commercial contract, such as the Convention's provisions on contract formation, interpretation and remedies.[1041] Likewise, *Schwenzer* posits that a framework agreement should in its entirety be governed by the CISG, provided that its sales part is preponderant.[1042] In her view, the CISG's provisions are suitable for service obligations as well as any kind of long-term obligations that may be part of a framework agreement.[1043]

To summarise, the proponents of this approach advocate that the CISG should apply to a framework agreement as a whole, provided that it contains a preponderant sales part.

c. *Preferable View: The CISG Is Applicable to the Entire Framework Agreement*

This study supports the second approach outlined above. The CISG should be applied to a framework agreement in its entirety, provided that it contains a preponderant sales part.[1044] Overall, the more persuasive arguments indicate that a unitary treatment of mixed contracts is preferable to a *dépeçage*, particularly in light of Art. 3(2) CISG.[1045]

1040. *Perales Viscasillas*, Extending the Scope, pp. 128, 129; *Perales Viscasillas*, Int'l Distribution Contracts and CISG, p. 55; cf. also CISG-AC, Op. 4 *Perales Viscasillas*, Comment 3.1.
1041. *Perales Viscasillas*, Extending the Scope, p. 129; *Perales Viscasillas*, Int'l Distribution Contracts and CISG, p. 55, further she states that 'it is important to mention not only the model legislative role the CISG plays in domestic, regional and international initiatives but also its analogous or supplementary application to other contracts made by courts and arbitral tribunals'.
1042. *Schwenzer*, Challenges of the 2020s, pp. 44, 45.
1043. *Schwenzer*, Challenges of the 2020s, pp. 44, 45; cf. also *Schwenzer/Ranetunge/Tafur*, (2019) 10 Indian J. Int'l Econ. L., pp. 185 et seq.; *Schwenzer/Ranetunge/Tafur*, (2019/20) 39 J. L. & Com., pp. 319 et seq.
1044. Cf. *Achilles*, Art. 3 CISG, para. 10; CISG-AC, Op. 4 *Perales Viscasillas*, Comment 3.1; Ferrari *et al./Saenger*, Art. 3 CISG, para. 7; *Honnold/Flechtner*, Art. 3 CISG, para. 79; Honsell/*Siehr*, Art. 3 CISG, para. 2; *Karner/Koziol*, para. 38; *Karollus*, p. 24; MüKoBGB/*Huber*, Art. 3 CISG, para. 17; MüKoHGB/*B. Köhler*, Art. 3 CISG, para. 16; *Perales Viscasillas*, Extending the Scope, pp. 128, 129; *Perales Viscasillas*, Int'l Distribution Contracts and CISG, p. 55; *Schlechtriem*, (2005) 36 V.U.W. L. Rev., p. 787; Schlechtriem/Schwenzer/Schroeter/*Ferrari*, 8th German ed., Art. 3 CISG, para. 16; *Schwenzer*, Challenges of the 2020s, pp. 44, 45; Staudinger/*Magnus*, Art. 3 CISG, para. 29; cf. also O.R., pp. 241, 242, para. 33 (*Reishofer*); *C. Witz*, paras 112.131, 112.132.
1045. In agreement: *Achilles*, Art. 3 CISG, para. 10; *Bell*, (1996) 1 Pace Int'l L. Rev., p. 252; CISG-AC, Op. 4 *Perales Viscasillas*, Comment 3.1; Ferrari *et al./Saenger*, Art. 3 CISG, para. 7; *Honnold/Flechtner*, Art. 3 CISG, para. 79; Honsell/*Siehr*, Art. 3 CISG, para. 2; *Karner/Koziol*, para. 38; *Karollus*, p. 24; MüKoBGB/*Huber*, Art. 3 CISG, para. 17; MüKoHGB/*B. Köhler*, Art. 3 CISG, para. 16; *Schlechtriem*, (2005) 36 V.U.W. L. Rev., p. 787; Schlechtriem/Schwenzer/Schroeter/*Ferrari*, 8th German ed., Art. 3 CISG, para. 16; Staudinger/*Magnus*, Art. 3 CISG, para. 29; cf. also O.R., pp. 241, 242, para. 33 (*Reishofer*); *C. Witz*, paras 112.131, 112.132; *contra*: *Torsello*, pp. 206–208.

i. *Literal Interpretation of Article 3(2) CISG*

First and foremost, the wording of Art. 3(2) CISG does not support a *dépeçage*-solution.[1046] This provision holds that the Convention does not apply to a mixed contract with a preponderant non-sales part. It does not distinguish between various elements of the contract, but rather refers to the agreement as a whole. Accordingly, a literal interpretation of Art. 3(2) CISG suggests that the Convention excludes mixed contracts in their entirety from its sphere of application if they include a preponderant non-sales part.[1047] Vice versa, the Convention should be applied to mixed contracts in their entirety if they contain a preponderant sales part.[1048] The same can be said of the general principle derived from this provision, which merely expands the legal consequences of Art. 3(2) CISG to comparable situations that are not explicitly covered by this provision.[1049]

ii. *Teleological Interpretation*

The preponderance test set forth by Art. 3(2) CISG presupposes that sales and non-sales obligations are combined in one single contract.[1050] It is thus necessary to initially determine whether the obligations agreed upon by the parties constitute one unified contract or whether they can be separated into two distinct contracts.[1051] In essence, this assessment boils down to a matter of contract interpretation.[1052] As the CISG autonomously determines its own scope of application, this interpretation should be governed by the Convention itself, in particular Art. 8 CISG.[1053]

1046. Cf. *Achilles*, Art. 3 CISG, para. 10; *Schlechtriem*, (2005) 36 V.U.W. L. Rev., p. 787; but *see Torsello*, pp. 207, 208.
1047. MüKoBGB/*Huber*, Art. 3 CISG, para. 16; *Piltz*, AnwBl 1990, p. 59; *Piltz*, para. 2-37; *Schlechtriem*, (2005) 36 V.U.W. L. Rev., p. 787; *C. Witz*, para. 112.131; but *see Torsello*, p. 208.
1048. Cf. only *Achilles*, Art. 3 CISG, para. 10; MüKoBGB/*Huber*, Art. 3 CISG, para. 17; *Piltz*, AnwBl 1990, p. 59; *Schlechtriem*, (2005) 36 V.U.W. L. Rev., p. 787; *C. Witz*, para. 112.131.
1049. Cf. from a methodical point of view on the concept of analogy: *Kramer*, pp. 229 et seq.; *Reimer*, paras 591, 592.
1050. *Gabriel*, para. 2.58; *Herber/Czerwenka*, Art. 3 CISG, para. 4; *Honnold/Flechtner*, Art. 3 CISG, para. 79; jurisPK-BGB/*Münch*, Art. 3 CISG, para. 8; *Karner/Koziol*, para. 17; Mankowski/*Mankowski*, Art. 3 CISG, para. 13; MüKoBGB/*Huber*, Art. 3 CISG, para. 11; MüKoHGB/*B. Köhler*, Art. 3 CISG, para. 16; *Piltz*, para. 2-35; Schlechtriem/Schwenzer/Schroeter/*Ferrari*, 8th German ed., Art. 3 CISG, para. 12; Schlechtriem/Schwenzer/Schroeter/*Hachem*, 5th English ed., Art. 3 CISG, para. 12; Staudinger/*Magnus*, Art. 3 CISG, para. 9; *C. Witz*, para. 112.131; Witz/Salger/Lorenz/*Lorenz*, Art. 3 CISG, para. 5; cf. also RB Den Haag, 8 November 2023, CISG-online 6814, para. 17: the Court rejected the argument that the parties had concluded a (mixed) distribution contract, instead assuming that there was a series of separate sales agreements.
1051. *Herber/Czerwenka*, Art. 3 CISG, para. 4; Kröll *et al./Mistelis/Raymond*, Art. 3 CISG, paras 21, 22; *Schroeter*, para. 107.
1052. CISG-AC, Op. 4 *Perales Viscasillas*, Comment 3.1; MüKoBGB/*Huber*, Art. 3 CISG, para. 11.
1053. Schlechtriem/Schwenzer/Schroeter/*Hachem*, Art. 3 CISG, para. 12; in agreement: BeckOK/*Saenger*, Art. 3 CISG, para. 1; Ferrari *et al./Saenger*, Art. 3 CISG, para. 1; *Honnold/Flechtner*, Art. 3 CISG, para. 80; *Herber/Czerwenka*, Art. 3 CISG, para. 4; Mankowski/*Mankowski*, Art. 3 CISG, para. 14; MüKoBGB/*Huber*, Art. 3 CISG, para. 11; Schlechtriem/Schwenzer/Schroeter/*Ferrari*, 8th German ed., Art. 3 CISG, para. 12; *C. Witz*,

Once it has been established that there is one unified mixed contract, the preponderance test essentially seeks to identify this agreement's centre of gravity.[1054] The mixed contract is to be submitted to (primarily) one legal regime corresponding to its centre of gravity.[1055] The rule enshrined in Art. 3(2) CISG is based on the presumption that the parties typically wish to submit their mixed contract to (primarily) a single legal regime, given that they have agreed on a single unified contract.[1056] In light of this presumption, the first approach is not persuasive, as the Convention rather assumes that the parties' intentions typically oppose a contractual *dépeçage*.[1057] It should be noted that the aforementioned considerations do not apply if the parties have explicitly stipulated that the CISG shall apply exclusively to the sales part of a mixed contract.[1058] This would constitute a partial exclusion of the Convention in accordance with Art. 6 CISG. However, in the absence of any contrary indication, a unified mixed contract should be governed by or excluded from the CISG as a whole in accordance with Art. 3(2) CISG or the general principle underlying this provision. This is supported by a teleological interpretation of the provision in Art. 3(2) CISG.

iii. Significant Relationship Between Contractual Obligations

Moreover, there will usually be a significant relationship between the sales and non-sales obligations, provided that they are combined in one unified contract.[1059] In light of this significant relationship, the entire agreement should be governed by the same law.[1060] Should a unified contract be divided into a sales-related part and a non-sales-related part, it is possible that inconsistencies may arise in the event of a dispute.[1061] There may be ambiguity with regard to the remedies; for instance, whether a breach of a non-sales obligation entitles the aggrieved party to avoid the entire agreement, including all other obligations, i.e., including the sales obligations.[1062] In

para. 112.131; more guardedly Witz/Salger/Lorenz/*Lorenz*, Art. 3 CISG, para. 5; but *see* Secretariat's Commentary, Art. 3, No. 3, holding that this question of interpretation should be resolved in accordance with the applicable domestic law.

1054. Cf. OLG Dresden, 11 June 2007, CISG-online 1720, paras 46 et seq.; *Karner/Koziol*, para. 2: the CISG adheres to the '*Absorptionstheorie*', a legal doctrine that is widely recognised in German-speaking jurisdictions; *Karollus*, p. 25; *C. Witz*, para. 112.61.
1055. Cf. *C. Witz*, paras 112.131, 112.132.
1056. Cf. *Achilles*, Art. 3 CISG, paras 10, 11; *Fogt*, IPRax 2003, p. 367; *Honnold/Flechtner*, Art. 3 CISG, para. 79 in footnote 17; *Schwenzer/Ranetunge/Tafur*, (2019) 10 Indian J. Int'l Econ. L., p. 185; *Schwenzer/Ranetunge/Tafur*, (2019/20) 39 J. L. & Com., p. 320; *C. Witz*, para. 112.132.
1057. *See Fogt*, IPRax 2003, p. 367; *Herber/Czerwenka*, Art. 3 CISG, para. 4; *Honnold/Flechtner*, Art. 3 CISG, para. 79 in footnote 17; cf. also *Schwenzer/Ranetunge/Tafur*, (2019) 10 Indian J. Int'l Econ. L., p. 185; *Schwenzer/Ranetunge/Tafur*, (2019/20) 39 J. L. & Com., p. 320.
1058. Ferrari *et al./Saenger*, Art. 3 CISG, para. 1; Staudinger/*Magnus*, Art. 3 CISG, para. 12; cf. also *Enderlein/Maskow*, Art. 3 CISG, note 1; *Herber/Czerwenka*, Art. 3 CISG, para. 4.
1059. *Fogt*, IPRax 2003, p. 367 ('*zusammenhängende Vertragsbeziehung*'); *Honnold/Flechtner*, Art. 3 CISG, para. 79 in footnote 17.
1060. Cf. *Fogt*, IPRax 2003, pp. 367, 368 (distinguishing between different scenarios); *Honnold/Flechtner*, Art. 3 CISG, para. 79; cf. also in a different context *Jayme*, p. 313.
1061. Ferrari *et al./Saenger*, Art. 3 CISG, para. 1; *Fogt*, IPRax 2003, p. 367; *Honnold/Flechtner*, Art. 3 CISG, para. 79; *Karner/Koziol*, para. 5.
1062. Similarly, *Honnold/Flechtner*, Art. 3 CISG, para. 79; cf. also *Fogt*, IPRax 2003, p. 367.

such a scenario, a uniform legal regime may be necessary to find consistent solutions.[1063]

It should be noted that the situation discussed here differs from a mere relationship between distinct contracts. While it is preferable to identify the law applicable to related contracts separately,[1064] the law applicable to a unified contract that combines various obligations should be found in a uniform manner.

Finally, the CISG is in fact largely suitable to govern service or other non-sales obligations.[1065] Hence, the application of the CISG to the non-sales obligations within a mixed framework agreement would not result in any unsatisfactory outcomes.[1066]

2. Applying the CISG to Non-sales Parts in Framework Agreements?

This study supports applying the CISG to a mixed framework agreement as a whole. Consequently, the Convention applies to the non-sales part contained in such an agreement, such as service obligations or other non-sales obligations (e.g., exclusivity obligations), provided that the prerequisites for its application are met.[1067]

However, it is essential to consider the fact that the CISG is by default fragmentary and non-exhaustive.[1068] The Convention will not provide an answer to all legal questions that may be raised by mixed framework agreements; in some cases, it may be necessary to resort to the applicable domestic law.[1069] This is particularly relevant given that CISG's provisions are not specifically tailored to service or other non-sales obligations, but rather to the sale of goods.[1070] Yet, before having recourse to domestic law, it is necessary to determine whether a specific matter falls within the CISG's substantive scope of application. Once this has been established, it may be necessary to rely on the mechanism set forth by Art. 7(2) CISG.[1071]

Framework agreements typically contain service obligations in the narrower sense as well as other non-sales obligations, such as exclusivity obligations or

1063. Cf. *Honnold/Flechtner*, Art. 3 CISG, para. 79 in footnote 17.
1064. *See* Ch. 3 V. 3. above.
1065. *Perales Viscasillas*, Extending the Scope, p. 129; *Perales Viscasillas*, Int'l Distribution Contracts and CISG, p. 55; Schlechtriem/Schwenzer/Schroeter/*Ferrari*, 8th German ed., Art. 3 CISG, para. 16; Schlechtriem/Schwenzer/Schroeter/*Hachem*, 5th English ed., Art. 3 CISG, para. 17; *Schwenzer*, Challenges of the 2020s, pp. 44, 45; *Schwenzer/Ranetunge/Tafur*, (2019) 10 Indian J. Int'l Econ. L., pp. 187 et seq.; *Schwenzer/Ranetunge/Tafur*, (2019/20) 39 J. L. & Com., pp. 322 et seq.; Staudinger/*Magnus*, Art. 3 CISG, para. 29.
1066. *See* Ch. 4 III. 2. below in more detail.
1067. On mixed contracts in general: *Achilles*, Art. 3 CISG, para. 10; *Bell*, (1996) 1 Pace Int'l L. Rev., p. 252; BeckOK/*Saenger*, Art. 3 CISG, para. 7; Ferrari *et al./Saenger*, Art. 3 CISG, para. 7; *Honnold/Flechtner*, Art. 3 CISG, para. 79; Honsell/*Siehr*, Art. 3 CISG, para. 2; *Karner/Koziol*, para. 38; *Karollus*, p. 24; MüKoBGB/*Huber*, Art. 3 CISG, para. 17; MüKoHGB/*B. Köhler*, Art. 3 CISG, para. 16; Schlechtriem/Schwenzer/Schroeter/*Ferrari*, 8th German ed., Art. 3 CISG, para. 16; Staudinger/*Magnus*, Art. 3 CISG, para. 29; *C. Witz*, para. 112.61; cf. also O.R., pp. 241, 242, para. 33 (*Reishofer*); but *see Torsello*, pp. 206 et seq.
1068. *Schroeter*, para. 92; *Torsello*, pp. 206, 207.
1069. *Schroeter*, para. 92.
1070. Cf. Schlechtriem/Schwenzer/Schroeter/*Hachem*, 5th English ed., Art. 3 CISG, para. 17; *Karner/Koziol*, para. 38.
1071. *See* Ch. 1 IV. 2. above.

non-competition clauses, which are of particular practical importance. The following part will commence with an analysis of the CISG's application to service obligations included in framework agreements in a general manner. So far, hardly any cases have dealt with these issues. The second section will address the frequently included exclusivity and non-competition obligations in framework agreements, which are of practical importance and have already been discussed in case law to some extent. The third section will outline issues that fall outside the CISG's substantive scope of application.

a. In General: Service Obligations

Framework agreements may contain service obligations in a narrower sense.[1072] In particular, distribution contracts frequently include service obligations, e.g., obligations to market, advertise and promote the goods, to provide technical assistance, to provide customer service and advice, and the like.[1073] The content of these service obligations is typically established by the contract or derived from a contract interpretation in accordance with Art. 8 CISG, or alternatively from practices and usages within the meaning of Art. 9 CISG.[1074]

The application of the CISG to service obligations raises a number of issues, particularly in relation to the question of which remedies are available to the aggrieved party in the event of a breach of the service obligations.[1075] It is submitted that the Convention's provisions, particularly those concerning remedies,[1076] are sufficiently flexible to deal with the breach of service obligations. If the CISG's provisions cannot be applied directly to a certain question, it is initially necessary to determine whether the discussed matter falls within the Convention's substantive scope. If it does fall within its ambit, the mechanism established by Art. 7(2) CSG applies.[1077] This means that it is necessary to identify whether there is a gap in the Convention that must be filled by analogy, in conformity with the Convention's general principles or, as a 'last

1072. *Grunewald*, p. 57; Schlechtriem/Schwenzer/Schroeter/*Schroeter*, 5th English ed., Intro Arts 14–24 CISG, para. 24; cf. also *Schwenzer/Ranetunge/Tafur*, (2019) 10 Indian J. Int'l Econ. L., p. 181, who characterise distribution contracts as service contracts altogether; *Schwenzer/Ranetunge/Tafur*, (2019/20) 39 J. L. & Com., p. 314.

1073. Cf. OLG Graz, 28 September 2000, CISG-online 798; OLG Köln, 15 February 2000, CISG-online 3036; *Grieser*, p. 126; *Perales Viscasillas*, Extending the Scope, p. 128; *Perović*, (2011) 59 Belgrade L. Rev., p. 189; Schlechtriem/Schwenzer/Schroeter/*Schroeter*, 5th English ed., Intro Arts 14–24 CISG, para. 24; *Schluep*, pp. 20 et seq.; *UNCITRAL et al.*, Legal Guide, para. 432.

1074. Schlechtriem/Schwenzer/*Schlechtriem*, 2nd English ed., Art. 7 CISG, para. 31; Schlechtriem/Schwenzer/Schroeter/*Hachem*, 5th English ed., Art. 7 CISG, para. 31.

1075. *Schlechtriem*, (2005) 36 V.U.W. L. Rev., p. 788; cf. also Schlechtriem/Schwenzer/Schroeter/*Hachem*, 5th English ed., Art. 7 CISG, para. 37.

1076. Cf. *Magnus*, Remedies, p. 259, who holds that 'most CISG remedies can be viewed as constituting general remedies, which apply to any breach of a CISG contract by either party'.

1077. Cf. also *Schlechtriem*, Symposium Vischer, p. 14; Schlechtriem/Schwenzer/*Schlechtriem*, 2nd English ed., Art. 7 CISG, para. 31; Schlechtriem/Schwenzer/Schroeter/*Hachem*, 5th English ed., Art. 7 CISG, para. 37.

resort', by having recourse to applicable domestic law in accordance with Art. 7(2) CISG.[1078]

In accordance with the structure of the CISG's remedies, the following part will distinguish between two scenarios: in the first scenario, the seller has not performed their service obligations at all. In the second scenario, the seller has performed their service obligations in a non-conforming manner.[1079]

i. *Non-performance of Service Obligations*

1) Specific Performance

The buyer may claim for specific performance as per Art. 46(1) CISG – this remedy can equally be applied to service obligations without any modifications.[1080] Under this provision, 'the buyer may require performance by the seller of his obligations [...]'. It is not limited to certain obligations of the seller and therefore may also refer to service obligations. In addition, there are no fundamental differences between the claim for specific performance of service obligations and the claim for specific performance of sales obligations.[1081] Consequently, this provision can be applied directly to service obligations. It should be noted that Art. 28 CISG must be considered in the context of a claim for specific performance of service obligations.[1082]

2) Reduction of the Price

A reduction of the price in accordance with Art. 50 CISG should also be possible if the seller has failed to perform their service obligation entirely.[1083] Upon initial examination, the provision enshrined in Art. 50 CISG appears to refer solely to non-conforming goods in the sense of Art. 35 CISG. It is contended that the Convention covers the matter of price reduction with regard to all types of obligations that may be included in a CISG contract, including service obligations. Yet, Art. 50 CISG does not explicitly address service obligations. Nevertheless, in order to fill this gap, this provision should be applied analogously or a general principle should be derived from it if service

1078. *See* Ch. 1 IV. 2. above.
1079. With the same distinction: *Schlechtriem*, Symposium Vischer, pp. 14 et seq.; cf. also *Karner/Koziol*, paras 69 et seq.
1080. *Karner/Koziol*, para. 74; *Schlechtriem*, Symposium Vischer, p. 14; Schlechtriem/Schwenzer/*Schlechtriem*, 2nd English ed., Art. 7 CISG, para. 31; Schlechtriem/Schwenzer/Schroeter/*Hachem*, 5th English ed., Art. 7 CISG, para. 37; *Schwenzer/Ranetunge/Tafur*, (2019) 10 Indian J. Int'l Econ. L., p. 192; *Schwenzer/Ranetunge/Tafur*, (2019/20) 39 J. L. & Com., p. 327; cf. also *Schwenzer*, Challenges of the 2020s, p. 45.
1081. Cf. *Karner/Koziol*, paras 74 et seq.
1082. *Schlechtriem*, Symposium Vischer, p. 14; Schlechtriem/Schwenzer/*Schlechtriem*, 2nd English ed., Art. 7 CISG, para. 31; Schlechtriem/Schwenzer/Schroeter/*Hachem*, 5th English ed., Art. 7 CISG, para. 37; *see also Schwenzer/Ranetunge/Tafur*, (2019) 10 Indian J. Int'l Econ. L., p. 191; *Schwenzer/Ranetunge/Tafur*, (2019/20) 39 J. L. & Com., p. 327.
1083. *Karner/Koziol*, para. 80; *Schlechtriem*, Symposium Vischer, p. 16; Schlechtriem/Schwenzer/*Schlechtriem*, 2nd English ed., Art. 7 CISG, para. 31; Schlechtriem/Schwenzer/Schroeter/*Hachem*, 5th English ed., Art. 7 CISG, para. 37.

obligations have not been performed. In this context, the non-performance of services may be considered a defect in quantity in accordance with Art. 35(1) CISG.[1084]

However, it may be challenging to calculate the proportionate value in the sense of Art. 50, sentence 1 CISG.[1085] In case of (total) non-performance, the overall price might arguably be reduced to the extent of the service obligation's entire value, provided that the overall price is the sum of the prices for sales and service obligations.[1086] In some cases, it may still be challenging or impossible to determine how the price under a contract has been composed.[1087] Although the buyer may claim the reduction of the price in theory, there may be practical obstacles to this remedy in the event of non-performance of service obligations.

3) Avoidance of the Agreement

The buyer should further be entitled to declare the contract avoided if the seller does not perform their service obligations in accordance with Art. 49(1) CISG[1088] or Art. 73 CISG. Both of these provisions are worded broadly and refer to the failure to perform 'any of his obligations'.[1089] In light of this wording, it is submitted that these provisions can be applied directly if the seller has failed to perform their service obligations under a mixed framework agreement.

In general, resort to the remedy of avoidance requires a fundamental breach within the meaning of Art. 25 CISG in accordance with Arts 49(1)(a) CISG[1090] and 73(1) or (2) CISG.[1091] This threshold could, for instance, be met if the service obligations were to be performed on a fixed date.[1092] Furthermore, the buyer should be entitled to avoid the agreement after the lapse of an additional period of time in the sense of Art. 49(1)(b) CISG, if the seller fails to perform their service obligations in full.[1093]

1084. *Schlechtriem*, Symposium Vischer, p. 16; Schlechtriem/Schwenzer/Schroeter/*Hachem*, 5th English ed., Art. 3 CISG, para. 17.
1085. Schlechtriem/Schwenzer/*Schlechtriem*, 2nd English ed., Art. 7 CISG, para. 31; Schlechtriem/Schwenzer/Schroeter/*Hachem*, 5th English ed., Art. 7 CISG, para. 37.
1086. *Karner/Koziol*, para. 80.
1087. Cf. LG Mainz, 26 November 1998, CISG-online 563.
1088. *Karner/Koziol*, para. 79; *Schlechtriem*, Symposium Vischer, p. 15; Schlechtriem/Schwenzer/Schroeter/*Hachem*, 5th English ed., Art. 3 CISG, para. 17; Schlechtriem/Schwenzer/Schroeter/*Hachem*, 5th English ed., Art. 7 CISG, para. 37; cf. also *Schwenzer/Ranetunge/Tafur*, (2019) 10 Indian J. Int'l Econ. L., p. 192; *Schwenzer/Ranetunge/Tafur*, (2019/20) 39 J. L. & Com., pp. 327, 328.
1089. Art. 49(1)(a) CISG: 'if the failure by the seller to perform any of his obligations [...]'; Art. 73(1) CISG: 'if the failure of one party to perform any of his obligations [...]'.
1090. *Schlechtriem*, Symposium Vischer, p. 15; Schlechtriem/Schwenzer/Schroeter/*Hachem*, 5th English ed., Art. 3 CISG, para. 17; Schlechtriem/Schwenzer/Schroeter/*Hachem*, 5th English ed., Art. 7 CISG, para. 37; cf. also *Magnus*, 59 (1995) RabelsZ, p. 483.
1091. It is important to note that Art. 73(2) CISG refers to an anticipated fundamental breach of contract, *see* Ch. 5 III. 5. below.
1092. Cf. *Schlechtriem*, Symposium Vischer, p. 15.
1093. Accord *Karner/Koziol*, para. 79; *Schlechtriem*, Symposium Vischer, p. 15; Schlechtriem/Schwenzer/Schroeter/*Hachem*, 5th English ed., Art. 3 CISG, para. 17; *Schwenzer/Ranetunge/Tafur*, (2019) 10 Indian J. Int'l Econ. L., pp. 192, 193; *Schwenzer/Ranetunge/Tafur*, (2019/20) 39 J. L. & Com., p. 328.

If the seller's non-performance exclusively concerns the services, while the goods are delivered in conformity with the contract, the mixed framework agreement should be separated with regard to the legal consequences.[1094] In such cases, avoidance in accordance with Art. 49(1)(a) or (b) CISG should be restricted to the service part of the mixed framework agreement, as the buyer will typically still be able to use the goods that have been delivered in conformity with the contract.[1095] This can be based on a general principle derived from Arts 51(1) and 73(1) CISG.[1096] This approach is in line with the *favor contractus* principle, which underlies the CISG.[1097] An exception to this rule should be made in cases where the non-performance of a service obligation fundamentally affects the entire framework agreement, i.e., the seller's non-performance of the service obligation causes the buyer to also lose their interest in the sales part of the agreement.[1098]

4) Damages

The buyer may also be interested in claiming damages if a service obligation under a mixed framework agreement has not been performed by the seller. They should be able to do so in accordance with Art. 45(1)(b) in conjunction with Art. 74 CISG.[1099] Art. 45(1) CISG is broadly worded and merely requires the seller's failure to perform 'any of his obligations'. The seller's non-performance of a service obligation constitutes such a failure to perform.[1100] Accordingly, the Convention's provisions on damages may be applied directly in cases where a service obligation has not been performed.

1094. On mixed sales contracts in general: *Schlechtriem*, Symposium Vischer, p. 15; Schlechtriem/Schwenzer/*Schlechtriem*, 2nd English ed., Art. 7 CISG, para. 31; Schlechtriem/Schwenzer/Schroeter/*Hachem*, 5th English ed., Art. 7 CISG, para. 37.
1095. On mixed sales contracts in general: *Schlechtriem*, Symposium Vischer, p. 15; Schlechtriem/Schwenzer/Schroeter/*Hachem*, 5th English ed., Art. 3 CISG, para. 17; Schlechtriem/Schwenzer/Schroeter/*Hachem*, 5th English ed., Art. 7 CISG, para. 37; *Schwenzer/Ranetunge/Tafur*, (2019) 10 Indian J. Int'l Econ. L., p. 192; *Schwenzer/Ranetunge/Tafur*, (2019/20) 39 J. L. & Com., p. 328; not mentioning a restriction of avoidance: *Karner/Koziol*, para. 79.
1096. *Schlechtriem*, Symposium Vischer, p. 15; Schlechtriem/Schwenzer/Schroeter/*Hachem*, 5th English ed., Art. 3 CISG, para. 17.
1097. *Favor contractus* is considered to be a general principle within the meaning of Art. 7(2) CISG: Bianca/Bonell/*Bonell*, Art. 7 CISG, note 2.3.2.2; *Ferrari*, IHR 2013, p. 193; Kröll *et al./Perales Viscasillas*, Art. 7 CISG, para. 65; *Magnus*, RabelsZ 95 (1995), p. 483; Schlechtriem/Schwenzer/Schroeter/*Ferrari*, 8th German ed., Art. 7 CISG, para. 54; Schlechtriem/Schwenzer/Schroeter/*Hachem*, 5th English ed., Art. 7 CISG, para. 34.
1098. Cf. *Schlechtriem*, Symposium Vischer, p. 15; cf. also Schlechtriem/Schwenzer/Schroeter/*Hachem*, 5th English ed., Art. 3 CISG, para. 17; Schlechtriem/Schwenzer/Schroeter/*Hachem*, 5th English ed., Art. 7 CISG, para. 37.
1099. *See Schlechtriem*, Symposium Vischer, pp. 14, 15; Schlechtriem/Schwenzer/*Schlechtriem*, 2nd English ed., Art. 7 CISG, para. 31; Schlechtriem/Schwenzer/Schroeter/*Hachem*, 5th English ed., Art. 7 CISG, para. 37; *Schwenzer/Ranetunge/Tafur*, (2019) 10 Indian J. Int'l Econ. L., p. 193; *Schwenzer/Ranetunge/Tafur*, (2019/20) 39 J. L. & Com., pp. 328, 329.
1100. Cf. *Magnus*, Remedies, p. 260: 'It does not matter which duty has been breached ("any of his obligations under the contract or the Convention"), including violations of additional duties that the parties have agreed on.'

With regard to the scope and calculation of damages, Art. 74 CISG is primarily of relevance.[1101] This also implies that the prerequisites of Art. 74 CISG must be met.[1102] Should these prerequisites be met, the claim for damages should typically not present any significant challenges in cases where the seller has not performed their service obligations; the claim for damages is equally appropriate in instances where service obligations have been breached, as it is when sales obligations have been breached.[1103]

5) Right to Withhold Performance

The CISG does not (explicitly) provide for a general right to withhold performance.[1104] The buyer should, nevertheless, be entitled to withhold payment of the purchase price in cases where the seller fails to perform contractual service obligations.[1105] The prevailing view holds that a general principle to withhold performance can be derived from the principle of simultaneous performance that underlies the provisions in Arts 58, 71, 81(2), 85, sentence 2 and 86(1), sentence 2 CISG.[1106] No modifications or adaptations are necessary when it comes to service obligations; the aforementioned general principle can be applied 'directly'. In fact, the right to withhold performance can readily be applied to any type of obligation under a synallagmatic (bilateral) contract.[1107]

The extent to which the buyer may exercise the right to withhold performance may be doubtful in cases where the non-performance is merely partial. To illustrate, the seller under a framework agreement may be obliged to advertise the goods and invest a certain amount for their promotion. Subsequently, the seller merely advertises the goods on a smaller scale and fails to invest the promised amount in their promotion.[1108] This may prompt the question whether the buyer should still be entitled to withhold their entire performance or merely a part of it. The preferable view is that

1101. *See Magnus*, Remedies, p. 263; Schlechtriem/Schwenzer/Schroeter/*Schwenzer*, 5th English ed., Art. 74 CISG, para. 1; *Schroeter*, paras 814 et seq.
1102. Regarding potentially problematic issues: *Karner/Koziol*, paras 90 et seq.
1103. *Schlechtriem*, Symposium Vischer, p. 14; *Schwenzer*, Challenges of the 2020s, p. 45; *Schwenzer/Ranetunge/Tafur*, (2019) 10 Indian J. Int'l Econ. L., p. 193; *Schwenzer/Ranetunge/Tafur*, (2019/20) 39 J. L. & Com., p. 329.
1104. Cf. only *Karner/Koziol*, paras 53, 72; *Schlechtriem*, Symposium Vischer, p. 16.
1105. OGH, 8 November 2005, CISG-online 1156; HGer Aargau, 10 March 2010, CISG-online 2176, para. 96; *Karner/Koziol*, para. 72; *Schlechtriem*, Symposium Vischer, p. 16; Schlechtriem/Schwenzer/*Schlechtriem*, 2nd English ed., Art. 7 CISG, para. 31; Schlechtriem/Schwenzer/Schroeter/*Hachem*, 5th English ed., Art. 7 CISG, para. 38.
1106. BGH, 24 September 2014, CISG-online 2545, para. 58; OGH, 8 November 2005, CISG-online 1156; HGer Aargau, 10 March 2010, CISG-online 2176, para. 96; *Fountoulakis*, IHR 2005, p. 247; *F. Hartmann*, IHR 2005, pp. 181 et seq.; *Kern*, ZEuP 2000, pp. 837 et seq.; Kröll *et al./Perales Viscasillas*, Art. 7 CISG, para. 64; *Schlechtriem*, Symposium Vischer, pp. 18, 19; Schlechtriem/Schwenzer/Schroeter/*Ferrari*, 8th German ed., Art. 7 CISG, para. 55; Schlechtriem/Schwenzer/Schroeter/*Hachem*, 5th English ed., Art. 7 CISG, para. 40; Staudinger/*Magnus*, Art. 4 CISG, para. 47a.
1107. *Karner/Koziol*, paras 72, 73; cf. also *Kern*, ZEuP 2000, p. 856.
1108. Cf. *Kern*, ZEuP 2000, p. 856.

the buyer should be entitled to withhold the entire performance, even if the non-performance of the service obligations may be considered partial.[1109] This approach yields clear and pragmatic solutions from a practical standpoint.[1110]

If the parties conclude a framework agreement with a two-tier structure, i.e., a distinction is made between the framework agreement and the individual sales contracts, another question may arise: can the buyer rely on a right to withhold performance if the seller has not performed one of their obligations under a different but related contract, either another individual sales contract or the framework agreement?[1111] The answer should be in the affirmative, provided that the relevant obligations are internal to the Convention, i.e., all contracts involved are governed by the CISG and the agreements are economically related.[1112] Consequently, the buyer should be able to withhold performance under an individual sales contract if the seller has not performed their obligations under the framework agreement or any other individual sales contract, and vice versa, as these contracts are economically related, provided that the CISG applies to both the framework agreement and all of the individual sales contracts.

ii. Non-conforming Supply of Services

In the second scenario mentioned above, the seller performs their service obligations but not in conformity with the parties' agreement.

1) Non-conforming Services?

Initially, it is necessary to determine whether the services rendered by the seller are 'non-conforming' under the Convention. The Convention, in general, intends to cover this matter, as evidenced by its provisions on non-conformity. The CISG's provisions on non-conformity, enshrined in Arts 35, 41 and 42 CISG, can also provide an answer to the question whether services are non-conforming.[1113] Although these provisions exclusively refer to the delivery of goods, they contain general principles that can be applied to the supply of services.[1114] Nevertheless, some complications may arise in

---

1109. *F. Hartmann*, IHR 2006, p. 187; *Kern*, ZEuP 2000, pp. 858, 859.
1110. *Kern*, ZEuP 2000, p. 859; in agreement but with a nuance: *F. Hartmann*, IHR 2006, p. 187.
1111. *See* on this question under domestic Swiss law: BSK OR-I/*Schroeter*, Art. 82 CO, para. 50; cf. also *C. Meyer*, pp. 278, 279; *Tritten*, paras 662 et seq. (with regard to 'linked contracts').
1112. Similarly, Staudinger/*Magnus*, Art. 4 CISG, para. 47a; regarding domestic Swiss law: BSK OR-I/*Schroeter*, Art. 82 CO, para. 50; cf. also *Tritten*, paras 662 et seq. (with regard to 'linked contracts').
1113. Schlechtriem/Schwenzer/*Schlechtriem*, 2nd English ed., Art. 7 CISG, para. 31; Schlechtriem/Schwenzer/Schroeter/*Hachem*, 5th English ed., Art. 7 CISG, para. 37; *Schwenzer/Ranetunge/Tafur*, (2019) 10 Indian J. Int'l Econ. L., pp. 187 et seq.; *Schwenzer/Ranetunge/Tafur*, (2019/20) 39 J. L. & Com., pp. 322 et seq.
1114. Cf. Schlechtriem/Schwenzer/*Schlechtriem*, 2nd English ed., Art. 7 CISG, para. 31; Schlechtriem/Schwenzer/Schroeter/*Hachem*, 5th English ed., Art. 7 CISG, para. 37 ('While the provisions are tailored to the delivery of goods, they nevertheless provide principles and

consideration of the different legal nature of service obligations in contrast to sales obligations.

a) *Obligations de Résultat* Versus *Obligations de Moyens*

Service obligations typically oblige the debtor to use reasonable skill and judgment when providing the services, not to achieve a certain result (*obligation de moyens*).[1115] Sales obligations, in contrast, oblige the seller to achieve a certain result (*obligation de résultat*).[1116] This distinction has implications for the determination of a breach of a contract. An *obligation de résultat* is breached when a specific result has not been achieved, regardless of whether the debtor has exercised reasonable skill and judgment.[1117] In contrast, an *obligation de moyens* is only breached when the debtor has not exercised reasonable skill and judgment in the performance of their obligation, regardless of the result.[1118] In light of the aforementioned, it could be argued that the CISG's provisions regarding non-conformity – which are tailored to sales obligations (*obligations de résultat*) – are not suitable to determine a breach of contract in cases involving the breach of service obligations, i.e., *obligations de moyens*.[1119]

However, it is submitted that these provisions or the principles underlying them may still be applied in the event of a breach of a service obligation under a CISG contract because, in certain instances, service obligations have been characterised as *obligations de résultat* in the context of domestic or regional laws.[1120] If this is also possible under the Convention, its provisions on non-conformity can be applied without significant difficulties, as the standard of liability is the same as for the breach of sales obligations (i.e., strict liability).[1121] Furthermore, it is contended here that in other cases, the principles derived from the CISG's provisions on non-conformity should be applied to service obligations by way of gap-filling pursuant to Art. 7(2) CISG.[1122] Consequently, a literal application of these provisions to service obligations is not necessary in such cases. The Convention's provisions on non-conformity may

standards applicable to this matter'); *Schwenzer/Ranetunge/Tafur*, (2019) 10 Indian J. Int'l Econ. L., p. 189; *Schwenzer/Ranetunge/Tafur*, (2019/20) 39 J. L. & Com., p. 324.

1115. *Karner/Koziol*, para. 65; *Schwenzer/Ranetunge/Tafur*, (2019) 10 Indian J. Int'l Econ. L., pp. 183, 184; *Schwenzer/Ranetunge/Tafur*, (2019/20) 39 J. L. & Com., pp. 317, 318.
1116. *Schwenzer/Ranetunge/Tafur*, (2019) 10 Indian J. Int'l Econ. L., p. 183; *Schwenzer/Ranetunge/Tafur*, (2019/20) 39 J. L. & Com., p. 317; cf. also *Karner/Koziol*, para. 65 (regarding contracts for work).
1117. *Schwenzer/Ranetunge/Tafur*, (2019) 10 Indian J. Int'l Econ. L., p. 183; *Schwenzer/Ranetunge/Tafur*, (2019/20) 39 J. L. & Com., p. 317.
1118. *Karner/Koziol*, para. 65; *Schwenzer/Ranetunge/Tafur*, (2019) 10 Indian J. Int'l Econ. L., p. 183; *Schwenzer/Ranetunge/Tafur*, (2019/20) 39 J. L. & Com., pp. 317, 318.
1119. Cf. *Karner/Koziol*, paras 60 et seq., 81, 89 (differentiating).
1120. *Schwenzer/Ranetunge/Tafur*, (2019) 10 Indian J. Int'l Econ. L., pp. 183, 184 with examples; *Schwenzer/Ranetunge/Tafur*, (2019/20) 39 J. L. & Com., p. 318 with examples.
1121. Cf. *Schwenzer/Ranetunge/Tafur*, (2019) 10 Indian J. Int'l Econ. L., pp. 188, 189; *Schwenzer/Ranetunge/Tafur*, (2019/20) 39 J. L. & Com., pp. 323, 324.
1122. Cf. Schlechtriem/Schwenzer/Schroeter/*Hachem*, 5th English ed., Art. 7 CISG, para. 37; *Schwenzer/Ranetunge/Tafur*, (2019) 10 Indian J. Int'l Econ. L., p. 189; *Schwenzer/Ranetunge/Tafur*, (2019/20) 39 J. L. & Com., p. 324.

therefore provide standards and principles that can be applied to establish liability in the event of a breach of a service obligation.[1123]

b) The CISG's Provisions on Non-conformity

Art. 35 CISG stipulates how to determine the conformity of the goods. This provision and the principles derived from it are also suitable to determine the conformity of services. The underlying principle of Art. 35(1) CISG can be applied to any kind of contract, including mixed framework agreements containing sales and service obligations, as this provision refers to the contractual stipulations agreed upon by the parties.[1124] It holds, *inter alia*, that the goods must be of the quantity and quality required by the contract ('subjective' standard of conformity). The same applies to services – they must be of the quality and quantity as agreed upon in the contract.[1125]

Similarly, the rationale or general principle behind Art. 35(2) CISG can also be applied to service obligations, as this provision at its core enshrines an objective standard of conformity.[1126] If the service obligations are classified as *obligations de résultat*, the standard set forth in Art. 35(2) CISG may be relied on directly to determine the conformity of the services in a manner similar to how it would be used to determine the conformity of the goods.[1127]

Art. 35(2) CISG may be equally applied if the service obligations take the form of an *obligation de moyens*, because this provision ultimately sets forth an objective fall-back standard to determine whether performance conforms with the contract if the parties have omitted contractual stipulations.[1128] If the debtor owes an *obligation de moyens*, the relevant question must be 'what degree of reasonable care and skill would be expected in these circumstances from an objectively reasonable perspective?'.[1129] The rationale for such an interpretation may be based on a general principle derived from Art. 35(2) CISG.[1130] Beyond that, the parties are free to derogate from any standard under Art. 35(2) CISG in accordance with Art. 6 CISG in instances where they

1123. Schlechtriem/Schwenzer/Schroeter/*Hachem*, 5th English ed., Art. 7 CISG, para. 37; *Schwenzer/Ranetunge/Tafur*, (2019) 10 Indian J. Int'l Econ. L., pp. 188, 189; *Schwenzer/Ranetunge/Tafur*, (2019/20) 39 J. L. & Com., p. 324; cf. also *Karner/Koziol*, para. 89, positing that the mixed contracts governed by the CISG are typically more result-oriented in comparison to other mixed service contracts; *C. Witz*, para. 112.61.

1124. *Schwenzer/Ranetunge/Tafur*, (2019) 10 Indian J. Int'l Econ. L., pp. 187, 188; *Schwenzer/Ranetunge/Tafur*, (2019/20) 39 J. L. & Com., p. 323; cf. *also Perales Viscasillas*, Extending the Scope, pp. 133 et seq.

1125. In more detail: *Schwenzer/Ranetunge/Tafur*, (2019) 10 Indian J. Int'l Econ. L., p. 188; *Schwenzer/Ranetunge/Tafur*, (2019/20) 39 J. L. & Com., p. 323; cf. also CA Lyon, 18 December 2003, CISG-online 871.

1126. *Schwenzer/Ranetunge/Tafur*, (2019) 10 Indian J. Int'l Econ. L., pp. 188, 189; *Schwenzer/Ranetunge/Tafur*, (2019/20) 39 J. L. & Com., pp. 323, 324.

1127. *Schwenzer/Ranetunge/Tafur*, (2019) 10 Indian J. Int'l Econ. L., pp. 188, 189; *Schwenzer/Ranetunge/Tafur*, (2019/20) 39 J. L. & Com., pp. 323, 324, who also indicate in which cases service obligations may be considered *obligations de résultat*.

1128. Cf. also *Schwenzer/Ranetunge/Tafur*, (2019) 10 Indian J. Int'l Econ. L., pp. 187, 189; *Schwenzer/Ranetunge/Tafur*, (2019/20) 39 J. L. & Com., pp. 322, 324.

1129. *Schwenzer/Ranetunge/Tafur*, (2019) 10 Indian J. Int'l Econ. L., p. 189; *Schwenzer/Ranetunge/Tafur*, (2019/20) 39 J. L. & Com., p. 324.

1130. *Schwenzer/Ranetunge/Tafur*, (2019) 10 Indian J. Int'l Econ. L., p. 189; *Schwenzer/Ranetunge/Tafur*, (2019/20) 39 J. L. & Com., p. 324.

incorporate service obligations into a framework agreement governed by the Convention.[1131]

Furthermore, Arts 41 and 42 CISG can be applied to service obligations, too: the seller must provide services free from third-party property rights or claims (Art. 41 CISG) and free from third-party intellectual property rights or claims (Art. 42 CISG).[1132] These provisions and the principles enshrined in them are sufficiently flexible to be applied to service obligations.

In conclusion, the CISG's provisions on non-conformity and third-party rights or claims may also be used to establish liability for the breach of service obligations, despite the fact that they are primarily tailored for sales obligations.[1133]

2) Obligation to Give Notice?

The CISG generally obliges the buyer to examine the goods (Art. 38 CISG) and give timely notice of any non-conformity (Art. 39 CISG) or third-party rights or claims within the meaning of Arts 41 and 42 CISG (Art. 43 CISG). According to Arts 39(1) and 43 CISG, failure to comply with this obligation results in the buyer's loss of the right to rely on the lack of conformity of the goods or on the provisions of Art. 41 or Art. 42 CISG. This prompts the question whether such a notice requirement also applies in the event of a breach of a service obligation.

a) Prevailing View: General Notice Requirement

The slightly prevailing view among scholars argues that the buyer should be obliged to give timely notice to the seller of any non-conformities based on a general principle derived from Arts 39(1) and 43 CISG.[1134] In order to reinforce the idea of a notice requirement under the CISG for a breach of a service obligation, *Schwenzer*, *Ranetunge* and *Tafur* draw a comparison to the EU Directive on Package Holidays and to the Principles of European Law on Service Contracts.[1135] Under Art. 5(4) of the EU Directive on Package Holidays, the consumer must, *inter alia*, communicate any failure in the performance of a service contract to the provider of the services. Similarly, the Principles of European Law on Service Contracts oblige the recipient of services to

1131. Cf. *Schwenzer/Ranetunge/Tafur*, (2019) 10 Indian J. Int'l Econ. L., pp. 189, 190; *Schwenzer/Ranetunge/Tafur*, (2019/20) 39 J. L. & Com., p. 324.

1132. *See Schwenzer/Ranetunge/Tafur*, (2019) 10 Indian J. Int'l Econ. L., pp. 189, 190; *Schwenzer/Ranetunge/Tafur*, (2019/20) 39 J. L. & Com., pp. 324, 325.

1133. Accord Schlechtriem/Schwenzer/Schroeter/*Hachem*, 5th English ed., Art. 3 CISG, para. 17; *Schwenzer/Ranetunge/Tafur*, (2019) 10 Indian J. Int'l Econ. L., pp. 188, 189; *Schwenzer/Ranetunge/Tafur*, (2019/20) 39 J. L. & Com., pp. 323, 324; more guardedly *Karner/Koziol*, para. 89.

1134. *Schlechtriem*, Symposium Vischer, p. 16; Schlechtriem/Schwenzer/*Schlechtriem*, 2nd English ed., Art. 7 CISG, para. 31; Schlechtriem/Schwenzer/Schroeter/*Hachem*, 5th English ed., Art. 7 CISG, para. 37; *Schwenzer*, Challenges of the 2020s, p. 45; *Schwenzer/Ranetunge/Tafur*, (2019) 10 Indian J. Int'l Econ. L., p. 190; *Schwenzer/Ranetunge/Tafur*, (2019/20) 39 J. L. & Com., pp. 325, 326.

1135. *Schwenzer/Ranetunge/Tafur*, (2019) 10 Indian J. Int'l Econ. L., p. 190; *Schwenzer/Ranetunge/Tafur*, (2019/20) 39 J. L. & Com., pp. 325, 326.

notify the service provider about any failure in the performance of a service contract.[1136] If the service recipient does not notify the service provider, they lose the right to rely on the non-conformity or must compensate the service provider. These rules illustrate that notice requirements may indeed apply to service contracts in certain circumstances, according to *Schwenzer*, *Ranetunge* and *Tafur*.[1137]

In addition, they note that the notice requirement is essentially 'nothing more than an expression of the principle of good faith and fair dealing in international commerce'.[1138] Moreover, the notice requirement has also been confirmed by a Belgian Commercial Court, which determined that Arts 38 and 39 CISG applied to the service obligations under a mixed sales contract governed by the Convention.[1139]

b) Opposing View: No General Notice Requirement

In contrast, the opposing view posits that Arts 38 and 39 CISG should generally not be applied in case of 'other' breaches of contract, without further distinction.[1140] This could be understood to mean that these provisions should also not be applied in case of a breach of a service obligation, such as the obligation to provide training for the buyer's staff.[1141]

Furthermore, the proponents of this view submit that an exception to the aforementioned rule should be made: Arts 38 and 39 CISG should apply to breaches of 'other' obligations, provided that these obligations are closely linked to the conformity of the goods.[1142] To illustrate, the goods may only become non-conforming as a consequence of their incorrect installation by the seller; in such cases, the obligation to examine the goods and give notice of defects should be applicable, according to this view.[1143]

c) Preferable View

This study supports the view that Arts 38, 39 and 43 CISG should not apply to the breach of service obligations for the following reasons: first of all, Arts 39 and 43 CISG are 'selective' provisions that pertain only to specific cases, namely cases where the

1136. Art. 1:113 Principles of European Law on Service Contracts: Failure to Notify for Non-conformity.
1137. *Schwenzer/Ranetunge/Tafur*, (2019) 10 Indian J. Int'l Econ. L., p. 190; *Schwenzer/Ranetunge/Tafur*, (2019/20) 39 J. L. & Com., pp. 325, 326.
1138. *Schwenzer/Ranetunge/Tafur*, (2019) 10 Indian J. Int'l Econ. L., p. 190; *Schwenzer/Ranetunge/Tafur*, (2019/20) 39 J. L. & Com., pp. 325, 326.
1139. RB Hasselt, 4 February 2004, CISG-online 863; *see also* LG Mainz, 26 November 1998, CISG-online 563, paras 21, 22.
1140. *Benedick*, para. 556; MüKoHGB/*Benicke*, Vor Art. 38 CISG, para. 11 (Arts 38 and 39 CISG do not apply to the breach of 'ancillary' obligations); Staudinger/*Magnus*, Art. 38 CISG, para. 9; Staudinger/*Magnus*, Art. 39 CISG, para. 12.
1141. Cf. Staudinger/*Magnus*, Art. 38 CISG, para. 9, explicitly referencing to a failure to provide training, etc.
1142. Schlechtriem/Schwenzer/Schroeter/*Schwenzer/Janssen*, 8th German ed., Art. 38 CISG, para. 13 (with regard to 'accessory obligations'); Staudinger/*Magnus*, Art. 38 CISG, para. 9; but *see* MüKoHGB/*Benicke*, Vor Art. 38, para. 11, who advocates for a more expansive application of Arts 38 and 39 CISG.
1143. Schlechtriem/Schwenzer/Schroeter/*Schwenzer/Janssen*, 8th German ed., Art. 38 CISG, para. 13; Staudinger/*Magnus*, Art. 38 CISG, para. 9.

seller has delivered non-conforming goods or goods that are not free from third-party rights or claims.[1144] In accordance with these provisions, the buyer is not obliged to give notice about any other breach of contract committed by the seller. If Art. 39 CISG were to enshrine a general principle, namely a general notice requirement in relation to any breaches of contract, there would have been no need to include Art. 43 CISG in the Convention, and vice versa. Therefore, these provisions should be considered selective exceptions and should not be extended to other breaches of contract.[1145]

Moreover, the rationale behind Arts 38, 39 and 43 CISG is not equally applicable in the event of a breach of service obligations. A key rationale underlying the notice requirement is, among others, to protect the seller from claims arising out of defects that fall within the buyer's sphere of risk.[1146] The seller is not equally deserving of protection with regard to their service obligations. In fact, service obligations are predominantly performed in the seller's sphere of risk in the majority of cases. For instance, the seller's obligation to market, advertise and promote the goods under mixed framework agreements is mainly performed in the seller's sphere of risk. Another rationale underlying the notice requirement is that the seller should be put into a position to prepare legal claims against their own supplier.[1147] Typically, there is no comparable need with regard to the seller's service obligations.

As framework agreements often contain long-term service obligations, it may also be unclear when, for example, the cut-off time limit under Art. 39(2) commences. The relevant points in time within the meaning of Arts 38, 39 and 43 CISG are difficult to determine with regard to long-term service obligations. This further suggests that these provisions should not be applied to the service part in mixed long-term framework agreements.

It would be reasonable to permit an exception to the aforementioned position in cases in which the conformity of the services is closely linked to the conformity of the goods.[1148] In such cases, the buyer should be obliged to give notice to the seller in accordance with Arts 38 and 39 CISG, despite the fact that the delivery may have conformed with the contract, because the non-conforming services may affect the conformity of the goods.[1149] Accordingly, non-conforming services may result in non-conforming goods, with the consequence that a clear distinction between the two is hardly possible. In such circumstances, the notice requirement should exceptionally be applied to instances of breach of service obligations.

3) Substitute Delivery and Repair

If the seller provides non-conforming services, the buyer may wish to resort to specific performance, which takes the form of substitute delivery and repair in cases of

1144. Cf. *Schroeter*, para. 477 (regarding Arts 38, 39).
1145. To that effect: MüKoHGB/*Benicke*, Vor Art. 38 CISG, para. 11; Staudinger/*Magnus*, Art. 39 CISG, para. 12.
1146. Cf. only Staudinger/*Magnus*, Art. 38 CISG, para. 3.
1147. Cf. Schlechtriem/Schwenzer/Schroeter/*Schwenzer*, 5th English ed., Art. 38 CISG, para. 4.
1148. MüKoHGB/*Benicke*, Vor Art. 38, para. 11; Staudinger/*Magnus*, Art. 38 CISG, para. 9.
1149. Cf. Staudinger/*Magnus*, Art. 38 CISG, para. 9.

non-conformity pursuant to Art. 46(2) and 46(3) CISG.[1150] Art. 46 CISG distinguishes between substitute delivery and repair in its paragraphs 2 and 3, which are subject to different prerequisites. The buyer may only demand substitute delivery if the lack of conformity constitutes a fundamental breach in the sense of Art. 25 CISG.[1151] The underlying rationale is to avoid unnecessary and costly transfers of the goods; this same rationale underlies the restricted right to avoid the contract under the Convention.[1152] In contrast, Art. 46(3) CISG does not require a fundamental breach.

Generally, the principles underlying the remedies of substitute delivery and repair should also be available to the buyer if the seller has provided non-conforming services.[1153] However, with regard to services, it may be difficult to distinguish between a completely new performance, i.e., substitute delivery (Art. 46(2) CISG), and repair (Art. 46(3) CISG).[1154] In light of the aforementioned considerations, *Schlechtriem* posits that the buyer's right to demand cure of the non-conforming services should not require a fundamental breach.[1155] The seller obliged to cure the services should only be permitted to invoke unreasonableness within the meaning of Art. 46(3) CISG as a defence against the buyer's claim.[1156]

This view is persuasive. The distinction between a 'substitute delivery' and a 'repair' of services is typically blurred. The buyer should therefore simply have one single claim for the cure of non-conforming services through gap-filling in accordance with Art. 7(2) CISG. The follow-up question is whether the prerequisites set out in Art. 46(2) or Art. 46(3) CISG should be applied to this claim. It is more convincing to apply Art. 46(3) CISG to the buyer's claim for the cure of non-conforming services.[1157] There is simply no necessity to restrict the buyer's claim to cases of fundamental breach (Art. 46(2) CISG). The rationale underlying Art. 46(2) CISG, which is to avoid unnecessary and costly transfers of the goods, is not transferable to the cases discussed here. Consequently, it is justifiable to entitle the buyer to demand the cure of non-conforming services, unless this is unreasonable for the seller in light of the specific circumstances in accordance with Art. 46(3) CISG.[1158]

1150. *Schwenzer/Ranetunge/Tafur*, (2019) 10 Indian J. Int'l Econ. L., p. 192; *Schwenzer/Ranetunge/Tafur*, (2019/20) 39 J. L. & Com., p. 327.
1151. CISG-AC, Op. 21 *Schwenzer/Beimel*, Comment 3.19; Kröll *et al./Huber*, Art. 46 CISG, para. 4.
1152. CISG-AC, Op. 21 *Schwenzer/Beimel*, Comment 3.19; Kröll *et al./Huber*, Art. 46 CISG, para. 33.
1153. Schlechtriem/Schwenzer/Schroeter/*Hachem*, 5th English ed., Art. 7 CISG para. 37; *Schwenzer/Ranetunge/Tafur*, (2019) 10 Indian J. Int'l Econ. L., p. 192; *Schwenzer/Ranetunge/Tafur*, (2019/20) 39 J. L. & Com., p. 327; cf. also CA Grenoble, 26 April 1995, CISG-online 154; more guardedly *Karner/Koziol*, paras 86 et seq.
1154. *Schlechtriem*, Symposium Vischer, pp. 16, 17.
1155. *Schlechtriem*, Symposium Vischer, p. 17.
1156. *Schlechtriem*, Symposium Vischer, p. 17; similarly, Schlechtriem/Schwenzer/Schroeter/*Hachem*, 5th English ed., Art. 7 CISG, para. 37.
1157. In agreement: *Schlechtriem*, Symposium Vischer, p. 17; Schlechtriem/Schwenzer/*Schlechtriem*, 2nd English ed., Art. 7 CISG, para. 31; Schlechtriem/Schwenzer/Schlechtriem/*Hachem*, 5th English ed., Art. 7 CISG, para. 37.
1158. To that effect: Schlechtriem/Schwenzer/*Schlechtriem*, 2nd English ed., Art. 7 CISG, para. 31; Schlechtriem/Schwenzer/Schroeter/*Hachem*, 5th English ed., Art. 7 CISG, para. 37.

4) Avoidance of the Agreement

If the services rendered by the seller are non-conforming, the buyer should also be entitled to avoid the contract in accordance with Art. 49(1) CISG[1159] or Art. 73 CISG. As these provisions merely refer to the failure to perform 'any of his obligations',[1160] they may even be applied directly to cases where the seller has provided non-conforming services under a mixed framework agreement.[1161] However, avoidance after the lapse of an additional period of time in accordance with Art. 49(1)(b) CISG is limited to cases of non-performance; it should not be extended to cases where the seller has rendered non-conforming services.[1162]

The avoidance of a mixed contract under the Convention requires a fundamental breach of the service obligations, as defined in Art. 25 CISG, in accordance with Art. 49(1)(a) CISG[1163] and Art. 73 CISG. Furthermore, avoidance should be limited to the service part of the mixed contract, as the buyer will often still be able to use the goods that have been delivered in conformity with the contract.[1164] This approach can be based on a general principle derived from Arts 51(1) and 73(1) CISG[1165] and is in accordance with the CISG's general principle of *favor contractus*. An exception to this approach should be considered in cases where the non-conforming services fundamentally affect the entire framework agreement, i.e., the non-conforming services cause the buyer to also lose their interest in the sales part of the agreement.[1166]

1159. *Schlechtriem*, Symposium Vischer, p. 17; Schlechtriem/Schwenzer/*Schlechtriem*, 2nd English ed., Art. 7 CISG, para. 31; Schlechtriem/Schwenzer/Schroeter/*Hachem*, 5th English ed., Art. 3 CISG, para. 17; Schlechtriem/Schwenzer/Schroeter/*Hachem*, 5th English ed., Art. 7 CISG, para. 37; *Schwenzer/Ranetunge/Tafur*, (2019) 10 Indian J. Int'l Econ. L., p. 192; *Schwenzer/Ranetunge/Tafur*, (2019/20) 39 J. L. & Com., pp. 327, 328.

1160. Art. 49(1)(a) CISG: 'if the failure by the seller to perform any of his obligations [...]'; Art. 73(1) CISG: 'if the failure of one party to perform any of his obligations [...]'.

1161. Cf. *Schwenzer/Ranetunge/Tafur*, (2019) 10 Indian J. Int'l Econ. L., p. 192; *Schwenzer/Ranetunge/Tafur*, (2019/20) 39 J. L. & Com., p. 328.

1162. *Schlechtriem*, Symposium Vischer, p. 17; Schlechtriem/Schwenzer/Schroeter/*Hachem*, 5th English ed., Art. 7 CISG, para. 37.

1163. *Schlechtriem*, Symposium Vischer, p. 17; Schlechtriem/Schwenzer/*Schlechtriem*, 2nd English ed., Art. 7 CISG, para. 31; Schlechtriem/Schwenzer/Schroeter/*Hachem*, 5th English ed., Art. 3 CISG, para. 17; Schlechtriem/Schwenzer/Schroeter/*Hachem*, 5th English ed., Art. 7 CISG, para. 37; *Schwenzer/Ranetunge/Tafur*, (2019) 10 Indian J. Int'l Econ. L., p. 192; *Schwenzer/Ranetunge/Tafur*, (2019/20) 39 J. L. & Com., p. 328; in ICC, 18203/2013, CISG-online 2973, the fundamental breach of an obligation to promote the goods was assumed (it should be noted that this obligation was part of the buyer's obligations and therefore the Tribunal relied on Art. 64(1)(a) CISG, rather than Art. 49(1)(a) CISG).

1164. *Schlechtriem*, Symposium Vischer, pp. 15, 17; Schlechtriem/Schwenzer/Schroeter/*Hachem*, 5th English ed., Art. 3 CISG, para. 17; Schlechtriem/Schwenzer/Schroeter/*Hachem*, 5th English ed., Art. 7 CISG, para. 37; *see* already Ch. 4 III. 2. a. i. 3) above.

1165. *Schlechtriem*, Symposium Vischer, p. 15; Schlechtriem/Schwenzer/Schroeter/*Hachem*, 5th English. ed., Art. 3 CISG, para. 17.

1166. Cf. *Schlechtriem*, Symposium Vischer, p. 15; cf. also Schlechtriem/Schwenzer/Schroeter/*Hachem*, 5th English ed., Art. 3 CISG, para. 17; Schlechtriem/Schwenzer/Schroeter/*Hachem*, 5th English ed., Art. 7 CISG, para. 37.

5) Other Remedies

The remaining remedies are generally the same as in cases of non-performance. The buyer should be entitled to claim a price reduction pursuant to Art. 50 CISG.[1167] This provision should be applied analogously or by deriving a general principle from it in instances where service obligations have been supplied in a non-conforming manner. There may, however, be practical obstacles to this remedy, given that it may be challenging to calculate the proportionate value of the non-conforming services.[1168]

The buyer should also be entitled to claim damages in accordance with Arts 45(1)(b) in conjunction with 74 CISG; these provisions may even be applied directly if services have been provided non-conformingly.[1169] Nevertheless, quantifying the claim for damages in the event of non-conforming services may be even more challenging than in cases of (total) non-performance.[1170] Finally, the buyer should also be entitled to withhold payment of the purchase price if the seller does not perform services in conformity with the contract.[1171]

iii. Service Obligations of the Buyer

In some instances, it is not the seller who undertakes the service obligations, but rather the buyer, particularly in distribution contracts.[1172] If the buyer breaches one of their service obligations under a framework agreement, the seller should generally be entitled to the same remedies as the buyer. This is due to the fact that the majority of CISG remedies are equally applicable to both parties of the contract, subject to the same requirements, regardless of which party breaches the contract.[1173] More precisely, the CISG's provisions on the seller's remedies (Arts 62–65 CISG) and the general principles underlying these provisions should be relied upon if the buyer fails to perform their service obligations.[1174] There are no significant differences between the buyer's remedies outlined above and those provisions and general principles. Consequently,

1167. *Schwenzer/Ranetunge/Tafur*, (2019) 10 Indian J. Int'l Econ. L., p. 194; *Schwenzer/Ranetunge/Tafur*, (2019/20) 39 J. L. & Com., p. 330; more guardedly *Karner/Koziol*, paras 81 et seq.
1168. *Karner/Koziol*, paras 81, 82; it is important to highlight that the absence of a market price for services does not impede the implementation of this remedy, as Art. 50 CISG is based on the specific value ratio stipulated in the relevant contract (proportionate value), rather than on a market price (*see*: *Schwenzer/Ranetunge/Tafur*, (2019) 10 Indian J. Int'l Econ. L., p. 194; *Schwenzer/Ranetunge/Tafur*, (2019/20) 39 J. L. & Com., p. 330).
1169. *See* Ch. 4 III. 2. a. i. 4) above.
1170. Cf. *Karner/Koziol*, paras 90 et seq.; *Kern*, ZEuP 2000, p. 858.
1171. *See* already Ch. 4 III. 2. a. i. 5) above; *Karner/Koziol*, para. 72; *Schlechtriem*, Symposium Vischer, pp. 16, 17 et seq.; Schlechtriem/Schwenzer/*Schlechtriem*, 2nd English ed., Art. 7 CISG, para. 31; Schlechtriem/Schwenzer/Schroeter/*Hachem*, 5th English ed., Art. 7 CISG, para. 38; cf. also OGH, 8 November 2005, CISG-online 1156; HGer Aargau, 10 March 2010, CISG-online 2176, para. 96.
1172. Cf. ICC, 18203/2013, CISG-online 2973 (with regard to the buyer's obligation to promote the goods); *Grieser*, p. 126; *Thieffry*, Dr. prat. com. int. 1993, p. 62; *Perales Viscasillas*, Extending the Scope, p. 128; *Perović*, (2011) 59 Belgrade L. Rev., p. 189; *UNCITRAL et al.*, Legal Guide, para. 432.
1173. *Magnus*, Remedies, p. 259.
1174. *See* ICC, 18203/2013, CISG-online 2973.

the seller should be entitled to claim specific performance of the services by the buyer (Art. 62 CISG), to avoid the mixed framework agreement under certain conditions (Art. 64 CISG), to claim damages (Art. 61(1)(b) CISG) and to withhold their own performance.[1175]

An arbitral award rendered by an ICC tribunal illustrates the application of Art. 64 CISG in the event of a breach of a service obligation by the buyer. In brief, the Arbitral tribunal decided that the seller was entitled to avoid a 'Distributor Agreement', since the buyer, *inter alia*, fundamentally breached their obligation to adequately promote the seller's products.[1176]

In addition to the aforementioned remedies, there are a number of buyer-specific remedies, for example, those set out in Art. 46(2) and (3) CISG. However, the seller should also be entitled to claim cure of non-conforming services, unless this is deemed unreasonable for the buyer based on a general principle derived from Art. 46(3) CISG.[1177] Although this remedy is technically available only to the buyer under the CISG, there is no reason to treat the parties differently with regard to the breach of service obligations under a mixed framework agreement governed by the Convention. Instead, both parties should be able to rely on the same remedies if it is the opposing party who undertook to provide services in addition to their sales obligations. In such instances, it could be argued that a comparable outcome could be achieved by invoking Art. 62 CISG, given that a distinction between the performance of outstanding services and the cure of non-conforming services will not always be clear.

iv. Particularities of Two-Tier Framework Agreements

In general, all of the above analysis applies regardless of whether the framework agreement adheres to a two-tier structure, i.e., a distinction is made between the framework agreement and individual sales contracts, or not. Nevertheless, it is worth noting that there is a particular feature of two-tier framework agreements governed by the CISG that merits further consideration: under such agreements, both parties may be obliged to conclude individual sales contracts, which constitute the (precontractual) sales part of these framework agreements. Consequently, it is strictly speaking not yet possible to distinguish between the seller's and the buyer's remedies. The parties will only assume their respective roles as seller and buyer under the individual sales contracts that are subsequently concluded.

Regardless of the framework agreement's structure, the buyer and seller should generally both be able to rely on the same remedies if the other party has breached their service obligations.[1178] This is unproblematic since the majority of CISG remedies are applicable to both parties of the contract, subject to the same requirements, regardless of which party breaches the contract.[1179] Furthermore, even buyer-specific remedies

1175. *See* ICC, 18203/2013, CISG-online 2973 (in reference to Art. 64 CISG).
1176. ICC, 18203/2013, CISG-online 2973, note 56.
1177. *See* Ch. 4 III. 2. a. ii. 3) above.
1178. *See* Ch. 4 III. 2. a. iii. above.
1179. *Magnus*, Remedies, p. 259.

can be granted to the seller if a buyer breaches service obligations; there is no reason for differentiating between the parties' remedies with regard to the breach of service obligations contained in a mixed framework agreement. In light of this, both parties should be entitled to claim specific performance (Arts 46(1), 62 CISG), cure of non-conforming services (Art. 46(3) CISG), damages (Arts 45(1)(b), 61(1)(b) in conjunction with Art. 74 CISG), avoidance of the agreement (Arts 49(1), 64(1), 73 in conjunction with Art. 25 CISG), and the right to withhold their performance. The only remedy that may not be applicable is the remedy of price reduction (Art. 50 CISG), which arguably does not align with two-tier framework agreements, given that there is no actual price under the framework agreement yet.[1180]

b. *In Particular: Exclusivity Obligations and Non-competition Clauses*

Framework agreements frequently include exclusivity obligations or non-competition clauses.[1181] Exclusivity obligations may take various forms: the seller may be obliged to only sell the goods to buyers that meet certain requirements, a group of buyers or to one buyer in a certain geographical area.[1182] In return, an exclusivity clause may also oblige the buyer to exclusively buy the goods from the seller.[1183] A non-competition clause may oblige the buyer, for instance, to refrain from (re-)selling the products under the contract in a specific market, thereby preventing competition, or alternatively, to generally refrain from distributing any products that may compete with those of the seller.[1184]

Occasionally, the distinct nature of such obligations in comparison to labour or service obligations in the sense of Art. 3(2) CISG has been highlighted.[1185] Nevertheless, it is submitted that the CISG's provisions are sufficiently flexible to govern exclusivity and non-competition obligations in the same way that they are suitable to govern service obligations. Therefore, reference can be made to the discussion of

1180. The price may be determined at a later stage, namely, once the individual sales contracts have been concluded.
1181. *UNCITRAL et al.*, Legal Guide, para. 432.
1182. Examples can be found in case law: OGH, 15 November 2012, CISG-online 2399, para. 4: the seller was obliged to sell their fashion products exclusively to the buyer within a specified geographical area; OLG Koblenz, 31 January 1997, CISG-online 256, para. 4: the seller was bound to sell their products exclusively to the buyer in Germany; cf. also OLG Frankfurt, 17 September 1991, CISG-online 28.
1183. CA Warsaw, 15 May 2015, CISG-online 2783: the buyer of a distribution contract agreed to purchase dietary products only from the seller; OLG Koblenz, 31 January 1997, CISG-online 256, para. 4: the buyer was obliged to buy blankets only from the seller; *Perales Viscasillas*, Extending the Scope, p. 126; *Perales Viscasillas*, Int'l Distribution Contracts and CISG, p. 52.
1184. *See* KGer St. Gallen, 13 May 2008, CISG-online 1768: the buyer was (allegedly) prohibited from supplying the goods to South Korea, as the seller's supplier was responsible for this market; CA Grenoble, 22 February 1995, CISG-online 151: the buyer was obliged to refrain from distributing the seller's products within the EU, as the seller had concluded exclusive distribution contracts with other parties within the EU; Martinek/Semler/Flohr/*Rahlmeyer/Duhe*, § 42, para. 3; Münch/Passadelis/Lehne/*Rohn*, para. 4.121.
1185. *Magnus*, FS Bonell, p. 1778; Staudinger/*Magnus*, Art. 3 CISG, para. 23; cf. also *Gillette/Walt*, p. 64; *see* Ch. 4 I. 2. a. ii. above.

service obligations above.[1186] The CISG's provisions, e.g., on non-conformity or on remedies, may again be applied directly, or alternatively, by relying on the general principles underlying these provisions in accordance with Art. 7(2) CISG.[1187]

From a practical standpoint, two questions are of particular interest in cases where an exclusivity obligation or non-competition clause has been breached by one of the parties: is it possible for the aggrieved party to avoid the framework agreement? And are they entitled to claim damages? The following section will examine these questions. It will not distinguish between the seller's and the buyer's remedies, as the Convention gives both parties a right to avoid the contract (Arts 49, 64 CISG) and claim damages (Arts 45, 61 in conjunction with Art. 74 CISG).

i. *Avoidance of the Agreement*

In accordance with Arts 49(1)(a) and 64(1)(a) CISG or Art. 73(1) CISG, contract avoidance generally requires a fundamental breach. The legal definition of a fundamental breach can be found in Art. 25 CISG.[1188] This provision holds that a breach is fundamental 'if it results in such detriment to the other party as substantially to deprive him of what he is entitled to expect under the contract, unless the party in breach did not foresee and a reasonable person of the same kind in the same circumstances would not have foreseen such a result'. A breach of any obligation under a CISG contract may be fundamental, including exclusivity obligations or non-competition clauses contained in a framework agreement that is governed by the Convention.[1189] The prerequisites set out by Art. 25 CISG must be fulfilled, i.e., the breach of an exclusivity obligation or non-competition clause must seriously impair the legitimate interests of the aggrieved party to the extent that they essentially lose their interest in the performance of the contract.[1190] The determination of this matter must be made on a case-by-case basis.[1191] Nevertheless, an examination of existing case law may prove beneficial for future cases.

1186. *See* Ch. 4 III. 2. above; cf. also *C. Witz*, para. 112.132.
1187. Cf. also MüKoBGB/*Huber*, Art. 53 CISG, para. 3.
1188. Schlechtriem/Schwenzer/Schroeter/*Schroeter*, 5th English ed., Art. 25 CISG, paras 1, 2.
1189. Schlechtriem/Schwenzer/Schroeter/*Schroeter*, 5th English ed., Art. 25 CISG, paras 264, 265; Schlechtriem/Schwenzer/Schroeter/*Schroeter*, 8th German ed., Art. 25 CISG, paras 243, 244; cf. also OLG Frankfurt, 17 September 1991, CISG-online 28, para. 18; BeckOK/*Saenger*, Art. 25 CISG, para. 10; Brunner/Gottlieb/*Brunner/Leisinger*, Art. 25 CISG, para. 20; Kröll *et al./Björklund*, Art. 25 CISG, para. 42; MüKoHGB/*Benicke*, Art. 25 CISG, para. 52; *Schlechtriem/Butler*, para. 114.
1190. Cf. BGH, 24 September 2014, CISG-online 2545, para. 23; OLG Frankfurt, 17 September 1991, CISG-online 28, para. 18; *Ferrari*, (2005) 389 Int'l Bus. L. J., p. 393.
1191. *See* only OGH, 15 November 2012, CISG-online 2399; *Ferrari*, (2005) 389 Int'l Bus. L. J., p. 392.

1) Case Law on (Non-)fundamental Breaches of Exclusivity Obligations or Non-competition Clauses

In a case before the Court of Appeal Frankfurt, the Court came to the conclusion that the Italian seller fundamentally breached a contract by violating their exclusivity obligation, thus entitling the German buyer to avoid the agreement.[1192] Similarly, the Court of Appeal Grenoble held that the US buyer had breached their contractual obligations by re-importing goods into the EU and failing to deliver them to the agreed destination outside of the EU.[1193] The parties in this case had agreed on a prohibition of re-importing the goods into the EU (a non-competition clause), and thus the buyer's breach was considered fundamental by the Court.[1194]

Moreover, the Court of Appeal Koblenz stated that the violation of an exclusivity obligation may, in general, be regarded as a fundamental breach in the sense of Art. 25 CISG, thereby entitling the aggrieved party to avoid the contract.[1195] However, in the case under consideration, the buyer had lost their right to declare the contract avoided, as they did not do so within a reasonable time after discovering the breach as required by Art. 49(2)(b)(i) CISG.[1196] In light of this, the Court ultimately left the question open as to whether the breach of the specific exclusivity obligation was fundamental.[1197]

In contrast, the Austrian Supreme Court decided that an Austrian seller's violation of an exclusive distribution agreement was not fundamental, given that the goods had been delivered to merely one single branch of the buyer's competitor within the same geographical area and for only a brief period of time.[1198] Consequently, the Court concluded that the buyer's chances of selling the goods were not 'destroyed' by the seller's breach of contract.[1199]

Similarly, the Court of First Instance No. 3 of Badalona denied the fundamental breach of a non-competition clause.[1200] The contract in question contained a 'fundamental condition' that required the buyer to resell the goods exclusively in countries within the Middle East, and not in other countries.[1201] Notwithstanding the fact that some of the goods under this contract had been detected outside the Middle East, the Court ruled that the buyer had not breached their non-competition obligation. It further elaborated that the buyer was not obliged to verify that their customers in the Middle East only sold the products in those countries.[1202]

1192. OLG Frankfurt, 17 September 1991, CISG-online 28.
1193. CA Grenoble, 22 February 1995, CISG-online 151.
1194. CA Grenoble, 22 February 1995, CISG-online 151.
1195. OLG Koblenz, 31 January 1997, CISG-online 256, para. 18.
1196. OLG Koblenz, 31 January 1997, CISG-online 256, para. 18.
1197. OLG Koblenz, 31 January 1997, CISG-online 256, para. 18.
1198. OGH, 15 November 2012, CISG-online 2399, para. 5.
1199. OGH, 15 November 2012, CISG-online 2399, para. 5.
1200. JPI Badalona No. 3, 22 May 2006, CISG-online 1391.
1201. JPI Badalona No. 3, 22 May 2006, CISG-online 1391.
1202. JPI Badalona No. 3, 22 May 2006, CISG-online 1391.

2) Conclusions

These cases reveal that the breach of exclusivity obligations or other non-competition obligations may be fundamental if the parties have placed particular emphasis on these obligations. This can be presumed to be the case if the framework agreement is designed as an exclusive distribution agreement.[1203] In such cases, it can typically be assumed that any breach of the parties' exclusivity obligations may be regarded as a fundamental breach.[1204] In general, exclusivity obligations are typically of considerable significance to the parties to a framework agreement; consequently, they are frequently regarded as a 'fundamental' obligation, particularly in the context of distribution agreements.[1205] Nevertheless, the specific circumstances of each case will ultimately be decisive in determining whether a breach of such obligations must be considered fundamental within the meaning of Art. 25 CISG.

Furthermore, Art. 49(1)(b) and Art. 64(1)(b) CISG should not be applicable in the event of a breach of an exclusivity obligation or non-competition clause, given that non-performance is unlikely in these scenarios.[1206] It may nonetheless be advisable for the aggrieved party to fix an additional period of time.[1207] Failure to properly perform the obligations within this additional period of time may indicate that the breach is in fact fundamental.[1208]

ii. Damages

Arts 45(1)(b) and 61(1)(b) CISG in conjunction with Art. 74 CISG entitle the aggrieved party to claim damages if the breaching party violates 'any of his obligations under the contract or this Convention'.[1209] The nature of the breached obligation is irrelevant; the aggrieved party is also entitled to claim damages if a non-sales obligation (or 'ancillary' obligation) has been breached under a CISG contract.[1210] The breaching party must not be at fault since the CISG adopts a strict liability approach.[1211] In addition, the claim for

1203. Schlechtriem/Schwenzer/Schroeter/*Schroeter*, 5th English ed., Art. 25 CISG, para. 265; Schlechtriem/Schwenzer/Schroeter/*Schroeter*, 8th German ed., Art. 25 CISG, para. 244.
1204. Schlechtriem/Schwenzer/Schroeter/*Schroeter*, 5th English ed., Art. 25 CISG, para. 265.
1205. Cf. Ch. 2 III. 4. above (important but not essential).
1206. Cf. MüKoBGB/*Gruber*, Art. 25 CISG, para. 33; *Schroeter*, para. 573.
1207. MüKoBGB/*Gruber*, Art. 25 CISG, para. 33.
1208. CA Grenoble, 22 February 1995, CISG-online 151; MüKoBGB/*Gruber*, Art. 25 CISG, para. 33.
1209. BeckOK/*Saenger*, Art. 45 CISG, para. 8; MüKoBGB/*Huber*, Art. 45 CISG, para. 13; MüKoBGB/*Huber*, Art. 61 CISG, para. 6; MüKoBGB/*Huber*, Art. 74 CISG, paras 3, 4; MüKoHGB/*Sommerfeld*, Art. 74 CISG, para. 5; Schlechtriem/Schwenzer/Schroeter/*Schwenzer*, 5th English ed., Art. 74 CISG, para. 11; Schlechtriem/Schwenzer/Schroeter/*Schwenzer/B. Köhler*, 8th German ed., Art. 74 CISG, paras 19, 20.
1210. BeckOK/*Saenger*, Art. 53 CISG, para. 2; MüKoBGB/*Huber*, Art. 45 CISG, para. 13; MüKoBGB/*Huber*, Art. 53 CISG, paras 3, 4; MüKoBGB/*Huber*, Art. 61 CISG, para. 6; MüKoBGB/*Huber*, Art. 74 CISG, para. 4; MüKoHGB/*Wertenbruch*, Art. 61 CISG, para. 4.
1211. BeckOK/*Saenger*, Art. 45 CISG, para. 8; MüKoBGB/*Huber*, Art. 45 CISG, para. 14; MüKoBGB/*Huber*, Art. 61 CISG, para. 6; MüKoBGB/*Huber*, Art. 74 CISG, para. 3; MüKoHGB/*Sommerfeld*, Art. 74 CISG, para. 5; Schlechtriem/Schwenzer/Schroeter/*Schwenzer*, 5th English ed., Art. 74 CISG, para. 12; Schlechtriem/Schwenzer/Schroeter/*Schwenzer/B. Köhler*, 8th German ed., Art. 74 CISG, para. 20.

damages does not require a fundamental breach of contract within the meaning of Art. 25 CISG.[1212]

It is possible to apply these provisions in cases where an exclusivity obligation or non-competition clause has been breached without encountering any difficulties.[1213] For instance, the Court of Appeal St. Gallen ruled that a seller was entitled to claim damages according to Art. 74 CISG, given that the buyer in the case had breached their obligation to not import the goods to Korea.[1214] The preceding analysis demonstrates that the CISG's provisions on damages are generally suitable and sufficiently flexible to deal with the breach of any obligations under an international framework agreement.[1215]

The parties involved in international commerce frequently take much more care in negotiating a framework agreement than they do in negotiating a 'simple' sales contract.[1216] Consequently, framework agreements typically contain more detailed provisions, including provisions on damages. They may, for example, include so-called indemnification clauses or penalty clauses.[1217] In general, the parties are at liberty to modify the non-mandatory provision set forth in Art. 74 CISG in accordance with Art. 6 CISG.[1218] The question whether a specific agreement between the parties is supposed to exclude other remedies, such as damages, is one of contract interpretation.[1219]

c. *Issues Outside the CISG's Scope of Application*

While the CISG contains general principles that may be able to govern a great number of issues raised by framework agreements, it may still be necessary to resort to the applicable domestic law with regard to some aspects.[1220] This is due to the fact that the CISG is, by default, fragmentary and non-exhaustive.[1221]

1212. MüKoBGB/*Huber*, Art. 74 CISG, para. 3; MüKoHGB/*Sommerfeld*, Art. 74 CISG, para. 5; Schlechtriem/Schwenzer/Schroeter/*Schwenzer*, 5th English ed., Art. 74 CISG, para. 11; Schlechtriem/Schwenzer/Schroeter/*Schwenzer/B. Köhler*, 8th German ed., Art. 74 CISG, para. 20.

1213. *See* Ch. 4 III. 2. b. above.

1214. KGer St. Gallen, 13 May 2008, CISG-online 1768, paras 27 et seq.

1215. *Schwenzer*, Challenges of the 2020s, p. 45; *Thieffry*, Dr. prat. com. int. 1993, p. 65 (also mentioning Art. 79 CISG).

1216. *Thieffry*, Dr. prat. com. int. 1993, p. 63.

1217. ICC, 1 November 2016, CISG-online 5988 (exclusive distribution contract that included a number of warranty and indemnification clauses); CA Warsaw, 15 May 2015, CISG-online 2783 (exclusive distribution contract that included a penalty clause).

1218. Schlechtriem/Schwenzer/Schroeter/*Schwenzer*, 5th English ed., Art. 74 CISG, paras 60 et seq.; Schlechtriem/Schwenzer/Schroeter/*Schwenzer/B. Köhler*, 8th German ed., Art. 74 CISG, paras 50 et seq.

1219. Schlechtriem/Schwenzer/Schroeter/*Schwenzer*, 5th English ed., Art. 74 CISG, para. 61 (with regard to agreed sums payable upon breach); Schlechtriem/Schwenzer/Schroeter/*Schwenzer/B. Köhler*, 8th German ed., Art. 74 CISG, para. 52 (with regard to agreed sums payable upon breach).

1220. *Schroeter*, para. 92; *C. Witz*, para. 112.61.

1221. *Schroeter*, para. 92; *Torsello*, pp. 206, 207.

As outlined above, Art. 4 CISG is of limited use to determine the borders of the CISG's substantive scope of application.[1222] Rather, this study will rely on the two-step test in this regard.[1223] Under this test, domestic law is pre-empted by the CISG if two criteria are cumulatively fulfilled: the domestic law rule must be triggered by the same set of facts as the CISG (factual criterion) and pertain to a legal matter that is also regulated by the Convention (legal criterion).[1224]

The following section will address selected issues that are likely to fall outside the CISG's substantive scope of application, in accordance with the two-step test. It will focus on those issues that appear to be particularly relevant when dealing with international framework agreements.

i. *Competition or Anti-trust Law*

Some terms contained in framework agreements may clash with the principle of open competition and violate domestic or regional competition or anti-trust laws.[1225] Examples of such terms include exclusivity obligations, non-competition clauses and price-fixing agreements.[1226] The relevant competition or anti-trust laws often render such clauses or even the entire agreement null or void, and may also provide for regulatory consequences imposed by the competent authorities.[1227]

An application of the two-step test indicates that domestic competition or anti-trust law provisions may occasionally be triggered by the same facts as the CISG (factual criterion), yet do not pertain to legal matters (legal criterion) governed by the Convention.[1228] This is because the CISG is generally not concerned with the violation of statutory prohibitions, which may include prohibitions that are based on competition or anti-trust considerations.[1229] Furthermore, the Convention does not attempt to

1222. *See* Ch. 1 IV. 1. a. above.
1223. Regarding the two-step test: *Schroeter*, Vill. L. Rev. 2013, pp. 563 et seq.; *Schroeter*, paras 160 et seq.; *see* Ch. 1 IV. 1. b. above.
1224. *Schroeter*, Vill. L. Rev. 2013, p. 563; *Schroeter*, para. 160.
1225. *Hoffbauer*, p. 122; Münch/Passadelis/Lehne/*Rohn*, para. 4.105; cf. BGH, 23 July 1997, CISG-online 276.
1226. *Heinemann/Schnyder*, p. 133; *Hoffbauer*, p. 122; Martinek/Semler/Flohr/*Rahlmeyer/Duhe*, § 42, para. 3; in detail: Münch/Passadelis/Lehne/*Rohn*, paras 4.109 et seq.; Reithmann/Martiny/*Fabig*, § 37, para. 37.3; cf. also BGH, 23 July 1997, CISG-online 276.
1227. Cf. BGH, 23 July 1997, CISG-online 267; *Hoffbauer*, pp. 122 et seq.; *Magnus*, IHR 2018, pp. 56, 57; Reithmann/Martiny/*Fabig*, § 37, para. 37.4.
1228. With the same result: BGH, 23 July 1997, CISG-online 276, para. 14; BeckOK/*Saenger*, Art. 4 CISG, para. 26; *Gillette/Walt*, pp. 80, 81 (competition law is 'not triggered by the same operative facts as the CISG'); *Honnold/Flechtner*, Art. 4 CISG, para. 89; *Perales Viscasillas*, Extending the Scope, p. 125; *Perales Viscasillas*, Int'l Distribution Contracts and CISG, p. 5; Schlechtriem/Schwenzer/Schroeter/*Hachem*, 5th English ed., Art. 4 CISG, para. 39; cf. also CISG-AC, Op. 23 *Beale*, Rule 3, Comment 3.14.
1229. BeckOK/*Saenger*, Art. 4 CISG, para. 26; Schlechtriem/Schwenzer/Schroeter/*Hachem*, 5th English ed., Art. 4 CISG, para. 39; in general with regard to statutory prohibitions: MüKoBGB/*Huber*, Art. 4 CISG, para. 17; MüKoHGB/*B. Köhler*, Art. 4 CISG, para. 8; Schlechtriem/Schwenzer/Schroeter/*Ferrari*, 8th German ed., Art. 4 CISG, para. 18; *Schroeter*, para. 202.

steer the economy,[1230] in contrast to domestic law provisions that relate to matters of open and fair competition.[1231]

Consequently, domestic competition or anti-trust laws should not be displaced by the CISG; they are in fact applicable alongside the Convention.[1232] This includes competition law provisions that deal with the admissibility of exclusivity or non-competition obligations.[1233] The result submitted by this study has been confirmed in the *Benetton II* case, in which the German Supreme Court, *inter alia*, held that the CISG does not address the validity of individual sales contracts in light of European Union or German competition laws.[1234]

The consequences of a framework agreement violating domestic competition law provisions thus depend on the applicable domestic law determined by the conflict of law rules of the forum.[1235] It is, naturally, necessary to assess whether domestic competition law is capable of applying to international transactions in the first place.[1236] In this context, it should be noted that certain domestic competition law provisions may be considered overriding mandatory provisions, e.g., as defined in Art. 9 Rome I Regulation.[1237] In such cases, these provisions must be taken into account under the CISG, even if they originate from the law of a third state rather than the *lex contractus*.[1238]

Finally, it is questionable whether the violation of competition law, e.g., through the inclusion of an inadmissible exclusivity obligation, may have consequences not only for the framework agreement, but also for the individual sales contracts concluded subsequently (in the case of a two-tier framework agreement). In this context, the German Supreme Court ruled in the *Benetton II* case that the potential invalidity of a franchise agreement based on a violation of German or EU competition laws does not affect the validity of the individual sales contracts that were governed by the CISG.[1239] In fact, the validity of the individual sales contracts in light of domestic or regional competition laws must be determined separately, given the distinction between these

---

1230. MüKoBGB/*Huber*, Art. 4 CISG, para. 17; MüKoHGB/*B. Köhler*, Art. 4 CISG, para. 8; Schlechtriem/Schwenzer/Schroeter/*Ferrari*, 8th German ed., Art. 4 CISG, para. 19; *Schroeter*, para. 202.
1231. Cf. *Stawski Distributing Co., Inc. v. Zywiec Breweries PLC*, US Dist. Ct. ND Illinois, 6 October 2003, CISG-online 1225.
1232. BGH, 23 July 1997, CISG-online 297, paras 14 et seq.; BeckOK/*Saenger*, Art. 4 CISG, para. 26; *Czerwenka*, p. 166; *Gillette/Walt*, pp. 80, 81; *Perales Viscasillas*, Extending the Scope, p. 125; *Perales Viscasillas*, Int'l Distribution Contracts and CISG, p. 51; Schlechtriem/Schwenzer/Schroeter/*Hachem*, 5th English ed., Art. 4 CISG, para. 39.
1233. Cf. *Czerwenka*, p. 166; *Thieffry*, Dr. prat. com. int. 1993, p. 63; *C. Witz*, para. 112.61.
1234. BGH, 23 July 1997, CISG-online 276, para. 14.
1235. *Czerwenka*, p. 166; cf. also BGH, 23 July 1997, CISG-online 297 (with regard to the individual sales contracts concluded in accordance with the terms of a distribution agreement).
1236. Cf. *Schlechtriem/Butler*, para. 34; in general, competition law is based on the 'effects doctrine' ('*Auswirkungsprinzip*'), providing more details: Münch/Passadelis/Lehne/*Rohn*, para. 4.106; Reithmann/Martiny/*Fabig*, § 37, para. 37.4.
1237. *Heinemann/Schnyder*, p. 133; Kronke *et al./Killias/Marzorati*, Teil G, para. 351; *Magnus*, IHR 2018, pp. 56, 57; Münch/Passadelis/Lehne/*Rohn*, para. 4.108.
1238. Brunner/Gottlieb/*Brunner/Murmann/Stucki*, Art. 4 CISG, paras 7, 8; MüKoBGB/*Huber*, Art. 4 CISG, para. 17; Staudinger/*Magnus*, Art. 4 CISG, para. 20.
1239. BGH, 23 July 1997, CISG-online 297, para. 14.

individual contracts and the framework agreement.[1240] Accordingly, the consequences arising out of a potential violation of domestic or regional competition laws must be determined separately with regard to the framework agreement and the individual sales contracts.[1241]

ii. Claims for Compensation after Termination of Distribution Agreements

A number of jurisdictions grant claims for compensation to the distributor (buyer) after a distribution agreement has been terminated, subject to certain conditions.[1242] The rationale for these claims for compensation is not that the supplier has caused damage to the distributor, but rather that the distributor should be compensated for the goodwill they have added to the supplier's business by (significantly) increasing the number of customers for the supplier's products. It is likely that the supplier will continue to benefit from these customers even after the distribution agreement has been terminated.[1243]

The CISG contains provisions on the effects of avoidance in Arts 81–84 CISG. These provisions also apply if a CISG contract has been terminated by mutual agreement or in accordance with a contractual right to terminate the contract.[1244] Consequently, claims for compensation from domestic laws may be triggered by the same factual circumstances as the Convention, namely the termination or avoidance of an international distribution agreement governed by the CISG.[1245] Accordingly, the first criterion – the factual criterion – could arguably be met under the two-step test.

However, domestic claims for compensation after termination do not pertain to legal matters that are governed by the CISG, i.e., the legal criterion is not met.[1246] This is due to the fact that the Convention is concerned solely with the benefits that have been derived from the goods themselves (Art. 84(2) CISG). It does not consider other benefits, such as those that may arise from expanding the customer base by distributing the goods. The CISG does not attempt to regulate or address compensation for this type of benefit. The subject of regulation differs between the domestic law provisions

1240. Cf. BGH, 23 July 1997, CISG-online 297, paras 14 et seq.
1241. To that effect: BGH, 23 July 1997, CISG-online 297, paras 14 et seq.
1242. Reithmann/Martiny/*Fabig*, § 37, paras 37.97 et seq. (comparing different jurisdictions); Belgium: Art. X.37 of the *Code de droit économique*; Germany: *see* only BGH, 5 February 2015, VII ZR 315/13; Martinek/Semler/Flohr/*Rösch/van der Moolen*, § 25, paras 1 et seq. with further references; Switzerland: BGer, 22 May 2008, BGE 134 III 497, with a note by *Fountoulakis*, recht 2008, pp. 222 et seq.; *Fountoulakis*, pp. 94 et seq.; *Groz/Zehner*, AJP 2024, pp. 398 et seq.; *C. Meyer*, ZVertriebsR 2017, pp. 19 et seq.; Kull/Wildhaber/*Wildhaber*, paras 806 et seq.; Austria: OGH, 22 April 2009, 3 Ob44/09f; *Moritz*, ZVertriebsR 2017, pp. 144 et seq.
1243. BGer, 22 May 2008, BGE 134 III 497 (highlighting that the compensation is not a claim for damages); *Fountoulakis*, pp. 82, 83 (with regard to agency contracts); *Fountoulakis*, recht 2008, p. 224; *Groz/Zehner*, AJP 2024, pp. 403, 404; *C. Meyer*, ZVertriebsR 2017, p. 19; *Oetiker/Weibel/Mata*, IHR 2022, p. 54; cf. also Art. X.37 *Code de droit économique* (Belgium).
1244. Each with further references: LG Dortmund, 21 April 2017, CISG-online 2801; Schlechtriem/Schwenzer/Schroeter/*Fountoulakis*, 5th English ed., Intro to Arts 81–84 CISG, para. 9; Staudinger/*Magnus*, Art. 81 CISG, para. 4.
1245. Cf. in a different context: *Schroeter*, para. 166.
1246. Accord *Schroeter*, para. 92.

and the CISG's provisions. Hence, the existence and calculation of claims for compensation of a distributor should be governed by the applicable domestic law and not be superseded by the CISG.[1247]

iii. 'Rupture Brutale'

Art. 442-1(2) of the French Commercial Code stipulates that the abrupt termination of a commercial relationship may entitle the aggrieved party to claim compensation. In essence, this provision holds that a party who terminates an existing business relationship of any kind without observing a notice period, which is to be regarded as reasonable in light of the overall circumstances (in particular, the duration of the business relationship), is liable and shall compensate the other party.[1248] The determination of the reasonableness of a notice period must be based solely on objective criteria, namely the overall circumstances, in particular the duration of the business relationship. The existence of a contractually agreed-upon shorter notice period is irrelevant in this respect.[1249] Art. 442-1(2) of the French Commercial Code is of particular relevance with regard to the termination of framework agreements.[1250] It has been noted that this provision bears resemblance to the aforementioned claim for compensation after termination of a distribution agreement, as found, for example, in German law.[1251]

In cases where business relationships were also, to some extent, subject to the CISG, the majority of French courts applied or referred to Art. 442-1(2) of the French Commercial Code alongside the CISG.[1252] It is once more necessary to assess the accuracy of this approach in light of the two-step test.

As with the claims for compensation after termination of a distribution agreement discussed above, factual scenarios that may give rise to a claim for compensation based on '*rupture brutale*' (Art. 442-1(2) of the French Commercial Code) may also trigger the CISG's application. This is because the CISG addresses the effects of avoidance (Arts 81–84 CISG).[1253] The Convention further entitles the aggrieved party to seek compensation for damages, provided that a breach of contract has occurred in accordance with Art. 45(1)(b) or Art. 61(1)(b) in conjunction with Art. 74 CISG.[1254] Art. 81(1), sentence 1 CISG explicitly states that any damages claims that may be due will

1247. *Schroeter*, para. 92.
1248. *Stade*, ZVertriebsR, pp. 294, 295; cf. also *Bauerreis*, FS C. Witz, pp. 62, 63; *Malaurie/Aynès/Stoffel-Munck*, pp. 217, 218.
1249. *Bauerreis*, FS C. Witz, p. 62; *Stade*, ZVertriebsR, p. 295.
1250. CA Paris, 6 September 2023, CISG-online 6562 (with regard to the termination of an exclusive distribution agreement); CA Paris, 5 March 2019, CISG-online 5765 (with regard to the termination of a framework 'logistics agreement'); Cour de Cassation, 20 February 2007, CISG-online 1492 (with regard to the termination of a distribution contract); *Bauerreis*, FS C. Witz, p. 62, holding that this provision was originally designed for distribution agreements.
1251. *Bauerreis*, FS C. Witz, p. 63.
1252. *See* CA Lyon, 18 February 2016, CISG-online 3054; CA Paris, 6 September 2023, CISG-online 6562; CA Paris, 5 March 2019, CISG-online 5765; Cour de Cassation, 20 February 2007, CISG-online 1492; cf. also CA Paris, 7 February 2024, CISG-online 6838.
1253. *See* Ch. 4 III. 2. c. ii. above.
1254. Cf. CA Douai, 1 February 2024, CISG-online 6805.

remain unaffected by the contract avoidance.[1255] Consequently, it can be argued that the factual criterion is met.

Art. 442-1(2) of the French Commercial Code, which penalises the sudden termination of an established commercial relationship,[1256] is designed to safeguard the interests of a party that is dependent on the other party and disinclined to terminate the business relationship.[1257] It considers the party's extent of dependency on the other party and aims to mitigate the adverse effects of a sudden termination of a long-standing business relationship.[1258] The CISG does not seek to regulate or address the adverse effects of a sudden termination of an established business relationship in its provisions on the effects of avoidance. It also does not seek to protect the interests of a party in a dependent relationship who is generally disinclined to terminate the relationship. Rather, the Convention merely upholds damages claims that may be due when the contract is terminated (Art. 81(1) CISG). Apart from this possibility of pursuing claims for damages based on a breach of contract, which is not a prerequisite for a claim based on *rupture brutale*, the CISG does not extend further on this matter. Consequently, the subject of regulation between Art. 442-1(2) of the French Commercial Code and the CISG's provisions differs. This result was confirmed by the Court of Appeal Grenoble, which held that the application of the CISG was not sufficient to exclude the application of Art. 442-6.I.5 (predecessor to Art. 442-1(2)) of the French Commercial Code, given that this provision is not concerned with substantive sales law but rather penalises the sudden termination of a commercial relationship.[1259]

iv. Form Requirements Related to Non-sales Obligations

Art. 11 CISG enshrines the principle of freedom of form. This principle is limited to matters explicitly addressed by the CISG, primarily those pertaining to sales; the principle of freedom of form does not extend to the non-sales obligations that may be included in mixed framework agreements governed by the CISG.[1260]

Non-competition clauses or exclusivity obligations that are frequently contained in framework agreements may be subject to form requirements under domestic laws in

1255. Schlechtriem/Schwenzer/Schroeter/*Fountoulakis*, 5th English ed., Art. 81 CISG, para. 15.
1256. CA Paris, 6 September 2023, CISG-online 6562, para. 26; CA Colmar, 23 November 2010, CISG-online 2593.
1257. Cf. CA Paris, 5 March 2019, CISG-online 5765, paras 100 et seq.; *Malaurie/Aynès/Stoffel-Munck*, p. 217.
1258. Cf. CA Paris, 5 March 2019, CISG-online 5765, para. 100 (with regard to the notice period); *Bauerreis*, FS C. Witz, pp. 62, 63; *Malaurie/Aynès/Stoffel-Munck*, p. 217.
1259. CA Colmar, 23 November 2010, CISG-online 2593: '*Attendu cependant que l'application de la Convention de Vienne, [...], ne suffit pas en soi pour écarter l'application de l'article L.442-6.I.5° du code de commerce qui ne régit pas le droit substantiel de la vente, mais qui vient sanctionner la rupture brutale de relations commerciales établies en droit interne français.*'
1260. Not specifically with regard to framework agreements: BeckOK/*Saenger*, Art. 11 CISG, para. 6; Brunner/Gottlieb/*Brunner/Balogh*, Art. 11 CISG, para. 2; MüKoBGB/*Gruber*, Art. 11 CISG, para. 5; MüKoHGB/*Ferrari*, Art. 11 CISG, para. 4; Schlechtriem/Schwenzer/Schroeter/*Schmidt-Kessel*, 5th English ed., Art. 11 CISG, para. 7; Staudinger/*Magnus*, Art. 11 CISG, para. 7; but *see* Kröll *et al.*/*Perales Viscasillas*, Art. 11 CISG, paras 11 et seq.

some jurisdictions.[1261] It can be argued that the CISG is not even triggered by such factual scenarios, since the principle of freedom of form is restricted to sales matters. In any case, as the principle of freedom of form does not apply to such non-sales matters, these domestic form requirements for non-competition clauses or exclusivity obligations are not superseded by Art. 11 CISG and its underlying principle.[1262] Consequently, the parties to a framework agreement must still comply with the relevant form requirements that may originate from the applicable domestic law, even if the contract falls within the scope of application of the CISG.[1263]

v. *Industry Specific Rules:* Stawski Distributing v. Zywiec Breweries

The US District Court for the Northern District of Illinois was required to determine whether the Illinois Beer Industry Fair Dealing Act ('IBIFDA') could be applied alongside the CISG or whether it was pre-empted by the Convention.[1264] The IBIFDA imposes several restrictions on the contractual relationship between brewers and beer wholesalers (primarily distribution agreements); this includes international distribution agreements which may be governed by the CISG.[1265] It, among other things, specifies in its sections three and four that a contractual relationship may be terminated or cancelled only if strict formal and substantive requirements are met.[1266] This was relevant to the case under consideration, given that the seller intended to terminate an exclusive distribution agreement which was potentially governed by the CISG.[1267] The Court eventually came to the conclusion that the IBIFDA was not displaced by the Convention.[1268]

Upon initial examination, it is possible that the IBIFDA was triggered by the same factual circumstances as the CISG, namely, the termination of an international distribution agreement.[1269] However, the IBIFDA's subject of regulation is not covered by the CISG. According to section 2(a) IBIFDA, the Act aims at promoting the public's interest in the fair, efficient and competitive distribution of malt beverages; this is

1261. Cf. BGH, 23 July 1997, CISG-online 276.
1262. BeckOK/*Saenger*, Art. 11 CISG, para. 6; Brunner/Gottlieb/*Brunner/Balogh*, Art. 11 CISG, para. 2; MüKoBGB/*Gruber*, Art. 11 CISG, para. 5; MüKoHGB/*Ferrari*, Art. 11 CISG, para. 4; Schlechtriem/Schwenzer/Schroeter/*Ferrari*, 8th German ed., Art. 4 CISG, para. 14; Schlechtriem/Schwenzer/Schroeter/*Schmidt-Kessel*, 5th English ed., Art. 11 CISG, para. 10; *Schroeter*, paras 92, 286; Staudinger/*Magnus*, Art. 11 CISG, para. 7.
1263. *Schroeter*, paras 92, 286.
1264. *Stawski Distributing Co., Inc. v. Zywiec Breweries PLC*, US Dist. Ct. ND Illinois, 6 October 2003, CISG-online 1225 with notes by *Schroeter*, (2013) 58 Vill. L. Rev., pp. 565 et seq.; *Schroeter*, para. 166.
1265. *Schroeter*, (2013) 58 Vill. L. Rev., p. 565.
1266. *See also Stawski Distributing Co., Inc. v. Zywiec Breweries PLC*, US Dist. Ct. ND Illinois, 6 October 2003, CISG-online 1225.
1267. *Stawski Distributing Co., Inc. v. Zywiec Breweries PLC*, US Dist. Ct. ND Illinois, 6 October 2003, CISG-online 1225 with notes by *Schroeter*, (2013) 58 Vill. L. Rev., pp. 565 et seq.; *Schroeter*, para. 166.
1268. *Stawski Distributing Co., Inc. v. Zywiec Breweries PLC*, US Dist. Ct. ND Illinois, 6 October 2003, CISG-online 1225 with notes by *Schroeter*, (2013) 58 Vill. L. Rev., pp. 565 et seq.; *Schroeter*, para. 166.
1269. *Schroeter*, (2013) 58 Vill. L. Rev., pp. 565, 566; *Schroeter*, para. 166.

achieved, for instance, by ensuring that the beer wholesaler is free to manage their business enterprise, including the wholesaler's right to independently establish their selling prices.[1270] The CISG does not intend to regulate the fair, efficient and competitive distribution in the beer industry or any other industry, and therefore it was correct for the Court to conclude that the IBIFIDA did not displace the Convention and both could be applied to the contract.[1271] It should be noted that in contrast to a number of domestic law provisions, the Convention generally does not attempt to make regulations that steer the economy.[1272]

IV. CONCLUSION

Framework agreements that contain sales obligations that fall within the CISG's scope as well as service or labour obligations that fall outside the CISG's scope are within the ambit of Art. 3(2) CISG. The same should apply to framework agreements that contain sales obligations as well as exclusivity and non-competition obligations. Although they may not fall directly within the scope of Art. 3(2) CISG, such contracts should still be considered to trigger the general principle underlying this provision and should thus be regarded as non-sales elements to be taken into account for the determination of the preponderant part. Art. 3(2) CISG and its underlying principle should equally be applied to preliminary agreements and framework agreements that contain an obligation to conclude individual sales contracts.[1273]

In general, there are two approaches to determine the preponderant part in mixed contracts under Art. 3(2) CISG. The first approach is the economic value test. Second, there is an overall assessment, which incorporates additional criteria, such as the parties' intentions and interests, the text of the contract, the weight given to the different obligations, the intended duration of the contract, the circumstances surrounding the contract conclusion, and the primary purpose of the contract. In the context of framework agreements, it is often not possible to determine the preponderant part solely based on the economic value test. Consequently, this study posits that the overall assessment with its supplementary criteria should be considered when determining the preponderant part in mixed framework agreements. The CISG's applicability will therefore depend on the particular circumstances of each case. This approach seems justified with regard to framework agreements, given the considerable heterogeneity of these contracts. Furthermore, it is not problematic that some framework agreements are structured in a two-tier manner. It is necessary to determine the preponderant part of the framework agreement itself, without having regard to the individual sales contracts.[1274]

It is submitted that if a mixed framework agreement contains a preponderant sales part, the CISG should be applied to the entire agreement, rather than just the sales

1270. *See also Schroeter*, (2013) 58 Vill. L. Rev., p. 568.
1271. Accord *Schroeter*, (2013) 58 Vill. L. Rev., pp. 567, 568; *Schroeter*, para. 166.
1272. *See* Ch. 4 III. 2. c. i. above.
1273. *See* Ch. 4 I. above.
1274. *See* Ch. 4 II. above.

part. This can be derived from a literal and purposive interpretation of Art. 3(2) CISG. Moreover, there are typically significant relationships between the different obligations if they are combined in one single framework agreement; this also suggests that the same law should be applied. The application of the CISG to the non-sales parts of framework agreements and any other mixed contracts does not result in unsatisfactory outcomes, given that the Convention's provisions are suitable and sufficiently flexible to also govern these issues.[1275]

To be more precise, the CISG's provisions and its underlying principles provide solutions if the seller does not perform their service obligations under a mixed framework agreement. The aggrieved buyer may pursue the remedies of specific performance, reduction of the price, avoidance and damages, provided that the respective prerequisites are met. The aggrieved party may also be entitled to withhold their own performance. The CISG's provisions on these matters may either be applied directly or, alternatively, general principles may be derived from them, thus resulting in these remedies being suitable and sufficiently flexible if service obligations have not been performed at all. The same applies in cases where service obligations have been performed in a non-conforming manner. Although service obligations are sometimes characterised as *obligations de moyens*, the Convention contains general principles that may be applied to establish liability for the breach of service obligations; it also contains remedies that are suitable and sufficiently flexible for such cases. Nevertheless, it is not appropriate to apply all of the CISG's provisions and its underlying principles to cases of breach of service obligations. In particular, the obligation to give notice should not be extended. The Convention may also be applied to cases where the buyer is the party who has undertaken service obligations and has breached those obligations. This is because the majority of CISG remedies apply equally to both parties of the contract, subject to the same requirements. Furthermore, the parties should generally have the same remedies if the opposing party breaches their service obligations, as a distinction does not seem justified in this context. The Convention's provisions and its underlying principles are also capable of addressing breaches of exclusivity or non-competition obligations, which are of particular practical importance. In such instances, case law has established that the aggrieved party may be entitled to claim damages and avoid the contract if such obligations have been breached.[1276]

It should, however, be kept in mind that the CISG is, by default, fragmentary and non-exhaustive. Thus, it will be necessary to resort to the applicable domestic law with regard to certain aspects. The CISG is, among other things, not concerned with issues of competition law, claims for compensation after termination of a distribution agreement, claims based on '*rupture brutale*', form requirements for exclusivity or non-competition clauses, and other industry-specific rules. This has been revealed by applying the two-step test. Instead, these matters should be governed by the applicable

1275. *See* Ch. 4 III. 1. above.
1276. *See* Ch. 4 III. 2. a., b. above.

domestic law. This demonstrates that the CISG's application to international framework agreements is without prejudice to specific domestic law rules.[1277]

1277. *See* Ch. 4 III. 2. c. above.

CHAPTER 5
Framework Agreements as Long-Term Contracts under the CISG

Framework agreements are commonly characterised as long-term contracts, as they are designed to regulate a supply relationship for an extended period of time.[1278] This time factor may potentially give rise to specific problems when dealing with framework agreements and other long-term contracts under the CISG.[1279] There appear to be little to no scholarly writings or case law that specifically address the challenges of long-term contracts under the CISG.[1280] In contrast, there has been a great deal of literature devoted to the subject of long-term contracts under domestic laws, e.g., German laws of obligations.[1281] The following part will establish a notion of long-term contracts derived from the CISG, outline the types of long-term contracts that may fall within the Convention's sphere of application and address the specific challenges long-term framework agreements as well as other long-term contracts governed by the CISG are faced with.

1278. OLG München, 18 June 2018, CISG-online 3080; BSK OR-I/*Amstutz/Morin*, Einl. vor Arts 184 ff. CO, para. 115; *Budde/Geks*, ZVertriebsR 2012, p. 37; *Fuchs-Wissemann*, p. 101; *Furrer/Lohri*, p. 24; *C. Meyer*, pp. 110, 111; *Gatsi*, paras 223 et seq.; *Hoffbauer*, p. 17; *Horn*, p. 563; Sayag/*Pollaud-Dulian*, para. 100; *Ulmer*, p. 301; *Weber*, ZSR 1987, p. 410; cf. also *Oetker*, pp. 119 et seq.

1279. *See* for an extensive discussion of these matters in the course of modernising the German BGB: *Horn*, pp. 557 et seq.

1280. Schlechtriem/Schwenzer/Schroeter/*Schroeter*, 8th German ed., Einleitung, para. 85, holding that long-term contracts are becoming increasingly prevalent in case law, yet there is virtually no literature on this type of contract under the CISG.

1281. *See* only: *Horn*, pp. 557 et seq.; *Oetker*, pp. 66 et seq.

I. NOTION OF LONG-TERM CONTRACTS

Generally, there seems to be no universal understanding of 'long-term contracts'.[1282] Moreover, the CISG does not explicitly refer to long-term contracts in its provisions.[1283]

1. Definition Derived from the CISG

Given the absence of any reference to them, the CISG naturally does not provide for an explicit definition of long-term contracts. In fact, the majority of its provisions were drafted with the intention of regulating one-off sales contracts.[1284] Nevertheless, Art. 73 CISG refers to 'a contract for delivery of goods by instalments'. A significant number of commentators have characterised such instalment contracts as long-term contracts.[1285] Thus, the definition of instalment contracts within the meaning of Art. 73 CISG may be employed as a starting point to develop an understanding of long-term contracts under the Convention.

The prevailing view among scholars defines instalment contracts within the meaning of Art. 73 CISG as agreements that provide for at least two successive deliveries at different points in time.[1286] This definition suggests that any long-term contract under the CISG involves a multitude of deliveries over an extended period of time.[1287] However, a multitude of deliveries is a specific characteristic of instalment contracts and not necessarily an element of all long-term contracts covered by the Convention.[1288] The CISG may also apply to long-term framework agreements which merely oblige the parties to conclude multiple individual sales contracts,[1289] i.e., do not themselves involve a multitude of deliveries.

1282. *Doralt*, pp. 60, 61 (with regard to German law); *Guo*, pp. 18, 19 with further references; *Oetker*, pp. 96 et seq. (no clear and universally accepted terminology in Germany); cf. also *Nicklisch*, p. 17, who asserts that there is no precise definition at all.
1283. *Doralt*, p. 86; Honsell/*Brunner/Hurni*, Art. 73 CISG, para. 9.
1284. Cf. *Doralt*, p. 86; *Schroeter*, RabelsZ 81 (2017), p. 64; *Torsello*, pp. 208, 209; with regard to contract avoidance: Schlechtriem/Schwenzer/Schroeter/*Schroeter*, 5th English ed., Art. 25 CISG, para. 104; Schlechtriem/Schwenzer/Schroeter/*Schroeter*, 8th German ed., Art. 25 CISG, para. 96.
1285. To that effect: Brunner/*Brunner/Boog/Schläpfer*, Art. 73 CISG, para. 19; Brunner/Gottlieb/*Brunner/Schläpfer/Boog*, Art. 73 CISG, para. 19; Kröll *et al./Saidov*, Art. 73 CISG, para. 4; Schlechtriem/Schwenzer/Schroeter/*Fountoulakis*, 5th English ed., Art. 73 CISG, para. 4; *von Scheven*, p. 104; employing a different terminology ('*Dauerschuldverhältnis*'): Honsell/*Brunner/Hurni*, Art. 73 CISG, para. 9; cf. with regard to German law: MüKoBGB/*Weber*, § 510 BGB, para. 11; *Oetker*, pp. 120, 121.
1286. Kröll *et al./Saidov*, Art. 73 CISG, para. 3; MüKoBGB/*Huber*, Art. 73 CISG, para. 2; MüKoHGB/*Sommerfeld*, Art. 73 CISG, para. 3; Schlechtriem/Schwenzer/Schroeter/*Fountoulakis*, 5th English ed., Art. 73 CISG, para. 7; Staudinger/*Magnus*, Art. 73 CISG, para. 6.
1287. Probably accord: Brunner/*Brunner/Boog/Schläpfer*, Art. 73 CISG, para. 19; Brunner/Gottlieb/*Brunner/Schläpfer/Boog*, Art. 73 CISG, para. 19.
1288. But *see* (relying on a 'general definition' of long-term contracts): Brunner/*Brunner/Boog/Schläpfer*, Art. 73 CISG, para. 19 in footnote 2616; Brunner/Gottlieb/*Brunner/Schläpfer/Boog*, Art. 73 CISG, para. 19 in footnote 2702.
1289. *See* Ch. 3 III. 1. b. above.

It is therefore proposed that only the time element contained in the definition of instalment contracts under Art. 73 CISG should be generalised for a definition of long-term contracts under the CISG.[1290] The time element can be interpreted to imply that long-term contracts under the CISG generally must be for an extended duration.[1291] This means that the obligations under such contracts are to be performed over a prolonged period of time.[1292] It is irrelevant whether the obligations must be performed regularly or irregularly over time.[1293] Furthermore, it is not possible to derive a minimum duration required for a contract to be characterised as a long-term contract.[1294] In contrast to one-off contracts that are to be performed at one singular point in time, any substantial duration should be sufficient, provided that the performance is 'stretched' over this period of time.[1295] The determination of whether there is a substantial duration depends on the individual circumstances of each case and may, for instance, differ according to the relevant industry.[1296]

2. Comparison with the Definition under the UPICC

A comparable definition of long-term contracts can be found within the UPICC. In contrast to the CISG, the UPICC explicitly mentions long-term contracts. Art. 1.11 UPICC contains the following definition:[1297]

> 'long-term contract' refers to a contract which is to be performed over a period of time and which normally involves, to a varying degree, complexity of the transaction and an ongoing relationship between the parties.

This definition includes three elements: the duration of the contract, an ongoing relationship between the parties, and the complexity of the transaction.[1298] Of these three elements, the duration of the contract is the essential one, while the other two elements are not necessarily required for a contract to be characterised as a long-term

1290. Similarly, with regard to German law: *Doralt*, pp. 214, 215; differently, *Dessemontet*, FS Schwenzer, pp. 396, 397.
1291. Cf. on German law: *Hoffbauer*, p. 16; *Horn*, pp. 560 et seq.; *Oetker*, pp. 99 et seq., who proposes a categorisation of contracts according to a temporal element ('*langfristiger Vertrag*' as an umbrella term).
1292. Art. 1.11 UPICC; *Horn*, p. 561 (with regard to German law); *Oetker*, p. 142 (with regard to German law); but *see Dessemontet*, FS Schwenzer, p. 396.
1293. Cf. *Hoffbauer*, p. 16; with regard to Art. 73 CISG: Brunner/Gottlieb/*Brunner/Schläpfer/Boog*, Art. 73 CISG, para. 2; MüKoHGB/*Sommerfeld*, Art. 73 CISG, para. 3; Staudinger/*Magnus*, Art. 73 CISG, para. 6.
1294. In a different context: *Guo*, p. 19 ('there is no precise stipulation regarding how long a contract should be in order for it to be considered as a long-term contract'); *Horn*, p. 562; but *see Dessemontet*, FS Schwenzer, p. 397, suggesting that a contract should be classified as 'long-term' if it lasted a minimum of eight years.
1295. *Oetker*, pp. 112 et seq., who distinguishes between one-off contracts ('*punktueller Austauschvertrag*') and long-term contracts ('*langfristiger Vertrag*'); cf. also *Guo*, p. 19; *Nicklisch*, p. 17; *von Bar/Clive*, p. 2426 (distribution contracts usually last for a substantial period of time).
1296. Cf. *Guo*, p. 19; *Horn*, p. 562.
1297. There is a debate as to whether this constitutes a definition or a mere description, *see Guo*, p. 33.
1298. Comment 3 on Art. 1.11 UPICC.

contract under the UPICC.[1299] This definition of long-term contracts confirms the assertion that the temporal factor, i.e., performance over an extended period of time, should be regarded as the essential element of long-term contracts.[1300] This aligns with the definition under the CISG proposed above. For the avoidance of doubt, it should be noted that this study does not attempt to interpret the CISG by reference to the UPICC. The UPICC's definition merely demonstrates that the definition proposed by this study is likely to be accepted internationally.[1301]

II. TYPES OF LONG-TERM CONTRACTS GOVERNED BY THE CISG

Before addressing the challenges that long-term contracts under the CISG are confronted with, it is first necessary to outline the types of long-term contracts that may fall within the Convention's sphere of application.

As evidenced by Art. 73 CISG, the Convention covers instalment contracts.[1302] The term 'instalment contracts' must be understood broadly within the context of the Convention.[1303] As previously stated, framework agreements that already contain the defining characteristics of a sales contract, namely sales obligations in *sensu stricto*, may also fall within the Convention's sphere of application[1304] and may be characterised as instalment contracts in the sense of Art. 73 CISG.[1305] Instalment contracts are typically performed over a substantial period of time, thus qualifying as long-term contracts within the meaning of the definition proposed by this study. Accordingly, instalment contracts are one type of long-term contract governed by the CISG.[1306]

1299. Comment 3 on Art. 1.11 UPICC; *see also* UNIDROIT working group on long-term contracts, Study L – Misc. 21, paras 5 et seq.
1300. Cf. also *B. Köhler*, Long-term contracts, p. 154.
1301. *See* Ch. 1 III. 2. b. above.
1302. *See, e.g.*, Cour de cassation, 12 January 2016, CISG-online 2698; Supr. Ct. Denmark, 17 October 2007, CISG-online 2014; OLG Jena, 8 December 2015, CISG-online 2664; HGer Zürich, 5 February 1997, CISG-online 327; ICC, 20 December 1999, CISG-online 1646.
1303. Cf. *Grunewald*, p. 84; Staudinger/*Magnus*, Art. 73 CISG, para. 6.
1304. ICC, 1 November 2016, CISG-online 5988; CA Reims, 4 September 2012, CISG-online 3141; Tribunale di Forli, 6 March 2012, CISG-online 2585, IHR 2013, pp. 198, 199; OLG Frankfurt, 20 November 2012, CISG-online 2481; CA Geneva, 20 May 2011, CISG-online 2429, note. 4; Supr. Ct. Poland, 27 January 2006, CISG-online 1399; Cour de Cassation, 30 June 2004, CISG-online 870; ICC, July 1999, CISG-online 707; LG München I, 9 December 1996, CISG-online 405, paras 14, 15.
1305. *Grieser*, pp. 125, 132, 133; Mankowski/*Dornis*, Art. 73 CISG, para. 3 (in reference to distribution agreements); MüKoHGB/*Sommerfeld*, Art. 73 CISG, para. 4; *Newhouse/Tanaka*, R.L.R. 2012, p. 18 (in reference to distribution agreements); Schlechtriem/Schwenzer/Schroeter/*Fountoulakis*, 5th English ed., Art. 73 CISG, para. 8; Schlechtriem/Schwenzer/Schroeter/*Fountoulakis*, 8th German ed., Art. 73 CISG, para. 9; Staudinger/*Magnus*, Art. 73 CISG, para. 7; cf. also OLG Jena, 8 December 2015, CISG-online 2664, para. 52.
1306. To that effect: Brunner/*Brunner/Boog/Schläpfer*, Art. 73 CISG, para. 19; Brunner/Gottlieb/*Brunner/Schläpfer/Boog*, Art. 73 CISG, para. 19; Kröll *et al./Saidov*, Art. 73 CISG, para. 4; Schlechtriem/Schwenzer/Schroeter/*Fountoulakis*, 5th English ed., Art. 73 CISG, para. 4; *von Scheven*, p. 104; more guardedly Honsell/*Brunner/Hurni*, Art. 73 CISG, para. 9; cf. also *Oetker*, pp. 120, 121 (with regard to German law).

Moreover, this study submits that framework agreements containing an obligation to conclude individual sales contracts may also be subject to the CISG.[1307] Given that such agreements are to be performed over an extended period of time, namely by concluding multiple individual sales contracts, they also fall within this study's definition of long-term contracts.[1308]

Finally, it is possible that other long-term contracts may exceptionally fall within the CISG's sphere of application. Mixed contracts may include one-off sales obligations, but they may also include long-term non-sales obligations which are to be performed over an extended period of time. This could, for instance, be the case if an agreement was concluded for the joint development of a product over an extended period of time, which is to be sold to one of the parties.[1309] If the CISG is applicable – which will mainly depend on the test under Art. 3(2) CISG[1310] or on a choice of law clause in favour of the Convention[1311] – such contracts will be considered to fall under this study's definition of long-term contracts, as they involve performance over an extended period of time.

III. CHALLENGES WHEN APPLYING THE CISG TO LONG-TERM FRAMEWORK AGREEMENTS

In general, long-term framework agreements and any other long-term contracts are largely subject to the same rules as one-off contracts under the CISG. In most cases, there is no need to treat such long-term contracts differently.[1312] For instance, the Convention's provisions on contract formation can be applied to long-term contracts without difficulty.[1313] However, there are some particularities that require specific attention.

In consideration of the temporal factor of long-term contracts, it is possible that various challenges may arise when dealing with such contracts.[1314] To begin with, the parties to a long-term framework agreement intend to establish a relationship that is

1307. *See* Ch. 3 III. 1. b. ii. above.
1308. In agreement with regard to German law: *Fuchs-Wissemann*, p. 21; *Hoffbauer*, p. 17; *Oetker*, pp. 120, 121; cf. also *Horn*, p. 563.
1309. Also mentioning this type of long-term contracts in the context of German domestic law: *Horn*, p. 562, who, however, employs a different terminology ('*Dauerschuldverhältnisse*' and '*langfristige Verträge*'); cf. SCC, 5 April 2007, CISG-online 1521: the parties agreed on the sale of sensors and on an ongoing licence to use (and integrate) these sensors.
1310. *See* Ch. 4 above.
1311. *See* Ch. 6 below.
1312. DiMatteo *et al./Cordero-Moss/DiMatteo*, Ch. 28, para. 30.
1313. Cf. DiMatteo *et al./Cordero-Moss/DiMatteo*, Ch. 28, para. 30.
1314. In 2015, UNIDROIT established a working group on long-term contracts with the objective of formulating proposals for potential amendments and additions to the black letter rules and comments of the UPICC 2010 regarding long-term contracts. The proposals and potential amendments have, for the most part, been incorporated into the UPICC 2016. The Working Group submitted drafts on the following topics: (a) the notion of long-term contracts; (b) termination for compelling reasons; (c) contracts with open terms; (d) restitution after ending contracts entered into for an indefinite period of time; (e) agreements to negotiate in good faith; (f) contracts with evolving terms; (g) supervening events; (h) cooperation between the parties; (i) post-contractual obligations.

supposed to last for an extended period of time.[1315] In order for the relationship to endure for an extended period of time, cooperation and trust may be crucial elements in some long-term contracts.[1316] This leads to the question of whether the parties to a long-term framework agreement are obliged to cooperate or to be loyal to each other under the CISG, and to what extent.

Furthermore, the extended duration may have a twofold impact on long-term framework agreements. First, the contract may require adaption in the course of its performance; its obligations may be of a somewhat 'evolutionary' nature.[1317] Second, long-term framework agreements are prone to changes in the surrounding circumstances based on their duration.[1318]

Moreover, a number of questions arise if one of the contracting parties wishes to sever ties under a long-term framework agreement, particularly in relation to the termination and avoidance of such contracts.[1319] It is, for example, debatable whether there is room for a right to terminate a long-term framework agreement for a compelling reason that is governed by the CISG.[1320] In addition to questions regarding termination or avoidance of a long-term framework agreement, there is a related issue of the effects that result from ending such a contract.[1321]

1. Cooperation and Trust Between the Parties

It is important to note at the outset that there appears to be no universal understanding of 'cooperation'. This study will refer to all types of cooperation obligations that bind the parties to work together in order to enable each other to perform their obligations

1315. Cf. OLG München, 18 June 2018, CISG-online 3080; BSK OR-I/*Amstutz/Morin*, Einl. vor Arts 184 ff. CO, para. 115; *Budde/Geks*, ZVertriebsR 2012, p. 37; *Fuchs-Wissemann*, p. 101; *Furrer/Lohri*, p. 24; *C. Meyer*, pp. 110, 111; *Gatsi*, paras 223 et seq.; *Hoffbauer*, p. 17; Sayag/*Pollaud-Dulian*, para. 100; *Ulmer*, p. 301; *Weber*, ZSR 1987, p. 410.
1316. *Campbell/Harris*, (1993) 20 (2) J. L. & Soc., p. 167; UNIDROIT 2014, Study L – Doc. 126, paras 31 et seq.; UNIDROIT 2016, Study L – Misc. 32, paras 64 et seq. (item (h) 'co-operation between the parties' of the report submitted by the working group on long-term contracts); cf. also *Hoffbauer*, pp. 13, 14; *Robertson*, (2010) 17 Austral. Int'l L. J., p. 187; Schlechtriem/Schwenzer/Schroeter/*Schroeter*, 5th English ed., Art. 25 CISG, para. 106; Schlechtriem/Schwenzer/Schroeter/*Schroeter*, 8th German ed., Art. 25 CISG, para. 96.
1317. Comment 3 on Art. 4.3 UPICC; UNIDROIT 2014, Study L – Doc. 126, paras 19 et seq.; UNIDROIT 2016, Study L – Misc. 32, paras 52 et seq. (item (f) of the report 'contracts with evolving terms').
1318. Cf. *Brunner*, p. 438; CISG-AC, Op. 20 *Muñoz*, Comment 7.12.; DiMatteo *et al./Cordero-Moss/DiMatteo*, Ch. 28, para. 31; *Gillette/Walt*, p. 302; *Guo*, pp. 22, 23; *Hoffbauer*, p. 127; *Horn*, pp. 559 et seq.; *Klotz*, p. 216; *Schwenzer*, (2008) 39 V.U.W. L. Rev., p. 709; UNIDROIT 2014, Study L – Doc. 126, paras 25 et seq.; UNIDROIT 2016, Study L – Misc. 32, paras 59 et seq. (item (g) of the report 'supervening events').
1319. In detail regarding the termination and avoidance of long-term contracts under German law: *Oetker*, pp. 248 et seq.
1320. With regard to the UPICC: UNIDROIT 2014, Study L – Doc. 126, paras 41, 42; UNIDROIT 2016, Study L – Misc. 32, paras 12 et seq. (item (b) of the report 'termination for compelling reasons').
1321. UNIDROIT 2014, Study L – Doc. 126, paras 36, 43 et seq.; UNIDROIT 2016, Study L – Misc. 32, paras 38 et seq., 73 et seq. (item (d) 'restitution after ending contracts entered into for an indefinite period of time' and item (i) of the report 'post-contractual obligations').

under the contract.[1322] The notion of enabling each other to perform encompasses not only refraining from actions that would hinder the other party from performing their obligation(s), but also taking active measures in this regard,[1323] such as applying for administrative authorisations or even informing the other party about certain circumstances.[1324] In the context of long-term contracts, cooperation is of particular importance.[1325] Consequently, obligations regarding the parties' cooperation and related obligations are frequently included in long-term framework agreements and any other long-term contracts.[1326]

Moreover, the parties to a long-term framework agreement typically aspire to enter into a relationship of trust.[1327] Therefore, the parties may also include obligations that are influenced by their unique relationship of trust in their contract, such as fiduciary or loyalty obligations.[1328] Such obligations are characterised by a deliberately granted possibility of one party to influence the financial interests of the other party, the obligation to act exclusively in the interests of this other party and an increased relationship of trust.[1329] Although it is uncertain whether this type of obligation occurs frequently in long-term framework agreements that are governed by the CISG,[1330] it is possible that confidentiality obligations may occur in CISG contracts; these confidentiality obligations may arguably be considered fiduciary obligations, or at least comparable to them.[1331]

One rationale behind all of these obligations is to mitigate the risk of opportunistic behaviour.[1332] As long-term contracts, particularly framework agreements, often contain open or indefinite terms, they leave some discretion to the parties, creating a potential for opportunistic behaviour.[1333] To address this risk, the parties may agree on clauses pertaining to cooperative or loyal behaviour in order to protect one another

1322. *See* Art. 5.1.3 UPICC; cf. also *Enderlein/Maskow*, Art. 7 CISG, note 9.1; *Fountoulakis*, p. 91 (regarding Swiss domestic law); Schlechtriem/Schwenzer/Schroeter/*Ferrari*, 8th German ed., Art. 7 CISG, para. 54.
1323. Comment 1 on Art. 5.1.3 UPICC; *Doralt*, pp. 224 et seq.
1324. Cf. Comment 1 on Art. 5.1.3 UPICC, Illustrations; *Doralt*, pp. 229 et seq.; *Fountoulakis*, p. 91.
1325. *Campbell/Harris*, (1993) 20 (2) J. L. & Soc., p. 167; *Doralt*, p. 228; cf. also *Fountoulakis*, p. 91 (with regard to distribution contracts under Swiss domestic law); *Hoffbauer*, pp. 13, 14; *Robertson*, (2010) 17 Austral. Int'l L. J., p. 187; Schlechtriem/Schwenzer/Schroeter/*Schroeter*, 5th English ed., Art. 25 CISG, para. 106; Schlechtriem/Schwenzer/Schroeter/*Schroeter*, 8th German ed., Art. 25 CISG, para. 96.
1326. Cf. *Hoffbauer*, p. 14; *Robertson*, (2010) 17 Austral. Int'l L. J., p. 187.
1327. Cf. *Hoffbauer*, pp. 13, 14; *Doralt*, p. 228.
1328. Providing further detail on fiduciary obligations and the CISG: *B. Köhler*, pp. 329 et seq.; providing a definition of fiduciary obligations with regard to English law: *Rusch*, pp. 31 et seq.; *see* further *Fountoulakis*, pp. 91 et seq.
1329. *Rusch*, pp. 31 et seq. (with regard to English law); *B. Köhler*, p. 330, who relies on a similar definition for a discussion in the context of the CISG.
1330. Cf. *B. Köhler*, pp. 330, 331.
1331. *See* OLG Jena, 8 December 2015, CISG-online 2664; SCC, 5 April 2007, CISG-online 1521; *B. Köhler*, p. 331.
1332. *Robertson*, (2010) 17 Austral. Int'l L. J., p. 187.
1333. *Doralt*, pp. 210, 247; *Robertson*, (2010) 17 Austral. Int'l L. J., pp. 186, 187; *Zuñiga Peralta*, (2021) 26 Unif. L. Rev., pp. 507, 508.

from opportunistic behaviour.[1334] From an economic perspective, long-term contracts pursue the objective of utility maximisation through cooperation over an extended period of time.[1335]

The following section will address cooperation and fiduciary obligations in long-term framework agreements governed by the CISG. The first part will deal with the incorporation of such obligations into CISG contracts. The second part will elaborate on the consequences in case such obligations have been breached.

a. Incorporation of Cooperation and Fiduciary Obligations

i. Contractual Agreements

In accordance with the principle of party autonomy (Art. 6 CISG), the parties are at liberty to incorporate obligations pertaining to their cooperation, such as information obligations[1336] or fiduciary obligations, into their contract governed by the CISG.[1337] This may particularly be the case in long-term framework agreements, which frequently contain so-called relational obligations that relate to the parties' cooperation and overall relationship.[1338] Examples of cooperation or fiduciary obligations in long-term framework agreements include confidentiality obligations, exclusivity obligations, loyalty obligations, information obligations and other obligations that may refer to the parties' cooperation.[1339]

The question of whether a framework agreement includes a certain cooperation or fiduciary obligation must be determined by way of contract interpretation in light of Art. 8 CISG.[1340] If a framework agreement is followed by individual sales contracts that are subsequently concluded (two-tier structure), it is necessary to interpret all of these contracts as a whole under Art. 8 CISG.[1341] Art. 8 CISG applies to the respective contracts, provided that each of them is governed by the Convention.[1342] Consequently, if a cooperation or fiduciary obligation is merely set out in a framework agreement, it may still extend its effects to the individual sales contracts that have been

1334. *Robertson*, (2010) 17 Austral. Int'l L. J., pp. 186, 187; *Zuñiga Peralta*, (2021) 26 Unif. L. Rev., pp. 508, 509 with a hypothetical example.
1335. *Campbell/Harris*, (1993) 20(2) J. L. & Soc., pp. 166 et seq.; cf. also *Zuñiga Peralta*, (2021) 26 Unif. L. Rev., pp. 507, 508.
1336. Cf. BeckOK/*Saenger*, Art. 30 CISG, para. 6; *Benedick*, paras 138, 139; Brunner/Gottlieb/*Brunner/Dimsey*, Art. 30 CISG, para. 15; Honsell/*Ernst/Lauko*, Art. 30 CISG, para. 17.
1337. Cf. BeckOK/*Saenger*, Art. 30 CISG, para. 6; Honsell/*Ernst/Lauko*, Art. 30 CISG, para. 17; *B. Köhler*, pp. 331, 332; Schlechtriem/Schwenzer/Schroeter/*Widmer Lüchinger*, 5th English ed., Art. 30 CISG, para. 12.
1338. *See* Ch. 2 III. 2. above; cf. also *Hoffbauer*, p. 13; *C. Meyer*, p. 57.
1339. *See Budde/Geks*, ZVertriebsR 2012, p. 37; *Hoffbauer*, pp. 12, 13; *B. Köhler*, pp. 330, 331; *Perales Viscasillas*, Extending the Scope, p. 128.
1340. The interpretation of contracts in accordance with Art. 8 CISG also applies to the non-sales elements in CISG contracts: MüKoBGB/*Gruber*, Art. 8 CISG, para. 6; Schlechtriem/Schwenzer/Schroeter/*Schmidt-Kessel*, 5th English ed., Art. 8 CISG, para. 6; Staudinger/*Magnus*, Art. 8 CISG, para. 7.
1341. Schlechtriem/Schwenzer/Schroeter/*Schmidt-Kessel*, 5th English ed., Art. 8 CISG, para. 31.
1342. MüKoBGB/*Gruber*, Art. 8 CISG, para. 6.

subsequently concluded, even if the relevant obligation has not been explicitly mentioned in the individual sales contracts governed by the CISG.[1343] Furthermore, cooperation and fiduciary obligations may arise from usages or practices established between the parties in the sense of Art. 9 CISG.[1344]

ii. The CISG as a Basis

If the parties do not incorporate cooperation or fiduciary obligations into their contract through an agreement, such obligations may (subsidiarily) be derived from the Convention itself.[1345] However, the CISG does not explicitly mention general cooperation obligations[1346] or fiduciary obligations. An exception may arguably be seen in a number of specific provisions that are based on the idea of cooperation, such as Art. 60(a) CISG (buyer has to enable the seller to make delivery).[1347]

Nevertheless, it appears to be the prevailing view in case law and among commentators that the parties to a CISG contract are generally obliged to cooperate with each other.[1348] In contrast, there is no similar view when it comes to fiduciary obligations in CISG contracts. This is because fiduciary rights and obligations become part of CISG contracts only through a party agreement.[1349] The Convention does not contain any elements that would allow for finding such obligations. In other words, fiduciary obligations may not be derived from the Convention itself.

Thus, the following part will focus on the question of whether the CISG can serve as a basis for cooperation obligations, i.e., whether there is a general obligation to cooperate under the Convention.

1343. Cf. OLG Hamburg, 5 October 1998, CISG-online 473 (with regard to a choice of law clause); Schlechtriem/Schwenzer/Schroeter/*Schmidt-Kessel*, 5th English ed., Art. 8 CISG, para. 31.
1344. *See* Brunner/Gottlieb/*Brunner/Dimsey*, Art. 30 CISG, para. 15; Kröll *et al./Piltz*, Art. 30 CISG, para. 27; Schlechtriem/Schwenzer/Schroeter/*Widmer Lüchinger*, 5th English ed., Art. 30 CISG, para. 12; with more detail on Art. 9 CISG: Schlechtriem/Schwenzer/Schroeter/*Schmidt-Kessel*, 5th English ed., Art. 9 CISG, paras 7 et seq.; Staudinger/*Magnus*, Art. 9 CISG, paras 6 et seq.
1345. Cf. BeckOK/*Saenger*, Art. 30 CISG, para. 6; *Gillette/Walt*, p. 119.
1346. Witz/Salger/Lorenz/*W. Witz*, Art. 30 CISG, para. 23.
1347. *Benedick*, para. 1014.
1348. CA Lyon, 9 February 2017, CISG-online 2823, para. 51; Cuban Court of International Trade Arbitration, 31 January 2014, CISG-online 2613, para. 27; BGH, 31 October 2001, CISG-online 617, para. 16; OLG Celle, 24 July 2009, CISG-online 1906, para. 19; OLG Köln, 21 December 2005, CISG-online 1201, para. 12; LG Neubrandenburg, 3 August 2005, CISG-online 1190, para. 26; *Achilles*, Art. 7 CISG, para. 10; BeckOGK/*Al-Debi'i*, Art. 30 CISG, para. 8; BeckOK/*Saenger*, Art. 7 CISG, para. 7; *Benedick*, paras 1014, 1015; Bianca/Bonell/*Bonell*, Art. 7 CISG, note 2.3.2.2.; Brunner/Gottlieb/*Brunner/Dimsey*, Art. 30 CISG, para. 15; Ferrari *et al./Saenger*, Art. 7 CISG, para. 7; *Honnold*, p. 139; *Honnold/Flechtner*, Art. 80 CISG, para. 595; *Magnus*, RabelsZ 59 (1995), p. 484; Mankowski/*Mankowski*, Art. 7 CISG, para. 17; MüKoBGB/*Gruber*, Art. 7 CISG, para. 39; MüKoHGB/*Ferrari*, Art. 7 CISG, para. 55; Schlechtriem/Schwenzer/Schroeter/*Ferrari*, 8th German ed., Art. 7 CISG, para. 54; Staudinger/*Magnus*, Art. 7 CISG, para. 47; Soergel/*Kreße*, Art. 7 CISG, para. 10.
1349. *See B. Köhler*, pp. 330 et seq.

1) Subsidiary Relevance of the Convention

Above all, contractual obligations must be derived from the contract itself or, alternatively, from established usages or practices between the parties in accordance with Arts 6 and 9 CISG.[1350] The obligations of a party to any CISG contract may also be derived from the Convention itself, but only to a subsidiary extent.[1351] This encompasses not only the Convention's explicit provisions but also the general principles on which it is based, given that they are an integral part of the CISG.[1352] Consequently, if the CISG were to provide for a general principle or obligation of cooperation, it may be possible to infer obligations for the parties to a framework agreement from the Convention itself.

2) General Obligation to Cooperate under the CISG?

The prevailing view in case law and among legal scholars is that there is a general obligation to cooperate with each other under the CISG.[1353] A number of reasons have been brought forward to explain the rationale behind such an obligation. One view holds that an obligation to cooperate and inform can be derived from the principle of good faith as per Art. 7(1) CISG.[1354] A different view posits that the cooperation obligation is a general principle within the meaning of Art. 7(2) CISG, which has been derived from multiple provisions in the Convention, namely Arts 32(2) (obligation to conclude an appropriate transportation contract), 34, 37, 48 (buyer has to accept a cure in performance), 60(a) (buyer has to enable the seller to make delivery), 77 (duty to

1350. *See Gillette/Walt*, pp. 119, 120; Kröll *et al./Piltz*, Art. 30 CISG, paras 27 et seq.
1351. *Gillette/Walt*, pp. 119, 120; Kröll *et al./Piltz*, Art. 30 CISG, paras 27 et seq.
1352. *Piltz*, para. 4-91; Witz/Salger/Lorenz/*W. Witz*, Art. 8 CISG, para. 3; cf. also Schlechtriem/Schwenzer/Schroeter/*Schmidt-Kessel*, 5th English ed., Art. 8 CISG, para. 28; *Schroeter*, paras 147 et seq. (regarding the substantive scope of the CISG).
1353. CA Lyon, 9 February 2017, CISG-online 2823, para. 51; Cuban Court of International Trade Arbitration, 31 January 2014, CISG-online 2613, para. 27; BGH, 31 October 2001, CISG-online 617, para. 16; OLG Celle, 24 July 2009, CISG-online 1906, para. 19; OLG Köln, 21 December 2005, CISG-online 1201, para. 12; LG Neubrandenburg, 3 August 2005, CISG-online 1190, para. 26; *Achilles*, Art. 7 CISG, para. 10; BeckOGK/*Al-Debi'i*, Art. 30 CISG, para. 8; BeckOK/*Saenger*, Art. 7 CISG, para. 7; *Benedick*, paras 1014, 1015; Bianca/Bonell/*Bonell*, Art. 7 CISG, note 2.3.2.2.; Brunner/Gottlieb/*Brunner/Dimsey*, Art. 30 CISG, para. 15; Ferrari *et al./Saenger*, Art. 7 CISG, para. 7; *Honnold*, p. 139; *Honnold/Flechtner*, Art. 80 CISG, para. 595; *Magnus*, RabelsZ 59 (1995), p. 484; Mankowski/*Mankowski*, Art. 7 CISG, para. 17; MüKoBGB/*Gruber*, Art. 7 CISG, para. 39; MüKoHGB/*Ferrari*, Art. 7 CISG, para. 55; *Neumann*, pp. 110 et seq.; Schlechtriem/Schwenzer/Schroeter/*Ferrari*, 8th German ed., Art. 7 CISG, para. 54; Schlechtriem/Schwenzer/Schroeter/*Mohs*, 5th English ed., Art. 53 CISG, para. 39; Staudinger/*Magnus*, Art. 7 CISG, para. 47; Staudinger/*Magnus*, Art. 30 CISG, para. 15; Soergel/*Kreße*, Art. 7 CISG, para. 10.
1354. BeckOGK/*Al-Debi'i*, Art. 30 CISG, para. 8 ('*Treu und Glauben*'); MüKoBGB/*Gruber*, Art. 7 CISG, para. 39; cf. also Schlechtriem/Schwenzer/Schroeter/*Mohs*, 5th English ed., Art. 53 CISG, para. 39, who bases the duty to cooperate and inform on Art. 60(a) in conjunction with Art. 7(1) CISG.

mitigate losses), 80 (exemption of the debtor if breach is caused by creditor), 85 and 86 (obligations relating to the preservation of goods) CISG.[1355]

However, the more compelling arguments militate against the assumption of a general cooperation obligation, either under Art. 7(1) CISG or under Art. 7(2) CISG.[1356] First, if Art. 7(1) CISG is read literally, it merely refers to the interpretation of the Convention. Therefore, it cannot serve as a foundation for a general rule of conduct for the parties to a CISG contract.[1357] Moreover, a general concept of good faith that would apply to the parties' contractual relationship was rejected during the drafting of the CISG.[1358] Those opposed to such a general concept expressed concern that it could lead judges and arbitrators to rely on their domestic understanding of good faith in the interpretation of CISG contracts, thereby endangering uniformity.[1359] Thus, a literal and historical interpretation of Art. 7(1) CISG suggests that no party obligations, such as the general obligation to cooperate, should be derived from this provision.

It is also not appropriate to infer the general obligation to cooperate under the CISG from a general principle within the meaning of Art. 7(2) CISG.[1360] This is because the CISG already stipulates multiple types of obligations that involve cooperation between the parties.[1361] This sophisticated and more specific system of cooperation set out in the Convention could be undermined by a general cooperation obligation that might overlap with it.[1362] Moreover, the substance of a general cooperation obligation appears to be difficult to predict in most cases and is open to diverging interpretations. In order to ensure legal certainty and predictability, the parties should be able to foresee their contractual obligations by taking into account the contract, any established usages or practices and the provisions within the CISG that may require

---

1355. *Benedick*, para. 1014 (mentioning Art. 60(a) CISG); *Honnold/Flechtner*, Art. 80 CISG, para. 595, primarily relying on Art. 80 CISG as a basis for a general principle of cooperation in the performance of a contract; *Magnus*, RabelsZ 59 (1995), p. 484; Mankowski/*Mankowski*, Art. 7 CISG, para. 17; Staudinger/*Magnus*, Art. 7 CISG, para. 47; mentioning merely Arts 32(2), 34, 37, 48, 77 CISG but not Arts 85 and 86 CISG: BeckOK/*Saenger*, Art. 7 CISG, para. 7; Ferrari *et al./Saenger*, Art. 7 CISG, para. 7; cf. also Bianca/Bonell/*Bonell*, Art. 7 CISG, note 2.3.2.2.; Soergel/*Kreße*, Art. 7 CISG, para. 10 (referring to Arts 32(2), 32(3) and 37 CISG).

1356. To that effect: Kröll *et al.*/Piltz, Art. 30 CISG, para. 29; Witz/Salger/Lorenz/*W. Witz*, Art. 30 CISG, para. 23.

1357. *Walt*, (2015) 33 B. U. Int'l L. J., p. 42; Witz/Salger/Lorenz/*W. Witz*, Art. 30 CISG, para. 23.

1358. *Bridge*, Int'l Sale of Goods, para. 10.42; *Bridge*, (2017) 22 Unif. L. Rev., p. 14; *Schroeter*, paras 137, 182; *Walt*, (2015) 33 B. U. Int'l L. J., p. 42.

1359. *Andersen*, (2014) 17 Int'l Trade & Bus. L. Rev., pp. 315 et seq.; *Bridge*, (2017) 22 Unif. L. Rev., p. 14; *Schroeter*, para. 137; *Walt*, (2015) 33 B. U. Int'l L. J., p. 42.

1360. Cf. Kröll *et al./Piltz*, Art. 30 CISG, para. 29, who cautions against the development of party obligations based on Art. 7 CISG.

1361. *See Neumann*, pp. 110, 111, holding that 'at least three groups require or presuppose certain cooperation' in relation to obligations of communication (Arts 19(2), 21(2), 26, 39(1), 48(2), 65, 68, 71(3), 72(2), 79(4), 88(1) CISG), rules regarding the preservation of the goods (Arts 85–89 CISG), and provisions requiring steps to enable the other party's performance (e.g., Arts 54, 60(a) CISG); *see also* for an overview: *Magnus*, RabelsZ 59 (1995), p. 484; Staudinger/*Magnus*, Art. 7 CISG, para. 47.

1362. Advancing a similar argument but in relation to a general information obligation under the CISG: *Schroeter*, para. 193; cf. also Witz/Salger/Lorenz/*W. Witz*, Art. 30 CISG, para. 23; this illustrates that there is a delicate balance to be struck between deriving general principles from the Convention's provisions and jeopardising its carefully crafted balancing of risks.

cooperation.[1363] As it is open to diverging interpretations, a general cooperation obligation may also create the risk that courts will read domestic concepts into it, such as ancillary obligations in the sense of §§ 241, 242 BGB.[1364] Finally, it is unclear whether a general cooperation obligation would qualify as a legal obligation in *sensu stricto* or as a non-actionable duty; the breach of such a non-actionable duty would not entitle the aggrieved party to rely on remedies, but would merely lead to a legal disadvantage for the breaching party.[1365]

For the avoidance of doubt, it should be noted that while there is no room to develop a general cooperation obligation under the CISG on the basis of Art. 7 CISG, cooperation obligations may nonetheless arise in specific contexts. Such obligations may be derived from the contract, either explicitly or implicitly.[1366] This may be particularly the case in the context of long-term framework agreements or any other long-term contracts, as they often entail a higher degree of cooperation between the parties during the performance.[1367] In this respect, it is necessary to consider Art. 8(3) CISG; specific cooperation or fiduciary obligations may be derived from the relevant circumstances in the sense of this provision. In framework agreements with a two-tier structure, such obligations may also extend their effects to the individual sales contracts without being mentioned again.[1368] Furthermore, cooperation obligations in a long-term framework agreement may arise from usages or practices established between the parties within the meaning of Art. 9(1) CISG.[1369] Similarly, there may be industry-specific cooperation obligations that apply by virtue of Art. 9(2) CISG to a long-term framework agreement.[1370] In addition, party obligations that require some form of cooperation may be derived from an interpretation of specific provisions of the Convention.[1371]

1363. Kröll *et al./Piltz*, Art. 30 CISG, para. 29 (seller should not 'be concerned that further obligations are constructed to his detriment' beyond the parties' agreement, usages and practices and the Convention's provisions); cf. also *Magnus*, RabelsZ 59 (1995), p. 484 (regarding a general information obligation).
1364. With regard to good faith as per Art. 7(1) CISG: *Ferrari*, IHR 2013, pp. 153, 154; *Schlechtriem*, (2004) 2 Pace Int'l L. Rev., pp. 292, 293; regarding § 241(2) BGB: Schlechtriem/Schwenzer/Schroeter/*Schroeter*, 5th English ed., Art. 25 CISG, para. 65; cf. also Witz/Salger/Lorenz/*W. Witz*, Art. 30 CISG, para. 23, noting that the CISG is not familiar with a provision comparable to § 242 BGB.
1365. Cf. on this distinction with regard to Art. 38 CISG: BeckOGK/*Hachem*, Art. 38 CISG, para. 5; Brunner/Gottlieb/*Brunner/Peter*, Art. 38 CISG, para. 3; Schlechtriem/Schwenzer/Schroeter/*Schwenzer*, 5th English ed., Art. 38 CISG, para. 5; Staudinger/*Magnus*, Art. 38 CISG, para. 12.
1366. Kröll *et al./Piltz*, Art. 30 CISG, para. 29; Witz/Salger/Lorenz/*W. Witz*, Art. 30 CISG, para. 23.
1367. Cf. Schlechtriem/Schwenzer/Schroeter/*Schroeter*, 5th English ed., Art. 25 CISG, para. 106; Schlechtriem/Schwenzer/Schroeter/*Schroeter*, 8th German ed., Art. 25 CISG, para. 96; UNIDROIT 2014, Study L – Doc. 126, paras 31 et seq. (on the UPICC).
1368. Cf. OLG Hamburg, 5 October 1998, CISG-online 473 (with regard to a choice of law clause); Schlechtriem/Schwenzer/Schroeter/*Schmidt-Kessel*, 5th English ed., Art. 8 CISG, para. 50.
1369. Kröll *et al./Piltz*, Art. 30 CISG, para. 29.
1370. With regard to this provision *see* only: Kröll *et al./Perales Viscasillas*, Art. 9 CISG, paras 17 et seq.; *Schroeter*, paras 275 et seq.; Schlechtriem/Schwenzer/Schroeter/*Schmidt-Kessel*, 5th English ed., Art. 9 CISG, paras 14 et seq.
1371. Cf. Witz/Salger/Lorenz/*W. Witz*, Art. 30 CISG, para. 23.

3) General Information Obligation?

Information obligations may be considered to be closely related to or even part of a general cooperation obligation,[1372] therefore, information obligations will also be briefly addressed here. Some proponents of the view that there is a general cooperation obligation under the CISG also propose that there should similarly be a general information obligation.[1373] According to this view, the parties have to inform each other about essential circumstances that are discernibly unknown to the other party in a reasonable, timely and adequate manner.[1374] Similar to the discussion above, the more compelling arguments militate against a general obligation to inform under the CISG.[1375] The allocation of information risks stipulated by the CISG should not be undermined by a general information obligation that is hardly predictable.[1376] Consequently, there should also be no general information obligation under the CISG. However, specific information obligations may arise under a long-term framework agreement based on the contract, established usages or practices or as part of certain CISG provisions.

iii. Domestic Law

In addition to the parties' contract, established usages or practices or specific provisions of the CISG, the question may arise as to whether cooperation or fiduciary obligations under a long-term framework agreement governed by the Convention may also be derived from domestic law rules. Methodologically, there are two ways in which this could be the case.

First, a specific provision within the Convention may contain a gap which might have to be filled in conformity with the applicable domestic law, provided that no general principles can be found in the sense of Art. 7(2) CISG. If the applicable domestic law stipulates cooperation or fiduciary obligations, they may apply to a framework agreement governed by the CISG. It is, however, important to conduct a careful analysis of which provisions contain such a gap that cannot be filled by recourse to general principles of the CISG.

1372. Cf. *Benedick*, para. 1015; MüKoBGB/*Gruber*, Art. 7 CISG, para. 39; MüKoHGB/*Ferrari*, Art. 7 CISG, para. 55; Schlechtriem/Schwenzer/Schroeter/*Ferrari*, 8th German ed., Art. 7 CISG, para. 54; Staudinger/*Magnus*, Art. 7 CISG, para. 48.

1373. CA Lyon, 9 February 2017, CISG-online 2823, para. 51; BGH, 31 October 2001, CISG-online 617, para. 16; OLG Celle, 24 July 2009, CISG-online 1906, para. 19; OLG Köln, 21 December 2005, CISG-online 1201, para. 12; LG Neubrandenburg, 3 August 2005, CISG-online 1190, para. 26; *Achilles*, Art. 7 CISG, para. 10; *Benedick*, paras 1014, 1015; Mankowski/*Mankowski*, Art. 7 CISG, para. 17; MüKoBGB/*Gruber*, Art. 7 CISG, para. 39; MüKoHGB/*Ferrari*, Art. 7 CISG, para. 55; Schlechtriem/Schwenzer/Schroeter/*Ferrari*, 8th German ed., Art. 7 CISG, para. 54; Schlechtriem/Schwenzer/Schroeter/*Mohs*, 5th English ed., Art. 53 CISG, para. 39; Staudinger/*Magnus*, Art. 7 CISG, para. 48.

1374. In detail *Benedick*, paras 1020 et seq.; cf. also Staudinger/*Magnus*, Art. 7 CISG, para. 48.

1375. To that effect: *Magnus*, RabelsZ 59 (1995), p. 484, who, however, appears to have modified his position, *see* Staudinger/*Magnus*, Art. 7 CISG, para. 48; *Schroeter*, para. 193; cf. also *C. Witz/B. Köhler*, IHR 2014, pp. 90, 91 (regarding an obligation to consult).

1376. *Schroeter*, para. 193.

Second, cooperation or fiduciary obligations may also be derived from domestic law rules if they relate to matters not governed by the CISG.[1377] The CISG does, for example, not deal with the legal limits on what to sell, for instance, whether certain goods are regarded as *res extra commercium* and restrictions imposed by competition laws or by export/import regulations.[1378] Domestic law rules may oblige the parties to cooperate in respect to such restrictions, e.g., to provide foreign parties with the necessary information to obtain an export/import licence. However, in some cases, a similar obligation may also be derived from the parties' contract, in particular a long-term framework agreement, or specific provisions of the CISG, such as Art. 80 CISG.[1379]

b. Consequences in Case of a Breach

If the Convention applies to a long-term framework agreement, it is generally applicable to the entire contract, including its non-sales part.[1380] Accordingly, the Convention governs the consequences of a breach of cooperation or fiduciary obligations that have been incorporated into a CISG contract. In this context, Arts 45 and 61 CISG mention the seller's or buyer's 'failure to perform any of his obligations under the contract or this Convention'. This demonstrates that the Convention does not differentiate between the type and nature of the obligation that has been breached in terms of the remedies available to the aggrieved party.[1381] An illustrative example can be found in a case decided by the Court of Appeal Jena:[1382] in this case, the Court essentially awarded damages to the seller in accordance with Art. 61 in conjunction with Art. 74 CISG, because the buyer had breached a confidentiality obligation set forth in a long-term contract for the production and sale of 'balancers' (car parts that reduce the movement and noise of motors).[1383]

In contrast, *B. Köhler* maintains that the CISG does not regulate the breach of fiduciary obligations, as the remedies of the Convention are tailored to obligations in sales contracts that are not characterised by a relationship of trust between the

1377. With regard to disclosure obligations: CISG-AC, Op. 23 *Beale*, Rule 3, Comments 6.3., 6.4.
1378. Schlechtriem/Schwenzer/Schroeter/*Hachem*, 5th English ed., Art. 4 CISG, para. 39; *Schroeter*, Unif. L. Rev. 2017, p. 58; *C. Witz*, para. 114.41; cf. the 'pesofication' as provided for under Argentinean law as an illustrative example: Argentinean National Commercial Court of Appeals, 19 October 2012, CISG-online 6574; Argentinean National Commercial Court of Appeals, 19 November 2008, CISG-online 4438.
1379. Schlechtriem/Schwenzer/Schroeter/*Schwenzer*, 5th English ed., Art. 80 CISG, para. 3.
1380. *See* Ch. 4 III. 1. c. above; cf. also *B. Köhler*, p. 333; *Perales Viscasillas*, Extending the Scope, pp. 128, 129.
1381. *See* Ch. 4 III. 2. above; cf. only *B. Köhler*, p. 333; *Magnus*, Remedies, pp. 259, 260; Schlechtriem/Schwenzer/Schroeter/*Müller-Chen*, 5th English ed., Art. 45 CISG, para. 3 (explicitly mentioning information obligations); Schlechtriem/Schwenzer/Schroeter/*Mohs*, 5th English ed., Art. 64 CISG, para. 4.
1382. OLG Jena, 8 December 2015, CISG-online 2664.
1383. OLG Jena, 8 December 2015, CISG-online 2664, paras 64 et seq.; cf. also SCC, 5 April 2007, CISG-online 1521, paras 147 et seq. (damages were awarded on the grounds of a breach of confidentiality provisions set forth in a contract for the supply and licensing of pressure sensors).

parties.[1384] He proposes that there is a gap in the sense of Art. 7(2) CISG, and that domestic law should apply as there are no general principles underlying the Convention to rely on.[1385] Alternatively, he suggests that the CISG's provisions do not purport to exhaustively govern the breach of fiduciary obligations; instead, concurrent domestic law rules should apply alongside the CISG.[1386]

This study posits that the CISG generally governs the consequences of a breach of fiduciary or cooperation obligations, as the Convention's remedies are based on the premise that it is not relevant which kind of obligations have been breached.[1387] The CISG's provisions on remedies are suitable and sufficiently flexible to govern the breach of non-sales obligations.[1388] They may either be applied directly or recourse must be had to the general principles underlying these remedy provisions.[1389]

This prompts the question of whether the CISG's remedies preclude the concurrent application of domestic remedies that may specifically arise if fiduciary obligations have been breached.[1390] In general, the CISG supersedes overlapping domestic law rules provided that a matter falls within its substantive scope of application.[1391] An exception to this rule has been assumed in cases where a certain domestic remedy is not only tied to a breach of contract but also sanctions an additional element that is not sanctioned by the CISG; this is exemplified by domestic remedies that are related to fraud.[1392] In light of this consideration, *B. Köhler* has put forward the argument that (special) domestic remedies for the breach of fiduciary obligations, such as disgorgement of profits, are not only tied to a breach of contract but also to the possibility of influencing the financial interests of the other party and the increased relationship of trust between the parties.[1393] This submission is convincing in that domestic remedies that specifically arise in the context of a breach of a fiduciary obligation also sanction the misuse of trust and influence, which is not sanctioned by the Convention. Consequently, a concurrent application of domestic remedies and the CISG's remedies appears to be appropriate in such cases.

c. *Summary*

In the context of long-term framework agreements, cooperation and trust are of particular importance. The parties are free to incorporate cooperation and fiduciary

1384. *B. Köhler*, pp. 333, 334; cf. also *Schroeter*, RabelsZ 81 (2017), p. 64.
1385. *B. Köhler*, pp. 333 et seq.
1386. *B. Köhler*, pp. 339, 340.
1387. Cf. *Magnus*, Remedies, pp. 259 et seq.; Schlechtriem/Schwenzer/Schroeter/*Müller-Chen*, 5th English ed., Art. 45 CISG, para. 3; Schlechtriem/Schwenzer/Schroeter/*Mohs*, 5th English ed., Art. 64 CISG, para. 4.
1388. *See* Ch. 4 III. 2. above.
1389. *See* Ch. 4 III. 2. above.
1390. *See B. Köhler*, p. 339.
1391. *Schroeter*, para. 169; *see also*: *B. Köhler*, p. 339; *B. Köhler*, Independent Development, p. 14.
1392. CISG-AC, Op. 23 *Beale*, Rule 3, Rule 9; *B. Köhler*, p. 340; *Schroeter*, paras 169, 238 (such domestic remedies impose sanctions on the parties' intentional misconduct, which is not sanctioned by the CISG).
1393. *B. Köhler*, pp. 339, 340.

obligations into their contract under the CISG. Such obligations may also be derived from usages or practices that have been established between the parties in the sense of Art. 9 CISG. A number of such clauses, such as confidentiality or exclusivity obligations, are particularly common in framework agreements.

The CISG does not explicitly mention cooperation or fiduciary obligations. The latter obligations may only be incorporated into a CISG contract through the agreement of the parties. Furthermore, there is a controversy as to whether a general cooperation obligation can be derived from Art. 7(1) or Art. 7(2) CISG. The preferable view is that no general cooperation obligation should be derived from the Convention. A literal and historical interpretation of Art. 7(1) CISG reveals that this provision does not impose any obligations on the parties to a CISG contract. Moreover, a general cooperation obligation should not be considered a general principle in the sense of Art. 7(2) CISG, as it would hardly be predictable, potentially undermine the CISG's existing cooperation system and create the risk of diverging interpretations.

Although they may not be derived from a general concept under the CISG, cooperation as well as fiduciary obligations may arise contextually. Either based on an interpretation of the contract (Art. 8 CISG), which may be the case particularly when it comes to long-term framework agreements, established usages or practices (Art. 9 CISG) or an interpretation of the CISG's provisions (in light of good faith, *see* Art. 7(1) CISG). Similarly, there is no general information obligation under the CISG, but specific information obligations may arise depending on the circumstances. Moreover, cooperation or fiduciary obligations may arise from domestic law rules in accordance with Art. 7(2) CISG, or if they are related to a matter outside the Convention's sphere of application, e.g., legal limits on what can be sold.

If fiduciary or cooperation obligations have been incorporated into a long-term framework agreement governed by the CISG, the Convention generally governs the consequences of a breach of these obligations. However, it has been convincingly argued that special domestic law remedies relating to the breach of fiduciary obligations (e.g., disgorgement of profits) should be applicable alongside the CISG if they are not merely linked to a breach of contract, but if they also sanction other aspects, such as misuse of trust or influence.

2. Evolving Terms

Long-term framework agreements and other long-term contracts may necessitate adaptation during the course of performance. Given their duration, they are of a somewhat 'evolutionary' nature.[1394] This fact has several implications. First, the parties' conduct may deviate from the contractual terms over time.[1395] Second, it may be controversial to determine the actual content of the contract after the lapse of time and in light of the parties' subsequent conduct.[1396] This raises the question of how the

1394. Comment 3 on Art. 4.3 UPICC; *Iliou*, ZVertriebsR 2023, p. 82.
1395. UNIDROIT 2014, Study L – Doc. 126, para. 19.
1396. Cf. UNIDROIT 2014, Study L – Doc. 126, para. 19.

parties' subsequent conduct affects the contract. Furthermore, the parties may incorporate a reference to external standards in order to deal with the evolutionary nature of their contractual relationship.[1397]

a. *Effects of the Parties' Subsequent Conduct*

Once a long-term framework agreement governed by the CISG has been concluded, the parties' subsequent conduct may be relevant in two distinct ways.[1398]

i. *Relevant Circumstance for Interpretation*

First, the parties' subsequent conduct may be considered a relevant circumstance in determining a party's intent or in interpreting a contract according to Art. 8(3) CISG.[1399] The conduct may provide an indication of how a declaration or the contract was understood originally, i.e., at the time it was made.[1400] In particular, the manner in which a contract is performed by the parties may permit the drawing of conclusions regarding their original understanding.[1401] It can typically be presumed that the parties act in accordance with the original understanding of the contract.[1402] This interpretative tool, namely the parties' subsequent conduct during contract performance, is particularly relevant for long-term contracts, such as framework agreements.[1403]

With regard to Art. 8 CISG, it is important to consider the specific features of framework agreements with a two-tier structure. These agreements set out contractual terms that are intended to apply to the individual sales contracts that are to be concluded under their umbrella.[1404] The objective is to ensure that all subsequent transactions are conducted under largely the same legal terms.[1405] If an individual sales contract concluded between the parties is based on the framework agreement, the contractual terms set out in the framework agreement are to be implemented into the

1397. UNIDROIT 2014, Study L – Doc. 126, para. 23.
1398. Cf. OGer Zug, 8 November 2011, CISG-online 2425, para. 16; Brunner/Gottlieb/*Brunner/Hurni/Kissling*, Art. 8 CISG, para. 18; MüKoHGB/*Ferrari*, Art. 8 CISG, para. 15; Schlechtriem/Schwenzer/Schroeter/*Schmidt-Kessel*, 5th English ed., Art. 8 CISG, para. 56; *Schroeter*, para. 267; Staudinger/*Magnus*, Art. 8 CISG, para. 25.
1399. Schlechtriem/Schwenzer/Schroeter/*Schmidt-Kessel*, 5th English ed., Art. 8 CISG, para. 56.
1400. OGer Zug, 8 November 2011, CISG-online 2425, para. 16; Brunner/Gottlieb/*Brunner/Hurni/Kissling*, Art. 8 CISG, para. 18; MüKoHGB/*Ferrari*, Art. 8 CISG, para. 15; Schlechtriem/Schwenzer/Schroeter/*Schmidt-Kessel*, 5th English ed., Art. 8 CISG, para. 56; *Schroeter*, para. 267; Staudinger/*Magnus*, Art. 8 CISG, para. 25.
1401. OGer Zug, 8 November 2011, CISG-online 2425, para. 16; Brunner/Gottlieb/*Brunner/Hurni/Kissling*, Art. 8 CISG, para. 18.
1402. OGer Zug, 8 November 2011, CISG-online 2425, para. 16; Brunner/Gottlieb/*Brunner/Hurni/Kissling*, Art. 8 CISG, para. 18.
1403. Brunner/Gottlieb/*Brunner/Hurni/Kissling*, Art. 8 CISG, para. 18 (although this interpretative tool is not exclusively pertinent to long-term contracts); cf. Comment 3 on Art. 4.3 UPICC.
1404. OLG München, 18 June 2018, CISG-online 3080, p. 10; *Budde/Geks*, ZVertriebsR 2012, p. 37; *Hoffbauer*, pp. 5, 45; *J. Schmidt*, (1983–1984) 6 Houst. J. Int'l L., p. 55.
1405. OLG München, 18 June 2018, CISG-online 3080; cf. also *Hoffbauer*, p. 46; *J. Schmidt*, (1983–1984) 6 Houst. J. Int'l L., p. 55.

sales contract. An explicit reference is not necessarily required.[1406] In view of this connection between the framework agreement and the individual sales contracts, an individual sales contract may have to be interpreted in light of the framework agreement under Art. 8 CISG.[1407] In doing so, the framework agreement may be regarded as a practice in the sense of Art. 8(3) CISG, thereby extending its effects, i.e., its terms, to the individual sales contracts.[1408] Conversely, the subsequent conduct of the parties under the individual sales contracts may be taken into consideration for an interpretation of the framework agreement itself.

ii. Contract Modification?

Second, the parties may agree to modify their contract in accordance with Art. 29(1) CISG by deviating from earlier statements.[1409] This can, for instance, be assumed if one of the parties performs their obligations in a particular manner and the other party accepts this performance without objection – the lack of objection can arguably be seen as acceptance of the performing party's (implicit) offer to modify the contract.[1410] However, it is not possible to modify a contract unilaterally; rather, there must be an agreement between the parties that is sufficiently recognisable.[1411]

Typically, contract modifications occur as a consequence of changes in the surrounding circumstances subsequent to the contract's conclusion.[1412] Framework agreements and other long-term contracts are particularly prone to changes in the surrounding circumstances based on their duration.[1413] Consequently, they may require modifications during the course of their performance.[1414] The parties are free to do so, as with any other CISG contract, in accordance with Art. 29 CISG. However, the interest in contract modification may conflict with the interest in continuity, which is inherent in framework agreements that have been concluded for an extended period of

1406. OLG München, 18 June 2018, CISG-online 3080; *Hoffbauer*, p. 46.
1407. *See* Ch. 3 III. 2. b. ii. above; cf. also Schlechtriem/Schwenzer/Schroeter/*Schmidt-Kessel*, 5th English ed., Art. 8 CISG, paras 31, 50; *Schroeter*, para. 94.
1408. OLG Hamburg, 5 October 1998, CISG-online 473 (with regard to a choice of law clause); Schlechtriem/Schwenzer/Schroeter/*Schmidt-Kessel*, 5th English ed., Art. 8 CISG, paras 31, 50; *Schroeter*, para. 94; cf. also Schlechtriem/Schwenzer/Schroeter/*Schroeter*, 5th English ed., Art. 29 CISG, para. 67 (with regard to form requirements).
1409. Brunner/Gottlieb/*Brunner/Hurni/Kissling*, Art. 8 CISG, para. 18; Staudinger/*Magnus*, Art. 8 CISG, para. 25; cf. also OGer Zug, 8 November 2011, CISG-online 2425, para. 16; MüKoHGB/*Ferrari*, Art. 8 CISG, para. 15; Schlechtriem/Schwenzer/Schroeter/*Schmidt-Kessel*, 5th English ed., Art. 8 CISG, para. 56; *Schroeter*, para. 267.
1410. Brunner/Gottlieb/*Brunner/Hurni/Kissling*, Art. 8 CISG, para. 18; cf. also Comment 3 on Art. 4.3 UPICC, Illustration 5.
1411. MüKoHGB/*Ferrari*, Art. 8 CISG, para. 15; Schlechtriem/Schwenzer/Schroeter/*Schmidt-Kessel*, 5th English ed., Art. 8 CISG, para. 56; Staudinger/*Magnus*, Art. 8 CISG, para. 25.
1412. Schlechtriem/Schwenzer/Schroeter/*Schroeter*, 5th English ed., Art. 29 CISG, para. 35; *Iliou*, ZVertriebsR 2023, p. 82 (with regard to German domestic law).
1413. Cf. DiMatteo *et al.*/*Cordero-Moss/DiMatteo*, Ch. 28, para. 31; *Gillette/Walt*, p. 302; *Guo*, pp. 22, 23; *Hoffbauer*, p. 127.
1414. Cf. Comment 3 on Art. 4.3 UPICC; *Iliou*, ZVertriebsR 2023, p. 82.

time in order to have planning reliability.[1415] Accordingly, it is submitted that there must be sufficient indications of the parties' concurrent will to modify their framework agreement. An implicit contract modification should not be assumed lightly.

Based on similar considerations, the parties may submit any modifications to a form requirement in accordance with Art. 29(2), sentence 1 CISG.[1416] This ensures that modifications to their framework agreement must meet a certain threshold. Furthermore, individual sales contracts may be subject to a form requirement based on a framework agreement that contains an explicit form requirement to be implemented in the individual contracts.[1417]

In addition, the parties to a long-term contract may stipulate further mechanisms for potential contract modifications in their agreement, in anticipation of potential contractual adaptions.[1418] To illustrate, the parties to framework agreements often agree on price escalation clauses.[1419] A price escalation clause enables the parties to modify the price in light of changed circumstances, such as an increase in the cost of raw materials.[1420] Price escalation clauses are particularly relevant in instances where the parties have agreed on a fixed price in their framework agreement, yet the supplier wishes to maintain a constant profit margin.[1421]

b. External Standards

In light of potential changes in the surrounding circumstances over time, it is more likely that long-term framework agreements or any other long-term contracts will incorporate external standards, as these standards provide for greater flexibility.[1422] Such external standards may either determine the essential elements of the contract or expand upon the performance of the parties' obligations.[1423]

Should a reference to external standards be included in order to determine the essential elements under a framework agreement, such as the purchase price or quantity of the goods, this may be deemed an issue of sufficient definiteness under the CISG. However, it has been submitted by this study that the Convention is generally based on a rather liberal standard of sufficient definiteness.[1424] In applying this liberal standard, a reference to external standards may arguably be considered a reference to objective factors, which would be sufficient under Art. 14(1), sentence 2 CISG ('makes

1415. *Iliou*, ZVertriebsR 2023, p. 82; with regard to this conflict in the context of long-term contracts in a general manner: *Horn*, pp. 563 et seq.
1416. In detail on this provision: Schlechtriem/Schwenzer/Schroeter/*Schroeter*, 5th English ed., Art. 29 CISG, paras 53 et seq.
1417. Schlechtriem/Schwenzer/Schroeter/*Schroeter*, 5th English ed., Art. 29 CISG, para. 67; *Wey*, para. 423 (relying on an analogy).
1418. Cf. Comment 3 on Art. 4.3 UPICC.
1419. *Budde/Geks*, ZVertriebsR 2012, p. 42; in detail: *Hoffbauer*, pp. 134 et seq.; Ostendorf/*Ostendorf/Sauthoff*, § 18, paras 222 et seq.; cf. also CISG-AC, Op. 20 *Muñoz*, Comment 1.10.
1420. *Budde/Geks*, ZVertriebsR 2012, p. 42; cf. also *Macauly*, (1963) 28 (1) Am. Soc. Rev., p. 56.
1421. *Budde/Geks*, ZVertriebsR 2012, p. 42.
1422. UNIDROIT 2014, Study L – Doc. 126, para. 23.
1423. Cf. UNIDROIT 2014, Study L – Doc. 126, para. 23.
1424. *See* Ch. 3 IV. above for more detail.

provisions for determining').[1425] Furthermore, the parties are at liberty to deviate from any standard set forth by the Convention in accordance with Art. 6 CISG,[1426] and may agree to determine, for instance, the purchase price under their framework agreement by reference to dynamic external standards (such as an index).[1427] Consequently, the parties are free to agree upon external standards in order to determine the essential elements under a long-term framework agreement governed by the CISG.

A long-term framework agreement may also require the seller to deliver goods in conformity with a particular external standard,[1428] either directly or by including this reference in the subsequently concluded individual sales contracts. The parties are free to do so in accordance with the principle of freedom of contract, which is enshrined in Art. 6 CISG and underlies Art. 35(1) CISG.[1429] The consequence of an external standard being part of the agreement is that the seller is in breach of contract if they do not comply with this specific standard.[1430] Such standards may be incorporated explicitly and refer to physical features of the goods; they may also be concerned with sustainability or ethical considerations in the manufacturing process.[1431] External standards relating to the goods' conformity may also be incorporated implicitly.[1432] However, this assumption should not be made lightly. There must be sufficiently clear circumstances indicating that the parties intended to do so in accordance with Art. 8 CISG.[1433]

In a framework agreement that follows a two-tier structure, a reference to an external standard may be explicitly mentioned in the framework agreement itself, but not in the individual sales contracts that are subsequently concluded. To illustrate, the framework agreement may point to the buyer's code of conduct, referring to recognised standards for the protection of the environment and respect for human rights, which is supposed to govern the entire supply relationship between the parties.[1434] In such a case, the aforementioned reference will typically extend its effects to the individual sales contracts concluded under the umbrella of the framework agreement in light of Art. 8 CISG.[1435]

In summary, references to external standards, such as those mentioned above, are admissible under the CISG. This applies to any CISG contract, whether a long-term framework agreement or a short-term sales contract. The duration of the contract is irrelevant in this respect. External standards are, however, particularly relevant for

1425. *See* Ch. 3 IV. 2. b. above.
1426. Schlechtriem/Schwenzer/Schroeter/*Schroeter*, 5th English ed., Art. 14 CISG, para. 78.
1427. Cf. *Brunner*, pp. 451, 452.
1428. Cf. CISG-AC, Op. 19 *Saidov*, Comment 3.1.
1429. CISG-AC, Op. 19 *Saidov*, Comment 3.1.
1430. CISG-AC, Op. 19 *Saidov*, Comment 3.1.
1431. *Butler*, pp. 302 et seq.; CISG-AC, Op. 19 *Saidov*, Comment 3.1.; Ostendorf/*Ostendorf/Sauthoff*, § 18, paras 224 et seq.
1432. CISG-AC, Op. 19 *Saidov*, Comment 3.2.
1433. CISG-AC, Op. 19 *Saidov*, Comments 3.2. et seq. with examples.
1434. Ostendorf/*Ostendorf/Sauthoff*, § 18, para. 226 (providing a sample clause); cf. also *Butler*, p. 305.
1435. Cf. Schlechtriem/Schwenzer/Schroeter/*Schmidt-Kessel*, 5th English ed., Art. 8 CISG, para. 50; *Schroeter*, para. 94; in a different context: OLG Hamburg, 5 October 1998, CISG-online 473.

long-term framework agreements and other long-term contracts as they are able to change in accordance with the surrounding circumstances.[1436]

c. *Summary*

Long-term contracts are prone to changes in their surrounding circumstances. As a consequence, the parties may deviate from the contractual terms through their subsequent conduct following the contract conclusion. The parties' subsequent conduct must be taken into account for the interpretation of any CISG contract. According to Art. 8(3) CISG, it is a relevant circumstance indicating the parties' intent. This interpretative tool is particularly relevant for long-term framework agreements and other long-term contracts. If a framework agreement follows a two-tier structure, the subsequently concluded individual sales contracts must be interpreted in light of the framework agreement and vice versa.

In addition, the parties may wish to subsequently modify their contract. They are free to do so in line with Art. 29 CISG, although there must be sufficient indications of an agreement between the parties in that regard. The parties may also agree on additional mechanisms for contract modifications in anticipation of potential adaptions. For instance, the parties to framework agreements commonly incorporate price escalation clauses into their contracts.

In light of changing surrounding circumstances, the parties may also agree on external standards regarding the essential elements of their long-term framework agreement or external standards expanding on the performance of their obligations. The CISG allows for a reference to objective factors, such as external standards, to satisfy the standard of sufficient definiteness. Furthermore, the parties may either explicitly or implicitly agree on an external standard defining the conformity of the goods (Art. 35(1) CISG). In a framework agreement with a two-tier structure, an external standard referred to in the framework agreement may also be relevant for the subsequently concluded individual sales contracts. Overall, all of these references to external standards are permitted under the CISG, irrespective of the contract's duration. They are, however, particularly relevant for long-term framework agreements and other long-term contracts as external standards are able to dynamically change in line with the surrounding circumstances.

3. Supervening Events (Force Majeure and Hardship)

As previously established, long-term framework agreements and other long-term contracts are prone to changes in the surrounding circumstances based on their duration.[1437] The temporal dimension renders any long-term contract more susceptible

1436. UNIDROIT 2014, Study L – Doc. 126, para. 23.
1437. Cf. *Brunner*, p. 438; CISG-AC, Op. 20 *Muñoz*, Comment 7.12.; DiMatteo *et al./Cordero-Moss/DiMatteo*, Ch. 28, para. 31; *Gillette/Walt*, p. 302; *Guo*, pp. 22, 23; *Hoffbauer*, p. 127; *Klotz*, p. 216; *Schwenzer*, (2008) 39 V.U.W. L. Rev., p. 709.

to economic, political or technological shifts compared to a short-term contract.[1438] Such changes may give rise to so-called supervening events, such as instances of force majeure or hardship, which are of particular relevance in the context of long-term contracts.[1439] The term 'force majeure' is generally used to describe exceptional events or circumstances that are beyond a party's control, unforeseeable, insurmountable, and cannot be attributed to either party.[1440] Typical cases of force majeure may occur in long-term framework agreements, such as trade embargos, natural disasters, epidemics (e.g., COVID-19)[1441] or war.[1442] More frequently, there are merely changes in economic circumstances, e.g., a significant rise in the production costs of the goods or a drastic currency depreciation, etc.[1443] Such issues are frequently discussed under the notion of (economic) hardship,[1444] which refers to situations where the contractual equilibrium has been fundamentally altered due to the occurrence of unforeseeable and uncontrollable events or circumstances that cannot be attributed to either party.[1445] It is also possible that the same factual situation can be considered to constitute both a case of force majeure and a case of hardship.[1446]

Although these issues have been extensively addressed under the CISG, the following section will provide a brief overview of the Convention's position on these matters, with particular attention to the specifics of long-term framework agreements.

a. *Force Majeure under the CISG*

The Convention addresses the occurrence of exceptional events or circumstances in Art. 79 CISG. According to this provision, 'a party is not liable for a failure to perform any of his obligations if he proves that the failure was due to an impediment beyond his control and that he could not reasonably be expected to have taken the impediment into account at the time of the conclusion of the contract or to have avoided or overcome it or its consequences'.

1438. *Brunner*, p. 438.
1439. Cf. Comment 5 on Art. 6.2.2 UPICC ('hardship normally relevant to long-term contracts'); Comment 5 on Art. 7.1.7 UPICC.
1440. Cf. only *Klotz*, pp. 205 et seq.
1441. Cf. *Janssen/Wahnschaffe*, EuZW 2020, pp. 410 et seq.
1442. *Hoffbauer*, p. 131; cf. also on typical cases of force majeure: *Brunner*, pp. 206 et seq.; Schlechtriem/Schwenzer/Schroeter/*Schwenzer*, 5th English ed., Art. 79 CISG, para. 17; Staudinger/*Magnus*, Art. 79 CISG, paras 27, 28.
1443. *Hoffbauer*, p. 131; *Vischer*, Lausanner Kolloquium, p. 177.
1444. Cf. *Brunner*, pp. 213 et seq.; Brunner/Gottlieb/*Brunner*, Art. 79 CISG, paras 26 et seq.; CISG-AC, Op. 20 *Muñoz*, Comments 7.12., 7.13.; for a definition of hardship *see* Art. 6.2.2 UPICC.
1445. Cf. *Lookofsky*, (2011) 29 J. L. & Com., pp. 156, 157; cf. also Art. 6.2.2 UPICC; *Flechtner*, p. 5, referencing Art. 6.2.2 UPICC.
1446. Comment 6 on Art. 6.2.2 UPICC; Comment 5 on Art. 7.1.7 UPICC.

i. *General Remarks*

In general, this provision undisputedly covers cases of force majeure (*'höhere Gewalt'*), provided that its prerequisites are met.[1447] Art. 79 CISG requires that there be an uncontrollable, unforeseeable and unavoidable impediment causing one of the parties to fail to perform.[1448] This implies that an 'impediment' to the performance must have arisen, which is outside the obligor's sphere of influence ('beyond his control').[1449] Furthermore, it is required that the obligor could not reasonably be expected to have taken the impediment into account at the time of contract conclusion (i.e., unforeseeable).[1450] Even an unforeseeable and uncontrollable impediment does not exempt the obligor if they could reasonably be expected to have avoided or overcome the impediment or its consequences.[1451] Finally, there must be a causal link between the unforeseeable and insuperable impediment and the obligor's failure to perform.[1452]

Should these requirements be met, the obligor is exempt from paying damages to the obligee in accordance with Art. 79(1) CISG.[1453] Furthermore, the prevailing view holds that the right to demand specific performance should also be excluded, at least in cases of objective impossibility – despite the existence of Art. 79(5) CISG, which states that 'nothing in this article prevents either party from exercising any right other than to claim damages under this Convention'.[1454] Moreover, it has been persuasively argued that the right to specific performance should be suspended or not enforceable as long as an impediment exists, even if the impediment does not qualify as an objective impossibility.[1455] This is because the exemption intended by Art. 79 CISG would be undermined if the right to specific performance were granted to the obligee.[1456]

1447. Schlechtriem/Schwenzer/Schroeter/*Schwenzer*, 5th English ed., Art. 79 CISG, para. 17; *Schroeter*, para. 764; cf. also Staudinger/*Magnus*, Art. 79 CISG, paras 27, 28.
1448. In more detail and with further references: Kröll *et al.*/*Atamer*, Art. 79 CISG, paras 43 et seq.; Schlechtriem/Schwenzer/Schroeter/*Schwenzer*, 5th English ed., Art. 79 CISG, paras 11 et seq.; *Schroeter*, paras 762 et seq.; Staudinger/*Magnus*, Art. 79 CISG, paras 15 et seq.
1449. *Flechtner*, p. 1; Kröll *et al.*/*Atamer*, Art. 79 CISG, paras 46 et seq.; Schlechtriem/Schwenzer/Schroeter/*Schwenzer*, 5th English ed., Art. 79 CISG, paras 12, 13; *Schroeter*, paras 764 et seq.; Staudinger/*Magnus*, Art. 79 CISG, paras 16 et seq.
1450. *Flechtner*, p. 1; Kröll *et al.*/*Atamer*, Art. 79 CISG, paras 50 et seq.; Schlechtriem/Schwenzer/Schroeter/*Schwenzer*, 5th English ed., Art. 79 CISG, para. 14; *Schroeter*, paras 774 et seq.; Staudinger/*Magnus*, Art. 79 CISG, paras 32, 33.
1451. *Flechtner*, p. 1; Kröll *et al.*/*Atamer*, Art. 79 CISG, paras 54 et seq. (distinguishing between avoiding and overcoming); Schlechtriem/Schwenzer/Schroeter/*Schwenzer*, 5th English ed., Art. 79 CISG, para. 15; *Schroeter*, paras 777 et seq.; Staudinger/*Magnus*, Art. 79 CISG, para. 34.
1452. Kröll *et al.*/*Atamer*, Art. 79 CISG, paras 58, 59; Schlechtriem/Schwenzer/Schroeter/*Schwenzer*, 5th English ed., Art. 79 CISG, para. 16; Staudinger/*Magnus*, Art. 79 CISG, para. 31.
1453. CISG-AC, Op. 20 *Muñoz*, Comment 9.2.; Schlechtriem/Schwenzer/Schroeter/*Schwenzer*, 5th English ed., Art. 79 CISG, paras 50 et seq.
1454. BeckOK/*Saenger*, Art. 79 CISG, para. 16; Schlechtriem/Schwenzer/Schroeter/*Schwenzer*, 5th English ed., Art. 79 CISG, paras 53 et seq.; Staudinger/*Magnus*, Art. 79 CISG, paras 57 et seq.; with different reasoning: *Atamer*, FS Schwenzer, pp. 92, 93; *Schroeter*, para. 759.
1455. CISG-AC, Op. 20 *Muñoz*, Comments 9.3., 9.4.; Schlechtriem/Schwenzer/Schroeter/*Schwenzer*, 5th English ed., Art. 79 CISG, para. 55.
1456. Schlechtriem/Schwenzer/Schroeter/*Schwenzer*, 5th English ed., Art. 79 CISG, para. 55; *Schwenzer*, (2008) 39 V.U.W. L. Rev., p. 720; cf. also *Schroeter*, para. 801 (with regard to hardship), relying on an interpretation of Arts 30 and 53 CISG in light of Art. 7(1) CISG.

ii. *Long-Term Framework Agreements in Particular*

Long-term framework agreements are also subject to Art. 79 CISG in the event of an uncontrollable, unforeseeable and unavoidable impediment that causes one of the parties to fail to perform their obligations. In general, the same prerequisites must be met regardless of the duration of the contract.[1457] If these prerequisites are met, the same consequences under Art. 79 CISG apply to long-term framework agreements and other long-term contracts. This means that the obligor is exempted from paying damages, and that the right to specific performance is excluded or at least suspended during the impediment's existence.[1458]

In deviation from Art. 79 CISG, long-term framework agreements and other long-term contracts frequently include force majeure clauses.[1459] Such clauses may contain a list of events that exempt the obligor, or provide for an option to terminate the contract under certain circumstances.[1460] It should be noted, however, that the parties to a long-term contract often wish to continue their contractual relationship rather than bring it to an end.[1461] This is because their relationship may have already lasted several years or because the parties may have made large initial investments, the value of which will only materialise over time.[1462] Thus, they may stipulate a procedure to be followed in the event of force majeure, which may permit them to continue their relationship and merely resort to contract termination as an *ultima ratio*.[1463]

For an example of such a clause, the International Chamber of Commerce ('ICC') provides a sample force majeure clause.[1464] This sample clause, among other things, defines force majeure, contains a list of events falling under force majeure and regulates the consequences of it, especially the remedies. This demonstrates that force majeure clauses generally regulate the prerequisites as well as the consequences in cases of the occurrence of exceptional events or circumstances.[1465] Consequently, the parties may agree to derogate from or modify the provision in Art. 79 CISG by incorporating such a clause into their contract.[1466] The parties are free to do so in

1457. In the context of hardship: CISG-AC, Op. 20 *Muñoz*, Comment 7.12.
1458. *See* Ch. 5 III. 3. a. i. above.
1459. *Flambouras*, (2001) 13 Pace Int'l L. Rev., pp. 278, 279; *Hoffbauer*, p. 131; *Guo*, p. 63; Schlechtriem/Schwenzer/Schroeter/*Schwenzer*, 5th English ed., Art. 79 CISG, para. 58.
1460. Cf. *Kumpers Composites GmbH & Co KG v. TPI Composites Inc.*, US Dist. Ct. Ariz., 25 February 2025, CISG-online 7294, para. 9; *Hoffbauer*, p. 131; Schlechtriem/Schwenzer/Schroeter/*Schwenzer*, 5th English ed., Art. 79 CISG, para. 58.
1461. Cf. Comment 5 on Art. 7.1.7 UPICC; UNIDROIT 2014, Study L – Doc. 126, paras 25 et seq.
1462. UNIDROIT 2014, Study L – Doc. 126, para. 25; Comment 5 on Art. 7.1.7 UPICC.
1463. Cf. Comment 5 on Art. 7.1.7 UPICC, Illustration 3; UNIDROIT 2014, Study L – Doc. 126, paras 25 et seq.
1464. ICC Force Majeure Clause 2020 (https://iccwbo.org/wp-content/uploads/sites/3/2020/03/icc-forcemajeure-hardship-clauses-march2020.pdf, last checked September 2025); further examples can be found in *Klotz*, pp. 205 et seq.
1465. *See* MKAC, 17 October 1995, CISG-online 207: the parties had agreed on an exhaustive list of circumstances that could be considered force majeure. However, the buyer's lack of foreign currency, which was invoked by the buyer, was not included on that list.
1466. *Flambouras*, (2001) 13 Pace Int'l L. Rev., p. 283; MüKoBGB/*Huber*, Art. 79 CISG, para. 34; MüKoHGB/*Sommerfeld*, Art. 79 CISG, para. 66; Schlechtriem/Schwenzer/Schroeter/*Schwenzer*, 5th English ed., Art. 79 CISG, para. 58; Staudinger/*Magnus*, Art. 79 CISG, para. 65.

accordance with Art. 6 CISG.[1467] The incorporation of force majeure clauses is subject to Arts 14–24 CISG, which are particularly relevant if they form part of the contract's standard terms.[1468] Conversely, their validity is governed by domestic law in accordance with Art. 4(a) CISG.[1469]

b. Hardship

i. Drafting History of Article 79 CISG

In contrast to cases of force majeure, there was a debate during its drafting as to whether the CISG should extend its coverage to cases of hardship.[1470] The wording of Art. 79(1) CISG was changed from its predecessor Art. 74(1) ULIS, and the term 'circumstances' was replaced with 'impediment'.[1471] This change was partly in response to concerns that a reference to 'circumstances' could exempt obligors if the performance merely became more difficult or unprofitable.[1472] Furthermore, at the Vienna Diplomatic Conference, a Norwegian proposal was put forth that a party should be exempted after a temporary impediment has ceased and the circumstances have radically changed, so that it would be unreasonable to hold the concerned party liable.[1473] This proposal was, *inter alia*, rejected on the grounds that it 'was tantamount to introducing a provision similar to the doctrine of frustration in English law [...]' and because it was feared that it would move the provision away from force majeure to the *théorie de l'imprévision* as known in French law.[1474] This drafting history has given rise to divergent interpretations, leading to a debate as to whether Art. 79 CISG should be applied in cases of (economic) hardship.[1475]

1467. *Flambouras*, (2001) 13 Pace Int'l L. Rev., p. 283; *Rösler*, ERPL 2007, p. 503; MüKoHGB/*Sommerfeld*, Art. 79 CISG, para. 66; Schlechtriem/Schwenzer/Schroeter/*Schwenzer*, 5th English ed., Art. 79 CISG, para. 58; Staudinger/*Magnus*, Art. 79 CISG, para. 65.
1468. MüKoBGB/*Huber*, Art. 79 CISG, para. 34; *see* generally on the incorporation of standard terms under the CISG: Schlechtriem/Schwenzer/Schroeter/*Schroeter*, 5th English ed., Art. 14 CISG, paras 125 et seq.
1469. MüKoBGB/*Huber*, Art. 79 CISG, para. 34; MüKoHGB/*Sommerfeld*, Art. 79 CISG, para. 67; Staudinger/*Magnus*, Art. 79 CISG, para. 65; on validity under German law: *Hoffbauer*, pp. 138 et seq.
1470. *Brunner*, p. 216; *Schroeter*, para. 797; cf. UNCITRAL Y.B. V (1974), pp. 66, 67; UNCITRAL Y.B. VI (1975), pp. 84, 85; UNCITRAL Y.B. VIII (1977), p. 135 para. 24, p. 160 para. 14.
1471. *Brunner*, p. 216; *Honnold/Flechtner*, Art. 79 CISG, para. 579; *Schroeter*, para. 797.
1472. *Brunner*, p. 216; *Honnold/Flechtner*, Art. 79 CISG, para. 579; cf. UNCITRAL Y.B. V (1974), p. 39.
1473. Official Records, p. 381, para. 52.
1474. Official Records, p. 381, paras 58 et seq.
1475. Providing a comprehensive overview of this controversy: CISG-AC, Op. 20 *Muñoz*, Comments 2.1. et seq.

ii. *Applicability of Article 79 CISG to Cases of Hardship*

Based on the drafting history mentioned above, some scholars have concluded that the CISG does not intend to regulate hardship or frustration of purpose at all.[1476] Further scholars have also rejected the applicability of the CISG (in particular Art. 79 CISG) to cases of hardship, with various arguments put forth.[1477] As an alternative, it has been proposed that recourse should be had to the applicable domestic law.[1478]

In contrast, the now prevailing view is that hardship is within the scope of Art. 79 CISG, again with various arguments being advanced in support of this position.[1479] Notably, a few proponents of this view also rely on the drafting history of Art. 79 CISG.[1480]

This illustrates that the drafting history is simply not sufficiently clear to permit any conclusions to be drawn regarding the CISG's coverage of hardship.[1481] Nevertheless, the more compelling arguments support the prevailing view, given that economic impediments can hardly be distinguished from factual impediments.[1482] In fact, an economic impediment may originate from a factual impediment if the latter can theoretically be overcome but only with exorbitant costs.[1483] It would therefore be inconsistent to exempt the obligor in cases where overcoming a factual impediment (or procuring the goods) would be associated with exorbitant costs, but not in cases where overcoming economic circumstances, such as extraordinary market changes or drastic currency depreciation, would be excessively more burdensome (i.e., associated with exorbitant costs).[1484] Given the similarities between these cases, similar solutions are required. Consequently, Art. 79 CISG should be applied to all of these cases. A literal

1476. *Nicholas*, § 5.03; *Rösler*, ERPL 2007, p. 503; cf. also Bianca/Bonell/*Tallon*, Art. 79 CISG, note 3.1.2.; *Zeller*, Damages, pp. 164, 165.
1477. *Audit*, p. 174; *Gillette/Walt*, pp. 309 et seq.; *Nicholas*, § 5.03; *Stoll*, p. 274; *Vischer*, Lausanner Kolloquium, pp. 176, 177; cf. also *Flambouras*, (2001) 13 Pace Int'l L. Rev., pp. 279, 280; *Lookofsky*, (2011) 29 J. L. & Com., pp. 161 et seq.
1478. *Flambouras*, (2001) 13 Pace Int'l L. Rev., pp. 280, 281; *Gillette/Walt*, p. 313; *Lookofsky*, (2011) 29 J. L. & Com., pp. 163 et seq.; *Vischer*, Lausanner Kolloquium, p. 177.
1479. *Brunner*, pp. 213 et seq.; Brunner/Gottlieb/*Brunner*, Art. 79 CISG, paras 26 et seq.; CISG-AC, Op. 7 *Garro*, Rule 3.1; CISG-AC, Op. 20 *Muñoz*, Comment 2.2.; *Honnold/Flechtner*, Art. 79 CISG, para. 579; Kröll *et al./Atamer*, Art. 79 CISG, paras 78 et seq.; MüKoBGB/*Huber*, Art. 79 CISG, para. 21; MüKoHGB/*Sommerfeld*, Art. 79 CISG, para. 40; Schlechtriem/Schwenzer/Schroeter/*Schwenzer*, 5th English ed., Art. 79 CISG, para. 31; Schlechtriem/Schwenzer/Schroeter/*Schwenzer/B. Köhler*, 8th German ed., Art. 79 CISG, para. 30; *Schroeter*, paras 797, 800; Staudinger/*Magnus*, Art. 79 CISG, paras 24, 24a; cf. also Supr. Ct. Belgium, 19 June 2009, CISG-online 1963; BeckOK/*Saenger*, Art. 79 CISG, para. 7.
1480. Brunner/Gottlieb/*Brunner*, Art. 79 CISG, para. 26; *Honnold/Flechtner*, Art. 79 CISG, para. 579; *Schroeter*, para. 797.
1481. Kröll *et al./Atamer*, Art. 79 CISG, para. 78; *Lookofsky*, (2011) 29 J. L. & Com., p. 157; cf. also CISG-AC, Op. 7 *Garro*, Comments 28 et seq.
1482. *Brunner*, p. 215; Brunner/Gottlieb/*Brunner*, Art. 79 CISG, para. 27; cf. already *Zweigert/Kötz*, p. 556 ('all these cases [impossibility, performance becoming more difficult and frustration of purpose] are closely interconnected').
1483. *Brunner*, p. 215; Brunner/Gottlieb/*Brunner*, Art. 79 CISG, para. 27; cf. also MüKoHGB/*Sommerfeld*, Art. 79 CISG, para. 40, noting that Art. 79 CISG is based on the concept of what is reasonable ('*zumutbar*') for the obligor.
1484. *Brunner*, pp. 215, 216; Brunner/Gottlieb/*Brunner*, Art. 79 CISG, paras 27, 28; Staudinger/*Magnus*, Art. 79 CISG, para. 24a.

interpretation of Art. 79 CISG supports this position. This provision is worded broadly, and hardship can indeed be considered an 'impediment beyond his control' in some cases.[1485] The aforementioned change in wording from 'circumstances' to 'impediment' is of no consequence, as the latter term is still neutral and open to a broad interpretation.[1486] Therefore, Art. 79 CISG should be applicable to cases of (economic) hardship.

iii. Requirements

1) General Remarks

In general, economic hardship must be particularly serious – the contractual equilibrium must be altered fundamentally.[1487] Furthermore, it is necessary to demonstrate that the event causing the hardship is beyond the control of the obligor, i.e., outside their sphere of risk.[1488] Hardship as an impediment can only exempt the obligor if the event causing the imbalance could not reasonably have been taken into account by the obligor at the time of contract conclusion (i.e., unforeseeable).[1489] In addition, it is necessary that the event causing the hardship cannot be reasonably avoided or overcome.[1490]

The question of whether the threshold for hardship has been met, in particular whether there has been a fundamental alteration of the contractual equilibrium, must be assessed on a case-by-case basis in light of the individual circumstances.[1491] Nevertheless, the CISG-Advisory Council Opinion No. 20 has proposed a non-exclusive list of elements that may be taken into account when determining whether a change of circumstances amounts to a fundamental alteration of the contract.[1492] The aforementioned elements are: (a) whether the risk of a change of circumstances was assumed by either party; (b) whether the contract is of speculative nature; (c) whether and to what extent there have been previous market fluctuations; (d) the duration of the contract;

1485. CISG-AC, Op. 7 *Garro*, Rule 3.1; CISG-AC, Op. 20 *Muñoz*, Comment 4.2.; *Honnold/Flechtner*, Art. 79 CISG, para. 579; *Schroeter*, para. 800; cf. also Kröll *et al./Atamer*, Art. 79 CISG, para. 80 (but relying on a different approach); but *see Stoll*, p. 274.
1486. Cf. *Honnold/Flechtner*, Art. 79 CISG, para. 579; *Schroeter*, para. 797.
1487. BeckOK/*Saenger*, Art. 79 CISG, para. 7; *Brunner*, p. 213 ('excessively onerous'); Brunner/Gottlieb/*Brunner*, Art. 79 CISG, para. 26 ('limit of sacrifice'); CISG-AC, Op. 20 *Muñoz*, Comments 4.1. et seq.; Kröll *et al./Atamer*, Art. 79 CISG, paras 81, 82; Schlechtriem/Schwenzer/Schroeter/*Schwenzer*, 5th English ed., Art. 79 CISG, para. 31 ('ultimate limit of sacrifice'); Schlechtriem/Schwenzer/Schroeter/*Schwenzer/B. Köhler*, 8th German ed., Art. 79 CISG, para. 30; *Schroeter*, para. 800; *Schwenzer*, (2008) 39 V.U.W. L. Rev., pp. 714, 715; Staudinger/*Magnus*, Art. 79 CISG, para. 24a.
1488. CISG-AC, Op. 20 *Muñoz*, Comments 4.3., 4.4.
1489. CISG-AC, Op. 20 *Muñoz*, Comment 4.5.; *Schwenzer*, (2008) 39 V.U.W. L. Rev., p. 719.
1490. CISG-AC, Op. 20 *Muñoz*, Comments 4.7., 4.8.; *Schroeter*, para. 800; *Schwenzer*, (2008) 39 V.U.W. L. Rev., p. 719.
1491. Brunner/Gottlieb/*Brunner*, Art. 79 CISG, paras 30, 31; CISG-AC, Op. 20 *Muñoz*, Comments 7.1. et seq.; Kröll *et al./Atamer*, Art. 79 CISG, para. 82.
1492. CISG-AC, Op. 20 *Muñoz*, Rule 7; accord Schlechtriem/Schwenzer/Schroeter/*Schwenzer*, 5th English ed., Art. 79 CISG, para. 31.

(e) whether the seller has obtained the goods from their supplier; (f) whether either party has hedged against market changes.[1493]

2) Duration of the Contract as Relevant Factor?

In the context of long-term framework agreements, it may be important to consider the relevance of element (d) 'duration of the contract'.[1494] In this regard, the CISG-AC Opinion persuasively holds that the same standards should apply 'irrespective of the duration of contracts'.[1495] Nevertheless, the Opinion additionally states that in exceptional cases, a lower threshold might apply if the disadvantaged party's financial ruin is imminent, especially with regard to a long-term contract.[1496]

However, each party is generally held accountable for their own financial situation under the CISG.[1497] Consequently, the financial difficulties of the obligor should not be considered in order to reduce the threshold for hardship in long-term framework agreements or other long-term contracts.[1498] There appears to be no compelling argument to deviate from this fundamental risk allocation on the basis of the contract's duration.

3) Further Particularities with Regard to Long-Term Framework Agreements

In addition to the aforementioned considerations, there are further particularities with regard to long-term framework agreements and other long-term contracts that should be taken into account when dealing with potential cases of hardship.

As the performance of a long-term contract including long-term framework agreements occurs over an extended period of time, it should be carefully assessed whether the parties have explicitly or implicitly allocated certain risks.[1499] This may be the case, for instance, if the parties have agreed upon a price escalation clause.[1500] In such instances, the risk of changed circumstances has been addressed by the parties, leaving no room for invoking hardship.[1501] Similarly, other specific risks may have been addressed in a long-term framework agreement, which excludes any recourse to hardship.[1502] The question of whether the parties have explicitly or implicitly addressed and allocated certain risks must be assessed on the basis of each specific

1493. In detail CISG-AC, Op. 20 *Muñoz*, Comments 7.1. et seq.
1494. Cf. also *Schwenzer*, (2008) 39 V.U.W. L. Rev., p. 716.
1495. CISG-AC, Op. 20 *Muñoz*, Comment 7.13.; accord *Brunner*, p. 438.
1496. CISG-AC, Op. 20 *Muñoz*, Comment 7.13.; in more detail *Brunner*, pp. 435 et seq.
1497. Court of Arbitration of the Hamburg CC, 21 March 1996, CISG-online 187, paras 30 et seq.; Schlechtriem/Schwenzer/Schroeter/*Schwenzer*, 5th English ed., Art. 79 CISG, para. 26; *Schroeter*, para. 772.
1498. But *see Brunner*, pp. 435 et seq.; CISG-AC, Op. 20 *Muñoz*, Comment 7.13.
1499. *Brunner*, pp. 439 et seq.
1500. *Brunner*, pp. 440, 441.
1501. *Brunner*, pp. 440, 441.
1502. *Brunner*, pp. 440 et seq.

contract and in light of the surrounding circumstances.[1503] It is more likely that the parties to a long-term framework agreement or other long-term contracts have drafted their contract in a more sophisticated manner and thus considered such risks, in contrast to short-term contracts.[1504]

Another peculiarity in long-term framework agreements and other long-term contracts is the point of reference for determining whether there has been a fundamental change of circumstances.[1505] In determining whether there has been a fundamental alteration of the equilibrium in a long-term framework agreement, it is necessary to consider the entire undertaking of a party under the relevant transaction.[1506] This means that past and future performances upon the contract's termination or expiration must be considered.[1507]

In this context, *Brunner* posits that 'depending on the circumstances, it may even be appropriate to extend this principle to *connected contracts*'.[1508] This raises the question of whether the subsequently concluded individual sales contracts may also be considered when assessing whether there has been a fundamental alteration of a framework agreement with a two-tier structure (and vice versa). It is submitted that this assessment must generally be done individually, given that these contracts are separate agreements.[1509] Nevertheless, the individual sales contracts may be considered relevant circumstances (Art. 8(3) CISG) for the interpretation of the framework agreement under the CISG and vice versa.[1510] In this respect, the individual sales contracts may influence the determination of whether there has been a fundamental alteration of the framework agreement, and the framework agreement may influence the same determination with regard to the individual sales contracts. Consequently, the related contracts may be deemed (indirectly) relevant for the assessment of whether there has been a fundamental alteration of a framework agreement or an individual sales contract.

iv. Consequences

1) Exemption from Damages and Specific Performance

If the prerequisites set out by Art. 79 CISG are met in a case of hardship, the obligor is primarily exempted from their obligation to pay damages during the period in which

1503. *Brunner*, p. 440.
1504. Cf. *Brunner*, pp. 439 et seq.
1505. In detail *Brunner*, pp. 461 et seq.
1506. Cf. *Brunner*, pp. 461 et seq.; CISG-AC, Op. 20 *Muñoz*, Comment 7.13.
1507. *Brunner*, pp. 461 et seq.; cf. also BGer, 3 November 1991, BGE 47 II 440, pp. 459 et seq. (on Swiss law).
1508. *Brunner*, p. 462.
1509. *See* Ch. 3 V. 3. b. above (the argument that different hardship standards may apply if different laws govern related contracts does not, in itself, provide a convincing rationale for applying the same law to all related contracts).
1510. *See* Ch. 3 III. 2. b. ii. above.

the impediment exists, in accordance with Art. 79(1), (3) and (5).[1511] In the event of force majeure, the right to require specific performance is deemed to be suspended or unenforceable as long as the impediment exists, according to the prevailing view.[1512] The right to require specific performance should similarly be suspended or unenforceable in cases of hardship, which is essentially just another type of impediment under Art. 79 CISG.[1513] Granting the right of specific performance to the obligee would undermine the exemption intended by Art. 79 CISG.[1514]

In contrast to the right to damages or specific performance, the obligee may exercise any other right under the Convention, as set out in Art. 79(5) CISG. These include the right to suspend performance (Art. 71(1) CISG), the right to reduce the price (Art. 50 CISG) and the right to avoid the contract (Arts 49(1) and 64(1) CISG),[1515] provided that the respective requirements are met.[1516] As the parties to a long-term framework agreement are frequently particularly interested in maintaining their relationship, they may also agree to suspend their right to avoid the contract for a specific period.[1517] Such an agreement would be permissible under Art. 6 CISG, given that Art. 79 CISG is subject to contractual modifications or derogations.[1518]

2) Mandated Contract Adaption or Termination?

Furthermore, it has been proposed that courts, arbitral tribunals or the parties themselves should be granted the authority or obligation to adapt the contract in order to restore the contractual equilibrium or, alternatively, to terminate the contract in cases of hardship under Art. 79 CISG.[1519] To justify this position, the principle of good faith (Art. 7(1) CISG) has been invoked.[1520] In addition, a general principle, as outlined

1511. CISG-AC, Op. 20 *Muñoz*, Comment 9.2.; cf. also CISG-AC, Op. 7 *Garro*, Rule 1; Kröll *et al./Atamer*, Art. 79 CISG, para. 13; Schlechtriem/Schwenzer/Schroeter/*Schwenzer*, 5th English ed., Art. 79 CISG, para. 50; *Schwenzer*, (2008) 39 V.U.W. L. Rev., p. 719.
1512. BeckOK/*Saenger*, Art. 79 CISG, para. 16; Schlechtriem/Schwenzer/Schroeter/*Schwenzer*, 5th English ed., Art. 79 CISG, paras 53 et seq.; *Schwenzer*, (2008) 39 V.U.W. L. Rev., p. 720; cf. also Kröll *et al./Atamer*, Art. 79 CISG, para. 27; MüKoBGB/*Huber*, Art. 79 CISG, para. 30 (not applying Art. 79 CISG but relying on a general principle under Art. 7(2) CISG); Staudinger/*Magnus*, Art. 79 CISG, paras 57 et seq.; *contra*: *Stoll*, pp. 271, 272.
1513. CISG-AC, Op. 20 *Muñoz*, Comment 9.3.; *Atamer*, FS Schwenzer, pp. 93 et seq. (with different reasoning); *Schroeter*, para. 801 (with different reasoning); *Schwenzer*, (2008) 39 V.U.W. L. Rev., pp. 715, 720; but *see Stoll*, p. 274.
1514. Schlechtriem/Schwenzer/Schroeter/*Schwenzer*, 5th English ed., Art. 79 CISG, para. 55; *Schwenzer*, (2008) 39 V.U.W. L. Rev., p. 720; cf. also *Schroeter*, para. 801, who relies on an interpretation of Arts 30 and 53 CISG in light of Art. 7(1) CISG; similarly, *Atamer*, FS Schwenzer, pp. 92 et seq. (invoking a gap in Art. 46(1) CISG).
1515. In more detail: CISG-AC, Op. 20 *Muñoz*, Comments 9.5. et seq.
1516. Cf. *Schwenzer*, (2008) 39 V.U.W. L. Rev., p. 720.
1517. Cf. Comment 5 on Art. 7.1.7 UPICC, Illustration 3.
1518. MüKoBGB/*Huber*, Art. 79 CISG, para. 34; MüKoHGB/*Sommerfeld*, Art. 79 CISG, para. 66; Staudinger/*Magnus*, Art. 79 CISG, para. 65.
1519. Brunner/Gottlieb/*Brunner*, Art. 79 CISG, para. 33; Kröll *et al./Atamer*, Art. 79 CISG, para. 86; MüKoBGB/*Huber*, Art. 79 CISG, para. 21.
1520. MüKoBGB/*Huber*, Art. 79 CISG, para. 21; cf. also Brunner/Gottlieb/*Brunner*, Art. 79 CISG, para. 33.

in Art. 7(2) CISG, has been employed in support of this view.[1521] It has also been argued that certain rules, in particular Art. 6.2.3(4) UPICC, should be characterised as an international usage in the sense of Art. 9(2) CISG.[1522]

However, the more compelling reasons suggest that it is not appropriate to derive such an authority or obligation from the CISG.[1523] First, it is doubtful whether rights and obligations of the parties can be derived from the principle of good faith enshrined in Art. 7(1) CISG.[1524] In addition, there is no gap in Art. 79 CISG that would require recourse to general principles in accordance with Art. 7(2) CISG.[1525] The creation of a distinct set of remedies for hardship in contrast to any other impediment under Art. 79 CISG would be inconsistent and unnecessary.[1526] For similar reasons to those previously outlined, the parties should not be obliged to renegotiate the contract in instances of hardship under the CISG.[1527]

Furthermore, the legal consequences in the event of hardship are exclusively addressed in Art. 79 CISG, which provides for exemption from damages and, at least temporarily, specific performance.[1528] Art. 79(5) CISG states that 'any right [...] under this Convention' is still available to either party. However, the CISG does not provide for an adaption or termination of the contract in the event of hardship.[1529] Proposals to introduce provisions that would empower courts or arbitral tribunals to adapt a contract in situations of hardship were explicitly rejected at the time of drafting.[1530]

Under the CISG, contract modification is only possible by agreement of the parties in accordance with Art. 29(1) CISG. The delegation of authority to a court or arbitral tribunal to adapt a contract in the event of hardship would be at odds with the CISG's approach and would necessitate the inclusion of an explicit provision in the Convention.[1531] The same applies to a termination or avoidance in cases of hardship, whether ordered by a court or arbitral tribunal or *ipso facto* (*ipso iure*). The CISG has opted for a solution that requires a declaration by the aggrieved party in order to avoid the contract.[1532] Granting a court or arbitral tribunal the power to terminate a contract or assuming an *ipso facto* termination in the event of hardship could not be reconciled

1521. Flechtner/*Schlechtriem*, (1999) 18 J. L. & Com., p. 236.
1522. Brunner/Gottlieb/*Brunner*, Art. 79 CISG, para. 33; Kröll *et al./Atamer*, Art. 79 CISG, para. 86.
1523. Accord CISG-AC, Op. 20 *Muñoz*, Comments 12.1. et seq.; *Honnold/Flechtner*, Art. 79 CISG, para. 589; *Schroeter*, para. 801; *Schwenzer*, (2008) 39 V.U.W. L. Rev., pp. 723 et seq.
1524. Both covering this controversy: *Ferrari*, IHR 2013, pp. 152 et seq.; *Schroeter*, (2018) 41 Loy. L.A. Int'l & Comp. L. Rev., pp. 25 et seq.
1525. CISG-AC, Op. 20 *Muñoz*, Comment 12.1.; *Flechtner*, p. 8; *Honnold/Flechtner*, Art. 79 CISG, para. 589; *Schroeter*, para. 801; *Schwenzer*, (2008) 39 V.U.W. L. Rev., p. 713.
1526. CISG-AC, Op. 20 *Muñoz*, Comment 12.3.
1527. Arriving at the same outcome: CISG-AC, Op. 20 *Muñoz*, Comments 11.1. et seq.; *Gillette/Walt*, pp. 312 et seq.; Kröll *et al./Atamer*, Art. 79 CISG, para. 84; MüKoHGB/*Sommerfeld*, Art. 79 CISG, para. 40; Schlechtriem/Schwenzer/Schroeter/*Schwenzer*, 5th English ed., Art. 79 CISG, para. 55; *Schroeter*, para. 801.
1528. *Flechtner*, pp. 8, 9; *Schroeter*, para. 801; cf. also CISG-AC, Op. 20 *Muñoz*, Comment 12.1.; *Honnold/Flechtner*, Art. 79 CISG, para. 589.
1529. CISG-AC, Op. 20 *Muñoz*, Comment 12.1.
1530. *Flechtner*, pp. 4, 5; *Honnold/Flechtner*, Art. 79 CISG, para. 589.
1531. Cf. CISG-AC, Op. 20 *Muñoz*, Comment 12.5.
1532. CISG-AC, Op. 20 *Muñoz*, Comments 13.1. et seq.; cf. also Staudinger/*Magnus*, Art. 79 CISG, para. 59 (in a different context).

with the Convention's approach.[1533] Finally, the concept of mandated contract adaption does not constitute an international trade usage in the sense of Art. 9(2) CISG, as this concept is not internationally accepted.[1534] Thus, there is no obligation or right on the part of the parties, nor a power of courts or arbitral tribunals, to adapt the contract in case of hardship. The same applies to a termination that is solely based on the existence of hardship. An aggrieved party may only avoid the contract if the prerequisites set out in Art. 49(1) or Art. 64(1) CISG are met under the specific circumstances.

3) Agreements Between the Parties

The parties are, of course, at liberty to voluntarily renegotiate their framework agreement in the event of hardship.[1535] Furthermore, the parties may include a hardship clause in their contract.[1536] Hardship clauses are particularly common in framework agreements and other long-term contracts.[1537] The parties are free to derogate from Art. 79 CISG in accordance with Art. 6 CISG by including such a clause.[1538] Hardship clauses may stipulate an obligation to renegotiate in the event of hardship, and frequently contain detailed provisions on this matter.[1539] They may also empower a court, an arbitral tribunal or the parties themselves to adapt or terminate the contract if a hardship event occurs.[1540] In addition, hardship clauses often stipulate the circumstances that qualify as hardship.[1541]

It is important to note that clauses which are not explicitly labelled as hardship clauses may also preclude the parties from relying on hardship, as they can be interpreted to mean that the parties assumed specific risks.[1542] To illustrate, price escalation clauses are frequently perceived to address the risk of changed circumstances (relating to the price), thereby excluding the invocation of hardship.[1543]

1533. CISG-AC, Op. 20 *Muñoz*, Comments 13.1. et seq.
1534. CISG-AC, Op. 20 *Muñoz*, Comment 12.7.; *Honnold/Flechtner*, Art. 79 CISG, para. 589: US law does not recognise the concept of mandated contract adaption; but *see* Kröll *et al./Atamer*, Art. 79 CISG, para. 86.
1535. Cf. CISG-AC, Op. 20 *Muñoz*, Comment 11.1.
1536. CISG-AC, Op. 20 *Muñoz*, Comment 11.2.; Kröll *et al./Atamer*, Art. 79 CISG, para. 94; Schlechtriem/Schwenzer/Schroeter/*Schwenzer*, 5th English ed., Art. 79 CISG, para. 55; cf. also MüKoHGB/*Sommerfeld*, Art. 79 CISG, para. 66.
1537. *Flambouras*, (2001) 13 Pace Int'l L. Rev., p. 284 (noting that force majeure clauses are used in one-off contracts, hardship clauses in long-term agreements); *Guo*, p. 63; *Hoffbauer*, pp. 134 et seq.; *Klotz*, p. 216; Kröll *et al./Atamer*, Art. 79 CISG, para. 94.
1538. *Flambouras*, (2001) 13 Pace Int'l L. Rev., p. 283; MüKoBGB/*Huber*, Art. 79 CISG, para. 34; Schlechtriem/Schwenzer/Schroeter/*Schwenzer*, 5th English ed., Art. 79 CISG, para. 58; Staudinger/*Magnus*, Art. 79 CISG, para. 65; cf. also *Hoffbauer*, pp. 175 et seq.
1539. Kröll *et al./Atamer*, Art. 79 CISG, para. 94; *Perillo*, (1997) 5 Tulane J. Int'l & Comp. L., p. 11; Schlechtriem/Schwenzer/Schroeter/*Schwenzer*, 5th English ed., Art. 79 CISG, para. 58.
1540. *Perillo*, (1997) 5 Tulane J. Int'l & Comp. L., p. 11; Schlechtriem/Schwenzer/Schroeter/*Schwenzer*, 5th English ed., Art. 79 CISG, para. 58.
1541. Schlechtriem/Schwenzer/Schroeter/*Schwenzer*, 5th English ed., Art. 79 CISG, para. 58; cf. also *Guo*, p. 64.
1542. Cf. *Brunner*, pp. 439 et seq.
1543. *See* Ch. 5 III. 3. b. iii. 2) above; *Brunner*, pp. 440, 441.

Given that the issue of hardship under the CISG remains a point of contention and that the Convention does not impose an obligation to renegotiate, adapt or terminate the contract in the event of hardship, the parties to a long-term framework agreement are well advised to incorporate hardship clauses into their contract if they wish to have more flexible remedies and greater predictability in this regard.[1544] The incorporation of hardship clauses, which are particularly relevant if they are part of standard terms,[1545] is governed by the CISG (Arts 14–24 CISG).[1546] However, the validity of such clauses is governed by domestic law in accordance with Art. 4(a) CISG.[1547]

4) Pre-emption of Domestic Solutions

In light of the Convention's provisions (potentially) being triggered by a change in circumstances, and in view of the CISG comprehensively regulating the impact of these changed circumstances on the parties' obligations, it can be concluded that the Convention pre-empts domestic law in this matter;[1548] the factual and legal criterion under the two-step test are met.[1549] Accordingly, domestic concepts that may be relevant to the same facts, such as frustration of purpose, *clausula rebus sic stantibus* or *Wegfall der Geschäftsgrundlage* (§ 313 BGB), cannot be applied to contracts governed by the CISG,[1550] including long-term framework agreements.

c. *Summary*

Long-term framework agreements and other long-term contracts are particularly susceptible to changes in the surrounding circumstances. They may be confronted with supervening events which raise the issues of force majeure and hardship. The CISG covers cases of force majeure in Art. 79 CISG. This provision requires an impediment beyond control that is unforeseeable and unavoidable, causing one of the parties to fail to perform. In such a case, the obligor is exempted from their liability to pay damages. Furthermore, the obligee's right to demand specific performance is suspended or unenforceable during the impediment's existence, which follows from a purposive interpretation of Art. 79 CISG. Framework agreements and other long-term contracts

1544. Kröll *et al.*/*Atamer*, Art. 79 CISG, para. 94; MüKoBGB/*Huber*, Art. 79 CISG, para. 34; Staudinger/*Magnus*, Art. 79 CISG, para. 65.
1545. On the incorporation of standard terms under the CISG in detail: Schlechtriem/Schwenzer/Schroeter/*Schroeter*, 5th English ed., Art. 14 CISG, paras 125 et seq.
1546. MüKoBGB/*Huber*, Art. 79 CISG, para. 34; cf. also Schlechtriem/Schwenzer/Schroeter/*Schwenzer*, 5th English ed., Art. 79 CISG, para. 58.
1547. MüKoBGB/*Huber*, Art. 79 CISG, para. 34; MüKoHGB/*Sommerfeld*, Art. 79 CISG, para. 67; Staudinger/*Magnus*, Art. 79 CISG, para. 65; on validity under German law: *Hoffbauer*, pp. 138 et seq.
1548. Accord CISG-AC, Op. 20 *Muñoz*, Comment 2.3.; *Flechtner*, p. 8; *Honnold/Flechtner*, Art. 79 CISG, para. 579; Staudinger/*Magnus*, Art. 4 CISG, para. 59; *contra*: *Lookofsky*, (2011) 29 J. L. & Com., pp. 156 et seq.
1549. *See* Ch. 1 IV. 1. b. above.
1550. CISG-AC, Op. 20 *Muñoz*, Comment 2.3.; for an overview of domestic solutions: *Perillo*, (1997) 5 Tulane J. Int'l & Comp. L., pp. 6 et seq.; *Schwenzer*, (2008) 39 V.U.W. L. Rev., pp. 710, 711.

are equally subject to this provision, with the same prerequisites applying and the same consequences following. Nevertheless, long-term agreements frequently include force majeure clauses which modify or derogate from Art. 79 CISG. The parties are free to incorporate such clauses into their contract in accordance with Art. 6 CISG.

Although there is still some controversy, the prevailing and more persuasive view is that Art. 79 CISG should also apply to cases of hardship. This follows from the fact that it would be inconsistent to exempt the obligor in cases where overcoming a factual impediment or procuring the goods would be associated with exorbitant costs, but not in cases where overcoming economic circumstances would be equally associated with exorbitant costs. In addition, the wording of Art. 79 CISG is broad and can also cover cases of hardship.

It is necessary that there be a fundamental alteration of the contractual equilibrium. Moreover, the event causing the imbalance must be beyond the control of the obligor, unforeseeable and insurmountable.

While the threshold for hardship should be assessed on a case-by-case basis, there are certain elements that may be taken into account. In contrast to the view of some scholars, the contract's duration is not such an element that should be taken into account. Nevertheless, it is important to note that there are other peculiarities with regard to long-term framework agreements that should be considered. It is necessary to assess whether the parties to such a contract have explicitly or implicitly addressed a certain risk, which would leave no room for invoking hardship. In addition, the point of reference to determine whether there has been a fundamental alteration of the contractual equilibrium is the entire framework agreement, including past and future performances. Although this assessment must be conducted separately for a framework agreement with a two-tier structure and the individual sales contracts, the latter may still influence this determination since they may be considered a relevant circumstance for the interpretation of the framework agreement and vice versa.

Should these requirements be met, the obligor is exempt from any claims for damages and specific performance (during the impediment's existence). The CISG does not empower tribunals or courts to adapt or terminate contracts. Similarly, the parties are not obliged or entitled to adapt or terminate their contract in the event of hardship. Furthermore, the Convention does not impose a duty on the parties to renegotiate their contract. The primary reason for this is that Art. 79 CISG does not contain a gap, and therefore the legal remedies should follow from this provision itself and not from the principle of good faith (Art. 7(1) CISG), general principles (Art. 7(2) CISG) or usages (Art. 9(1) CISG).

It is, of course, open to the parties to voluntarily renegotiate, adapt or terminate their contract. Furthermore, the parties may incorporate hardship clauses into their long-term framework agreement. The incorporation of such clauses is subject to the CISG (Arts 14–24 CISG), whereas their validity is governed by the applicable domestic law (Art. 4(a) CISG).

4. Termination under the CISG Versus Domestic Law Rules

As time passes, one or both of the parties involved in a long-term supply relationship such as a framework agreement may become interested in terminating it.[1551] There are many potential reasons for this course of action; one such reason is that the parties involved may recognise that the premises on which their contractual relationship was established will not materialise in the near future.[1552] This raises the general question of what circumstances may allow the termination of framework agreements or other long-term contracts under the Convention. The following part will analyse the issue of termination of such contracts under the CISG. It will also consider the impact of domestic law rules that provide for a right to terminate long-term contracts and examine how these rules interact with the CISG's provisions.

a. *Termination by Expiration*

A long-term framework agreement may be constrained to a specific period of time, with the duration being defined by the parties involved.[1553] Under Swiss and German domestic law, any long-term contract is automatically terminated as soon as the defined time limit has elapsed.[1554] With regard to the length of the contractual duration, the parties must observe certain limitations imposed by various domestic law provisions. Overly extensive durations of a long-term framework agreement may give rise to concerns under domestic competition laws, the violation of morality (*Sittenwidrigkeit*) and (where applicable) the control of standard terms.[1555]

The Convention mentions contract termination in Art. 29(1) CISG which states that 'a contract may be modified or terminated by the mere agreement of the parties'.[1556] The existence of such an agreement must be determined in accordance with the Convention, notably Arts 8 and 14–24 CISG.[1557] If the parties establish a time limit for their long-term framework agreement, this may typically be interpreted as an indication that they anticipate the termination of their contract upon the expiration of this time limit. In essence, such a time limit may be regarded as an agreement to terminate the contract in the future, contingent upon the expiration of the time limit. There is nothing in Art. 29 CISG that would prevent this form of agreement to

1551. *See Lange*, NJOZ 2013, p. 577.
1552. *Lange*, NJOZ 2013, p. 577.
1553. High Ct. Singapore, 13 March 2019, CISG-online 4108, (clause (b) of the agreement); OLG Jena, 8 December 2015, CISG-online 2664; *Hoffbauer*, p. 190; *Gebhardt*, p. 28; *C. Meyer*, ZVertriebsR 2017, p. 15; Kull/Wildhaber/*Wildhaber*, paras 630 et seq.; *Muhl/Lüthge*, GWR 2016, p. 27.
1554. German law: *Hoffbauer*, p. 190; *Martinek*, p. 84; *Muhl/Lüthge*, GWR 2016, p. 27; Swiss law: *C. Meyer*, Alleinvertrieb, p. 332; *C. Meyer*, ZVertriebsR 2017, p. 14.
1555. With more detail: *Doralt*, pp. 295 et seq.; *Hoffbauer*, pp. 191 et seq.; Kull/Wildhaber/*Wildhaber*, paras 632, 633.
1556. With regard to the CISG's differentiation between contract termination (an agreement between the parties) and avoidance (a unilateral right to end a contract), *see*: Schlechtriem/Schwenzer/Schroeter/*Schroeter*, 5th English ed., Art. 29 CISG, para. 47.
1557. Schlechtriem/Schwenzer/Schroeter/*Schroeter*, 5th English ed., Art. 29 CISG, para. 10; *Schroeter*, para. 362.

terminate. It is therefore submitted that the parties to a long-term framework contract are at liberty to agree on termination by expiration in light of Art. 29 CISG. In any event, they are free to do so in line with Art. 6 CISG.[1558] However, the applicable domestic law governs the question of whether a specific contractual duration is admissible or appropriate, as the Convention is not concerned with this matter in the sense of Art. 4(a) CISG.[1559] The Convention's intention to be applicable to this set of facts may remain debatable; however, the Convention certainly does not aim to regulate the underlying issue concerning the contractual maximum binding period.

In addition to stipulating the duration of a long-term framework agreement, the parties may agree on a so-called renewal clause.[1560] Such clauses are usually incorporated in order to 'automatically' renew the contract as soon as its original duration expires.[1561] In this situation, the agreement is not terminated by expiration. Nevertheless, the parties may terminate the agreement under certain conditions (e.g., within a specific period),[1562] the exact prerequisites of which will depend on the specific clause agreed upon by the parties. The parties are free to agree on renewal clauses under the CISG. Their incorporation is subject to Arts 14–24 CISG, whereas their validity is governed by the applicable domestic law (Art. 4(a) CISG).[1563]

If the parties to a long-term framework agreement or any other long-term contract agree on a time limit for their agreement, Art. 73 CISG is not necessarily excluded.[1564] Although the parties may express their intention to exclude other possibilities to terminate or avoid the contract apart from the termination by expiration,[1565] it should still be possible to prematurely 'end' – i.e., unilaterally avoid – the contract if there is a particularly grave breach of contract.[1566] Consequently, Art. 73 CISG remains open to the parties provided that its requisite conditions are met.[1567]

1558. Cf. also CA Warsaw, 20 November 2008, CISG-online 2539.
1559. Staudinger/*Magnus*, Art. 73 CISG, para. 1; the maximum duration of a long-term framework agreement may be constrained by a number of domestic law rules, *see Hoffbauer*, pp. 191 et seq. (regarding German law).
1560. *See* CA Luxembourg, 27 January 2010, CISG-online 4887, para. 4, where the contract in question contained the following clause: 'This contract is fix and cannot be cancelled by one of the parties before end of contract period. Contract has to be cancelled in writing by one of the parties latest 12 months before end of contract duration. In case contract is not cancelled by one of the parties, contract will continue for one more year each.'; cf. also *Hoffbauer*, p. 195.
1561. CA Luxembourg, 27 January 2010, CISG-online 4887; *Hoffbauer*, p. 195.
1562. CA Luxembourg, 27 January 2010, CISG-online 4887; *Hoffbauer*, p. 195.
1563. Staudinger/*Magnus*, Art. 73 CISG, para. 1; with regard to the validity of renewal clauses under German law: *Hoffbauer*, p. 195.
1564. Staudinger/*Magnus*, Art. 73 CISG, para. 38; cf. also BeckOK/*Saenger*, Art. 73 CISG, para. 1.
1565. Cf. CA Warsaw, 20 November 2008, CISG-online 2539; *Hoffbauer*, p. 190.
1566. Staudinger/*Magnus*, Art. 73 CISG, para. 38.
1567. *See* Ch. 5 III. 5. b. below.

b. *General Right to Terminate an Indefinite Long-Term Contract*

In some instances, the parties to a long-term contract may fail to explicitly or implicitly define the contract's duration.[1568] Similarly, the parties may simply continue to perform their contractual obligations after the agreement has expired; alternatively, they may explicitly stipulate that the contract is of indefinite duration.[1569]

Under Swiss and German domestic law, scholars frequently hold that there is a general right to terminate any long-term contract with an indefinite duration.[1570] A similar right is also found in Art. 5.1.8 UPICC.[1571] This right is generally available to both parties under all types of long-term contracts with an indefinite duration.[1572] This right allows the parties to unilaterally terminate the indefinite contract, which must comply with certain time limitations.[1573] In contrast to the CISG's provisions, an agreement between the parties[1574] or a breach of contract[1575] is not a prerequisite for the general right to terminate the contract. This could potentially lead to a conflict between such domestic law provisions and the Convention

i. *The CISG's Position*

A number of commentators point out that the CISG does not provide for a general right of termination.[1576] The CISG indeed does not recognise such a right, nor does it (explicitly or implicitly) mention one in its provisions, and there is no underlying

1568. Comment 1 on Art. 5.1.8 UPICC; *Hoffbauer*, p. 196; *Lange*, NJOZ 2013, p. 579; *C. Meyer*, Jusletter 2 May 2016, para. 26; *C. Meyer*, ZVertriebsR 2017, p. 15.
1569. CA Warsaw, 15 May 2015, CISG-online 2783 (the contract in question was concluded for an indefinite period with a 12-month notice termination clause); Comment 1 on Art. 5.1.8 UPICC; *Gebhardt*, p. 28; *C. Meyer*, Alleinvertrieb, pp. 332, 333; *C. Meyer*, Jusletter 2 May 2016, para. 26; *C. Meyer*, ZVertriebsR 2017, p. 15.
1570. German law: *Hoffbauer*, pp. 196, 197; *Horn*, p. 573; *Lange*, NJOZ 2013, p. 579; *Oetker*, pp. 272 et seq.; *von Scheven*, p. 129; Swiss law: *C. Meyer*, Alleinvertrieb, pp. 334 et seq.; *C. Meyer*, ZVertriebsR 2017, p. 15.
1571. Art. 5.1.8 UPICC: 'A contract for an indefinite period may be terminated by either party by giving notice a reasonable time in advance.'; cf. also § 2-309(2) UCC: 'Where the contract provides for successive performances but is indefinite in duration it is valid for a reasonable time but unless otherwise agreed may be terminated at any time by either party.'
1572. Art. 5.1.8 UPICC (indefinite contract 'may be terminated by either party'); *Hoffbauer*, p. 196; *Oetker*, p. 275, adding that the end of the contract must not be susceptible to objective determination (e.g., through the fulfilment of a resolutive condition, etc.); with a more nuanced approach: *Doralt*, pp. 295 et seq.; drawing an analogy with regard to distribution contracts (which are not explicitly regulated in Swiss law): BSK OR-I/*Amstutz/Morin*, Einl. vor Arts 184 ff. CO, para. 123; *C. Meyer*, ZVertriebsR 2017, p. 15; cf. also § 2-309(2) UCC (indefinite contract 'may be terminated […] by either party'); Comment 1 on Art. 5.1.8 UPICC.
1573. *See* Art. 5.1.8 UPICC: 'by giving notice a reasonable time in advance'; cf. also § 2-309(3) UCC: 'Termination of a contract by one party […] requires that reasonable notification be received by the other party […]'; *Hoffbauer*, p. 196.
1574. Art. 29 CISG (termination).
1575. For example, Arts 49(1)(a) and 64(1)(a) CISG (in conjunction with Art. 25 CISG).
1576. BeckOGK/*Schmidt-Ahrendts*, Art. 73 CISG, para. 2.1; Brunner/*Brunner/Boog/Schläpfer*, Art. 73 CISG, para. 20; Brunner/Gottlieb/*Brunner/Schläpfer/Boog*, Art. 73 CISG, para. 20; Honsell/*Brunner/Hurni*, Art. 73 CISG, para. 9; MüKoHGB/*Sommerfeld*, Art. 73 CISG, para. 1; Staudinger/*Magnus*, Art. 73 CISG, para. 1.

general principle that would justify it. Consequently, the Convention itself does not entitle the parties to terminate an indefinite long-term contract.

However, it is possible to question whether this is a matter that the CISG regulates or whether there is room to have recourse to domestic law rules. The relevant question is whether this matter falls within the CISG's substantive scope. As stated above, this study relies on the two-step test to determine the limits of the Convention's substantive scope.[1577] Accordingly, the two-step test will be applied to assess whether domestic law rules that provide a right to terminate an indefinite long-term contract are superseded by the CISG or whether they should apply alongside the Convention. The first step in this test is to determine whether a factual situation triggers both the CISG and the relevant domestic law rules (the factual criterion).[1578] In a second step, it is necessary to assess whether the CISG addresses the particular risk in question in an exhaustive manner (the legal criterion).[1579] If both criteria are cumulatively met, the CISG will supersede the overlapping domestic law rules.[1580]

Both the CISG and the aforementioned domestic law rules cover factual situations in which one of the parties wishes to unilaterally sever ties under a long-term framework agreement or any other long-term contract that falls within the Convention's sphere of application. Therefore, the factual criterion is met. In a second step, the subject matter of the relevant domestic law rules must be contrasted with that of the CISG.[1581] In this context, it is important to note that the focus is on the subject matter of a regulation and not on the legal means by which it seeks to achieve this subject matter.[1582]

Upon initial examination, it would appear that the relevant domestic law rules refer to the termination of indefinite long-term contracts, which is a matter governed by the CISG. The Convention intends to comprehensively regulate the termination and avoidance of contracts within its sphere of application, thereby superseding any domestic law rules pertaining to that matter. It does not differentiate based on the duration of a contract. However, this approach would not sufficiently consider the regulatory matter of the relevant rules, according to this study. The general right to terminate long-term contracts with an indefinite duration, as recognised in some domestic laws and Art. 5.1.8 UPICC, is, *inter alia*, based on the consideration that the parties may not bind themselves indefinitely and that they should be able to opt out of an 'eternal' contract.[1583] Under Swiss and German law, an eternal contract may contravene the parties' personal rights and their economic freedom.[1584] In contrast, the

1577. *See* Ch. 1 IV. 1. b. above; in detail on the two-step test: *Schroeter*, (2013) 58 Vill. L. Rev., pp. 556 et seq.; *Schroeter*, paras 160 et seq.
1578. *Schroeter*, Vill. L. Rev. 2013, pp. 563, 564; *Schroeter*, paras 161 et seq.
1579. *Schroeter*, Vill. L. Rev. 2013, pp. 566 et seq.; *Schroeter*, paras 165 et seq.
1580. *Schroeter*, (2013) 58 Vill. L. Rev., p. 563.
1581. *Schroeter*, (2013) 58 Vill. L. Rev., p. 567; *Schroeter*, para. 165.
1582. *Schroeter*, para. 167 *in fine*.
1583. Cf. Comment 1 on Art. 5.1.8 UPICC; *Hoffbauer*, p. 196 (German law); *Oetker*, pp. 272 et seq., 460; *Schwenzer/Fountoulakis*, para. 32.24 (Swiss law); but *see Doralt*, pp. 295 et seq., employing a more nuanced approach in the context of German law.
1584. Under Swiss law this may constitute a violation of Art. 27 of the Swiss Civil Code, *see*: BGer, 21 June 1988, BGE 114 II 159; *Schwenzer/Fountoulakis*, para. 32.24; on German law: *Doralt*,

CISG does not seek to regulate the admissible duration of contractual bindings.[1585] Although domestic law rules that provide for a general right to terminate may relate to the avoidance or termination of a CISG contract, they are concerned with a substantive matter that the Convention does not attempt to regulate: the question of whether the parties may bind themselves indefinitely. Therefore, this study proposes that the general right to terminate indefinite long-term contracts should be applicable alongside the Convention, given that it falls outside the CISG's substantive scope (Art. 4(a) CISG).[1586]

With regard to other domestic law rules that provide for a general right to terminate long-term contracts based on a different regulatory objective, it may well be that they are superseded by the CISG.[1587] Once more, the two-step test must be employed in order to ascertain whether this is indeed the case.

ii. Contractual Agreements

Furthermore, the parties are at liberty to agree upon a general right to terminate a long-term contract (e.g., a framework agreement) that is governed by the CISG within specified time limits.[1588] For instance, in a case before the Court of Appeal Graz, a long-term framework agreement, *inter alia*, included a provision according to which each party had the right to terminate the contract within three months of the end of the month.[1589] The parties are free to include such clauses in their contract in accordance with Art. 6 CISG.[1590] Furthermore, the parties may agree on a right to terminate the contract in conjunction with a renewal clause; in such an instance, the contract will automatically renew itself if the parties do not terminate it within a specific period of time.[1591]

pp. 333 et seq., who enumerates four potential reasons that may contradict the existence of eternal contracts under certain circumstances, namely personal freedom, economic freedom of movement, public interests (e.g., protection of competition) and paternalistic protection; *Hoffbauer*, p. 196; *Iliou*, ZVertriebsR 2023, p. 82; *Oetker*, pp. 272, 275 (right of self-determination).

1585. Probably accord Staudinger/*Magnus*, Art. 73 CISG, para. 1 (the admissible duration of such contracts is a question of validity (Art. 4(a) CISG)).
1586. Staudinger/*Magnus*, Art. 73 CISG, para. 1.
1587. A number of commentators maintain that the CISG does not recognise a general right to terminate long-term contracts, without explicitly addressing the role of domestic law: BeckOGK/*Schmidt-Ahrendts*, Art. 73 CISG, para. 2.1; Brunner/*Brunner/Boog/Schläpfer*, Art. 73 CISG, para. 20; Brunner/Gottlieb/*Brunner/Schläpfer/Boog*, Art. 73 CISG, para. 20, mentioning that 'this stands in contrast to German or Swiss law'; Honsell/*Brunner/Hurni*, Art. 73 CISG, para. 9; MüKoHGB/*Sommerfeld*, Art. 73 CISG, para. 1; Staudinger/*Magnus*, Art. 73 CISG, para. 1.
1588. CA Warsaw, 15 May 2015, CISG-online 2783 (indefinite contract with a 12-month notice termination clause); cf. also BeckOGK/*Schmidt-Ahrendts*, Art. 73 CISG, para. 2.1; BeckOK/*Saenger*, Art. 73 CISG, para. 1; Staudinger/*Magnus*, Art. 73 CISG, para. 38.
1589. OLG Graz, 28 September 2000, CISG-online 798, para. 2 (clause 7b): '*Danach kann jede der Parteien den Vertrag mit einer Frist von drei Monaten zu Monatsende kündigen*'.
1590. Cf. OLG Graz, 28 September 2000, CISG-online 798, para. 42, although with regard to a different clause.
1591. CA Luxembourg, 27 January 2010, CISG-online 4887; cf. also *Martinek*, p. 84.

As is customary in such agreements, notices of termination are primarily subject to the 'default rule' enshrined in Art. 27 CISG (dispatch principle), unless the parties have agreed otherwise.[1592] The question of whether the parties have agreed otherwise is essentially a matter of contract interpretation under Art. 8 CISG.[1593] In this regard, a decision rendered by the Court of Appeal Luxembourg is illustrative.[1594] In that case, it was disputed whether the notice of termination was sent in a timely manner in accordance with a termination clause (more specifically, a renewal clause).[1595] As the clause did not specify the medium or method required for the submission of a notice of termination, the Court was confronted with the question of whether Art. 27 CISG shall apply.[1596] The Court concluded that the parties had derogated from this provision based on their contractual agreement and the surrounding circumstances (Art. 8 CISG), such that the timeliness of the termination notice was ultimately dependent on its receipt, rather than its dispatch.[1597]

Moreover, in instances where the parties have agreed on a specific notice period for a general right to terminate a long-term framework agreement that is subject to the CISG and French law, it is necessary to consider Art. 442-1(2) of the French Commercial Code. This is because a contractually agreed-upon notice period may be deemed to be objectively unreasonable when viewed in light of the criteria mentioned in Art. 442-1(2) of the French Commercial Code. Consequently, this may give rise to a claim for compensation based on the concept of '*rupture brutale*'.[1598]

c. *Termination for a Compelling Reason*

In addition to the general right to terminate indefinite long-term contracts, a so-called right to terminate for a compelling reason (or alternatively, 'right to terminate for just cause')[1599] is frequently discussed in the context of long-term framework agreements under domestic laws.[1600] The introduction of such a right was also discussed (but

1592. BeckOK/*Saenger*, Art. 27 CISG, para. 2; *Enderlein/Maskow*, Art. 27 CISG, note 4.1; *Herber/Czerwenka*, Art. 27 CISG, para. 6; MüKoBGB/*Gruber*, Art. 27 CISG, para. 8; Schlechtriem/Schwenzer/Schroeter/*Schroeter*, 5th English ed., Art. 27 CISG, para. 12; Staudinger/*Magnus*, Art. 27 CISG, para. 12.
1593. Schlechtriem/Schwenzer/Schroeter/*Schroeter*, 5th English ed., Art. 27 CISG, para. 12.
1594. CA Luxembourg, 27 January 2010, CISG-online 4887, para. 4: 'This contract is fix and cannot be cancelled by one of the parties before end of contract period. Contract has to be cancelled in writing by one of the parties latest 12 months before end of contract duration. In case contract is not cancelled by one of the parties, contract will continue for one more year each.'
1595. CA Luxembourg, 27 January 2010, CISG-online 4887.
1596. CA Luxembourg, 27 January 2010, CISG-online 4887, paras 24 et seq.
1597. CA Luxembourg, 27 January 2010, CISG-online 4887, paras 24 et seq.
1598. *See* Ch. 4 III. 2. c. iii. above.
1599. The UNIDROIT working group on long-term contracts selected the term 'termination for a compelling reason' (alternatively: 'termination for compelling reasons') over the term 'termination for (just) cause' on the grounds that the former term more accurately reflected the exceptional nature of this remedy, *see*: UNIDROIT 2015, Study L – Misc. 31, paras 76 et seq.
1600. Cf. only on Austrian domestic law: OGH, 12 July 2023, CISG-online 6628, para. 32; on Swiss domestic law: BSK OR-I/*Amstutz/Morin*, Einl. vor Arts 184 ff. CO, para. 124; CHK/*Jacobs*, Innominatverträge/AVV, para. 43; German domestic law: *Hoffbauer*, pp. 197 et seq.; *Lange*, NJOZ 2013, p. 580.

rejected) under the UPICC.[1601] In contrast, the Convention does not recognise a right to terminate long-term framework agreements or other long-term contracts for a compelling reason or for just cause, apart from its provisions on contract termination or avoidance. This may, once more, indicate a potential conflict between respective domestic law provisions and the provisions of the CISG.

i. *Discussions with Regard to the UPICC*

Prior to examining domestic laws, it is pertinent from an international perspective to consider the discussions with regard to the UPICC. These discussions, which spanned multiple occasions, addressed the question of whether the UPICC should introduce a general right to terminate any long-term contract for a compelling reason. Originally, this matter was discussed by a working group tasked with the preparation of the UPICC 2010 edition.[1602] However, the working group decided not to pursue this task and deferred it to a future edition of the UPICC.[1603] The issue was subsequently revisited by a working group on long-term contracts in 2014.[1604]

One of the primary considerations was that long-term contracts 'are subject not only to the usual risks of a breach by one of the parties or of supervening events making performance impossible or excessively more onerous, but also to the risk of an irreparable breakdown of the parties' mutual trust and confidence making the continuation of their relationship, at least for one of the parties, no longer sustainable'.[1605] In other words, it was agreed that this remedy was necessary since the provisions on force majeure, hardship and fundamental non-performance, which were already part of the UPICC, were considered to be inadequate in addressing the situation of irreparable harm to the relationship between parties to a long-term contract.[1606] Thus, the latest proposal issued by the working group on long-term contracts from 2016 suggested the addition of Art. 6.3.1 and 6.3.2 to Chapter 6 of the UPICC.[1607] The proposed Art. 6.3.1 UPICC contained a right to terminate a long-term contract for a compelling reason, while the proposed Art. 6.3.2 UPICC dealt with the effects of a termination for a compelling reason.[1608]

1601. In detail: *Guo*, (2018) 21 Int'l Trade & Bus. L. Rev., pp. 1 et seq.
1602. UNIDROIT 2007, Study L – Doc. 104, pp. 3 et seq.; UNIDROIT 2009, Study L – Doc. 109, pp. 1 et seq. ('Draft Chapter on Termination of Long Term Contracts for Just Cause').
1603. UNIDROIT 2009, Study L – Misc. 29, paras 105 et seq.; UNIDROIT 2014, Study L – Doc. 126, para. 42; *see also B. Köhler*, Long-term contracts, p. 157; *Dessemontet*, FS Schwenzer, pp. 396, 397.
1604. UNIDROIT 2014, Study L – Doc. 126, paras 41 et seq.; UNIDROIT 2015, Study L – Doc. 135, Annex 10; UNIDROIT 2016, Study L – Doc. 135 rev., Annex 10; UNIDROIT 2016, Study L – Misc. 32, paras 12 et seq.
1605. UNIDROIT 2014, Study L – Doc. 126, para. 41; cf. also UNIDROIT 2015, Study L – Doc. 135, Annex 10, Comment 2; UNIDROIT 2016, Study L – Doc. 135 rev., Annex 10, Comment 2.
1606. UNIDROIT 2016, Study L – Doc. 135 rev., Annex 10, Comment 2; cf. also *Dessemontet*, FS Schwenzer, pp. 398, 399.
1607. *See* UNIDROIT 2016, Study L – Misc. 32, para. 24; UNIDROIT 2016, Study L – Doc. 135 rev., Annex 10; previous draft: UNIDROIT 2015, Study L – Doc. 135, Annex 10.
1608. In detail UNIDROIT 2016, Study L – Doc. 135 rev., Annex 10.

However, in May 2016, the UNIDROIT Governing Council unexpectedly decided not to adopt the new provisions on termination for a compelling reason.[1609] A clear majority of the members of the Governing Council were against the introduction of these provisions.[1610] They reasoned that the introduction of a right to terminate for a compelling reason 'might be seen as a radical departure from established principles in many legal systems', thereby having a negative impact on the acceptance of the UPICC on a global scale.[1611] Moreover, it was argued that this right would potentially lead to abusive practices due to its ambiguity.[1612] In addition, it was noted that the introduction of similar provisions has been discussed but rejected in the past.[1613]

Nevertheless, the working group's endeavours demonstrate that it may be necessary to discuss the role of the right to terminate long-term contracts for a compelling reason in international commercial trade.[1614] The working group's considerations indicate that the right to terminate for a compelling reason may have a role to play even if a set of rules already addresses non-performance, force majeure and hardship, such as the UPICC or likewise the CISG.

ii. Swiss and German Domestic Law

Swiss and German domestic law both generally provide for a right to terminate long-term contracts for a compelling reason.[1615] While German domestic law addresses this issue explicitly in § 314 of the BGB, the right to terminate for a compelling reason is based on a general principle under Swiss law.[1616] In both jurisdictions, the continuation of the contractual relationship must be unreasonable ('*unzumutbar*') for one of

1609. UNIDROIT 2016, C.D. (95) Misc. 2, para. 5 (in contrast, the Governing Council decided to adopt all other amendments and additions to the UPICC recommended by the working group on long-term contracts); cf. also *Doralt*, p. 440.
1610. UNIDROIT 2016, C.D. (95) 15, pp. 13 et seq.; cf. also *Guo*, (2018) 21 Int'l Trade & Bus. L. Rev., pp. 5, 6.
1611. UNIDROIT 2016, C.D. (95) 15, pp. 13 et seq.
1612. UNIDROIT 2016, C.D. (95) 15, p. 14.
1613. UNIDROIT 2016, C.D. (95) 15, p. 14.
1614. Cf. also *Doralt*, p. 441; *Guo*, (2018) 21 Int'l Trade & Bus. L. Rev., p. 16; *B. Köhler*, Long-term contracts, p. 158.
1615. Swiss law: BGer, 5 June 1996, BGE 122 III 262, consid. 2a)aa); BGer, 5 April 2012, BGE 138 III 304, consid. 7; BSK OR-I/*Amstutz/Morin*, Einl. vor Arts 184 ff. CO, para. 124; CHK/*Jacobs*, Innominatverträge/AVV, para. 43; *C. Meyer*, Alleinvertrieb, pp. 338, 339; with a critical perspective on the general right to terminate distribution agreements for a compelling reason under Swiss law, *C. Meyer*, ZVertriebsR 2017, pp. 15 et seq.; German law: § 314 BGB; *Doralt*, pp. 409 et seq.; *Hoffbauer*, p. 197; *Lange*, NJOZ 2013, p. 580; *Martinek*, p. 87 (prior to the introduction of § 314 BGB); *Oetker*, pp. 265 et seq. (prior to the introduction of § 314 BGB); cf. also Art. 1211 French Code Civile; OGH, 12 July 2023, CISG-online 6628, para. 32 (Austrian domestic law).
1616. German law: § 314(1) BGB (unofficial translation): 'Each party may terminate a contract for the performance of a continuing obligation for a compelling reason without a notice period. There is a compelling reason if the terminating party, taking into account all the circumstances of the specific case and weighing the interests of both parties, cannot reasonably be expected to continue the contractual relationship until the agreed end or until the expiry of a notice period'; *see also Hoffbauer*, p. 197; *Lange*, NJOZ 2013, p. 580; Swiss law: BGer, 5 June 1996, BGE 122 III 262, consid. 2a)aa); BGer, 3 April 2002, BGE 128 III 428; BGer, 5 April 2012, BGE 138 III 304, consid. 7; BSK OR-I/*Amstutz/Morin*, Einl. vor Arts 184 ff. CO, para. 124;

the parties from an objective standpoint.[1617] The right of termination for a compelling reason is not subject to the same time limits as the general right to terminate a long-term contract with indefinite duration.[1618] Furthermore, it cannot be excluded by a contractual agreement between the parties; the right to terminate for a compelling reason is mandatory under both Swiss and German domestic law.[1619] The parties may merely limit or extend the right as long as it is not completely undermined.[1620] They may also include an illustrative, exemplary (but not exhaustive) list of compelling reasons in their agreement.[1621]

The right to terminate long-term contracts for a compelling reason, specifically with regard to long-term supply contracts or framework agreements, has been discussed and affirmed in the following cases: in general, a party is entitled to terminate a long-term contract if there are particularly grave or repeated breaches of contract.[1622] In the event of a two-tier framework agreement, the aggrieved party may also be entitled to avoid the framework agreement if one or multiple individual sales contracts have been breached in a grave or repeated manner.[1623] Furthermore, a right to terminate for a compelling reason has also been affirmed in the case of one of the parties to a distribution contract – i.e., a framework agreement – falling into bankruptcy.[1624] Moreover, a party may rely on the right to terminate a long-term contract for a compelling reason if the contractual equilibrium has been fundamentally altered due to the occurrence of unforeseeable and uncontrollable events or circumstances, which may also fall under the category of economic hardship.[1625] Additionally, a right to

CHK/*Jacobs*, Innominatverträge/AVV, para. 43; *C. Meyer*, Alleinvertrieb, pp. 338, 339; *Schwenzer/Fountoulakis*, para. 3.27; Kull/Wildhaber/*Wildhaber*, para. 658 (on distribution contracts).

1617. § 314(1) BGB; *Doralt*, pp. 413, 414; *Lange*, NJOZ 2013, p. 580; BGer, 5 June 1996, BGE 122 III 262, consid. 2a)aa); BGer, 3 April 2002, BGE 128 III 428, consid. 3c) and 4; BGer, 5 April 2012, BGE 138 III 304, consid. 7; *C. Meyer*, Alleinvertrieb, p. 339; *Oetker*, pp. 264, 265.

1618. Cf. § 314(1) BGB; *Hoffbauer*, p. 198; BGer, 5 April 2012, BGE 138 III 304, consid. 7; *Oetker*, p. 264; but *see Doralt*, pp. 424 et seq.; Kull/Wildhaber/*Wildhaber*, para. 659.

1619. BGer, 22 January 1963, BGE 89 II 35, consid. 5a); CHK/*Jacobs*, Innominatverträge/AVV, para. 43; *Doralt*, p. 411; *Hoffbauer*, p. 198; *Iliou*, ZVertriebsR 2023, p. 82; *Martinek*, p. 88; *C. Meyer*, Alleinvertrieb, p. 340; cf. also Honsell/*Brunner/Hurni*, Art. 73 CISG, para. 9.

1620. *Hoffbauer*, pp. 198, 199; *Doralt*, p. 411; *see also* BGer, 22 January 1963, BGE 89 II 35, consid. 5a); *C. Meyer*, Alleinvertrieb, pp. 340, 341.

1621. BGer, 22 January 1963, BGE 89 II 35, consid. 5a); *Hoffbauer*, pp. 199 et seq.; *Doralt*, p. 411; Kull/Wildhaber/*Wildhaber*, paras 650, 660.

1622. BGer, 5 April 2012, BGE 138 III 304, consid. 7; *Hoffbauer*, pp. 200, 201; *Lange*, NJOZ 2013, p. 581; *Martinek*, p. 89; a comparable case group (termination based on the other party's conduct) is also referenced by Brunner/*Brunner/Boog/Schläpfer*, Art. 73 CISG, para. 20; Brunner/Gottlieb/*Brunner/Schläpfer/Boog*, Art. 73 CISG, para. 20; with regard to breaches of contract as compelling reason under § 314 BGB: *Doralt*, pp. 416 et seq.; MüKoBGB/*Gaier*, § 314 BGB, paras 26 et seq.

1623. *Hoffbauer*, p. 116; *C. Meyer*, Alleinvertrieb, pp. 342 et seq.

1624. BSK OR-I/*Amstutz/Morin*, Einl. vor Arts 184 ff. CO, para. 124; CHK/*Jacobs*, Innominatverträge/AVV, para. 43; *Hoffbauer*, p. 201; cf. also *Lange*, NJOZ 2013, p. 581.

1625. *Lange*, NJOZ 2013, p. 581; MüKoBGB/*Gaier*, § 314 BGB, paras 32 et seq., analysing the relationship between § 313 and § 314 BGB; cf. also the case group (termination based on change of circumstances) proposed by Brunner/*Brunner/Boog/Schläpfer*, Art. 73 CISG, para. 21; Brunner/Gottlieb/*Brunner/Schläpfer/Boog*, Art. 73 CISG, para. 21; Honsell/*Brunner/Hurni*, Art. 73 CISG, para. 9.

terminate for a compelling reason has been affirmed if any long-term contract requires intensive cooperation between the parties and there has been a serious disruption of the personal relationship between the parties.[1626]

iii. The CISG's Position

The CISG does not explicitly address the issue of a general right to terminate for a compelling reason beyond its provisions on contract termination and avoidance.[1627] Similarly, there is no indication to suggest that there is a general principle in the sense of Art. 7(2) CISG that provides for such a right.[1628] Once more, it is possible to question whether the CISG even regulates this matter at all, or whether there is room to have recourse to domestic law in this regard.

1) Distinguishing Between Different Cases

In order to ascertain whether the aforementioned domestic rules on termination for a compelling reason are superseded by the CISG, the two-step test will again be applied.[1629] Accordingly, it will be determined whether the factual and legal criteria have been met.[1630]

The right to terminate for a compelling reason, as provided for in Swiss and German domestic law, generally requires that the continuation of the contractual relationship would be unreasonable (*'unzumutbar'*) for one of the parties from an objective standpoint.[1631] While the ultimate determination of this assessment must be based on the specific circumstances of each case, certain cases have been identified as typically qualifying as compelling reasons.[1632] Given the broad range of cases covered by the right to terminate for a compelling reason under domestic law, it appears to be more accurate to address these cases separately in applying the two-step test. Thus, this study will distinguish between different case groups in order to determine whether domestic law rules that include a right to terminate for a compelling reason are superseded by the CISG.

a) Breaches of Contract

A right to terminate a long-term supply contract or framework agreement for a compelling reason has been affirmed under Swiss and German domestic law in the

1626. BeckOK/*Lorenz*, § 314 BGB, para. 14; *Doralt*, pp. 419 et seq., who references the case group 'lost and ruined trust' (*'Verlorenes und zerstörtes Vertrauen'*).
1627. OGH, 12 July 2023, CISG-online 6628, para. 27.
1628. But *see* OGH, 12 July 2023, CISG-online 6628, paras 27 et seq.
1629. *See* Ch. 1 IV. 1. b. above.
1630. In detail: *Schroeter*, (2013) 58 Vill. L. Rev., pp. 563 et seq.; *Schroeter*, paras 160 et seq.
1631. § 314(1) BGB; *Doralt*, pp. 413, 414; *Lange*, NJOZ 2013, p. 580; BGer, 5 June 1996, BGE 122 III 262, consid. 2a)aa); BGer, 3 April 2002, BGE 128 III 428, consid. 3c) and 4; BGer, 5 April 2012, BGE 138 III 304, consid. 7; *C. Meyer*, Alleinvertrieb, p. 339; *Oetker*, pp. 264, 265.
1632. BeckOK/*Lorenz*, § 314 BGB, para. 12.

event of particularly grave or repeated breaches of contract.[1633] The CISG and the domestic law rules both address the situation in which one of the parties to a long-term framework agreement commits breaches of contract and the opposing party wishes to avoid the contract; the factual criterion is met.

The Austrian Supreme Court reached a similar conclusion in a case where one of the questions was whether the Austrian seller was entitled to terminate a distribution agreement governed by the CISG based on the Belgian buyer's violation of a confidentiality obligation.[1634] In its assessment, the Court made reference to the CISG's provisions (e.g., Arts 73(2), 49(1)(a) and 25 CISG), as well as the right to terminate for a compelling reason under Austrian domestic law.[1635] This confirms that the factual criterion was indeed met. However, the Court did not elaborate on the relationship between these rules. It simply held that there was insufficient evidence to grant a provisional measure in favour of the seller[1636] without discussing the legal criterion under the two-step test. The following section aims to fill this lacuna and to elucidate the legal criterion in the cases discussed here.

i) Framework Agreements Containing Sales Obligations

If long-term framework agreements, such as distribution contracts, already contain the defining characteristics of a sales contract, i.e., sales obligations in *sensu stricto*, they may be characterised as instalment contracts in the sense of Art. 73 CISG.[1637] In such cases, Art. 73 CISG addresses situations in which one of the parties wishes to avoid an instalment contract based on one or multiple breaches of contract committed by the other party.[1638]

Art. 73(2) CISG particularly grants the aggrieved party the right to avoid the contract *ex nunc* if there are grounds for the assumption that a future fundamental breach of contract will occur based on a current breach of contract.[1639] Such grounds

1633. BGer, 5 April 2012, BGE 138 III 304, consid. 7; *Doralt*, pp. 416 et seq.; *Hoffbauer*, pp. 200, 201; *Lange*, NJOZ 2013, p. 581; a similar case group (termination based on the other party's conduct) is also mentioned by Brunner/*Brunner/Boog/Schläpfer*, Art. 73 CISG, para. 20; Brunner/Gottlieb/*Brunner/Schläpfer/Boog*, Art. 73 CISG, para. 20; cf. also OGH, 12 July 2023, CISG-online 6628, para. 32; *Dessemontet*, FS Schwenzer, p. 403.

1634. OGH, 12 July 2023, CISG-online 6628, paras 20 et seq.

1635. OGH, 12 July 2023, CISG-online 6628, paras 27 et seq.

1636. OGH, 12 July 2023, CISG-online 6628, para. 34; it is important to note that this decision was subsequently overturned by the Austrian Supreme Court, which considered there to be sufficient evidence to grant a provisional measure in favour of the seller. However, the Supreme Court did not elaborate further on the relationship between the CISG and domestic law, *see* OGH, 21 November 2023, CISG-online 6656, paras 14 et seq.

1637. *Grieser*, pp. 125, 132, 133; Mankowski/*Dornis*, Art. 73 CISG, para. 3 (referring to distribution agreements); MüKoHGB/*Sommerfeld*, Art. 73 CISG, para. 4; *Newhouse/Tanaka*, R.L.R. 2012, p. 18 (referring to distribution agreements); Schlechtriem/Schwenzer/Schroeter/*Fountou lakis*, 5th English ed., Art. 73 CISG, para. 8; Schlechtriem/Schwenzer/Schroeter/*Fountoulakis*, 8th German ed., Art. 73 CISG, para. 9; Staudinger/*Magnus*, Art. 73 CISG, para. 7.

1638. Brunner/*Brunner/Boog/Schläpfer*, Art. 73 CISG, para. 20; Brunner/Gottlieb/*Brunner/Schläpfer/Boog*, Art. 73 CISG, para. 20; cf. also *Grunewald*, p. 85; Honsell/*Brunner/Hurni*, Art. 73 CISG, para. 9.

1639. Cf. Brunner/*Brunner/Boog/Schläpfer*, Art. 73 CISG, para. 20; Brunner/Gottlieb/*Brunner/Schläpfer/Boog*, Art. 73 CISG, para. 20; Honsell/*Brunner/Hurni*, Art. 73 CISG, para. 9; in detail

may exist if one of the parties commits a series of non-fundamental breaches of contract with regard to several individual deliveries.[1640] In this context, *Grunewald* correctly asserts that this provision encompasses an essential group of cases that would fall within the scope of the right to terminate for a compelling reason under German law.[1641] Consequently, Art. 73(2) CISG effectively contains a functional equivalent to domestic law rules that provide for a right to terminate for a compelling reason in the event of breaches of contract.[1642] A particularly grave breach of contract with regard to a single individual delivery may entitle the aggrieved party to avoid the contract with respect to this specific instalment under Art. 73(1) CISG, provided that it is fundamental in the sense of Art. 25 CISG.[1643] In certain instances, such a grave breach may also satisfy the criteria set forth in Art. 73(2) CISG if it allows for the prediction of a future fundamental breach of contract.[1644] Furthermore, if one or multiple breaches of contract constitute a fundamental breach of the entire framework agreement, the aggrieved party may also be able to invoke Art. 49 or 64 CISG.[1645]

The CISG, thus, addresses the risk of a continuation of the contractual relationship becoming unreasonable for one of the parties due to one or multiple breaches of contract.[1646] In light of the fulfilment of both criteria under the two-step test, the Convention supersedes any domestic law rule that provides for a right to terminate a long-term framework agreement containing sales obligations for a compelling reason based on breaches of contract.[1647] If the prerequisites of the CISG's provisions on

on Art. 73(2) CISG: Schlechtriem/Schwenzer/Schroeter/*Fountoulakis*, 5th English ed., Art. 73 CISG, paras 20 et seq.; Staudinger/*Magnus*, Art. 73 CISG, paras 17 et seq.

1640. Bianca/Bonell/*Benett*, Art. 73 CISG, note 2.7.; MüKoHGB/*Sommerfeld*, Art. 73 CISG, para. 11; Schlechtriem/Schwenzer/Schroeter/*Fountoulakis*, 5th English ed., Art. 73 CISG, para. 21; Staudinger/*Magnus*, Art. 73 CISG, para. 18; cf. also CA Grenoble, 22 February 1995, CISG-online 151.

1641. *Grunewald*, p. 85: '*Damit erfasst die Norm eine wesentliche Fallgruppe der Kündigung aus wichtigem Grund nach deutschem Recht*'.

1642. Cf. also Brunner/Gottlieb/*Brunner/Schläpfer/Boog*, Art. 73 CISG, para. 20; Brunner/*Brunner/Boog/Schläpfer*, Art. 73 CISG, para. 20, suggesting to have recourse to Art. 73 CISG in matters that would fall under the right to terminate for a compelling reason under domestic law.

1643. Cf. on this prerequisite: BeckOK/*Saenger*, Art. 73 CISG, para. 4; Kröll *et al./Saidov*, Art. 73 CISG, para. 10; MüKoBGB/*Huber*, Art. 73 CISG, para. 6; Schlechtriem/Schwenzer/Schroeter/*Fountoulakis*, 5th English ed., Art. 73 CISG, paras 12 et seq.; Staudinger/*Magnus*, Art. 73 CISG, para. 12.

1644. Cf. HGer Zürich, 5 February 1997, CISG-online 327 (good grounds to conclude that a future fundamental breach of contract is likely to occur, given the seller's failure to make the initial delivery).

1645. Cf. *Honnold/Flechtner*, Art. 73 CISG, para. 531; Staudinger/*Magnus*, Art. 73 CISG, para. 1.

1646. Cf. also ICC, 11849/2003, CISG-online 1421: in this case, the sole arbitrator was, *inter alia*, tasked with determining whether the Convention regulates the termination of a distribution agreement governed by the CISG based on a breach of the payment obligation. The arbitrator rejected the buyer's argument that Italian domestic law should be applied to this question and instead relied on the CISG's provisions. However, they ultimately concluded that the seller was not entitled to terminate the distribution agreement under the Convention; OLG Hamburg, 14 December 1994, CISG-online 216, para. 55 ('*Art. 49 UN-KaufR regelt das Recht zu Vetragsaufhebung unter Anknüpfung an die Verletzung vertraglicher Pflichten umfassend*').

1647. Differently, *Karollus*, p. 162, who asserts that Art. 73 CISG does not generally supersede the right to terminate for a compelling reason as known under Austrian law.

avoidance, in particular Art. 73 CISG, are not met, there is no room for an additional right to avoid or terminate such a framework agreement governed by the CISG.[1648]

ii) Framework Agreements with a Two-Tier Structure

The situation becomes more complex when considering framework agreements with a two-tier structure, which merely oblige the parties to conclude individual sales contracts. In such cases, it is necessary to distinguish between the framework agreement and the individual sales contracts that are subsequently concluded.[1649] If the framework agreement itself is breached, the CISG once again determines whether the contract may be avoided based on any breaches of contract (e.g., grave or repeated breaches of contract), most notably in Arts 49 and 64 CISG. Consequently, the risk of breaches of contract is exhaustively governed by the CISG.[1650] Thus, the legal criterion is met.

However, it is necessary to distinguish another group of cases from the previous one. In a typical situation, the aggrieved party may wish to avoid the framework agreement if the breaching party commits a particularly 'grave' breach of an individual sales contract or repeated breaches of the individual sales contracts.[1651] As the aggrieved party would normally be obliged under the framework agreement to conclude further individual sales contracts in the future, they may wish to not only avoid the individual sales contracts that have been breached but also the framework agreement.[1652] Nevertheless, a breach of sales obligations under the individual sales contracts does not typically violate the obligations set out in the framework agreement, as it merely binds the parties to conclude individual sales contracts without containing any actual sales obligations.[1653] However, there appears to be agreement under German and Swiss domestic law that the aggrieved party may be entitled to terminate a framework agreement for a compelling reason if the individual sales contracts have

1648. Cf. also Brunner/*Brunner/Boog/Schläpfer*, Art. 73 CISG, para. 20; Brunner/Gottlieb/*Brunner/Schläpfer/Boog*, Art. 73 CISG, para. 20.
1649. With regard to this two-tier structure: Art. 1111 French Cc; OLG München, 18 June 2018, CISG-online 3080; Supr. Ct. Italy, 20 September 2004, CISG-online 1015; OLG Düsseldorf, 11 July 1996, CISG-online 201; BeckOGK/*Möslein*, § 145 BGB, para. 79; BK OR/*Kramer*, Art. 22 CO, para. 76; BSK OR-I/*Zellweger-Gutknecht*, Vor Art. 1-40f CO, para. 40; BSK OR-I/*Zellweger-Gutknecht*, Art. 22 CO, para. 29; *Bucher*, p. 109; *Budde/Geks*, ZVertriebsR 2012, p. 37; *Furrer/Lohri*, pp. 23, 24; *Gass/Lange*, pp. 14, 15; *Henrich*, p. 117; *Hoffbauer*, p. 6; Jauernig/*Stadler*, § 311 BGB, para. 22; KuKo OR/*Herzog*, Art. 22 CO, para. 7; Martinek/Semler/Flohr/*Budde/Eckhoff*, § 40, para. 9; *Muhl/Lüthge*, GWR 2016, p. 26; *Schlechtriem/Butler*, para. 24a; *Ulmer*, p. 300; *von der Crone*, pp. 245, 246; *Weber*, ZSR 1987, p. 410; ZK OR/*Schönle*, Art. 184 CO, para. 104; ZK OR/*Schönle*, Vorbem. Arts 184–551 CO, para. 32.
1650. Probably accord Brunner/*Brunner/Boog/Schläpfer*, Art. 73 CISG, para. 20; Brunner/Gottlieb/*Brunner/Schläpfer/Boog*, Art. 73 CISG, para. 20; Honsell/*Brunner/Hurni*, Art. 73 CISG, para. 9; cf. also *Schlechtriem*, Lausanner Kolloquium, p. 162.
1651. *Hoffbauer*, pp. 115, 116.
1652. Cf. *Hoffbauer*, pp. 115, 116.
1653. Cf. *Fuchs-Wissemann*, pp. 220, 221; *Hoffbauer*, pp. 114, 115; cf. also BGH, 23 July 1997, CISG-online 276, where the Court ruled that the invalidity of the framework agreement does not affect the validity of the individual sales contracts.

been breached in a serious or repeated manner.[1654] The rationale for this position is that such breaches of the individual sales contracts may result in a loss of trust, which is deemed to be a compelling reason to terminate the framework agreement.[1655]

In such cases, the factual criterion is met. With regard to the legal criterion under the two-step approach, it might be concluded once more that the risk of breaches of contract is exhaustively governed by the CISG. However, the cases to be analysed here differ in certain aspects: primarily, the avoidance of a framework agreement is based on the breach of another contract, namely, breaches of the individual sales contracts. It is uncertain whether the CISG regulates the consequences of 'cross-contractual' breaches of contract, and if so, to what extent. More importantly, domestic law rules that permit termination for a compelling reason in such instances are based on a loss of trust, rendering the continuation of the framework agreement unreasonable;[1656] they are not (merely) linked to a breach of the framework agreement, which arguably does not even occur.[1657] It is submitted that the CISG does not address the risk of loss of trust within a contractual relationship, particularly in instances where such a loss is not exclusively attributable to a breach of the contract in question. In response, one might argue that the Convention may consider such circumstances to be irrelevant and therefore insufficient grounds to sever ties under a contractual relationship.[1658] However, it appears more probable that the CISG simply does not intend to regulate the loss of trust within a contractual relationship, particularly in the absence of a breach of contract.[1659] Consequently, the legal criterion is not met. It is not appropriate for the CISG to supersede domestic law rules that permit the termination of a contract for a compelling reason in such circumstances.

b) Insolvency

Furthermore, the right to terminate a long-term framework agreement for a compelling reason has been affirmed if one of the parties has fallen into insolvency or bankruptcy.[1660] The CISG and the relevant domestic law rules are both triggered when a party to an international long-term framework agreement becomes insolvent and the other party then seeks to withdraw from the contract. Thus, the factual criterion under the two-step test is met.

1654. *Fuchs-Wissemann*, p. 221; *Hoffbauer*, p. 116; *Gebhardt*, pp. 43, 44; *C. Meyer*, Alleinvertrieb, pp. 342, 343; *Saxinger*, pp. 176, 177; cf. also Kull/Wildhaber/*Wildhaber*, para. 660 (with regard to distribution contracts).

1655. *See Fuchs-Wissemann*, p. 221; *Hoffbauer*, p. 116; *Saxinger*, p. 176; cf. also *Gebhardt*, pp. 43, 44 (endangerment of the contract's purpose).

1656. Cf. *Fuchs-Wissemann*, p. 221; *Hoffbauer*, p. 116; *Saxinger*, p. 176.

1657. But *see Fuchs-Wissemann*, p. 221 and *Saxinger*, p. 176, maintaining that a breach of the individual sales contracts necessarily constitutes a breach of the framework agreement; cf. also *Hoffbauer*, p. 116 (more guardedly).

1658. Similarly *Schlechtriem*, Lausanner Kolloquium, p. 162.

1659. Cf. *Doralt*, pp. 441 et seq., who notes that the UPICC does not extend coverage to cases of loss of trust (without a breach of contract) that would fall under § 314 BGB.

1660. BSK OR-I/*Amstutz/Morin*, Einl. vor Arts 184 ff. CO, para. 124; CHK/*Jacobs*, Innominatverträge/AVV, para. 43; Kull/Wildhaber/*Wildhaber*, paras 650, 660; cf. also *Hoffbauer*, p. 201, arguing that even the commencement of insolvency proceedings suffices; *Lange*, NJOZ 2013, p. 581.

The risk of insolvency is addressed in a number of provisions of the Convention. First, the opening of insolvency proceedings may constitute 'a serious deficiency [...] in his creditworthiness' in the sense of Art. 71(1)(a) CISG.[1661] This provision confers upon one of the parties the right to suspend their performance 'if, after contract conclusion, it becomes apparent that other party will not perform a substantial part of his obligations' due to a substantial deficiency in their creditworthiness.[1662] Consequently, the CISG stipulates that a right of suspension may be exercised if one of the parties becomes insolvent or bankrupt.

Moreover, it is necessary to consider the relationship between Art. 71 CISG and Arts 72 and 73 CISG.[1663] Art. 72(1) CISG stipulates that each party may declare the contract avoided if, prior to performance, it is clear that the other party will commit a fundamental breach of contract (anticipatory breach of contract). The prevailing view is that the insolvency of one party may constitute potential grounds for such a future breach of contract, which entitles the other party to avoid the contract.[1664] If the insolvent party has already committed a breach of contract, e.g., by not paying outstanding invoices, Art. 73(2) CISG may be applicable.[1665] The current breach of contract in conjunction with the breaching party's insolvency may be regarded as 'good grounds to conclude that a fundamental breach of contract will occur', thereby entitling the other party to avoid the long-term contract *ex nunc* in accordance with Art. 73(2) CISG.[1666] However, in the absence of a current breach of contract, a party may not rely on the opposing party's lack of creditworthiness or inability to pay under Art. 73(2) CISG, given that this provision necessitates the existence of a breach of contract.[1667]

1661. OGH, 12 February 1998, CISG-online 349; Brunner/Gottlieb/*Brunner/Berchtold*, Art. 71 CISG, para. 22; Mankowski/*Dornis*, Art. 71 CISG, para. 11; MüKoBGB/*Huber*, Art. 71 CISG, para. 8; MüKoHGB/*Sommerfeld*, Art. 71 CISG, para. 14; Schlechtriem/Schwenzer/Schroeter/*Fountoulakis*, 5th English ed., Art. 71 CISG, para. 23; Staudinger/*Magnus*, Art. 71 CISG, para. 25.
1662. With regard to the requirements under Art. 71 CISG, cf. only Brunner/Gottlieb/*Brunner/Berchtold*, Art. 71 CISG, paras 17 et seq.; Schlechtriem/Schwenzer/Schroeter/*Fountoulakis*, 5th English ed., Art. 71 CISG, paras 18 et seq.; Staudinger/*Magnus*, Art. 71 CISG, paras 14 et seq.
1663. Schlechtriem/Schwenzer/Schroeter/*Fountoulakis*, 5th English ed., Art. 71 CISG, para. 3.
1664. Brunner/Gottlieb/*Brunner/Altenkirch*, Art. 72 CISG, para. 6; MüKoBGB/*Huber*, Art. 72 CISG, para. 9; MüKoHGB/*Sommerfeld*, Art. 72 CISG, para. 8; *Schlechtriem*, Lausanner Kolloquium, pp. 157 et seq.; Schlechtriem/Schwenzer/Schroeter/*Fountoulakis*, 5th English ed., Art. 72 CISG, para. 13; Staudinger/*Magnus*, Art. 72 CISG, para. 11; with the same result but (questionably) relying on Art. 64 in conjunction with Art. 25 CISG: *Roder Zelt- und Hallenkonstruktionen GmbH v. Rosedown Park Pty Ltd*, Federal Ct. of Australia, 28 April 1995, CISG-online 281; but *see* Kröll *et al.*/*Saidov*, Art. 72 CISG, para. 9.
1665. With regard to the distinction between Art. 73(2) and Art. 72 CISG: BeckOGK/*Schmidt-Ahrendts*, Art. 73 CISG, para. 31; Schlechtriem/Schwenzer/Schroeter/*Fountoulakis*, 5th English ed., Art. 73 CISG, para. 32.
1666. Cf. Schlechtriem/Schwenzer/Schroeter/*Fountoulakis*, 5th English ed., Art. 73 CISG, para. 21: 'Sporadic delays in delivery or payment may constitute good grounds for a future fundamental breach if [...] there are other disturbing factors that indicate that the debtor will commit a fundamental breach with regard to future instalments'; but *see* Bianca/Bonell/*Bennett*, Art. 73 CISG, note 3.3., who is sceptical as to whether bankruptcy can be considered good grounds for the purposes of Art. 73(2) CISG.
1667. MüKoHGB/*Sommerfeld*, Art. 73 CISG, para. 11.

In light of the aforementioned considerations, it can be concluded that the CISG addresses the risk of one party becoming insolvent in a number of provisions, which provide for a right of suspension and a right to avoid the contract if certain prerequisites are met. Consequently, the CISG aims to regulate these matters in an exhaustive manner. Therefore, the legal criterion under the two-step test is also met. As both criteria are met, the CISG supersedes domestic law rules which allow for the termination of a long-term framework agreement or any other long-term contract for a compelling reason in cases of insolvency.[1668]

c) Economic Hardship

The right to terminate a contract for a compelling reason under domestic law has also been discussed in cases of fundamental alteration of the contractual equilibrium.[1669] Thus, this right may also be available in cases that have been referenced above under the notion of economic hardship.[1670] The CISG and the aforementioned domestic law rules are both triggered by a situation where the economic circumstances surrounding a long-term framework agreement change significantly. Consequently, the factual criterion is met.

As discussed above,[1671] the CISG provides a comprehensive regulation of the impact of changed economic circumstances on the parties' obligations, primarily in Art. 79 CISG.[1672] According to this provision and its underlying rationale, the obligor may be exempted from any claims for damages and specific performance, provided that the requisite conditions are met.[1673] However, the Convention does not empower tribunals or courts to adapt or terminate the contract in such cases. Similarly, the parties are not obliged to adapt or terminate their contract in the event of hardship.[1674] As the Convention addresses the risks of changed economic circumstances, the legal criterion is also fulfilled. Consequently, there is no room to invoke domestic law rules that provide for a right to terminate a long-term framework agreement for a compelling reason in such cases.

Furthermore, *Brunner, Schläpfer* and *Boog* propose that in cases 'where the desire to terminate is based on the circumstances (e.g., cases of *clausula rebus sic stantibus*), interpretation of the contract or contractual gap-filling according to the parties'

1668. Cf. also *Schlechtriem*, Lausanner Kolloquium, p. 153, arguing that there is no room to invoke domestic law remedies in cases that fall under Art. 71 CISG.
1669. *Lange*, NJOZ 2013, p. 581; MüKoBGB/*Gaier*, § 314 BGB, paras 32 et seq.; cf. also the case group (termination based on change of circumstances) referenced by Brunner/*Brunner/Boog/Schläpfer*, Art. 73 CISG, para. 21; Brunner/Gottlieb/*Brunner/Schläpfer/Boog*, Art. 73 CISG, para. 21; nevertheless, a distinction has been proposed under the UPICC, *see* UNIDROIT 2016, Study L – Doc. 135 rev., Annex 10, Comment 2 and Illustration 3.
1670. MüKoBGB/*Gaier*, § 314 BGB, para. 33; but *see* BeckOK/*Lorenz*, § 314 BGB, para. 7, proposing a distinction between §§ 313 and 314 BGB.
1671. *See* Ch. 5 III. 3. above.
1672. Accord CISG-AC, Op. 20 *Muñoz*, Comment 2.3.; *Flechtner*, p. 8; *Honnold/Flechtner*, Art. 79 CISG, para. 579; Staudinger/*Magnus*, Art. 4 CISG, para. 59; *contra*: *Lookofsky*, (2011) 29 J. L. & Com., pp. 156 et seq.
1673. Brunner/*Brunner/Boog/Schläpfer*, Art. 73 CISG, para. 21; Brunner/Gottlieb/*Brunner/Schläpfer/Boog*, Art. 73 CISG, para. 21.
1674. *See* Ch. 5 III. 3. b. iv. above.

hypothetical intent may lead to an appropriate solution (cf. Art. 8)'.[1675] They argue that the determining court should inquire as to what avoidance or termination clause the parties would have agreed upon at the time of contract conclusion had they foreseen the subsequent developments.[1676] However, this view is not entirely persuasive for two main reasons. Primarily, this approach would exceed the boundaries of judicial contract supplementation under the Convention. While judicial supplementation of a contract may be permissible under the CISG, it is essential to observe certain limits.[1677] A contract governed by the CISG should be supplemented solely through dispositive law, usages and practices, general principles in the sense of Art. 7(2) CISG or an *ex aequo et bono* decision of a court or tribunal, provided that the court or tribunal is authorised to do so.[1678] A right to terminate the contract for a compelling reason in the event of changed circumstances arguably does not fall within any of the aforementioned categories – unless the parties authorise a court or tribunal to supplement the agreement *ex aequo et bono*. Should a court or tribunal be permitted to supplement a long-term framework agreement governed by the CISG without such an authorisation and by reference to concepts that arguably originate in domestic law, uniformity within the meaning of Art. 7(1) CISG would be placed at risk.[1679] Second, the possibility of adapting or terminating a long-term framework agreement or other long-term contracts, by implying a right of termination for a compelling reason, appears to conflict with the Convention's regulation on changed economic circumstances. As previously stated, the CISG exhaustively addresses the impact of changed economic circumstances on the parties' obligations.[1680] Therefore, it would be incongruous to read such a possibility of adapting or terminating into the contract through judicial contract supplementation.

d) Disruption of Personal Relationship

A right to terminate for a compelling reason may also arise under domestic laws if long-term framework agreements or other long-term contracts require trusting cooperation between the parties and there has been a serious disruption of the parties' (personal) relationship.[1681] Even if a long-term contract does not necessitate trusting

1675. Brunner/*Brunner/Boog/Schläpfer*, Art. 73 CISG, para. 21; Brunner/Gottlieb/*Brunner/Schläpfer/Boog*, Art. 73 CISG, para. 21, although noting that this method should be applied with caution, as it constitutes a severe intervention in the contract; cf. also Honsell/*Brunner/Hurni*, Art. 73 CISG, para. 9 ('*Allenfalls kann auch die Vertragsauslegung oder vertragliche Lückenfüllung (vgl. Art. 8) zu einem sachgerechten Ergebnis führen*'); *Karollus*, p. 162.
1676. Brunner/*Brunner/Boog/Schläpfer*, Art. 73 CISG, para. 21; Brunner/Gottlieb/*Brunner/Schläpfer/Boog*, Art. 73 CISG, para. 21.
1677. Schlechtriem/Schwenzer/Schroeter/*Schmidt-Kessel*, 5th English ed., Art. 8 CISG, para. 28; Schlechtriem/Schwenzer/Schroeter/*Schmidt-Kessel*, 8th German ed., Art. 8 CISG, para. 26; cf. also *Schwenzer/Muñoz*, para. 26.71 (in agreement that contract supplementation under the CISG is possible).
1678. Schlechtriem/Schwenzer/Schroeter/*Schmidt-Kessel*, 5th English ed., Art. 8 CISG, para. 28; Schlechtriem/Schwenzer/Schroeter/*Schmidt-Kessel*, 8th German ed., Art. 8 CISG, para. 26.
1679. Cf. Schlechtriem/Schwenzer/Schroeter/*Schmidt-Kessel*, 5th English ed., Art. 8 CISG, para. 28.
1680. *See* Ch. 5 III. 3. above.
1681. BeckOK/*Lorenz*, § 314 BGB, para. 14; *Brunner*, pp. 520, 521; *Doralt*, pp. 419 et seq.; MüKoBGB/*Gaier*, § 314 BGB, para. 30; cf. also *Bremenkamp*, ZVertriebsR 2023, pp. 208, 209;

cooperation between the parties and thus a rupture of the personal relationship would not compromise the contract's purpose, a right to terminate for a compelling reason has been affirmed in certain instances, e.g., if one of the parties commits an intentional criminal act against the other party.[1682] While the CISG is primarily concerned with international commercial contracts between legal entities, it may also apply to natural persons (unless the exception of Art. 2(a) CISG applies). In addition, the contractual relationship between legal entities, such as companies, may also entail trusting cooperation.[1683]

Consequently, should a party seek to avoid a long-term framework agreement that falls within the CISG's sphere of application on the grounds of a disruption of the parties' personal relationship, both the Convention and the relevant domestic law rules will be invoked. Although the CISG does not explicitly mention the disruption of the parties' personal relationship as grounds for avoiding or terminating a contract, it may cover this factual scenario.[1684] The factual criterion is therefore fulfilled.

With regard to the legal criterion, the CISG does not address the risk of a disruption of the parties' personal relationship. This issue is not addressed in the Convention's provisions on contract avoidance or termination, nor in the provisions that have been mentioned in the context of insolvency and economic hardship. This is particularly relevant in cases where the disruption of the personal relationship occurs without the contract being breached.[1685] Initially, one might conclude that the CISG deems a disruption of the parties' personal relationship to be inconsequential and thus not a sufficient basis for avoiding a contract within its sphere of application. In a similar vein, *Schlechtriem* asserts that the purpose of a CISG contract is typically not jeopardised by a disruption of the parties' personal relationship and that there is no basis for invoking a domestic law right to terminate the contract in such instances.[1686] He posits that international sales contracts governed by the Convention are of a purely economic nature.[1687]

However, it is submitted that the CISG simply does not seek to regulate the consequences of a disruption of the parties' personal relationship under a long-term framework agreement.[1688] In such instances, the continuation of the contractual relationship becomes untenable for the aggrieved party due to factors that impact the aggrieved party's personality.[1689] Such considerations are not taken into account under the CISG. Based on this, *Schlechtriem* concludes that the Convention's provisions are

---

Schlechtriem, Lausanner Kolloquium, p. 162; but *see Oetker*, pp. 270, 271 (right to terminate for a compelling reason does not require a particular relationship of trust).

1682. BeckOK/*Lorenz*, § 314 BGB, para. 14; MüKoBGB/*Gaier*, § 314 BGB, para. 30.
1683. Cf. OLG Jena, 8 December 2015, CISG-online 2664; *B. Köhler*, pp. 329 et seq.
1684. Cf. *Schlechtriem*, Lausanner Kolloquium, p. 162; in the context of negligent misrepresentation but with a similar argument: *Schroeter*, (2013) 58 Vill. L. Rev., p. 581.
1685. *See Doralt*, pp. 419, 420.
1686. *See Schlechtriem*, Lausanner Kolloquium, p. 162.
1687. *Schlechtriem*, Lausanner Kolloquium, p. 162.
1688. With a different approach but similar outcome: *Karollus*, p. 162.
1689. Cf. *Oetker*, p. 264, positing that there is an immanent barrier to the right of self-determination; distinguishing these cases from cases of economic hardship: *Brunner*, pp. 520, 521; Honsell/*Brunner/Hurni*, Art. 73 CISG, para. 9; cf. also *Karollus*, p. 162.

exhaustive (Art. 73 CISG) in this regard, as the CISG does not cover contracts in which the parties' personal relationship is of relevance.[1690] However, the Convention may in fact be applicable to long-term framework agreements and other contracts that are not solely of an economic nature and that may establish a relationship of trust.[1691] Thus, the preferable view is that the Convention does not seek to regulate this matter in an exhaustive manner. The CISG is not equipped to deal with all matters that may arise in conjunction with the termination or avoidance of long-term framework agreements or other long-term contracts, given that most of its provisions were drafted with short-term contracts in mind.[1692] Consequently, this study argues that the legal criterion is not met; the CISG does not supersede domestic law rules that provide for a right to terminate for a compelling reason under such circumstances.

e) Change of Control

The right to terminate for a compelling reason may also be of interest if there is a change of control of one of the parties.[1693] This may, for example, be the case if one of the parties is acquired by a third party.[1694] Such a change of control may entitle the other party to avoid the contract for a compelling reason under domestic laws, for instance: if the third party is a direct competitor, if the change of control results in a partial shutdown, if the third party cannot guarantee the same quality, or if the third party acts recklessly towards the aggrieved party so that they cannot reasonably be expected to continue the contractual relationship with the third party.[1695]

A factual situation in which one of the parties intends to avoid a long-term framework agreement based on a change of control of the other party triggers both the CISG and domestic law rules that provide for a right to terminate for a compelling reason. Accordingly, the factual criterion under the two-step test is met.

It is debatable whether the CISG addresses the risk of a change of control in any of its provisions. The Convention's provisions on contract avoidance or termination are not concerned with this risk, as it is more based on a loss of trust rather than a breach of contract.[1696] Similarly, the provisions mentioned above in the context of insolvency and economic hardship do not address the risk of a change of control of one of the parties. Arguably, this could mean that the CISG considers changes of control to be irrelevant, and thus not a circumstance to be considered in the context of contract avoidance or termination. However, it seems more probable that the Convention simply does not regulate this matter at all, and it does not intend to do so, given that there are no indications to the contrary.[1697] In light of the aforementioned, this study

1690. Cf. *Schlechtriem*, Lausanner Kolloquium, p. 162.
1691. Cf. Ch. 5 II. above.
1692. Schlechtriem/Schwenzer/Schroeter/*Schroeter*, 5th English ed., Art. 29 CISG, para. 104.
1693. Cf. *Hoffbauer*, pp. 201, 202; Kull/Wildhaber/*Wildhaber*, para. 660; providing a slightly different example: *Doralt*, p. 442.
1694. UNIDROIT 2016, Study L - Doc. 135 rev., Annex 10, Illustration 1; cf. also *Doralt*, p. 442.
1695. Cf. *Hoffbauer*, p. 202; *Karollus*, p. 162; UNIDROIT 2016, Study L - Doc. 135 rev., Annex 10, Illustration 1.
1696. Cf. *Doralt*, pp. 442, 443.
1697. Cf. also *Karollus*, p. 162.

proposes that a right to terminate for a compelling reason based on a change of control should be applicable alongside the Convention.

f) Interim Conclusion

In contrast to some domestic laws, the CISG does not explicitly mention a right to terminate a long-term framework agreement or other long-term contracts for a compelling reason. Given the broad range of cases covered by the right to terminate for a compelling reason under domestic law, this study suggests distinguishing between different case groups in order to determine whether domestic law rules that provide for a right to terminate for a compelling reason are superseded by the CISG. This study proposes relying on the two-step test. The first case group concerns breaches of contract. The CISG covers these factual scenarios and addresses the legal risks in these cases exhaustively in its provisions on contract avoidance (Arts 49, 64 and 73 CISG) if the breach relates to the framework agreements themselves. This is the case irrespective of the structure of the framework agreement. Consequently, there is no basis for invoking a domestic law right to terminate a long-term framework agreement, which is subject to the CISG, for a compelling reason in such circumstances. The same applies to cases of insolvency and economic hardship. The Convention addresses the legal risks in these factual scenarios and regulates them exhaustively, specifically in Arts 71, 72, 73 and 79 CISG. Thus, any right to terminate for a compelling reason that may arise under domestic law is superseded by the Convention in these case groups.

However, a different approach should be taken in cases in which the aggrieved party wishes to avoid a two-tier framework agreement based on breaches of the individual sales contracts. This is essentially a matter of lost trust, which is not intended to be covered by the CISG. In such instances, the aggrieved party may therefore rely on domestic law rules that provide for a right to terminate for a compelling reason. The same should apply to cases in which a serious disruption of the parties' personal relationship occurred and cases in which the control of one of the parties changes. Although the Convention is also triggered by these factual scenarios, it does not attempt to regulate the legal risks in such cases – unlike the right to terminate for a compelling reason, which is recognised under some domestic laws. Consequently, the aggrieved party is entitled to invoke domestic law rules that provide for a right to terminate for a compelling reason in such cases.

2) Contractual Agreements

The CISG's provisions on contract termination and avoidance are subject to modification and derogation in accordance with Art. 6 CISG.[1698] Accordingly, the parties are at liberty to agree upon rights to avoid or terminate their long-term contract based on 'compelling reasons'. For instance, the parties may describe the specific grounds that

1698. (Questionably) referencing domestic law when analysing a 'termination for convenience' clause: *Kumpers Composites GmbH & Co KG v. TPI Composites Inc.*, US Dist. Ct. Ariz., 25 February 2025, CISG-online 7294, paras 34 et seq.

entitle one of them to terminate the entire long-term framework agreement.[1699] To illustrate, in a case before the Milan Chamber of Arbitration, the parties to a distribution agreement governed by the CISG agreed upon a contractual right of 'early termination' if the distributor (buyer) repeatedly breached their payment obligations or 'materially' breached any of their other obligations.[1700] Similarly, in a case before the Court of Appeal Graz, a framework agreement governed by the CISG provided for a right to terminate the contract for compelling reasons and contained an exemplary list of such compelling reasons.[1701] This exemplary list mentioned a default in payment despite a reminder that sets a deadline, a party becoming unable to pay or entering into insolvency or other settlement proceedings and a default in delivery of the goods despite a reminder that sets a deadline.[1702] The Court held that the parties were permitted to agree on such a clause in accordance with Art. 6 CISG and that the buyer was entitled to terminate the contract based on a default in the delivery of the goods.[1703] In the interest of certainty, the parties may wish to include a clause in the contract that additionally allows either party to terminate the contract in the event of a change of ownership of one of the parties (so-called change of control clause).[1704]

Should the parties decide to exclude any form of avoidance or termination before the contract's duration expires, issues of validity may arise under the otherwise applicable domestic law.[1705] In addition, agreements on a unilateral right to terminate the contract based on specific grounds may be declared invalid under some domestic law provisions that are concerned with the control of the content of contractual clauses, such as § 307 of the BGB – in particular, if they are part of standard terms.[1706] Such rules are applicable alongside the CISG, as the Convention is not concerned with the control of the content of contractual clauses, particularly in relation to standard terms.[1707] For instance, in a case before the Court of Appeal Koblenz, the distribution agreement, which was governed by the CISG and German law, stipulated in clause 9.2 that the manufacturer of the goods (seller) had an 'extraordinary right of termination'

1699. *Doralt*, p. 411 (German law); *Hoffbauer*, pp. 199 et seq. (German law); *B. Köhler*, Sustainable Supply Chains, pp. 352, 353; sceptical Kull/Wildhaber/*Wildhaber*, paras 671, 672 (Swiss law).
1700. Milan Chamber of Arbitration, 15 January 2020, CISG-online 5554, para. 51 (Art. 15 of the distribution agreement); cf. also District Court Tokyo, 16 June 2020, CISG-online 5648.
1701. OLG Graz, 28 September 2000, CISG-online 798, para. 2, clause 7b).
1702. OLG Graz, 28 September 2000, CISG-online 798, para. 2, clause 7b): '*Unabhängig davon ist jede Partei berechtigt, den Vertrag fristlos zu kündigen, falls ein wichtiger Grund vorliegt, der ihr die Fortsetzung des Vertrages unzumutbar macht. Als wichtiger Grund gilt insbesondere Zahlungsverzug trotz Mahnung mit Fristsetzung, Zahlungsunfähigkeit oder Antrag auf Eröffnung von Vergleichs- oder Konkursverfahren, Lieferverzug trotz Mahnung mit Fristsetzung.*'
1703. OLG Graz, 28 September 2000, CISG-online 798, paras 42 et seq.
1704. *Hoffbauer*, pp. 201, 202.
1705. Putting emphasis on the fact that the right to terminate for a compelling reason is mandatory under Swiss and German domestic law and therefore cannot be excluded by contractual agreement: BGer, 22 January 1963, BGE 89 II 30, consid. 5a); CHK/*Jacobs*, Innominatverträge/AVV, para. 43; *Hoffbauer*, pp. 198, 199.
1706. With more detail on German law: *Hoffbauer*, pp. 199 et seq.; cf. also Kull/Wildhaber/*Wildhaber*, paras 671, 672 (Swiss law).
1707. Schlechtriem/Schwenzer/Schroeter/*Schroeter*, 5th English ed., Intro Arts 14–24 CISG, para. 35.

if the distributor (buyer) failed to meet a certain minimum turnover that was agreed upon in the contract.[1708] The Court of Appeal deemed this clause to be invalid under § 307 BGB, as it constituted an unreasonable disadvantage for the distributor to link a right for termination or avoidance of the contract to a minimum turnover to be achieved.[1709]

d. *Summary*

As time passes, the termination (or avoidance) of long-term framework agreements or any other long-term contract becomes a matter of particular interest to the parties. The CISG as well as domestic law rules provide for multiple ways to bring such contracts to an end.

Long-term framework agreements are frequently limited in time, and the parties intend to terminate the contract with the expiration of its duration. Such agreements are possible under the CISG and arguably constitute a termination agreement in the sense of Art. 29(1) CISG, after the expiration of a certain period of time. However, the admissibility of specific contractual durations is subject to domestic law (Art. 4(a) CISG). The parties are also free to agree on so-called renewal clauses, the incorporation of which is subject to Arts 14–24 CISG, whereas their validity is again governed by domestic law.

Some domestic laws provide for a right to unilaterally terminate any long-term contract in compliance with certain time limits, provided that the agreement is of indefinite duration. Applying the two-step test reveals that the CISG may cover these factual scenarios, but it does not intend to regulate this subject matter. The general right to terminate indefinite long-term contracts is, *inter alia*, based on the consideration that the parties should not be able to contractually bind themselves eternally. This risk is not addressed by the CISG. Therefore, domestic law rules that provide for a general right to terminate indefinite long-term contracts should be applicable alongside the Convention and should not be superseded by the latter. In addition, the parties are free to contractually agree upon such a right under a long-term framework agreement that is subject to the CISG. In the absence of any contrary agreements, the CISG will apply to the modalities of a contractual termination clause, e.g., Art. 27 CISG.

In contrast to certain domestic laws, the CISG does not explicitly mention a right to terminate a long-term contract for a compelling reason. Given the extensive range of cases covered by the right to terminate for a compelling reason under domestic laws, it is necessary to distinguish between different case groups in order to determine whether domestic law rules that provide for a right to terminate for a compelling reason are superseded by the CISG. Applying the two-step test to these case groups reveals that there is no straightforward answer to the question of whether the CISG overrides such domestic law rules. The Convention provides exhaustive regulation of cases of breaches of contract with regard to the framework agreement itself, insolvency and

1708. OLG Koblenz, 22 April 2010, CISG-online 2163, para. 19.
1709. OLG Koblenz, 22 April 2010, CISG-online 2163, para. 20.

economic hardship. These matters are particularly addressed by the provisions set forth in Arts 49, 64, 71, 72, 73 and 79 CISG. Consequently, there is no room for invoking domestic law provisions that permit the termination for compelling reasons under such circumstances. In contrast, this study posits that domestic law rules that provide for a right to terminate for a compelling reason should be applied alongside the CISG in cases of 'cross-contractual' breaches (termination of a framework agreement based on breaches of individual sales contracts), cases of disruption of the parties' personal relationship, and cases of change of control. Although the Convention covers these factual scenarios, it does not address the underlying risks nor attempt to regulate them. Thus, the legal criterion under the two-step test is not fulfilled, and consequently, the CISG should not supersede domestic law rules that provide for a right to terminate for a compelling reason in such cases.

Furthermore, the parties are at liberty to agree on a right to terminate their contract for specified reasons in accordance with Art. 6 CISG. It should be noted that such agreements, particularly if they are part of standard terms, may be deemed invalid by some domestic rules on contract validity. These domestic rules must also be taken into account when dealing with a long-term framework agreement under the Convention in accordance with Art. 4(a) CISG.

5. Avoidance Based on Breaches of Contract under the CISG

The avoidance of long-term framework agreements under the CISG has already been discussed above in the context of contract termination, as there are partial overlaps with domestic law provisions on termination for a compelling reason.[1710] Nevertheless, the avoidance of long-term framework agreements under the CISG will be presented in a separate section below because certain unique aspects of framework agreements deserve particular attention. Prior to this, the particularities of long-term framework agreements in light of Art. 25 CISG will be outlined, as this provision is of paramount importance for the avoidance of any contract under the Convention.[1711]

a. Particularities under Article 25 CISG

In the majority of cases, a fundamental breach of contract is required to avoid a contract under the Convention, as evidenced by Arts 49(1)(a), 64(1)(a), 72(1) and 73(1)(2) CISG.[1712] Art. 25 CISG defines a fundamental breach of contract.[1713] According to this provision, 'a breach of contract committed by one of the parties is fundamental if it results in such detriment to the other party as substantially to deprive him of what

1710. *See* Ch. 5 III. 4. c. above.
1711. Cf. only Schlechtriem/Schwenzer/Schroeter/*Schroeter*, 5th English ed., Art. 25 CISG, para. 1; Staudinger/*Magnus*, Art. 25 CISG, para. 2.
1712. Cf. Kröll *et al.*/Björklund, Art. 25 CISG, para. 1; MüKoBGB/*Huber*, Art. 25 CISG, paras 1 et seq.; MüKoHGB/*Benicke*, Art. 25 CISG, para. 1; Schlechtriem/Schwenzer/Schroeter/*Schroeter*, 5th English ed., Art. 25 CISG, paras 5, 6; Staudinger/*Magnus*, Art. 25 CISG, para. 1.
1713. Schlechtriem/Schwenzer/Schroeter/*Schroeter*, 5th English ed., Art. 25 CISG, paras 1, 2.

he is entitled to expect under the contract [...]'.[1714] Consequently, the non-breaching party must essentially lose their interest in contract performance.[1715] The question of whether this is the case should be resolved objectively, taking into account the non-breaching party's expectations as set out in the contract.[1716] It is therefore necessary to determine whether the parties have intended to attribute particular importance to certain obligations in their agreement by way of contract interpretation (Art. 8 CISG).[1717] If contract interpretation does not lead to clear outcomes, the non-breaching party's expectations must be determined from the perspective of a reasonable third person (Art. 8(2) CISG) in light of the specific contract.[1718] This assessment essentially involves an objective balancing of both parties' interests, taking into account the contract in question.[1719] In determining whether there has been a fundamental breach in the sense of Art. 25 CISG, it is necessary to consider the specific features of long-term framework agreements.[1720] The interests to be considered in such agreements may vary from those in short-term contracts, and the intention of the breaching party may play a role.

i. *Interests to Be Considered*

Long-term framework agreements frequently include non-sales obligations, particularly those pertaining to the parties' overall cooperation and relationship.[1721] The avoidance of a long-term framework agreement based on a fundamental breach of contract typically results in the termination not only of the sales obligations but also of those non-sales obligations.[1722] Consequently, the interests underlying the non-sales obligations must also be taken into account in objectively balancing both parties' interests.[1723] Under a framework, a buyer may, for example, have an 'objective'

1714. In detail on the prerequisites under Art. 25 CISG: Kröll *et al./Björklund*, Art. 25 CISG, paras 9 et seq.; Schlechtriem/Schwenzer/Schroeter/*Schroeter*, 5th English ed., Art. 25 CISG, paras 54 et seq.; Staudinger/*Magnus*, Art. 25 CISG, paras 9 et seq.
1715. *See* only BGH, 24 September 2014, CISG-online 2545, para. 23; OGH, 22 November 2011, CISG-online 2239, para. 24; BeckOK/*Saenger*, Art. 25 CISG, para. 4; Schlechtriem/Schwenzer/Schroeter/*Schroeter*, 5th English ed., Art. 25 CISG, para. 87; Staudinger/*Magnus*, Art. 25 CISG, para. 13.
1716. Schlechtriem/Schwenzer/Schroeter/*Schroeter*, 5th English ed., Art. 25 CISG, para. 85.
1717. BeckOK/*Saenger*, Art. 25 CISG, para. 4; MüKoHGB/*Benicke*, Art. 25 CISG, paras 16, 17; Schlechtriem/Schwenzer/Schroeter/*Schroeter*, 5th English ed., Art. 25 CISG, paras 88 et seq.; Staudinger/*Magnus*, Art. 25 CISG, para. 13.
1718. Schlechtriem/Schwenzer/Schroeter/*Schroeter*, 5th English ed., Art. 25 CISG, para. 95; cf. also Staudinger/*Magnus*, Art. 25 CISG, para. 13.
1719. Cf. only OGH, 15 November 2012, CISG-online 2399, para. 2; Schlechtriem/Schwenzer/Schroeter/*Schroeter*, 5th English ed., Art. 25 CISG, paras 96, 97.
1720. Schlechtriem/Schwenzer/Schroeter/*Schroeter*, 5th English ed., Art. 25 CISG, para. 104; Schlechtriem/Schwenzer/Schroeter/*Schroeter*, 8th German ed., Art. 25 CISG, para. 96.
1721. Schlechtriem/Schwenzer/Schroeter/*Schroeter*, 5th English ed., Art. 25 CISG, para. 105; Schlechtriem/Schwenzer/Schroeter/*Schroeter*, 8th German ed., Art. 25 CISG, para. 96.
1722. Schlechtriem/Schwenzer/Schroeter/*Schroeter*, 5th English ed., Art. 25 CISG, para. 105; Schlechtriem/Schwenzer/Schroeter/*Schroeter*, 8th German ed., Art. 25 CISG, para. 96.
1723. Schlechtriem/Schwenzer/Schroeter/*Schroeter*, 5th English ed., Art. 25 CISG, para. 105; Schlechtriem/Schwenzer/Schroeter/*Schroeter*, 8th German ed., Art. 25 CISG, para. 96.

interest[1724] in maintaining their sales potential if the contract contains an exclusivity obligation.[1725] Whereas a seller may, for instance, have an objective interest in retaining or increasing their market shares if the contract contains an obligation to promote the goods.[1726] Similarly, they may have an interest in avoiding competition with their own business or the businesses of their distributors if the contract includes a non-competition agreement.[1727] All of these interests should be considered when objectively balancing the parties' interests under Art. 25 CISG; thus, the interests to be taken into consideration differ somewhat from those underlying short-term contracts.[1728] It is important to note that similar considerations might apply to other mixed contracts governed by the Convention which do not qualify as long-term contracts.

ii. Intention of the Breaching Party

The intention of the breaching party in and of itself does not transform a breach into a fundamental breach within the meaning of Art. 25 CISG.[1729] However, the breaching party's intentional conduct may be relevant if it results in the non-breaching party being deprived of their contractual expectations.[1730] Long-term framework agreements often oblige the parties to cooperate with each other.[1731] Therefore, it can reasonably be assumed that the parties to such a contract are frequently entitled to expect trust and

1724. Cf. only Schlechtriem/Schwenzer/Schroeter/*Schroeter*, 5th English ed., Art. 25 CISG, para. 85.
1725. Schlechtriem/Schwenzer/Schroeter/*Schroeter*, 5th English ed., Art. 25 CISG, para. 105; Schlechtriem/Schwenzer/Schroeter/*Schroeter*, 8th German ed., Art. 25 CISG, para. 96; *see* the following case law: OGH, 15 November 2012, CISG-online 2399, para. 5 (a fundamental breach of an exclusivity obligation was discussed but denied); OLG Koblenz, 31 January 1997, CISG-online 256, para. 18 (a fundamental breach of an exclusivity obligation was discussed but left open); OLG Frankfurt, 17 September 1991, CISG-online 28 (a fundamental breach of an exclusivity obligation had occurred).
1726. ICC, 18203/2013, CISG-online 2973, para. 56 (fundamental breach of the buyer's obligation to promote the goods); Schlechtriem/Schwenzer/Schroeter/*Schroeter*, 5th English ed., Art. 25 CISG, para. 105.
1727. JPI Badalona No. 3, 22 May 2006, CISG-online 1391 (fundamental breach denied: the contract included a 'fundamental condition' that the buyer was only permitted to resell the goods in countries of the Middle East. However, the buyer was not obliged to verify that their customers in the Middle East were only selling the products in those countries); CA Grenoble, 22 February 1995, CISG-online 151 (fundamental breach of non-competition clause established); Schlechtriem/Schwenzer/Schroeter/*Schroeter*, 8th German ed., Art. 25 CISG, para. 96.
1728. Schlechtriem/Schwenzer/Schroeter/*Schroeter*, 5th English ed., Art. 25 CISG, para. 105; Schlechtriem/Schwenzer/Schroeter/*Schroeter*, 8th German ed., Art. 25 CISG, para. 96.
1729. BeckOGK/*Schmidt-Ahrendts*, Art. 25 CISG, para. 12; Ferrari *et al.*/Ferrari, Art. 25 CISG, para. 23; MüKoBGB/*Gruber*, Art. 25 CISG, para. 13; MüKoHGB/*Benicke*, Art. 25 CISG, para. 53; Kröll *et al.*/*Björklund*, Art. 25 CISG, para. 15; Schlechtriem/Schwenzer/Schroeter/*Schroeter*, 5th English ed., Art. 25 CISG, paras 65 et seq.; Schlechtriem/Schwenzer/Schroeter/*Schroeter*, 8th German ed., Art. 25 CISG, para. 62.
1730. Ferrari *et al.*/Ferrari, Art. 25 CISG, para. 23; MüKoBGB/*Gruber*, Art. 25 CISG, para. 13; Schlechtriem/Schwenzer/Schroeter/*Schroeter*, 5th English ed., Art. 25 CISG, para. 68; Schlechtriem/Schwenzer/Schroeter/*Schroeter*, 8th German ed., Art. 25 CISG, para. 62a; cf. also Kröll *et al.*/*Björklund*, Art. 25 CISG, para. 15; Staudinger/*Magnus*, Art. 25 CISG, para. 9.
1731. Cooperation obligations may be derived from a contractual agreement, usages and established practices, or from the interpretation of specific provisions of the CISG, *see* Ch. 5 III. 1. a. above.

reliability from each other.[1732] Consequently, the intentional conduct of the breaching party may result in the non-breaching party being deprived of their expectations of trust and reliability under a long-term framework agreement, in particular with regard to the performance of the remaining part of the contract.[1733] In order for the aforementioned to be the case, it is necessary that the breaching party acts in a deceitful manner ('*betrügerisches Verhalten*') and that the contract has not yet been fully performed.[1734] If so, there may be a fundamental breach of contract which would entitle the aggrieved party to avoid the contract (Arts 49, 64, 72, 73 CISG).[1735] Conversely, the situation is usually different with regard to short-term contracts for two main reasons.[1736] First, the parties are less likely to be entitled to expect trust and reliability from each other under a short-term contract. Second, instances where the contract has not yet been fully performed are more likely to be found in the context of long-term contracts. Consequently, deceitful breaches of long-term framework agreements may occasionally result in fundamental breaches, in accordance with the aforementioned criteria, whereas this is less probable in the case of short-term contracts.

In conclusion, the specific features of long-term framework agreements must be taken into consideration under Art. 25 CISG. This primarily (but not exhaustively) concerns the specific interests to be considered in objectively balancing both parties' interests, which differ somewhat from those to be considered under short-term contracts. Furthermore, the importance of trust and reliability is increased in long-term framework agreements. Thus, the intentional conduct of the breaching party may play a role in certain circumstances when determining whether there has been a fundamental breach within the meaning of Art. 25 CISG.

The following section will provide an overview of the possibilities to avoid framework agreements under the CISG. A distinction will be made in accordance with the two structures of framework agreements that have been identified throughout the

1732. Cf. MüKoHGB/*Benicke*, Art. 25 CISG, para. 53; Schlechtriem/Schwenzer/Schroeter/*Schroeter*, 5th English ed., Art. 25 CISG, para. 68; Schlechtriem/Schwenzer/Schroeter/*Schroeter*, 8th German ed., Art. 25 CISG, para. 62a.

1733. With regard to long-term contracts in general: BGer, 2 April 2015, CISG-online 2592, paras 139, 140; Schlechtriem/Schwenzer/Schroeter/*Schroeter*, 5th English ed., Art. 25 CISG, para. 68; Schlechtriem/Schwenzer/Schroeter/*Schroeter*, 8th German ed., Art. 25 CISG, para. 62a; cf. also BeckOGK/*Schmidt-Ahrendts*, Art. 25 CISG, paras 12, 12.1; MüKoHGB/*Benicke*, Art. 25 CISG, para. 53 (mentioning instalment contracts); Staudinger/*Magnus*, Art. 25 CISG, para. 9.

1734. BGer, 2 April 2015, CISG-online 2592, para. 140; MüKoHGB/*Benicke*, Art. 25 CISG, para. 53; Schlechtriem/Schwenzer/Schroeter/*Schroeter*, 5th English ed., Art. 25 CISG, para. 68; Schlechtriem/Schwenzer/Schroeter/*Schroeter*, 8th German ed., Art. 25 CISG, para. 62a; cf. also BeckOGK/*Schmidt-Ahrendts*, Art. 25 CISG, para. 12.1; BeckOK/*Saenger*, Art. 25 CISG, para. 10; MüKoBGB/*Gruber*, Art. 25 CISG, para. 13; Ferrari *et al.*/*Ferrari*, Art. 25 CISG, para. 23.

1735. *See, e.g.*, ICC, 2020, CISG-online 5519, paras 35 et seq., where the seller intentionally deceived the buyer by providing falsified certificates concerning the goods and by concealing the true facts.

1736. Cf. also with regard to 'one-off sales contracts': Schlechtriem/Schwenzer/Schroeter/*Schroeter*, 5th English ed., Art. 25 CISG, para. 68 *in fine*; Schlechtriem/Schwenzer/Schroeter/*Schroeter*, 8th German ed., Art. 25 CISG, para. 62a *in fine*.

course of this study, namely, framework agreements containing sales obligations in *sensu stricto* and framework agreements with a two-tier structure.[1737]

b. Framework Agreements Containing Sales Obligations Stricto Sensu

A framework agreement, such as a distribution contract, that contains sales obligations in *sensu stricto* is typically subject to Art. 73 CISG.[1738] In the event of a breach of such a framework agreement, the specific rules on contract avoidance enshrined in Art. 73 CISG become relevant.[1739] This provision distinguishes between three different scenarios. In accordance with Art. 73(1) CISG, the aggrieved party is entitled to avoid the contract with regard to one instalment if the contract has been fundamentally breached with regard to that instalment.[1740] This presupposes the existence of a fundamental breach of contract in the sense of Art. 25 CISG.[1741]

Art. 73(2) CISG grants the aggrieved party the right to avoid the contract *ex nunc* if there are grounds for the assumption that a future fundamental breach of contract will occur based on a current breach of contract.[1742] This necessitates the existence of a current but not necessarily fundamental breach of contract with regard to one or multiple instalments that allows for the prediction of a future fundamental breach of contract.[1743] To illustrate, this provision has been applied in case law where one of the parties refused to guarantee that they would comply with their exclusivity obligation under a sales contract.[1744]

Art. 73(3) CISG grants the buyer a right to avoid the entire contract *ex tunc* if the seller has committed a fundamental breach of contract with regard to one instalment that also renders past or future instalments useless.[1745] The prerequisites for this right are that the seller has committed a fundamental breach of contract with regard to one

1737. *See* Ch. 3 III. 1. a. above.
1738. *Grieser*, pp. 125, 132, 133; Mankowski/*Dornis*, Art. 73 CISG, para. 3 (regarding distribution agreements); MüKoHGB/*Sommerfeld*, Art. 73 CISG, para. 4; *Newhouse/Tanaka*, R.L.R. 2012, p. 18 (regarding distribution agreements); Schlechtriem/Schwenzer/Schroeter/*Fountoulakis*, 5th English ed., Art. 73 CISG, para. 8; Schlechtriem/Schwenzer/Schroeter/*Fountoulakis*, 8th German ed., Art. 73 CISG, para. 9; Staudinger/*Magnus*, Art. 73 CISG, para. 7; cf. also ICC, July 1999, CISG-online 707; Court of Arbitration of the Hamburg CC, 21 March 1996, CISG-online 187, paras 39 et seq.
1739. Cf. Schlechtriem/Schwenzer/Schroeter/*Fountoulakis*, 5th English ed., Art. 73 CISG, para. 1; Staudinger/*Magnus*, Art. 73 CISG, para. 1: Art. 73 CISG is generally considered to be *lex specialis* in relation to Art. 49 CISG.
1740. *See* the overview provided by Schlechtriem/Schwenzer/Schroeter/*Fountoulakis*, 5th English ed., Art. 73 CISG, para. 1.
1741. In more detail: BeckOK/*Saenger*, Art. 73 CISG, para. 4; Kröll *et al.*/Saidov, Art. 73 CISG, paras 9, 10; MüKoBGB/*Huber*, Art. 73 CISG, para. 6; Schlechtriem/Schwenzer/Schroeter/*Fountoulakis*, 5th English ed., Art. 73 CISG, paras 12 et seq.; Staudinger/*Magnus*, Art. 73 CISG, paras 12 et seq.
1742. Cf. Brunner/*Brunner/Boog/Schläpfer*, Art. 73 CISG, para. 20; Brunner/Gottlieb/*Brunner/Schläpfer/Boog*, Art. 73 CISG, para. 20.
1743. In detail on Art. 73(2) CISG: Schlechtriem/Schwenzer/Schroeter/*Fountoulakis*, 5th English ed., Art. 73 CISG, paras 20 et seq.; Staudinger/*Magnus*, Art. 73 CISG, paras 17 et seq.
1744. CA Grenoble, 22 February 1995, CISG-online 151.
1745. Schlechtriem/Schwenzer/Schroeter/*Fountoulakis*, 5th English ed., Art. 73 CISG, paras 34 et seq.; Staudinger/*Magnus*, Art. 73 CISG, paras 29 et seq.

instalment – i.e., a scenario to which Art. 73(1) CISG would apply – and that, as a consequence of this and the interdependence of the contract's instalments, the entire contract, or at least a substantial part of it, is impaired.[1746]

In general, Art. 73 CISG is the *lex specialis* in relation to the other provisions on contract avoidance under the Convention, specifically Arts 49 and 64 CISG.[1747] However, if the entire framework agreement is affected by a fundamental breach of contract, the aggrieved party should also be able to invoke Art. 49 or 64 CISG, provided that the respective prerequisites are met.[1748] Furthermore, if it becomes evident prior to performance of the framework agreement that the other party will commit a fundamental breach (anticipatory breach of contract), each party is entitled to declare the contract avoided in accordance with Art. 72(1) CISG.[1749]

c. *Framework Agreements with a Two-Tier Structure*

The situation may be different when it comes to framework agreements that follow a two-tier structure, i.e., there is a distinction between the framework agreement and the individual sales contracts subsequently concluded. This study posits that the CISG may also be applicable to such agreements, provided that they contain an obligation to conclude individual sales contracts and that they do not include a preponderant non-sales part.[1750] Notwithstanding the applicability of the CISG to the framework agreement, the individual sales contracts may still fall within the Convention's sphere of application.[1751]

i. *Distinction Between Framework Agreement and Individual Sales Contracts*

When it comes to the avoidance of such agreements, it is crucial to differentiate between the framework agreement and the individual sales contracts. Initially, it is necessary to determine whether a breach occurred with regard to one or multiple individual sales contracts or with regard to the framework agreement itself.[1752] This is achieved by delineating the obligations under the individual sales contracts from the obligations under the framework agreement.[1753] A comparable approach has been adopted in international case law, whereby courts and tribunals have frequently

1746. In detail: Schlechtriem/Schwenzer/Schroeter/*Fountoulakis*, 5th English ed., Art. 73 CISG, paras 34 et seq.
1747. MüKoBGB/*Huber*, Art. 73 CISG, para. 27; Staudinger/*Magnus*, Art. 73 CISG, para. 1.
1748. Cf. *Honnold/Flechtner*, Art. 73 CISG, para. 531; Staudinger/*Magnus*, Art. 73 CISG, para. 1.
1749. Cf. Schlechtriem/Schwenzer/Schroeter/*Fountoulakis*, 5th English ed., Art. 73 CISG, para. 17.
1750. *See* Ch. 3 III. and Ch. 4 above.
1751. *See, e.g.*, Ch. 3 V. above.
1752. With regard to German domestic law: *Hoffbauer*, p. 114; *Gebhardt*, p. 43; *Saxinger*, p. 176; but *see Bucher*, p. 109, who posits that in the context of dispute resolution, both the framework contract and the individual contract should be regarded as forming a 'single, unified contractual basis' ('*gemeinschaftliche Vertragsgrundlage*').
1753. Cf. *Hoffbauer*, p. 114; *C. Meyer*, Alleinvertrieb, pp. 328, 329; *Perović*, (2011) 59 Belgrade L. Rev., pp. 190, 191.

considered whether a claim pertained to the obligations set forth in the individual sales contracts or those in the framework agreement.[1754]

If a claim relates to the violation of sales obligations in *sensu stricto* (e.g., a violation of payment obligations), it is founded on a breach of the sales obligations under the individual sales contracts.[1755] In such instances, the legal basis for any claims resulting from the breach is the relevant individual sales contract.[1756] Consequently, the individual sales contract may be avoided in accordance with Arts 49 and 64 CISG, provided that the respective prerequisites are met.[1757] This may be the case if one of the parties commits a fundamental breach of contract within the meaning of Art. 25 CISG. In such cases, avoidance is restricted to the individual sales contract that has been fundamentally breached.[1758] The other individual sales contracts and the framework agreement remain unaltered.[1759]

In the event of a breach of an individual sales contract, the framework agreement may still be considered relevant. It may contain provisions on the prerequisites for a breach of contract and on the remedies available for such a breach.[1760] Such provisions may subsequently be incorporated into the individual sales contract. This may, for instance, be the case if the parties have made an explicit reference to the terms of the framework agreement in their individual sales contract; they may also be incorporated implicitly. The question of whether the framework agreement's terms have become part of the individual sales contracts is essentially one of contract interpretation (Art. 8 CISG). In this context, the individual sales contract may have to be interpreted

1754. *See* Milan Chamber of Arbitration, 15 January 2020, CISG-online 5554: the payment claims were based on the 'individual purchase orders'; Supr. Ct. Norway, 6 February 2019, CISG-online 4318: the dispute pertained to a right of stoppage under an individual sales contract; *Gruppo Essenziero Italiano, S.p.A. v. Aromi D'Italia, Inc.*, US Dist. Ct. Mary., 27 July 2011, CISG-online 2223: the buyer sought compensation (damages) for the wrongful termination of an exclusive distribution agreement, which was deemed to be related to the distribution contract and not the individual sales contracts; OLG Köln, 29 January 2010, CISG-online 2172: the claim for payment of the outstanding purchase price was considered to be related to the individual sales contracts, whereas the other claims were deemed to be related to the distribution contract; Foreign Trade Court of Arbitration of the CC and Industry of Serbia, 28 January 2009, CISG-online 1856: the Court determined that the seller's claim for payment of the purchase price was based on the individual transactions, rather than the framework agreement as a whole; Supr. Ct. China, 21 September 2005, CISG-online 1611: the Court ruled that only disputes that originated from the 'placing of orders or thereafter' are pertinent to the sales relationship; Supr. Ct. Italy, 20 September 2004, CISG-online 1015: the claim for performance was based on the individual sales contracts; Court of Arbitration of the Hamburg CC, 21 March 1996, CISG-online 187: in its decision, the Court distinguished between the claims for damages based on the individual sales contracts and the claims for damages based on the framework agreement (although the exact characterisation of this contract remains unclear).

1755. Cf. Milan Chamber of Arbitration, 15 January 2020, CISG-online 5554; Supr. Ct. Norway, 6 February 2019, CISG-online 4318; Foreign Trade Ct. of Arbitration of the CC and Industry of Serbia, 28 January 2009, CISG-online 1856; Supr. Ct. China, 21 September 2005, CISG-online 1611; Supr. Ct. Italy, 20 September 2004, CISG-online 1015.

1756. OLG Köln, 29 January 2010, CISG-online 2172; *Hoffbauer*, p. 114; *Saxinger*, p. 176; but *see Bucher*, p. 109.

1757. Similar with regard to German law: *Hoffbauer*, p. 114.

1758. In a different context but with a similar approach: *C. Meyer*, Alleinvertrieb, p. 329.

1759. Cf. *Hoffbauer*, p. 115; *Saxinger*, p. 176.

1760. *Hoffbauer*, pp. 114, 115; *Saxinger*, p. 176.

in light of the framework agreement.[1761] In doing so, the framework agreement may be considered a practice in the sense of Art. 8(3) CISG and extend its effects, i.e., its terms, to the individual sales contracts.[1762] Thus, the framework agreement must still be taken into account when examining a breach of an individual sales contract.

In contrast, breaches that relate to the obligations set out in the framework agreement entitle the aggrieved party to seek remedies solely in relation to this contract.[1763] To illustrate, one of the parties may refuse to conclude individual sales contracts.[1764] In such a case, the aggrieved party may be entitled to avoid this agreement, provided that the prerequisites under the Convention are met (Arts 49 and 64 CISG). This will typically be determined by whether such a refusal can be regarded as a fundamental breach in the sense of Art. 25 CISG. Moreover, the breach of other obligations under a framework agreement may also be regarded as a fundamental breach, thereby entitling the aggrieved party to avoid the contract.[1765] This may, for instance, be the case if one of the parties has breached an obligation to adequately promote the goods,[1766] an exclusivity obligation[1767] or a non-competition agreement.[1768]

In contrast to framework agreements that already contain the defining characteristics of a sales contract,[1769] Art. 73 CISG generally does not apply if there is a distinction between the framework agreement and the subsequently concluded individual sales contracts.[1770] This is because Art. 73 CISG requires that there be a single uniform contract in order for it to be applicable.[1771] The specific remedies set forth in

1761. *See* Ch. 3 III. 2. b. ii. above; Schlechtriem/Schwenzer/Schroeter/*Schmidt-Kessel*, 5th English ed., Art. 8 CISG, paras 31, 50; *Schroeter*, para. 94.
1762. OLG Hamburg, 5 October 1998, CISG-online 473 (with regard to a choice of law clause); Schlechtriem/Schwenzer/Schroeter/*Schmidt-Kessel*, 5th English ed., Art. 8 CISG, paras 31, 50; *Schroeter*, para. 94; cf. also Schlechtriem/Schwenzer/Schroeter/*Schroeter*, 5th English ed., Art. 29 CISG, para. 67 (with regard to form requirements).
1763. Cf. *Gebhardt*, p. 43; *Hoffbauer*, p. 114.
1764. *Hoffbauer*, pp. 112, 113; cf. also *Torsello*, p. 235 with regard to preliminary agreements.
1765. *See* Ch. 4 III. 2. above; cf. also Schlechtriem/Schwenzer/Schroeter/*Schroeter*, 5th English ed., Art. 25 CISG, paras 264, 265; Schlechtriem/Schwenzer/Schroeter/*Schroeter*, 8th German ed., Art. 25 CISG, paras 243, 244.
1766. ICC, 18203/2013, CISG-online 2973.
1767. OGH, 15 November 2012, CISG-online 2399, para. 5 (non-fundamental breach of exclusivity obligation in a regular sales contract); OLG Koblenz, 31 January 1997, CISG-online 256, para. 18 (the Court did not determine whether a breach of an exclusivity obligation in a regular sales contract was fundamental); OLG Frankfurt, 17 September 1991, CISG-online 28 (a fundamental breach of the exclusivity obligation set out in a regular sales contract was established).
1768. JPI Badalona No. 3, 22 May 2006, CISG-online 1391 (fundamental breach of non-competition agreement denied); CA Grenoble, 22 February 1995, CISG-online 151 (a fundamental breach of a non-competition agreement was established).
1769. *See* Ch. 2 III. 1. above.
1770. Cf. JPI Badalona No. 3, 22 May 2006, CISG-online 1391 (no recourse to Art. 73(2) CISG, given that the contracts in question were separate individual contracts, rather than constituting a single, uniform instalment contract); MüKoHGB/*Sommerfeld*, Art. 73 CISG, para. 4; Soergel/*Lutzi*, Art. 73 CISG, para. 2; Witz/Salger/Lorenz/*Lorenz*, Art. 73 CISG, paras 6, 8.
1771. *Achilles*, Art. 73 CISG, para. 2; Brunner/Gottlieb/*Brunner/Schläpfer/Boog*, Art. 73 CISG, para. 3; Honsell/*Brunner/Hurni*, Art. 73 CISG, para. 3; MüKoHGB/*Sommerfeld*, Art. 73 CISG, para. 4; Schlechtriem/Schwenzer/Schroeter/*Fountoulakis*, 5th English ed., Art. 73 CISG, para. 11; Schlechtriem/Schwenzer/Schroeter/*Fountoulakis*, 8th German ed., Art. 73 CISG, para. 12;

this provision are based on the premise that although the individual deliveries are somewhat separable,[1772] they are still connected through one uniform contract.[1773] Given that the individual deliveries are connected through a uniform contract and thus interrelated, Art. 73(2) and (3) CISG entitle the aggrieved party to avoid the entire contract in certain circumstances. The situation is distinct with regard to the framework agreements discussed here, as such agreements and the individual sales contracts are not connected through one uniform agreement. Rather, they are merely economically related but separate contracts.[1774]

Consequently, the remedy of avoidance is generally confined to the contract that has been (fundamentally) breached, namely one or multiple individual sales contracts or the framework agreement. However, there may be instances where an individual sales contract has been breached, and the aggrieved party is not only interested in avoiding the individual sales contract but also the framework agreement.[1775]

ii. Avoidance of Framework Agreement Based on Breach of Individual Sales Contract

A typical situation in which the aggrieved party may wish to avoid all contractual relationships between the parties may occur if the breaching party commits a particularly 'grave' breach of an individual sales contract or repeatedly breaches the individual sales contracts.[1776] As the aggrieved party would normally be obliged to conclude further individual sales contracts in the future as part of their obligations under the framework agreement, they may wish to avoid not only the individual sales contracts that have been breached but also the framework agreement.[1777]

In general, a fundamental breach of the framework agreement is required to entitle the aggrieved party to avoid this contract under the CISG.[1778] Conversely, a breach of sales obligations set out in the individual sales contracts generally does not violate the obligations set out in the framework agreement, as the framework agreement merely binds the parties to conclude individual sales contracts without containing actual sales obligations.[1779] Art. 73 CISG cannot be applied to such cases.[1780]

Soergel/*Lutzi*, Art. 73 CISG, para. 2; Staudinger/*Magnus*, Art. 73 CISG, para. 7; cf. also Kröll *et al./Saidov*, Art. 73 CISG, paras 6, 7.

1772. Netherlands Arbitration Institute, 15 October 2002, CISG-online 740, para. 134; Kröll *et al./Saidov*, Art. 73 CISG, para. 3; Schlechtriem/Schwenzer/Schroeter/*Fountoulakis*, 5th English ed., Art. 73 CISG, para. 7.
1773. MüKoHGB/*Sommerfeld*, Art. 73 CISG, para. 4; cf. also *Enderlein/Maskow*, Art. 73 CISG, note 1; Witz/Salger/Lorenz/*Lorenz*, Art. 73 CISG, para. 6.
1774. Cf. also Witz/Salger/Lorenz/*Lorenz*, Art. 73 CISG, para. 8.
1775. Cf. *Hoffbauer*, pp. 115 et seq.; *C. Meyer*, Alleinvertrieb, pp. 342 et seq.; *Saxinger*, pp. 176, 177.
1776. *See* Ch. 5 III. 4. c. iii. 1) a) ii) above.
1777. Cf. *Hoffbauer*, pp. 115, 116.
1778. *See* Ch. 5 III. 5. a. above; on domestic German and Swiss domestic law: *Hoffbauer*, p. 116; *C. Meyer*, Alleinvertrieb, p. 342, 343; *Saxinger*, p. 176.
1779. Cf. *Hoffbauer*, pp. 114, 115; this approach of separating the individual sales contracts from the framework agreement was adopted by the German Supreme Court, although in a different context: *see* BGH, 23 July 1997, CISG-online 276, where the Court ruled that the invalidity of the framework agreement did not affect the validity of the individual sales contracts.

Consequently, breaches relating to the individual sales contracts do not concern the framework agreement; therefore, the aggrieved party is generally not entitled to avoid the framework agreement based on a breach of the individual sales contracts under the CISG. Nevertheless, as argued above, the aggrieved party may be able to invoke domestic law rules that permit termination of the framework agreement for a compelling reason under such circumstances.[1781]

In addition, Arts 71 and 72 CISG may be applicable to related contracts, provided that the respective prerequisites are met.[1782] This is supported by the broad wording of these provisions.[1783] Consequently, if one party breaches their obligations under an individual sales contract, the aggrieved party may be entitled to suspend their performance or even avoid other individual sales contracts that have already been concluded in accordance with Art. 71 or Art. 72 CISG. It is, however, questionable whether the same applies in view of the framework agreement. A breach of an individual sales contract does not make it 'apparent' or 'clear' that the other party will not perform their obligations under the framework agreement, since the obligations under these contracts differ from each other.[1784] The individual sales contracts contain sales obligations in *sensu stricto*, whereas the framework agreement obliges the parties to conclude further contracts.[1785] Accordingly, the aggrieved party should primarily rely on domestic law provisions if they wish to avoid the framework agreement based on breaches of the individual sales contracts. It is also possible to invoke a contractual agreement if a clause has been incorporated into the framework agreement (Art. 6 CISG) according to which the aggrieved party is entitled to avoid the entire framework agreement based on breaches of individual sales contracts.[1786]

d. Summary

The avoidance of long-term framework agreements governed by the CISG is generally subject to the Convention's provisions on contract avoidance, in particular Arts 25, 49, 64, 72 and 73 CISG. However, there are some particularities when determining whether the breaching party has fundamentally breached the contract in the sense of Art. 25 CISG. It is important to consider a multitude of interests when attempting to objectively balance both parties' interests, since framework agreements often entail obligations

1780. *See* Ch. 5 III. 5. c. i. above.
1781. *See* Ch. 5 III. 4. c. iii. 1) a) ii) above.
1782. CA Paris, 2 October 2023, CISG-online 6569 (Art. 71 CISG applied to related sales contracts); OLG Köln, 14 January 1994, CISG-online 119 (Art. 72 CISG applied to related contracts) with a comment by *Schroeter*, para. 730; CISG-AC, Op. 9 *Bridge*, Comment 3.4; *Enderlein/Maskow*, Art. 73 CISG, note 1 (mentioning Art. 72 CISG); *Schroeter*, para. 729; Witz/Salger/Lorenz/*Lorenz*, Art. 73 CISG, para. 8.
1783. Cf. CISG-AC, Op. 9 *Bridge*, Comment 3.4; *Schroeter*, para. 729.
1784. Cf. *Fuchs-Wissemann*, pp. 220, 221; *Hoffbauer*, p. 116; probably different: CISG-AC, Op. 9 *Bridge*, Comment 3.4.
1785. *See* Ch. 2 III. 2. above.
1786. Cf. District Court Tokyo, 16 June 2020, CISG-online 5648; OGH, 28 September 2000, CISG-online 798, para. 2 (clause 7d); CISG-AC, Op. 9 *Bridge*, Comment 3.4 ('cross-default clauses').

relating to the parties' overall relationship and cooperation. Therefore, the interests to be taken into account are somewhat different to those of short-term contracts. In addition, the importance of trust and reliability is heightened in long-term framework agreements. Consequently, deceitful conduct of the breaching party may give rise to doubts about their reliability and trustworthiness, thereby influencing the assessment of whether there has been a fundamental breach within the meaning of Art. 25 CISG.

The avoidance of framework agreements that already contain the defining characteristics of a sales contract is primarily subject to Art. 73 CISG. Furthermore, Arts 49 and 64 CISG might be of relevance.

The avoidance of framework agreements with a two-tier structure is a more complex issue. In such cases, it is necessary to differentiate between the framework agreement and the individual sales contracts when dealing with disputes. In a first step, one must determine which obligations have been breached: those under the individual sales contracts or those under the framework agreement. If there has been a fundamental breach of any obligations, the remedy of avoidance is limited to the contract in which the fundamental breach occurred. In certain instances, however, the aggrieved party may be motivated to sever all ties with the breaching party, extending beyond the avoidance of an individual sales contract to encompass the framework agreement that would otherwise oblige them to conclude additional contracts with the breaching party. In general, the breach of individual sales contracts does not entitle the aggrieved party to avoid the framework agreement under the CISG. Nevertheless, the aggrieved party may be able to invoke Art. 71 or 72 CISG in order to suspend or avoid related individual sales contracts based on a breach of another individual sales contract. Furthermore, they may be able to invoke domestic law provisions that provide for a right to terminate the framework agreement for a compelling reason based on breaches of the individual sales contracts.

6. Effects of Avoidance or Termination of Long-Term Framework Agreements

The following section will address the effects of avoiding or terminating a long-term framework agreement under the CISG. However, it should be noted that this section will not cover all aspects of this issue; rather, it will address selected questions that are of particular importance when it comes to long-term framework agreements.

a. Scope of Avoidance and Termination

In general, restitution is addressed in Arts 81–84 CISG. These provisions also apply, by way of gap-filling in the sense of Art. 7(2) CISG, if the parties agree to terminate a contract.[1787]

1787. *See* only LG Dortmund, 21 April 2017, CISG-online 2801; Ferrari *et al./Ferrari*, Art. 81 CISG, para. 5; Kröll *et al./Bridge*, Art. 81 CISG, para. 14; MüKoBGB/*Huber*, Art. 81 CISG, para. 2; Schlechtriem/Schwenzer/Schroeter/*Fountoulakis*, 5th English ed., Intro Arts 81–84 CISG,

If a framework agreement already contains the defining characteristics of a sales contract, the avoidance of such a contract is primarily governed by Art. 73 CISG. In accordance with Art. 73(1) CISG, the avoidance is limited to a single instalment under the contract. Consequently, restitution as per Arts 81–84 CISG is similarly limited to that instalment; the remainder of the contract is otherwise unaffected.[1788] Art. 73(2) CISG entitles the aggrieved party to avoid the contract *ex nunc*, i.e., for the future, in certain circumstances.[1789] The other part of the contract that has already been performed remains unaffected by such an avoidance.[1790] With regard to the future part of the contract, the parties are released from their obligations in accordance with Art. 81(1) CISG.[1791] It is not necessary to make a restitution since the parties have not yet performed the future part of the contract. If the parties have made preparations for the performance of the entire contract, such as the provision of basic equipment or advance payments, etc., a restitution may exceptionally be required.[1792] In cases covered by Art. 73(3) CISG, restitution may also be required. This is because the aforementioned provision entitles the aggrieved party to partially or completely avoid the contract, including parts of the contract that have already been performed.[1793] The same may apply in instances where Art. 49 or 64 CISG is applicable.[1794] If the parties terminate their contract by mutual agreement, they are free to determine whether the contract shall be ineffective *ex tunc* or *ex nunc* in accordance with Art. 6 CISG.[1795]

Should there be a distinction between a framework agreement and the individual sales contracts, the avoidance of the framework agreement generally has no impact on the individual sales contracts.[1796] The individual sales contracts may have been concluded on the basis of the framework agreement, but they are independent sales contracts.[1797] Consequently, the parties are not obliged to make restitution of the goods or refund the purchase price under these individual sales contracts if the framework agreement has been avoided. Attempting to make restitution in the sense of Arts 81–84 CISG with regard to the framework agreement that has been avoided is futile, as it does

paras 9, 10; Schlechtriem/Schwenzer/Schroeter/*Schroeter*, 5th English ed., Art. 29 CISG, para. 52; Staudinger/*Magnus*, Art. 81 CISG, para. 4.

1788. BeckOGK/*Schmidt-Ahrendts*, Art. 73 CISG, para. 15; MüKoBGB/*Huber*, Art. 73 CISG, paras 9, 10; MüKoHGB/*Sommerfeld*, Art. 73 CISG, para. 9; Schlechtriem/Schwenzer/Schroeter/*Fountoulakis*, 5th English ed., Art. 73 CISG, para. 18; cf. also Staudinger/*Magnus*, Art. 73 CISG, paras 16, 16a.
1789. *See* Ch. 5 III. 5. b. above.
1790. BeckOGK/*Schmidt-Ahrendts*, Art. 73 CISG, para. 30; BeckOK/*Saenger*, Art. 73 CISG, para. 10; MüKoBGB/*Huber*, Art. 73 CISG, para. 17; MüKoHGB/*Sommerfeld*, Art. 73 CISG, para. 18; Schlechtriem/Schwenzer/Schroeter/*Fountoulakis*, 5th English ed., Art. 73 CISG, para. 31; Staudinger/*Magnus*, Art. 73 CISG, para. 27.
1791. BeckOGK/*Schmidt-Ahrendts*, Art. 73 CISG, para. 30; cf. also BeckOK/*Saenger*, Art. 73 CISG, para. 10; MüKoBGB/*Huber*, Art. 73 CISG, para. 17.
1792. MüKoBGB/*Huber*, Art. 73 CISG, para. 17; Schlechtriem/Schwenzer/Schroeter/*Fountoulakis*, 5th English ed., Art. 73 CISG, para. 31; Staudinger/*Magnus*, Art. 73 CISG, para. 27.
1793. *See* MüKoBGB/*Huber*, Art. 73 CISG, para. 26; Schlechtriem/Schwenzer/Schroeter/*Fountoulakis*, 5th English ed., Art. 73 CISG, paras 39 et seq.
1794. Cf. only Schlechtriem/Schwenzer/Schroeter/*Müller-Chen*, 5th English ed., Art. 49 CISG, para. 43; Schlechtriem/Schwenzer/Schroeter/*Mohs*, 5th English ed., Art. 64 CISG, para. 33.
1795. Schlechtriem/Schwenzer/Schroeter/*Schroeter*, 5th English ed., Art. 29 CISG, para. 52.
1796. *Hoffbauer*, p. 203.
1797. *Hoffbauer*, p. 203; *see* Ch. 2 III. 1. above.

not involve the exchange of goods against payment, which is a fundamental premise of the aforementioned provisions, as evidenced in Art. 82 or 84 CISG. In such cases, avoidance primarily affects the future, in that the parties will not be obliged to conclude further individual sales contracts. In contrast, if an individual sales contract that has already been performed is avoided, restitution will typically be required. However, avoidance in such cases is limited to the relevant individual sales contract. The other individual sales contracts remain unaffected, unless Art. 72(1) CISG applies, which presupposes that it must be 'clear' that the breaching parties will commit a fundamental breach of another individual sales contract.[1798]

b. Claims for Compensation of Investments

It is not uncommon for the parties to a framework agreement to make significant initial investments, which are only recouped over time.[1799] This may particularly be the case in instances where the seller has oriented their production towards the buyer, for example, where the seller is obliged to sell a significant amount of their output to the buyer.[1800] In such cases, the investing party may wish to be compensated for their investments once the framework agreement or any other long-term contract has been avoided or terminated.[1801]

Under the CISG, the aggrieved party may be entitled to rely on Art. 45(1)(b) or 61(1)(b) in conjunction with Art. 74 CISG.[1802] These provisions permit the aggrieved party to be compensated for frustrated expenses in certain instances.[1803] It can be argued that the investments discussed here may be considered as such frustrated expenses.[1804] In order for this to be the case, it is necessary for the investments to have been made in reliance on the contract, for them to have been rendered useless, and for them to have been appropriate and reasonable for the performance of the contract from the viewpoint of a reasonable third person (Art. 8(2) CISG).[1805] It is only if these prerequisites are met that the investing party will be entitled to be compensated under Art. 45(1)(b) or 61(1)(b) in conjunction with Art. 74 CISG. In practice, it might be

1798. *See* Ch. 5 III. 5. c. ii. above.
1799. *See* OLG Jena, 8 December 2015, CISG-online 2664, para. 6; cf. also Comment 5 on Art. 7.1.7 UPICC; *Hoffbauer*, p. 209; *Martinek*, p. 90; *Oetker*, pp. 43 et seq.; *Saxinger*, pp. 232, 233; UNIDROIT 2014, Study L – Doc. 126, paras 25 et seq.
1800. Cf. *Hoffbauer*, p. 209; *Saxinger*, pp. 233, 238.
1801. *Hoffbauer*, p. 209; *Saxinger*, pp. 232 et seq.; *see* the case in OLG Jena, 8 December 2015, CISG-online 2664.
1802. OLG Jena, 8 December 2015, CISG-online 2664, para. 54; cf. *Bremenkamp*, ZVertriebsR 2023, pp. 210, 211 (with regard to German domestic law).
1803. OGH, 14 January 2002, CISG-online 643, para. 47; *Delchi Carrier, SpA v. Rotorex Corp.*, US Ct. App. (2nd Cir.), 6 December 1995, CISG-online 140; Schlechtriem/Schwenzer/Schroeter/*Schwenzer*, 5th English ed., Art. 74 CISG, para. 40; *Schroeter*, para. 850; Staudinger/*Magnus*, Art. 74 CISG, para. 53; providing a detailed analysis of the compensation of frustrated expenses in case of unwinding failed contracts under the CISG: *Schmidt-Ahrendts*, IHR 2006, pp. 67 et seq.
1804. With a similar idea under German domestic law: *Hoffbauer*, pp. 210, 211.
1805. Cf. OGH, 14 January 2002, CISG-online 643, para. 47; *Schroeter*, para. 850; Staudinger/*Magnus*, Art. 74 CISG, para. 53.

challenging to prove that the investments were made in reliance on a specific framework agreement.[1806]

The case of *MITEC Automotive AG v. Ford Motor Company*, which was decided by the German District Court Meiningen and the Court of Appeal Jena, is illustrative in this context.[1807] In this case, the parties concluded a long-term contract for the production and sale of 'balancers' (car parts that reduce movement and noise of motors). This contract was limited in time to five years.[1808] The seller, however, made investments in reliance on the parties' discussions and the buyer's conduct, which allegedly suggested that the contract might be renewed for another year.[1809] Consequently, they sought compensation for these investments based on Art. 61(1)(b) in conjunction with Art. 74 CISG. The Court of Appeal held that the seller was not entitled to assume that the contract would be extended for another year.[1810] Thus, the seller's claim for damages was rejected.[1811] In essence, the seller's costs were not considered to be foreseeable for the buyer in the sense of Art. 74 CISG.[1812]

Furthermore, parties to a distribution agreement may be entitled to claim compensation based on different grounds subsequent to the termination of the contract. As stated above, the CISG is not concerned with such considerations, which is why domestic law should apply in that regard.[1813]

c. *Post-contractual Obligations*

Framework agreements frequently necessitate a high degree of collaboration between the parties involved. Consequently, there is a possibility that confidential business information may be disclosed between them.[1814] For this reason, the parties to a framework agreement frequently agree on clauses regarding confidentiality or the sharing of know-how.[1815] Art. 81(1) CISG explicitly states that 'avoidance does not affect any provision of the contract for the settlement of disputes or any other provision of the contract governing the rights and obligations of the parties consequent upon the

1806. *Hoffbauer*, p. 211.
1807. The entire case history includes: LG Meiningen, 25 March 2010, CISG-online 3065; OLG Jena, 10 November 2010, CISG-online 2216; BGH, 5 July 2011, CISG-online 3082 (no decision on the merits); LG Meiningen, 29 November 2012, CISG-online 3076; OLG Jena, 8 December 2015, CISG-online 2664; LG Meiningen, 22 November 2018, CISG-online 4671.
1808. OLG Jena, 8 December 2015, CISG-online 2664, para. 8.
1809. OLG Jena, 8 December 2015, CISG-online 2664, para. 6.
1810. OLG Jena, 8 December 2015, CISG-online 2664, paras 51 et seq.
1811. OLG Jena, 8 December 2015, CISG-online 2664, paras 51 et seq.; cf. also LG Meiningen, 22 November 2018, CISG-online 4671, paras 48 et seq.; differently, CA Lithuania, 26 February 2015, CISG-online 5138, where the Court, *inter alia*, awarded damages to the buyer for investments under Art. 74 CISG, following the (allegedly unlawful) termination of a distribution agreement, in particular for the marketing expenses incurred by the buyer under the distribution agreement.
1812. Cf. LG Meiningen, 22 November 2018, CISG-online 4671, paras 50, 51.
1813. *See* Ch. 4 III. 2. c. ii., iii. above.
1814. *Saxinger*, p. 241.
1815. Cf. *Saxinger*, p. 241; Schlechtriem/Schwenzer/Schroeter/*Fountoulakis*, 5th English ed., Art. 73 CISG, para. 8.

avoidance of the contract'. This may include confidentiality and related obligations.[1816] Thus, contractual confidentiality obligations may also apply subsequent to the termination or avoidance of a framework agreement. In order for this to be the case, it is necessary for the parties to intend for these clauses to survive.[1817] This is essentially a question of contract interpretation that will turn on the circumstances of each case.[1818] The question of whether the content of such contractual obligations has been validly agreed upon is determined by the applicable domestic law.[1819]

d. Summary

The effects of avoidance and termination of a long-term framework agreement are contingent upon the parties' agreement and the remedy sought by the aggrieved party. With regard to framework agreements that already contain the defining characteristics of a sales contract, Art. 73 CISG is of significance. In accordance with Art. 73(1) CISG, avoidance and, if applicable, restitution (Arts 81 et seq. CISG) is restricted to a single instalment under the contract. Conversely, Art. 73(2) CISG may entitle the aggrieved party to avoid a framework agreement *ex nunc*, without affecting the part of the contract that has already been performed. In accordance with Art. 73(3) CISG, the aggrieved party may be entitled to avoid the framework agreement in its entirety, thereby necessitating restitution. If the parties agree to terminate their contract, they are at liberty to determine whether the contract shall be ineffective *ex tunc* or *ex nunc* (Art. 6 CISG).

The situation is distinct when considering framework agreements that adhere to a two-tier structure. The avoidance of such agreements typically does not impact the individual sales contracts that are concluded under its umbrella. Furthermore, restitution in the sense of Arts 81 et seq. CISG is normally not necessary in such contracts, as they do not involve the exchange of goods for money (in contrast to the individual sales contracts). The avoidance of such framework agreements primarily has implications for the future, as the parties will not be obliged to conclude further individual sales contracts. Conversely, the avoidance of individual sales contracts may require restitution. In certain instances, the breach of an individual sales contract may entitle the aggrieved party to avoid further individual sales contracts in accordance with Art. 72(1) CISG.

As the parties to long-term framework agreements frequently make substantial initial investments that are recouped over time, they may be interested in being compensated for their investments if the contract is avoided or terminated. Under the CISG, they may be able to do so pursuant to Art. 45(1)(b) or 61(1)(b) in conjunction with Art. 74 CISG. For such investments to be eligible for compensation, they must

1816. CISG-AC, Op. 9 *Bridge*, Comment 3.3; Schlechtriem/Schwenzer/Schroeter/*Fountoulakis*, 5th English ed., Art. 81 CISG, para. 14; Staudinger/*Magnus*, Art. 81 CISG, para. 8; cf. also Kull/Wildhaber/*Kull*, paras 689 et seq. (on post-contractual confidentiality clauses under Swiss domestic law).
1817. CISG-AC, Op. 9 *Bridge*, Comment 3.3.
1818. Cf. CISG-AC, Op. 9 *Bridge*, Comment 3.3.
1819. Staudinger/*Magnus*, Art. 81 CISG, para. 8.

have been made in reliance on the contract, rendered useless, and considered appropriate and reasonable for the performance of the contract from the viewpoint of a reasonable third person (Art. 8(2) CISG). In other words, the investments must qualify as frustrated expenses.

Some obligations that are part of a long-term framework agreement may survive its avoidance or termination in accordance with Art. 81(1), sentence 2 CISG. The prerequisite is that the parties intended for a clause to govern their entire relationship, including the post-contractual stages. This may be the case for confidentiality clauses or the like. Essentially, the parties' intentions must be determined by way of contract interpretation.

IV. CONCLUSION

A 'long-term contract' is defined as any contract that must be performed over an extended (significant) period of time, as per this study. The CISG covers long-term contracts, most notably framework agreements and instalment contracts.[1820] The temporal aspect of such contracts presents specific problems in certain contexts but not in a general manner.

One such problem is the role of cooperation and trust in long-term framework agreements. The parties are free to incorporate cooperation and fiduciary obligations into their contract under the CISG. However, it has been submitted by this study that no general cooperation or information obligations may be derived from the CISG (in particular Art. 7(1) or (2) CISG). Nevertheless, cooperation or fiduciary obligations may arise from an interpretation of the contract (Art. 8 CISG), established usages or practices (Art. 9 CISG) or an interpretation of specific provisions of the CISG in light of good faith (Art. 7(1) CISG). In addition, they may follow from domestic law rules in accordance with Art. 7(2) CISG, or if they are related to a matter outside the Convention's sphere of application. If fiduciary or cooperation obligations have been incorporated into a long-term framework agreement governed by the CISG, the breach of such obligations shall be governed by the Convention. However, domestic law remedies shall apply alongside the CISG, provided that they are not only linked to a breach of contract but also to other aspects, such as the parties' specific relationship of trust.[1821]

Long-term framework agreements are susceptible to alterations in the surrounding circumstances. Consequently, the parties may diverge from the contractual terms through their actual conduct following contract conclusion. The parties' subsequent conduct must be taken into account for the interpretation of any CISG contract in accordance with Art. 8(3) CISG. This interpretative tool is particularly pertinent to long-term framework agreements and other long-term contracts. Furthermore, the parties may wish to modify their framework agreement at a later stage (Art. 29 CISG).

1820. *See* Ch. 5 I., II. above.
1821. *See* Ch. 5 III. 1. above.

They may also agree on additional mechanisms for contract modifications in anticipation of potential changes, such as price escalation clauses, which are common in framework agreements, or external standards. The latter may stipulate the essential elements of a long-term framework agreement (e.g., price) or expand on the performance of their obligations (e.g., specify the conformity of the goods).[1822]

Long-term framework agreements may also be subject to supervening events, which are frequently discussed under the notion of force majeure or hardship. The CISG should encompass instances of both force majeure and hardship (Art. 79 CISG). Framework agreements and other long-term contracts are also generally subject to this provision, with the same prerequisites applying and the same consequences ensuing. Nevertheless, such contracts frequently diverge from the aforementioned provision by including force majeure or hardship clauses. Furthermore, such contracts are more likely to explicitly or implicitly address certain risks, thereby limiting the possibility of hardship. In addition, the point of reference for determining whether there has been a fundamental alteration of the contractual equilibrium is the entire framework agreement, including past and future performances. It is crucial to note that this assessment must be conducted separately for a framework agreement with a two-tier structure and the individual sales contracts. Nevertheless, it is possible that these contracts may influence the interpretation of each other, which could affect the assessment of whether there has been a fundamental alteration of the contract in question.[1823]

Long-term framework agreements are frequently limited in time, and the parties intend to terminate the contract upon its expiration. Such arrangements may be agreed upon under the CISG (Art. 29 CISG). The admissibility of specific contractual durations is subject to domestic law (Art. 4(a) CISG). Some domestic laws provide for a right to unilaterally terminate any long-term contract (including framework agreements) within a specific timeframe, provided that the contract is of indefinite duration. An application of the two-step test indicates that the CISG may cover these factual scenarios, but it does not intend to govern this subject matter. The general right to terminate indefinite long-term contracts is, *inter alia*, based on the consideration that the parties should not be able to contractually bind themselves eternally. This risk is not addressed by the CISG. Therefore, domestic law rules that provide for a general right to terminate indefinite long-term contracts should be applicable alongside the Convention.[1824]

The CISG differs from some domestic laws in that it does not mention a right to terminate a long-term framework agreement or other long-term contracts for a compelling reason. Once more, this study proposes that the two-step test should be relied upon. In this context, it is necessary to differentiate between different cases. The Convention exhaustively governs cases of breach of contract (Arts 49, 64, 73 CISG), cases of insolvency (Arts 71, 72, 73 CISG) and cases of hardship (Art. 79 CISG). Therefore, there is no room to have recourse to domestic law rules. In contrast, domestic law rules that provide for a right to terminate for a compelling reason should

1822. *See* Ch. 5 III. 2. above.
1823. *See* Ch. 5 III. 3. above.
1824. *See* Ch. 5 III. 4. a., b. above.

be applied alongside the CISG in cases of 'cross-contractual' breaches (termination of a framework agreement based on breach of individual sales contracts), cases of disruption of the parties' personal relationship and cases of change of control. While the Convention covers these factual scenarios, it does not address the underlying risks, nor does it attempt to regulate them.[1825]

The avoidance of long-term framework agreements governed by the CISG is generally subject to the Convention's provisions on contract avoidance. In the context of framework agreements, it may be necessary to consider the parties' multifaceted interests and their contractual expectation of reliable and trustworthy conduct in the context of the balancing act required by Art. 25 CISG. The avoidance of framework agreements that already contain the defining characteristics of a sales contract is primarily subject to Art. 73 CISG, and where applicable Arts 49 and 64 CISG. The avoidance of framework agreements with a two-tier structure is a more complex issue. In general, the right to avoid is limited to the contract that has been fundamentally breached. Nevertheless, in certain instances, the aggrieved party may be interested in avoiding not only an individual sales contract but also the framework agreement itself. As a general rule, the breach of an individual sales contract does not entitle the aggrieved party to avoid the framework agreement under the CISG. Yet, the aggrieved party may be entitled to rely on domestic law provisions that provide for a right to terminate for a compelling reason in such cases. In addition, they may be able to invoke Art. 71 or 72 CISG in order to suspend or avoid related individual sales contracts based on a breach of another individual sales contract.[1826]

The effects of avoidance or termination of a long-term framework agreement governed by the CISG are largely set out in the Convention. Art. 73(1) CISG restricts the possibility of avoidance and restitution to a single instalment under the contract. Art. 73(2) CISG, however, may entitle the aggrieved party to avoid a framework agreement *ex nunc* without affecting the part of the contract that has already been performed in the past. Art. 73(3) CISG may entitle the aggrieved party to avoid the entire framework agreement, thereby necessitating restitution. Different rules apply to framework agreements with a two-tier structure. The avoidance of these agreements typically does not affect the individual sales contracts concluded under their umbrella. Furthermore, restitution, as outlined in Arts 81 et seq. CISG, is normally not necessary in such contracts, as they do not involve the exchange of goods for money. The avoidance of such framework agreements primarily has *ex nunc* effects, as the parties are no longer obliged to conclude further individual sales contracts. Furthermore, following the avoidance or termination of a framework agreement, the parties may be interested in compensation for investments that have been made, which would have materialised over time. Under the CISG, such a course of action may be pursued in accordance with Art. 45(1)(b) or 61(b) CISG in conjunction with Art. 74 CISG. Finally, some obligations that are part of a long-term framework agreement may survive its avoidance or termination in accordance with Art. 81(1), sentence 2 CISG.[1827]

1825. *See* Ch. 5 III. 4. c. above.
1826. *See* Ch. 5 III. 5. above.
1827. *See* Ch. 5 III. 6. above.

Chapter 6

Choice of Law Clauses in Framework Agreements

Parties to a framework agreement may incorporate a choice of law clause into their framework agreement. This may help to avoid uncertainties and provide clarity regarding the law applicable to the agreement.[1828] Such a choice of law clause may also affect the CISG's applicability to the contract.

A review of existing case law suggests that the parties to a framework agreement frequently agree on choice of law clauses in favour of the CISG.[1829] This can be attributed to the general advantages of the CISG, for instance, that it is a 'neutral' law that is detached from a domestic context.[1830] Moreover, the CISG's applicability to framework agreements may be uncertain, and thus a choice of law clause could serve to clarify the situation.[1831] The CISG's applicability may be uncertain from a territorial perspective, particularly in cases where it is not entirely clear whether the Convention will apply pursuant to Art. 1(1)(a) or Art. 1(1)(b) CISG.[1832] Furthermore, it may also be

1828. In general: MüKoHGB/*B. Köhler*, Art. 6 CISG, para. 16; Ostendorf/*Ostendorf*, § 13, para. 2.
1829. *See McHugh et al. v. Vertical Partners West, LLC et al.*, US Dist. Ct. Idaho, 19 April 2021, CISG-online 6003, para. 16 ('exclusive supply agreement'); High Ct. Singapore, 13 March 2019, CISG-online 4108 (arbitral award: ICC, 10 December 2015, CISG-online 4106); CA Toulouse, 25 February 2015, CISG-online 5188; ICC, 18203/2013, CISG-online 2973; *FPM Financial Services, LLC v. Redline Products Ltd.*, US Dist. Ct. NJ, 17 September 2013, CISG-online 2849 (choice of the CISG, provided that the conditions set forth in Art. 1(1)(a) CISG are met); High Ct. Singapore, 14 August 2012, CISG-online 2725 (arbitral award: ICC, 11 November 2011, CISG-online 1851); OLG Koblenz, 22 April 2010, CISG-online 2163, para. 16; *Chemische Fabrik Budenheim KG v. Bavaria Corp. Int'l*, US Dist. Ct. MD Florida, 8 July 2009, CISG-online 4578; ICC, 11849/2003, CISG-online 1421.
1830. In detail *Fountoulakis*, EJLR 2005, pp. 313 et seq.; Schlechtriem/Schwenzer/Schroeter/*Schroeter*, 8th German ed., Einleitung, paras 42 et seq.; cf. also *Gillette/Walt*, p. 74.
1831. Cf. *Perales Viscasillas*, Extending the Scope, p. 118; *Perales Viscasillas*, Int'l Distribution Contracts and CISG, p. 46; *Perović*, (2011) 59 Belgrade L. Rev., p. 191; Schlechtriem/Schwenzer/Schroeter/*Schroeter*, 8th German ed., Einleitung, para. 75.
1832. Cf. ICC, 18203/2013, CISG-online 2973, where both parties had their place of business in the United Arab Emirates.

uncertain whether a specific framework agreement falls within the material scope of the Convention, particularly in light of Arts 1 and 3 CISG.[1833] This raises the questions of whether parties may choose the CISG in cases where a framework agreement does not fall within its territorial or material scope of application, and what consequences follow from such a choice of law clause. The subsequent part will analyse the effects of choice of law clauses in framework agreements with regard to the CISG's applicability. In this context, this study will distinguish between a 'direct' or 'isolated' choice of the CISG without reference to any other laws and a choice of domestic law.[1834]

I. DIRECT OR ISOLATED CHOICE OF THE CONVENTION

A direct choice of the Convention as the law applicable to a framework agreement is unproblematic if the contract would be subject to the CISG per se. Such a clause serves only to reaffirm what already applies in accordance with Arts 1–6 CISG.[1835] This type of choice of law clause presents no particular challenges and has no independent significance.[1836]

An isolated or direct choice of the CISG without reference to domestic law is a more complex matter when one of the prerequisites for the Convention's application, as set out in Arts 1–6 CISG, is not met. The Convention does not apply in such cases in accordance with its own terms. It is questionable whether a choice of the Convention is still admissible in such circumstances.

1. Admissibility

The CISG itself is silent on the issue of opting in, in contrast to its predecessor, namely Art. 4 of the ULIS.[1837] The CISG merely addresses the issue of opting out in Art. 6 CISG. Despite its silence on this matter, the prevailing view among scholars is that the CISG does not prevent the parties from opting into the Convention.[1838]

1833. *See* Chs 3 and 4 above on Arts 1 and 3 CISG in the context of framework agreements; cf. also Staudinger/*Magnus*, Art. 6 CISG, para. 68, noting that a clarifying choice of law is advisable with regard to Art. 3 CISG.
1834. With a similar distinction: *Lohmann*, pp. 309 et seq.; cf. also MüKoBGB/*Huber*, Art. 6 CISG, para. 32.
1835. *Lohmann*, p. 332; *Schroeter*, para. 83.
1836. *Schroeter*, para. 83.
1837. *Bridge*, Int'l Sale of Goods, para. 10.53; *Gillette/Walt*, p. 73; Kröll *et al./Mistelis*, Art. 6 CISG, para. 27; *Lohmann*, p. 311; MüKoBGB/*Huber*, Art. 6 CISG, para. 31; Schlechtriem/Schwenzer/Schroeter/*Ferrari*, 8th German ed., Art. 6 CISG, para. 39; Staudinger/*Magnus*, Art. 6 CISG, para. 62; cf. also *Flechtner/Brand*, p. 111.
1838. *Enderlein/Maskow*, Art. 6 CISG, note 3.2; *Gillette/Walt*, p. 73; *Herber/Czerwenka*, Art. 6 CISG, para. 19; Kröll *et al./Mistelis*, Art. 6 CISG, para. 27; *Lindbach*, pp. 185 et seq.; *Lohmann*, p. 311; MüKoBGB/*Huber*, Art. 6 CISG, para. 31; Schlechtriem/Schwenzer/Schroeter/*Ferrari*, 8th German ed., Art. 6 CISG, para. 39; Schlechtriem/Schwenzer/Schroeter/*Hachem*, 5th English ed., Art. 6 CISG, para. 32.

With regard to the admissibility of a direct choice of the CISG, most scholars distinguish between opting in on a conflict of laws level and on a substantive level.[1839] Whether the parties intended for a choice of law clause to operate at the level of conflict of laws or at a substantive level must be determined by interpretation in accordance with the applicable domestic law rules.[1840]

The practical difference between these two levels primarily lies in the fact that a choice of law on a conflict of laws level results in mandatory domestic law provisions being superseded by the CISG, with the exception of so-called overriding mandatory provisions.[1841] A choice of law on a substantive level, however, must remain within the limits of party autonomy granted by the otherwise applicable domestic law.[1842] Consequently, mandatory domestic law provisions still take precedence over the Convention's provisions in the event of a conflict.[1843]

a. *Substantive Level*

It is undisputed that selecting the CISG on a substantive level is unproblematic.[1844] The admissibility of such a choice of law is to be determined by the domestic law applicable by virtue of international private law rules (*lex contractus*).[1845] If the applicable

1839. BeckOK/*Saenger*, Art. 6 CISG, para. 7; *Lindbach*, pp. 180 et seq.; MüKoBGB/*Huber*, Art. 6 CISG, paras 32 et seq.; MüKoHGB/*B. Köhler*, Art. 6 CISG, paras 16 et seq.; Schlechtriem/Schwenzer/Schroeter/*Ferrari*, 8th German ed., Art. 6 CISG, para. 40; Schlechtriem/Schwenzer/Schroeter/*Hachem*, 5th English ed., Art. 6 CISG, para. 32; *Schroeter*, paras 83 et seq.; cf. also Brunner/Gottlieb/*Manner/Schmitt*, Art. 6 CISG, para. 12; Staudinger/*Magnus*, Art. 6 CISG, paras 62 et seq.
1840. Schlechtriem/Schwenzer/Schroeter/*Ferrari*, 8th German ed., Art. 6 CISG, para. 40; Schlechtriem/Schwenzer/Schroeter/*Hachem*, 5th English ed., Art. 6 CISG, para. 32.
1841. Brunner/Gottlieb/*Manner/Schmitt*, Art. 6 CISG, para. 12; MüKoBGB/*Huber*, Art. 6 CISG, para. 34; *Lohmann*, pp. 135, 136 (in general on this distinction); *Roth*, FS Jayme, p. 759; *Schroeter*, para. 85; cf. also Honsell/*Siehr*, Art. 6 CISG, para. 15; Schlechtriem/Schwenzer/Schroeter/*Hachem*, 5th English ed., Art. 6 CISG, paras 32, 37.
1842. *Bridge*, Choice of Law, p. 72; *Fawcett/Harris/Bridge*, para. 13.89; *Lindbach*, p. 180; *Schroeter*, para. 84; Schlechtriem/Schwenzer/Schroeter/*Ferrari*, 8th German ed., Art. 6 CISG, para. 41; Staudinger/*Magnus*, Art. 6 CISG, para. 65.
1843. BeckOK/*Saenger*, Art. 6 CISG, para. 7; *Bridge*, Choice of Law, p. 72; Brunner/Gottlieb/*Manner/Schmitt*, Art. 6 CISG, para. 12; *Herber/Czerwenka*, Art. 6 CISG, para. 19; *Lohmann*, p. 136; MüKoBGB/*Huber*, Art. 6 CISG, para. 33; MüKoHGB/*B. Köhler*, Art. 6 CISG, para. 19; Schlechtriem/Schwenzer/Schroeter/*Ferrari*, 8th German ed., Art. 6 CISG, para. 41; Schlechtriem/Schwenzer/Schroeter/*Hachem*, 5th English ed., Art. 6 CISG, para. 32; *Schroeter*, paras 84, 85; Staudinger/*Magnus*, Art. 6 CISG, paras 62, 65.
1844. BeckOK/*Saenger*, Art. 6 CISG, para. 7; Bianca/Bonell/*Bonell*, Art. 6 CISG, notes 3.5.1. et seq.; *Bridge*, Choice of Law, p. 72; *Bridge*, Int'l Sale of Goods, para. 10.54; Brunner/Gottlieb/*Manner/Schmitt*, Art. 6 CISG, para. 12; *Fawcett/Harris/Bridge*, para. 13.89; *Lindbach*, p. 180; Schlechtriem/Schwenzer/Schroeter/*Ferrari*, 8th German ed., Art. 6 CISG, para. 41; Schlechtriem/Schwenzer/Schroeter/*Hachem*, 5th English ed., Art. 6 CISG, para. 32; *Schroeter*, para. 84; Staudinger/*Magnus*, Art. 6 CISG, para. 62; cf. also *Gillette/Walt*, p. 74; *Lohmann*, pp. 136, 137 (in reference to the CISG's drafting history).
1845. *Bridge*, Choice of Law, p. 72; *Bridge*, Int'l Sale of Goods, para. 10.54; *Fawcett/Harris/Bridge*, para. 13.89; *Lindbach*, p. 180; MüKoHGB/*B. Köhler*, Art. 6 CISG, para. 19; Schlechtriem/Schwenzer/Schroeter/*Ferrari*, 8th German ed., Art. 6 CISG, para. 41; *Schroeter*, para. 84; Staudinger/*Magnus*, Art. 6 CISG, para. 65; cf. also MüKoBGB/*Huber*, Art. 6 CISG, para. 33; Schlechtriem/Schwenzer/Schroeter/*Hachem*, 5th English ed., Art. 6 CISG, para. 32.

domestic law permits the parties to displace its own provisions, they are at liberty to subject their contract, such as a framework agreement,[1846] to the CISG, despite the fact that it would not apply in accordance with its own terms.[1847] Consequently, the parties to a framework agreement are free to choose the CISG as the law governing their contract on a substantive level, provided that the applicable domestic law does not restrict their autonomy.[1848]

In such cases, the CISG's provisions are incorporated as a series of contractual terms, comparable to standard terms,[1849] into the framework agreement that is governed by another (domestic) law.[1850] This eliminates the necessity for the parties to replicate each provision of the CISG term by term in their agreement.[1851]

b. *Conflict of Laws Level*

The question of whether the CISG may be chosen on a conflict of laws level is a matter of greater controversy. The admissibility of such a choice of law in a framework agreement or any other contract must be determined in accordance with the relevant international private law rules.[1852] The following section will address the relevant international private law rules within the European Union and Switzerland.

i. *Rome I Regulation*

In the European Union, the law applicable to any contractual obligations is regulated by the Rome I Regulation. Art. 3(1) Rome I Regulation states that the parties are generally free to choose the law applicable to their contract. However, this provision is subject to controversy among legal scholars, who debate which kinds of laws can be selected by the parties and whether the CISG is one of them.

1846. Also mentioning this example: *Schroeter*, para. 84.
1847. Cf. *Bridge*, Int'l Sale of Goods, para. 10.54; *Fawcett/Harris/Bridge*, para. 13.89; *Karollus*, p. 40; MüKoHGB/*B. Köhler*, Art. 6 CISG, para. 19; Schlechtriem/Schwenzer/Schroeter/*Ferrari*, 8th German ed., Art. 6 CISG, paras 40, 41; *Schroeter*, para. 84; Staudinger/*Magnus*, Art. 6 CISG, para. 65.
1848. Cf. also *Schroeter*, para. 84.
1849. Using the same comparison: Brunner/Gottlieb/*Manner/Schmitt*, Art. 6 CISG, para. 12; MüKoHGB/*B. Köhler*, Art. 6 CISG, para. 19; Schlechtriem/Schwenzer/Schroeter/*Ferrari*, 8th German ed., Art. 6 CISG, para. 41; Staudinger/*Magnus*, Art. 6 CISG, para. 64.
1850. Not specifically with regard to framework agreements: BeckOK/*Saenger*, Art. 6 CISG, para. 7; Brunner/Gottlieb/*Manner/Schmitt*, Art. 6 CISG, para. 12; *Fawcett/Harris/Bridge*, para. 13.89; MüKoHGB/*B. Köhler*, Art. 6 CISG, para. 19; MüKoBGB/*Huber*, Art. 6 CISG, para. 33; Schlechtriem/Schwenzer/Schroeter/*Ferrari*, 8th German ed., Art. 6 CISG, para. 41; Staudinger/*Magnus*, Art. 6 CISG, para. 64.
1851. *Fawcett/Harris/Bridge*, para. 13.89; *Gillette/Walt*, p. 74.
1852. BeckOK/*Saenger*, Art. 6 CISG, para. 7; *Fawcett/Harris/Bridge*, para. 13.88; *Karollus*, p. 39; *Lindbach*, pp. 192, 193; *Lohmann*, p. 322; MüKoBGB/*Huber*, Art. 6 CISG, para. 32; MüKoHGB/*B. Köhler*, Art. 6 CISG, para. 19; Schlechtriem/Schwenzer/Schroeter/*Ferrari*, 8th German ed., Art. 6 CISG, para. 42; Schlechtriem/Schwenzer/Schroeter/*Hachem*, 5th English ed., Art. 6 CISG, para. 35; *Schroeter*, para. 85; Staudinger/*Magnus*, Art. 6 CISG, para. 65; cf. also *Bridge*, Choice of Law, pp. 71, 72; *Bridge*, Int'l Sale of Goods, para. 10.39; Brunner/Gottlieb/*Manner/Schmitt*, Art. 6 CISG, para. 12; *Gillette/Walt*, p. 74.

1) Prevailing View

The prevailing view in scholarly writings is that the parties are merely free to choose the domestic law of a state on a conflict of laws level under Art. 3(1) Rome I Regulation.[1853] This view is based on a systematic interpretation of the Regulation, which mainly refers to domestic state laws in its provisions.[1854] Moreover, the most prominent argument is based on a historical interpretation of Art. 3 Rome I Regulation. The proposal for the Rome I Regulation included an explicit provision (Art. 3(2)) that permitted the parties to select 'non-state law', i.e., rules other than the domestic law of a state; however, this provision was not included in the final text.[1855] It was presumed that there was a lack of clarity surrounding the issue of which non-state law could be selected by the parties and who should be responsible for determining this, which would have resulted in legal uncertainty.[1856] In light of this genesis, a significant number of scholars have reached the conclusion that non-state law cannot be chosen on a conflict of laws level.[1857] Although recital 13 of the Rome I Regulation[1858] refers to a 'non-state body of law or an international convention', the majority of commentators interpret this recital as a reference to a choice of law on a substantive level, rather than on a conflict of laws level.[1859]

1853. BeckOGK/*Wendland*, Art. 3 Rome I Regulation, para. 65; BeckOK/*Spickhoff*, Art. 3 Rome I Regulation, para. 7; Calliess/Renner/*Calliess*, Art. 3 Rome I Regulation, para. 34; Ferrari *et al./Ferrari*, Art. 3 Rome I Regulation, para. 18; Magnus/Mankowski/*Mankowski*, Art. 3 Rome I Regulation, paras 247 et seq.; MüKoBGB/*Huber*, Art. 6 CISG, para. 33; MüKoBGB/*Martiny*, Art. 3 Rome I Regulation, para. 29; MüKoHGB/*B. Köhler*, Art. 6 CISG, para. 19; Ostendorf/*Ostendorf*, § 13, para. 23; Rauscher/*von Hein*, Art. 3 Rome I Regulation, para. 51; *Rühl*, FS Kropholler, p. 189; Staudinger/*Magnus*, Art. 3 Rome I Regulation, para. 40; *von Hein/Vuattoux-Bock*, ZEuS 2023, pp. 488, 489; *Wegen/Asbrand*, RIW 2016, p. 558.

1854. BeckOK/*Spickhoff*, Art. 3 Rome I Regulation, para. 7; MüKoBGB/*Martiny*, Art. 3 Rome I Regulation, para. 29; Ostendorf/*Ostendorf*, § 13, para. 23; Rauscher/*von Hein*, Art. 3 Rome I Regulation, para. 51; *Rühl*, FS Kropholler, p. 190; Staudinger/*Magnus*, Art. 3 Rome I Regulation, para. 40; *Wegen/Asbrand*, RIW 2016, p. 558.

1855. BeckOK/*Spickhoff*, Art. 3 Rome I Regulation, para. 11; Calliess/Renner/*Calliess*, Art. 3 Rome I Regulation, para. 20; Ferrari *et al./Ferrari*, Art. 3 Rome I Regulation, para. 21; Magnus/Mankowski/*Mankowski*, Art. 3 Rome I Regulation, paras 248 et seq.; *Mankowski*, IHR 2008, p. 136; MüKoBGB/*Martiny*, Art. 3 Rome I Regulation, para. 29; Rauscher/*von Hein*, Art. 3 Rome I Regulation, para. 52; *Rühl*, FS Kropholler, pp. 189, 190; Staudinger/*Magnus*, Art. 3 Rome I Regulation, para. 40; *Wegen/Asbrand*, RIW 2016, p. 558; *Wilderspin*, para. 6-013.

1856. Magnus/Mankowski/*Mankowski*, Art. 3 Rome I Regulation, para. 250; *Mankowski*, IHR 2008, p. 136; *Mankowski*, IPRax 2006, p. 102; Rauscher/*von Hein*, Art. 3 Rome I Regulation, para. 52; *Wegen/Asbrand*, RIW 2016, p. 558.

1857. BeckOK/*Spickhoff*, Art. 3 Rome I Regulation, paras 11, 12; Ferrari *et al./Ferrari*, Art. 3 Rome I Regulation, para. 21; Magnus/Mankowski/*Mankowski*, Art. 3 Rome I Regulation, paras 248 et seq.; *Mankowski*, IHR 2008, p. 136; MüKoBGB/*Martiny*, Art. 3 Rome I Regulation, para. 29; Rauscher/*von Hein*, Art. 3 Rome I Regulation, para. 52; *Rühl*, FS Kropholler, pp. 189, 190; Staudinger/*Magnus*, Art. 3 Rome I Regulation, para. 40; *Wegen/Asbrand*, RIW 2016, p. 558; *Wilderspin*, para. 6-013.

1858. 'This Regulation does not preclude parties from incorporating by reference into their contract a non-State body of law or an international convention.'

1859. Calliess/Renner/*Calliess*, Art. 3 Rome I Regulation, para. 21; Magnus/Mankowski/*Mankowski*, Art. 3 Rome I Regulation, paras 262 et seq.; MüKoBGB/*Martiny*, Art. 3 Rome I Regulation, para. 33; Rauscher/*von Hein*, Art. 3 Rome I Regulation, para. 54; *Rühl*, FS

With regard to the CISG, the drafting history of Art. 3 Rome I Regulation is also invoked to justify that it cannot be chosen on a conflict of laws level.[1860] Scholars take the view that the CISG cannot be characterised as the domestic law of a state.[1861] In fact, it is considered to be merely a (non-independent) part of the domestic law of each state that has ratified it.[1862] Some proponents of this view additionally posit that the Convention lacks independent legitimacy and authority beyond its designated sphere of application;[1863] it can essentially be regarded as non-state law beyond its designated sphere of application.[1864] Furthermore, the fragmentary nature of the CISG has been identified as a practical obstacle to choosing the Convention. If the parties were to select the CISG as the applicable law without reference to any other law, recourse to domestic law would still be necessary.[1865]

2) Preferable View

Nevertheless, the more compelling arguments suggest that Art. 3 Rome I Regulation should be interpreted to permit the parties to choose the CISG as the applicable law on a conflict of laws level.[1866] While the drafting history may indeed indicate that

---

Kropholler, p. 190; *Wegen/Asbrand*, RIW 2016, p. 559; *Wilderspin*, para. 6-108; more guardedly Staudinger/*Magnus*, Art. 3 Rome I Regulation, para. 40.

1860. BeckOGK/*Wendland*, Art. 3 Rome I Regulation, paras 105, 105.1; BeckOK/*Spickhoff*, Art. 3 Rome I Regulation, para. 12; Brunner/Gottlieb/*Manner/Schmitt*, Art. 6 CISG, para. 12; Magnus/Mankowski/*Mankowski*, Art. 3 Rome I Regulation, para. 282; Ostendorf/*Ostendorf*, § 13, para. 23; Rauscher/*von Hein*, Art. 3 Rome I Regulation, para. 62; *Wegen/Asbrand*, RIW 2016, p. 559.
1861. BeckOGK/*Wendland*, Art. 3 Rome I Regulation, para. 105; BeckOK/*Saenger*, Art. 6 CISG, para. 7; BeckOK/*Spickhoff*, Art. 3 Rome I Regulation, para. 12; Brunner/Gottlieb/*Manner/Schmitt*, Art. 6 CISG, para. 12; Magnus/Mankowski/*Mankowski*, Art. 3 Rome I Regulation, paras 282, 283; *Wegen/Asbrand*, RIW 2016, p. 559; cf. also *Bridge*, Choice of Law, p. 71 (on the 1980 Rome Convention); *Fawcett/Harris/Bridge*, para. 13.88 (on the 1980 Rome Convention); *Gillette/Walt*, p. 75.
1862. BeckOGK/*Wendland*, Art. 3 Rome I Regulation, para. 105; *Bridge*, Choice of Law, p. 71; *Fawcett/Harris/Bridge*, para. 13.88 (on the 1980 Rome Convention); MüKoHGB/*B. Köhler*, Art. 6 CISG, para. 19; Rauscher/*von Hein*, Art. 3 Rome I Regulation, para. 63; Staudinger/*Magnus*, Art. 6 CISG, para. 65.
1863. BeckOGK/*Wendland*, Art. 3 Rome I Regulation, para. 105; BeckOK/*Spickhoff*, Art. 3 Rome I Regulation, para. 12; Magnus/Mankowski/*Mankowski*, Art. 3 Rome I Regulation, paras 282, 283; Rauscher/*von Hein*, Art. 3 Rome I Regulation, para. 63; Staudinger/*Magnus*, Art. 6 CISG, para. 65.
1864. BeckOGK/*Wendland*, Art. 3 Rome I Regulation, para. 105; BeckOK/*Spickhoff*, Art. 3 Rome I Regulation, para. 12.
1865. BeckOGK/*Wendland*, Art. 3 Rome I Regulation, para. 105; Staudinger/*Magnus*, Art. 3 Rome I Regulation, para. 62; cf. also *MPI*, RabelsZ 68 (2004), p. 31 (with regard to international conventions in general).
1866. Accord Honsell/*Siehr*, Art. 6 CISG, para. 15; *Lindbach*, pp. 196 et seq. (with regard to the German EGBGB); Schlechtriem/Schwenzer/Schroeter/*Hachem*, 5th English ed., Art. 6 CISG, paras 35, 36; *Schroeter*, para. 86; cf. also OLG Jena, 26 May 1998, CISG-online 513, the Court determined that a choice of the CISG was valid under German conflict of law rules, which are similar to the 1980 Rome Convention; *Fountoulakis*, EJLR 2005, p. 314 ('From a conflict of law rules perspective, the choice of the CISG does not raise any difficulties'); *Lohmann*, pp. 327 et seq. (with regard to the 1980 Rome Convention); Witz/Salger/Lorenz/*Lorenz*, Art. 6 CISG, para. 21.

non-state law, such as the UPICC or PECL, may not be chosen on a conflict of laws level,[1867] this does not apply to the CISG.[1868] Although the Convention was explicitly addressed in the Commission's Green Paper,[1869] it was not mentioned again in Art. 3(2) of the proposal for a Rome I Regulation.[1870] In contrast to the view of some scholars,[1871] the rejection of the proposed Art. 3(2), which would have explicitly allowed the parties to select non-state law, is not a relevant factor with regard to the CISG.[1872] Furthermore, the majority of objections to the possibility of choosing non-state law on a conflict of laws level do not equally apply to a choice of the Convention, as it is, for instance, undisputed that the CISG has the required 'quality' of a 'law'[1873] and contains sufficiently[1874] clear provisions.[1875]

Moreover, the Convention is essentially the specific law for international sales contracts in 97 Contracting States.[1876] In this respect, it is to be considered having the same authority as any other state law.[1877] The Convention's lack of independent authority beyond its designated sphere of application does also not present an obstacle to a choice of the CISG. This is because the same can be said of any 'foreign' state law, which can undoubtedly be chosen on a conflict of laws level in accordance with the Rome I Regulation; outside its own territorial sphere of application, the domestic law

1867. Generally advocating for the possibility to choose non-state law on a conflict of laws level: Callies/Renner/*Callies*, Art. 3 Rome I Regulation, para. 20; *Hellgardt*, RabelsZ 82 (2018), pp. 676 et seq. (at least in cases, where an unrestricted choice of foreign law is also possible).
1868. Cf. *Schroeter*, para. 86.
1869. Green Paper on the Conversion of the Rome Convention of 1980 on the law applicable to contractual obligations into a Community instrument and its modernisation, COM(2002) 654 final, pp. 22, 23.
1870. BeckOGK/*Wendland*, Art. 3 Rome I Regulation, para. 105.1; Magnus/Mankowski/*Mankowski*, Art. 3 Rome I Regulation, para. 282; Rauscher/*von Hein*, Art. 3 Rome I Regulation, para. 62.
1871. BeckOGK/*Wendland*, Art. 3 Rome I Regulation, para. 105.1 (highlighting that the proposal was intended to encompass international conventions, with particular reference to recital 13 of the Rome I Regulation); Magnus/Mankowski/*Mankowski*, Art. 3 Rome I Regulation, para. 282 (emphasising that uniform law was not even included in the proposal, but was likely to be encompassed – with the failure of the proposal 'any further discussions' became 'obsolete'); Rauscher/*von Hein*, Art. 3 Rome I Regulation, para. 62 (reaching a similar conclusion to that of the previous scholar).
1872. Similarly, *Schroeter*, para. 86; cf. also *Roth*, FS Jayme, p. 771, in his view a clarification in a revised 1980 Rome Convention would be possible, but not necessary. Instead, he considered the parties' possibility to choose international conventions, such as the CISG, to be unproblematic.
1873. Critical of this criterion *Hellgardt*, RabelsZ 82 (2018), pp. 693, 694; for more detail: *MPI*, RabelsZ 68 (2004), pp. 32, 33; cf. also Schlechtriem/Schwenzer/Schroeter/*Hachem*, 5th English ed., paras 34 et seq.
1874. *Lindbach*, pp. 199, 200; *Roth*, FS Jayme, pp. 765, 766.
1875. *Roth*, FS Jayme, p. 770; *Schroeter*, para. 86; this has even been conceded by proponents of the opposing view: BeckOGK/*Wendland*, Art. 3 Rome I Regulation, para. 105; Staudinger/*Magnus*, Art. 3 Rome I Regulation, para. 60.
1876. *See* https://uncitral.un.org/en/texts/salegoods/conventions/sale_of_goods/cisg/status, last checked October 2025.
1877. Cf. *Fountoulakis*, EJLR 2005, p. 314; Honsell/*Siehr*, Art. 6 CISG, para. 15; *Lohmann*, p. 329; *Schroeter*, para. 86.

of any state lacks authority or 'legitimacy' through a state legislator.[1878] In fact, the application of the CISG, as well as the domestic law of a state, in the cases discussed here is based on the fundamental principle of party autonomy, rather than its authority or 'legitimacy'.[1879]

Furthermore, it should be noted that Art. 3(1), sentence 3 Rome I Regulation explicitly states that the parties 'can select the law applicable [...] to part only of the contract'. Such a partial choice of law still has effects on a conflict of laws level.[1880] A choice of the CISG is comparable to a partial choice of a domestic law under Art. 3(1), sentence 3 Rome I Regulation for two main reasons.[1881] First, the CISG also refers to a specific, definable set of questions pertaining to a contract,[1882] namely matters that fall within its substantive scope of application.[1883] Second, the applicable law to the remaining legal questions under the contract must be determined in the absence of a choice, which is also the case when a partial choice of law has been made.[1884] Consequently, the CISG's fragmentary character is not a barrier to it being selected on a conflict of laws level, given that the Rome I Regulation permits a partial choice of law.[1885]

In light of the aforementioned considerations, the parties should be permitted to choose the CISG as the law applicable to their framework agreement and any other contract on a conflict of laws level under Art. 3(1) Rome I Regulation.

ii. Swiss Private International Law Rules

1) PILA

In Switzerland, the law applicable to contractual obligations is primarily regulated within the Swiss PILA. Art. 116(1) PILA states that the contract shall be governed by the law chosen by the parties. As with the Rome I Regulation, there is a debate among

1878. In more detail: *Hellgardt*, RabelsZ 82 (2018), pp. 680 et seq. (with regard to non-state law in general); cf. also *Lindbach*, pp. 198, 199; Witz/Salger/Lorenz/*Lorenz*, Art. 6 CISG, para. 21, maintaining that the rationale for treating the CISG differently from any other domestic law is unclear.

1879. Cf. *Lindbach*, pp. 198, 199; *Roth*, FS Jayme, p. 770; with regard to non-state law: *Hellgardt*, RabelsZ 82 (2018), pp. 681, 682; *Vischer*, Unidroit, p. 206; *Vischer/Huber/Oser*, para. 123.

1880. *See* Ch. 6 I. 2. below on the consequences of choosing the CISG.

1881. Accord *Lohmann*, pp. 329 et seq.; *Roth*, FS Jayme, p. 767; *Schroeter*, para. 86.

1882. *See* MüKoBGB/*Martiny*, Art. 3 Rome I Regulation, para. 67 ('*bestimmte Fragen eines Vertragsverhältnisses*'); cf. also *Roth*, FS Jayme, p. 767.

1883. *Lohmann*, pp. 332, 333; cf. also Honsell/*Siehr*, Art. 6 CISG, para. 15.

1884. With regard to a partial choice of law under the Rome I Regulation: BeckOK/*Spickhoff*, Art. 3 Rome I Regulation, para. 30; Ferrari *et al.*/*Ferrari*, Art. 3 Rome I Regulation, paras 36 et seq.; *Lohmann*, p. 331 (with regard to the 1980 Rome Convention); *Magnus*, IHR 2018, p. 52 (with regard to distribution contracts); MüKoBGB/*Martiny*, Art. 3 Rome I Regulation, paras 66 et seq.; Staudinger/*Magnus*, Art. 3 Rome I Regulation, paras 104 et seq.

1885. *Lohmann*, p. 333; *Schroeter*, para. 86; cf. also *Fawcett/Harris/Bridge*, para. 13.90; *Hellgardt*, RabelsZ 82 (2018), p. 693; *Lindbach*, p. 199 (with regard to the German EGBGB); *Roth*, FS Jayme, p. 767.

scholars as to whether the parties are free to select non-state law to govern their contract on a conflict of laws level under Art. 116 PILA.[1886]

It has been argued that the parties may choose only domestic law that has been enacted by a state or a community of states.[1887] Moreover, some scholars have pointed out that non-state law is often incomplete and lacks sufficient predictability.[1888] Furthermore, in a leading case, the Swiss Supreme Court determined that the rules and regulations of private organisations, particularly those of FIFA, do not qualify as 'law' in the sense of Art. 116(1) PILA and may not be selected on a conflict of laws level.[1889]

In contrast, *Vischer* has forcefully argued that non-state law may be chosen under Art. 116(1) PILA, provided that the non-state law 'is [a] clear and stable codification created by an approved international organization'; in other words, the non-state law must essentially be comparable to domestic law codifications.[1890] As an illustration, he primarily mentions the UPICC.[1891] This view has gained considerable support among scholars in recent years.[1892]

The question of whether the parties are free to select the UPICC is not addressed here. However, this study proposes that the CISG may be chosen under Art. 116(1) PILA.[1893] The CISG is part of the domestic law of all of its Contracting States and, as such, has the same authority as any other state law.[1894] However, its application in the cases discussed here is based on the fundamental principle of party autonomy, rather than its 'authority'.[1895] It is hard to fathom why the parties should be permitted to

1886. BGer, 20 December 2005, BGE 132 III 285, consid. 1.2; BSK IPRG/*Amstutz/Wang/Gohari*, Art. 116 PILA, para. 21; OFK/*Kren Kostkiewicz*, Art. 116 PILA, para. 8; *Vischer*, Unidroit, pp. 204 et seq., who provides a general overview of the controversy, with a particular focus on the UPICC; *Vischer/Huber/Oser*, paras 118 et seq.; ZK IPRG/*Kren Kostkiewicz*, Art. 116 PILA, para. 18.
1887. Cf. *Spickhoff*, RabelsZ 52 (1992), p. 128; von *Bar/Mankowski*, § 2, para. 72; presenting this argument followed by a refutation of it: *Vischer*, Unidroit, pp. 204, 205; *Vischer/Huber/Oser*, para. 118.
1888. CHK/*Möcklin-Doss/Schnyder*, Art. 116 PILA, para. 4; ZK IPRG/*Kren Kostkiewicz*, Art. 116 PILA, para. 18; cf. also *Vischer*, Unidroit, p. 205; *Vischer/Huber/Oser*, paras 119, 120.
1889. BGer, 20 December 2005, BGE 132 III 285, consid. 1.1 et seq.
1890. With detailed reasoning: *Vischer*, EJLR 1999, pp. 211, 212; *Vischer*, Unidroit, pp. 206 et seq.; *Vischer/Huber/Oser*, paras 120 et seq.
1891. *See Vischer*, EJLR 1999, p. 211; *Vischer*, Unidroit, p. 206; *Vischer/Huber/Oser*, para. 120.
1892. CHK/*Möcklin-Doss/Schnyder*, Art. 116 PILA, para. 4; OFK/*Kren Kostkiewicz*, Art. 116 PILA, para. 8; *Schnyder/Liatowitsch*, para. 728; ZK IPRG/*Kren Kostkiewicz*, Art. 116 PILA, para. 18; cf. also *Siehr*, FS Keller, pp. 501, 502 (adopting a different line of reasoning).
1893. BSK IPRG/*Amstutz/Wang/Gohari*, Art. 116 PILA, para. 21; Honsell/*Siehr*, Art. 6 CISG, para. 15; *Siehr*, FS Keller, pp. 501, 502 (explicitly referring to the CISG in footnote 101); cf. also *Vischer*, Unidroit, p. 207; *Vischer/Huber/Oser*, para. 356, who posit that the CISG's provisions on contract formation may be applied to any contract; but *see* Brunner/Gottlieb/*Manner/Schmitt*, Art. 6 CISG, para. 12.
1894. Cf. BSK IPRG/*Amstutz/Wang/Gohari*, Art. 116 PILA, para. 21; *Fountoulakis*, EJLR 2005, p. 314; Honsell/*Siehr*, Art. 6 CISG, para. 15; *Lohmann*, p. 329; *Schroeter*, para. 86.
1895. *Lindbach*, pp. 198, 199; *Roth*, FS Jayme, p. 770; with regard to non-state law in a general manner: *Hellgardt*, RabelsZ 82 (2018), pp. 681, 682; *Vischer*, Unidroit, p. 206; *Vischer/Huber/Oser*, para. 123.

choose any domestic state law – 'however distant'[1896] – but not the CISG.[1897] The Convention represents a clear and balanced (partial) codification of international sales law.[1898] In contrast to less clear rules, such as a so-called *lex mercatoria*, it does not lack sufficient predictability.[1899] Consequently, there are no substantive concerns against the possibility of choosing the Convention.[1900]

The CISG's fragmentary character does not present an obstacle to its selection on a conflict of laws level, as a partial choice of law is permitted under the Swiss PILA, according to the prevailing view.[1901] It is therefore unproblematic that the law applicable to matters outside the CISG's substantive scope of application may have to be determined in the absence of a choice.[1902]

Finally, it should be noted that the decision rendered by the Swiss Supreme Court may indeed exclude the choice of rules, regulations and standards by private organisations. However, this does not provide a reason to draw any conclusions regarding the question whether the CISG can be chosen under Art. 116(1) PILA.[1903] In light of the aforementioned considerations, the parties should be at liberty to select the CISG on a conflict of laws level under Art. 116(1) PILA.

2) 1955 Hague Convention

In Switzerland, it is possible for additional conflict of laws rules to be relevant. With regard to the sale of movable goods, Art. 118(1) PILA states that the 1955 Hague Convention on the Law Applicable to International Sale of Goods is applicable. The 1955 Hague Convention's material sphere of application largely overlaps with that of the CISG.[1904] Consequently, framework agreements that do not fall within the CISG's

1896. *Vischer*, EJLR 1999, p. 211.
1897. With regard to the UPICC: *Vischer*, EJLR 1999, pp. 211, 212; *Vischer*, Unidroit, p. 206; *Vischer/Huber/Oser*, para. 123; cf. also Witz/Salger/Lorenz/*Lorenz*, Art. 6 CISG, para. 21 (with regard to the Rome I Regulation).
1898. BeckOGK/*Wendland*, Art. 3 Rome I Regulation, para. 105; *Lindbach*, p. 198; *Schroeter*, para. 86; Staudinger/*Magnus*, Art. 3 Rome I Regulation, para. 62.
1899. Schlechtriem/Schwenzer/Schroeter/*Hachem*, 5th English ed., Art. 6 CISG, para. 36; positing that the UPICC and the CISG represent 'more of a counterpoint to the *lex mercatoria* than element of it': *Vischer*, EJLR 1999, p. 208; *Vischer*, Unidroit, pp. 203, 204; *Vischer/Huber/Oser*, para. 122.
1900. *See also* BeckOGK/*Wendland*, Art. 3 Rome I Regulation, para. 105; *Schroeter*, para. 86; Staudinger/*Magnus*, Art. 3 Rome I Regulation, para. 62; cf. also *Roth*, FS Jayme, pp. 765, 766.
1901. BSK IPRG/*Amstutz/Wang/Gohari*, Art. 116 PILA, para. 13; CHK/*Möcklin-Doss/Schnyder*, Art. 116 PILA, para. 3; *Siehr*, FS Keller, pp. 498, 499; ZK IPRG/*Kren Kostkiewicz*, Art. 116 PILA, paras 82 et seq.
1902. Honsell/*Siehr*, Art. 6 CISG, para. 15; *Schroeter*, para. 86.
1903. Concluding from the Supreme Court's decision that only rules and regulations of private organisations cannot be chosen under Art. 116(1) PILA: BSK IPRG/*Amstutz/Wang/Gohari*, Art. 116 PILA, para. 21, who, however, also conclude that the same result is likely to apply to a *lex mercatoria*; OFK/*Kren Kostkiewicz*, Art. 116 PILA, para. 8; *Schnyder/Liatowitsch*, para. 728; ZK IPRG/*Kren Kostkiewicz*, Art. 116 PILA, paras 18, 19 ('*Die Rechtsprechung des Bundesgerichts kann folglich nicht als Absage an die kollisionsrechtliche Wahl von sämtlichen nicht staatlichen Regelwerken verstanden werden.*'); *see* BGer, 20 December 2005, BGE 132 III 285, consid. 1.3, 1.4.
1904. Brunner/Gottlieb/*Brunner*, Introduction, para. 15.

material scope of application will typically also not fall within the 1955 Hague Convention's ambit. Rather, they may be subject to the conflict of laws rule enshrined in Art. 116 PILA (or Art. 117 PILA).

Nevertheless, there may be a few instances where a framework agreement containing a choice of law clause in favour of the CISG falls within the 1955 Hague Convention's ambit but not within the Convention's sphere of application. If so, Art. 2(1) of the 1955 Hague Convention states that 'a sale shall be governed by the domestic law of the country designated by the Contracting Parties'. The wording of this provision illustrates that the parties must designate a country of which the chosen law is part of.[1905] It is therefore not possible to select the CISG in isolation as the law applicable to a framework agreement on a conflict of laws level under the 1955 Hague Convention. The Convention is part of the law of each Contracting State; however, it is unclear under which country's law the CISG is to be applied in such cases.[1906] It is necessary for the parties to clarify as part of which state's legal system the Convention is to be chosen.[1907] Otherwise, a choice of law in favour of the CISG will have effects only on a substantive level.[1908] Consequently, a choice of the CISG without referring to a domestic law is not admissible under the 1955 Hague Convention.

iii. Extension of Material Scope of Application?

A few scholars argue that a choice of the CISG at a conflict of laws level should be permitted only in instances where the Convention's temporal or territorial scope of application is being extended.[1909] This view maintains that it is not admissible to extend the Convention's material scope of application by relying on a choice of the CISG.[1910] This is based on the premise that the CISG is not an actual substantive law.[1911] Furthermore, it has been emphasised that the characterisation of a contract is a matter for domestic substantive law – the parties should not be able to circumvent the limits of this law by choosing the CISG as the law applicable to their contract.[1912] If one were to adopt this view, the CISG could not be selected as the applicable law for framework

1905. *Lohmann*, p. 322.
1906. Cf. *Lindbach*, p. 196; *Lohmann*, p. 322.
1907. *Lohmann*, p. 322.
1908. *Lohmann*, p. 322; cf. also Schlechtriem/Schwenzer/Schroeter/*Ferrari*, 8th German ed., Art. 6 CISG, para. 42, who maintains that the CISG generally cannot be selected on a conflict of laws level under the 1955 Hague Convention; but *see* Schlechtriem/Schwenzer/Schroeter/*Hachem*, 5th English ed., Art. 6 CISG, paras 35, 36, who notes that the situation is disputed under the 1955 Hague Convention and then 'generally' advocates for the possibility of choosing the CISG at the level of conflict of laws.
1909. *Karollus*, p. 39 (it is only possible to extend the temporal scope of application); *Neumayer/Ming*, Art. 6 CISG, note 9. (it is only possible to extend the territorial scope of application); cf. also *Lohmann*, pp. 376 et seq. (it is possible to extend the CISG's scope of application in the sense of Arts 1-6 CISG, with the mere exception of cases where Art. 3(2) CISG leads to the Convention's non-applicability).
1910. *Karollus*, p. 39; cf. also Bianca/Bonell/*Bonell*, Art. 6 CISG, note 3.5.1. (if a contract is excluded from the Convention's sphere of application, the selection of the CISG must be considered a choice on a substantive level); *Lohmann*, p. 415 (with regard to Art. 3(2) CISG).
1911. *Karollus*, p. 39.
1912. Cf. *Lohmann*, p. 415.

agreements that fall outside the Convention's material scope of application, e.g., based on Art. 1 or 3(2) CISG.

The preferable view is that it should not make a difference whether the Convention's material, territorial or temporal scope of application is extended by virtue of a choice of the CISG.[1913] In all of these situations, the parties' interests are worth acknowledging in line with the principle of party autonomy.[1914] Moreover, the parties are free to 'create' a non-existent substantive law by selecting and combining the rules of different jurisdictions, thereby relying on a partial choice of multiple domestic laws.[1915] Ultimately, the answer to the question whether the CISG may be selected must be determined solely in accordance with the relevant international private law rules.[1916] As previously stated, the parties should be free to select the CISG as the law applicable to any contract, including framework agreements, under the relevant international private law rules in the European Union and Switzerland. In this regard, the CISG may be regarded as a body of substantive law that may be the subject of a choice of law.[1917]

Furthermore, the international private law rules in Switzerland and the European Union do not differentiate based on whether the CISG's territorial, material or temporal scope of application is being extended.[1918] The limitations to the freedom of choice may be exclusively derived from the relevant international private law rules, for instance, with regard to consumer contracts (Art. 6 Rome I Regulation; Art. 120 PILA).[1919] Characterisations under domestic substantive law, however, are irrelevant in this regard.

Consequently, the CISG's material scope of application can be extended to framework agreements that would usually not fall within its ambit, provided that the relevant international private law rules acknowledge the possibility of choosing the Convention at the level of conflict of laws.[1920] This may be of particular relevance in instances where the assessment under Art. 3(2) CISG does not yield clear results or even appears to militate for the applicability of domestic law.[1921]

iv. Arbitration Proceedings

The controversies outlined above primarily relate to state court litigation. With regard to arbitration proceedings, the prevailing view is that the parties are at liberty to select

1913. Honsell/*Siehr*, Art. 6 CISG, para. 16; *Lindbach*, pp. 204 et seq.; Schlechtriem/Schwenzer/Schroeter/*Hachem*, 5th English ed., Art. 6 CISG, paras 30, 31; cf. also MüKoHGB/*B. Köhler*, Art. 6 CISG, para. 18.
1914. Cf. *Lindbach*, p. 210.
1915. *Lindbach*, p. 210; cf. also *Hellgardt*, RabelsZ 82 (2018), p. 690.
1916. *Lindbach*, p. 210.
1917. *Lindbach*, p. 210; *see* Ch. 6 I. 1. b. i., ii. above.
1918. *Lindbach*, p. 210 (with regard to the German EGBGB).
1919. Honsell/*Siehr*, Art. 6 CISG, para. 16; *Lindbach*, p. 210.
1920. Accord *Lindbach*, pp. 207 et seq.
1921. Cf. Staudinger/*Magnus*, Art. 6 CISG, para. 68.

the CISG – and even any other non-state rules[1922] – on a conflict of laws level.[1923] This is due to the fact that the majority of arbitration rules and the specific conflict of law rules that apply to arbitration proceedings generally grant the parties greater freedom in choosing the law that will govern their contract.[1924] Consequently, it is less problematic to choose the CISG as the applicable law in a framework agreement on a conflict of laws level in arbitration proceedings.[1925]

An illustrative example can be found in an ICC case involving a framework agreement for the supply of food.[1926] In clause 10.1 of the framework agreement, the parties explicitly agreed that 'the Agreement is to be governed by the "rules of the Vienna Convention on Contracts for the International Sale of Goods ('the CISG')"'.[1927] The arbitral tribunal and the state court that considered a motion to set the award aside both gave effect to this choice of law and, *inter alia*, interpreted the contract in accordance with Art. 8 CISG.[1928]

Similarly, in another ICC case, the parties agreed on the following choice of law clause within their distribution agreement: 'The Arbitrator shall apply the 1980 UN Convention on the International Sale of Goods for what is not expressly or implicitly provided for under the contract. Letters of Credit shall be governed by the Uniform Customs and Practices for Documentary Credits (1993 Revision), International Chamber of Commerce Publication no. 500.'[1929] However, the buyer in this case was insistent upon the application of Italian law on the grounds that the CISG does not cover distribution contracts and that its application would be inappropriate in the case of complex long-term contracts. The buyer further asserted that the CISG may be applicable only to the individual sales contracts concluded under the umbrella of the distribution agreement.[1930] The seller, however, argued in favour of the CISG's

1922. *Fountoulakis*, EJLR 2005, pp. 325, 328 (in reference to the UPICC, PECL and *lex mercatoria*); Ostendorf/*Ostendorf*, § 13, para. 74; Staudinger/*Magnus*, Art. 3 Rome I Regulation, para. 41 (UPICC); *Vischer*, EJRL 1999, p. 206 (*lex mercatoria*); with regard to non-state law in general: *Roth*, FS Jayme, p. 760; *Vischer*, Unidroit, p. 202; *von Hein/Vuattoux-Bock*, ZEuS 2023, pp. 490, 491; *Wegen/Asbrand*, RIW 2016, pp. 559, 560.
1923. Bianca/Bonell/*Bonell*, Art. 6 CISG, note 3.5.3.; *Bridge*, Choice of law, p. 73; *Bridge*, Int'l Sale of Goods, paras 10.38, 10.54; Brunner/Gottlieb/*Manner/Schmitt*, Art. 6 CISG, para. 12; *Gillette/Walt*, pp. 74, 75; *Lindbach*, pp. 184, 185; *Lohmann*, p. 72; Schlechtriem/Schwenzer/Schroeter/*Hachem*, 5th English ed., Art. 6 CISG, para. 35; *Schroeter*, para. 87; *Schwenzer/Jaeger*, IWRZ 2016, pp. 100, 101; *Wegen/Asbrand*, RIW 2016, p. 561; but *see* MüKoBGB/*Huber*, Art. 6 CISG, para. 37.
1924. Bianca/Bonell/*Bonell*, Art. 6 CISG, note 3.5.3.; Brunner/Gottlieb/*Manner/Schmitt*, Art. 6 CISG, para. 12; *Fountoulakis*, EJRL 2005, p. 325, who refers to the UNCITRAL Model Law on International Commercial Arbitration from 1985; *Gillette/Walt*, p. 74; *Lindbach*, p. 185; *Schroeter*, para. 87, mentioning § 1051(1) of the German code of civil procedure; cf. also *von Hein/Vuattoux-Bock*, ZEuS 2023, pp. 490, 491.
1925. *See Schwenzer/Jaeger*, IWRZ 2016, p. 101, who propose to agree upon a choice of law in framework agreements.
1926. ICC, 10 December, CISG-online 4106, full text available: High Ct. Singapore, 13 March 2019, CISG-online 4108, where an application to set the award aside was rejected.
1927. *See* High Ct. Singapore, 13 March 2019, CISG-online 4108, para. 4.
1928. High Ct. Singapore, 13 March 2019, CISG-online 4108, paras 23, 89; ICC, 10 December 2015, CISG-online 4106 (summarised in the decision by the High Ct. Singapore).
1929. ICC, 11849/2003, CISG-online 1421.
1930. ICC, 11849/2003, CISG-online 1421.

application.[1931] The sole arbitrator determined that the CISG was applicable as the parties had clearly expressed their intention for their contract to be governed by a neutral law, rather than the domestic law of either party; they reached this conclusion, despite holding that the CISG would generally not apply to long-term distribution contracts.[1932] Furthermore, the arbitrator ruled that the parties had expressed their intention to submit the entire framework agreement to the Convention, rather than just the individual sales contracts.[1933]

In another ICC case, it was not entirely evident whether the parties had intended to choose the CISG as the applicable law for their distribution agreement.[1934] The distribution agreement in this case included a choice of law clause stipulating that 'this agreement shall be governed by laws as defined by the EEC (European Economic Community) [...]'.[1935] As both parties were situated within the same non-Contracting State (United Arab Emirates), the Convention would not have been applicable in accordance with its own terms (Art. 1(1) CISG). The precise nature and characterisation of the distribution agreement remain unknown based on the available information, but the arbitrator appeared to assume that there was at least a mixed sales contract.[1936] With regard to the choice of law clause, the sole arbitrator concluded that this 'could mean or at least encompass' the CISG.[1937] In support of this interpretation, the arbitrator noted that the CISG is part of the laws of most countries in the European Union, including those that were formerly part of the European Economic Community (EEC).[1938] Moreover, the arbitrator ruled that the parties are at liberty to choose the CISG indirectly, namely as part of the 'laws as defined by the EEC', in accordance with the ICC rules and the domestic rules on arbitration on the basis of the principle of party autonomy, despite the fact that both parties were situated in the United Arab Emirates, which is not a CISG Contracting State.[1939]

Despite the differences between these cases, it can be concluded that arbitral tribunals typically give effect to choice of law clauses in favour of the CISG that have been included in framework agreements, even if those framework agreements would not per se be covered by the CISG. It could therefore be advisable for the parties to agree on arbitration that is more liberal than state courts with regard to party autonomy in order to ensure that their choice of law is being respected.

1931. ICC, 11849/2003, CISG-online 1421.
1932. ICC, 11849/2003, CISG-online 1421.
1933. ICC, 11849/2003, CISG-online 1421.
1934. ICC, 18203/2013, CISG-online 2973.
1935. ICC, 18203/2013, CISG-online 2973, paras 13 et seq.
1936. ICC, 18203/2013, CISG-online 2973, paras 31 ('as the CISG is meant to govern international sales of goods, which is the case of the Distributor Agreement'), 37 ('the above remains true, even if part of the Distributor Agreement pertains not to items or goods *per se* but also, and to a certain and limited extent, to services').
1937. ICC, 18203/2013, CISG-online 2973, para. 28.
1938. ICC, 18203/2013, CISG-online 2973, paras 29, 30.
1939. ICC, 18203/2013, CISG-online 2973, paras 32 et seq.

2. Consequences

This study has postulated that the CISG may be chosen on a conflict of laws level under the international private law rules in Switzerland and the European Union.[1940] Consequently, the Convention should generally be applied to a framework agreement in its entirety, provided that the parties effectively include a corresponding choice of law clause in their contract. In this regard, the parties are at liberty to extend the CISG's applicability to framework agreements that would otherwise fall outside the scope of the Convention, such as framework agreements that are not binding with regard to the individual transactions or framework agreements that contain a preponderant non-sales part.[1941] Accordingly, the Convention overrides any overlapping domestic law rules that may apply to such agreements, regardless of whether these rules are mandatory in nature – this would be exactly as would be the case if the Convention were to apply in accordance with its own terms.[1942]

a. Application Within the CISG's Substantive Scope

Nevertheless, although the parties are free to extend the Convention's territorial or material sphere of application, the CISG will continue to apply solely to matters that are within its substantive scope.[1943] The law applicable to matters outside the Convention's substantive scope must be determined in the absence of a choice in accordance with the relevant international private law rules, e.g., pursuant to Art. 4 Rome I Regulation, Art. 117 PILA or Art. 3 of the 1955 Hague Convention (*see* Art. 118 PILA).[1944] It is therefore crucial to ascertain the boundaries of the CISG's substantive scope of application in instances where the parties have agreed to its applicability through the use of a choice of law clause.[1945]

With regard to framework agreements, it is possible that there may be, e.g., mandatory domestic law provisions with regard to competition law.[1946] However, as outlined above, the majority of these matters are not regulated by the CISG, including form requirements that relate to non-sales matters, provisions on competition, general rights to terminate indefinite framework agreements or claims for compensation after a distribution contract has been ended.[1947] Consequently, there is no inherent conflict between these domestic law rules and the CISG's provisions in the first place.

1940. *See* Ch. 6 I. 1. b. above.
1941. *See* Ch. 3 III. 2. b., Ch. 4 above.
1942. In general on the pre-emption of domestic law if the CISG is applicable: *ThyssenKrupp Metallurgical Prods. GmbH v. Energy Coal, S.p.A.*, Supr. Ct. NY, 14 October 2015, CISG-online 2793, para. 20; *Piltz*, ZVertriebsR 2017, p. 138.
1943. *Lohmann*, pp. 332, 333; cf. also Honsell/*Siehr*, Art. 6 CISG, para. 15; *Schroeter*, para. 86; slightly different: *Schwenzer/Fountoulakis/Dimsey*, p. 701, stating that 'the CISG should apply to the extent its provisions are apt to govern the question at issue'.
1944. Honsell/*Siehr*, Art. 6 CISG, para. 15; *Lohmann*, pp. 332, 333; *Schroeter*, para. 86.
1945. Cf. Honsell/*Siehr*, Art. 6 CISG, para. 15; *see* Ch. 1 IV. 1. above (on how to ascertain the boundaries of the CISG's substantive scope).
1946. *See* Ch. 4 III. 2. c. i. above.
1947. *See* Ch. 4 III. 2. c., Ch. 5 III. 4. above.

In the event of a conflict between mandatory domestic law provisions on framework agreements and the CISG's provisions, the latter would generally prevail, provided that the parties have selected the Convention on a conflict of laws level. Nevertheless, mandatory provisions may prevail over those of the CISG if they qualify as overriding mandatory provisions (*see* Art. 9 Rome I Regulation).[1948] Provisions on competition law may be considered overriding mandatory provisions and apply to international framework agreements, in particular, distribution contracts.[1949] It should also be noted that in Belgium and Germany, provisions on the claim for compensation after a distribution agreement has been terminated are regarded as overriding mandatory provisions in certain circumstances.[1950] However, as this study posited that both of these matters fall outside the CISG's substantive scope, it is the otherwise applicable domestic law that will be superseded by these overriding mandatory provisions.

Once it has been established that a specific matter is within the CISG's substantive scope, Art. 7(2) CISG is also relevant in cases where the Convention is chosen as the law applicable to a framework agreement.[1951] In this regard, a case decided by the OLG Graz and the Austrian Supreme Court provides an illustrative example.[1952] In this case, the parties agreed on the CISG's applicability to an international distribution agreement.[1953] The Court of Appeal Graz emphasised that any gaps in the CISG must primarily be filled by having recourse to the general principles underlying the Convention, and only subsidiarily in conformity with the otherwise applicable domestic law.[1954] In light of this consideration, the Court, *inter alia*, concluded that the CISG does not expressly provide for a right to terminate distribution agreements for a compelling reason, yet it does regulate the avoidance of contracts due to breaches of contract.[1955] While the Court's approach is commendable, it would have been more methodologically sound for the Court to first determine whether the disputed matter fell under the CISG's substantive scope at all before turning to the mechanism enshrined in Art. 7(2) CISG.[1956]

1948. Brunner/Gottlieb/*Manner/Schmitt*, Art. 6 CISG, para. 12; MüKoBGB/*Huber*, Art. 6 CISG, para. 34; *Lohmann*, pp. 135, 136 (in general on this distinction); *Roth*, FS Jayme, p. 759; *Schroeter*, para. 85; cf. also Honsell/*Siehr*, Art. 6 CISG, para. 15; Schlechtriem/Schwenzer/Schroeter/*Hachem*, 5th English ed., Art. 6 CISG, paras 32, 37.
1949. BeckOGK/A. *Köhler*, Art. 4 Rome I Regulation, para. 119; *Magnus*, IHR 2018, p. 56; Staudinger/*Magnus*, Art. 4 Rome I Regulation, paras 82, 83; Ostendorf/*Ostendorf*, § 19, paras 32 et seq.
1950. Belgium: Art. X.37 and Art. X.39 of the *Code de droit économique*; Ostendorf/*Ostendorf*, § 19, para. 39; Germany: *Magnus*, IHR 2018, pp. 56, 57; in more detail: *Fabig*, IHR 2019, pp. 1 et seq.; but *see* Ostendorf/*Ostendorf*, § 19, para. 29 footnote 45.
1951. *Lindbach*, p. 211; *Schroeter*, para. 86.
1952. OGH, 21 November 2023, CISG-online 6656; OLG Graz, 12 July 2023, CISG-online 6628 (Court of Second Instance); LG Klagenfurt, 14 December 2022, CISG-online 6588 (Court of First Instance).
1953. OGH, 21 November 2023, CISG-online 6656, para. 7: '*Der vorliegende Vertrag unterliegt dem internationalen Kaufvertragsrecht, wobei das Wiener Kaufvertragsrecht zur Anwendung gelangt*'; OLG Graz, 12 July 2023, CISG-online 6628, paras 15 et seq.
1954. OLG Graz, 12 July 2023, CISG-online 6628, paras 16, 17.
1955. OLG Graz, 12 July 2023, CISG-online 6628, paras 27 et seq. (the Court, however, also referred to Austrian domestic law in order to emphasise that the result would be the same regardless of the applicable law).
1956. *See* Ch. 1 IV. 1., 2. above.

b. *Substantive Choice of the CISG*

Should the parties not be permitted to select the CISG on a conflict of laws level under the applicable international private law rules, the choice of law clause may still be interpreted as a choice of the Convention at the level of substantive law.[1957] Furthermore, the parties may deliberately intend for the CISG to apply only on a substantive level to their framework agreement.[1958]

If this is the case, mandatory provisions from the otherwise applicable domestic law will prevail over those of the Convention if they conflict with each other.[1959] This applies despite the fact that a matter would theoretically fall within the CISG's substantive scope. The CISG's provisions are essentially contractual terms of the framework agreement in such cases and merely displace non-mandatory domestic law.[1960] Consequently, the parties' freedom may be limited not only by overriding mandatory provisions but also by mandatory rules of the otherwise applicable domestic law.[1961]

It is noteworthy that instances of conflict between mandatory domestic law provisions and those set out in the CISG are relatively uncommon.[1962] Mandatory domestic law provisions frequently relate to matters that are not regulated by the Convention,[1963] particularly in the context of framework agreements.[1964] Therefore, the implications of differentiating between a choice of the CISG at the level of substantive law and at the level of conflict of laws are relatively insignificant in practice.

1957. *Fawcett/Harris/Bridge*, para. 13.89; MüKoBGB/*Huber*, Art. 6 CISG, para. 33; Schlechtriem/Schwenzer/Schroeter/*Hachem*, 5th English ed., Art. 6 CISG, para. 37.
1958. This is a matter of interpretation that must be settled in accordance with the applicable domestic law rules, cf. Schlechtriem/Schwenzer/Schroeter/*Ferrari*, 8th German ed., Art. 6 CISG, para. 40; Schlechtriem/Schwenzer/Schroeter/*Hachem*, 5th English ed., Art. 6 CISG, para. 32.
1959. BeckOK/*Saenger*, Art. 6 CISG, para. 7; Bianca/Bonell/*Bonell*, Art. 6 CISG, note 3.5.1.; *Bridge*, Choice of Law, p. 72; *Herber/Czerwenka*, Art. 6 CISG, para. 19; *Kritzer*, p. 103; *Lindbach*, pp. 180, 181; MüKoBGB/*Huber*, Art. 6 CISG, para. 33; MüKoHGB/*B. Köhler*, Art. 6 CISG, para. 19; *Neumayer/Ming*, Art. 6 CISG, note 9; Schlechtriem/Schwenzer/Schroeter/*Hachem*, 5th English ed., Art. 6 CISG, para. 32; *Schroeter*, paras 84, 85; Staudinger/*Magnus*, Art. 6 CISG, para. 65; cf. also Schlechtriem/Schwenzer/Schroeter/*Ferrari*, 8th German ed., Art. 6 CISG, para. 41.
1960. Cf. BeckOK/*Saenger*, Art. 6 CISG, para. 7; *Bridge*, Int'l Sale of Goods, para. 10.54 ('exclusion of non-mandatory national rules'); Brunner/Gottlieb/*Manner/Schmitt*, Art. 6 CISG, para. 12; *Herber/Czerwenka*, Art. 6 CISG, para. 19; *Karollus*, p. 40; *Lindbach*, p. 180; *Lohmann*, p. 135; MüKoBGB/*Huber*, Art. 6 CISG, para. 33; MüKoHGB/*B. Köhler*, Art. 6 CISG, para. 19; Schlechtriem/Schwenzer/Schroeter/*Hachem*, 5th English ed., Art. 6 CISG, para. 32; *Schroeter*, paras 84, 85.
1961. Cf. Staudinger/*Magnus*, Art. 6 CISG, para. 65.
1962. Cf. *Bridge*, Choice of Law, p. 72 ('if the sales rules of the applicable law were mandatory, which is unlikely, given the paucity of such mandatory rules in sales law'); Witz/Salger/Lorenz/*Lorenz*, Art. 6 CISG, para. 21; but *see* Schlechtriem/Schwenzer/Schroeter/*Ferrari*, 8th German ed., Art. 6 CISG, para. 41, noting that form requirements set forth by domestic may displace Art. 11 CISG.
1963. Witz/Salger/Lorenz/*Lorenz*, Art. 6 CISG, para. 21.
1964. *See* Ch. 4 III. 2. c., Ch. 5 III. 4. above.

3. Interplay Between Framework Agreement and Individual Sales Contracts?

If the parties conclude a framework agreement with a two-tier structure, it is important that the independence of the framework agreement and the individual sales contracts be taken into account when choosing the applicable law under the Rome I Regulation and Swiss PILA.[1965] A choice of law in either the framework agreement or the individual sales contracts does not necessarily apply to the other contract(s).[1966] If the parties select the CISG as the law applicable to their framework agreement, the choice of law does not apply by default to the individual sales contracts, nor vice versa.

Nevertheless, the parties may explicitly extend a choice of law clause included in the framework agreement to the individual sales contracts.[1967] It should be noted that the individual sales contracts concluded under the umbrella of the framework agreement will often per se be within the CISG's sphere of application.[1968] In such cases, a choice of the CISG is unproblematic and merely has confirmatory effects for the individual sales contracts.[1969] Even if the individual sales contracts fall outside the CISG's sphere of application, the parties should be permitted to select the CISG on a conflict of laws level under the relevant international private law rules in Switzerland and the European Union. This generally applies to any contract, unless the conflict of laws rules impose limitations on the parties' freedom of choice, as, for example, in Art. 6 Rome I Regulation.[1970] Consequently, the parties are at liberty to extend the effects of their choice of the CISG in the framework agreement to the individual sales contracts, even if the latter fall outside the Convention's sphere of application.[1971]

A more complex situation may arise in instances where the parties select the CISG as the law applicable merely to their framework agreement, without explicitly choosing the law applicable to the individual sales contracts. In general, the choice of law included in the framework agreement does not apply by default to the individual sales contracts.[1972] Nevertheless, the presence of a choice of law clause in the framework

1965. *Magnus*, IHR 2018, p. 52; Magnus/Mankowski/*Magnus*, Art. 4 Rome I Regulation, para. 134; Ostendorf/*Ostendorf*, § 19, para. 26; Reithmann/Martiny/*Fabig*, para. 37.146; Staudinger/*Magnus*, Art. 4 Rome I Regulation, para. 76; cf. also *Vischer/Huber/Oser*, para. 669.
1966. BeckOGK/*A. Köhler*, Art. 4 Rome I Regulation, paras 121, 122; *Magnus*, IHR 2018, p. 52; Magnus/Mankowski/*Magnus*, Art. 4 Rome I Regulation, para. 134; Staudinger/*Magnus*, Art. 4 Rome I Regulation, para. 76.
1967. *Audit*, p. 40; *Hoffbauer*, p. 48; Ostendorf/*Ostendorf*, § 19, para. 26; Reithmann/Martiny/*Fabig*, para. 37.146 (with regard to non-unified domestic law).
1968. From a conflict of laws perspective: *Magnus*, IHR 2018, p. 51; Magnus/Mankowski/*Magnus*, Art. 4 Rome I Regulation, para. 131; MüKoBGB/*Martiny*, Art. 4 Rome I Regulation, para. 158; Ostendorf/*Ostendorf*, § 19, para. 27; Reithmann/Martiny/*Fabig*, paras 37.66, 37.147; *Thume*, IHR 2009, p. 145.
1969. *See* Ch. 6 I. above.
1970. *See* Ch. 6 I. 1. iii. above.
1971. But *see* Reithmann/Martiny/*Fabig*, para. 37.146, who merely notes that the parties may extend the application of non-unified domestic law from the framework agreement to the individual sales contracts.
1972. Cf. OLG Hamburg, 5 October 1998, CISG-online 473, consid. 1; BeckOGK/*A. Köhler*, Art. 4 Rome I Regulation, paras 121, 122; *Magnus*, IHR 2018, p. 52; Magnus/Mankowski/*Magnus*, Art. 4 Rome I Regulation, para. 134; Staudinger/*Magnus*, Art. 4 Rome I Regulation, para. 76.

agreement may be interpreted as an indication of an implicit choice of law with regard to the individual sales contracts.[1973] However, it is typically necessary to identify additional indications that demonstrate the parties' intention to apply the governing law of the framework agreement to the individual sales contracts.[1974] This may be the case, for instance, if the parties express the intention that their entire contractual relationship should be governed by a 'neutral law', rather than the domestic law of either party.[1975] In such a scenario, the CISG may again apply to the individual sales contracts in accordance with its own terms. If this is the case, a choice of the CISG has no independent significance for the individual sales contracts. In instances where the individual sales contracts do not satisfy the prerequisites for the Convention's application, it is necessary to ascertain further indications of the parties' intention to select the CISG not only as the law applicable to the framework agreement but also to the individual contracts.

In certain cases, only the individual sales contracts may include a choice of law clause, while the framework agreement does not. The inclusion of such a choice of law in the individual sales contracts may be interpreted as an indication that the framework agreement is to be governed by the same law.[1976] This is essentially again a question of interpretation.[1977] Consequently, if the parties exclusively select the CISG as the law applicable to the individual sales contracts, they may also intend for the Convention to govern the framework agreement. However, there must be sufficient indications that the parties intended to do so, which will depend on the specific circumstances of each case. It is crucial to differentiate between the aforementioned cases and instances where the parties have agreed upon a choice of law clause in their framework agreement, stipulating that the CISG shall govern solely the individual sales contracts.[1978] In such instances, the parties typically indicate that the Convention shall be applied to the individual sales contracts and not to the framework agreement itself.[1979]

1973. OLG Hamburg, 5 October 1998, CISG-online 473, consid. 1; LG Bielefeld, 31 October 2003, CISG-online 907, para. 16; *Magnus*, IHR 2018, p. 53; MüKoBGB/*Martiny*, Art. 4 Rome I Regulation, para. 158; Ostendorf/*Ostendorf*, § 19, para. 26; Reithmann/Martiny/*Fabig*, para. 37.146 (in the sense of Art. 3(1), sentence 2 Rome I Regulation); Staudinger/*Magnus*, Art. 4 Rome I Regulation, para. 76; *Thume*, IHR 2009, p. 146; more guardedly BeckOGK/*A. Köhler*, Art. 4 Rome I Regulation, para. 122.

1974. BeckOGK/*A. Köhler*, Art. 4 Rome I Regulation, para. 122; Staudinger/*Magnus*, Art. 4 Rome I Regulation, para. 76; more liberal *Thume*, IHR 2009, pp. 145, 146, who argues that the parties will typically be interested in agreeing on a single legal system to govern both the framework agreement and the individual sales contracts.

1975. Cf. ICC, 11849/2003, CISG-online 1421.

1976. *Magnus*, IHR 2018, p. 53; Reithmann/Martiny/*Fabig*, para. 37.145; Staudinger/*Magnus*, Art. 4 Rome I Regulation, para. 76; *Thume*, IHR 2008, p. 145; to that effect CA Paris, 5 March 2019, CISG-online 5765, paras 82 et seq.

1977. Cf. Reithmann/Martiny/*Fabig*, para. 37.145; with regard to the controversial question of which law governs the interpretation of a choice of law clause under the Rome I Regulation: *Magnus*, IHR 2018, pp. 52, 53.

1978. *Casaceli v. Natuzzi S.p.A.*, Federal Ct. of Australia, 29 June 2012, CISG-online 6045, paras 27, 30 (a franchise agreement was subject to Italian law, while the individual sales contracts were subject to the CISG); AP Barcelona, 14 September 2010, CISG-online 3915; *Audit*, p. 40.

1979. Cf. *Casaceli v. Natuzzi S.p.A.*, Federal Court of Australia, 29 June 2012, CISG-online 6045; AP Barcelona, 14 September 2010, CISG-online 3915.

II. CHOICE OF DOMESTIC LAW

The parties to a framework agreement may alternatively agree on the applicability of domestic law. In this context, it is necessary to distinguish between situations in which the parties choose the domestic law of a Contracting State, the domestic law of a non-Contracting State or domestic law in combination with the CISG.

1. Domestic Law of a Contracting State

If the parties select the domestic law of a Contracting State as the law applicable to their framework agreement, the CISG's applicability to this contract will depend on the question whether the contract is per se within the Convention's sphere of application. If the framework agreement falls within the CISG's sphere of application,[1980] the choice of the domestic law of a Contracting State must generally be understood to mean that it includes the Convention.[1981] In the context of arbitration proceedings, such a choice of law clause will in fact typically constitute the starting point in determining the applicability of the CISG.[1982]

An illustrative example can be found in an ICC case, where the parties agreed on the applicability of Swiss law to a 'Frame Contract'.[1983] The arbitral tribunal characterised the parties' 'Frame Contract' as a purchase agreement, given that its non-sales elements were subordinated to the sales elements. Based on the choice of law clause and the contract's characterisation, the tribunal concluded that the CISG was applicable to this agreement.[1984]

In contrast, if a framework agreement per se falls outside the CISG's sphere of application, the choice of the domestic law of a Contracting State will not result in the Convention's applicability.[1985] This is because such a choice of law may include the CISG, but only to the extent that the requirements for its applicability are met.[1986]

It should be noted that the CISG's non-applicability to the framework agreement does not generally affect the CISG's applicability to the individual sales contracts, as the

1980. *See* in particular Chs 3 and 4 above.
1981. ICC, 1 November 2016, CISG-online 5988, paras 116 et seq. (the choice of Austrian law in a 'Distribution Agreement' was interpreted to include the CISG); ICC, 12173/2004, CISG-online 2066 (the choice of Swiss law in a 'Frame Contract' was interpreted to include the CISG); Court of First Instance Basel-Stadt, 1 March 2002, CISG-online 729 (the choice of Swiss law in a 'Supply Agreement' was interpreted to include the CISG); OLG Graz, 28 September 2000, CISG-online 798, paras 37 et seq. (the choice of German law in a framework agreement was interpreted to include the CISG); cf. also BGer, 18 April 2024, CISG-online 6978 (the applicability of the CISG was left open due to the fact that both parties and the lower court assumed the applicability of the Swiss CO, *see* para. 14).
1982. In detail: Brunner/Gottlieb/*Manner/Schmitt*, Art. 1 CISG, paras 16, 18; Schlechtriem/Schwenzer/Schroeter/*Hachem*, 5th English ed., Intro Arts 1–6 CISG, paras 11, 12.
1983. ICC, 12173/2004, CISG-online 2066, para. 17.
1984. ICC, 12173/2004, CISG-online 2066, paras 16, 17.
1985. OLG Hamburg, 5 October 1998, CISG-online 473, consid. 1; *Magnus*, IHR 2018, p. 52; cf. also LG Bielefeld, 31 October 2003, CISG-online 907; *Rehbinder*, IPRax 1982, p. 8 (with regard to the ULIS and ULF); *Thume*, IHR 2009, p. 145.
1986. Cf. OLG Hamburg, 5 October 1998, CISG-online 473, consid. 1.

applicable law is to be determined separately.[1987] In certain instances, a choice of the domestic law of a Contracting State included in a framework agreement that is not governed by the CISG may, in conjunction with additional indications, be interpreted as an implicit choice of law with regard to the individual sales contracts.[1988] Notwithstanding the fact that the Convention does not apply to the framework agreement in such cases, it may still apply to the individual sales contracts provided that the additional prerequisites for its application are met and that the parties did not exclude its application by other means.[1989]

Put another way, the explicit choice of the domestic law of a Contracting State in a framework agreement that is not governed by the CISG should not, in and of itself, be construed as an exclusion of the CISG for the individual sales contracts.[1990] This is of particular relevance in state court proceedings in a Contracting State, in which cases the competent court is under an obligation to apply the CISG.[1991] The aforementioned interpretation is consistent with the prevailing view that the mere choice of the domestic law of a Contracting State is insufficient to exclude the CISG's applicability in accordance with Art. 6 CISG.[1992] Consequently, should the parties intend to have domestic law govern both the framework agreement and the individual sales contracts, they must clarify their intention beyond the mere choice of the law of a Contracting State in their framework agreement.[1993]

2. Domestic Law of a Non-contracting State

Alternatively, the parties to a framework agreement may agree on the domestic law of a non-Contracting State of the Convention as the law applicable to their contract. If a framework agreement with such a choice of law clause falls outside the CISG's sphere

1987. *See* Ch. 3 V. above.
1988. *See* OLG Hamburg, 5 October 1998, CISG-online 473, consid. 1; LG Bielefeld, 31 October 2003, CISG-online 907, paras 16, 17.
1989. Cf. OLG Hamburg, 5 October 1998, CISG-online 473, consid. 1; OLG Koblenz, 17 September 1993, CISG-online 91, paras 38 et seq.; LG Bielefeld, 31 October 2003, CISG-online 907, paras 16, 17; Reithmann/Martiny/*Fabig*, para. 37.148; *Thume*, IHR 2009, p. 145.
1990. *Magnus*, IHR 2018, p. 53; Reithmann/Martiny/*Fabig*, paras 37.147, 37.148; *Thume*, IHR 2009, p. 145; cf. also BeckOGK/*A. Köhler*, Art. 4 Rome I Regulation, para. 121; but *see* OLG Düsseldorf, 16 December 2010, CISG-online 2856, paras 64, 65, where the Court (unconvincingly) interpreted the choice of German law contained in a distribution agreement as an implicit exclusion of the CISG for the individual sales contracts; *Rehbinder*, IPRax 1982, p. 8 (with regard to the ULIS and ULF).
1991. Brunner/Gottlieb/*Manner/Schmitt*, Art. 1 CISG, para. 2; Schlechtriem/Schwenzer/Schroeter/*Hachem*, 5th English ed., Intro Arts 1–6 CISG, para. 3.
1992. *See* only Gerechtshof Arnhem-Leeuwarden, 19 July 2022, CISG-online 6452, paras 22, 23; KGer Zug, 24 February 2022, CISG-online 6285, paras 35, 36; Commercial Court Vienna, 3 January 2022, CISG-online 6229, para. 73; BGH, 11 May 2010, CISG-online 2125, para. 15; *Easom Automation Systems, Inc. v. ThyssenKrupp Fabco, Corp.*, US Dist. Ct. Mich., 28 September 2007, CISG-online 1601; CISG-AC, Op. 16 *Spagnolo*, Rule 4(b)(i); Kröll *et al./Mistelis*, Art. 6 CISG, para. 18; MüKoBGB/*Huber*, Art. 6 CISG, para. 12; MüKoHGB/*B. Köhler*, Art. 6 CISG, para. 7; Reithmann/Martniy/*Fabig*, paras 37.147, 37.148; Schlechtriem/Schwenzer/Schroeter/*Hachem*, 5th English ed., Art. 6 CISG, paras 14 et seq.; Staudinger/*Magnus*, Art. 6 CISG, para. 24.
1993. Cf. also Reithmann/Martiny/*Fabig*, para. 37.148.

of application, there are no indications that the parties intend to opt into the Convention. A similar result may be arrived at in the context of arbitral proceedings and state court proceedings in non-Contracting states, in the absence of an obligation to apply the CISG.

In instances where a framework agreement containing such a choice of law falls within the CISG's sphere of application and the competent court is generally bound to apply the Convention, the question whether this amounts to an exclusion of the Convention in accordance with Art. 6 CISG is one of interpretation under Art. 8 CISG.[1994] The prevailing view is that the parties typically intend to exclude the CISG if they choose the domestic law of a non-Contracting State.[1995] However, this may be different if the parties wish to choose the domestic law solely as a supplementary law.[1996] The question of whether this is the case must again be determined through interpretation and should not be assumed lightly.[1997] All of the above must also apply with regard to framework agreements that contain a choice of law clause in favour of the domestic law of a non-Contracting State; even if such contracts are within the CISG's ambit, the choice of the law of a non-Contracting State will usually result in the exclusion of the Convention in accordance with Art. 6 CISG (or not lead to its application in the first place).

A choice of the law of a non-Contracting State in a framework agreement does, in principle, not affect the law applicable to the individual sales contracts. Consequently, even if such a choice of law results in the exclusion of the CISG or does not lead to its application in the first place with regard to the framework agreement, the Convention may still apply to the individual sales contracts if the requirements for its application are met. However, in certain instances, the choice of law set forth in the framework agreement, when coupled with additional indications, may be interpreted as an implicit choice of law with regard to the individual sales contracts.[1998] If this is the case, the choice of the domestic law of a non-Contracting State may result in the exclusion of the CISG's applicability to the individual sales contracts, or alternatively, not lead to its application to begin with.

1994. Schlechtriem/Schwenzer/Schroeter/*Hachem*, 5th English ed., Art. 6 CISG, para. 13; Staudinger/*Magnus*, Art. 6 CISG, para. 23; cf. also *Juhasz*, IHR 2021, p. 89; *Schroeter*, paras 71 et seq.
1995. OLG Linz, 23 January 2006, CISG-online 1377, para. 73; Tribunale di Padova, 11 January 2005, CISG-online 967, para. 29; Tribunale Cantonal du Jura, 3 November 2004, CISG-online 965, para. 18; CISG-AC, Op. 16 *Spagnolo*, Rule 4(a)(ii); Kröll *et al.*/*Mistelis*, Art. 6 CISG, para. 17; MüKoBGB/*Huber*, Art. 6 CISG, para. 14; MüKoHGB/*B. Köhler*, Art. 6 CISG, para. 10; Schlechtriem/Schwenzer/Schroeter/*Ferrari*, 8th German ed., Art. 6 CISG, para. 20; Schlechtriem/Schwenzer/Schroeter/*Hachem*, 5th English ed., Art. 6 CISG, para. 13; *Schroeter*, para. 72; Staudinger/*Magnus*, Art. 6 CISG, para. 23.
1996. CISG-AC, Op. 16 *Spagnolo*, Comment 4.11; MüKoBGB/*Huber*, Art. 6 CISG, para. 14; MüKoHGB/*B. Köhler*, Art. 6 CISG, para. 10; Schlechtriem/Schwenzer/Schroeter/*Ferrari*, 8th German ed., Art. 6 CISG, para. 20; Schlechtriem/Schwenzer/Schroeter/*Hachem*, 5th English ed., Art. 6 CISG, para. 13; Staudinger/*Magnus*, Art. 6 CISG, para. 23.
1997. Cf. CISG-AC, Op. 16 *Spagnolo*, Comment 4.11; MüKoHGB/*B. Köhler*, Art. 6 CISG, para. 10; Schlechtriem/Schwenzer/Schroeter/*Hachem*, 5th English ed., Art. 6 CISG, para. 13 ('rare exception'); Staudinger/*Magnus*, Art. 6 CISG, para. 23.
1998. *See* Ch. 6 I. 3. above.

3. Domestic Law in Conjunction with the CISG

Finally, there may be instances where the parties choose a domestic law, either that of a Contracting or a non-Contracting State, in conjunction with the CISG as the law applicable to their framework agreement. To illustrate, in an ICC case, the parties to a distributorship agreement agreed upon the applicability of the CISG and Italian law.[1999] The tribunal interpreted the parties' choice of law clause to mean that the CISG should be applicable as long as the contract falls under its sphere of application; otherwise, Italian law should govern the contract.[2000] As the tribunal considered the parties' framework agreement to fall outside the CISG's sphere of application, it reached the conclusion that the Convention was not applicable. The competent state court upheld this award when it was challenged.[2001] In other cases where the parties consented to the CISG's applicability to a framework agreement in conjunction with domestic law, the applicability of the Convention was not subjected to a comprehensive examination.[2002]

In essence, the meaning of such a clause depends on an interpretation of the respective wording of the clause.[2003] Should the framework agreement itself fall within the CISG's sphere of application, it is probable that such a clause will result in the Convention being applied. If the framework agreement is not per se governed by the CISG, it is possible to arrive at a similar outcome as that of the arbitral tribunal outlined above.

However, it is equally plausible to put forward an alternative interpretation of the choice of law clause in this case. The parties agreed that their distribution agreement is to be governed by the CISG 'and where not applicable by Italian law'.[2004] This choice of law could also imply that the CISG should be applied to the distribution agreement, unless a matter does not fall within the Convention's substantive scope, or there is a gap which must be settled in conformity with domestic law (Art. 7(2) CISG). In other words, the CISG should apply to the distribution agreement, which might not fall within its sphere of application, but only to the extent that it regulates specific legal matters.[2005] If it does not regulate a matter or Art. 7(2) CISG requires recourse to

1999. ICC, 11 November 2011, CISG-online 1851; the arbitral award was subsequently challenged, *see* High Ct. Singapore, 14 August 2012, CISG-online 2725.
2000. Cf. High Ct. Singapore, 14 August 2012, CISG-online 2725, para. 38 (reciting the Arbitral Tribunal).
2001. High Ct. Singapore, 14 August 2012, CISG-online 2725, paras 39, 40; cf. also *FPM Financial Services, LLC v. Redline Products Ltd.*, US Dist. Ct. NJ, 17 September 2013, CISG-online 2489, where the parties had explicitly agreed that the CISG should apply within the limits set out in Art. 1(1)(a) CISG.
2002. *McHugh et al. v. Vertical Partners West, LLC et al.*, US Dist. Ct. Idaho, 19 April 2021, CISG-online 6003, para. 16; *Chemische Fabrik Budenheim KG v. Bavaria Corp. Int'l*, US Dist. Ct. MD Florida, 8 July 2009, CISG-online 4578.
2003. Cf. CISG-AC, Op. 16 *Spagnolo*, Comment 4.11.
2004. High Ct. Singapore, 14 August 2012, CISG-online 2725, para. 38.
2005. With regard to the question of whether the choice of domestic law of a non-Contracting State may be interpreted in a similar way: CISG-AC, Op. 16 *Spagnolo*, Comment 4.11, who mentions 'franchise or distribution agreements where domestic laws dealing with agency or validity are chosen'; MüKoBGB/*Huber*, Art. 6 CISG, para. 14; MüKoHGB/*B. Köhler*, Art. 6 CISG, para. 10; Staudinger/*Magnus*, Art. 6 CISG, para. 23.

domestic law, the parties have clarified their intention that Italian law should apply subsidiarily. This interpretation appears to be just as reasonable as the result reached by the arbitral tribunal,[2006] particularly given that the parties in arbitral proceedings have the freedom to choose the CISG as the law applicable to their framework agreement, even if it does not fall within the Convention's scope of application.[2007]

While it would be unwise to generalise about the interpretation of specific choice of law clauses, the interpretation put forth by this study should not be dismissed without further consideration. Ultimately, the circumstances of each individual case will be decisive for the interpretation of a choice of law clause in favour of the CISG in conjunction with domestic law and thus the Convention's applicability. If the CISG is not applicable in accordance with its own terms, or generally within the context of arbitral proceedings,[2008] it is essential to consider that the question of opting in must be determined in light of the relevant international private law rules.[2009]

III. CONCLUSION

A choice of the CISG on a substantive level is subject to the law applicable by virtue of international private law rules. Such a choice is typically unproblematic, provided that the applicable domestic law permits the parties to displace its own provisions; consequently, the parties are free to do so in a framework agreement. The admissibility of a choice of the CISG on a conflict of laws level must be determined in accordance with the relevant international private law rules. This study advocates that the parties should be permitted to do so under Art. 3 Rome I Regulation and Art. 117 PILA, whereas Art. 2(1) of the 1955 Hague Convention requires the designation of a domestic law in conjunction with the CISG.[2010]

The consequence of a choice of the CISG on a conflict of laws level is that the CISG will apply to matters that are within its substantive scope and supersede mandatory domestic law in this regard. The situation is distinct with regard to overriding mandatory provisions (*see* Art. 9 Rome I Regulation), which always prevail over the applicable law, i.e., the CISG. If the parties to a framework agreement have opted for the application of the CISG at the level of substantive law, mandatory provisions from the otherwise applicable domestic law will prevail over those of the Convention if they conflict with each other, even if a matter would theoretically be covered by the CISG's substantive scope.[2011]

It is possible for the choice of law clause included in the framework agreement to impact the law applicable to the individual sales contracts, and vice versa. In general, the applicable law to these contracts must be determined separately. However, the

2006. As the arbitral award is not publicly available, it cannot be ruled out that there were further circumstances which might have influenced the arbitral tribunal's interpretation.
2007. *See* Ch. 6 I. 1. b. iv. above.
2008. Cf. only Schlechtriem/Schwenzer/Schroeter/*Hachem*, 5th English ed., Intro Arts 1–6 CISG, paras 11, 12.
2009. *See* Ch. 6 I. 1. b. above.
2010. *See* Ch. 6 I. 1. above.
2011. *See* Ch. 6 I. 2. above.

parties may explicitly agree to extend the choice of the CISG contained in a framework agreement to the individual sales contracts. Furthermore, even if the parties select the CISG merely as the law applicable to the framework agreement, this may be interpreted as an indication that the Convention is also intended to govern the individual sales contracts. However, there must be additional indications that demonstrate the parties' intention to agree on an implicit choice of law. A choice of the CISG included in the individual sales contracts may also be considered an indication that the same law should apply to the framework agreement if there are sufficient indications in this regard.[2012]

If the parties to a framework agreement agree on domestic law as the governing law, it is necessary to distinguish between different scenarios. If they select the domestic law of a Contracting State, the CISG's applicability to the framework agreement will depend on the question of whether this contract per se falls within the scope of the Convention. If the parties to a framework agreement agree on the applicability of the domestic law of a non-Contracting State, the CISG will typically not be applicable. Furthermore, the parties to a framework agreement may opt for the applicability of a domestic law in conjunction with the CISG. The consequences of such a choice of law clause are a matter of interpretation and will depend on the specific circumstances of each case. This type of choice of law may be interpreted to mean that the CISG shall apply to matters within its substantive scope, whereas the chosen domestic law shall apply to matters outside the Convention's substantive scope, or if Art. 7(2) CISG requires, to have recourse to domestic law. In all of these scenarios, it is important to consider the potential interplay between choice of law clauses in framework agreements and the law applicable to the individual sales contracts, or vice versa.[2013]

2012. *See* Ch. 6 I. 3. above.
2013. *See* Ch. 6 II. above.

CHAPTER 7

Conclusions and Results

The analysis conducted by this study has revealed that the CISG may indeed be applicable to framework agreements, including distribution contracts, in some (but not all) cases. In order to determine whether the CISG is applicable, it is necessary to examine each individual framework agreement, along with the surrounding circumstances. Framework agreements that either contain sales obligations in *sensu stricto* or oblige the parties to conclude individual sales contracts should generally fall within the Convention's sphere of application. Furthermore, in order for the CISG to be applicable, it is necessary that the preponderant part of the contract does not consist of non-sales elements. The fact that framework agreements are long-term contracts and may contain open terms does not present an obstacle to the Convention's applicability.

In addition to considerations of applicability, this study has demonstrated that the CISG's actual application to framework agreements yields satisfactory results. The CISG's substantive provisions and its underlying principles are, for the most part, suitable and sufficiently flexible to deal with framework agreements that may contain non-sales elements and are to be performed over an extended period of time. Nevertheless, the Convention does not address all potential questions that may arise in the context of such contracts; some questions may be related to matters that fall outside the CISG's substantive scope of application. It is therefore crucial to determine the boundaries of the CISG's substantive scope in the context of long-term framework agreements. The findings of this study include the following results.

I. NOTION OF FRAMEWORK AGREEMENTS (CHAPTER 2)

The commercial rationale underlying framework agreements is, among other things, to combine the parties' interest in planning reliability with their interest in flexibility. Furthermore, framework agreements standardise and simplify contractual supply relationships. However, the CISG does not define or make any reference to this type of contract.

A comparable understanding of framework agreements can be found in Germany, Switzerland and France, where this type of contract sets out a general frame for an ongoing supply relationship between two parties. Framework agreements compromise selected terms pertaining to the sale of goods, which shall be incorporated into a series of sales contracts concluded at a later point in time. This understanding demonstrates that there is usually a distinction between the framework agreement itself and the subsequently concluded individual sales contracts (two-tier structure). A framework agreement usually includes an obligation to incorporate predetermined terms into the individual sales contracts. In addition, such an agreement often includes obligations pertaining to the overall cooperation between the parties, such as confidentiality or exclusivity obligations. The question of whether framework agreements must contain an obligation to conclude individual sales contracts is disputed in all three jurisdictions. Moreover, framework agreements are characterised as long-term contracts, as they are designed to regulate an ongoing supply relationship.

In contrast, there is no comparable concept of framework agreements or related discussions under US law. One such discussion that has been conducted pertains to contracts that leave several terms open for later determination, which may bear some resemblance to framework agreements in the sense of the European notion. In the past, US courts have been reluctant to validate such open term contracts due to concerns about their insufficient definiteness. However, this stance has evolved over time, with the UCC now expressly recognising the validity of open term contracts and providing gap-filling provisions. Furthermore, in the US, distribution contracts are characterised as hybrid transactions to which sales law (i.e., the UCC) is applied because of their predominant sales aspect. In contrast to Germany, Switzerland and France, a distinction between the framework agreement and individual sales contracts is not typically mentioned, with the exception of cases that relate to the CISG. The lack of definiteness and completeness of framework agreements does not present an obstacle in light of the UCC's liberal approach to open term contracts.

In the absence of a universal notion and in order to find an internationally acceptable solution, this study has employed a broad notion of framework agreements. Framework agreements are contracts designed to provide an umbrella for a series of individual sales transactions to be conducted over an extended period of time. In certain cases, there may be a distinction between the framework agreement and the individual sales contracts (two-tier structure). The parties are at liberty to structure their contract in accordance with their preferences (freedom of contract), and there may be justifiable reasons for a two-tier structure, for instance, if there are valid reasons for delaying the immediate conclusion of individual sales.

Framework agreements will typically set out terms to be incorporated into the individual sales contracts, provided that there is a two-tier structure. Furthermore, such framework agreements may – but do not have to – include an obligation to conclude individual sales contracts. Framework agreements may also contain sales obligations in *sensu stricto*. In addition to sales elements, framework agreements may include non-sales elements of various kinds. As they are to be performed over an extended period of time, framework agreements further qualify as long-term contracts.

This study considers distribution contracts as a subtype of framework agreements, which are of particular practical importance.

II. FRAMEWORK AGREEMENTS AS SALES CONTRACTS (CHAPTER 3)

Despite the absence of an express definition, sales contracts within the meaning of Art. 1 CISG are commonly defined by reference to the obligations enshrined in Arts 30 and 53 CISG. Consequently, a sales contract under the CISG generally includes rights and obligations to deliver goods, transfer property in them and pay the purchase price.

This definition is, however, not exhaustive as the Convention also encompasses contracts that do not adhere to this structure, specifically agreements to modify or terminate sales contracts (Art. 29 CISG). It is possible that such agreements may not resemble a typical sales contract but nevertheless fall under the purview of the Convention. This study has proposed that a general principle may be derived from this example, according to which the CISG covers closely related or linked contracts. In order for this principle to be applicable, it is necessary that these related or linked contracts either establish or directly affect the parties' rights and obligations under one or multiple CISG contracts.

In light of this principle, the CISG should also cover preliminary agreements in certain circumstances. Preliminary agreements that oblige the parties to conclude a sales contract governed by the CISG may themselves not fit within the definition of sales contract derived from Art. 1 in conjunction with Arts 30 and 53 CISG. Nevertheless, such agreements, in substance, establish rights and obligations under a CISG contract. Indeed, the main purpose of such contracts is to establish rights and obligations under a sales contract by binding the parties to conclude a final sales contract in the future. Conversely, the Convention should not apply to non-binding preliminary agreements and preliminary agreements that merely relate to the negotiations between the parties. It is possible that such agreements may still be relevant for the interpretation of a CISG contract under Art. 8(3) CISG, despite the fact that they remain outside the Convention's sphere of application.

In light of the aforementioned considerations, this study posited that the CISG should be applicable to framework agreements that are binding with regard to the individual transactions. In this context, it is necessary to distinguish between framework agreements containing sales obligations in *sensu stricto* and framework agreements that contain an obligation to conclude individual sales obligations. If such contracts contain sales obligations in *sensu stricto*, the CISG is applicable given that they essentially resemble sales contracts within the meaning of Art. 1 in conjunction with Arts 30 and 53 CISG. There is no provision in the Convention that would militate against this interpretation. Moreover, the characterisation of such agreements under domestic law is irrelevant, as the Convention determines its sphere of applicability autonomously.

Furthermore, the Convention should be applicable to framework agreements that contain an obligation to conclude individual sales contracts. This type of framework agreement is essentially comparable to preliminary agreements that oblige one or both parties to conclude a sales contract. Consequently, they effectively establish rights and obligations under one or multiple CISG contracts. Accordingly, they trigger the general principle according to which the Convention is applicable to related or closely linked contracts, provided that they establish the parties' rights and obligations under a CISG contract. Moreover, the practical differences between such a framework agreement and a framework agreement containing actual sales obligations are relatively insignificant, which is why they should be treated equally with regard to the Convention's applicability. The CISG's provisions are sufficiently flexible to accommodate both types of framework agreements, including instances where the obligation to conclude individual sales contracts and the like has been breached.

In contrast to this, this study has argued that framework agreements which are not binding with regard to the individual transactions should not be governed by the CISG. Even though they may predetermine several terms to be incorporated into the individual sales contracts (comparable to standard terms), they do not directly affect the parties' rights and obligations under these CISG contracts, as the parties need to find an additional agreement in order to incorporate these terms. Furthermore, such agreements do not establish rights and obligations, as both parties may still choose not to conclude individual sales contracts at all without any legal consequences. However, the CISG may still be indirectly relevant for such framework agreements, which, as such, remain outside its sphere of application. This is because, should the parties decide to enter into individual sales contracts under the umbrella of the framework agreement, the individual sales contracts may be subject to the Convention. The framework agreement may then be relevant for the interpretation of the individual sales contracts (Art. 8(3) CISG). It may further be considered a practice within the meaning of Art. 9(1) CISG or constitute a derogation from certain provisions of the Convention, for example, Art. 18(1) CISG.

Some scholars, and in particular US case law, have held that framework agreements do not fall within the Convention's sphere of application due to their insufficient definiteness (Art. 14(1) CISG). However, a thorough interpretation of Art. 14(1), sentence 1 CISG has revealed that it does not set a strict but rather a liberal standard of sufficient definiteness. This view is, therefore, not persuasive and fails to consider the Convention's full sphere of application. It is not a barrier to the CISG's applicability if framework agreements leave certain terms open or indefinite. For the purposes of Art. 14(1) CISG, it is sufficient if the minimum content is stipulated only in the individual orders or even in the individual sales contracts. In any case, the parties are at liberty to deviate from the standard of definiteness set out in Art. 14(1) CISG in accordance with Art. 6 CISG.

Furthermore, this debate fails to address the pivotal issue: the pertinent question is whether framework agreements fall within the CISG's sphere of application. The CISG does not restrict its application to contracts containing sufficiently definite terms; it is, in fact, rather flexible in that regard. Consequently, the 'sufficient definiteness' requirement is not directly related to the CISG's sphere of application. Art. 14(1) CISG is not an 'invalidating provision'.

The conclusions of this study may imply a correlation between the governing law of the framework agreement and that of the individual sales contracts. A similar argument has also been presented in legal writings on the CISG and private international law rules in the European Union and Switzerland. Based on the relationship between the framework agreement and the individual sales contracts, it can be argued that they should generally be governed by the same law. However, the preferable approach is that the law applicable to the framework agreement and that to the individual sales contracts should generally be determined independently. This allows for the specific circumstances of each case to be taken into account. Even if a framework agreement is closely related to the individual sales contracts, it may contain additional non-sales elements that shift its focus.

The approach proposed by this study leads to the conclusion that the applicability of the CISG will depend on whether a framework agreement is binding with regard to the individual transactions. The presence of a requirement clause or a minimum purchase requirement indicates that the parties are bound to carry out the individual transactions. Conversely, the presence of a forecast clause indicates that the parties did not bind themselves with regard to the individual transactions. With regard to exclusivity clauses, the commitment by the parties may depend on the specific nature of the exclusivity obligation contained in the respective framework agreement. Ultimately, the specific circumstances of each case will be determinative in resolving this question of characterisation, which is to be determined in accordance with the CISG, in particular Art. 8 CISG.

III. FRAMEWORK AGREEMENTS AS MIXED CONTRACTS (CHAPTER 4)

An additional challenge for framework agreements arises from the fact that they frequently contain various non-sales obligations. In this regard, Art. 3(2) CISG is of pivotal importance for the Convention's applicability. This is because framework agreements that contain sales obligations within the CISG's scope as well as service or labour obligations outside the CISG's scope are generally within the ambit of Art. 3(2) CISG. The same should apply to framework agreements that contain sales obligations and exclusivity or non-competition obligations. Although they may not directly fall within the ambit of Art. 3(2) CISG, such contracts should still trigger the general principle underlying this provision. Art. 3(2) CISG and its underlying principle should equally apply to preliminary agreements as well as framework agreements that contain an obligation to conclude individual sales contracts.

In the context of mixed contracts under Art. 3(2) CISG, there are two principal approaches to determine the preponderant part. The first is the economic value test, which compares the value ratio of the sales part to the value ratio of the non-sales part. Second, there is an overall assessment, which incorporates additional criteria, such as the parties' intentions and interests, the text of the contract, the weight given to the different obligations, the intended duration of the contract, the circumstances surrounding the contract conclusion, and the primary purpose of the contract. With regard to framework agreements, it is often not possible to determine the preponderant part based solely on the economic value test, given that such contracts frequently contain open terms and the value of their non-sales part is difficult to ascertain. Therefore, this study has concluded that it is preferable to rely on the overall assessment. The CISG's applicability to framework agreements will then depend on the particular circumstances of each case. This approach appears to be justified in the context of framework agreements, which are inherently heterogenous. Moreover, the fact that some framework agreements are structured in a two-tier manner does not present any issues. The preponderant part of the framework agreement must be determined by itself independently of the individual sales contracts.

In case a mixed framework agreement contains a preponderant sales part, this study has supported the position that the CISG should be applied to the entire agreement, rather than solely to the sales part. This conclusion is derived from a literal and purposive interpretation of Art. 3 (2) CISG. Moreover, there are usually significant relationships between the different obligations if they are merged into one single framework agreement, which further prompts the application of the same law.

The application of the CISG to the non-sales parts in framework agreements and any other mixed contracts results in satisfactory outcomes. The Convention's provisions are suitable and sufficiently flexible to govern issues that may arise in such cases. To be more specific, the CISG's provisions and its underlying principles provide solutions if the seller fails to perform their service obligations under a mixed framework agreement. In such cases, the aggrieved buyer may seek redress through the remedies of specific performance, reduction of the price, avoidance or damages, provided that the respective prerequisites are met. Furthermore, the aggrieved party may be entitled to withhold their own performance.

The same applies in cases where service obligations have been performed in a non-conforming manner. Although service obligations are sometimes characterised as *obligations de moyens*, the Convention contains general principles that may be applied to establish liability for the breach of such obligations. However, this study posits that not all of the CISG's provisions and underlying principles should be applied in a 'blind' manner to cases of breach of service obligations. In particular, the obligation to give notice of non-conformity should not be applied beyond the delivery of goods. The Convention equally contains sufficient solutions if the buyer is the party who is to provide the services and breaches their obligations. The majority of CISG remedies apply to both parties of the contract under the same or similar requirements. Furthermore, the parties should generally have the same remedies in respect of the breach of service obligations, as a distinction between seller and buyer does not appear to be reasonable in this context. It is of particular importance to note that the Convention's provisions and its underlying principles are able to address the breach of exclusivity or non-competition obligations, which are frequently included in distribution contracts in practice.

It should be noted that the Convention is, by default, fragmentary and non-exhaustive. Consequently, there will still be a need to resort to the applicable domestic law with regard to certain aspects. This study has relied on the two-step test to determine the boundaries of the Convention's substantive scope of application. Under this test, a factual and legal criterion must be applied. An application of this test has revealed that the CISG is, *inter alia*, not concerned with issues of competition law, claims for compensation after termination of a distribution agreement, claims based on '*rupture brutale*', form requirements for exclusivity or non-competition clauses, and other industry-specific rules. Rather, these matters should be governed by the applicable domestic law. This demonstrates that the CISG's application to international framework agreements is without prejudice to specific domestic law rules that fall outside the Convention's substantive scope.

IV. FRAMEWORK AGREEMENTS AS LONG-TERM CONTRACTS (CHAPTER 5)

The fact that framework agreements are considered to be long-term contracts raises further questions. This study has referred to 'long-term contracts' in regard to any contract that must be performed over an extended period of time. The temporal aspect of such contracts contextually gives rise to specific issues, although not in a universal manner.

One of those issues is the role of cooperation and trust in long-term framework agreements. The parties are free to incorporate cooperation and fiduciary obligations into their contract under the CISG. Such obligations may also be derived from usages or practices established between the parties (Art. 9 CISG). However, it has been submitted by this study that no general cooperation or information obligations may be derived from the CISG, in particular from Art. 7(1) or (2) CISG. It is still possible that certain provisions of the CISG may involve an element of cooperation or information. In addition, cooperation or fiduciary obligations may arise from domestic law rules pursuant to Art. 7(2) CISG, or if they are related to matters outside the Convention's substantive scope of application. If fiduciary or cooperation obligations have been incorporated into a long-term framework agreement governed by the CISG, their breach is, in principle, governed by the Convention. Nevertheless, domestic law remedies shall apply alongside the CISG, provided that they are not only linked to a breach of contract but also to other aspects, such as the parties' specific relationship of trust.

Long-term framework agreements are susceptible to changes in the surrounding circumstances. The parties may deviate from the contractual terms through their actual conduct following contract conclusion. The parties' subsequent conduct must be taken into account for the interpretation of any CISG contract according to Art. 8(3) CISG. This interpretative tool is particularly relevant for long-term framework agreements and other long-term contracts. The individual sales contracts that have been concluded under the umbrella of a two-tier framework agreement should be interpreted in light of the latter, and vice versa (Art. 8(3) CISG). Furthermore, the parties may wish to subsequently modify their framework agreement (Art. 29 CISG). The parties may also agree on additional mechanisms for contract modifications in anticipation of potential changes. Such mechanisms may include price escalation clauses, which are common in framework agreements, or references to external standards that stipulate essential elements of their contract (e.g., the price by reference to an index) or expand on their performance (e.g., specifying the requirements for the conformity of goods).

It is also possible that changes in the surrounding circumstances may lead to problems of force majeure or hardship in long-term framework agreements. This study posited that the CISG should cover both cases of force majeure and hardship (Art. 79 CISG). In this respect, there are no fundamental differences between framework agreements or other long-term contracts in comparison to one-off contracts; the same prerequisites apply, and the same legal consequences follow. Nevertheless, the parties to a framework agreement frequently diverge from the CISG's provisions by including force majeure or hardship clauses (Art. 6 CISG). Moreover, framework agreements are more likely to implicitly or explicitly address certain risks, thereby not leaving much room for hardship. Additionally, the assessment of whether there has been a fundamental alteration of the contractual equilibrium may be more challenging as the point of reference is the entire agreement, including past and future performances under a long-term framework agreement. Although this assessment must be conducted separately for framework agreements with a two-tier structure and the individual sales contracts, it is possible that these contracts may influence the interpretation of each other, and, to this extent, indirectly the assessment in question.

Long-term framework agreements may be limited in time, which could be considered a form of termination agreement in the sense of Art. 29(1) CISG. The admissibility of a specific duration of a contract is subject to the relevant domestic law (Art. 4(a) CISG). The parties are also free to agree on so-called renewal clauses; their incorporation is subject to Arts 14–24 CISG, whereas their validity is governed by the applicable domestic law.

Furthermore, certain domestic laws provide for a right to unilaterally terminate any long-term contract (including framework agreements) in compliance with certain time limits, provided that the contract is of indefinite duration. An application of the two-step test has revealed that the CISG may cover these factual scenarios, but it does not intend to govern this subject matter. The general right to terminate indefinite long-term contracts under domestic laws is, *inter alia*, based on the consideration that the parties should not be able to contractually bind themselves eternally. This risk is not addressed by the CISG. Consequently, domestic law rules that provide for a general right to terminate indefinite long-term contracts should be applicable alongside the Convention. The parties are also at liberty to contractually agree upon a similar right within their framework agreement, which is subject to the CISG.

In contrast to certain domestic laws, the CISG does not include a right to terminate long-term framework agreements or other long-term contracts for a compelling reason. Given the extensive range of cases covered by the right to terminate for a compelling reason under domestic laws, this study has distinguished between different case groups, leading to a nuanced conclusion. The Convention addresses the risks involved in cases of breaches of contract (*see* Arts 49, 64, 73 CISG), cases of insolvency (*see* Arts 71, 72, 73 CISG) and cases of hardship (Art. 79 CISG) – and should, therefore, exhaustively govern these cases. Conversely, this study has posited that domestic law rules that provide for a right to terminate for a compelling reason should be applicable alongside the CISG in cases of 'cross-contractual' breaches (termination of a frame work agreement based on breach(es) of individual sales contracts), cases of disruption of the parties' personal relationship and cases of change of control. While the Convention also covers these factual scenarios, it does not address the underlying risks nor attempt to regulate them. The parties are once again at liberty to contractually agree upon such a right to terminate their framework agreement for a compelling reason (Art. 6 CISG), although the limits of validity set out by the applicable domestic law must be taken into account.

The avoidance of long-term framework agreements governed by the CISG is subject to the Convention's provisions on contract avoidance. In the context of framework agreements, it may be necessary to take the parties' multitude of interests and their contractual expectation of loyal behaviour into account under the balancing act that is required by Art. 25 CISG. The avoidance of framework agreements that already contain the defining characteristics of a sales contract is primarily subject to Art. 73 CISG and, where applicable, to Arts 49 and 64 CISG. A more challenging issue is that of avoiding framework agreements with a two-tier structure. Such avoidance is generally restricted to the contract that has been fundamentally breached, i.e., either the framework agreement or one or multiple individual sales contracts. A 'cross-contractual' right to avoid a contract does not follow from the CISG but may be derived from domestic law rules that permit a party to terminate a contract for a compelling reason in such circumstances. The aggrieved party may additionally invoke Art. 71 or 72 CISG in order to suspend or avoid related individual sales contracts based on a breach of another individual sales contract.

In accordance with Art. 73(1) CISG, avoidance and restitution are permitted in relation to a single instalment under the contract. Art. 73(2) CISG, however, may entitle the aggrieved party to avoid a framework agreement *ex nunc* without affecting parts of the contract that have already been performed in the past. Art. 73(3) CISG may entitle the aggrieved party to avoid a framework agreement in its entirety, necessitating restitution. The avoidance of a framework agreement with a two-tier structure does not affect the individual sales contracts concluded under its umbrella. Furthermore, after avoiding such contracts, restitution in the sense of Arts 81 et seq. CISG will not typically be necessary, as the contracts in question do not involve the exchange of goods against money. The avoidance of such framework agreements primarily has effects for the future, in that the parties will not be obliged to conclude further individual sales contracts. Conversely, the avoidance of individual sales contracts concluded under framework agreements with a two-tier structure may make restitution necessary. Once the framework agreement has ended, the parties may wish to be compensated for their investments. Under the CISG, an aggrieved party is entitled to pursue such a claim if these investments qualify as frustrated expenses that fall within the scope of a claim for damages (Art. 45(1)(b) or 61(1)(b) in conjunction with Art. 74 CISG).

V. CHOICE OF LAW CLAUSES IN FRAMEWORK AGREEMENTS (CHAPTER 6)

Finally, the parties may wish to choose the CISG as the law applicable to their framework agreement. A choice of the CISG on a substantive level is subject to the law applicable by virtue of international private law rules and is typically unproblematic, at least within the limits granted by the applicable domestic law. Furthermore, this study has reached the conclusion that the parties should be permitted to select the CISG as the law applicable to their contract under the relevant international private law rules in Switzerland (at least under Art. 117 PILA) and the European Union (Art. 3 Rome I Regulation). Consequently, the parties are free to agree upon the CISG's applicability even if a framework agreement would not per se be covered by the Convention. Even then, the Convention should apply only within its substantive scope of application and not govern all matters that may arise in connection with a framework agreement.

Furthermore, there may be an interplay between a choice of law clause that is contained in the framework agreement and the law applicable to the individual sales contracts, and vice versa. In general, the law applicable to these contracts must be determined separately. Nevertheless, the parties may explicitly agree to extend the choice of the CISG contained in a framework agreement to the individual sales contracts. Moreover, even if the parties merely selected the CISG as the applicable law for the framework agreement, this may be interpreted as an indication that the Convention is also intended to govern the individual sales contracts. Nevertheless, there must be further indications that reveal the parties' intentions to agree on such an implicit choice of law. A choice of the CISG contained in the individual sales contracts may also be considered an indication that the same law should apply to the framework agreement, which also requires additional indications.

In the context of a choice of domestic law, it is necessary to distinguish between various scenarios. In cases where the parties to a framework agreement agree on the domestic law of a Contracting State, the CISG's applicability to the framework agreement will depend on whether the contract per se falls within the Convention's sphere of application. As a general rule, the choice of the domestic law of a Contracting State typically also includes the CISG as part of this law. If the parties to a framework agreement agree on the applicability of the domestic law of a non-Contracting State, the CISG will usually not be applicable. In instances where the parties have consented to the applicability of the CISG in conjunction with domestic law, the interpretation of the specific choice of law clause will be pivotal. One potential interpretation put forth by this study was that the parties may have selected the CISG's applicability, whereas the chosen domestic law should govern matters that fall outside the Convention's substantive scope of application. In all of these scenarios, it is important to consider potential interplays between the law applicable to the framework agreement and that to the individual sales contracts.

Bibliography

Achilles, Wilhelm-Albrecht: Kommentar zum UN-Kaufrechtsübereinkommen (CISG), 2nd ed., Köln: Carl Heymanns Verlag/Wolters Kluwer (2018).

American Law Institute: Uniform Commercial Code, Official Text and Comments, 2010-2011 ed., St. Paul: West (2010) (cited: *American Law Institute*, §, note).

Andersen, Camilla Baasch: Good Faith? Good Grief!, (2014) 17 Int'l Trade & Bus. L. Rev., pp. 310–321.

Atamer, Yeşim M.: Availability of Remedies Other Than Damages in Case of Exemption According to Art. 79 CISG, in: Büchler, Andrea/Müller-Chen, Markus (eds), Private Law: National - Global - Comparative, Festschrift für Ingeborg Schwenzer zum 60. Geburtstag, Bern: Stämpfli (2011), pp. 83–98 (cited: *Atamer*, FS Schwenzer, p.).

Audit, Bernard: La vente internationale de marchandises, Convention des Nations-Unies du 11 avril 1980, Paris: Librairie générale de droit et de jurisprudence (1990).

Bauerreis, Jochen: La rupture brutale des relations commerciales établies dans les contrats internationaux, in: Mélanges en l'honneur du Professeur Claude Witz, Paris: LexisNexis (2018), pp. 61–72 (cited: *Bauerreis*, FS C. Witz, p.).

Beale, Hugh G. (ed.): Chitty on Contracts, Vol. I, 35th ed., London: Sweet Maxwell/Thomson Reuters (2024) (cited: *Chitty on contracts*, para.).

Bell, Gary F.: The Sphere of Application of the Vienna Convention on Contracts for the International Sale of Goods, (1996) 1 Pace Int'l L. Rev., pp. 237–258 https://doi.org/10.58948/2331-3536.1288, last checked October 2025.

Ben-Shahar, Omri: 'Agreeing to Disagree': Filling Gaps in Deliberately Incomplete Contracts, (2004) 389 Wis. L. Rev., pp. 390–428.

Bénabent, Alain: Droit des obligations, 19th ed., Paris: Librairie générale de droit et de jurisprudence (2021).

Benedick, Gilles: Die Informationspflichten im UN-Kaufrecht (CISG) und ihre Verletzung, unter Berücksichtigung des Zusammenspiels mit dem nationalen schweizerischen Recht, Bern/München: Stämpfli Verlag AG/Sellier. European Law Publishers (2008).

Bens, Tess: Application of the CISG to Mixed Contract/Non-conformity of Services Accessory to the Sale of Goods, IHR 2022, pp. 63–64.

Bianca, Cesare Massimo/Bonell, Michael Joachim (eds): Commentary on the International Sales Law the 1980 Vienna Sales Convention, Milan: Giuffrè (1987) (cited: Bianca/Bonell/*Author*, Art., note).

Bonell, Michael Joachim: Vertragsverhandlungen und culpa in contrahendo nach dem Wiener Kaufrechtsübereinkommen, RIW 1990, pp. 693–702.

Bremenkamp, Fernanda Luisa: Rechtliche Governance von Zulieferverträgen, eine vergleichende Untersuchung in der Automobilindustrie zum deutschen, italienischen und englischen Recht, Tübingen: Mohr Siebeck (2020).

Bremenkamp, Fernanda Luisa: Vorzeitige Beendigung kooperativer Zulieferverträge und ihre Grenzen, ZVertriebsR 2023, pp. 206–212.

Bridge, Michael G.: Choice of Law and the CISG: Opting In and Opting Out, in: Flechtner, Harry M./Brand, Ronald A./Walter, Mark S. (eds), Drafting Contracts under the CISG, New York: Oxford University Press (2008) (cited: *Bridge*, Choice of Law and the CISG, p.).

Bridge, Michael G.: Good Faith, Common Law and the CISG, (2017) 22 Unif. L. Rev., pp. 1–16 https://doi.org/10.1093/ulr/unw059 last checked October 2025.

Bridge, Michael G.: The International Sale of Goods, 5th ed., Oxford: Oxford University Press (2023) (cited: *Bridge*, Int'l Sale of Goods, para.).

Brunner, Christoph: Force Majeure and Hardship under General Contract Principles: Exemption for Non-performance in International Arbitration, Austin: Wolters Kluwer (2009).

Brunner, Christoph (ed.): UN-Kaufrecht: CISG, Kommentar zum Übereinkommen der Vereinten Nationen über Verträge über den internationalen Warenkauf von 1980, 2nd ed., Bern: Stämpfli AG (2014) (cited: Brunner/*Author*, Art., para.).

Brunner, Christoph/Gottlieb, Benjamin (eds): Commentary on the UN Sales Law (CISG), Alphen aan den Rijn: Wolters Kluwer (2019) (cited: Brunner/Gottlieb/*Author*, Art., para.).

Bucher, Eugen: Schweizerisches Obligationenrecht, Allgemeiner Teil ohne Deliktsrecht, 2nd ed., Zürich: Schulthess Polygraphischer Verlag (1988).

Bucher, Andreas/Guillaume, Florence (eds): Commentaire Romand, Loi sur le droit international privé, Convention de Lugano, 2nd ed., Basel: Helbing Lichtenhahn Verlag (2024) (cited: CR LDIP/*Author*, Art., para.).

Budde, Robert/Geks, Victoria: Rahmenlieferverträge: ein Instrument zur Verstetigung von Vertriebsbeziehungen, ZVertriebsR 2012, pp. 37–47.

Buffelan-Lanore, Yvaine/Larribau-Ternyere, Virginie: Droit civil, Les obligations, 16th ed., Paris: Dalloz Sirey (2018).

Butler, Petra: The CISG: A Secret Weapon in the Fight for a Fairer World?, in: Schwenzer, Ingeborg (ed.), 35 Years CISG and Beyond, The Hague: Eleven International Publishing (2016).

Calliess, Gralf-Peter/Renner, Moritz (eds): Rome Regulations, Commentary, 3rd ed., Aalphen aan den Rijn: Wolters Kluwer (2020) (cited: Calliess/Renner/*Author*, Art., para.).

Campbell, David/Harris, Donald: Flexibility in Long-Term Contractual Relationships: The Role of Cooperation, (1993) 20(2) J. L. & Soc., pp. 166–191 https://doi.org/10.2307/1410166, last checked October 2025.

Canaris, Claus-Wilhelm: Die Feststellung von Lücken im Gesetz, Eine methodologische Studie über Voraussetzungen und Grenzen der richterlichen Rechtsfortbildung *praeter legem*, 2th ed., Berlin: Duncker & Humblot (1983) (cited: *Canaris*, Lücken, p.).

Canaris, Claus-Wilhelm: Handelsrecht, 24th ed., München: C.H. Beck (2006).

Christou, Richard: International Agency, Distribution and Licensing Agreements, 6th ed., London: Thomson Reuters (2011).

CISG-AC Opinion No. 4, Contracts for the Sale of Goods to Be Manufactured or Produced and Mixed Contracts: Article 3 CISG, 24 October 2004, Rapporteur: Perales Viscasillas, Pilar (cited: CISG-AC, Op. 4 *Perales Viscasillas*).

CISG-AC Opinion No. 7, Exemption of Liability for Damages under Article 79 of the CISG, 12 October 2007, Rapporteur: Garro, Alejandro (cited: CISG-AC, Op. 7 *Garro*).

CISG-AC Opinion No. 9, Consequences of Avoidance of the Contract, 15 November 2008, Rapporteur: Bridge, Michael G. (cited: CISG-AC, Op. 9 *Bridge*).

CISG-AC Opinion No. 16, Exclusion of the CISG under Article 6, 30 May 2014, Rapporteur: Spagnolo, Lisa (cited: CISG-AC, Op. 16 *Spagnolo*).

CISG-AC Opinion No. 19, Standards and Conformity of the Goods under Article 35 CISG, 25 November 2018, Rapporteur: Saidov, Djakhongir (cited: CISG-AC, Op. 19 *Saidov*).

CISG-AC Opinion No. 20, Hardship under the CISG, 2–5 February 2020, Rapporteur: Muñoz, Edgardo (cited: CISG-AC, Op. 20 *Muñoz*).

CISG-AC Opinion No. 21, Delivery of Substitute Goods and Repair under the CISG, 3 and 4 February 2020, Rapporteurs: Schwenzer, Ingeborg/Beimel, Ilka H. (cited: CISG-AC, Op. 21 *Schwenzer/Beimel*).

CISG-AC Opinion No. 23, Mistake, Fraud, Misrepresentation and Initial Impossibility in CISG Contracts, 12–14 December 2023, Rapporteur: Beale, Hugh G. (cited: CISG-AC, Op. 23 *Beale*).

Crockett, Matt: The Law of Sales under the Uniform Commercial Code, Danvers: Thomson Reuters (2021).

Czerwenka, Beate: Rechtsanwendungsprobleme im internationalen Kaufrecht, Das Kollisionsrecht bei grenzüberschreitenden Kaufverträgen und der Anwendungsbereich der internationalen Kaufrechtsübereinkommen, Berlin: Duncker & Humboldt (1988).

Dessemontet, François: Sanctity of Contracts vs. Termination for Cause: Why Is UNIDROIT Afraid of the Big Bad § 314 BGB?, in: Büchler, Andrea/Müller-Chen, Markus (eds), Private law – national – global – comparative, Festschrift für Ingeborg Schwenzer zum 60. Geburtstag, Bern: Stämpfli (2011), pp. 395–407 (cited: *Dessemontet*, FS Schwenzer, p.).

DiMatteo, Larry A./et al. (eds): International Sales Law, Contracts, Principles & Practice, Baden-Baden: C.H. Beck/Hart/Nomos (2016) (cited: DiMatteo *et al./Author*, Ch., para.).

Dörr, Oliver/Schmalenbach, Kirsten (eds): Vienna Convention on the Law of Treaties, A Commentary, 2nd ed., Berlin/Heidelberg: Springer-Verlag (2018) (cited: Dörr/Schmalenbach/*Author*).

Doralt, Walter: Langzeitverträge, Tübingen: Mohr Siebeck (2018).

Drescher, Ingo/Fleischer, Holger/Schmidt, Karsten (eds): Münchener Kommentar zum HGB, 6th ed., München: C.H. Beck (2025) (cited: MüKoHGB/*Author*).

Ebenroth, Carsten Thomas: Absatzmittlungsverträge im Spannungsverhältnis von Kartell- und Zivilrecht, Konstanz: Universitätsverlag Konstanz (1980).

Eiselen, Sieg: Literal Interpretation: The Meaning of the Words, in: Janssen, André/Meyer, Olaf (eds), CISG Methodology, München: Sellier. European Law Publishers (2009).

Enderlein, Fritz/Maskow, Dietrich: International Sales Law, United Nations Convention on Contracts for the International Sale of Goods, Convention on the Limitation Period in the International Sale of Goods, Commentary, New York/London: Oceana Publications (1992) (cited: *Enderlein/Maskow*, Art., note).

Fabig, Philine: Der Vertragshändlerausgleich in internationalen Verträgen, IHR 2019, pp. 1–11.

Farnsworth, Allan: Farnsworth on Contracts, 3rd ed., New York: Aspen Publishers (2004).

Farnsworth, Allan: Precontractual Liability and Preliminary Agreements: Fair Dealing and Failed Negotiations, (1987) 87 Col. L. Rev., pp. 217–294 https://doi.org/10.2307/1122561 last checked October 2025.

Fawcett, James/Harris, Jonathan/Bridge, Michael G. (eds): International Sale of Goods in the Conflict of Laws, Oxford: Oxford University Press (2005).

Ferrari, Franco: Contrat de vente internationale, Applicabilité et applications de la Convention de Vienne sur les contrats de vente internationale de marchandises, 2nd ed., Basel/Geneva/München: Helbing & Lichtenhahn Verlag (2005).

Ferrari, Franco: Der Vertriebsvertrag als vom UN-Kaufrechtsübereinkommen (nicht) erfasster Vertragstyp, EuLF 2000/2001, pp. 7–12.

Ferrari, Franco: Fundamental Breach of Contract under the UN Sales Convention: 25 Years Article 25 CISG, (2005) 389 Int'l Bus. L. J., pp. 389–400.

Ferrari, Franco: The CISG's Interpretative Goals, Its Interpretative Method and Its General Principles in Case Law, Part I & II, IHR 2013, pp. 137–155 & IHR 2013, pp. 181–196.

Ferrari, Franco/et al. (eds): Internationales Vertragsrecht, Rom I-VO, CISG, CMR, FactÜ, Kommentar, 3rd ed., München: C.H. Beck (2018) (cited: Ferrari *et al./Author*, Art., para.).

Fikentscher, Wolfgang/Heinemann, Andrea: Schuldrecht: Allgemeiner und Besonderer Teil, 12th ed., Berlin/Boston: Walter de Gruyter GmbH (2022).

Flambouras, Dionysios P.: The Doctrines of Impossibility of Performance and Clausula Rebus Sic Stantibus in the 1980 Convention on Contracts for the International Sale of Goods and the Principles of European Contract Law: A Comparative Analysis, (2001) 13 Pace Int'l L. Rev., pp. 262–293 https://doi.org/10.58948/2331-3536.1212, last checked October 2025.

Flechtner, Harry M.: The Exemption Provisions of the Sales Convention, Including Comments on 'Hardship' Doctrine and the 19th June 2009 Decision of the Belgian Supreme Court, Working Paper (cited: *Flechtner*, p.).

Flechtner, Harry M. (ed.): Transcript of a Workshop on the Sales Convention: Leading Scholars Discuss Contract Formation, Validity, Excuse for Hardship, Avoidance, *Nachfrist*, Contract Interpretation, Parol Evidence, Analogical Application and Much More, (1999) 18 J. L. & Com., pp. 191–258 (cited: Flechtner/*Speaker*, (1999) 18 J. L. & Com., p.).

Flechtner, Harry M./Brand, Roland A.: Opting In to the CISG: Avoiding the Redline Products Problems, in: Andersen, Mads Bryde/Henschel, René Franz (eds), A Tribute to Joseph M. Lookofsky, Copenhagen: Djøf Publishing (2015).

Fogt, Morten M.: Contract Formation under the CISG: The Need for a Reform, in: DiMatteo, Larry A. (ed.), International Sales Law, A Global Challenge, New York: Cambridge University Press (2014).

Fogt, Morten M.: Einheitlicher Vertrag oder Aufspaltung nach Art. 3 Abs. 2 CISG, IPRax 2003, pp. 364–369.

Fonseca, John R./Fonseca, Patricia F. (eds): Williston on Sales, 5th ed., Danvers: Thomson Reuters (2023) (cited: *Williston on Sales*, §, p.).

Fountoulakis, Christiana: Agentur- und Fachhändlerverträge: jüngere Rechtsprechung und aktuelle Probleme, in: Arter, Oliver (ed.), Vertriebsverträge, Bern: Stämpfli Verlag (2007).

Fountoulakis, Christiana: The Parties' Choice of Neutral Law in International Commercial Sales Contracts, EJLR 2005, pp. 303–330.

Fountoulakis, Christiana: Zur Kundschaftsentschädigung bei Beendigung eines Alleinvertriebsvertrages (Vertragshändlervertrages), recht 2008, pp. 222–226.

Fountoulakis, Christiana: Zurückbehaltungsrecht bei nicht ausgestellter Quittung im UN-Kaufrecht, IHR 2005, pp. 244–249.

Fuchs-Wissemann, Georg: Die Abgrenzung des Rahmenvertrages vom Sukzessivlieferungsvertrag, Marburg: Fotodruck Symon und Wagner OHG (1980).

Furrer, Andreas/Lohri, Gino: Die Anwendung kaufrechtlicher Bestimmungen auf langfristige Lieferungs- und Bezugsverträge, in: Arter, Oliver (ed.), Vertriebsverträge, Bern: Stämpfli Verlag (2007).

Furrer, Andreas/Girsberger, Daniel/Müller-Chen, Markus (eds): Handkommentar zum Schweizer Privatrecht, Internationales Privatrecht, Art. 1–200 PILA, 4th ed., Zürich: Schulthess Juristische Medien AG (2024) (cited: CHK/*Author*, Art., para.).

Gabriel, Henry D.: Contracts fort the Sale of Goods: A Comparison of U.S. and International Law, 3rd ed., Oxford: Oxford University Press (2022).

Gass, Wolfram/Lange, Knut Werner: Rahmenverträge für moderne Produktionsformen, Einführung und Gestaltung, München: C.H. Beck (1999).

Gatsi, Jean: Le contrat-cadre, Paris: Libraire générale de droit et de jurisprudence (1996).

Gauch, Peter (ed.): Zürcher Kommentar, Volume No. V/2a, Kauf und Schenkung, Erste Lieferung, Art. 184–191 OR, 3rd ed., Zürich: Schulthess Polygraphischer Verlag (1993) (cited: ZK OR/*Author*, Art., para.).

Gebhardt, Hans-Peter: Der Zuliefervertrag, Köln/Berlin/Bonn/München: Carl Heymanns Verlag KG (1994).

Genys, Victoria: Blazing a Trail in the 'New Frontier' of the CISG: Helen Kaminski Pty. Ltd. V. Marketing Australian Products, Inc., (1997/98) 17 J. L. & Com., pp. 415–426.

Gillette, Clayton P./Walt, Steven D.: The UN Convention on Contracts for the International Sale of Goods, Theory and Practice, 2nd ed., New York: Cambridge University Press (2016).

Grieser, Simon Gottlieb: Die Behandlung von atypischen Kaufverträgen im UN-Kaufrecht, Frankfurt: Peter Lang (2003).

Grolimund, Pascal/Loacker, Leander D./Schnyder, Anton K. (eds): Basler Kommentar, Internationales Privatrecht, 4th ed., Basel: Helbing Lichtenhahn Verlag (2021) (cited: BSK IPRG/*Auhor*, Art., para.).

Groz, Philipp/Zehner, Alisa: Zur Kundschaftsentschädigung beim Alleinvertriebsvertrag, AJP 2024, pp. 398–407.

Gruber, Urs Peter: Methoden des internationalen Einheitsrechts, Tübingen: Mohr Siebeck (2004).

Grunewald, Barbara: Handbuch des Schuldrechts, Kaufrecht, Tübingen: Mohr Siebeck (2006).

Gsell, Beate/et al. (eds): Beck-online Grosskommentar, Zivilrecht (periodically updated online commentary, last checked September 2025) (cited: BeckOGK/*Author*, §/Art., para.).

Guo, Peng: Good Faith in Long-Term Supply Relational Supply Contracts in the Context of Hardship from a Comparative Perspective, Singapore: Springer (2022).

Guo, Peng: Termination for a Compelling Reason under the UNIDROIT Principles: The Status Quo and a Way Forward, (2018) 21 Int'l Trade & Bus. L. Rev., pp. 1–18.

Harjani, Sunil R.: The Convention on Contracts for the International Sale of Goods in United States Courts, (2004) 23:1 Houst. J. Int'l L., pp. 50–84.

Hartmann, Felix: Ungeschriebene Zurückbehaltungsrechte im UN-Kaufrecht, IHR 2006, pp. 181–191 (cited: *F. Hartmann*, IHR 2006, p.).

Hartmann, Jürg: Vertriebsverträge im internationalen Kontext, Alleinvertriebsvertrag und verwandte Verträge (Selektiver Vertrieb, Franchise-Vertrag) unter Berücksichtigung des schweizerischen und des EU-Wettbewerbsrechts, Zürich/Basel/Genf: Schulthess Juristische Medien (2007) (cited: *J. Hartmann*, p.).

Hartnell, Helen Elizabeth: Rousing the Sleeping Dog: The Validity Exception to the Convention on Contracts for the International Sale of Goods, (1993) 18 Yale J. Int'l L., pp. 1–93.

Hau, Wolfgang/Poseck, Roman (eds): Beck'scher Online Kommentar BGB, 75th ed., München: C.H. Beck (2025) (cited: BeckOK/*Author*, §/Art., para.).

Hayward, Benjamin: To Boldy Go, Part I: Developing a Specific Legal Framework for Assessing the Regulations of International Data Trade under the CISG, UNSW L. J. 2021, pp. 878–918.

Heinemann, Andreas/Schnyder, Anton K.: Internationales Wirtschaftsrecht in a nutshell, Zürich: Dike Verlag (2017).

Hellgardt, Alexander: Das Verbot der kollisionsrechtlichen Wahl nichtstaatlichen Rechts und das Unionsgrundrecht der Privatautonomie, RabelsZ 82 (2018), pp. 655–695.

Henrich, Dieter: Vorvertrag, Optionsvertrag, Vorrechtsvertrag, Tübingen: J.C.B. Mohr (Paul Siebeck) (1965).

Herber, Rolf: Anwendungsbereich des UNCITRAL-Übereinkommens, in: Doralt, Peter (ed.), Das UNCITRAL-Kaufrecht im Vergleich zum österreichischen Recht, Referate und Diskussionen des Symposiums in Baden bei Wien 17.–19. April 1983, Wien: Manz Verlag (1985), pp. 28–55.

Herber, Rolf/Czerwenka, Beate (eds): Internationales Kaufrecht: Kommentar zu dem Übereinkommen der Vereinten Nationen vom 11. April 1980 über Verträge über den Internationalen Warenkauf, München: C.H. Beck (1991) (cited: *Herber/Czerwenka*, Art., para.).

Herberger, Maximilian/et al. (eds): Juris PraxisKommentar BGB, Band 6: Internationales Privatrecht und UN-Kaufrecht, 10th ed., Saarbrücken: juris GmbH (2023) (cited: jurisPK-BGB/*Author*, Art., para.).

Himmen, Tatjana: Die Lückenfüllung anhand allgemeiner Grundsätze im UN-Kaufrecht (Art. 7 Abs. 2 CISG), Jena: Jenaer Wissenschaftliche Verlagsgesellschaft (2007).

Hochstrasser, Michael/Huber-Purtschert, Tina/Maissen, Eva (eds): Handkommentar zum schweizerischen Privatrecht, Obligationenrecht, Einzelne Vertragsverhältnisse, Art. 184–529 OR und Innominatverträge, 4th ed., Zürich: Schulthess Juristische Medien AG (2023) (cited: CHK/*Author*, Art., para.).

Hoffbauer, Christiane: Der Rahmenvertrag in der Lieferbeziehung, Berlin: Logos Verlag Berlin (2010).

Höß, Stefan: Der gegenständliche Anwendungsbereich des UN-Kaufrechts: 'contracts to which the CISG is applicable' (Diss. Augsburg 1995).

Honnold, John O.: Uniform Words and Unform Application. The 1980 Sales Convention and International Juridical Practice, in: Schlechtriem, Peter (ed.), Einheitliches Kaufrecht und nationales Obligationenrecht, Referate und Diskussionen der Fachtagung Einheitliches Kaufrecht am 16.-17.2.1987, Baden-Baden: Nomos Verlagsgesellschaft (1987).

Honnold, John O./Flechtner, Harry M.: Honnold's Uniform Law for International Sales under the 1980 United Nations Convention, 5th ed., Alphen aan den Rijn: Wolters Kluwer (2021).

Honsell, Heinrich (ed.): Kommentar zum UN-Kaufrecht, Übereinkommen der Vereinten Nationen über Verträge über den Internationalen Warenkauf (CISG), 2nd ed., Heidelberg/Dordrecht/New York/London: Springer (2010) (cited: Honsell/*Author*, Art., para.).

Honsell, Heinrich (ed.): Kurzkommentar Obligationenrecht, Basel: Helbing Lichtenhahn Verlag (2014) (KuKo OR/*Author*, Art., para.).

Hopt, Klaus (ed.): Handelsgesetzbuch mit GmbH & Co., Handelsklauseln, Bank- und Kapitalmarktrecht, Transportrecht (ohne Seerecht), 44th ed., München: C.H. Beck (2025) (cited: Hopt/*Author*, §, para.).

Horn, Norbert: Vertragsdauer, Die Vertragsdauer als schuldrechtliches Regelungsproblem, empfiehlt sich eine zusammenfassende Regelung der Sonderprobleme von Dauerschuldverhältnissen und langfristigen Verträgen?, in: Bundesministerium der Justiz (ed.), Gutachten und Vorschläge zur Überarbeitung des Schuldrechts, Band I, Köln: Bundesanzeiger (1981).

Huber, Peter/Mulis, Alastair: The CISG, A New Textbook for Students and Practitioners, München: Sellier. European Law Publishers (2007) (cited: Huber/Mulis/*Author*, p.).

Huguenin, Claire: Obligationenrecht, Allgemeiner und Besonderer Teil, 3rd ed., Zürich/Basel/Genf: Schulthess Juristische Medien AG (2019).

Iliou, Christopher: Rahmenverträge: Selbstdisziplinierung möglich oder Flexibilität unumgänglich?, ZVertriebsR 2023, pp. 81–82.

Janssen, André: Die Bedeutung der Rechtsvergleichung für die deutsche Zivilrechtslandschaft im 21. Jahrhundert, in: Janssen, André/Schulte-Nölke, Hans (eds), Researches in European Private Law and Beyond, Contributions in Honour of Reiner Schulze's Seventieth Birthday, Baden-Baden: Nomos (2020), pp. 299–324.

Janssen, André/Ahuja, Navin G.: The Imperfect International Sales Law: Revamp, Supplement or Leave it Alone?, IHR 2020, pp. 1–9.

Janssen, André/Kiene, Sörren Claas: The CISG and its General Principles, in: Janssen, André/Meyer, Olaf (eds), CISG Methodology, München: Sellier. European Law Publishers (2009).

Janssen, André/Wahnschaffe, Christian Johannes: Der internationale Warenkauf in Zeiten der Pandemie, EuZW 2020, pp. 410–415.

Janssen, André/Wahnschaffe, Christian Johannes: Von Impfstoffen und Einheitsrecht: Zur verkannten Rolle des UN-Kaufrechts im Rechtsstreit der Europäischen Union mit AstraZeneca, EuZW 2021, pp. 877–883.

Jayme, Erik: Kollisionsrechtliche Techniken für Langzeitverträge mit Auslandsberührung, in: Nicklisch, Fritz (ed.), Der komplexe Langzeitvertrag, Strukturen und Internationale Schiedsgerichtsbarkeit: The Complex Long-Term Contract, Structures and International Arbitration, Heidelberg: C.F. Müller Juristischer Verlag (1987).

Jiang, Zuoli: In Favor of Appropriate Dynamic Interpretation for the CISG's Legal Uniformity, in: Modernizing International Trade Law to Support Innovation and Sustainable Development: Proceedings of the Congress of the United Nations Commission on International Trade Law, Vienna, 4–6 July 2017, Volume 4: Papers presented at the Congress, Vienna: United Nations (2017), pp. 343–351.

Juhasz, Julian: Stillschweigender Ausschluss des UN-Kaufrechts im Prozess, IHR 2021, pp. 89–95.

Juhasz, Julian: Rahmenverträge in internationalen Lieferbeziehungen und das CISG, IHR 2025, 41–48.

Karner, Ernst/Koziol, Helmut: Zur Anwendbarkeit des UN-Kaufrechts bei Werk- und Dienstleistungen, Am Beispiel der Maschinen- und Industrieanlagenlieferungsverträge, Wien: Jan Sramek Verlag (2015).

Karollus, Martin: UN-Kaufrecht, Eine systematische Darstellung für Studium und Praxis, Wien/New York: Springer-Verlag (1991).

Kern, Christoph: Ein einheitliches Zurückbehaltungsrecht im UN-Kaufrecht?, ZEuP 2000, pp. 837–859.

Kilian, Monica: CISG and the Problem with Common Law Jurisdictions, (2011) 11 Transnat. L. & Pol'y, pp. 217–241.

Klima, Peter: Anwendbarkeit des CISG auf Rahmenvereinbarungen in Vertragshändlerverträgen, RIW 1996, pp. 1035–1036.

Klotz, James M.: International Sales Agreements, an Annotated Drafting and Negotiation Guide, 3rd ed., Alphen aan den Rijn: Kluwer Law International B.V. (2018).

Knapp, Charles: Enforcing the Contract to Bargain, (1969) 44 N.Y.U. L. Rev., pp. 673–728.

Kock, Annette: Nebenpflichten im UN-Kaufrecht, dargestellt am Beispiel des Verkäufers, Regensburg: S. Roderer (1995).

Köhler, Ben: Die Vorteils- und Gewinnherausgabe im CISG, Zugleich ein Beitrag zu Zulässigkeit und Grenzen der eigenständigen Weiterentwicklung des Übereinkommens, Tübingen: Mohr Siebeck (2021) (cited: *B. Köhler*, p.).

Köhler, Ben: For an Independent Development of the CISG Beyond Article 7(2): A Stocktake and a Proposal, in: Meškić, Zlatan/et al. (eds), Balkan Yearbook of European and International Law 2020, Cham: Springer (2021), pp. 3–39 (cited: *B. Köhler*, Independent Development, p.).

Köhler, Ben: The CISG in the Age of Sustainable Supply Chains, in: Gulati, Rishi/John, Thomas/Köhler, Ben (eds), The Elgar Companion to UNCITRAL, Cheltenham: Edward Elgar (2023), pp. 339–355 (cited: *B. Köhler*, Sustainable Supply Chains, p.).

Köhler, Ben: Long-Term Contracts in the 2016 UNIDROIT Principles of International Commercial Contracts, in: Gulati, Rishi/John, Thomas/Köhler, Ben (eds), The Elgar Companion to UNIDROIT, Cheltenham/Northampton: Edward Elgar (2024), pp. 151–164 (cited: *B. Köhler*, Long-term contracts, p.).

Kramer, Ernst A.: Juristische Methodenlehre, 6th ed., Bern: Stämpfli Verlag (2019).

Kren Kostkiewicz, Jolanta: IPRG/LugÜ, Orell Füssli Kommentar, Bundesgesetz über das Internationale Privatrecht, Lugano-Übereinkommen und weitere Erlasse, Zürich: Orell Füssli (2019) (cited: OFK/*Kren Kostkiewicz*, Art., para.).

Kritzer, Albert H.: Guide to Practical Applications of the United Nations Convention on Contracts for the International Sale of Goods, Denver/Bosten: Kluwer Law/Taxation Publishers (1989).

Kröll, Stefan/Mistelis, Loukas/Perales Viscasillas, Pilar (eds): UN Convention on Contracts for the International Sale of Goods (CISG), A Commentary, 2nd ed., München/Oxford/Baden-Baden: C.H. Beck/Hart/Nomos (2018) (cited: Kröll *et al./Author*, Art., para.).

Kronke, Herbert/Melis, Werner/Kuhn, Hans (eds): Handbuch Internationales Wirtschaftsrecht, 2nd ed., Köln: Verlag Dr. Otto Schmidt KG (2017) (cited: Kronke *et al./Author*, Teil, para.).

Kropholler, Jan: Internationales Einheitsrecht, Allgemeine Lehren, Tübingen: Mohr Siebeck (1975).

Kull, Michael/Wildhaber, Christoph (eds): Schweizer Vertriebsrecht, Ein Handbuch für Praktiker, Zürich/St. Gallen: Dike Verlag (2008) (cited: Kull/Wildhaber/*Author*, para.).

Lange, Frank-Holger: Laufzeit, Anpassung und Beendigung von Belieferungsverträgen am Beispiel der Kfz-Zulieferindustrie, NJOZ 2013, pp. 577–581.

Lindbach, Jochen: Rechtswahl im Einheitsrecht am Beispiel des Wiener UN-Kaufrechts, Aachen: Shaker Verlag (1996).

Lohmann, Arnd: Parteiautonomie und UN-Kaufrecht, Zugleich ein Beitrag zum Anwendungsbereich des Wiener Kaufrechtsübereinkommens der Vereinten Nationen vom 11. April 1980, Tübingen: Mohr Siebeck (2005).

Lookofsky, Joseph: Not Running Wild with the CISG, (2011) 29 J. L. & Com., pp. 141–169 https://doi.org/10.5195/jlc.2011.27, last checked October 2025.

Lookofsky, Joseph: The 1980 United Nations Convention on Contracts for the International Sale of Goods (CISG), 3rd ed., Alphen aan den Rijn: Wolters Kluwer (2016).

Lookofsky, Joseph: Understanding the CISG: A Compact Guide to the 1980 United Nations Convention on Contracts for the International Sale of Goods, 6th ed., Alphen aan den Rijn/Copenhagen: Wolters Kluwer/Djøf Publishing (2022) (cited: *Lookofsky*, Understanding the CISG, §).

Lord, Richard A. (ed.): A Treatise on the Law of Contracts, by Samuel Williston, Vol. 1, 4th ed., Eagan: Thomson/West (2007) (cited: *Williston on Contracts*, §, p.).

Macauly, Stewart: Non-contractual Relations in Business: A Preliminary Study, (1963) 28(1) Am. Soc. Rev., pp. 55–67 https://doi.org/10.2307/2090458 last checked October 2025.

Magnus, Ulrich: Borderline Problems of the CISG, in: UNIDROIT (ed.), *Eppur si move*: The Age of Uniform Law, Essays in Honour Michael Joachim Bonell to Celebrate His 70th birthday, Vol. 2, Rome: UNIDROIT (2016) (cited: *Magnus*, FS Bonell, p.).

Magnus, Ulrich: Das UN-Kaufrecht: Fragen und Probleme seiner praktischen Bewährung, ZEuP 1997, pp. 823–846.

Magnus, Ulrich: Die allgemeinen Grundsätze im UN-Kaufrecht, RabelsZ 59 (1995), pp. 469–494.

Magnus, Ulrich: Grenzüberschreitende Vertriebsverträge, IHR 2018, pp. 49–60.

Magnus, Ulrich: Remedies: Damages, Price Reduction, Avoidance, Mitigation, and Preservation, Part IV – Remedies and Damages, in: DiMatteo, Larry A. (ed.), International Sales Law: A Global Challenge, New York: Cambridge University Press (2014) (cited: *Magnus*, Remedies, p.).

Magnus, Ulrich: Tracing Methodology in the CISG: Dogmatic Foundations, in: Janssen, André/Meyer, Olaf (eds), CISG Methodology, München: Sellier. European Law Publishers (2009) (cited: *Magnus*, Tracing Methodology, p.).

Magnus, Ulrich: Wesentliche Fragen des UN-Kaufrechts, ZEuP 1999, pp. 642–662.

Magnus, Ulrich/Mankowski, Peter (eds): European Commentaries on Private International Law, ECPIL, Vol. II, Rome I Regulation, Köln: Otto Schmidt (2017) (cited: Magnus/Mankowski/*Author*, Art., para.).

Mahnken, Volker: Anlagenverträge und UN-Kaufrecht, IHR 2020, pp. 237–246.

Maier-Lohmann, Till: Property in Goods and the CISG, Frankfurt am Main: Fachmedien Recht und Wirtschaft, dfv Mediengruppe (2024).

Malaurie, Philippe/Aynès, Laurent/Stoffel-Munck, Philippe: Droit des obligations, 12th ed., Paris: Librairie générale de droit et de jurisprudence (2022).

Mankowski, Peter (ed.): Commercial Law, Article-by-Article Commentary, Baden-Baden: Nomos Verlagsgesellschaft (2019) (cited: Mankowski/*Author*, Art., para.).

Mankowski, Peter: Die Rom I-Verordnung: Änderungen im europäischen IPR für Schuldverträge, IHR 2008, pp. 133–152.

Mankowski, Peter: Der Vorschlag für die Rom I-Verordnung, IPRax 2006, pp. 101–113.

Martinek, Michael: Zulieferverträge und Qualitätssicherung, Köln: Verlag Kommunikationsform GmbH (1991).

Martinek, Michael/Semler, Franz-Jörg/Flohr, Eckhard: Handbuch des Vertriebsrechts, 5th ed., München: C.H. Beck (2025) (cited: Martinek/Semler/Flohr/*Author*, §, para.).

Martinez-Luna, William Fernando: Applicable Law to Distribution Contracts in the European Union Regulation 593/2008 (Rome I), Rev. Col. Der. Int. (2016), pp. 247–281.

Max Planck Institute for Foreign Private and Private International Law: Comments on the European Commission's Green Paper on the Conversion of the Rome Convention of 1980 on the Law Applicable to Contractual Obligations into a Community Instrument and Its Modernization, RabelsZ 68 (2004), pp. 1–97 (cited: *MPI*, RabelsZ 68 (2004), p.).

Meier-Hayoz, Arthur (ed.): Berner Kommentar Schweizerisches Zivilgesetzbuch, das Obligationenrecht, Allgemeinen Bestimmungen, Vol. VI/1/2/1a, Bern: Stämpfli Verlag (1991) (cited: BK OR/*Author*, Art., para.).

Memmo, Daniela: Il contrato di vendita internazionale nel diritto uniforme, Riv. Trim. Dir. Proced. Civ. 1983, pp. 180–214.

Meyer, Christian Alexander: Agentur- und Vertragsbeendigung in der Schweiz, ZVertriebsR 2017, pp. 14–24 (cited: *C. Meyer*, ZVertriebsR 2017, p.).

Meyer, Christian Alexander: Der Alleinvertriebsvertrag, ein Handbuch für Praktiker, 2nd ed., St. Gallen: Sogetes Verlag (1992) (cited: *C. Meyer*, p.).

Meyer, Christian Alexander: Der Alleinvertrieb: Typus, vertragsrechtliche Probleme und Qualifikation im IPR, St. Gallen: Sogetes Verlag (1990) (cited: *C. Meyer*, Alleinvertrieb, p.).

Meyer, Christian Alexander: Gedanken zum Vertriebsrecht, Jusletter 2 May 2016, pp. 1–46 (cited: C. Meyer, Jusletter 2 May 2016, para.).

Meyer, Olaf: Constructive Interpretation: Applying the CISG in 21st Century, in: Janssen, André/Meyer, Olaf (eds), CISG Methodology, München: Sellier. European Law Publishers (2009) (cited: *O. Meyer*, Constructive Interpretation, p.).

Moritz, Wendelin: Beendigungsansprüche eines Vertragshändlers in Österreich: eine Bestandaufnahme, ZVertriebsR 2017, pp. 143–149.

Mousseron, Jean-Marc/Seube, Alain: A propos des contrats d'assistance et fourniture, D. 1973, pp. 197–206.

Müller-Chen, Markus/Widmer Lüchinger, Corinne (eds): Zürcher Kommentar zum IPRG, Band II, Art. 108a–200, 3rd ed., Zürich/Basel/Genf: Schulthess Juristische Medien AG (2018) (cited: ZK IPRG/*Author*, Art., para.).

Münch, Peter/Passadelis, Nicolas/Lehne, Jens (eds): Handbuch Internationales Handels- und Wirtschaftsrecht, Basel: Helbing Lichtenhahn Verlag (2015) (cited: Münch/Passadelis/Lehne/*Author*, para.).

Muhl, Felix/Lüthge, Benedikt: Rahmenverträge in Lieferbeziehungen: Struktur, Beendigung und Rechtsfolgen, GWR 2016, p. 26.

Muñoz, Edgardo: Software Technology in CISG Contracts, (2019) 24 Unif. L. Rev., pp. 281–301 https://doi.org/10.1093/ulr/unz016, last checked October 2025.

Murray, Carole/Holloway, David/Timson-Hunt, Daren (eds): Schmitthoff's the Law and Practice of International Trade, 12th ed., London: Sweet & Maxwell (2012) (cited: *Murray/Holloway/Timson-Hunt*, Schmitthoff's Law and Practice, para.).

Neumann, Thomas: The Duty to Cooperate in International Sales, The Scope and Role of Article 80 CISG, München: Sellier. European Law Publishers (2012).

Neumann, Thomas: Dominant Control: A Proposal for the Classification of International Transactions of Modern Software, 21 VJ, pp. 109–128.

Neumayer, Karl H./Ming, Catherine: Convention de Vienne sur les contrats de vente internationale de marchandises, Commentaire, Lausanne: Centre du droit de l'entreprise de l'Université de Lausanne (1993) (cited: *Neumayer/Ming*, Art., note).

Neuner, Jörg: Allgemeiner Teil des Bürgerlichen Rechts, 13th ed., München: C.H. Beck (2023).

Newhouse, Adam/Tanaka, Tsuneyoshi: CISG: A Tool for Globalization (1): American and Japanese Perspectives, R.L.R. 2012, pp. 1–41.

Nicholas, Barry: Chapter 5: Impracticability and Impossibility in the U.N. Convention on Contracts for the International Sale of Goods, in: Galston, Nina M./Smit, Hans (eds), International Sales, The United Nations Convention on Contracts for the International Sale of Goods, New York: Matthew Bender (1984).

Nicklisch, Fritz: Vorteile einer Dogmatik für komplexe Langzeitverträge, in: Nicklisch, Fritz (ed.), Der komplexe Langzeitvertrag, Strukturen und Internationale Schiedsgerichtsbarkeit: The Complex Long-Term Contract, Structures and International Arbitration, Heidelberg: C.F. Müller Juristischer Verlag (1987).

Nicolai, Philip: Der Vertragstyp des UN-Kaufrechts, in: Santos, Francisco Javier Andrés/Baldus, Christian/Dedek, Helge (eds), Vertragstypen in Europa, Historische Entwicklungen und europäische Perspektiven, München: Sellier. European Law Publishers (2011), pp. 259–294.

Oertel, Roberta Ribeiro (ed.): Les contrat international de distribution, Concession et Franchise, Comparaison France-Brésil, Bruxelles: Bruylant (2016) (cited: Oertel/*Author*, p.).

Oetiker, Christian/Weibel, Thomas/Mata, Aline: Die Kundschaftsentschädigung bei Agentur- und Alleinvertriebsverträgen, IHR 2022, pp. 52–59.

Oetker, Hartmut: Das Dauerschuldverhältnis und seine Beendigung, Bestandsaufname und kritische Würdigung einer tradierten Figur der Schuldrechtsdogmatik, Tübingen: Mohr Siebeck (1994).

Ostendorf, Patrick (ed.): Internationale Wirtschaftsverträge, Exportkontrolle, Kartellrecht, Freistellung, Haftungsbeschränkung, Abtretungsverbote, Rechtswahl, Vertragsbeendigung, Streitbeilegung, Versicherung, internationale Liefer- und

Anlagenbauverträge, Vertriebs- und Lizenzvereinbarungen u.v.m., 3rd ed., München: C.H. Beck (2023) (cited: Ostendorf/*Author*, §, para.).

Padovini, Fabio: La Vendita Internazionale Dalle Convenzioni Della'a alla Convenzione di Vienna, Riv. Dir. Int. Priv. Proc. 1987, pp. 47–58.

Palumbo, Alissa: Modern Law of Sales in the United States, The Hague: Eleven International Publishing (2015).

Pavic, Vladimir/Djordjevic, Milena: The Scope and Sphere of Application of the CISG in the Balkans, in: Stamm, Jürgen (ed.), Festschrift für Helmut Rüßmann, Saarbrücken: Juris GmbH (2013), pp. 887–916 (cited: *Pavic/Djordjevic*, FS Rüßmann, p.).

Perales Viscasillas, Pilar: Extending the Scope of the 1980 Vienna Convention on the International Sale of Goods to Framework Distribution Contracts, in: Schwenzer, Ingeborg (ed.), 35 years CISG and beyond, The Hague: Eleven International Publishing (2016), pp. 115–138 (cited: *Perales Viscasillas*, Extending the Scope, p.).

Perales Viscasillas, Pilar: International Distribution Contracts and CISG, in: Schwenzer, Ingeborg/Atamer, Yeşim M./Butler, Petra (eds), Current Issues in the CISG and Arbitration, The Hague: Eleven International Publishing (2014), pp. 43–57 (cited: *Perales Viscasillas*, Int'l Distribution Contracts and CISG, p.).

Perillo, Joseph: Force Majeure and Hardship under the UNIDROIT Principles of International Commercial Contracts, (1997) 5 Tulane J. Int'l & Comp. L., pp. 6–28.

Perović, Jelena: Selected Critical Issues Regarding the Sphere of Application of the CISG, (2011) 59 Belgrade L. Rev., pp. 181–195.

Piltz, Burghard: Der Anwendungsbereich des UN-Kaufrechts, AnwBl 1991, pp. 57–62.

Piltz, Burghard: Internationales Kaufrecht, Das UN-Kaufrecht in praxisorientierter Darstellung, 2nd ed., München: C.H. Beck (2008).

Piltz, Burghard: Münchener Anwaltshandbuch, Internationales Wirtschaftsrecht, München: C.H. Beck (2017) (cited: *Piltz*, Int. Wirtschaftsrecht, §, para.).

Piltz, Burghard: Neue Entwicklungen im UN-Kaufrecht, NJW 2003, pp. 2056–2062.

Piltz, Burghard: Rahmen-Einkaufsvertrag nach CISG, in: Beck'sche Online-Formulare, Internationales Handels- und Vertriebsrecht, Formular 2.2.3.1.1., 13th ed., C.H. Beck (2025) (cited: *Piltz*, Rahmen-Einkaufsvertrag, para.).

Piltz, Burghard: Rahmen-Verkaufsvertrag nach CISG, in: Beck'sche Online-Formulare, Internationales Handels- und Vertriebsrecht, Formular 2.2.3.2.1., 13th ed., C.H. Beck (2025) (cited: Piltz, Rahmen-Verkaufsvertrag, para.).

Piltz, Burghard: UN-Kaufrecht/CISG: Was spricht dagegen?, ZVertriebsR 2017, pp. 138–142.

Ragno, Francesca: The CISG and Choice of Law: Two Worlds Apart?, (2019/20) 38 J. L. & Com., pp. 245–272 https://doi.org/10.5195/jlc.2020.188, last checked October 2025.

Rauscher, Thomas (ed.): Europäisches Zivilprozessrecht und Kollisionsrecht EuZPR/EuIPR, Kommentar, Band III: Rom I-VO & Rom II-VO, 5th ed., Köln: Verlag Dr. Otto Schmidt KG (2022) (cited: Rauscher/*Author*, Art., para.).

Rehbinder, Eckard: Alleinvertriebsverträge im Einheitskauf- und Kartellrecht, IPRax 1982, pp. 7–9.

Reimer, Franz: Juristische Methodenlehre, 2nd ed., Baden-Baden: Nomos Verlag (2020).

Reithmann, Christoph/Martiny, Dieter (eds): Internationales Vertragsrecht, Das internationale Privatrecht der Schuldverträge, 9th ed., Köln: Verlag Dr. Otto Schmid KG (2021) (cited: Reithmann/Martiny/*Author*, para.).

Ritzinger, Horst: Der Vorvertrag in der notariellen Praxis, NJW 1990, pp. 1201–1208.

Robertson, Donald: Symposium Paper: Long-Term Relational Contracts and the UNIDROIT Principles of International Commercial Contracts, (2010) 17 Austral. Int'l L. J., pp. 185–192.

Rösler, Hannes: Hardship in German Codified Private Law: In Comparative Perspective to English, French and International Contract Law, ERPL 2007, pp. 483–513.

Roth, Wulf-Henning: Zur Wählbarkeit nichtstaatlichen Rechts, in: Mansel, Heinz-Peter/Pfeiffer, Thomas/Kronke, Herbert (eds), Festschrift für Erik Jayme, Band I, München: Sellier. European Law Publishers (2004) (cited: *Roth*, FS Jayme, p.).

Rother, Werner: Der Vertrag als Vertragsgegenstand, in: Paulus, Gotthard/Diedrichsen, Uwe/Canaris, Claus-Wilhelm (eds), Festschrift für Karl Larenz zum 70. Geburtstag, München: C.H. Beck'sche Verlagsbuchhandlung (1973), pp. 435–454 (cited: *Rother*, FS Larenz, p.).

Rothermel, Martin: Internationales Kauf-, Liefer- und Vertriebsrecht, 2nd ed., Frankfurt: Deutscher Fachverlag GmbH, Fachmedien Recht und Wirtschaft (2021).

Rusch, Konrad: Gewinnhaftung bei Verletzung von Treuepflichten, Tübingen: Mohr Siebeck (2003).

Säcker, Franz Jürgen/Rixecker, Roland/Oetker, Hartmut/Limperg, Bettina (eds): Münchener Kommentar zum Bürgerlichen Gesetzbuch, 9th ed., München: C.H. Beck (2024) (cited: MüKoBGB/*Author*).

Saxinger, Andreas: Zulieferverträge im deutschen Recht, Zugleich eine Abhandlung zu den Besonderheiten langfristiger Schuldverhältnisse, Baden-Baden: Nomos (1993).

Sayag, Alain (ed.): Le contrat-cadre, 1. Exploration comparative, Paris: Creda (1994) (cited: Sayag/*Author*, para.).

Schlechtriem, Peter: CISG: Auslegung, Lückenfüllung und Weiterentwicklung, Vortrag gehalten auf eine Symposium zu Ehren von Dr. iur. Dr. h.c. Frank Vischer am 11. Mai 2004 in Basel (cited: *Schlechtriem*, Symposium Vischer, p.).

Schlechtriem, Peter: Gemeinsame Bestimmungen über Verpflichten des Verkäufers und des Käufers, in: Schweizerisches Institut für Rechtsvergleichung (ed.), Wiener Übereinkommen von 1980 über den internationalen Warenkauf, Lausanner Kolloquium vom 19. und 20. November 1984, Zürich: Schulthess Polygraphischer Verlag (1985) (cited: *Schlechtriem*, Lausanner Kolloquium, p.).

Schlechtriem, Peter: Internationales UN-Kaufrecht, 4th ed., Tübingen: Mohr Siebeck (2007) (cited: *Schlechtriem*, 4th ed., para.).

Schlechtriem, Peter: Interpretation, Gap-Filling and Further Development of the U.N. Sales Convention, (2004) 2 Pace Int'l L. Rev., pp. 281–306 https://doi.org/10.58948/2331-3536.1165, last checked October 2025.

Schlechtriem, Peter: Requirements of Applicability and Sphere of Applicability of the CISG, (2005) 36 V.U.W. L. Rev., pp. 781–794 https://doi.org/10.26686/vuwlr.v36i4.5625 last checked October 2025.

Schlechtriem, Peter/Butler, Petra: UN Law on International Sales, the UN Convention on the International Sale of Goods, Heidelberg: Springer (2008).

Schlechtriem, Peter/Schwenzer, Ingeborg (eds): Commentary on the UN Convention on the International Sale of Goods, 2nd ed., Oxford: Oxford University Press (2005) (cited: Schlechtriem/Schwenzer/*Author*, 2nd English ed., Art., para.).

Schlechtriem, Peter/Schwenzer, Ingeborg/Schroeter, Ulrich G. (eds): Kommentar zum UN-Kaufrecht (CISG), 8th ed., München/Basel: C.H. Beck/Helbing Lichtenhahn/LexisNexis (2025) (cited: Schlechtriem/Schwenzer/Schroeter/*Author*, 8th German ed., Art., para.).

Schlechtriem, Peter/Schwenzer, Ingeborg/Schroeter, Ulrich G. (eds): Schlechtriem & Schwenzer: Commentary on the UN Convention on the International Sale of Goods, 5th ed., Oxford: Oxford University Press (2022) (cited: Schlechtriem/Schwenzer/Schroeter/*Author*, 5th English ed., Art., para.).

Schluep, Walter R.: Der Alleinvertriebsvertrag, Marktstein der EWG-Kartellpolitik, Bern: Stämpfli Verlag (1966).

Schmidt, Joanna: Preliminary Agreements in International Contract Negotiation, (1983–94) 6 Houst. J. Int'l L., pp. 37–62 (cited: *J. Schmidt*, (1983–1984) 6 Houst. J. Int'l L., p.).

Schmidt, Karsten: Handelsrecht, Unternehmensrecht I, 6th ed., Köln: Carl Heymanns Verlag (2014) (cited: *K. Schmidt*, §, para.).

Schnyder, Anton K./Liatowitsch, Manuel: Internationales Privat- und Zivilverfahrensrecht, 4th ed., Zürich: Schulthess (2017).

Schroeter, Ulrich G.: Contract Validity and the CISG, (2017) Unif. L. Rev., pp. 47–71.

Schroeter, Ulrich G.: Defining the Borders of Uniform International Contract Law: The CISG and Remedies for Innocent, Negligent, or Fraudulent Misrepresentation, (2013) 58 Vill. L. Rev., pp. 553–587.

Schroeter, Ulrich G.: Does the 1980 Vienna Sales Convention Reflect Universal Values? The Use of the CISG as a Model for Law Reform and Regional Specificities, (2018) 41 Loy. L.A. Int'l & Comp. L. Rev., pp. 1–50.

Schroeter, Ulrich G.: Gegenwart und Zukunft des Einheitsrechts, RabelsZ 81 (2017), pp. 33–76.

Schroeter, Ulrich G.: Internationales UN-Kaufrecht, 7th ed., Tübingen: Mohr Siebeck (2022).

Schroeter, Ulrich G.: UN-Kaufrecht und Europäisches Gemeinschaftsrecht, Verhältnis und Wechselwirkungen, München: Sellier. European Law Publishers (2005) (cited: *Schroeter*, UN-Kaufrecht und Europ. Gemeinschaftsrecht, §, para.).

Schroeter, Ulrich G.: Vienna Sales Convention: Applicability to 'Mixed Contracts' and Interactions with the 1968 Brussels Convention, (2005) 5 VJ, pp. 74–86.

Schumacher, Florian: Kaufoptionsvertrag und Verwendungsrisiko im UN-Kaufrecht, IHR 2005, pp. 147–151.

Schwartz, Alan/Scott, Robert E.: The Law and Economics of Preliminary Agreements, (2007) 661 Harv. L. Rev., pp. 1 et seq.

Schwenzer, Ingeborg: Force Majeure and Hardship in International Sales Contracts, (2008) 39 V.U.W. L. Rev., pp. 709–725 https://doi.org/10.26686/vuwlr.v39i4.5487, last checked October 2025.

Schwenzer, Ingeborg: CISG: Challenges of the 2020s, in: UNCITRAL/Department of Justice of the Hong Kong SAR of the People's Republic of China/Asian Academy of International Law (eds), Celebrating the 40th Anniversary of the CISG: CISG as a Tool for Global Trade – Theory and Practice, Hong Kong: Asian Academy of International Law (cited: *Schwenzer*, Challenges of the 2020s, p.).

Schwenzer, Ingeborg: Interpretation and Gap-Filling under the CISG, in: Schwenzer, Ingeborg/Atamer, Yeşim M./Butler, Petra (eds), Current Issues in the CISG and Arbitration, The Hague: Eleven International Publishing (2014), pp. 109–118 (cited: *Schwenzer*, Interpretation and gap-filling, p.).

Schwenzer, Ingeborg/Fountoulakis, Christiana: Schweizerisches Obligationenrecht, Allgemeiner Teil, 8th ed., Bern: Stämpfli Verlag (2020).

Schwenzer, Ingeborg/Fountoulakis, Christiana/Dimsey, Mariel: International Sales Law: A Guide to the CISG, 3rd ed., Oxford/London/New York/New Delhi/Sidney: Hart (2019) (cited: *Schwenzer/Fountoulakis/Dimsey*, p.).

Schwenzer, Ingeborg/Jaeger, Florence: Das CISG im Schiedsverfahren, Die Tücken des anwendbaren Rechts materiellen Rechts im Schiedsverfahren, IWRZ 2016, pp. 99–106.

Schwenzer, Ingeborg/Mohs, Florian: Old Habits Die Hard: Traditional Contract Formation in a Modern World, IHR 2006, pp. 239–246.

Schwenzer, Ingeborg/Muñoz, Edgardo: Global Sales and Contract Law, 2nd ed., Oxford: Oxford University Press (2022).

Schwenzer, Ingeborg/Ranetunge, Julian/Tafur, Fernando: Service Contracts and the CISG, (2019) 10 Indian J. Int'l Econ. L., pp. 172–196.

Schwenzer, Ingeborg/Ranetunge, Julian/Tafur, Fernando: Service Contracts and the CISG, (2019/20) 39 J. L. & Com., pp. 305–332 https://doi.org/10.5195/jlc.2020.200, last checked October 2025.

Secretariat's Commentary on the Draft Convention on Contracts for the International Sale of Goods (1979) (A/CONF. 97/5), Official Records, pp. 14–66 (cited: Secretariat's Commentary, Art., No.).

Siehr, Kurt: Die Parteiautonomie Im Internationalen Privatrecht, in: Forstmoser, Peter/Heini, Anton/Giger, Hans/Schluep, Walter R. (eds), Festschrift für Max Keller zum 65. Geburtstag, Beiträge zum Familien- und Vormundschaftsrecht, Schuldrecht, Internationalen Privatrecht, Verfahrens-, Banken-, Gesellschafts-, und Unternehmensrecht, zur Rechtsgeschichte und zum Steuerrecht, Zürich: Schulthess Polygraphischer Verlag (1989), pp. 485–510 (cited: *Siehr*, FS Keller, p.).

Soergel, Hans-Theodor: Kommentar zum Bürgerlichen Gesetzbuch mit Einführungsgesetz und Nebengesetzen, Band 11, Schuldrecht 9, Übereinkommen der Vereinten Nationen über den internationalen Warenkauf (CISG), 14th ed., Stuttgart: Kohlhammer (2021) (cited: Soergel/*Author*, Art., para.).

Spickhoff, Andreas: Internationales Handelsrecht vor Schiedsgerichten und staatlichen Gerichten, RabelsZ 52 (1992), pp. 116–141.

Stade, Stefan: Rechtliche Fallstricke im Frankreichgeschäft, ZVertriebsR 2017, pp. 293–297.

Staudinger, Julius: Julius von Staudingers Kommentar zum Bürgerlichen Gesetzbuch: Buch 1: Allgemeiner Teil: §§ 139–163 (Teilnichtigkeit, Anfechtung, Vertrag, Bedingung und Zeitbestimmung), revised ed., Berlin: Sellier/de Gruyter (2020) (cited: Staudinger/*Author*, §, para.).

Staudinger, Julius: Julius von Staudingers Kommentar zum Bürgerlichen Gesetzbuch: Buch 2: Recht der Schuldverhältnisse: Wiener UN-Kaufrecht (CISG), revised ed., Berlin: Sellier/de Gruyter (2025) (cited: Staudinger/*Magnus*, Art., para.).

Stoll, Hans: Inhalt und Grenzen der Schadenersatzpflicht sowie Befreiung von der Haftung im UN-Kaufrecht im Vergleich zu EKG und BGB, in: Schlechtriem, Peter (ed.), Einheitliches Kaufrecht und nationales Obligationenrecht, Referate und Diskussionen der Fachtagung Einheitliches Kaufrecht am 16.-17.2.1987, Baden-Baden: Nomos Verlagsgesellschaft (1987).

Stürner, Rolf (ed.): Jauernig, Bürgerliches Gesetzbuch, mit Rom-I-VO, Rom-II-VO, Rom-III-VO, EGH-UnthVO/HUntProt und EuErbVO, 19th ed., München: C.H. Beck (2023) (cited: Jauernig/*Author*, §, para.).

Tallon, Denis: Chapter 7: The Buyer's Obligations under the Convention on Contracts for the International Sale of Goods, in: Galston, Nina M./Smit, Hans (eds), International Sales, The United Nations Convention on Contracts for the International Sale of Goods, New York: Matthew Bender (1984).

Thieffry, Jean: La convention de Vienne et les contrats de distribution, (1993) Dr. Prat. Com. Int., pp. 62–68.

Thiele, Christian: Das UN-Kaufrecht vor US-amerikanischen Gerichten: zugleich Anmerkung zu Viva Vino Import Corp. v. Farnese Vini S.r.l. (E.D. Pa. 2000), IHR 2002, pp. 8–14.

Thume, Karl-Heinz: Grenzüberschreitende Vertriebsverträge, IHR 2009, pp. 141–153.

Torsello, Marco: Preliminary Agreements and CISG Contracts, in: Flechtner, Harry M./Brand, Ronald A./Walter, Mark S. (eds), Drafting Contracts under the CISG, New York: Oxford University Press (2008).

Tritten, Melanie: Les contrats complexes et les complexes de contrats, étude sur les contrats liés en droit suisse, Geneva/Zürich: Schulthess Médias Juridiques (2024).

Ulmer, Peter: Der Vertragshändler, Tatsachen und Rechtsfragen kaufmännischer Geschäftsbesorgung beim Absatz von Markenwaren, München: C.H. Beck (1969).

UNCITRAL/HCCH/UNIDROIT: Legal Guide to Uniform Instruments in the Area of International Commercial Contracts, with a Focus on Sales (2021) (cited: *UNCITRAL et al.*, Legal Guide, para.).

van Alstine, Michael P.: Dynamic Treaty Interpretation, (1998) 146 U. Pa. L. Rev., pp. 687–793 https://doi.org/10.2307/3312609, last checked October 2025.

van Houtte, Hans: The Law of International Trade, 2nd ed., London: Sweet & Maxwell (2002).

Vischer, Frank: Die kollisionsrechtliche Bedeutung der Wahl einer nichtstaatlichen Ordnung für den staatlichen Richter am Beispiel der Unidroit Principles of

International Commercial Contracts, in: Widmer Lüchinger, Corinne/Geiser, Thomas/Sutter-Somm, Thomas (eds), Recht im Wandel, Ausgewählte Schriften von Frank Vischer zu seinem 90. Geburtstag, Zürich: Schulthess Juristische Medien AG (2013) (cited: *Vischer*, Unidroit, p.).

Vischer, Frank: Gemeinsame Bestimmungen über Verpflichtungen des Verkäufers und des Käufers, in: Schweizerisches Institut für Rechtsvergleichung (ed.), Wiener Übereinkommen von 1980 über den internationalen Warenkauf, Lausanner Kolloquium vom 19. und 20. November 1984, Zürich: Schulthess Polygraphischer Verlag (1985) (cited: *Vischer*, Lausanner Kolloquium, p.).

Vischer, Frank: The Relevance of the UNIDROIT Principles for Judges and Arbitrators in Disputes Arising out of International Contracts, EJLR 1999, pp. 203–216.

Vischer, Frank/Huber, Lucius/Oser, David: Internationales Vertragsrecht, 2nd ed., Bern: Stämpfli Verlag (2000).

von Bar, Christian/Clive, Eric: Principles, Definitions and Model Rules of European Law, Draft Common Frame of Reference (DCFR), Full edition, München: Sellier. European Law Publishers (2009).

von Bar, Christian/Mankowski, Peter: Internationales Privatrecht, Band I: Allgemeine Lehren, 2nd ed., München: C.H. Beck (2003).

von der Crone, Hans Caspar: Rahmenverträge, Vertragsrecht: Systemtheorie – Ökonomie, Zürich: Schulthess Polygraphischer Verlag (1993).

von Hein, Jan/Vuattoux-Bock, Samuel: Die *Conforama*-Entscheidung der französischen *Cour de cassation* zur kollisionsrechtlichen Vereinbarung der UNIDROIT-Prinzipien für Internationale Handelsverträge, ZEuS 4/2023, pp. 482–501.

von Scheven, Michael: Der Sukzessivlieferungsvertrag, Eine rechtsvergleichende Untersuchung zum deutschen Recht, zum Haager Einheitlichen Kaufrecht und zum UN-Kaufrecht, Frankfurt a.M./Bern/New York: Peter Lang (1985).

Walt, Steven D.: The Modest Role of Good Faith in Uniform Sales Law, (2015) 33 B. U. Int'l L. J., pp. 38–70.

Walt, Steven D.: Sales Law: Domestic and International, Cases, Problems, and Materials, 3rd ed., St. Paul: West Academic (2021).

Weber, Rolf H.: Rahmenverträge als Mittel zur rechtlichen Ordnung langfristiger Geschäftsbeziehungen, ZSR 1987, Volume I, pp. 403–434.

Wegen, Gerhard/Asbrand, Dominik: Nichtstaatliches Recht als Gegenstand einer Rechtswahlklausel?, RIW 2016, pp. 557–564.

Wellenhofer-Klein, Marina: Zulieferverträge im Privat- und Wirtschaftsrecht, München: Beck (1998).

Westermann, Harm Peter/Grunewald, Barbara/Maier-Reimer, Georg (eds): Erman, BGB Handkommentar mit AGG, EGBGB, ErbbauRG, LPartG, ProdhaftG, VBVG, VersAusglG, WEG und ausgewählten Rechtsquellen des IPR. In 2 Bänden, 17th ed., Köln: Verlag Dr. Otto Schmidt (2023) (cited: Erman/*Author*, §, para.).

Wey, Marc: Der Vertragsabschluss beim internationalen Warenkauf nach UNCITRAL- und schweizerischem Recht: mit Einschluss der Anwendungs- und allgemeinen Bestimmungen des Übereinkommens der Vereinten Nationen über den internationalen Warenkauf (Diss. Basel 1984).

White, James J./Summers, Robert S./Barnhizer, Daniel D./Barnes, Wayne/Snyder, Franklin G.: Uniform Commercial Code, 7th ed., St. Paul: West Academic Publishing (2022) (cited: *White/Summers et al.*, §, p.).

Widmer Lüchinger, Corinne/Oser, David (eds): Basler Kommentar, Obligationenrecht I, Art. 1–529, 7th ed., Basel: Helbing Lichtenhahn Verlag (2019) (cited: BSK OR-I/*Author*, Art., para.).

Wilderspin, Michael: The European Private International Law of Obligations, 5th ed., London: Sweet & Maxwell/Thomson Reuters (2020).

Witz, Claude: Vente Internationale de Marchandises, Conventions de Vienne et de New York Contrat: Prescription, 2nd ed., Paris: Dalloz (2023) (cited: *C. Witz*, para.).

Witz, Claude/Köhler, Ben: Der neueste Beitrag der französischen Gerichte zur Auslegung des CISG, IHR 2014, pp. 89–98 (cited: *C. Witz/B. Köhler*, IHR 2014, p.).

Witz, Wolfgang/Salger, Hanns-Christian/Lorenz, Manuel (eds): International Einheitliches Kaufrecht, Praktiker-Kommentar und Vertragsgestaltung zum CISG, 2nd ed., Frankfurt a.M.: Deutscher Fachverlag GmbH (2016) (cited: Witz/Salger/Lorenz/*Author*, Art., para.).

Wójtowicz, Ewa: Law Applicable to Distribution Contracts and Contracts of Sale: Relationship Between Framework Agreement and Application Contracts, ERCL 2018, pp. 138–156.

Zeller, Bruno: Damages under the Convention on Contracts for the International Sale of Goods, 2nd ed., Oxford: Oxford University Press (2009) (cited: *Zeller*, Damages).

Zeller, Bruno: Four-Corner: The Methodology for Interpretation and Application of the UN Convention on Contracts for the International Sale of Goods, Working Paper, Pace Law School (2003) (cited: *Zeller*, Ch.).

Zubović, Antonija/Filipović, Mihaela Braut: Significance of the CISG for Franchising and Distribution Agreements in the EU Market, in: Kandzija, Vinko/Kumar, Andrej (eds), Economic Integrations, Competitions and Cooperation, Accession of the Western Balkan Countries to the European Union, Rijeka: Rijeka University Press (2013).

Zuñiga Peralta, Raul F.: Long-Term Contracts and the UNIDROIT PICC: Towards a Realistic Regulation, (2021) 26 Unif. L. Rev., pp. 492–523 https://doi.org/10.1093/ulr/unab026, last checked October 2025.

Zweigert, Konrad/Kötz, Hein: An Introduction to Comparative Law, 2nd ed., New York/Oxford: Clarendon Press/Oxford University Press (1987).

GLOBAL TRADE LAW SERIES

1. Emmanuel T. Laryea, *Paperless Trade: Opportunities, Challenges and Solutions,* 2002 (ISBN 90-411-9897-0).
2. Xiang Gao, *The Fraud Rule in the Law of Letters of Credit: A Comparative Study,* 2002 (ISBN 90-411-9898-9).
3. Yuwa Wei, *Comparative Corporate Governance: A Chinese Perspective,* 2003 (ISBN 90-411-9908-X).
4. Ross P. Buckley (ed.), *The WTO and the Doha Round: The Changing Face of World Trade,* 2003 (ISBN 90-411-9947-0).
5. Bradley J. Condon, Joyce C. Sadka & Tapen Sinha (eds), *Insurance Regulation in North America: Integrating American, Canadian and Mexican Markets,* 2003 (ISBN 90-411-2301-6).
6. Jan Hoogmartens, *EC Trade Law Following China's Accession to the WTO,* 2004 (ISBN 90-411-2301-6).
7. Yang Guohua, Bryan Mercurio & Li Yongjie, *WTO Dispute Settlement Understanding: A Detailed Interpretation,* 2005 (ISBN 90-411-2361-X).
8. Jan Job de Vries Robbé, Paul U. Ali, *Securitisation of Derivatives and Alternative Asset Classes, Yearbook,* 2005 (ISBN 90-411-2375-X).
9. Markus W. Gehring, Marie-Claire Cordonier Segger, *Sustainable Development in World Trade Law,* 2005 (ISBN 90-411-2366-0).
10. Yann Aubin & Arnaud Idiart, *Export Control Law and Regulations Handbook: A Practical Guide to Military and Dual-Use Goods Trade Restrictions and Compliance,* 2007 (ISBN 90-411-2601-5).
11. Henry Kibet Mutai, *Compliance with International Trade Obligations: The Common Market for Eastern and Southern Africa,* 2007 (ISBN 978-90-411-2664-1).
12. Yong-Shik Lee, *Economic Development through World Trade: A Developing World Perspective,* 2007 (ISBN 978-90-411-2681-8).
13. Yanning Yu, *Circumvention and Anti-Circumvention Measures: The Impact on Anti-Dumping Practice in International Trade,* 2007 (ISBN 978-90-411-2686-3).
14. Ross Buckley, Vai Io Lo & Laurence Boulle, *Challenges to Multilateral Trade: The Impact of Bilateral, Preferential and Regional Agreements,* 2008 (ISBN 978-90-411-2711-2).
15. K.D. Raju, *World Trade Organization Agreement on Anti-dumping: A GATT/ WTO and Indian Jurisprudence,* 2008 (ISBN 978-90-411-2780-8).
16. Xiaochen Wu, *Anti-dumping Law and Practice in China,* 2008 (ISBN 978-90-411-2790-7).
17. Amin Alavi, *Legalization of Development in the WTO: Between Law and Politics,* 2008 (ISBN 978-90-411-2795-2).
18. Henrik Andersen, *EU Dumping Determinations and WTO Law,* 2009 (ISBN 978-90-411-2827-0).

19. Sherzod Shadikhodjaev, *Retaliation in the WTO Dispute Settlement System*, 2009 (ISBN 978-90-411-2811-9).
20. Yi Shin Tang, *The International Trade Policy for Technology Transfers: Legal and Economic Dilemmas on Multilateralism versus Bilateralism*, 2009 (ISBN 978-90-411-2825-6).
21. Reem Anwar Ahmed Raslan, *Antidumping: A Developing Country Perspective*, 2009 (ISBN 978-90-411-3128-7).
22. Pietro Poretti, *The Regulation of Subsidies within the General Agreement on Trade in Services of the WTO: Problems and Prospects*, 2009 (ISBN 978-90-411-3162-1).
23. Esther Lam, *China and the WTO: A Long March towards the Rule of Law*, 2009 (ISBN 978-90-411-3144-7).
24. Jorge Alberto Huerta-Goldman, *Mexico in the WTO and NAFTA: Litigating International Trade Disputes*, 2009 (ISBN 978-90-411-3169-0).
25. Laurence Boulle, *The Law of Globalization: An Introduction*, 2009 (ISBN 978-90-411-2828-7).
26. Daniel Lovric, *Deference to the Legislature in WTO Challenges to Legislation*, 2010 (ISBN 978-90-411-3145-4).
27. Gregory W. Bowman, Nick Covelli, David A. Gantz & Ihn Ho Uhm, *Trade Remedies in North America*, 2010 (ISBN 978-90-411-2840-9).
28. Madalina Diaconu, *International Trade in Gambling Services*, 2010 (ISBN 978-90-411-3248-2).
29. Mohamed Ramadan Hassanien, *United States Bilateral Free Trade Agreements: Consistencies or Conflicts with Norms in the Middle East?*, 2010 (ISBN 978-90-411-3281-9).
30. Marie-Claire Cordonier Segger, Markus W Gehring & Andrew Newcombe, *Sustainable Development in World Investment Law*, 2011 (ISBN 978-90-411-3166-9).
31. Nellie Munin, *Legal Guide to GATS*, 2010 (ISBN 978-90-411-2824-9).
32. Thomas G. Kelch, *Globalization and Animal Law: Comparative Law, International Law and International Trade*, 2011 (ISBN 978-90-411-3338-0).
33. Yann Aubin & Arnaud Idiart (eds), *Export Control Law and Regulations Handbook: A Practical Guide to Military and Dual-Use Goods Trade Restrictions and Compliance*, Third Edition, 2016 (ISBN 978-90-411-5443-9).
34. Yulia Selivanova (ed.), *Regulation of Energy in International Trade Law: WTO, NAFTA and Energy Charter*, 2011 (ISBN 978-90-411-3264-2).
35. Germano Franceschin & Francesco Misuraca, *India: Commercial Law, Customs and Taxation*, 2011 (ISBN 978-90-411-2836-2).
36. Humberto Zúñiga Schroder, *Harmonization, Equivalence and Mutual Recognition of Standards in WTO Law*, 2011 (ISBN 978-90-411-3657-2).
37. Kati Kulovesi, *The WTO Dispute Settlement System: Challenges of the Environment, Legitimacy and Fragmentation*, 2011 (ISBN 978-90-411-3406-6).
38. Martín Molinuevo, *Protecting Investment in Services: Investor-State Arbitration versus WTO Dispute Settlement*, 2012 (ISBN 978-90-411-3827-9).
39. Joachim Åhman, *Trade, Health, and the Burden of Proof in WTO Law*, 2012 (ISBN 978-90-411-3825-5).

40. Umair Hafeez Ghori, *Global Textiles and Clothing Trade: Trade Policy Perspectives*, 2012 (ISBN 978-90-411-3875-0).
41. Yenkong Ngangjoh Hodu, *Theories and Practices of Compliance with WTO Law*, 2012 (ISBN 978-90-411-3228-4).
42. Dan Wei & Fernando M. Furlan, *Brazil in World Trade: Contingent Protection Measures*, 2012 (ISBN 978-90-411-3335-9).
43. Jorge A. Huerta-Goldman, Antoine Romanetti & Franz X. Stirnimann (eds), *WTO Litigation, Investment Arbitration, and Commercial Arbitration*, 2013 (ISBN 978-90-411-4686-1).
44. Gilles Muller, *Liberalization of Trade in Legal Services*, 2013 (ISBN 978-90-411-4853-7).
45. Christian Struck, *Product Regulations and Standards in WTO Law*, 2014 (ISBN 978-90-411-4950-3).
46. Gonzalo Villalta Puig, *Economic Relations between Australia and the European Union: Law and Policy*, 2014 (ISBN 978-90-411-3405-9).
47. Maurizio Gambardella, Davide Rovetta & Simon van Cutsem, *Remission and Repayment of Customs Duties in the EU*, 2014 (ISBN 978-90-411-4764-6).
48. Lisa Spagnolo, *CISG Exclusion and Legal Efficiency*, 2014 (ISBN 978-90-411-5407-1).
49. Dennis Ndonga, *Single Windows and Trade Facilitation: A Tool for Development*, 2015 (ISBN 978-90-411-5834-5).
50. Malebakeng Agnes Forere, *The Relationship of WTO Law and Regional Trade Agreements in Dispute Settlement: From Fragmentation to Coherence*, 2015 (ISBN 978-90-411-6274-8).
51. Julien Chaisse & Jiaxiang Hu (eds), *International Economic Law and the Challenges of the Free Zones*, 2019 (ISBN 978-94-035-0893-1).
52. Boris Praštalo, *Uniformity in the Application of the CISG: Analysis of the Problem and Recommendations for the Future*, 2020 (ISBN 978-94-035-2072-8).
53. Manuel A.J. Teehankee, *Trade and Environment Governance at the World Trade Organization Committee on Trade and Environment*, 2020 (ISBN 978-94-035-2202-9).
54. Marco Tulio Molina Tejeda (ed.), *Practical Aspects of WTO Litigation*, 2020 (ISBN 978-90-411-8596-9).
55. James J. Nedumpara, Satwik Shekhar & Akshaya Venkataraman (eds), *Handbook on Product Standards and International Trade: Navigating the Regulatory Landscape in India*, 2021 (ISBN 978-94-035-3413-8).
56. José Rijo, *Customs Law in the European Union: Legal, Doctrinal and Jurisprudential Framework*, 2022 (ISBN 978-94-035-3811-2).
57. Lauri Railas, *Incoterms® 2020 Handbook: Effecting Deliveries in Challenging Times*, 2023 (ISBN 978-94-035-2076-6).
58. Mark K. Neville, Jr., *The Customs Valuation Agreement: Origin, Standards and Interpretations*, 2023 (ISBN 978-94-035-3096-3).
59. María Moreno Sancho, *Trade Remedy Laws: The Trojan Horse in the Multilateral Trading System*, 2025 (ISBN 978-94-035-3929-4).

60. Marie-Claire Cordonier Segger, Ilaria Espa & Nico Schrijver (eds), *Natural Resources, Sustainable Development and International Law*, 2026 (ISBN 978-94-035-4155-6).
61. Julian Juhasz, *Framework Agreements Regarding the International Supply of Goods and the CISG*, 2026 (ISBN 978-94-035-2079-7).

www.ingramcontent.com/pod-product-compliance
Lightning Source LLC
LaVergne TN
LVHW020643300926
849161LV00004B/796
* 9 7 8 9 4 0 3 5 2 0 7 9 7 *